Contesting Nation

Contesting Nation

Gendered Violence in South Asia:
Notes on the Postcolonial Present

Edited by

ANGANA P. CHATTERJI
and
LUBNA NAZIR CHAUDHRY

zubaan

ZUBAAN
128 B Shahpur Jat, 1st floor
NEW DELHI 110 049
Email: contact@zubaanbooks.com
Website: www.zubaanbooks.com

First published by Zubaan 2012

10 9 8 7 6 5 4 3 2

ISBN 978 81 89013 37 0

Zubaan is an independent feminist publishing house based in New Delhi with a strong academic and general list. It was set up as an imprint of India's first feminist publishing house, Kali for Women, and carries forward Kali's tradition of publishing world quality books to high editorial and production standards. *Zubaan* means tongue, voice, language, speech in Hindustani. Zubaan publishes in the areas of the humanities, social sciences, as well as in fiction, general non-fiction, and books for children and young adults under its Young Zubaan imprint.

Typeset by Jojy Philip, New Delhi 110 015
Printed in India by Repro India Ltd., Navi Mumbai

Contents

Acknowledgements

An intellectual and political obligation to speak to structural and personal inequities, borders and margins, nation and gender, and speech/silence has shaped this collection. The essays elaborate on a myriad of issues that bind South Asia in the historical present. As institutions of state and majoritarian and heteronormative nation-making fracture and frame cultural and political community, how are these processes productive of social violence in general, and gendered violence in particular?

We are privileged that this collection includes the work of feminists who are diverse in history and heritage, scholarship and disciplinary affiliations, acutely aware that collaborations on South Asia are often dominated by scholarship of India. Situated in South Asia and in the diaspora, these women bring powerful and varied experiences and insights to questions of violence, nation and nationalisms, rights, justice and resistance across issues of gender and ethnicity, class and identity, and community and culture in Afghanistan, Bangladesh, India, Kashmir, Nepal, Pakistan and Sri Lanka.

The friendships and solidarities that emerged through this process are precious and we hope will endure. Our collaboration permitted thinking the shared and divergent histories that shape us, and differing legacies of 'nation'. We remain grateful to the contributors; Huma Ahmed-Ghosh, Srimati Basu, Meghna Guhathakurta, Lamia Karim, Nyla Ali Khan, Rita Manchanda, Kavita Panjabi, Jyoti Puri, Darini Rajasingham-Senanayake, Usha Zacharias, for the care and commitment that produced this scholarship. To Sukanya Banerjee, Manali Desai, Saadia

Toor, our heartfelt thanks for shaping the introduction, and to Kamala Visweswaran, for her generous contributions in enabling the process and the first version of this volume (see below). Working with each one of you has been an invitation to learn and be challenged. Shefali Chandra, Meenakshi Ganguly, Saba Gul Khattak, Chandra Talpade Mohanty, Sujata Moorti, Nimanthi Rajasingham, Yasmin Saikia, thank you for your thoughtful and astute counsel. We owe a great debt to Richard Shapiro for his alliance, advice and intellect. We are obliged to Rajib Akhter for diligent and caring support. We sincerely appreciate the editorial assistance offered by Annie Paradise and Mia Houtermans. We thank Pei Wu for her help with research checks and Heidi Andréa Restrepo Rhodes for assistance with proof-reading. To Shweta Vachani, Preeti Gill and other colleagues at Zubaan, thank you for your expertise and labour. Most of all, our warmest thanks to Urvashi Butalia, whose formidable work and solidarity made this publication possible.

The essays in this collection were written between 2004 and 2007. Much has transpired since, across South Asia and elsewhere. We embarked on this project through the 32nd South Asia Conference at the University of Wisconsin-Madison in 2003, where a few of us convened a pre-conference on 'Gender, Violence and Community'. Our exchanges facilitated complex reflections on our work as feminists immersed in scholarship-activism on South Asia and its diasporas. Following the pre-conference, Kamala Visweswaran offered an invitation to assemble a double issue for *Cultural Dynamics*, of which she was the North American Editor. We are thankful to her, to Guha Sankar, Fern Bryant, Janet Defreitas, Catherine Gibbons, and others at *Cultural Dynamics* for making possible that publication, which appeared in October 2004. We thank Sage Publications, especially Huw Alexander, for permission to reproduce the material published in *Cultural Dynamics*. This book is an amplification of that endeavour. An iteration of the collectively-authored introduction and articles authored by Angana P. Chatterji, Lubna Nazir Chaudhry, Meghna Guhathakurta, Lamia Karim, Rita Manchanda, Darini Rajasingham-Senanayake and Usha Zacharias were first published in *Cultural Dynamics* (2004, 16[2/3]: 319–72). In addition, Srimati Basu's article first appeared in 'Playing Off Courts: The Negotiation of Divorce and Violence in Plural Legal Settings in Kolkata, India' (*Journal of Legal Pluralism and Unofficial Law*, 2007, 52: 41–75). Nyla Khan's article first appeared in 'The Land of Lalla-Ded: Politicization of Kashmir and Construction of the Kashmiri Woman' (*Journal of International Women's Studies*, 2007, 9[1]: 22–41).

We remain hopeful that histories, both violent and kind, can allow transformations and can power our becoming amid hybrid and non-normalizing worlds, in-between here and there, at home and in homelessness. We offer this, accepting that even as the concerns raised here are critical, too much is left unsaid.

Angana P. Chatterji and Lubna Nazir Chaudhry
April 2012

Introduction

Engendering Violence

Boundaries, Histories, and the Everyday

Sukanya Banerjee, Angana P. Chatterji, Lubna Nazir Chaudhry, Manali Desai, Saadia Toor[1]

BORDERS/BOUNDARIES

This volume addresses how borders violently mark women's bodies in wars of direct and indirect conquest, and how women's agency is constituted in these times. How is gendered violence inscribed through the spectacular and in everyday life? What is the role of war or armed conflict in transforming women's spheres of agency? As we write about this issue, we are struck by the historical paradox that we women in/from South Asia inhabit. Anti-colonial struggles that achieved independence and formed postcolonial nation-states have consolidated themselves through prodigious violence that defined and divided communities, memories and futures. Promises betrayed reverberate across the very borders such violation enshrines. This violence was inscribed upon women's bodies in very specific ways, as they became, to borrow from Gayle Rubin (1975), the 'vile and precious merchandise' that was literally and figuratively exchanged as boundaries were imposed and enforced. As Veena Das evocatively states, we have been unable 'to name that which died when autonomous citizens...[of India]...were simultaneously born as monsters' (2003: 332). This can be said of South Asia in its entirety.

The literature on state and nation formation in South Asia has yet to grasp the significance of the 'intimate' gendering of this double birth. Whether we are speaking of the first partition of India in 1947,[2] the second partition of Bangladesh/Pakistan in 1971, ethnic wars in Sri Lanka, ethnic and imperial wars in Afghanistan, insurgency and wars in Kashmir or Nepal, the troubled convulsions of postcolonial births have too often been understood in frameworks that restrict their formative events to the 'public sphere'; that is, the decisions of elite colonial officials and native leaders, the ebbs and flows of politicking, negotiations, round tables and conferences, of class conflicts, states and parties.[3] Although there exists a growing body of feminist research that includes women's narratives of these events, the considerable scope of scholarship on state and nation formation that examines its sexual politics, and the forced micro-dynamics of boundary formations, remains underappreciated (Bacchetta 2001; Chatterjee and Jeganathan 2000; Parker et al. 1992; Puri 2004).

Ideologies of nationhood have of course always been inescapably gendered (Kandiyoti 1997; Yuval-Davis and Anthias 1989; Moghadam 1994) and have precipitated in South Asia, as Ahmed-Ghosh, Rajasingham-Senanayake and Chaudhry point out in their essays, iconic forms of womanhood, which, in metaphorizing women as symbolic bearers of national identity, have rendered the materiality of women's lives and bodies all the more vulnerable to forms of violence and violent exclusion.

These acts of violence and 'boundary-making' that marked women as signifiers of cultural essence and (racial) purity are not confined to the historical moment of decolonization. Continued in an era of transnational capital, which professes to have exceeded the nation-state in both material and conceptual terms, gendered identities are constantly deployed to mediate the incommensurate between global capital and national particularisms. While the overwhelming sense of *trans*-nationalism permeating the current global scenario has led many to conjecture the demise of the nation-state, in reality it is far from 'dead'. As Aihwa Ong points out, 'despite frequent assertions about the demise of the state, the issue of the state remains central when it comes to the rearrangements of global spaces, and the restructuring of social and political relations' (Ong 2003: 40; see also Ong 1987). In fact, Ong alerts us to be vigilant to the 'mutations' of political and social power, of the ways in which the nation-state, far from receding into obsolescence, *remorphs* itself.

We are concerned with these very mutations and reincarnations in biopolitical states (Foucault 1978a, 1978b, 1994). Aware of the ways in which the authority of the state rearticulates itself through consolidations of cultural nationalisms and majority identity-formations, we wish to foreground the gendered contours in which this resurgence is effected, situating it within shifting global, national and local power relations.

Gendered violence is hardly the preserve of South Asia; globally, ethnic violence, wars, colonialism, economic policy, religion and communitarian brutality, and state-sanctioned terror have affected women in highly specific ways. Here we outline some of the words and events that highlight the importance of a gendered analysis of violence in South Asia. In doing so we seek to break the divisions between the public and private, political and sexual, that have pervaded the study of violence, arguing for reflexive scholarship and practice as powerful and necessary intervention. As we approach these questions in a shrinking post-9/11 world, in the eye of the most rapid process of globalization and expansion of Empire yet known, our framing is, out of necessity, broader—the 'older' questions of nation and state formation are now imbued with new significance and form as wars are led by new Empire (the United States), and as various fundamentalisms and chauvinisms find fuel.

In a prescient piece on the rise of violence against women in Asia, Bina Agarwal, following Amrita Chhachhi's argument, explains that 'the spread of religious fundamentalism' is due to its emphasis on the ideology of female exclusion which provides further justification for male chastisement of women who 'transgress' into public spaces of predominantly male presence, giving social and legal sanction to husbands and relatives to physically chastise women for their behaviour. This results in a crucial shift: 'whereas earlier the exercise of patriarchal authority rested only with *particular* men—fathers, brothers, husbands and extended family kin—*what is significant about state-sponsored religious fundamentalism is that it not only reinforces this patriarchal control, but more importantly, shifts the right of control to all men*' giving 'every and any man on the street the legitimate right to stop any woman who does not conform to the "traditional and proper" role assigned to her' (Agarwal 1998: 20–21). Agarwal points out that Chhachhi's explanation

> ...misses out on the crucial role that *the community* (religious, ethnic, clan, caste...) and not just family and extended kin, has always played (and continues to play) as a mediator between the state and the individual and

household in enforcing conformity to specific norms of behaviour, action and dress, and in the delineation of which the community's economically and politically influential members typically have a significant hand. Even when social legislation passed by the state has been progressive in a given context... this has seldom been strictly enforceable where community norms are to the contrary[4]... What appears to be happening today in much of South and South-East Asia is the *convergence* of state and community-dictated patriarchal norms. (1998: 22)

These acts, projects, processes should not be misunderstood as remnants of the past—testifying to South Asia's incomplete modernization, or looked upon uncritically as a contest between tradition and modernity—but as part of the process and experience of modernity. Scholars (Ahmad 2002) and social movements[5] have pointed to the consolidation and intensification of the global economy in the form of neo-liberalism/imperialism, and its attendant economic, political and social effects, as major contributors to the increase in communal politics. Nira Yuval-Davis and Floya Anthias show how 'central dimensions of the roles of women are constituted around the relationships of collectivities to the state and that equally central dimensions of the relationships between collectivities and the state are constituted around the roles of women' (1989).

These events share the traumas and dislocations of people caught in the seemingly endless repetition of colonial, neo-colonial/imperialist and local power configurations. A gendered analysis of the violence—everyday, symbolic or sudden—shows most of all that what women share is the way in which they *experience* this violence, holding in common the destructive reality of sexual brutalization, displacement, death, loss of loved ones, property, homes, and futures. These events shift subjectivities and create new forms of agency in the process. The question of women's agency looms large, pushing against the growing intractability of the networks of violence that constitute the state and nation in South Asia. Many of the articles in this volume propose a more nuanced understanding of these forms of agency. As Darini Rajasingham-Senanayake writes in this collection, 'women's agency in war or peace, or to use a term more commonly found in development discourse, women's "empowerment" is complex, non-linear and rarely un-ambivalent'. And as Huma Ahmed-Ghosh points out, western and fundamentalist interventions on women's bodies in times of violence and war continue the misogynist and racist regimes of the past.

State formation in each of the South Asian cases has been premised on political investments in forms of violence, and their intersection with the daily, economic violence of poverty and systemic disenfranchisement. The state in South Asia emerges quite literally as the primary regulator of the means of violence. Its investment in the mechanism and language of war, in structures of inequality, in the glorification of military cultures, and nuclearization only reinforce violence, and gendered violence in particular. We have yet to *systematically* trace the mechanisms that link the state in South Asia to gendered violence in its various registers, shaping, as Angana Chatterji explores in this collection, the 'genealogy of violence before violence in the making of "nation"'. The postcolonial state's direct responsibility for carnage, and for its perpetuation of a genocidal culture, is a starting point, perhaps, for a fuller accounting of the South Asian state's regularized and cumulative violence against women.

Jyoti Puri focuses on the role of 'state institutions in perpetrating social injustice through law and its enforcement... from the lens of sexuality'. Srimati Basu looks at domestic violence complaints in negotiating diverse forums for gender justice. Nyla Ali Khan outlines the collision of nationalisms and militarization in India-held Kashmir that structure routine, spectacular, and gendered violence. Kavita Panjabi elaborates on how Gujarat in 2002 brought to the fore state collusion— with its police, bureaucracy, judiciary, legislative, and executive branches party to, involved in, and complicit with the perpetration of violence.[6] Gujarat in 2002, and similarly Karachi through the 1990s and beyond, the monumental violence against Sikhs in Delhi in 1984, the violent partition in Bangladesh in 1971, the ethnic violence in Sri Lanka and Maoist insurgency in Nepal, and the war in Kashmir and Afghanistan, have particular and general histories. The growth and continuance of ethnic violence in the post-independence decades, religious violence and regional wars between India and Pakistan, or Pakistan and Bangladesh, have long lineages that refuse to die in popular memory/ practice. We cannot, however, detach them from their shared colonial histories. The imagined and real transfer of large numbers of people (larger than populations of most European countries) to unfamiliar new territories that ensued in the two partitions attest powerfully to a racist, colonial imaginary in shaping South Asia. We still live in the symbolic and material grip of this past.

HISTORIES/SPECIFICITIES

Violence against women, from dowry deaths and rapes to tribal traditions such as *karo kari*[7] is justified in the name of tradition. We are interested in understanding particular forms of 'pathological' violence that women experience via their signification as repositories of tradition and culture, and suffer at the hands of their 'own' or rival communities. We use the term community to refer to different social units at multiple levels of social organization—community here can mean *biradaris*, tribes, ethnic, sectarian and religious groups, or nation-states. It must be noted that there are 'family resemblances' between varying levels of 'community'—in effect imagined as 'kin groups'. Part of this kinship structure is the patriarchal designation of women as property—both literally and symbolically.[8] The Punjabi adage of *zar, zan, zameen* references three traditional forms of feudal property—gold, woman, land. When Levi-Strauss argued that kinship systems are actually structured around the exchange of women he was also saying that women thus become the means through which kin communities are consolidated.[9] By mapping ideas of honour and shame onto women's bodies, communities create extremely violent *moral* economies through which they differentiate themselves from one another. A stark example of the exchange of women as a means to consolidate national communities and differentiate them from one another is the exchange of abducted women between India and Pakistan that took place following Partition in 1947. Contemporary debates over this issue in the Indian parliament[10] reveal the moral anxieties over delineating the boundaries of the nation-state. More importantly, in the discourse of national honour/shame lives the idea of reclaiming one's property. To concede the ownership rights to personal or community property (here, the women) to a rival—especially when the property was 'abducted'—is to bring shame on oneself and one's 'kin community'—in this case the nation.[11]

The example of abducted women and their 'return' (on the basis of exchange for women of other communities) underscores the intersection of gender, polity and violence within specific communities, and between different communities. Women experience violence and commoditization *as the gendered property of their community, and repositories of its honour*, both within their own communities as well as from men of other communities. The strong identification of women with their community (as property and as signifier) makes them vulnerable to violence, especially at times of social instability, and cultural and moral anxiety. The forced seclusion of Afghan women in refugee camps (prior to the rise and fall of the

Taliban), the abduction of women in tribal vendettas, rape within the context of war,[12] and the recent sexualized violence against Muslim women in Gujarat, all exemplify the inscription of cultural identity and honour upon the bodies of women, turning them—as embodied signs—into literal and figurative battlefields.

The objectification of women formulates the body, as site of female difference, as the locus of violence. Rape is a mechanism of this violence, as is parading women of the 'other' naked. Khan records the use of rape in India's military subjugation of Kashmir. Panjabi documents extreme cases (in Gujarat and as during the Partition riots) where there is sexual mutilation, the severing of breasts, the tearing open of vaginas and wombs, and—distinctively, tragically, in Gujarat—the forced abortion of foetuses and their display on *trishuls*.[13] Embodied violence is perpetrated in different contexts. We refer here to war and conflict situations, chronic or otherwise, where women's displacement (literal and psychological) and the trauma of losing one's home, male family head and security, are augmented by the added responsibility of child rearing and caring for the aged and infirm, often without any support. Afghan refugees in Pakistan attest to this. Families are divided and decimated as women are disallowed outside the camps or family tents by surviving male family, even if it denotes a loss in income. Reports on the status of refugee women have noted high levels of trauma, depression and frustration, as Lubna Chaudhry has found in her work with Mohajir survivors of ethnic conflict in Pakistan in this volume. Echoes of this can be seen in Kashmir where fundamentalist groups have increasingly pressured women to adopt purdah, as described by Khan. As Huma Ahmed-Ghosh reminds us in her article, the status of women in Afghanistan under the Taliban needs no recapitulation: what we need to acknowledge and address is the devastation wrought on families by the United States' attacks, and the fact that Afghan women continue to be targeted by the new forces in power.

THE EVERYDAY IN THE POSTCOLONIAL PRESENT

What does it mean to inhabit the postcolonial present? The 'post', we have been cautioned, should not be taken too literally, for it is concomitant with neo-colonialism (Visweswaran 1997), conjoined with the nation-state, a largely masculinist enterprise (McClintock et al. 1997). Indeed, the frame/condition 'postcolonial' used in its descriptive sense poses challenges for feminist inquiry, for as Kumkum Sangari and

Sudesh Vaid have reminded us, 'the social and political developments of the past two decades have shattered postcolonial complacency about the improving status of women' (1989: 2). What, then, is at stake for us as we chart a feminist inquiry of the 'postcolonial present' (see Alexander and Mohanty 1997; Mohanty, 2004)? It encapsulates both the descriptive and analytical, calling for a methodology that disrupts linearity, and refuses to make monolithic struggle and emancipation. Emphasizing the interlocking nature of historical moments, the interrelations of multiple axes of power, the 'postcolonial present' emerges as a frame that implicates as it describes.

Everyday aspects of life in postcolonial South Asia are inextricably intertwined with larger processes of development and legacies of colonialism, even as the physical reality of place becomes a player in, and is impacted by, globalization. As an era of globalization[14] promises geosynchronicity (During 2000: 389), we would like to push for a reading, as others have done, that recognizes the unevenness and disjunctures in globalization (Dissanayake and Wilson 1996: 5). Thus even as the 'local' is bound with the 'global', it is crucial to examine the ways in which the local is reworked and becomes an important constituent of the global order as Angana Chatterji and Lamia Karim describe, focusing respectively on the ways that Hindu and Islamic nationalism in India and in Bangladesh are embedded in the twin projects of globalization and development. It is not just the fear of the local being effaced by the relentless strides of a global modernity that precipitates an obsessive surveillance (as evidenced in the 'policing' of couples on Valentine's Day in certain parts of India). Rather, as Usha Zacharias's article suggests, the particular forms in which the 'local' is imbricated with the 'global' concern us, not the least because it operates through the construction, reification and manipulation of gendered identities.

A word or two about the relationship between the everyday 'normal' violence and 'sudden events'. How do everyday forms of violence against women that do not requite enumeration facilitate large-scale events of gendered violence? How do such eruptions of violence reconstitute communities and subject formations? Das and Kleinman write about the everyday forms of violence, the 'soft knife of policies' and other symbolic forms that are often considered 'uneventful' (Das et al. 2001). The recurrent forms of violence against women—domestic violence, dowry deaths, acid throwing, and honour killings—link to the necessary devaluation of female life that occurs when women are targeted in riots and pogroms, and await feminist analytical and political attention.

Violence also *constitutes* communities after sundering them, as Gyanendra Pandey (2001) has forcefully argued. Too often, we are not told enough about how this constitution involves women, nor how women help the radical reconstitution of communities.

It is necessary to move away from normative notions of what constitutes violence that tend to spectacularize, drawing attention away from its more daily or 'banal' functions. The essays in this collection focus on violence affected by state formation and state authority, contoured by its affinity to ethnic or religious identities. Some of the articles reconceptualize violence in ways that reveal the linkages between acts of violence on a 'national' stage and those enacted in the practices of everyday life; between violence enacted in the name of religious or ethnic identity and that absorbed by rapid consumerism. Chatterji chronicles the multiple contexts at work in promoting Hindu majoritarianism as episodic and systematic across caste, class, gender, and minority groupings to institutionalize violence. Meghna Guhathakurta's and Lamia Karim's articles help us address forms of violence embedded in the elite women of micro-credit lending and the poor women enmeshed in those institutions, forcing attention to the class divisions in feminist politics that occur at local levels of a particular region: between Dhaka-based feminists and indigenous feminists of the impoverished Chittagong Hill Tracts in Bangladesh, between urban-based feminists and poor, rural women in areas serviced by non-governmental organizations (NGOs). Puri draws our attention to the ways in which the state's criminalization of same-sex sexual practices are constitutive of heteronormative gender and sexuality. Basu situates the multivariate forces that organize domestic violence within post/colonial contexts of inequity. Lubna Nazir Chaudhry speaks to Mohajir women's attempts to reconstitute selves and lives in ongoing structural violence and in the aftermath of conflict-generated cruelty in Pakistan of the 1990s. Together, they help us rethink the distinctions between the 'public' and 'private', the 'religious' and the 'secular', the 'spectacular' and 'mundane'. They help us conceptualize what Pradeep Jeganathan has termed 'a space for violence' that does not see violence only in sudden and episodic terms of 'fury' or 'eruption' (2000: 42); or imply that acknowledging the 'everyday-ness' of violence alone creates this space or analytic. We envisage an understanding of violence as something that is contiguous and contingent, not analytically isolated in terms of ideology, locality or history, as a call for a systematic approach that views violence as *process*, to create openings for intervention.

Viewing violence as a category of analysis, rather than viewing it in terms of its effects alone, as Rita Manchanda points outs in this volume, enables a fuller critique of militarism and its effects on women. As Cynthia Enloe has noted in a more general context:

> If the condition of women themselves is not part of the *explanation* of militarism, but only part of the litany of victims of militarism, women's experiences can be ghettoized as 'women's issues', to be assigned significance by male disarmament leaders only as they broaden the base of the movement's public support. (1983: 210)

Militarization in contemporary South Asia has been accompanied by a strident hierarchization as a structuring principle of civil society. The nuclear arms race in South Asia has been matched by the popularization of the rhetoric of majoritarianism (in India), for instance. It is imperative, then, to examine the gendered processes and effects of militarism. The study of gendered violence, we propose, should operate not just as shorthand for understanding violence on and against women, but also as an analytical category that is equally attentive to the ways in which normative ideas of masculinity and heterosexuality are disseminated amidst a pervasive context of militarism.

This can be seen in the rise of Hindu militancy and within Islamic fundamentalism, and its interesting manifestations are found in the militant roles of women cadres of the Hindutva movement, the role of women in the Maoist revolution in Nepal, and the role of female members of the elite suicide squad of the LTTE. While there has been some scholarship on women of the LTTE, by scholars like Neloufer de Mel (2001), that shows how discourses of honour specifically defined or framed women's decision to join the suicide squads, much less has been written on women in radical political movements in Nepal. In this respect, Rita Manchanda's article on 'Maoist Insurgency in Nepal: Radicalizing Gendered Narratives' is a long-awaited addition to our understanding of the contradictory positions of agency for women in the Maoist insurgency in Nepal. Meghna Guhathakurta's article also breaks new ground in looking at the appeal of militancy for indigenous women in Bangladesh, while Darini Rajasingham-Senanayake advances the discussion by examining the range of subject positions produced through the war for diverse groups of women, from female LTTE cadre to widows who are paradoxically freed from certain forms of patriarchal social control as a result of wartime violence and displacement.

CONTRIBUTIONS/QUESTIONS

Our scholarship as feminists is vibrantly focused on the diverse ways gender is constructed, mobilized and contested in South Asia. Religious majoritarianism, nation building and corporate dominated globalization produce myriad forms of violence, disproportionately enacted on the bodies and lives of women and children, mediated by class, ethnicity, caste, religion, sexuality, and region. The use of violence in the gendered production of culture and community escalates in historical moments marked by breakdown, rupture, assertion, and reinvention of 'tradition', transition and dislocation. Such periods are also productive of prolific resistance to oppression, political alliance, and local and global organization.

Even as some of us have been working on issues of gendered violence for some time, we felt that a more sustained and collaborative intervention was necessary after Gujarat. The timing, following 9/11 and the war in Afghanistan by a few months, and subsequently the invasion of Iraq, signified the rapidity with which violent events are encompassing women globally. As feminist scholar-activists, we have elaborated on the role of gendered and sexualized violence within South Asia. An examination of civil wars in Afghanistan and Sri Lanka, of ethnic conflict in India and Pakistan, or of class conflict in Nepal and Bangladesh, reveals with horrifying specificity the ways women are discursively framed and socially targeted. What enables majoritarian identity formation and religious nationalism through Hindutva in India, the Taliban in Afghanistan, Islamization in Pakistan or Bangladesh, and Sinhala nationalism in Sri Lanka? What are our own roles as members of majority communities in studying the problematics and possibilities of minority projects of cultural reassertion such as Muslims in India, Shias in Pakistan, Hindus in Bangladesh, Hazaras or Tajiks in Afghanistan, and Tamils/Christians/Muslims in Sri Lanka?

While the articles in this issue do not yet address all of these concerns, they represent an important step in that direction. Certain compelling, but intersecting themes emerge in this collection, and many of the essays share a common method. The articles by Zacharias, Basu, Karim, Panjabi, Chaudhry, Puri, and Guhathakurta undertake close readings of particular events to help us understand the gendering of local politics on the ground: the abduction and killing of a feminist activist, the disruption of a women's rally, the engendering of genocidal violence, or the conflict between two local communities over a relatively small incident; while the articles by Rajasingham-Senanayake, Khan and Ahmed-Ghosh seek to understand the logic of discursive structures underpinning our very comprehension of women's agency. Usha Zacharias's article examines how the gendering of violence shifts the very space through which violence shapes cultural citizenship; and the ways in which gender is crucial for even making violence intelligible. In turn, Meghna Guhathakurta examines the ways in which violence as political action reshapes social structures. Guhathakurta, Chatterji and Manchanda help us to understand how indigenous peoples of India, Nepal and Bangladesh, who have been sidelined or brutally repressed by the processes of development in those nation-states, are drawn into militant movements. Chatterji and Zacharias show how marginalized groups within Indian society, Dalit fisherfolk in Kerala and Adivasis in Orissa,[15] are lured into the mobilizational strategies of the Hindu nationalist movement. Ahmed-Ghosh and Chaudhry look at how different groups of refugee women, Mohajirs of the 1947 partition and Afghans fleeing successive repressive regimes, are positioned differently in contemporary Pakistani society. Basu and Puri elaborate on institutional arrangements of power, highlighting the law to gender analyses of violence and resistance in Kolkata and through the Delhi High Court ruling against a public interest litigation challenging the scope of Section 377, the 'sodomy law' that '*criminalizes sexual practices*'. Many of the articles move between descriptions of women as survivors of violence to document the ongoing conditions of violence, even in what, as Darini Rajasingham-Senanayake points out, is falsely understood to be 'peace'.

This collection enters into disputed representations of gendered violence in South Asia with small hope that knowledge itself, always partial and shifting, might act as an intervention to suffering. We acknowledge that the contested scholarship of this volume requires continual, self-reflexive scrutiny concerned with the politics and ethics of research, writing and representation. We are aware that an exploration of the relations of power and difference that shape enduring/provisional alliances and accountability must extend beyond justificatory and disjunctive critiques of academic practice as 'failure'. In bearing witness, how are we challenged to (re)define our role as scholar-activists? How do we support the development of scholarship in intimate relation to the horror of our times, seeking difficult lives of proximity to communities of practice? As postcoloniality interrogates knowledge-making, disciplinary/ scholarly practice is/must be reshaped with and at the margins. It will require that we repeatedly confront our own capacity building towards producing 'knowledge' allied with the marginalized. Scholarship, then, is an invitation to think our struggles as an ethics of response in solidarity with worlds that matter. How might such practice reflect the political commitments we carry, questioning the essentializing of truth, identity, thinking and action that organizes the production of knowledge? The legitimacy of relevant knowledge must hinge on the consequences that result, birthing language through relation and association. Such legitimacy is meaningful yet dangerous. Complex power dynamics intensify through such practice, rather than evaporate. Assessment of the effects of knowledge production requires diverse voices, and an ear attuned to inevitable silences (Chatterji and Shapiro 2011).

Nation making and nationalism in South Asia proceed in relation to the particular histories and discontinuities of colonization, internal and external structural inequities, and the strategic relations that shape regional and global interactions. Within the broader context of its implementation, nation making, in its diverse and shifting imaginary, intersects with projects of cultural assertion, modernization, development, and globalization. A diverse constituency of stakeholders seek acknowledgement, justice, cultural survival, and livelihood security. Debates on nation making raise strategic questions related to citizens in dissent, structural violence, and the responsibility of states to subaltern constituencies. These concerns, across Kashmir, Bhubaneswar and Jaffna, Kabul and Karachi, Kathmandu and the Chittagong Hill Tracts, reside in events marked by contested aspirations and inadequate commitments to producing non-violent futures. To dissect the historical, political and cultural dynamics productive of the present, through rigorous critique attentive to alliance for change, is an affirmation of thought and action at once necessary and (im)possible.

NOTES

1. We would like to acknowledge Kamala Visweswaran for her contributions to this introduction as one of the co-authors of the first version published in *Cultural Dynamics*, 2004, volume 16, numbers 2/3, pp. 125–40.
2. A small but growing and exemplary literature that examines women's experiences and memories of the partition of 1947 includes Butalia (2000) and Menon and Bhasin (1998).
3. Again, exceptions include Hasan (1994); Jalal (1995); Jayawardena and de Alwis (1996); Kumar (1993).
4. In Pakistan, for example, the issue of honour killings and the rights of women to choose their own life partners are two examples of community or

traditional tribal/feudal norms trumping even Islamic injunctions, much less the Pakistan Penal Code.

5. Such as the Narmada Bachao Andolan (Save the Narmada Movement). See www.narmada.org (URL consulted July 2004).

6. In ostensible revenge for the burning of a train carriage in the town of Godhra by Muslims, organized Hindus engaged in a well-orchestrated murder of Muslim women and men in the days that followed. Almost 2,000 Muslims were killed, and hundreds of thousands displaced from their homes, languishing in sordid relief camps for months after. Of particular note is the 'semiotics of terror', to use Tanika Sarkar's term, which surpassed anything ever imagined before. Centring gender in our understanding of the rapes and horrific sexual abuse visited upon women by mobs of Hindu men indicates that the forms of brutality (even if we would resist the impulse to chart a range for the unspeakable) reached new heights. As the report *Threatened Existence* (International Initiative for Justice [2003]) makes clear, these were genocidal acts: Gujarat is the sign of new and brutal imaginations of gendered violence that does not require the conditions of rupture, dislocation, or war to be realized; also see Sarkar (2002).

7. Karo kari is a traditional form of honour killing in Sindh (karo and kari both mean 'black') where traditionally both the man (karo) and the woman (kari) accused of illicit sexual relations are killed, but as some have pointed out, men have more mobility and they can also buy their lives through blood-money. Nafisa Shah notes:

> Karo Kari is a symbolic term, and the ritual, at every stage—from the execution of the adulterous couple to the settlement of disputes—operates through symbols. Traditional, shared community resources, like land, money and water are used as symbols of power and honour. The axe, an implement that hacks and cuts off one part of the body from another, is the symbol of retribution that brings death through dismemberment to the body that violates the honour code. (Shah 1997: 244)

Menon and Bhasin also talk about the 'brutal logic of reprisal': 'The form this violence takes—disfigurement, mutilation, disembowelment, castration, branding—are part of its pathology and must be recognized for their symbolic meaning' (1998: 39). The role of violence and its exchange between communities needs to itself be examined. Some social scientists have called this the 'language of feud'. Citing Veena Das and Ashis Nandy (1985), Menon and Bhasin state that

> ...feud may be defined as a 'pact of violence' between social groups in such a way that the 'definition of the self and the other emerges through an exchange of violence'. In this exchange, victims of feud are simply 'bearers of the status of their group, the means through which the pact of violence continues to be executed.' (1998: 39)

8. There is also the issue of women and property which feeds a political economy in which control over women becomes crucial given the imperatives of patriliny. In cultures where women can inherit, this ironically results in control over who they can marry, and this is one of the main underlying reasons for the upsurge in debates over the rights of adult Muslim women to marry without the consent of their *wali* in contemporary Pakistan, many cases of which end in harassment and even murder of the woman by her family. It is also responsible for other forms of control over women as an aspect of control over family property—*haq bakshwana*, forcible marriage to family members despite large age differences.

9. See Rubin (1975: 157–210).

10. Curiously, Pakistan was not a willing or active participant in this exchange.

11. This issue has of course been addressed in great detail by Ritu Menon and Kamala Bhasin in their book *Borders and Boundaries: Women in India's Partition* (1998) as well as a number of essays, as also by Urvashi Butalia in *The Other Side of Silence: Voices from the Partition of India* (2000).

12. Such as the rape of Kashmiri women by the Indian army, and the especially brutal experiment in 'eugenics' launched by the Pakistan army in what was then East Pakistan where the purpose was to 'purify' the insufficiently Muslim Bengali population (Pakistani army leadership is on record stating this). It is noteworthy that the UN only recently recognized rape legally as a war crime.

13. Trishul/trident is used as a symbol of militant Hinduism. The figure of the marauding Muslim features heavily in the discourse of Hindutva, and one of the defining and enduring myths from its beginnings has been the abduction of Hindu women by Muslim men in the wake of the Muslim invasion of India. Such myths—which take on the stature of history—no doubt underlie the targeting of Muslim women, understood now as an act of reprisal for past wrongs, and not of aggression against innocents.

14. Which, as Stuart Hall reminds us is not new, but has only taken on 'new forms' and 'new rhythms' (1997: 73).

15. Adivasi (tribal), Dalit ('lower', erstwhile 'untouchable', groups).

REFERENCES

Agarwal, Bina (1998). *Structures of Patriarchy: State, Community and Household in Modernizing Asia*. London: Zed Books.

Alexander, M. Jacqui and Chandra Talpade Mohanty (eds) (1997). *Feminist Genealogies, Colonial Legacies, Democratic Futures*. New York: Routledge.

Ahmad, Aijaz (2002). *On Communalism and Globalization: Offensives of the Far Right*. New Delhi: Three Essays Press.

Bacchetta, Paola (2001). 'Extraordinary Alliances in Crisis Situations: Women against Hindu Nationalism in India', in Kathleen M. Blee and France

Winddance Twine (eds), *Feminism and Antiracism:International Struggles for Justice*, pp. 220–49. New York: New York University Press.

Butalia, Urvashi (2000). *The Other Side of Silence: Voices from the Partition of India*. New Delhi: Kali for Women.

Chatterjee, Partha and Pradeep Jeganathan (eds) (2000). *Community, Gender and Violence. Subaltern Studies XI*. New York: Columbia University Press.

Chatterji, Angana P. and Richard Shapiro (2011). 'Knowledge Making as Intervention: The Academy and Social Change', in Bunyan Bryant (ed.), *A Collection on Environmental Justice and Human Rights*, pp. 169–92. Garden City: Morgan James Publishing.

Das, Veena (2003). 'Language and Body: Transactions in the Construction of Pain', in Nancy Scheper Hughes and Philippe Bourgois (eds), *Violence in War and Peace: An Anthology, Part VIII: Gendered Violence*, pp. 327–33. Oxford: Blackwell Press.

Das, Veena and Ashis Nandy (1985). 'Violence, Victimhood and the Language of Silence', *Contributions to Indian Sociology*, 19(1): 177–94.

Das, Veena, Arthur Kleinman, Margaret Lock, Mamphela Ramphele and Pamela Reynolds (eds) (2001). *Remaking a World: Violence, Social Suffering, and Recovery*. Berkeley: University of California Press.

De Mel, Neloufer (2001). *Women and the Nation's Narrative: Gender and Nationalism in Twentieth Century Sri Lanka*. Lanham, MD: Rowman & Littlefield.

Dissanayake, Wimal and Rob Wilson (1996). 'Introduction', in Wimal Dissanayake and Rob Wilson (eds), *Global/Local: Cultural Production and the Transnational Imaginary*, pp. 1–18. Durham, NC, and London: Duke University Press.

During, Simon (2000). 'Postcolonialism and Globalization: Towards a Historicization of their Inter Relation', *Cultural Studies*, 14(3/4): 385–404.

Enloe, Cynthia (1983). *Does Khaki Become You? The Militarization of Women's Lives*. Boston, MA: South End Press.

Foucault, Michel (1978a). *Discipline and Punish*. New York: Pantheon Press.

——— (1978b). *The History of Sexuality*, vol. I, *An Introduction*. New York: Random House.

——— (1994). 'Governmentality', in James Faubion (ed.), *Power: Essential Works of Michel Foucault, 1894–1954*, pp. 201–22. New York: New Press.

Hall, Stuart (1997). 'The Local and the Global', in Anne McClintock, Aamir Mufti and Ella Shohat (eds), *Dangerous Liaisons: Gender, Nation and Postcolonial Perspectives*. Minneapolis: University of Minnesota Press.

Hasan, Zoya (ed.) (1994). *Forging Identities: Gender, Communities and the State in India*. New Delhi: Kali for Women.

International Initiative for Justice (2003). *Threatened Existence: A Feminist Analysis of the Genocide in Gujarat*. Report by the International Initiative for Justice. Available at: http://www.onlinevolunteers.org/gujarat/reports/iijg/2003/. Last accessed June 2004.

Jalal, Ayesha (1995). *Democracy and Authoritarianism in South Asia: A Comparative and Historical Perspective*. Cambridge: Cambridge University Press.

Jayawardena, Kumari and Malathi de Alwis (eds) (1996). *Embodied Violence: Communalizing Women's Sexuality in South Asia*. London: Zed Books.

Jeganathan, Pradeep (2000). 'A Space for Violence', in Partha Chatterjee and Pradeep Jeganathan (eds), *Community, Gender and Violence. Subaltern Studies XI*, pp. 37–65. New York: Columbia University Press.

Kandiyoti, Deniz (1997). 'Bargaining with Patriarchy', in Nalini Visvanathan, Lynn Duggan, Laurie Nisonoff and N. Wiegersma (eds), *The Women, Gender and Development Reader*, pp. 86–92. London: Zed Books.

Kumar, Radha (1993) *The History of Doing: An Illustrated Account of Movements for Women's Rights and Feminism in India, 1800–1900*. New Delhi: Kali for Women.

McClintock, Anne, Aamir Mufti and Ella Shohat (eds) (1997). *Dangerous Liaisons: Gender, Nation and Postcolonial Perspectives*. Minneapolis: University of Minnesota Press.

Menon, Ritu and Kamala Bhasin (1998). *Borders and Boundaries: Women in India's Partition*. New Brunswick, NJ: Rutgers University Press.

Moghadam, Valentine (ed.) (1994). *Identity Politics and Women: Cultural Reassertions and Feminisms in International Perspective*. Oxford: Westview Press.

Mohanty, Chandra Talpade (2004). *Feminism Without Borders: Decolonizing Theory, Practicing Solidarity*. Durham: Duke University Press.

Ong, Aihwa (1987). *Spirits of Resistance and Capitalist Discipline: Factory Women in Malaysia*. New York: State University of New York Press.

———— (2003). 'Zones of New Sovereignty in Southeast Asia', in Richard Perry and Bill Maurer (eds), *Globalization under Construction: Governmentality, Law, and Identity*, pp. 39–69. Minneapolis: University of Minnesota Press.

Pandey, Gyanendra (2001). *Remembering Partition*. New York: Cambridge University Press.

Parker, Andrew, Mary Russo, Doris Summer and Patricia Yaeger (eds) (1992). *Nationalisms and Sexualities*. New York: Routledge.

Puri, Jyoti (2004). *Encountering Nationalism*. Malden, MA: Blackwell Publishers.

Rubin, Gayle (1975). 'The Traffic in Women: Notes on the Political Economy of Sex', in Rayna Peiter (ed.), *Toward an Anthropology of Women*, pp. 157–210. New York: Monthly Review Press.

Sangari, Kumkum and Sudesh Vaid (eds) (1989). *Recasting Women: Essays in Colonial History*. New Delhi: Kali for Women.

Sarkar, Tanika (2002). 'Semiotics of Terror', *Economic and Political Weekly*, 13 July.

Shah, Nafisa (1997). *A Story in Black. Karo Kari Killings in Upper Sindh*. Reuter Foundation, Paper 100. Oxford: Reuter Foundation.

Visweswaran, Kamala (1997). 'Postcolonialism', in *Encyclopaedia of Cultural Anthropology*, vol. 3, pp. 988–93. New York: Henry Holt.

Yuval-Davis, Nira and Floya Anthias (eds) (1989). *Woman, Nation, State*. New York: St. Martin's Press.

1

Between Reality and Representation

Women's Agency in War and Post-Conflict Sri Lanka[*]
Darini Rajasingham-Senanayake

We are in a no war, no peace, process. Much has changed and yet nothing has changed. People are not dying, that is good, and we can move about now, but the conditions are the same. Displaced people still can't go home because of high security zones, and military occupation… You ask about women's roles. How have they changed after the ceasefire? They have not because... because we do not have real peace in any case. They say there is the peace process and all the international community has promised funds for reconstruction, but nothing has changed, we are doing the same things.

– A woman activist in Jaffna, northern Sri Lanka. August 2003,
eighteen months after the ceasefire.

Images of child soldiers, women suicide bombers and women in battle fatigues carrying guns have become signifiers of how 'new wars' in the Global South blur gender roles as well as conventional distinctions between military and civilian actors. However, women living in conflict situations in South Asia continue to be represented, if not explicitly, then, implicitly, as doubly victimized. Not only are women living in conflict situations in the region victims of patriarchal structures that are found in most societies in the world, but patriarchy is seen to be exacerbated by caste and religious practices that are peculiar to the

---

[*] A version of this article appeared in Thiruchandran (1999), and in Manchanda (2001).

subcontinent. Additionally, after several decades of silence, an important and growing feminist literature on partition has traced the extent to which women and girls were the targets of rape, communal mutilation and humiliation in nationalist violence in South Asia (Butalia 1998; Menon and Bhasin 1998).[1]

It is perhaps because of this focus on women's suffering at the hands of their ethno-national communities that, despite women's active role as armed combatants in postcolonial armed conflicts in Sri Lanka and Nepal, the double victim image of women in South Asia's war zones remains compelling. By and large, feminist analysis has had difficulty coming to terms with nationalist women's agency in situations of conflict and peace.

The argument that women's agency cannot be realized within the parameters of nationalist projects (Liberation Tigers of Tamil Eelam, LTTE, or Bharatiya Janata Party, BJP) resonates with an older debate between Marxist and radical feminists. For radical feminists, Marxism rather than enabling of women's liberation was an obstacle to feminist transformation. Socialist feminism was the compromise. In my view, poststructuralist and postcolonial critique (for example, Spivak 1988) has rendered the issue of women's liberation far more complex by pointing to the ambivalent and contradictory constitution of agency and its interpretation, disallowing the presumption of linear progress towards a solid state of liberation or transcendental reason. As such, the issue of whether women can achieve greater autonomy within nationalist discourse is a moot point. This case disrupts the political correctness of liberal humanism as well as feminism.

Women political leaders seem to have had little success in bringing about significant improvement in the lives of women in the South Asian region or in building bridges across ethno-religious lines. Women heads of state have, however, moderated the more extreme misogynist cultural practices in a region where honour killings of women by their family members for defying the rules of whom 'she may or may not love', as Roy (1998) put it so evocatively, have been practised. This was arguably the case with Pakistan under Benazir Bhutto, where the more negative interpretations of Sharia law were not practised against women to the same extent as under many male rulers.

In reality and representation South Asian women have 'greatness' thrust upon them. South Asian women are rarely born great, though they may be born of great families, and they rarely achieve greatness without great men. The phenomenon of women from powerful political dynasties becoming president or prime minister literally over the dead bodies of their husbands and fathers is also a telling reflection and indictment of the gendered realities of political power and violence in the subcontinent. For, while postcolonial South Asia has had the highest regional concentration of women heads of state in the world—Benazir Bhutto in Pakistan, Khalida Zia and Sheikh Hasina in Bangladesh, Sirimavo and Chandrika Bandaranaike in Sri Lanka, and Indira Gandhi in India—they are all widows and/or bereaved daughters of male presidents and prime ministers. These women in power have rarely succeeded in stemming the violent trends in South Asian politics or in chalking out an alternative vision and course for their conflicted countries. By and large even women heads of state who once had an alternative secular vision of communal and ethnic peace, such as President Chandrika Bandaranaike, remain captive to the violent political forces, structures and processes that in the first instance thrust them to power—a metaphor of women's ambivalent agency. In short, even powerful South Asian women rarely appear to be agents of their destinies—in war or in peacetime. In the few cases where they hold formal power they appear to do so by virtue of dynastic tendencies in South Asian political processes and the legitimacy of party political lineage.

During the war years, Sri Lanka, with its lead on women's social indicators[2] in the South Asian region, had more widowed heads of state and widows contending for the post of head of state than any of its larger neighbours. Family, motherhood and widowhood were the symbols mobilized by women who sought political power as well as women activists in their struggles for and ascent to political power in a country ravaged by multiple political conflicts and violence. In Sri Lanka, widowhood, which bears a stigma in Hindu and to a lesser extent Buddhist culture, has been powerfully reconfigured by the Bandaranaikes (mother and daughter), and other widows of presidents and party leaders, such as Mrs. Premadasa and Mrs. Gamini Dissanayake. Notably, it was Chandrika Bandaranaike who took the unprecedented step among politicians of distancing herself from playing ethnic politics and Sinhala majoritarian chauvinism by calling for peace with justice for the minorities as a means to end the armed conflict between successive Sri Lankan governments and the LTTE fighting for a separate state. She was unable to fulfil that promise, caught up in the violent game of political survival and unable to transcend it—a metaphor for the ambivalent achievement of women in a period of social and political turmoil that has cast women in new roles in the subcontinent. As in the case of Sarojini Yogeswaran of the moderate

Tamil United Liberation Front (TULF), who became the first elected woman mayor in 1998 in the northern capital Jaffna's local government election and was shot dead by militants at her residence, other widowed women in these new roles have frequently not survived the violence.

Given the significant role of women in the LTTE, the lack of women at the Track 1 level of peace negotiations between the Government of Sri Lanka (GoSL) and the LTTE, facilitated by Norwegian diplomats during the two-year-old peace process in Sri Lanka, was conspicuous. The only woman at the negotiating table was the Australian wife of the LTTE spokesman, who has also been a driving force in the articulation of Tamil nationalist feminism, while the then Sri Lankan woman president was sidelined by the government. Ann Adele is however not representative of most Tamil women. After lobbying by women's groups in the south and upon the insistence of the international donor community that had pledged $4.5 billion for post-conflict reconstruction, it was agreed that a women's sub-committee would be set up to enable women from the two sides to exchange views and insert women's issues into the formal peace process. This has effectively meant the ghettoization of women's concerns and a limited conceptualization of what a truly gendered peace and post-conflict reconstruction process may mean, largely due to flaws in the structure of the Sri Lanka peace process itself.

Both Indian and Sri Lankan records show that incorporating women in leadership positions without fundamental cultural and structural changes in society and polity rarely results in the advancement of women. It is why South Asian women activists now advocate at least 33 per cent reservation for women in parliament in order to begin to change gender imbalances in politics and society. At the same time, the case of Hindu women activists of the BJP in India and women in the LTTE might indicate that for too long pro-peace secular feminist analysis has denied nationalist women their agency and their place in the sun. For, ironically, it is arguable that the recent South Asian picture of women entering new public spaces in peacetime, as well as due to war, indicates that women's agency and rights might be more effectively advanced within a nationalist framework due to the dominance of cultural nationalism in the region. In India and Sri Lanka it would appear that women's rights have been most systematically advanced within an ethno-nationalist framework. Of course, the Hindu nationalist BJP women are calling for a uniform civil code to enhance the rights of Muslim women vis-à-vis Muslim men, in a clearly ideologically biased manner, while Tamil women who dissented from the LTTE project paid heavily, in some cases with their lives.[3]

This article focuses on the lives of far less prominent women and their roles in the conflict-peace continuum in Sri Lanka. It explores new spaces of women's agency in the twenty-five-year-long conflict in the north and east of the country and asks if and how the return of peace may affect women's agency and empowerment. During the war years in the island, women carved for themselves new spaces of agency and new roles as armed combatants, a number of women took on new roles as principal income generator and head of household, but the question remains: will they be pushed back 'into the kitchen' with the return to peace? A generation of feminist analyses of women in conflict has suggested that return to peace is often signified as a return to the pre-war gender status quo.[4] That analysis was, however, based on the study of an older generation of conventional inter-state wars between militaries in Europe, as well as decolonization struggles and revolutions in Asia (for instance, in Vietnam and China). Rather, I suggest that the 'new war' in Sri Lanka, sustained and subsidized by a network of local-global actors—developmental, humanitarian, criminal, and diasporic—thrust women into new roles, enabling them to subtly and creatively craft their identities and destinies. This has often entailed manipulating the 'victim' identity assigned to them in the humanitarian and post-conflict policy discourse as they are displaced or widowed.

I suggest that the conflict that generated its own internal political economy and restructured society has subtly but irreversibly transformed gender roles and identities. Based on ethnographic fieldwork in the northeast conflict zones of Sri Lanka as well as analysis of the political economy of the armed conflict that began in 1983, and the early peace process between the GoSL and the LTTE in the northeast of the island (Rajasingham-Senanayake 1999, 2002, 2003), this article suggests that the structure of the 'new war' of international engagement and large-scale population displacement is such that a return to a pre-war gender status quo may not be possible, contrary to nationalist imaginaries and a significant literature on women in war.

I trace how spaces of women's agency and empowerment are configured by the macro structures and patterns of violence, as well as the local and international discourses (including human rights and humanitarian discourses) that respond to such violence, emergent in Sri Lanka and other 'new wars' in the Global South. As such, I bring a political economic analysis of the armed conflict between the LTTE and GoSL in the northeast of Sri Lanka (Rajasingham-Senanayake 1999, 2001a, 2001b) to bear on the interpretation of women's narratives that I recorded during nearly a decade of fieldwork in the conflict zones. This article reads women's empowerment in the conflict and post-conflict situation as an effect of the acceptance of and legitimacy conferred by wider society upon the new roles that women have begun to perform during the conflict years. It deliberately sidesteps much of the tendentious debate regarding the interpretation of agency and subjectivity that has characterized postcolonial analysis of subaltern identity politics. Rather, it draws on political economic analyses of the 'new wars' in the Global South and the work of Kaldor (1999) who has suggested that new or postmodern wars in the Balkans and Africa that involve the targeting and participation of large numbers of civilians, and extensive international engagement, present a fundamental challenge to how we may conceptualize war and peace. Violence is no longer merely the business of male combatants and trained militaries. One of the characteristics of modern wars in Asia, as in Africa, has been the targeting of civilians, who have become victims and perpetrators, sometimes seemingly in equal measure, as during the violence in Rwanda. Often the new wars have been fought not in battlefields but in multicultural urban or rural spaces and neighbourhoods between those of different ethno-religious or linguistic communities who once were neighbours. As such, the new wars where civilians are deliberately targeted have entailed the radical disruption/displacement/destruction and transformation of historically multicultural societies (Mamdani 2001; Rajasingham-Senanayake 2001a, 2001b). The armed conflict in northeast Sri Lanka has resulted in the death of 65,000 people in the official version, and the displacement overseas and to other parts of the country of over a million people at various times in the two decades of conflict and détente. The conflict zones have also recorded a demographic change in male-female ratios due to male deaths and out-migration.

Yet the changes that war has wrought on women's lives and the social and cultural fabric of family and communities in the conflict zones may give us clues towards developing creative strategies to 'empower' women and enhance their position and capacities for leadership and peace building in (post-) conflict societies. Studies of women in conflict situations have only recently begun to address the deeper social and economic transformations that armed conflicts entail, and their implications for political empowerment. In opening up new spaces for women's agency and leadership within changing family and community structures, this conflict has simultaneously destroyed previous spaces of agency, and placed a double burden on many women. I trace the transformations that the armed conflict in Sri Lanka has wrought on many civilian women in often subtle but significant ways by thrusting them into positions of power and decision within their families and communities in war-affected regions.

In this context, the argument that over two decades of war and uncertain peace may result in the unintended empowerment of women (sometimes at the expense of their menfolk) in Sri Lanka is dangerous and disturbing for those of us who believe in and advocate the peaceful resolution of conflicts arising from social injustice. Peace we still conceptualize as a 'return to things as they were' and this also includes, in the case of Tamil women, caste structures that buttress the (gender) status quo. For, after all, the gender hierarchy is one of the old established institutions of society, and as Chatterjee (1989) noted of women in the colonial period, they are frequently constructed as the central purveyors of a community's 'culture' and 'tradition', ironically precisely at a time that their lives and social roles might be undergoing great transformations. Chatterjee's argument pertained to the colonial and Indian nationalist construction of women. Moreover, as numerous feminist analyses have pointed out, in periods of violent nationalist conflict, women often are constructed as the bearers of a threatened national culture and tradition. Hence, often a return to peace is indexed by the return to the traditional gender status quo—and even women revolutionaries are pushed back into the kitchen. In this context, the LTTE's attempt to straddle Tamil cultural puritanism with a radical disregard for traditional caste and gender hierarchies has provided contradictory spaces for women's agency in northeast Sri Lanka.

Social scientists, development workers and activists have hesitated to address the issue of how social structural transformations wrought by long-term armed conflicts might have also brought desirable changes to entrenched social hierarchies and inequalities, such as caste and gender, among people exposed to these changes. We have grown wary of analysing the unintended transformations brought by war, of seeing positives in violence, lest we be branded 'warmongers'. Yet for many women who have lost family members peace can never be a simple return to the past. Rather, peace necessarily constitutes a creative remaking of cultural meanings and agency—a third space between a familiar, often romanticized, past and the traumatic present.

Failure to conceptualize and assist the dynamic of social transformation in conflict and peace building might also impede recovery from traumatic experiences, particularly since women (and men), who have to take on new non-traditional roles as a result of the conflict, might suffer secondary victimization arising from the new roles that they perform. This is particularly the case with a growing number of young Tamil women who have been widowed in the course of the armed conflict, and who are challenging conventional Hindu constructions of the 'good woman' as one who is married and auspicious (*samangali*). Increasingly, many young widows who have to go out to work to sustain young families are redefining the perception of widows (and to a lesser extent unmarried women) as inauspicious beings (*amangali*) by refusing to be socially and culturally marginalized and ostracized because they have lost husbands. Contemporary language still lacks the vocabulary for women to articulate the transformations that they have experienced, and many feel ashamed, guilty and/or traumatized by their changed circumstances and gender roles arising from conflict.

THE 'NO WAR, NO PEACE PROCESS'

As the woman quoted at the beginning of this article noted, in northeast Sri Lanka (as in many parts of Africa and Asia where internationally brokered 'peace processes' and post-conflict reconstruction are ongoing) the reality is that of a 'neither war, nor peace' impasse. Although since writing this article, the LTTE has been defeated and the United People's Freedom Alliance (UPFA) government and the Tamil National Alliance (TNA) are engaged in ongoing bilateral talks on a viable political solution, many of the structures of terror, taxation and displacement that sustained the political economy of war remain in place.[5] Moreover, in the Sri Lanka peace process, it is the men, despite the fact that the LTTE had a significant female fighting force, who have dominated the negotiations between the GoSL and the LTTE. Although a gender sub-committee was formed after lobbying by women's groups, women were not present at the Track 1 negotiation process. As a result, women's concerns have tended to be ghettoized and there has been little public discussion of how an adequately gendered peace may be achieved.

A 'real peace' or substantive peace contoured by the concerns and voices of the affected civilian communities remains elusive, even as the Ceasefire Agreement (CFA) overseen and monitored by Scandinavian peace monitors enables a minimalist or formal peace. This article suggests the need to conceptualize a substantive peace that recognizes and legitimizes new spaces of civilian women's agency in conflict situations and post-conflict reconstruction. It also suggests women's agency in war or peace, or to use a term more commonly found in development discourse, women's 'empowerment', is complex, non- linear and ambivalent, and as such requires that we develop a new language to think about gender identities and roles in peacetime.

The restructuring of war and peace challenges our conceptions of women's agency, which is rarely unambivalent—in war or peace. Likewise, as Jeffery has argued, 'agency is not wholly encompassed by political activism' (1998: 222). Yet it would appear that too many South Asian women's initiatives have neglected the social structural transformations to pre-existing family, kin group and caste hierarchies wrought by political violence. The overwhelming emphasis by women's groups as well as by women in relief and development programmes continues to be on seeing women as victims who need to be brought into peace processes or positions of political leadership in order to foster women's participation in governance and in legal reforms beneficial to women. This has been the case despite the fact that, ironically, the recent South Asian picture of women's advancement seems also to show that women's rights are often advanced within an ethno-nationalist framework, an issue to which I will return.

This article considers the changing shape of women's agency in the midst of armed conflict and its aftermath by exploring the new roles that women increasingly perform in their everyday activities in the north and east of the island where the armed conflict was fought bitterly and transformed social structures. Women from less politically powerful families than the Bandaranaikes have taken on many new and unaccustomed roles, such as head of household and principal income generator, mainly due to loss of male family members and displacement arising from the conflict. At the same time many women and girls have been rendered barely functional after suffering the violence of bombing, shelling, loss of family members, fragmentation of extended family, and displacement. Moreover, due to the security situation and the fact and perception that men are more likely to be 'terrorists', civilian women from families affected by the armed conflict in the northeastern war zones of the island have begun to play new public roles while simultaneously negotiating the duress brought on by these factors. Women in the former war zones deal with the authorities, from the government agent, to the military, to the humanitarian aid agencies. They file documents, plead their cases and implement decisions in public and private, in the presence or absence of their menfolk who have either disappeared or are increasingly disempowered.

Women's agency/empowerment in war or peace is not a 'zero sum' game, achieved at the expense of men. War places different burdens on men, for men and boys are the ones mainly targeted to fight and defend their nation, community, family and the honour of their women. It is largely men who are conscripted into paramilitaries to fight. Thus it follows that it is also men and boys who are more easily perceived as a security threat, particularly if they are of the 'wrong' ethnic or religious community. And they are the ones more likely to be killed. On the other hand, men who refuse to fight or who are forced to live off humanitarian aid in refugee camps suffer from emasculation because they cannot fulfil the socially prescribed role of protector and breadwinner of the family. The result is low self-esteem and a sense of failure that can lead to suicidal tendencies among men and boys. The psychological ramifications of this are supported by reports from those living in refugee camps: alcoholism is high, as is increased domestic violence. Clearly, there is a need for a systematic study of the impact of war and ensuing social and gender transformation among boys and men, and the cultural construction of masculinity, although this is not within the scope of this article.

I start from the premise that conflict affects women differently, depending on religion, caste, class, ethnicity, location, political affiliation and a variety of overlapping factors. But conflict also reveals a certain commonality in women's experience. Women experience the particularly gendered forms of violence, of rape, the fear of rape, of body searches and the persistent threat of other sexual violence, as well as the social stigmas that afflict women who have been the targets of sexual violence. Moreover, the fear of sexual violence that the situation of insecurity in armed conflict entails limits and inhibits most women's mobility and hence their livelihoods, choices and realities. At the same time, women react differently to nationalist armed violence: some, like the women cadres of the LTTE, or the women cadres of the Sri Lanka Army and Air Force, were radicalized and took up guns and weaponry for their respective nationalist struggles (De Mel 2001). Others have become political and social activists for peace, seeking to build alliances across ethnic, cultural and regional borders (Mother's Front, Mothers and Daughters of Lanka, Mothers of the Disappeared, Women for Peace, and Women's Coalition for Peace). This article examines (*i*) women who have had to take on new roles as head of household[6] and (*ii*) women engaged in peace and human rights work. Hence the second part assesses the implications of women's transformed roles for humanitarian interventions and development work in war and peacetime. The article also attempts to map militant and civilian women's agency in moments of violent social transformation and cultural change, to configure a more complex picture of women's agency, as well as their languages of resistance and empowerment in conflict. It also takes a critical look at how the construct of Sri Lankan women as a double 'victim' of wartime conflict, as well as of caste, culture and society in peacetime, might obscure and indeed impede an understanding of women's agency and empowerment in conflicts.

I draw from ethnographic field research conducted during several fieldwork stints over a number of years (1996–2000) among communities in the 'border areas' (both 'cleared' and 'uncleared' areas as they have come to be termed in the media and popular culture). This border constituted the shifting 'forward defence line' that demarcated land held by the Sri Lanka military and the LTTE. Land held by the military was referred to as 'cleared areas' while land controlled by the LTTE was termed 'uncleared'. Roughly, the border ran from the main eastern town of Batticaloa in the east, to Vavuniya at the centre, to Mannar in the west. It encompasses most of the eastern and north-central provinces of the island that experienced cycles of violent armed conflict, including repeated bombing and shelling of civilian populations.

My observations on displaced women are drawn from interviews conducted with women living in three different settings of displacement:

1. Welfare centres or refugee camps where people are housed in sheds, schools or shelters constructed by the United Nations High Commissioner for Refugees (UNHCR) and other relief agencies working with the government.

2. Residents of border villages, who have been displaced many times by the fighting, shelling and bombing, but chose to return to their villages rather than remain in refugee camps. These people live in constant fear of attack and displacement again, but since the majority are farmers, they choose to return to their land.

3. New settlements in the border areas of the Vanni, where the Sri Lanka government settles landless displaced families from the same province in a new plot of land. These new settlements are part of the rehabilitation and reconstruction programme in Vavuniya. In particular, I draw from interviews with young women heads of households in Siddambarapuram camp, which is located just outside the town of Vavuniya in the north-central province. This particular camp received a large number of displaced persons and families from Jaffna and the Vanni who had fled to India in the early 1990s and were

subsequently repatriated. I also draw from interviews conducted with women heads of households in the new settlement scheme adjacent to Siddambarapuram camp.

THE VICTIM AND HER MASKS

The tendency to view women as 'victims' in the armed conflict is fuelled by a number of popular and specialist discourses concerning several brutal rapes committed by members of the Sri Lanka Army, as well as the Indian Peace Keeping Forces (IPKF) when they controlled the conflict zones.[7] Human rights discourse and humanitarian interventions have also significantly contributed to the tendency to view women as 'victims'. The various and systematic forms of violence that civilian women experience at the hands of armed combatants, whether state armies or paramilitary personnel, in situations of armed conflict and displacement, have been extensively documented and highlighted in the former Yugoslavia, Rwanda and other parts of Africa and Asia. This process culminated in the UN resolution that established rape as a war crime and saw the appointment of Sri Lankan lawyer Radhika Coomaraswamy as the first UN Special Rapporteur on Violence against Women in 1997 (Coomaraswamy 1997a). Highlighting gross violations of women's bodies and lives in situations of conflict and displacement has been part of an important intervention by feminists and activists to promote women's rights as human rights internationally.

The focus on women as 'victims' of war and patriarchal culture has also arguably resulted in the elision of how long-term social upheaval might have additionally transformed women's (often subordinate) gender roles, lives and position in non-obvious ways. At the same time, in secular feminist analysis, women's political violence is often the uncomfortable black hole wherein women's agency, because it is violent, becomes a male patriarchal project. The claim is often made that women who enter new spaces as militants in nationalist armed struggle, such as the LTTE women, remain finally pawns and victims in the discourse of nationalist patriarchy, and it is hence that they are pushed back into the kitchen after the revolution/war. Likewise, it is argued that civilian women who take on new roles as head of household, principal income generator and decision-makers in the absence of their menfolk are really merely carrying a double burden. While there is little doubt that women in a war's interregnum carry a double burden, viewing women as merely victims of their culture, or of war and patriarchy, elides women's agency in violence. Positioning women as victims might also mean that they are subject to secondary victimization, since victimhood also often entails carrying the burden of a social stigma. Women who are widowed and or raped are particularly vulnerable to the double complex of stigmatized victim unless their suffering is recognized and treated sympathetically in the wider society, and recompense and restitution enabled by existing health and legal institutions.

But the construct of the Sri Lankan Tamil woman as 'victim' also draws from another genealogy. Anthropological, sociological and literary ethnography has tended to represent Tamil women as living within a highly patriarchal caste-ridden Hindu cultural ethos, particularly in comparison to Sinhala women whose lives are seen to be less circumscribed by caste ideologies and purity/pollution concepts and practices (Daniel 1997; Silva 2003). The troubling figure of the LTTE woman soldier—the armed virgin—stands as one of the few highly problematic exceptions to the representation of Tamil women as victims. Of course, the representation of Tamil woman in relation to caste and family is not entirely monochrome in the anthropological literature, which is split on the subject. For many anthropologists have also emphasized the strong matrilineal and matrilocal tendencies in Sri Lankan Tamil society (McGilvray 1989), where women inherit property in the maternal line according to customary Thesawalamai law and enjoy claims on natal families, in contrast to the rigidly patriarchal cultures of north India, where patrilineal descent and inheritance are the norm (Wadley 1991). Feminist ethnography, on the other hand, has emphasized the subordinate status of Tamil women in the Hindu caste structure, while frequently noting the split between the ideology of Shakti or female power as the primary generative force of the universe (also associated with the pantheon of powerful Hindu goddesses) and the reality of women's apparent powerlessness in everyday life (Thiruchandran 1997). Both schools, however, emphasize the generally restrictive nature of the Sri Lankan Tamil Hindu caste system on women and often tend to see caste and gender relations as culturally rather than historically determined. Nonetheless, by and large, women have rarely been centred in debates on caste, and when they have been, they are more often than not constructed as victims rather than agents of culture.[8]

More recently, historians have argued that colonialism permeated by British Victorian patriarchal culture (and, later, the enforcement of Brahminical north Indian imagination of state) eroded the status of women in the south Indian societies that follow a matrilineal Dravidian kinship pattern, where property is passed in the women's line, from mother to daughter—a practice which usually indicates the relatively high status of women in society, despite male structures of control. They have highlighted how colonial legal systems might have eroded the rights and freedoms that women had under customary law, particularly in matrilineal societies, while emphasizing the historically changing circumstances of family, kinship, caste and gender relations (Arunima 2003; Nair 1996). In this vein, this article looks at how over twenty years of armed conflict, displacement and humanitarian relief and development interventions might have altered the structure of family, caste, land rights, and gender status quo among communities in the border areas affected by the conflict.

THE STRUCTURE OF ARMED CONFLICT AND WOMEN AS NATIONALIST FIGHTERS

A friend and I met and interviewed Dhanu and her deputy Akhila in Jaffna at the headquarters of the LTTE in July 1987, soon after a peace accord was negotiated by the Indian government, and the IPKF was to arrive in north Sri Lanka. A few months later the LTTE rejected the Indian-brokered peace accord and commenced fighting with the IPKF and GoSL. Dhanu was the then commander of the women's wing of the LTTE. Our meeting took place two years before she assassinated former Indian prime minister Rajiv Gandhi in a suicide attack. When I met her she was the highest-ranking woman officer in the LTTE, and a frontline fighter, with many battle honours. We interviewed her in the LTTE headquarters, soon after Gandhi had dispatched Indian peacekeeping troops to bolster a ceasefire in Sri Lanka in 1987. In the course of our two-hour meeting, Dhanu, a highly intelligent and articulate woman, listed an account of violence committed by the state and the Sri Lanka military against her community. She insisted that she was fighting for the honour and liberation of her people. I had gone to interview her regarding the position of women in the LTTE. She told me that women's liberation was necessary but could only be achieved after the war for Eelam (the homeland of the Tamil people) was won. The woman problem would detract from focusing on the cause and could hence only be sorted out later.

The figure of the LTTE woman soldier, the armed virgin, the nationalist mother and/or queen of Sinhala legend who craved the blood of Tamils, and women in the armed forces stand as some of the few problematic exceptions to the representation of women as victims of war and their culture. LTTE women have been portrayed by the wife of an LTTE spokesman as enlightened (Adele 1993; Coomaraswamy 1997b; Schalk 1992) functionaries of the male leadership of the LTTE. The reality of LTTE women is probably somewhere in between. For while they may have broken out of the confines of their allotted domesticity and taken on new roles as fighters, it is indeed arguable that they are captive both to the patriarchal nationalist project of the LTTE leader Prabakaran, and the history and experience of oppression by the Sri Lankan military. However, to deny these Tamil nationalist women their agency because they are nationalist is to once again position them within the 'victim' complex, where the militant woman is denied her agency and perceived to be acting out a patriarchal plot. The minutely calculated and coordinated actions of Dhanu, who passed prime ministerial level security on her death march to Rajiv Gandhi in Madras (now Chennai), India, in 1989, cannot be explained in terms of false consciousness or economic rationality. Rather, Dhanu was a modern political agent fighting for a nation state and the right of her community's self-determination, in the language of the modern nation state, albeit an ethnically coded nation state. But then, what modern nation state is not ethnically coded?

Arguably, the LTTE line on the women question might have evolved beyond the first phase of the nationalist struggle when LTTE women seemed unable and unwilling to raise the question of gender inequality lest they be accused of fostering division in the Eelam nationalist cause. In the second phase of armed struggle in the 1990s, when the LTTE maintained a quasi-state in the 'uncleared areas', non-combatant women played new roles, albeit in a highly war traumatized and transformed society.

Almost twelve years after my meeting with Dhanu and Akhila, in January 1999, on a visit to the LTTE-held 'uncleared area' near the northeastern town of Trincomallee, I learned of the existence of a de facto LTTE policy on domestic violence. During a conversation with several members from a local community-based organization (CBO), one young woman said that women who suffer domestic violence and are physically abused by their spouses now complain to the LTTE cadres who take appropriate action. At the first complaint, the abusive spouse is given a warning, on the second he is fined and if there is a third complaint, he might end up in the LTTE jail. There are also reports that women now sit at LTTE local courts and arbitrate local disputes in the 'uncleared areas'. The respect that women LTTE cadres command in the wider Tamil society constituted an alternative if militarized role model for young women in northeast Sri Lanka. The possibility of violence that the militant woman represented facilitated wider society's regard of women through a slightly altered cultural lens. What this suggests is that even if women did not sit at the Track 1 negotiations, they could still be actively involved in post-conflict rehabilitation and reconstruction of the community. Moreover, given the demographic as well as social changes that have occurred, it is more likely that some women would be involved in the post-conflict policy process, even as others return to the kitchen. Finally, it is arguable that the numbers of women in the LTTE and the position accorded to them in the organization are a principal reason that rape has not been practised by the parties in the armed conflict in Sri Lanka—where the parameters of dirty war violence were largely set by the LTTE.

SPACES OF EMPOWERMENT: DISPLACING GENDER AND CASTE HIERARCHIES

Since the armed conflict commenced in Sri Lanka, the population of displaced people has fluctuated from half a million to 1.2 million, or between a tenth and a fifth of the country's population, at various points in the conflict. At the end of December 1995, the Ministry of Rehabilitation and Reconstruction in Sri Lanka estimated that there were 1,017,181 internally displaced people in Sri Lanka while 140,000 were displaced overseas (some of the latter have sought asylum status). Figures of displaced persons are, however, controversial. The University Teachers for Human Rights, Jaffna (1993), estimated that half a million Tamils had become refugees overseas. The decennial census of Sri Lanka scheduled for 1991 was not taken due to the conflict. Estimates cite that 78 per cent of the internally displaced are ethnic Tamils, 13 per cent Muslims and 8 per cent Sinhalese (Gomez 1994). Many displaced people, Tamils, Muslims[9] and Sinhalese alike, fled Sri Lanka Army and LTTE brutalities.

Displacement and camp life also provided spaces of empowerment for several Tamil women who had taken on the role of head of household for various reasons. In this section, I outline some of the processes of transformation in the lives of young and single, as also widowed, women whom I met at the Siddambarapuram camp and adjacent new settlement scheme. Siddambarapuram was located a few miles outside Vavuniya, the largest town in the north-central Vanni region. It had received a large influx of refugees from the north. In many ways the facilities, location and environmental/climatic conditions at that camp and the adjoining new settlements were exceptionally propitious. The relative prosperity of the locale and its residents was evident in the fact that the market in the camp was a vibrant and happening place that had become a shopping centre for nearby old (*purana*) villagers as well.

At Siddambarapuram, the sense of independence, empowerment and mobility of many women heads of household was tangible and remarkable in contrast to other women I met in camps in less favourable settings. Thulasi, a resident of the camp, told me:

> I used to work as a seamstress but after I was married I stopped work because my husband did not wish me to go out to work and I got pregnant, now that he is no more I have started to go to work in a tailor shop in Vavuniya town and it is with that money and the dry rations that I can bring up my children ... There are so many of us who have lost our husbands, many now do not follow the old ways, where widows were not supposed to dress nicely and go about. We wear the *pottu* [auspicious mark] and do what we need to do for our children and families. Sometimes come home very late after work.

Such narratives are explainable in terms of the camp's location close to the larger town of Vavuniya where women could find employment, particularly in the service sector. This is, of course, not an option for displaced women in other less conveniently located camps.

Siddambarapuram camp was initially constructed as a transit camp by UNHCR for refugees returning to Jaffna from India in 1991, who were subsequently stranded when the conflict started again in what is known as the second Eelam War. Many of the people in the camp had been residents for more than five years. One of the oldest refugee camps in Vavuniya, in many respects, the camp was exceptionally well located and serviced. Several young Tamil widows I interviewed in the camp and the adjoining new settlement noted that while they had initially had a hard time adjusting to displacement, camp life and the burdens of caring for their young families, they also had gained freedom to work outside the household, and increasingly enjoyed the role of being the head of the household and its principle decision-maker.

Several mothers with young children said that they had little desire to remarry, mainly due to anxiety that their children might not be well cared for by a second husband. Several women commented that previously their husbands would not permit them to work outside the household, even if they had done so prior to marriage. Of course, one of the principle reasons for these women's newly found sense of control was the fact that they were able to secure employment outside the household and the camp. Women in service and non-governmental organization (NGO) sectors had the best success.

It is arguable that the erosion of caste ideology and practice, particularly among the younger generation in the camps, had contributed to women's mobility and sense of empowerment. With the exception of the highly Westernized urban Tamil women professionals, caste has historically provided the mainstay of the Hindu Tamil gender status quo, since caste belonging often determines women's mobility, and seclusion, particularly among the high castes, is a sign of high status. Unlike in Jaffna, where village settlement was caste and region based, in the camp it was difficult to maintain social and spatial segregation, caste hierarchies and purity pollution taboos for a number of reasons. This is particularly true for members of the younger generation, who simply refused to adhere to caste inhibitions. As one mother speaking about the disruption of caste hierarchies in displacement observed:

> ... because we are poor here as displaced people, we only have two glasses to drink from, so when a visitor from another caste comes we have to use the same glass. Now my daughter refuses to observe the separate utensils and she is friendly with boys we wouldn't consider at home. Everything is changing with the younger generation because they are growing up all mixed up because we are displaced and living on top of each other in a camp ...

This mother went on to detail how it was difficult to keep girls and boys separate in the camp situation. She thought that the freer mingling of youth meant there would be more inter-caste marriages and, hence, an erosion of caste. Presumably this also meant that girls had more choice over who might be their partners.

The reconstitution of displaced families around women who had lost male kin curiously resonates with an older gender status quo: that of the pre-colonial Dravidian matrilineal family and kinship system where women would remain with their natal families after marriage, and were customarily entitled to lay claim on the resources of the matri-clan, enjoying a relatively higher status in comparison with women in strictly patrilineal societies. As Agarwal (1994) has pointed out, the existence of matrilineal systems where matrilineal descent, matrilocal residence and/ or bi-lateral inheritance is practised is usually an indicator of the relatively higher status of women when compared to the status of women in patrilineal groups. Similar observations concerning the status of women in matrilineal communities have been made by anthropologists who have studied the Nayars of Kerala as well as the Sinhalas, Tamils and Muslims of the east coast of Sri Lanka, where bi-lateral and matrilineal forms of inheritance are the norm (Menon 1994; Yalman 1967). These are also societies where social indicators have been consistently good, with high levels of female literacy, education and health care in South Asia.

During the colonial period in Sri Lanka, there was, however, a general erosion of matrilineal and bi-lateral descent practices, despite general provision being made for customary common law for indigenous communities (for example, Thesawalamai, Tamil customary law, Kandian Sinhala law and Muslim personal law). In the same period, the modernizing tendency towards the nuclear family, enshrined in secular European, Dutch and British law, also privileged male inheritance, thereby reducing the power of women within their families. The switch from matrilineal, matrilocal, to virilocal forms of residence and inheritance, where women take only movable property to their affinal household, might also be traced to various postcolonial land distribution schemes, wherein title deeds for land were invested in male heads of household, with the injunction against the further division of land due to land fragmentation, which set a precedent for male inheritance of the entirety of the family's land. The result has been the tendency towards male primogeniture—with the eldest son inheriting the land and daughters being disinherited from land ownership. Unfortunately, a similar pattern of title deeds being invested in male heads of households is still evident in the new settlement and land distribution schemes for landless, displaced populations that are taking place in Vavuniya under the rehabilitation and reconstruction project. In these projects, it is only where the male head of household is presumed dead that title deeds are invested in women. Women whose husbands have either left them or whose location cannot be ascertained are not deemed eligible for land grants. Clearly, in the case of Tamil inheritance patterns, customary practices are more liberal than that of postcolonial development practice.

What all of this indicates is that there are changes in cultural practices and structures impacting women's roles in situations of armed conflict. However, these changes do not manifest themselves in the same degree or even in the same way among all women. For while Tamil women have begun to play various unaccustomed public roles, the evidence from the war zones also suggests that conflict has restricted the mobility of

Muslim women in conflict zones and in the areas in which they have been displaced.

RETHINKING DISPLACEMENT: CHANGING ROLES OF WOMEN IN CONFLICT AND THE HUMANITARIAN CHALLENGE

Currently, there is growing recognition among those involved in humanitarian relief and rehabilitation work that women frequently bear the material and psychological brunt of armed conflict, and, hence, there is a need for gender-sensitive relief and rehabilitation work. Yet, few programmes have systematically explored how relief might aid recovery from individual trauma and social suffering, and facilitate women's empowerment in and through conflict. Thus, many gender programmes organized by the government's relief and rehabilitation authority and NGOs still remain within conventional development thinking rather than attempting to work out *culturally* appropriate and effective strategies for women's empowerment in the context of the social transformations that have occurred over years of armed conflict and displacement. These questions are further complicated in light of the devastation wrought by the tsunami in Sri Lanka in December 2004, leaving thousands dead and hundreds of thousands displaced.

Popular romanticizations of home, as well as constructions of internally displaced people as victims (the Sinhala term, *anathagatha kattiya*, literally means the abandoned people, while the Tamil term, *Veedu attavargal*, means people without a home), like the victim discourse concerning women in conflict in the human rights field, often obscure the realities of living at home in conflict. There is growing evidence to suggest that despite the psychosocial traumas that displacement entails, long-term displacement has provided windows of opportunity for greater personal and group autonomy as well as experiments with identity and leadership for displaced people, particularly for women (see the work of the Institute of Agriculture and Women in Development, a Sri Lankan NGO). Certainly this has been the case for many displaced Tamil women, many of whom have lost husbands and sons in the conflict. It is now time for humanitarian relief efforts to be conceptualized in terms of: (*i*) sustainability; (*ii*) maintaining local orders of ethnic co-existence and empowerment between displaced people and their local hosts; and (*iii*) empowerment of women within community and family structures dramatically different from the pre-conflict situation. In Sri Lanka, this is particularly necessary if the ethnic conflict is not to spread to new areas where the displaced have found refuge, and are often perceived to be in competition with poor local populations.

Many internally displaced women who have given up the dream of return are in the paradoxical position of being materially and psychologically displaced by the humanitarian interventions and human rights discourses, and practices that define them as victims who need to be returned to their original homelands for their protection and for the restoration of national and international order and peace.[10] The assumption of return is a fundamental premise of state, international and NGO policies vis-à-vis internally displaced people. The fact is that these policies might be contributing to prolonging the conflict as well as causing trauma for people who fled their home over a decade ago, or even two decades ago. This is particularly true of women for whom restrictions on mobility are difficult. Many of these women who wish to settle in the place where they have found refuge are being kept dependent on relief handouts rather than being assisted to build new lives and livelihoods. Thus, ironically, relief might be drawing out and perpetuating the trauma of the very people it is supposed to assist.

Under these circumstances, an approach which conceptualizes humanitarian work as part of a development continuum with gender-sensitive post-conflict intervention is especially necessary in instances where armed conflicts have lasted for several years with communities experiencing cycles of war, peace and displacement. While for some women there has only been trauma, for others the conflict has provided windows of opportunity for greater personal and group autonomy as well as experiments with identity and leadership. Certainly this has been the case for many displaced Tamil women, many of whom have lost husbands and sons in the conflict.[11] It is therefore important that relief aid should be conceptualized to sustain women's empowerment and leadership roles that initially arose as an effect of conflict within an altered family structure.

Clearly, the process of a woman becoming head of household is not transparent, unambivalent or free of guilt, and this was evident in many young widows' uncertainty about whether they should return home if and when the conflict ended. For them, displacement clearly constituted a space of such ambivalence: the place that marked the distress of dislocation concurrently represented a place of regeneration and the hope for a future unfettered by the past, loss and trauma. They were also concerned that return home would mean a return to the pre-war caste and gender status quo. Of course, anxiety about return was also related to qualms about personal security and trauma. Anxiety about return was clearest among young women heads of households at Siddambarapuram who had integrated into the local economy, and among those who had previously been landless.

LANGUAGES OF EMPOWERMENT: RECASTING WIDOWHOOD

A generation of young Tamil war widows who have been displaced to the border areas and have been living there for many years seem to be increasingly challenging conventional Hindu constructions of widowhood as a negative, polluting and inauspicious condition (*amangali*) that bars their participation in many aspects of community life. Several young widows working in Vavuniya town but resident in the camp, displayed their sense of independence by wearing the red *pottu*, the auspicious mark reserved for married Hindu women, despite being widows or women whose husbands had abandoned them. Likewise in Batticaloa, several women who had lost husbands to death, displacement or family fragmentation in the course of armed conflict and flight from bombing and shelling, increasingly refused to erase the signs of *sumangali* (particularly the auspicious red pottu) they wore when married, and refuse to be socially and culturally marginalized and ostracized simply because they lack husbands and children. Displacement, along with the fragmentation and reconstitution of families around women in a conflict, where men frequently have had to flee to avoid being killed or inducted by the armed groups, appears to have provided a space to redefine traditional Hindu Tamil perceptions of widows and single women as inauspicious (*amangali*) beings.

Of course, the demographic fact of a large number of young widows who are unwilling to take on the role of the traditional Hindu widow, who may not participate in auspicious social rituals such as wedding ceremonies and who are generally socially ostracized, facilitates the transformation of negative cultural patterns. Yet these young women's response to their changed circumstances marks the space for redefinition of what it means to be an unmarried or widowed woman in the more orthodox Hindu tradition. Consciously and unconsciously, they appear to be redefining conceptions of the 'good woman' as one who lives within the traditional confines of caste, kin group and village. As they struggle with new gender roles and identities, many of these young widows also struggle to find a language and cultural idiom to speak of their changed roles. They refuse to wear the prescribed garb of widowhood and appear to break with the ideology of Kanaki (Paththini), the exemplary faithful wife and widow of Tamil mythology and ideology. Rather, they seem to evoke the sign of the *devadasi*[12]—Kanaki's alter ego—who transcended conventional gender roles; the professional woman married to immortality for her talent and skill, most familiar to South Asian audiences in the name of the famed dancer and courtesan, Madhavi, of the Tamil Hindu-Buddhist epic, *Sillapaddikaram*.[13]

Yet, with the exception of the young Tamil widows who have found more freedom in the conflict, women still seem to lack a language to articulate this process of transformation and clearly feel guilty about expressing their new-found confidence. But one woman directly told me: 'It is a relief now that he [her husband] is not with me. He used to drink and beat me up.' While she worries for her personal safety and that of her children in the absence of her husband, particularly at night, she said that she had to support the children mainly on her own anyway, even when her husband was with her.

The victim ideology that pervades relief and rehabilitation as well as social health and trauma interventions for women in conflict situations needs to be problematized, especially as it may be internalized by some women with damaging consequences. Non-combatant women who have found spaces of empowerment in the conflict need sustained assistance to maintain their new-found mobility and independence in the face of sometimes virulently nationalist assertions of patriarchal cultural tradition and practices during the conflict and in the period of post-war reconstruction. The return to peace should not mean a return to the pre-war gender status quo. It follows that humanitarian and development interventions must creatively support and sustain positive changes to the status of civilian women living in conflict.

In the north and east of Sri Lanka the reality of war for women has been the loss of their menfolk, threats to their physical safety, psychological insecurity and a struggle for survival and to sustain the family. In short, they have had a double burden of keeping themselves and their families fed and sheltered while often assuming the sole responsibility for the vulnerable and weak: the children, the elderly and the disabled. As a result, women have crossed the private/public barriers to contend with the military, to compete in the market, to survive economically. Many women, who have been forced to take on various new roles within their families and communities during the years of armed conflict, have also gained greater self-confidence and decision-making power in the process. Over time, women have gone through a process of transformation, despite and because of the difficulty of taking on the added burden of traditionally male roles (head of household/ principal income generator). A backlash against women's changing roles and patterns of mobility is arguably one of the reasons for increased levels of violence against women.

BEYOND NATIONALISM? WOMEN'S ROLE IN POLITICAL CONFLICT AND PEACE BUILDING

Over two decades of armed conflict and the culture of ethno-nationalist and political polarization have also meant that activist women and secular women's groups have made little progress in peace building across ethnic lines. Though analyses of women's activism have sometimes privileged women's peace movements (Samuel 1998), most women's groups are mobilized by and large along ethnic lines with a few exceptions in Sri Lanka. The most powerful and oldest women's groups were anyway formed within a religious ethno-nationalist framework opposed to colonialism, such as the Young Women's Buddhist Association (YMBA). While these early women's organizations were anti-colonial rather than ethno-nationalist, they have over the years become increasingly ethno-nationalist. Seva Vanitha, the army unit that works for the bereaved families of armed forces personnel, is explicitly nationalist.

At the same time, secular women leaders like Chandrika Bandaranaike, who try to transcend ethno-religious divides, fall pray less to patriarchal nationalism than to the politics of survival in an increasingly violent political culture. Less high profile women have also had limited success reaching beyond their immediate circle and striking a common chord among the people at the national level, partly due to the lack of access to political party machinery which dominates national political processes. On the other hand, many local women's organizations have done and continue to do important work to improve the condition of women and to build bridges across ethnic-religious nationalist lines. Women's groups like the Suriya Women's Centre, founded in Batticaloa, in the east of Sri Lanka in 1990, have been actively engaged in human rights work, advocacy and peace education.

Several of the founding members of this group fled Jaffna after the LTTE killed one of the members, Rajini Thiranagama, also a senior lecturer at the University of Jaffna, for her outspoken stand on the LTTE's abuses of human rights. On the other hand, women's groups which had the potential to impact national level politics, such as the Mother's Front, have been appropriated by traditional party politicians and armed militant groups, who have used women's contributions and support to achieve positions of power, but who have rarely invested women with political power in the process.

When alliances across ethnic lines were struck, it was over particular issues, such as the Mothers' Front, which came together to stop the disappearances of family members arising from military violence and state brutality. However, these organizations have been subsequently co-opted by various political parties. By and large, it is arguable that this co-option was primarily due to the hostile ethno-nationalist climate in which secular women's groups operate, and made possible based on the reactive nature of the groups. Arguably, the absence of a proactive vision for strategic action has made secular groups vulnerable to co-option. This was largely the case with the secular Colombo-based group, Women for Peace, that convened in 1983 after the ethnic riots and dissolved in 1997, when it succumbed to the difficulties of working across ethnic lines in a time when the language of peace had been appropriated by a state intent on waging a 'war for peace'.

Clearly, there is a need to look elsewhere for women's agency and activism in armed conflict and peace building. Historically, women who took on various non-traditional gender roles in situations of social stress, conflict, war and revolution, have been 'pushed back into the kitchen after the revolution' as part of a return to everyday life (Enloe 1983; Jayawardena 1986). Arguably, one of the primary reasons that the return to peace often meant a return to the gender status quo was the lack of social recognition and a culturally appropriate idiom to articulate, legitimate and support women's transformed roles and empowerment in the midst of conflict, trauma and social disruption. This article attempts to distinguish between the kinds of transformations that have occurred by exploring their long-term impact. For social transformation to be sustained there needs to be cultural transformation, contingent on the acceptance of the legitimacy of women performing their new roles. And it is consequently arguable that the great threat and the greater challenge to the gender status quo comes less from the women in fatigues who might be asked to do desk jobs after the conflict, and more from the women who refuse to erase the red pottu, the unsung civilian women who daily struggle to sustain their families and themselves.

Unlike in Afghanistan where the situation of women has unambiguously deteriorated due to conflict and the victory of the Taliban, in Sri Lanka the evidence suggests, despite many women's experiences of traumatic violence and displacement, that some changes to the gender status quo wrought by armed conflict might have empowered women whose freedom and mobility were restricted by patriarchal cultural mores, morality and convention in peacetime. Several women who have faced the traumatic loss and scattering of family members due to displacement, conflict and the breakdown of family structures have also assumed new roles which were thrust upon them as a result of the disruption of peacetime community organization, social structures and patriarchal values. I do not wish to suggest that this is a general story that might be told of women living in conflict and displacement. Rather this article has focused on some women's agency at moments when they seem most victimized, to excavate some hidden moments and routes of women's agency in the situation of conflict.

This article seeks to develop an alternative framework for analysing women's agency and ambiguous empowerment in conflict situations while analysing changing gender relations. This has meant exploring gender relations outside the scripted frames of nationalist women's mobilization as well as gender analyses of women in politics. For it seems to me that the arena of politics proper in South Asia is a violent one, resulting in the stripping and humiliation of women politicians, as has repeatedly occurred at election time in Sri Lankan politics in the last decade. In Sri Lanka, which celebrated fifty years of democracy and was considered a mature democracy with free, fair and non-violent elections until recently, the crisis is acute.

I have argued elsewhere that nationalist women and women combatants in nationalist struggles waged by groups like the LTTE, or the nationalist women in Ireland or Palestine, are imbricated in ultra-conservative 'nationalist constructions of women' and tend to subordinate their gender identities to the nationalist cause (Rajasingham 1995). Suicide bombing is but the extreme version of this phenomenon, which might, in Durkheimian terms, be glossed as altruistic suicide, when individual autonomy and personal agency is completely subsumed in the national cause. The question might well be raised as to whether women would be more inclined than men to altruistic suicide, given their socialization in patriarchal Asian cultures, where girl children and women are more often than not taught to put themselves second, and their male folk, family and community honour first. Clearly, non-combatant women are differently imbricated in nationalist discourses, and the return to peacetime, which entails the reassertion of the (gender) status quo, is as problematic for them as it is for combatant women, but for different reasons.

Women's politics that crosses ethnic lines might be the best and last bulwark against growing ethnic chauvinism that is being built up by democratic politicians, intent on shoring up vote banks and personal power at the cost of national peace. Moreover, left liberal feminist positions that seek to transcend ethno-religious differences seem less likely to succeed in advancing women's rights than nationalist politics. Given that ethnic identity politics is increasingly co-terminous with politics proper, it is arguable that women will have to forge new spaces for activism—outside the sphere of politics proper and by exploiting the social and cultural spaces that have thrust women into new roles. Violent deaths and armed conflict open up ambiguous spaces of agency and empowerment for women within their families and communities who have not been directly engaged in violence.

Thus, this article also attempts to trace languages and patterns of empowerment in the generally tragic story of displaced women's lives towards recognizing and promoting positive changes wrought in conflict. The new spaces of cultural or ideological struggle opened by the social structural transformations engendered by long-term armed conflict also enable the agents and ideologues of violence, and recently invented nationalist 'tradition', often oppressive to women. Sometimes, for strategic reasons, those who advocate peace have tended to exaggerate the violence, and seen it as all-encompassing. Analysis has been the victim of such an approach to the study of gendered violence in war and peace. It is hence that this article has tried to rethink some of the gender dynamics of a return to peace by analysing women's new roles and the cultural frameworks that enable or disable them. For unless the cultural frameworks that denigrate (widowed) women are challenged and transformed, women and men who are coping and trying to recover from the wounds of war will carry a double burden, rather than be empowered in the new roles thrust upon them. This article charts the shifting terrain of women's ambivalent agency in armed conflict and peace building, the new spaces opened, the old spaces closed, and the changing structure of gender relations, in the war-affected northeast of Sri Lanka.

The notion that wars disrupt social, political and gender hierarchies in unexpected ways and benefit marginal groups and individuals, while obvious, is yet unexplored. This lacuna in the understanding of conflict and its effects has much to do with how we conceptualize peace—as a return to the (gender) status quo. Peace we still think constitutes a return to things the way they used to be: the certainties of familiar, older, ways of being and doing. But, to conceptualize peace thus is another kind of (epistemic) violence. For women, wives and mothers who have lost a head of household or seen him 'disappear' in the violence, there is no return to the old certainties of the nuclear family, headed by the father, the patriarch. For the war widows, for those who have lived intimately with war, the changes wrought by almost two decades of armed conflict and uncertain peace in Sri Lanka are too deep, too complex, structural and fundamental. They force us to challenge our certainties about war and peace. In this context, peace is necessarily a third place divorced from the past, utopia perhaps, somewhere arguably between the old and the existing, the past and the present.

NOTES

1. Butalia notes, 'if colonialism provided Indian men the rational for constructing and reconstructing the identity of the Hindu woman as a "bhadramahila"… Independence and its dark "other" Partition provided the rationale for making women into symbols of the nation's honour' (1998: 192).
2. In literacy, health, education. See UNDP Human Development Reports.
3. In Sri Lanka, the debate over secular and personal law as it applies to women is somewhat different and it is arguable that customary law in the case of Tamil Thesawalame and Kandian Sinhala Law is more favourable to women than is secular law on many matters. However, this is not entirely the case for Muslim personal law in Sri Lanka.
4. Recently this picture has changed, as the role of girls and women combatants is recognized and women are being pressed to take on a role in peace processes and post-conflict reconstruction.
5. See Rajasingham-Senanayake (1999, 2001a, 2001b) for details and examples of this political economy.
6. The social role of women, of holding the family together, of caring for children, tending the sick and the elderly, makes women the worst sufferers during conflict.
7. There are exceptions to the perspective of women as victims in activist and academic scholarship. Recent literature that centres precisely on the question of women, agency and war includes Manchanda (2001) who takes up the issue in the context of South Asia, as well as Moser and Clark (2001) who have a global focus. As early as 1998, several articles in Lorentzen and Turpin

(1998) addressed the uncomfortable issue of women in armed combat. However, the general trend in donor-driven research and reports compiled for humanitarian agencies continue to position women as victims. See, for instance, Rehn and Sirleaf (2002) and Mertus (2000), who despite taking into account contextual differences in women's lives, present a monolithic image of women victimized by violence.

8. Colonial evolutionary classifications of (primitive) societies presumed that fewer restrictions on women's freedom indicated a more primitive stage of civilizational advance.

9. While most Muslims are Tamil-speaking, they do not necessarily identify as Tamils.

10. For those in the conflict regions, the right to set up residence in an area of one's choice and the right to movement are seriously restricted by the LTTE and the GoSL's security regimes. While the Sri Lanka government restricts the movement of Tamils displaced southward, the LTTE will not permit Sinhalas to move or settle in the north. In fact, both the LTTE and the Sri Lankan government have used displaced persons as security shields or buffers during military campaigns. The Sri Lankan government's restrictions on the mobility of persons, and their confinement to camps, have other implications for youth and children. Militant groups who infiltrate camps have very little difficulty in recruiting new cadres from deeply frustrated and resentful youth, men and women, and girls and boys.

11. Among internally displaced Muslim women, however, the pattern is slightly different. Depending on the location of camps and the resources that families had, some women feel they have gained autonomy in their new situations while others complain of greater segregation.

12. The *devadasi* (lit. Slave of the Lord) was typically a young girl dedicated to the temple as a dancer who entertained upper-caste patrons. See Nair (1994).

13. The text is dated anywhere between the second and ninth centuries.

REFERENCES

Adele, Ann (1993). *Women Fighters of Liberation.* Jaffna: Publication Section LTTE/ Thasan Printers.

Agarwal, Bina (1994). *A Field of One's Own: Gender and Land Rights in South Asia.* Cambridge: Cambridge University Press.

Arunima, G. (2003). *There Comes Papa: Colonialism and the Transformation of Matriliny in Kerala, Malabar c. 1850–1940.* New Delhi: Orient Longman.

Butalia, Urvashi (1998). *The Other Side of Silence: Voices from the Partition of India.* Delhi: Penguin.

Chatterjee, Partha (1989). 'The Nationalist Resolution of the Women's Question', in Kumkum Sangari and Sudesh Vaid (eds), *Recasting Women: Essays in Colonial History*, pp. 233–53. New Delhi: Kali for Women.

Coomaraswamy, Radhika (1997a). *Violence against Women: Its Causes and Consequences: Preliminary Report*. New York: UN Human Rights Commission.

———— (1997b). 'Women of the LTTE', *Frontline*, Chennai, 10 January, pp. 61–64.

Daniel, E. Valentine (1997). *Chapters in an Anthropography of Violence. Sri Lankans, Sinhalas, and Tamils*. New Delhi: Oxford University Press.

De Mel, Neloufer (2001). *Women and the Nation's Narrative: Gender and Nationalism in Twentieth Century Sri Lanka*. Lanham, MD: Rowman and Littlefield.

Enloe, Cynthia (1983). *Does Khaki Become You? The Militarization of Women's Lives*. London: South End Press.

Gomez, Mario (1994). *Sri Lanka: State of Human Rights*. Colombo: Law and Society Trust.

Jayawardena, Kumari (1986). *Feminism and Nationalism in the Third World*. London: Zed Books.

Jeffery, Patricia (1998). 'Agency, Activism and Agendas', in Patricia Jeffery and Amrita Basu (eds), *Appropriating Gender: Women's Activism and Politicised Religion in South Asia*, pp. 221–44. New York and London: Routledge.

Kaldor, Mary (1999). *New and Old Wars: Organized Violence in a Global Era*. Stanford, CA: Stanford University Press.

Lorentzen, L.A. and J. Turpin (eds) (1998). *The Woman and War Reader*. New York and London: New York University Press.

McGilvray, Dennis (1989). 'Arabs, Moors and Muslims: Sri Lankan Muslim Ethnicity in Regional Perspective', in Veena Das, Dipankar Gupta and Patricia Uberoi (eds), *Tradition, Pluralism and Identity: In Honour of T.N. Madan*, pp. 192–235. New Delhi: Sage Publications.

Mamdani, Mahmood (2001). *When Victims become Killers: Colonialism, Nativism, and the Genocide in Rwanda*. Princeton, NJ: Princeton University Press.

Manchanda, Rita (ed.) (2001). *Women, War, and Peace in South Asia: Beyond Victimhood to Agency*. New Delhi: Sage Publications.

Menon, Leela Dmodara (1994). 'From Mothers to Daughters: Matrilineal Families in Kerala', *Manushi*, available at: http://free.freespeech.org/manushi/gallery/matriliny.html. Last accessed June 2004.

Menon, R. and K. Bhasin (1998). *Borders and Boundaries: Women in India's Partition*. New Delhi: Kali for Women.

Mertus, Julie A. (2000). *War's Offensive on Women: The Humanitarian Challenge in Bosnia, Kosovo, and Afghanistan*. Bloomfield, CT: Kumarian Press.

Moser, C.O.N. and F.C. Clark (eds) (2001). *Victims, Perpetrators, or Actors? Gender, Armed Violence, and Political Violence*. New Delhi: Kali for Women.

Nair, Janaki (1994). 'Devadasi, Dharma, and the State', *Economic and Political Weekly*, vol. 29, 10 December.

———— (1996). *Women and Law in Colonial India: A Social History*. New Delhi: Kali for Women.

Rajasingham, Darini (1995). 'On Mediating Multiple Identities: The Shifting Field of Women's Sexualities in the Community, State and Nation', in Margaret A. Schuler (ed.), *From Basic Needs to Basic Rights: Women's Claim to Human Rights*, pp. 233–48. Washington, DC: Women, Law and Development International.

——— (1999). 'The Hidden Economies of Conflict', in Robert Rotberg (ed.), *Creating Peace in Sri Lanka: Civil War and Reconciliation*, pp. 57–70. Washington, DC: Brookings Institution Press.

——— (2001a). *Dysfunctional Democracy and Dirty War in Sri Lanka*, East-West Centre Asia Pacific Issues Paper, 52. Honolulu, HI: East-West Centre.

——— (2001b) 'Transformation of Legitimate Violence and Civil-Military Relations', in Muthiah Allgappa (ed.), *Coercion and Governance: The Declining Political Role of the Military in Asia*, pp. 294–314. Stanford, CA: Stanford University Press.

——— (2002). 'Identity on the Borderline: The Colonial Census, Violence, and New Ethnicities', *Identité, Culture et Politique*, 3(2): 25–50.

——— (2003). 'Beyond Institution and Constitution Building: Linking Post/Conflict Reconstruction and Deep Democracy', in Markus Mayer, Darini Rajasingham-Senanayake and Yuvi Thangarajah (eds), *Building Local Capacities for Peace: Rethinking Conflict and Development in Sri Lanka*, pp. 107–31. New Delhi: Macmillan.

Rehn, E. and E.J. Sirleaf (2002). *Women, War, Peace: Progress of the World's Women 2002*, vol. 1. New York: United Nations Development Fund for Women (UNIFEM).

Roy, Arundhati (1998). *The God of Small Things*. Scranton, PA: HarperCollins.

Samuel, Kumudhini (1998). 'Women's Activism and Peace Initiatives in Sri Lanka', Paper presented at the Women in Conflict Zones meeting, Social Scientists' Association, Colombo, Sri Lanka.

Schalk, Peter (1992). 'Birds of Independence: On the Participation of Tamil Women in Armed Struggle', *Lanka*, vol. 7, pp. 44–142.

Silva, Neluka (ed.) (2003). *The Hybrid Island: Culture Crossings and the Invention of Identity in Sri Lanka*. London: Palgrave.

Spivak, Gayatri Chakravorty (1988). 'Can the Subaltern Speak?', in Cary Nelson and Lawrence Grossberg (eds), *Marxism and the Interpretation of Culture*, pp. 271–313. Urbana and Chicago, IL: University of Illinois Press.

Thiruchandran, Selvy (1997). *Ideology, Caste, Class and Gender*. Delhi: Vikas.

——— (ed.) (1999). *Women, Nation, and Narration*. Colombo: South Asia Books.

Wadley, Susan (ed.) (1991). *The Powers of Tamil Women*. New Delhi. Manohar.

Yalman, Nur (1967). *Under the Bo Tree: Studies in Caste, Kinship, and Marriage in the Interior of Ceylon*. Los Angeles and Berkeley, CA: University of CA Press.

2

Intelligible Violence

Gender, Citizenship and Visual Culture

Usha Zacharias

This article analyses media narrations of an incident of Hindu/Muslim communal conflict in Kerala, India. Depicting women as victims and agents of communal violence, the media visualized them in narratives of violation and retribution that are part of ready-made scripts of 'communities at war'. The narration of violence does not precede or follow gender politics. Rather, scripts of violence become intelligible through the logic of gender relations. The ideologies that thread together gender, violence and community, this article argues, critically underwrite the battle for cultural and political citizenship. Drawing on media representations of communal conflict among communities organized around religious groupings, I trace how the cultural act of making sense of communal violence is mediated by gender ideologies. The logics of violence are worked out through the cultural intelligibility of gender, and through the production of gender difference within ready-made scripts of communities at war, such as 'Muslim vs Hindu'. Regional and communal conflict becomes intelligible through the tropes of gender difference, that of 'Hindu wound', 'Islamic terrorism' and 'violated womanhood'. The gendering of violence serves to shift the space in which the violence occurs into the arena of cultural citizenship. In other words, this article addresses the question: through which representational logics of gender are violence, and its counterpart, retribution, normalized? How does the social sanction given to the logic of violence and retribution translate into questions of cultural citizenship and social power? I trace the way the intelligibility of communal violence is rendered into cultural sense through media representations and visual narratives of an incident of 'Hindu'/'Muslim' violence in the fishing village of Marad on the northern coast of Kerala, south India. I reformulate Butler's (1990: 22–25) notion of cultural intelligibility (that of coherence between sex, gender and desire) to indicate the signifying patterns in which community identities become crafted on to gender-coded bodies.

The Marad conflict occurred in the aftermath of the genocide of Muslims in Gujarat in February 2002 that had marked a moment of triumph for the nationalist, right-wing Hindutva (Hindu nationalist) movement and its anti-Muslim agenda. As a movement that gained hegemony through the 1990s, Hindutva is sustained by a range of organizations—including India's (until recently ruling) Hindu nationalist Bharatiya Janata Party (BJP), the cultural/political organization, Vishwa Hindu Parishad (VHP), and the paramilitary Bajrang Dal—that are ideologically allied to the shadowy Rashtriya Swayamsevak Sangh (RSS).[1] The RSS espouses a fascistic nationalist ideology of racial and civilizational supremacy, aiming at the creation of a Hindu-Aryan state that would transform all minority, non-Hindu groups into second-class citizens (for a brief analysis of the rise of Hindutva in the context of globalization, see Patnaik 2002). The communal violence in the fishing village of Marad, located in the northern Kerala district of Kozhikode, revealed how both the RSS and its Muslim fundamentalist adversaries, including the National Development Front (NDF), had succeeded in consolidating their power bases among the economically marginalized fisherfolk through a highlighting of religious divisions. Around 60 per cent of Marad's population is largely from the Araya ('Hindu') fishing community,[2] who, bureaucratically marked as 'Other Eligible Category' (OEC) for state welfare, are on the fringes of mainstream 'Hindu' society in Kerala, and the other 40 per cent are largely from the Muslim community.[3] In Kerala, the electoral balancing act between left and centrist coalitions has long held Hindutva politics at bay; however, since 1991 the state has seen the growth of fundamentalist forces, both Hindu and Muslim, following the Hindutva groups' demolition of the Babri Masjid (Krishnakumar 1998).

From May to October 2003, Marad was transformed into the scene of a prolonged political conflict between 'Muslim' and Araya ('Hindu') communities that I summarize here from an estimated 200 news reports running through this period that form the larger archive of this article.[4] The Marad conflict is significant for three reasons. First, occurring as it did in the aftermath of the Gujarat genocide, Marad showed how swiftly regional conflicts could be swept up into hegemonic, national and transnational plays of warring communities. The discourse around Marad, as I will show, was cast all too soon into ideological sense-making frameworks of violation and revenge between 'Hindus' and 'Muslims'. The first round of violence occurred in January 2002 when five persons (three Muslims, two Araya) were killed and fishing boats and huts were set ablaze after a false rumour broke out about a boy of one community molesting a girl of another community during the New Year celebrations (Sajeevan 2003). This incident invited the 'retaliatory' violence of 3 May 2003, when nine men, reportedly affiliated with the RSS, were killed on the beach at sunset, allegedly by a Muslim extremist organization, possibly the NDF (*Mathrubhoomi* 2003a). Alleging that the Muslim gang was allied with the Islamic extremist groups in Pakistan/Kashmir, the RSS and its electoral sibling, the BJP, demanded a national Central Bureau of Intelligence (CBI) inquiry, which the Kerala state government rejected (*Mathrubhoomi* 2003c; *New Indian Express* 2003b). The ruling coalition also refused to respond to accusations against the IUML minister, K. Kunjhalikutty (whose name has been linked to a variety of underhand enterprises ranging from running a sex racket to securing deals for the tourism industry) who was the immediate target of the Hindutva political attack at Marad. The way in which an 'Araya' could be metonymically transformed into 'Hindu'—the 'same' Hindu of 'Kashmir' and 'Gujarat'—and the north Kerala Muslim male is collapsed into the post-9/11 'Islamic terrorist' shows how the discourses of community and the bodies enacting violence are constructed as inseparable. Such a development was particularly surprising in Marad since the fishing community of the Arayas, whose RSS supporters were purportedly targeted by the Islamic groups, is not part of mainstream Hindu castes. The economically backward 'Araya' fisherfolk, as victims of the May 2003 violence, became representative of the 'Hindu wound', giving political mileage to the Hindutva leadership at the negotiating tables with the state government.

Second, the Hindutva group's strategy in Gujarat of using economically, culturally and politically marginalized communities to physically carry out their agendas of aggression (Balagopal 2002) seems to have been recreated in Marad in a different context. Fearing police harassment and revenge killings after the violence, over 1,500 Muslims fled the area en masse (*Madhyamam* 2003a). Arguably, this flight also had to do with the role that women in the community played by sheltering the attackers, who hid in the local mosque when the police arrived, a point that the RSS raised.[5] Stranded Muslim women, children and the elderly were accommodated in refugee camps within the Kozhikode district set up by political parties. As these families remained displaced from their homes, the Hindutva groups proceeded to battle the government on the political front by persisting in the demand for the CBI probe, and on the local front by blocking the return of Muslim families to Marad (*Madhyamam* 2003e). Aggrieved Araya women and families looted abandoned Muslim homes, carried away or destroyed consumer items such as television sets and kitchen appliances, and polluted wells with garbage, literally acting as the frontlines of the community (Gita 2003). Using Araya women as boundary-keepers to ward off Muslim families and to physically fence off the area for five months, the Marad RSS was able to win a major ideological triumph for Hindutva groups in Kerala, even as the ruling coalition held out against the CBI probe (*Mathrubhoomi* 2003c).

Third, the Hindutva strategy in Marad, which involved creating a closed, exclusionary 'Araya' community at the local level, necessarily involved an attack on the political citizenship of Muslims. Unable to return to the hostile locality for the next five months, women, children and the elderly remained uprooted in refugee camps and men disappeared under threat of arrests, until the state government reached an accord with the Hindutva groups while failing to reach a conclusion regarding the source of the violence itself (*Mathrubhoomi* 2003d).[6] The male leadership of Hindutva could trust the Araya women to perform the 'labour' of maintaining a hostile environment for Muslim families, as the state looked on. The gender intelligibility of violence, or the social sense-making of violence in gendered terms as rendered in the media, concealed a class politics in which 'Hindus' won symbolic gains in special citizenship through the bodies of lower-caste women who waged the physical struggle for them in Marad. This is not to state that Muslim families/women were purely victims uninvolved in the history of the struggle. It is to argue that this special citizenship is wrested from marginal figures: the Muslim woman is transformed into the political refugee asking for state charity, and the Muslim man, acquiring new, transnational dimensions after 9/11, into the 'Islamic terrorist'. And the political citizenship of Marad Muslims was sacrificed at the bargaining table between Hindutva forces and the state, which sought to protect its IUML partner's interests.

ENGENDERING VIOLENCE

By the feminist concept 'engendering' I underline my assumption, drawn from Scott (1988), that gender does not precede or follow its political context as a cultural ground or as ideological superstructure, but is embedded in the way that power relations are signified. Analysing the feminist writing of history, Scott shows how 'herstory', or the careful recovery of women's experiential voices, ends up asserting the uniqueness and difference of women, while traditional social history, or the writing of women's lives back into the fabric of political economy, becomes overly integrationist (ibid.: 18–22). Both miss, in her view, the 'silent and hidden operations of gender' or the way that gender signifies relations of power (ibid.: 42). I see Scott's insights as particularly useful for both reconstructing and interrogating history-in-the-making within the terms of the anti-capitalist, anti-fundamentalist feminist project that Alexander and Mohanty outline (1997: xlii). Alexander and Mohanty see religious fundamentalism as part of the processes of recolonization, inseparable from the nexus of state and capital (ibid.: xxv). The overall effort in this article from a feminist standpoint is to think through the intertwined immediacy of gender, power and violence that forms such a critical part of the logic of religious fundamentalism.

Such a perspective that critically examines the logic of gender and the logic of violence together is particularly relevant after Gujarat 2002 becomes available as a semiotically meaningful point of reference in public speech acts and in modes of representation. Even as progressive political forces termed Gujarat 'genocide', Hindutva had constructed its own triumphal narrative of Gujarat, one that projected it as an overdue victory of the violated 'Hindu'. The intertwined immediacy of gender, power and violence was particularly evident in the political contextualization of Marad. The discourses of community identities of 'Hindu' and 'Muslim' were territorialized through the imaginative geopolitics of gender (DeKoven 2001). Rather than view geographical features as inanimate entities, feminist scholars have shown how cultural codes of gender are interwoven into the language through which geography itself is articulated. Spaces and places are rhetorically framed in terms of gender difference and gender hierarchies that in turn sanction particular modes of action, such as conquest, occupation or development. In the rhetorical appeal of Hindutva leadership references to Marad, Kashmir and Gujarat play gendered roles of reference. Projected in Hindutva rhetoric as a national 'failure',

Kashmir is a sign of repeated defeat, an area colonized by Pakistan and by Islamic militant groups. After the Hindutva-organized genocide of Muslims, Gujarat, in contrast, represents the Hindu who refused to become a 'victim', or rather, one who responded effectively to the Muslim threat. In the symbolism of gendered geography generated by Hindutva leaders, Marad oscillated within the Kashmir/Gujarat gender code. Hindutva groups stated that Islamic terrorists were trying to turn Kerala into a 'Kashmir'[7] while Gujarat indicated the space where the Hindu had recaptured their rightful place, as evidenced in VHP leader, Praveen Togadia's speech in Marad that 'Muslims would not dare to do this in Gujarat' (*The Hindu* 2003).

In visual representations of Marad, the pictures of weeping, bereaved Araya women were embedded in news texts that referred to the possibly guilty Islamic 'terrorist' male (for example, *New Indian Express* 2003a). The Hindu male's emasculated status was silently referenced through the projection of Kashmir, as in the Union Home Minister L. K. Advani's statement that the Hindu 'minority' was being threatened in Marad the same way they were being intimidated in Kashmir (*Kerala Kaumudi* 2003). In terms of discursive geography, Marad was produced as a new site of violation of the Hindu, which then became a discursive field for engaging a logic of just retribution.

The idea of just retribution against the Muslim fundamentalists and their families formed the fuel for Araya women's mobilization in Marad. In this logic of violence and just retribution, Araya women played a key role that could expand our understanding of the role of women in right-wing organizations. Writers in a series of anthologies edited by Sarkar and Butalia (1995), Jayawardena and de Alwis (1996), and Jeffrey and Basu (1999) have analysed the appeal of Hindutva ideology and its promise of cultural identifications for women members. In Marad, we do not encounter the typical middle-class woman, the subject of Hindu cultural ideologies and identifications, who is analysed in feminist writings (Basu 1995; Sarkar 1995; Setalvad 1995). Instead, we see women of excluded, disempowered castes, who, as temporary pawns of Hindutva gender politics, were positioned to heighten the social and cultural intelligibility of the communal struggles. Methodologically, my focus on the media leads to a different emphasis from that of writers who have conducted ethnographic studies that explore the rationale of women's loyalties to Hindutva. The analysis of a communal conflict through its narrative logics shows the intertwined relations of gender, violence and citizenship, rather than the aspirations and agency of the women in the movement.

In the media, the women of Marad appeared to defend their families and their communities, their aggression apparently justified by the act of violence that preceded it. Once positioned as victims of the Muslim male attack, they played a critical role in the expansion of Hindu citizenship by granting power to male-dominated political bargaining groups. Since men of both communities were physically absent in the battle over the locality, newspaper reports appeared to feminize the battle between the communities. The state could conveniently remain a witness rather than an actor in the battle, since taking action would mean restraining Araya women who represented a bereaved, grieving community. The presence of the Araya women made the political citizenship of the Muslim community a non-issue. The engendering of the communal battle was thus directly tied into the political battle for citizenship.

The questions that this article asks are partly motivated by the occasion that prompted its writing. After Gujarat 2002, several of us, South Asian women scholars in the United States, decided to come together to work collectively on issues of gender, violence and community. We wondered how we could study the gender politics of South Asia after the rise of post-9/11 American imperialism, capitalist fundamentalism and religious militarism so as to remap our own multiple projects for social transformation. Given this context, this article explores the following questions: How do the discourses of Islamic terrorism and the acts of violence (imagined, threatened and real) help to mobilize and expand the scope of Hindu citizenship? How does state-sanctioned violence play into the transformations in cultural and political citizenship? How is gender critical to the project of the invisible, race-like[8] privileges of violence that Hindu groups can gain by rhetorically drawing on the 'global' fear of the Muslim? How is Muslim citizenship redefined in a way that politically marginalized the community? The theme that runs through this article is that of the gender intelligibility of community-coded violence and its victims, and how that intelligibility is constituted through narratives of violation and retribution implicated in unfolding agendas of power. The ideologies that tie together gender, violence and community, I hope to show, are intimately linked to practices of citizenship. The article is structured in three dramatic units that follow the chronology of the events: the act of violation, the act of retribution, and the return of order.

To illustrate these events, I am drawing from news photographs and around 200 news items that depict the three stages which appeared in three major Malayalam language newspapers of Kerala, the Muslim-sympathetic *Madhyamam*, the largely liberal *Mathrubhoomi*, and the conservative *Manorama*, and the national English newspaper, *New Indian Express*. Discursive practices are tested against events, assumed to be co-extensive or constitutive of the symbolic and real logic of events. I focus especially on the news photographs because they dramatically foreground the gender politics and cultural intelligibility of the events as they were coded into meaningful terms of gender difference. In doing so, I draw on Butler's insights into how gender works to 'produce' intelligibility: what is and is not intelligible, what will or will not signify, she writes, is itself established through moves of power that produce the 'field of appearances' through *foreclosure*, *erasure* and *negation* (1992: 19).

ACT OF VIOLATION: FEMINIZING GRIEF

Perhaps the act of violation could be reconstructed to begin with the newspaper photographs of the men killed at Marad. The attack that killed nine men who sat smoking and playing cards next to the Marad beach temple made front-page headlines in the Malayalam and English press. A news photo featured four dhoti-clad dead bodies laid out simply on the bare floor[9]: not yet Hindu in the sense that they would become in the next few months. As the media reflected the shock of events following the horrifying attack, curiously, visual culture translated the gender of grief as exclusively feminine. The living community was represented in newspaper photographs primarily through the distraught women whose sorrow overcame the self-consciousness of representation. Female relatives clung to each other in photographs, bodies close, intertwined, seeking support from those who had only helplessness to give.[10] Typically, caption writers glossed over the gender of the feminine bodies with headings such as 'relatives burst into tears as the bodies of victims are brought back to Marad beach' which accompanied a visual of women wailing (*Madhyamam* 2003a). The feminization of grief was evident later, too, as men remained completely invisible: one could wonder, did not the dead men have brothers, fathers, grandfathers, sons? Yet none of these was visible. In the stillness after the funerals, the picture showed women, lost in the numb liminal space between life and death, sitting amidst unknowing, playful children (*Madhyamam* 2003b).

The visit of politicians of various hues reinforced the feminization of the Hindu community through the figures of its women. During the week of 5–12 May, as upper-caste male politicians arrived at the homes of this Dalit community to console the women, their body postures, relative to one another, replayed sedimented ideologies of caste politics. Since most of Kerala's non-Brahmin communities are fish-eaters, the women selling fish are constant visitors to middle-class homes and colonies, where they are known for their bargaining powers. The women of the fishing community who normally appear at kitchen doors to sell fish are rarely allowed inside homes; often they occupy the steps just outside the door, signifying their own space at the threshold that marks the boundary between the upper castes and marginalized communities. Upper-caste men enjoy a distinctive freedom in dealing with the fish-sellers that is directly connected to the gendered context of trade. The news photos of male politicians visiting Marad followed this representational convention of the gendered ordering of vertical space within the photo: upright male politicians looked on in concern at weeping women crouched on the floor in two photos (*Madhyamam* 2003d; *New Indian Express* 2003a) and women on a bed in another, producing a strange sense of broken barriers (*Madhyamam* 2003b; *Madhyamam* 2003d).

Another photo, captioned, 'Healing Touch', showed the BJP union minister and Hindutva leader, I.D. Swami, reaching out a hand to touch the head of a suppliant, half-bent woman.[11] A similar photograph showed a grieving woman lying at the feet of BJP union minister O. Rajagopal.[12] The 'Hindu woman's' appealing posture to Hindu male leaders continued even months later, where a sobbing woman, wife of a local RSS leader who had died in the attack, appeared with arms folded as if before a deity to the deputy prime minister and Hindutva leader L.K. Advani.[13] In a photo captioned 'Ceaseless Mourning', the chief minister, A.K. Anthony, and his all-male entourage loomed above women whose arms were outstretched in gestures of helplessness, appeal and accusation (*Mathrubhoomi* 2003a). To all appearances, it seemed as if the victims of Muslim violence at Marad were visibly women, with men of the community or male relatives of victims never positioned to plead before the male politicians.

THE 'ISLAMIC TERRORIST'

If the affected Hindu males of Marad were absent, the Muslim male occupied a curious status of visibility. Physically absent from pictures like his Hindu counterpart, the Muslim male nevertheless appeared, synecdochically, in the form of numerous arms and weapons unearthed by the police in Marad (*Madhyamam* 2003c; *New Indian Express* 2003c; Prashanth 2003). Even as political parties blamed the state for turning a blind eye to the growth of Muslim extremist groups in the state, the photographs of long knives, swords and gelatine bombs arranged in vertical lines for the media reappeared in news visuals such as that in *India Today Malayalam*.[14] The weapons were found in a deserted house belonging to a Muslim man, and from inside the Marad mosque, and some, in an unusual move, after excavating the mosque grounds. These photographs were accompanied by the discursive projection of the Muslim extremist which political parties across the board quickly held responsible for the incident. The BJP leader, O. Rajagopal, accused a Muslim League minister of involvement in the event and compared the attack to a Kashmir-type plot to 'eliminate Hindus' (*Madhyamam* 2003d). The RSS immediately asked for a CBI inquiry because the attacks, in their view, were an act of 'ethnic cleansing' adopted by Islamic extremist groups in Kashmir (*New Indian Express* 2003a). RSS state secretary A.R. Mohanan said that the incident was a deliberate and pre-planned attempt by Muslim fundamentalist organizations to create safe pockets in the strategic coastal areas, while the RSS press release accused Pakistan's Inter-Services Intelligence (ISI) of fomenting a conspiracy to capture the coastlines (RSS 2003).[15]

Cast into a post-9/11 political context, the symbolic figure of the Muslim male appeared to proliferate transnational, coast-to-coast connections that ran horizontally from Kerala to the Middle Eastern nations, and north to Kashmiri and Pakistani extremist groups. Kerala's ancient coastline that once attracted Portuguese, Dutch, German, Christian, Jewish and Arab traders now became geopolitically significant for the hypothetical sea links to the Middle East. These statements also drew on the fact that many north Kerala Muslim homes have immigrant kin in nations such as the UAE, Saudi Arabia, Bahrain and Kuwait. The shadowy projection of the para-national Muslim extremist in turn positioned the community on the borderlines of the nation state. The array of long swords and knives that formed the discursive body of the threatening Muslim male constituted the visual logic for the disenfranchisement of the community that was to follow. In the subsequent days, over 150 Muslim men were arrested, many fled the area, and Friday prayers were held in mosques all over Calicut city with police presence, following the discovery of arms at the Marad Juma Masjid (*New Indian Express* 2003d).

The visualization of Hindu/Araya community through the grief-stricken bodies of the Araya women, the significant and consistent absence of the men, and the projection of the Islamic male extremist formed the germinating elements for the structuring of what could be termed the act of violation. Engendering grief heightened the outrage against the aggressors, even as it enabled the Hindutva's rhetorical projection of the Hindus as an effeminate, besieged community under threat. Discursively, a 'Hindu' community was constituted from the traditionally marginalized Araya groups through the gendered narrative of violation: the bereaved wives, mothers, sisters, and grandmothers framed against the invisible 'Islamic militant'. The invisibility of Araya/ RSS men also conveniently blanketed the issue of the murders in January 2002. The running theme of a 'revenge killing' was overshadowed by the police discovery of an extraordinary amount of unearthed weapons and crude bombs, which suggested a larger plan of attack on a scale unprecedented in the state (ibid.). The Hindu community, visually represented by its vulnerable women, rhetorically appeared as present and potential targets of Islamic terrorism. The narrative of violation gathered intelligibility through the visual depiction of victims and perpetrators. Curiously, the logic of the unfolding events left untouched the real acts of everyday male mobilization and training that the Hindu fundamentalist organization, RSS, has been organizing for the last thirty years in Kerala, and which the Muslim militant organizations in various forms have been carrying out in Kerala since the 1990s (Krishnakumar 1998). While NDF's political patronage by Muslim League ministers was called into question, the RSS was cloaked safely in the rhetoric of Hindu victimhood. The state compensated for its law and order 'failure' with a communal balancing act whose dimensions only grew with the developing events, and which, as I hope to show, resulted in the expansion of Hindu citizenship.

ACT OF RETRIBUTION: WOMEN AT THE FRONTLINES

In retrospect, a single photograph seems to have had a prophetic quality in its uncanny ability to predict the strategic turn of events after the initial shock of the Marad killings. The photograph contrasted with the gender conventions described earlier: it showed a dramatically defiant Uma Unni, the BJP city secretary, holding her arms outstretched to physically block the chief minister from visiting her injured husband and son, who were still at the Calicut hospital. Around her milled hospital staff, policemen and male politicians or leaders witnessing this event not daring to bypass her or to make room for the head of the state government.[16] This striking gesture from a female politician and the space that she could occupy with sanction from her political party foreshadowed the tactic that the Hindutva parties were about to deploy in Marad: in the coming months from the end of May through October 2003, women were at the forefront of the community, appearing as the active vanguard of the Hindutva mobilization in the locality. However, they were invariably absent from the public sphere outside the locality; the leadership at the Marad Hindu Raksha Samiti meeting in Calicut city was visibly comprised of upper-caste, older Hindu men and religious leaders as seen in one newspaper photo.[17] All authoritative speakers representing the 'mind' of the community in the press were male; the women appeared, stereotypically enough, as the 'body' that was enforcing the effects of male speech. In other words, male leaders produced ideologies that overwrote the actions of the women, so to speak, on the ground. For example, VHP organizing secretary and Hindu Aikyavedi general secretary Kummanam Rajasekharan appeared behind his office desk with photographs of divinities such as Rama, Shiva-Parvati and RSS ideologues, comfortably seated in his own self-created environment. In the interview, he argued that the Muslim families could not return to Marad until the Hindu 'wound' had healed (Ajayan 2003: 12–15).

The highlights of this 'phase of retribution' for the 'wound' included Araya women's organized opposition to two initiatives by the state. The first, which took place two months after the killings, was the staged and failed resettlement of Mariayambi, an older Muslim woman who attempted to reoccupy her own home with police assistance and was ousted by a militant group of 500 Araya/Hindu women (*Madhyamam* 2003f). The second was Araya women's success in blocking the state authorities' efforts to clean up the wrecked homes and surrounding areas of Muslim families before the resettlement took place. The Hindutva groups, deploying a gender strategy, countered both these state initiatives. Using women at the forefront to resist the state-sponsored initiatives, the RSS cloaked its male leadership with a female visage even as it effectively expanded its control over the locality through the bodies of its women volunteers.

The visual representation of the communal crisis underwent a radical shift as images of angry women mobs confronting police and state officials made their dramatic appearance in the press. The scenes of the feminized, grief-struck community were now replaced with the images of the rage of the violated community, again represented through its women members. The first targets of this rage were six Muslim women and their two children who were resettled back into their Marad homes. After fifty-five days at the refugee camp, these women returned with the protection of a 200-strong police force at 11:15 am on 25 June. Until 7.40 that night, their homes were surrounded by a raging mob of 500 Hindu women who shouted obscenities and laid waste the outside property as the police watched (Soman 2003). Finding the situation intolerable, one of the families returned to the Muslim refugee camp, while Mariayambi and her daughter-in-law, Nabisa, stayed on, inviting fresh wrath from the Araya women. Juxtaposed photos showed the contrasting demeanour of the Muslim and Hindu women, so that the entire event appeared as if it were purely a battle between women. One photograph depicted a sorrowful Mariayambi being escorted into her home by the police; just next to it stood a crowd of outraged women, one of them furiously gesticulating at a police officer (*Mathrubhoomi* 2003e). Another juxtaposed pair showed the small tiled house that Mariayambi had just entered, with Hindu women milling around the police demanding that the Muslim women be sent back immediately, according to the caption (*Madhyamam* 2003e). Paired with this was the photo of Mariayambi and Nabisa, carrying the two babies, and standing inside their house with windows barred.

Within a day the mob of Araya women had become even more impatient. Around fifty women who tried to break into Mariayambi's house when lunch was brought for the family were stopped by the police force, including women police officers. When Mariayambi came out to use the toilet, located outside as it is in many Kerala homes, a host of women tried to force their way in. When they were blocked by the police, the frustrated group, led by Uma Unni, then laid the property waste, pulling down plantain trees, and in a move with more immediate implications, breaking the door of the outside toilet. A photograph showed women about to pull down a small tree in the background, even as some women dragged out a broken down plantain tree to the mass of the uprooted vegetation that already filled the small plot around the home and the drinking water well (*Madhyamam* 2003f). The accompanying news report said that the police did nothing to prevent the destruction of property, and did not stop the women who were making off with the door of the toilet (ibid.). The women were only responsive to the Araya male leadership who checked further attack through commands via cell phones that women leaders were carrying. Bolstered by this performance, the Araya groups in turn boycotted the state government's negotiations set up for the resettlement of Muslim families.

On the night of 30 June, three days after she was 'resettled', Mariayambi, her daughter-in-law Nabisa, and her children left again for the Muslim refugee colony, after giving the government a statement that she was unable to survive in her own house, where she had lived for twenty-five years (*Madhyamam* 2003g). While Araya Samajam women workers harassed Mariayambi, their male counterparts boycotted government negotiating tables and refused to participate in the political process of reconcilement until their demands were conceded. With women presenting an aggressive front, and the men boycotting the negotiations, the community as a whole circumvented any process of dialogue.

Simultaneously, the RSS and VHP rhetorically drew on the metaphor of the 'wound' of the Hindu. VHP state organizing secretary, Kummanam Rajasekharan, said in two interviews that the attackers had castrated the Hindu men who were killed in Marad (Ajayan 2003). The language of the 'wound' that would not heal until a CBI inquiry was in place (that would concede the implicit para-national status of the attack) appeared to call for direct physical retribution. As Muslim women and children continued to live in refugee camps with twenty or thirty in a room, the VHP general secretary, Praveen Togadia, who visited the area, branded all Muslim families who fled the areas as 'criminals' who wanted to convert Kerala into Kashmir. Drawing on a familiar rhetorical ploy of Hindutva, he called for the re-masculinization of the Hindu community, as demonstrated by Gujarat where Muslims would not 'dare' to repeat any outrageous acts (*The Hindu* 2003). The criminalization of the entire Muslim community, especially those who had fled the area and were living in refugee camps, continued throughout the subsequent months. Although the Muslim male extremist seemed to be the perpetrator of the crime, the women and children in refugee camps now were invisible under his shadow. As the Hindu community was feminized in the rhetoric of victimhood, the Muslim community appeared to be represented by the paradoxical absence of the male Muslim, with the women seeming to provide a safe haven for them. The Muslim community appeared to be masculinized in the visual rhetoric of the unearthed weapons. With the Muslim male identified as the direct agent of violence, the Muslim women were silently implicated as those who had protected and sheltered the men.

MUSLIM WOMEN'S LOSS OF CITIZENSHIP

The feminization of the Hindu community and the masculinization of the Muslim community marginalized the fate of the Muslim women who formed the bulk of the 500 people living in the cramped refugee camps. With sixty-five Muslim men arrested the day of the killings, and over 150 arrested over the next week, the visual representation of the Muslim community was confined to its female members as victims of the conflict. Photographs showed Muslim women with knapsacks and loads on their heads, carrying their belongings with them on their way out of Marad, in some cases, with police escort.[18] Muslim men were conspicuous in their absence; visual representations of the women carrying heavy loads bore testimony to the men who had fled the area. This absence also meant women had to shoulder most of the work of resettlement, including childcare and education of the older children, who had to be moved out of Muslim-majority schools in the area due to fears of retaliation (*New Indian Express* 2003e). The victim photographs obscured the history of the communal conflict, and the role that Muslim women had played in sustaining community identity, although not as aggressively as their Hindu counterparts.

Muslim women who said they had nothing to do with the actual killings gained the maximum coverage in the press. 'We found our house destroyed and furniture damaged. How could I send my seven-year-old child to school?' asked Subaida, who moved out of Marad in fear after her home was ransacked by Hindu families (ibid.). The ransacking of abandoned Muslim homes continued sporadically during the five-month period of the 'just retribution' that was instigated by the RSS. As late as July, an informally constituted women's commission (whose members, drawn from groups associated with the opposition Left Democratic Front, convened to address the resettlement issue in the wake of government inaction) reported that the looting of deserted homes was continuing even in the area of Chulliyanvalappu, where there was not even a single person who was associated with the killings. When the homes of forty-eight Muslim families who lived in the area were first checked, it was found that the electronic items and household gadgets had all been stolen. The looters then came back to carry away all the furniture in the house, including beds and tables. Finally, they even dismantled and took away the wooden doors and window frames.

The women's commission's efforts to contact the BJP women leaders and the women of the Araya Samajam to join in negotiations were all unsuccessful. Muslim women like Kadisha, speaking from the Pallithodi refugee camp, said:

> Two and a half months have passed now. By the time a decision is reached, will there be anything left for us in Marad? The homes have all been vandalized with the collaboration of the police. Now they are dismantling the doors and windows. When will the government reach a decision? (*Madhyamam* 2003h)

After four months in refugee camps, a group of six Muslim women met the regional government officials to settle on a date for rehabilitation. By this time, there were around 2,000 individuals from over 300 families dispersed in three refugee camps run by the Marxist party and the Muslim League (*New Indian Express* 2003g). The women stated that as many as twenty-four families were living in a small room and they were unable to continue like this for much longer. 'Why should we be punished for the crimes committed by a few?' asked Jameela, who led the small delegation (*New Indian Express* 2003f). As a camp coordinator pointed out, the crime branch had already arrested all those who were responsible for the killings, and the displaced Muslim families were even ready to keep out any close relatives whose involvement was suspected by the BJP-RSS (*New Indian Express* 2003g).

The stalemate of the refugee camps and Marad blockade continued even after a court order in August clearly held the state responsible for the resettlement of the Muslim families; the state then passed on this responsibility to local agencies and officials (*Mathrubhoomi* 2003b). In response to a petition filed by Cheriyambi, a Muslim woman living at the refugee camp, the court stated that the state was obliged to fulfil its duty to protect the rights of all citizens. Despite this court order in August, the state did not use police force to resettle families; instead, they continued to woo Hindutva parties for a political settlement. In a similar and recurrent acquiescence of agency, the state's move to facilitate rehabilitation by cleaning wells and repairing structural damages on Muslim property was again challenged and forced to a halt by militant mobs of women (*New Indian Express* 2003h, 2003i).

The more active role played by several Muslim women and the legal initiatives they took did not gain space in the visual representations of the conflict. Most of the reports concerning Muslim women in the refugee camps were published by *Madhyamam*, the pro-Muslim daily. Living in refugee camps, Muslim women bore the brunt of maintaining families even as roughly 150 Muslim men were held in jail on charges yet to be substantiated. Powerful Hindu groups bargained with the state for a CBI inquiry; an equally powerful Muslim lobby exerted pressure against it, prompting the state to keep the issue unresolved. This battle of interests however primarily disinherited the Muslim families who were forced to abandon their homes and become economic refugees without political rights. As Azara said in helplessness in an interview at the camp: 'The state has made us into beggars' (*Deshabhimani* 2003).

THE RETURN OF ORDER, OR A PHOTO-OP ENDING

In the view of increasing pressure for rehabilitation of the refugees, including cases filed by the Muslim women, the state government finally negotiated a tripartite settlement involving Muslim and Hindu leaders. It was agreed that the state would look into the possibility of a CBI inquiry. The accord granted unprecedented compensation amounts to the kin of victims, and assured state government employment for the dependants of each victim. Thrown in was a special development package for Marad including healthcare, potable water, and road, electricity, and seawall construction—all this being especially suspect in the context of the state's own thrust to 'develop' the coastlines for tourism. All cases registered in connection with the agitators at Marad were to be withdrawn (*Mathrubhoomi* 2003d). Hindutva men and women remained outside the jurisdiction of the law, as the state openly played community cards to settle the issues. The photograph of the accord signing once again exclusively featured the male gender: politicians from Hindu and Muslim communities with the chief minister.[19] Another photograph was equally revealing: Araya Samajam secretary Thekkedathu Suresh arriving to address the women members' meeting to explain the accord to them. The photo showed a roomful of women waiting, seated, as Suresh entered the gathering. He asked the women to cooperate with the rehabilitation measures since their 'struggle to get justice' had finally yielded results (*New Indian Express* 2003j). The success of the Samajam, he said, was the 'result of the suffering our women have endured'. Even as the photo laid bare the gender hierarchy within the Araya Samajam, it also appropriated women into the success story of the RSS's first political experiment in Kerala.

The Hindutva groups savoured victory, and the state had its own moment of triumph for the restoration of secular co-existence within a tension-filled area. Colour photographs of Hindu-Muslim reunions appeared on the front pages of the major dailies. Titled 'The New Sweetness of Oneness', a photograph depicted an Araya/Hindu woman, Shailaja, serving tea to her three Muslim women neighbours who had returned to the area (*Mathrubhoomi* 2003e). Notably, these women were from an area where not a single family had been connected to the killings. The Hindu woman thus appeared as the gracious neighbour in the photo, with the Muslim women cast as the recipients of hospitality, possibly suggesting the new power relations that could colour the local relationships. Another photograph translated the bitterly fought political battle into a sentimental teenage reunion. In the photo, a Muslim girl, taller or possibly older, held a Hindu girl close to her. Their religious identities were clearly marked through the headscarf and sandalwood paste.[20] Their upturned faces were directed towards the camera. The caption read, 'The Reunion of Innocence', although the religious markings on the two girls proclaimed the rigidity of this innocence that had to be carefully coded in separate religious markings.

The harmonious front-page spreads of reunion were accompanied by smaller pictures: one showed the registration counter where returning Muslims, again women and children, were checking in before occupying their own homes.[21] Another, more grim set of photos, showed grief-struck Muslim women, many of whom had left behind families in camps who had yet not gathered the courage to return to Marad; another showed a woman fainting in shock as she saw her bare home.[22] The incompleteness of the resettlement project was even more distressing: around 300 women, children and elderly who were brought all the way back from the camp were temporarily housed in miserable conditions at the school near the beach. Clearly, the incoming families were filtered in through a local net that was not scanning Muslims alone, but targeting particular households and people from particular localities (*Deshabhimani* 2003).

CONCLUSION: VIOLENCE AND CITIZENSHIP

This article arose out of a South Asian feminist scholar collective's effort to evolve ways of understanding the connections of gender, violence and community following Gujarat 2002 even as we plan strategies for future collaboration and effective intervention. Through the analysis of media representations of a communal conflict in Kerala, I have attempted to show how communal violence makes 'sense' or becomes 'intelligible' often through the mediation of gender ideologies. The media representations of gender difference—the visibility of women's grief vs the invisibility of male grief; the visibility of women's anger vs the invisibility of male collaborators/organizers; the visibility of women's vulnerability vs the visibility of male aggressors in the form of arms and weapons—are not unconventional. However, by weaving these largely traditional patterns of gender difference into narratives of violation and retribution, the media inevitably intertwined the gender logic of these representations with the logic of violence. Gender ideologies mediate the very act of making cultural sense out of violence and the logic of violence/retribution.

The Marad incident also forms an example of the discursive production of a community in and through acts of violence; arguably one that forms the barely hidden agenda of Hindutva, starting with the demolition of the Babri Masjid in 1991, but more radically asserted in Gujarat. The way in which Araya women were consumed by Hindutva's political agenda shows how community loyalties are discursively produced in times of political conflict, often in ways that tear away at solidarity between women of the same class. The fisherwomen, who despite marginalization represent a vocal presence in their own localities, formed a powerful resource for Hindutva to redefine extreme forms of community solidarity. At the frontlines of the community, the Araya women also played a critical part in reconstituting what the sanctioned or socially tolerable limits of violence might be, especially violence towards those temporarily weaker than themselves. This scenario means that some of the concepts that guided feminist analyses of women's participation in Hindutva, such as that of traditional gender socialization into proper Hindu social roles of mother/wife (see essays in Sarkar and Butalia 1995), may not be as powerful a factor amongst the socio-economic classes that now form the right's new asset. The violence/retribution cycle as it occurred in Marad was not the end product of a process of community formation or socialization, where, for example, the community slowly melts into Hindutva politics, and is then swept up into extreme acts of violence. Instead, the incident effectively demonstrated that communities can be constituted through real and imagined violations. The cultural intelligibility of such communities rests on narratives of violation that make sense through gender relations: the loss of sons, husbands, fathers, and kin, or the actual or narrated rape of women (Kannabiran 1996), or even simply symbolic losses, such as loss of 'Hindu pride' evidenced in Kashmir posing a threat to the Araya folk in south India. Written into ready-made scripts of communities at war, the media representations of these narratives show how they function as powerful cultural logics for retribution. In this cycle of violation/retribution, violence does not precede or follow gender politics, but is manifested through the cultural intelligibility of gender relations. As seen in Marad, the logic of violence and retribution is expressed visibly as a battle between Hindu and Muslim women in ways that left the state's responsibility out of the picture. The logic of violence and retribution directly cast questions of minority citizenship into a predatory chain where the weak attack the weak. The interlinked logics of gender, violence and community are also questions of citizenship, where displacement and marginalization of communities stripped of political citizenship merely appear as cultural acts of community identity confrontations. It must be noted that Muslim women too acted in the interests of their family, kin and community, thus reinforcing the logic of communalism. Politicizing the cultural logic of fundamentalism is thus critical for confronting its deployment of gender.

This article also reveals the importance of the media in constituting and reflecting the logic of communal violence. As I have pointed out, the media used 'everyday' conventions of the representation of gender difference (visibility/invisibility of women; male/female power hierarchies) that in turn provided the logic of violation and retribution so essential to the popular understanding of conflict. The role of the media, in their various guises, raises important questions for feminist organizing. How might we develop a media strategy that analyses and counters dominant tropes of communal violation and conflict? How can feminist groups build strategies for alliances with media workers committed to gender justice to ensure that we have live veins of communication and solidarity in times of crisis, and in times of order? The everyday representational politics of gender in times of order, as we have seen, are inseparable from those in times of violence, indeed, in ways that call into question the very distinction between order and violence that Jeganathan (2000) has problematized. How may we manoeuvre spaces of representations within prominent media outlets to ensure that the cultural determinations of gender and the social order they underpin may be rewritten in terms that challenge the binaries of order and violence? What kinds of community can we form that would disarticulate the alliances (of state, capital and religio-patriarchal community) built through structures of gendered violence and through promises of power for women, in our work and in our lives within institutions?

ACKNOWLEDGEMENTS

I thank my father, K.T. Zacharias, for encouraging me to work on Kerala politics and culture and my mother, Annie George, for making sure that I did. Without the 'Madison Collective 2003'— Saadia Toor, Kamala Visweswaran, Angana Chatterji, Lubna Chaudhry, Sujata Moorti, Manali Desai, and Sukanya Banerjee—this article would not have been completed; without Angana's and Lubna's superb editing, it could not have been reshaped. From Kerala, Shahina, Bindu, Reshma, Devika, and Jayan stepped in at critical moments to help with facts and fiction. K. Ajitha who heads Anweshi, the Kerala women's organization, helped me immensely with feedback, as did Manu and Chandran. Thampy Kakkanadan's promptness in sending me sharp and relevant material as well as careful documentation work by Lal Lukose and Mansoor provided the ground for the news analysis.

NOTES

1. Started in 1925, the RSS is only open to Hindu males of the upper castes. As the authors of a campaign that investigated the foreign funding sources of the organization note, the RSS 'maintains no membership records; it has resisted being registered with the Government of India as a public/charitable trust; it has no bank accounts and pays no income tax'. The RSS plays a key role in the production of Hindutva ideologies in particular localities through its *shakha*s (cells) which train male *swayamsevak*s (volunteers) who will then continue to work for the Sangh (as the RSS is broadly known). The Sangh has created and propagated organizations in every facet of socio-political life in India—from political parties to children's centres, trade unions and militias (see *The Foreign Exchange of Hate: IDRF and the American Funding of Hindutva*, Sabrang Communications and South Asia Citizens Web, 2002, at www.stopfundinghate.org).

2. The Arayas are traditionally a fishing community settled in various areas along Kerala's coastline whose labour-related history predates that of modern caste politics. Given Kerala's rich coastline, the fisher folk took on various caste and religious hues. Today, Kerala's fisherfolk include Hindus, Christians and Muslims; all these communities are on the margins of mainstream society in terms of developmental indices such as education, health and income.

3. The growth of fundamentalist organizations in Kerala, which is noted for its achievements in literacy and education, has largely occurred in the last decade. While the RSS and the Communist Party of India (Marxist) or CPI (M) have a running feud in Kannur district, by and large Kerala is free of communal conflict. The state's caste lines are so strongly drawn into

electoral polarizations that it has been impossible for Hindutva parties to forge a unity based on Hindu identity. Until the May 2004 elections they had not managed to capture even a single assembly seat in Kerala. Since the Hindutva-led demolition of the Babri Masjid in 1991, Islamic organizations ranging from the militant to secular have grown in northern Kerala, often overlapping membership with the Indian Union Muslim League (IUML). The tension in Marad reflected the larger polarization of Hindu/Muslim alliances in northern Kerala, which has a significant Muslim population (almost 40 per cent). Although the northern Kerala Muslim community is socio-economically marginalized, the remittances from expatriates in west Asia (Middle East for the US) to their families have invited resentment from Hindu-related castes in the area (despite the fact that such inflows began to decline after the Gulf war). The Muslim community itself saw the Congress and the Communists as failing to protect them in the aftermath of the Babri Masjid, leading to the growth of a range of organizations, among which was the banned Islamic Sevak Sangh (ISS), a mirror organization, it would appear, of the RSS. While the ISS was banned along with the RSS, it appears to have regrouped under various other organizations, one of which is the NDF. The RSS-NDF battle at Marad thus reflected the political trends in fundamentalist organizing that had been taking shape in northern Kerala since 1991 (synthesized from Krishnakumar 1998, 2003).

4. The news reports are mainly drawn from the Malayalam newspapers, *Malayala Manorama, Mathrubhoomi, Madhyamam,* and detailed citations for incidents follow in each section of the article.

5. Interview with Suresh Thekkedath, Marad RSS leader, June 2004.

6. The main terms of the accord were that (*i*) the government would look into the possibility of a CBI inquiry even while a Crime Branch inquiry was underway; (*ii*) one of the dependents of those killed in Marad would get a government job; (*iii*) the government would pay a compensation of about $20,000 each to the bereaved families.

7. Such statements came from top Hindutva leaders, such as the VHP's Praveen Togadia, as in *Malayala Manorama* (2003); as well as the RSS ideologue, P. Parameswaran (2003), in the *Organiser*, the official publication of the RSS.

8. I make comparisons between power structures built on the differences amid racial communities in the West and community/caste/religion-based differences in India that sanction privileges for dominant communities.

9. *Madhyamam*, 3 May 2003, p. 9.

10. *Madhyamam*, 3 May 2003, p. 1; *New Indian Express*, 4 May 2003, p. 1.

11. *New Indian Express*, 6 May 2003, p. 1.

12. *Mathrubhoomi*, 7 May 2003.

13. *New Indian Express*, 25 September 2003, p. 1.

14. 21 May 2003, p. 40.

15. 'Spreading Tentacles of the ISI in Kerala', RSS press release, 9 May 2003. Available at: http://www.hvk.org/articles/0503/111.html.

16. *Madhyamam* 7 May 2003, p. 1.
17. *New Indian Express*, 21 May 2003, p. 1.
18. *Madhyamam*, 21 May 2003, p. 1 and 4 May 2003, p. 3.
19. *Mathrubhoomi*, 6 October 2003, p. 1.
20. *Madhyamam* 11 October 2003, p. 1.
21. *Madhyamam*, 11 October 2003, p. 1.
22. *Madhyamam*, 11 October 2003, p. 9.

REFERENCES

Ajayan, M.E. (2003). 'Hindu Hridayangalile Murivunakkiyittu Mathi Punaradhivasam', *Keralasabdam*, 10 August, pp. 12–15.

Alexander, M. Jacqui and Chandra Talpade Mohanty (1997). 'Introduction: Genealogies, Legacies, Movements', in M.J. Alexander and C.T. Mohanty (eds), *Feminist Genealogies, Colonial Legacies, Democratic Futures*, pp. xiii–xlii. New York and London: Routledge.

Balagopal, K. (2002). 'Reflections on "Gujarat Pradesh" of "Hindu Rashtra"', *Economic and Political Weekly*, pp. 2117–19.

Basu, Amrita (1995). 'Feminism Inverted: The Gendered Imaginary and Real Women of Hindu Nationalism', in Tanika Sarkar and Urvashi Butalia (eds), *Women and the Hindu Right*, pp. 158–80. New Delhi: Kali for Women.

Butler, Judith (1990). *Gender Trouble: Feminism and the Subversion of Identity*. London and New York: Routledge.

——— (1992). 'Contingent Foundations', in J. Butler and J.W. Scott (eds), *Feminists Theorize the Political*, pp. 3–21. New York and London: Routledge.

DeKoven, Marianne (ed.) (2001). *Feminist Locations: Global and Local, Theory and Practice*. New Brunswick, NJ: Rutgers University Press.

Deshabhimani (2003). 'Sarkar Njangale Thendikalakki', 13 October, p. 1.

Gita (2003). 'Kurukkanum Kunjadum', *Madhyamam*, 14 November, pp. 28–29.

Jayawardena, Kumari and Malathi de Alwis (eds) (1996). *Embodied Violence: Communalising Women's Sexuality in South Asia*. London: Zed Books.

Jeffrey, Patricia and Amrita Basu (1999). *Resisting the Sacred and the Secular: Women's Activism and Politicized Religion in South Asia*. New Delhi: Kali for Women.

Jeganathan, Pradeep (2000). 'A Space for Violence', in P. Chatterjee and P. Jeganathan (eds), *Subaltern Studies XI: Community, Gender and Violence*, pp. 37–65. New Delhi: Permanent Black.

Kannabiran, Kalpana (1996). 'Rape and the Construction of Communal Identity', in Kumari Jayawardena and Malathi de Alwis (eds), *Embodied Violence*, pp. 28–43. London: Zed Books.

Krishnakumar, R. (1998). 'Concern in Kerala', *Frontline*, 20 March. Available at: http://www.flonnet.com/fl1505/15051230.htm

——— (2003). 'An Emerging Threat', *Frontline*, 28 February. Available at: http://www.flonnet.com/fl2004/stories/20030228003704000.htm

Parameswaran, P. (2003). 'Marad is a Warning', *Organizer*, 8 June. Available at: http://www.hvk.org/articles/0703/138.html

Patnaik, Prabhat (2002). 'A Decade of Reaction', *Akhbar*, 5 December. Available at: http://www.indowindow.com/akhbar/article.php?article=136&category=2&issue=19.

Prashanth, M. P. (2003). 'Motive Was to Ignite A Riot', *New Indian Express*, 5 May, p. 1.

Sajeevan (2003). 'Marad: Oru Kimvadanthiyil Polinjathu 14 Jeevithangal', *Kerala Kaumudi*, 5 May, p. 5.

Sarkar, Tanika (1995). 'Heroic Women, Mother Goddesses: Family and Organization in Hindutva Politics', in Tanika Sarkar and Urvashi Butalia (eds), *Women and the Hindu Right*, pp. 181–215. New Delhi: Kali for Women.

Sarkar, Tanika and Urvashi Butalia (eds) (1995). *Women and the Hindu Right*. New Delhi: Kali for Women.

Scott, Joan W. (1988). *Gender and the Politics of History*. New York: Columbia Press.

Setalvad, Teesta (1995). 'The Woman Shiv Sainik and Her Sister Swayamsevika', in Tanika Sarkar and Urvashi Butalia (eds), *Women and the Hindu Right*, pp. 233–44. New Delhi: Kali for Women.

Soman, T. (2003). 'Maradu Ashantiyude Mulmunayil Punaradhivasam, *Mathrubhoomi*, 26 June, p. 1.

NEWSPAPERS

Kerala Kaumudi (2003), 'Koottakkolakku Pinnil NDF: Advani', 7 May, 1.

Madhyamam (2003a). 'Kootta Palayanam', 4 May, p. 3.

Madhyamam (2003b). 'Maradu CBI Answeshanam Nadathanam', 5 May, p. 12.

Madhyamam (2003c). 'Marad: Judicial Anweshanam Nadathum; Veendum Ayudha Sekharam Kandethi', 8 May, p. 1.

Madhyamam (2003d). 'Marad Akramatthil League Manthrikku Panku: Rajagopal', 12 May, p. 1.

Madhyamam (2003e). 'Maradu Punaradhivasippicha Kudumbangale Uparodhichu', 26 June, p. 1.

Madhyamam (2003f). 'Punaradhivasippicha Veettilekku Erachu Kayaran Sramam', 27 June, p. 1.

Madhyamam (2003g). 'Thengaladakki Mariaymbiyum Kudumbavum Padiyirangi', 30 June, p. 1.

Madhyamam (2003h). 'Punaradhivasam Neelunnathil Kudumbangalkku Rosham', 3 July, p. 1.

Malayala Manorama (2003). 'Marad Punaradhivasam Sammathikkilla: Togadia', 9 July, p. 3.

Mathrubhoomi (2003a). 'Maradu Veendum Akramam', 3 May, p. 1.

Mathrubhoomi (2003b). 'Marad Madangunnavarude Avakasam Samrakshikkanam', 2 August, p. 1.

Mathrubhoomi (2003c). 'Marad; CBI Anweshanam Avashyappettu Hindu Aikyavediyude Van Prakatanam', 31 August, p. 1.

Mathrubhoomi (2003d). 'Maradu Othutheerpayi', 6 October, p. 1.

Mathrubhoomi (2003e). 'Orumayude Puthuma', 11 October, p. 1.

New Indian Express (2003a). 'RSS Demands CBI Probe', 5 May, p. 1.

New Indian Express (2003b). 'BJP Reiterates Demand for CBI Probe', 9 May, p. 5.

New Indian Express (2003c). '6 More Arrested, Bombs Seized', 11 May, p. 1.

New Indian Express (2003d). 'Mosque Issue Snowballing in Marad', 15 May, p. 1.

New Indian Express (2003e). 'Muslim Students Fleeing Marad Schools', 27 May, p. 1.

New Indian Express (2003f). 'Marad Women Get No Word from RDO', 2 September, p. 4.

New Indian Express (2003g). 'Refugees' Hopes Fade as Talks Fail', 5 September, p. 1.

New Indian Express (2003h). 'Authorities Prevented from Cleaning Wells', 19 September, p. 1.

New Indian Express (2003i). 'Marad Women Block Repair Works for Second Day', 20 September, p. 1.

New Indian Express (2003j). 'Araya Samajam Briefs Women on Pact', 8 October, p. 5.

The Hindu (2003). 'Togadia Threatens to Block Marad Rehabilitation', 9 July, p. 4.

3

Maoist Insurgency in Nepal

Radicalizing Gendered Narratives

Rita Manchanda

The Maoist insurgency, to effect a revolutionary transformation in Nepal, has produced various women's narratives. Alongside the dominant narrative of victimhood, there are the radical narratives of civilian women in the midst of the societal upheaval following on conflict or 'internally stuck' in situations of conflict-induced displacement (when the men have fled), obliged to take on new roles with implications for unintended structural social change.[1] Here, too, are the narratives of women in the Maoist movement as propagandists and mobilizers, party cadres and district secretaries, and, above all, as guerrillas in the front ranks of the fighting. It is a problematic narrative for feminist politics for it posits the possibility of emancipatory politics in the crucible of a militarized, hierarchical, authoritarian culture of violent politics. These narratives acknowledge the political opportunity that the mobilization of women in revolutionary armed struggle creates, but equally they fundamentally question whether the visibility of women can translate into protagonism[2] and the power to shape a gendered programmatic agenda.

Feminist scholarship has explored the intersection of gender and state building in South Asia—the agentive moments made possible in the necessity to mobilize women; the construction (and violent containment) of woman as bearer of community/national identity's 'best values' and the closure of a certain feminist moment by the patriarchal state. In

South Asia, both nation state-building projects and armed revolutionary class struggles have seen the mobilization of women and its corollary, the subsuming of the women's question in nationalist or socialist projects and ideological strictures that in the aftermath pull women back to the gender discriminatory regimes of the personal sphere.[3] This article argues that the Maoist vision of a revolutionized Nepal opens up space for the articulation of a potentially transformative politics, though not without contradictions and paradoxes. The article examines the gender dynamics in the Maoist revolution in Nepal. It probes the tension between a near critical mass of women in the Maoist movement and a male leadership ambivalent about redefining gender relations. What does the 'empowerment' of women through participation in authoritarian and violently destructive struggles mean for the development of freedom? What questions does it raise about accountability for human rights abuses?

CONTEXT

The narratives of the Maoist conflict prompt the following set of questions: (*a*) Why are so many women joining the Maoist movement? Why are women from the Janjati (indigenous peoples) communities,[4] in particular, drawn to the movement? The Maoist leadership claims that nearly 30 per cent of the Maoists in their heartland are women. In the political reassertion of the identity of ethnic nationalities and territories in the conflict, how are Janjati women's identities being reconstructed? (*b*) What are the paradoxes inherent in the emancipatory possibilities of the Maoist ideology that provide political opportunities for women's involvement in violent revolutionary politics? Is there a subsuming of the women's question in overcoming class oppression? (*c*) What are the intended and unintended socio-cultural effects of the Maoist conflict in radicalizing the social agenda and specifically the women's question in Nepal? What are the implications of the Maoist ideology and its production of altered gender roles on the dominant model of Hindu upper-caste religiously sanctified cultural identity? What is its differential impact on myriad cultural identities of caste, ethnicity and religion?[5] (*d*) Can we pick out a gendered continuum of violence—from women's passive experience of structural violence in 'peace' time to nascent active roles or protagonist positions in violent politics during times of conflict? (*e*) How does the construction of violent and 'terrorist' politics affect social and national dynamics? How has the presence of women altered the character, culture and hierarchy of militant organizations?

These are questions that have engaged feminist scholars in myriad conflict areas—Sri Lanka, India (Tebhaga and Telegana), Vietnam, Guatemala, Chiapas-Mexico, El Salvador and Peru[6]—and the analytical frameworks and comparative insights derived from their research provide a rich resource in exploring the specific situation of Nepal. In this article, sustained observations drive the theoretical stance and thus the treatment is consciously exploratory.

It is beyond the scope of the article to engage with all these questions, rather my purpose is to explore the emancipatory potential of the participation of women in an authoritarian, militarized movement and to examine its impact on the transformation of cultural identities and the radicalization of the social agenda in Nepal.

Nearly six years ago, I was one of a group of six women journalists who visited the two districts most affected by the People's War. The experience inspired three of us to co-author 'Where there are No Men: Women in the Maoist Insurgency in Nepal' (Gautam et al. 2001). Nine years after the Maoists launched the revolution, I am prompted to revisit the sites of our conversations with the women in view of the tumultuous changes that have taken place. Since then, the reach of the People's War and the Royal Nepal Army's deployment has created a civil war situation with the Maoists in control of rural Nepal.

Subsequently, there has been greater exigency to recruit women. Wars expectedly have provoked population shifts; in Nepal, conflict-induced displacement is becoming an increasingly gendered phenomenon, with girls and women representing the largest percentage of the 'internally stuck'. The pro-active recruitment of women raises questions about the implications of a near critical mass of women in a militarized movement (Global IDP Project 2003; Manchanda 2003b; Martinez 2002). Many more critical voices of women Maoist leaders are available for analysis. At the time when we wrote 'Where there are No Men', women were just beginning to join the movement. Indeed, the chairperson of the Communist Party of Nepal (Maoist), Prachanda candidly admitted in an interview that in the early days they were overwhelmed by the unexpected response of the women in the movement (Onesto 2000). Moreover, the revisit provides the opportunity of a longitudinal view of how the roles of the women in the movement have consolidated or shifted, witness many more critical voices of Maoist women leaders. These are now available in print, as well as the published interviews of the male leaders. And although it is premature to make any substantive assessment about the production of new cultural identities and social structures, already it is possible to gauge the imprint on the radicalization of the social agenda in Nepal.

To inform my revisit, I draw upon our earlier collective empirical research, my subsequent field visits as a journalist to the districts of Rolpa (2002) and Sindhupalchowk (2001) and encounters with two top Maoist leaders, Baburam Bhattarai and Krishna Prasad Mahara during the interregnum of the Ceasefire II in 2003. In addition, the last couple of years have seen a spate of articles and scholarly research on the gender dimension of the Maoist movement that has inspired me to a fresh appraisal of an uncomfortable area of feminist politics, to make visible an agentive moment with all its contradictions and to participate in a discourse that shores up the ambivalent 'gains' of conflict (Maycock 2003; Parvati 2003b; Pettigrew and Shneiderman 2004; Shakhya 2003; Thapa 2004; Thapa and Sijapati 2003). Also, it is hoped that this exploration will contribute to the development of more gender-sensitive Disarmament, Demobilization and Reintegration (DDR) policy processes following a ceasefire.

HISTORICAL SNAPSHOT

Nepal's dominant historical narrative is structured around the Shah dynasty's establishment of a Hindu kingdom through reunification of the petty principalities of the territory of Nepal nearly two and a half centuries ago. Nepal's palace history is presided over through a lineage that spans the Shahs as conqueror, the hereditary Rana prime ministers as usurpers, the king as absolute ruler and then as constitutional monarch in a multi-party democracy and then as proactive ruler exercising de facto executive power in the name of a constitution that former king Gyanendra had rendered defunct. Power remains monopolized by a minority governing elite of Hindu upper-caste Brahmins and Chettri families with co-optation of some Buddhist Newar merchants and Sanskritized ethnic Magars. The democratic mobilization of the 1990 movement had seen the mass participation of Nepal's Janjati and other ethnic groups but once multi-party democracy was established they were excluded from the power structure (Gellner and Bhattachan 1999).

The confluence of regional, cultural, linguistic and religious discrimination and deprivation is common in those regions considered the most backward and most underdeveloped where the indigenous and ethnic groups are a majority. These disadvantaged communities make up a substantial support base for the Maoists. The epicentre of the Maoist insurgency, Rolpa, Rukum and Jajarkot, is in the backward mid-western hills, predominantly populated by the peoples. It was from here that the Communist Party of Nepal (Maoist) launched the 'People's War' in February 1996.[7] Since then it has spread to all of Nepal's seventy-five districts and virtually created a state within a state, as the writ of the government does not extend beyond the Kathmandu valley, the urban centres, the district headquarters and sections of the arterial highways.

VISIBILITY OF WOMEN IN THE MAOIST MOVEMENT

> The women have more to gain than the men from the People's War. That is why the women, especially the Tibeto-Burman and non-Aryan women constitute such an important part of the movement.[8]

Striking images of young women in fatigues, rifles hoisted on their shoulders, purposefully marching forward stare back at you when you click on the Communist Party of Nepal (Maoist) website. It reflects how central the woman guerrilla is in the public projection of the Maoist movement. Arguably, it also exemplifies the limits of the space reserved for women in the movement and the leverage of the woman's question in the movement. In the consciously balanced negotiating team that the Maoists put together for the peace talks in 2003, the Janjati and Madhesia constituencies were represented but there were no women delegates.

Mobilizing Women

In a rural community where one in every two households is involved in seasonal migration, where women form the majority, the subsistence agroeconomy is run by women. There can be no agrarian revolution without mobilizing women and putting them in guerrilla fatigues. The Revolutionary Internationalist Movement (RIM) organ, *The Worker*, in its focus on women, titled 'Fury of Women Unleashed', celebrated the participation of women at all levels, ranging 'from party committee secretaries [to] guerrilla squad commanders to local volunteers and propagandists' (Parvati 2003a).[9] The participation of women was promoted through an active propaganda network. Publicists spun a folklore that eulogized the exploits of women guerrilla leaders like Shanti Shrestha and Kamla Bhatta and cast them in a heroic, though gender-reinforcing, self-sacrificing and self-effacing, mode. To instil grit, determination and revolutionary fervour among raw recruits, much play was given to the heroic defiance of Comrade Devi Khadka. Even after she was gang-raped by the police her spirit was not broken. She vowed to fight on and take revenge (Gautam et al. 2001: 233–39).

Writing in the *Kantipur* daily on 23 February 2004, top Maoist woman leader Hsila Yami explained that the party recruited women because 'women make up the biggest segment of the population in the downtrodden communities', adding: 'Since women have suffered class and sexual oppression they have double the capacity to revolt.' When the People's War was initiated in 1996, the CPN (M) leadership made it mandatory to include two women in every unit of nine to eleven members, especially in the fighting ranks. It served as a check against excesses against women. Hsila Yami told me that in the Maoist strongholds every third guerrilla was a woman. In the new districts where the Maoist influence was spreading, every tenth combatant was a woman.[10]

An independent survey by IHRICON in 2001 estimated that in the Maoist-controlled districts of Rolpa, Rukum and Jajarkot, at the lowest level of the fighting ranks, in the people's militia women make up 40–50 per cent of the cadres, at the squad level 35 per cent, at the platoon level 20–30 per cent, and, at the highest level, a total of about nine women were reported (Gautam 2001). With the launch of an all-out civil war and increasing out-migration/displacement of men and boys, these numbers are likely to increase.

Comrade Parvati (an alias), a member of the CPN (M) Central Committee, and a spokesperson for the Maoists on the woman's question, maintained there were several women in the central committee, dozens at the regional level and even larger numbers at the district and cell levels. Women were included to prevent counter-revolution, as women are assumed to be more reliable (Parvati 2003a). Hsila Yami reinforced this faith in women's commitment, because for women return is not a ready option.

> Sons will be welcomed back with open arms, but for the daughters, can there be a return? When they become guerrillas, the women set themselves free from patriarchal bonds. How can they go back? That is why the women are more committed.[11]

Evidence of the growing number of women in the Maoist movement can be gauged in the rising casualties of women. The death toll of women killed in the first two years of the insurgency was six, three by the police and three by the Maoists. According to INSEC estimates, in 2003 the total number killed was 1,308, of which 159 were women. The security forces accounted for 138 killings and the Maoists twenty-one. Some 154 bodies remain sex unidentifiable. Since the People's War began in February 1996 through to December 2003, out of an estimated total of 8,265 killed, 561 have been women. Of the total number of men and women killed, Janjatis make up the largest group with 21 per cent. A gender segregation reveals that, among women, the percentage of Janjatis killed is much higher, at 28 per cent (INSEC 2004). It supports the claim that Janjati women have been drawn to the movement in large numbers.

Maoist women leader Hsila Yami maintains that a majority of the women in the movement are poor peasants from the Tibeto-Burman and non-Aryan communities, for example, Magars, Tamang, Kamis, and Gurungs. The People's War began from three districts in the western hills where the majority of the population are Janjatis. The failure of the dominant political processes of multi-party democracy to include the secular political claims of the oppressed nationalities has intensified their unsatisfied claims to an identity with dignity and left them full of revolutionary potential (De Sales 2003). The expansion of the Maoist power base into the eastern *terai* also has been buttressed by the support of the oppressed castes, Dalits and Tharus. The recent decision of the CPN (M) to flag off an outcrop of ethnic autonomous regions portends an ethnicization of the struggle. This affirmation of identity politics has implications for the construction of the Janjati women's identity within and outside the movement.

Illiterate or neo-literate girls and women constitute the bulk of the female backing of the movement. *Girls as young as twelve or thirteen are involved within the party (Thapa and Sijapati 2003: 180).* Adult neo-literate women and schoolgirls in Gorkha district were identified, in our earlier study, as a core group joining the movement in that district (Gautam et al. 2001: 243–46). While the Maoist movement has welcomed some educated women, the leadership has warned against the bourgeois proclivities of the urban educated. This is reflected in Prachanda's ambivalence towards 'bourgeois intellectuals'.[12] Parvati consolidates this position:

> ...because of their class background [educated women] may be more sensitive to gender issues than to class issues... if not checked this may lead to reformism or right deviation...hence the party should counter this danger by bringing class elements into the picture when debating the leading role of the women's movement. (2003b: 180)

Why Are Women Joining the Maoist Movement?

Arguably, there has been both voluntary and coercive recruitment of young girls, though given a pervasive geography of fear, the distinction is not particularly meaningful. Moreover, what capacity exists for young girls to make an informed choice? However, the question remains: why are so many girls and women choosing to get involved in such dangerous politics? Is the motivation for women different from that of men? Is the pull of emancipatory politics intersected by the gender gap? Is the motivation for Janjati women different from that of Janjati men?

Maoist women leaders—Comrade Parvati and Hsila Yami as well as RIM publicist, Li Onesto—emphasize the emancipatory impulse that is driving hundreds of thousands of women to join the movement. Hsila Yami, wife of Maoist leader and ideologue Baburam Bhattarai, frames women's involvement in the movement as liberating them from the oppressive feudal patriarchal system.

> Women are the most deprived in the existing feudal system despite their role in Nepal's agroeconomy. They are denied parental property although they run rural households on their own when their husbands are away earning money. When the men return they marry other women and the wives are forced to leave ... If the women marry someone else, they become outcastes.... The CPN Maoist is reversing this feudal practice through its People's War. It is leading the new revolution to implement ideas like equal rights for parental property and tillers as landowners. Women are fascinated with this change. The People's War has liberated women who otherwise had to spend their lives solely on domestic matters. Because of Hindu philosophy, girls are married off at an early age. They become grandmothers even before they reach menopause. The People's War has brought women out of the vicious cycle of living as reproductive machines... Rural women who were once deprived of their rights are now at the forefront of the People's War fighting as commanders. Now women are deciding not only when they live but also when they die...[13]

The romantic descriptions of Li Onesto's sojourn in Nepal among the Maoists between 1999 and 2000 have been particularly influential in casting the Maoist movement as opening the 'prison gates' for Nepali women. There is her cameo of Rachna (eighteen years of age), a peasant girl denied the opportunity to go to school like her brothers. Now in the movement, she tells Onesto: '[I] never had time to study but in the People's Army I have time to study, to read and to write and other comrades help me. I can read newspapers and write letters now' (Onesto 1999: 167). The Nepali writer Manjushree Thapa, in a far more critical account of her encounters with girls in the Maoist movement, quotes a young teenage girl explaining why she joined: 'You see, there used to only be sickles and grass in the hands of girls like us. And now there are automatic rifles' (Thapa 2003).

The girls are keener to join the armed ranks than they are to join the propaganda or party committees. It appears that the liberating opportunities of life in a 'squad' are more alluring than staying on in the village and at home where gender roles have changed far less. Within the productivity and propaganda teams and the political wing, traditional gender prescriptive relations still prevail. Thapa, in her conversations with Comrade Binita (seventeen years old) and Comrade Jumna (probably fifteen years old), emphasized their self- perception of uselessness before joining the party. What was she doing before? 'Nothing', said Binita. Now, she worked in a team of motivators, moving from house to house in Surkhet district. Unlike Binita, Jumna had never gone to school, though one of her brothers was a graduate and another was studying in the seventh standard. For her, life had been a drudgery of housework and working in the field. Was her work in a team that rears chicken and grows crops that different? 'We must not feel discouraged', Thapa quotes her saying.

Binita and Jumna's brothers had not joined the party, only the girls had, and with the backing of their parents. This supports reports in the media that in the rural areas, when the Maoists come calling for one child per family to join the movement, families are increasingly sending daughters, more expendable than sons.

The abject status of women in Nepal—albeit mediated by differences of class, caste and ethnicity—is reflected in a Nepali saying: 'If my next life is to be a dog's life and I can choose, I'd rather be a dog than a bitch.' The faces of Nepalese women are of women trafficked, of anaemic women who die neglected in childbirth, of poor and illiterate women behind bars for miscarriages or abortions, of menstruating women sequestered in cold and unhygienic *cauchholoo* sheds, of women without a son abandoned or supplanted in a polygamous marriage, and of culturally disadvantaged girl children burdened with a 1:4 ratio of labour load in comparison with their brothers.

The gender profile of Nepal reveals that women suffer from twenty-three discriminatory laws (NNAGT 2003). A woman's lifespan is shorter than a man's by two and a half years. More than 40 per cent of girls are married off by age fifteen and have their first child by nineteen. Nepal's maternity death rate, 905 out of 100,000, is matched only by Afghanistan. Women watch one in every ninth child die under the age of five. The literacy rate is 21 per cent for females. Dowry, polygamy, wife beating, and mass trafficking are common. Citizenship is through the male line and rights to ancestral property are restricted to unmarried daughters.

Gender inequalities vary according to different social groupings and regions. It is upper-caste Hindu women who are most subject to religiously sanctified 'exclusions', which span the household to the state level and cover political, economic and cultural domains. It is this Hindu patriarchal model that shapes Nepal's state building and developmental policies. Given the geographic and economic isolation of the hill districts, acculturation to dominant Hindu beliefs and customs has been slow but growing, thus undermining the relative autonomy of the women from the Tibeto-Burman communities like the Magars, Gurungs and Rais. The Janjatis have fewer religio-cultural restrictions as their identity is defined in a secular idiom: widow remarriage is possible and divorce does not entail a loss of ritual status. Thus while the Janjatis are excluded along other axes based on class, caste and ethnicity, they simultaneously enjoy freedoms unavailable to Hindu women.

Similarly, Magar women have access to a variety of economic options that give them a degree of socio-economic independence. Informal entrepreneurial activity, like the sale of *raski* (country liquor), is centred on women. Augusta Molnar, in an ethnographic study (1981) of the Kham Magar women of Thabang, Rolpa, argued that although women are denied legal right to land and family property, in the economic sphere they hold a position of complementary authority. It is a status they retain on divorce or widowhood. Women have primary responsibility for agriculture and animal husbandry, while ploughing is done by men, and seed selection is the responsibility of women.

With one in two households involved in seasonal migration as we saw earlier, women are obliged to make decisions in the absence of men. The informal institutions of women's work groups prop up a wageless labour exchange and foster small entrepreneurial activity. These 'work groups' provide women, more than men, access to information and informal political power. Indeed the traditional esteem enjoyed by the Magar women in society has made it socially acceptable for young educated Magar women to compete with males for posts as village officials (ibid.). It also locates the Magar women's participation in the Maoist movement as not one of sudden agency but made possible by larger socio-cultural structures that have (un)regulated these women's lives.

Even while it is useful to analytically factor in continuity as well as change in the possibility of agency of Janjati women, Seira Tamang, a Nepali political scientist, adds an important caveat. In today's Nepal, she argues, the traditional arenas of agency for Janjati women have shrunk because the twin processes of state building and development have promoted a specific form of Hindu patriarchy. In short, modernity may have limited the choices for Janjati women (Tamang 2002) and attracted them to the emancipatory potential of the Maoist ideology that promises equality with dignity for the marginalized and an agenda committed to uprooting gender discriminatory customary practices and social abuses, including alcoholism and gambling.

An understanding of why so many women, especially poor peasant women from the oppressed nationalities, are participating in a dangerous, brutally violent struggle may lie in the structural violence that is all around them in the form of domestic violence, social violence and the violence of the state apparatus. Violence and death as familiars breed a fatalism that the socio-religious culture reinforces. The Maoists have radicalized this sentiment: 'You've got to die sometime so why not die for a new order?' Fatalism acquires a paradoxically empowering nuance in the talk of a 'meaningful death'; there is unconscious irony in Hsila Yami's assertion that 'the People's War gives all of them (women) a meaningful life and a meaningful death; it allows them to prove their worth is equal to the men'.[14]

PROBLEMATICS AND EMANCIPATORY POSSIBILITIES OF THE MAOIST MOVEMENT

'I feel powerful with a gun.'
— A Maoist girl cadre

Traditionally, socialist ideology has recognized women's oppression. Within the revolutionary struggle gender discrimination is usually treated as something that dissolves when primary questions of feudal exploitation and class oppression are resolved. In short, gender oppression will melt away as women and men make more radical commitments. Leftist armed resistance movements subsume the women's question or postpone it until after the revolution.

Is the Maoist movement in Nepal the exception? Analysis of the role of women in the 'Shining Path', the acknowledged model for Nepal's People's War, suggests that, despite the fact that women achieved an important presence at all levels within the movement, the 'Shining Path established an instrumental relationship with its female members that reproduced patriarchal relations to benefit the party' (Cordero 1998). In Nepal the Maoist vision of a revolutionary nation has provided women with a political opportunity, but has their participation in the movement structured a field of the possible for articulating the woman's question? Or, as in the case of militarized struggles in Guatemala or in Sri Lanka, has the rhetoric been belied by practices that continue to reproduce stereotypical gender relations?

The Maoists in no. 19 of their forty-point memorandum had taken on board the women's question. 'Patriarchal exploitation and discrimination against women should be stopped. The daughter should be allowed access to property.' The problem of property largely relates to the social relations that surround property issues, which consolidate women's subordinate position. But Hsila Yami, in an article in a leading Nepali daily, exhorts women to place first the anti-feudal struggle against the monarchy, declaring 'the liberty of women is possible only after the freedom of all other communities and classes'. The struggle for women's emancipation can not 'be limited only to gender'.[15] This emphasis reflects the tension in the movement on the issue of subsuming gender oppression in class oppression. It echoes an earlier interview with me in which Yami said:

> ...since the NDR is anti feudal, it will at once remove feudal Brahminical Hindu rule which sees women in relationship to men. The anti imperialist nature of NDR will discourage unequal trade relations with imperialist and expansionist forces, thus saving women from sweat shops where they are exploited sexually and economically. It will prepare the ground for removing prostitution, consumerism and commoditization of women in Nepal.[16]

Beyond the rhetoric, what is the leverage of the women's question in shaping the programmatic agenda of the Maoist movement? What has been its impact in challenging patriarchal relations within the movement and producing a social revolution in religiously sanctified cultural identities and relations? Curiously, the writings of Maoist ideologue Baburam Bhattarai and the CPN chairperson Prachanda (alias) rarely engage seriously with the women's question. Much is made of Prachanda's comments on the women's question to Li Onesto where he acknowledges the party running to keep up with the overwhelming response of the women to the political opportunity opened up by the

Maoist ideology and its unintended social consequences. In 1997, in Rolpa, a year after the initiation, Prachanda claimed:

> The people were not only fighting with the police or reactionary feudal agents but they were also breaking the chains of exploitation and oppression and a whole cultural revolution was going on among the people. Questions of marriage, questions of love, questions of family, questions of relations between people. All of these things were being turned upside down and changed in the rural areas. (Onesto 2000: 195)

Before exploring at the ground level the credibility of these assertions of a social revolution, it is useful to keep in mind Comrade Parvati's criticism that women's issues are rarely taken up as a central issue and the party 'neglects to implement programmes developed by women's mass fronts'. Structurally speaking, the Prachanda Path, initiated in 2001, created a women's department in the Central Committee in recognition of the women's constituency in the Maoist movement, but has it enabled a sharper focus on the women's question or has it ghettoized it?

In the earlier study (Gautam et al. 2001), we acknowledged the marginal space given to the gender question in the programmatic framework articulated by the leadership. However, at the time we argued that

> ...there is a counter reality of how women in the movement have reshaped the ideology of the movement and ensured that at the ground level the women's question is not postponed. In the Maoist stronghold areas, many of the mass actions reportedly were related to getting women justice, punishing rapists, wresting back the usurped land of single women, punishing men for polygamy and mass action against liquor dealers.

Within Maoist propaganda, *Jan Adalats* or 'People's Courts' are lauded as upholding the rights of women on issues of social and domestic violence. 'A school teacher was known to exploit women sexually... he was brought before the People's Court and was made to stand up and sit down, holding his ears for several minutes...before being let off' (Parvati 2003b: 172). The Maoist organ *The Worker* claims:

> Women own land for the first time... Arranged marriages, polygamy and other feudal traditions oppressive to women are no longer practiced. Wife beating and rape are severely punished by the People's Courts. Women are given the right to divorce, go to school, are equal participants in the new economic, political, and social life of the villages.[17]

Nine years after the Maoist revolution was launched, newspapers are full of reports from the rural areas of Maoists taking action against dowry, wife beaters, rapists, polygamists, husbands who abandon their wives, and even a thirty-three-year-old man who married a thirteen-year-old girl. The All Nepalese Women's Association (Revolutionary) or ANWA(R), the party's mass women's organization, had spearheaded a nation-wide campaign to ban alcohol as a major social evil, especially in the hill areas. Local Maoist leaders claimed that they had put an end to the practice of segregating women from ritually pure places (kitchen) when they are menstruating and after they have given birth (Thapa 2003).

In an effort to get behind the propaganda narratives about the Maoist revolution opening up a field of possibilities for ending discrimination and transforming social relations, it may be useful to probe the revolution's engagement with the women's question by focusing on certain key sites of resistance and assertion. An obvious index to the redefining of gender relations is the leadership profile of women in the movement and their capacity to shape and define the culture and agenda of the movement. Has it produced new and more empowering cultural identities for women both within and outside the party that cut across class, caste and ethnicity? In nationalist discourses we have seen the (violent) construction of an 'acceptable' and homogenized women's identity in support of the state-building project, one that often ends up undermining women's autonomy. Who is defining the ethnic Magar, Limbu or Kirati women's identities in the Maoist dominated Magrat, Limbuwan and Khumbbuwan?

WOMEN'S QUESTION: SITES OF CONTESTATION AND RESISTANCE

Anti-Alcohol Campaign

The anti-alcohol campaign was projected as a major programmatic initiative driven by the women's agenda (Shah 2002). It needs, however, to be qualified that, among the Janjatis also called Matwalis (alcohol drinkers), alcohol or the home brew raski has symbolic and ritual value. For many young women the brewing of raski was a source of economic independence. Consequently, was the campaign mired in ambivalence as Pettigrew and Shneiderman argue (2004)? Did it alienate rather than attract the women? Conversations with civilian women in Mirule and Thawang villages in Rolpa district in 1998 revealed enthusiastic support for the anti-alcohol campaign and disgust at, and rejection of, the habitually drunk local officials (as in the case of the schoolteacher) and ostracism of one of the village women known to be still brewing liquor.

The campaign to ban alcohol peaked in 2001 at a time when the representatives of the Maoists and government (all male) were bogged down in the first round of ceasefire peace talks. From the point of view of the power games being played at the negotiating table, the timing may have been inopportune. The ANWA(R)-driven campaign demonstrated determination and capacity to push the male leadership. The campaign, albeit involving the use of force, eventually forced the government to begin regulating its open liquor policy.

Looking back, how effective has the anti-liquor ban been in the Maoist-controlled areas? In 2002, when I visited Sullichaur, an important quasi-urban market town in Rolpa district, liquor was again available but not over the counter; the campaign had driven the consumption of alcohol underground. It may be, as Pettigrew and Shneiderman argue, that because the anti-alcohol movement had different implications for different cultural groups it has slipped off the priority agenda. It may be, as Comrade Parvati reminds us, that male Maoist leaders rarely have time to consider 'women's issues'.

Sexuality and Reproductive Rights

Nationalist discourses usually produce normative ideas about sexuality and elaborate ideological strictures on sexual control, especially when belonging is determined by ethnic/religious identities. Revolutionary class struggles too take very seriously the party custodianship of the 'sexual morality' of the sisters and brothers of the revolution. In Nepal, on the issue of sexuality and reproductive rights, especially the criminal ban on abortion—illegal in Nepal up until 2003—the party appears on the defensive. To some extent, the conservatism has been prompted by propaganda about sexual licence among the young cadres. With young people becoming *farar* (absconding) and living together in the jungle, there has been a great deal of adverse publicity about licentious behaviour and the sexual exploitation of girl cadres.[18]

Sujita Shakhya of the dominant parliamentary left party (UML) claims that the Maoists have 'ill-treated' women and used rape within the party as a means of control: 'In the Maoist party ... cases of rape and sexual exploitation are apparently common, and incidents are heard in which women were raped because they held a different opinion in the party' (2003: 395). Notwithstanding Shakhya's critique, there appear to be few reports of sexual violence by the Maoists. That the people's courts take very seriously transgressions of sexual morality was confirmed by *Le Monde* journalist Cedric Gouvernor, in his account of his travels in the Maoists stronghold of Rukum in 2003. He cites one makeshift jail that he came across where a third of the fifteen inmates were being punished for 'sex before marriage and extra marital sex' (personal communication).

The issue of sexuality is a particularly explosive one in a conservative society like Nepal, although, among the non-Aryan ethnic groups, 'virginity' is not considered as sacrosanct. The sexuality of the widow is not seen as ritually dangerous and widow remarriage is possible. It could be argued that the party, by imposing a uniform disciplinary code of sexual conduct on party cadres, is doing violence to cultural groups that have a different sexual morality. According to Hsila Yami, 'a code of conduct is formulated for women and men, particularly for the combatants, so that sexuality leads to marriage, if both partners are not married', she said. 'If one or both are married, they are warned and punished', she added.

How seriously the issue of the 'morality' of the brothers and sisters of the revolution is regarded in the People's War was demonstrated with exemplarity when a top leader of the mass political front of the party, Pampa Bushal, was punished for sexual misconduct with a married comrade, 'Badal'. Pampa was suspended and sent to an obscure village post, for re-education. Badal was dropped from the central leadership and since has climbed back to become the military head of the party. Pampa Bushal too is back as a member of the Central Committee though the climb back took much longer (Gautam et al. 2001: 236).

Marriage and Family

Most female Maoist cadres in the rural areas are under twenty years old. An analysis by Pettigrew and Shneiderman suggests that the majority of Maoist women are unmarried at the time they join the movement. Marriage, they argue, is a means of controlling female cadres and making it difficult for them to leave the party. This is substantiated by Parvati who complains that Maoist women soon face internal party pressure to 'get married covertly or overtly as unmarried women draw lots of suspicion from men as well as women for their unmarried status. This results in marriages against their wishes or before they are ready to get married'. She denounces marriage as 'robbing the movement of promising women leaders' and perpetuating men's hegemony in property relations (Parvati 2003a: 3).

Evidently, the ideological position on the People's War regarding women's access to property has not fundamentally altered the patriarchal discourse or practise on marriage and family. Parvati is among those who denounce marriage, including those fostered by the party, as an institution that supports discrimination in property rights, arguing '[it] is an alliance for men to perpetuate hegemony through property relations. For women the same alliance in fact marginalizes them to domestic slavery' (ibid.: 3). The social revolution effected by the People's War remains tethered in the patriarchal values of 'protecting' or, as Parvati comments, 'overprotecting' women.

Moreover, participation in the movement is limited to young girls, and women tend to be discriminated against. Shneiderman in the course of her fieldwork found that young girls, fourteen to eighteen years old, were particularly targeted by the Maoists for recruitment, while women between eighteen and thirty tended to be overlooked. She argues that the logistical demand of maintaining a network of village household providers of food may have discouraged the Maoists from recruiting these women (Pettigrew and Shneiderman 2004). In the process, the party tended to reinscribe gendered roles.

Parenting too remains gendered, with women taking primary responsibility, though Li Onesto had remarked on emerging collective structures of child care. Parvati's description that, 'with the birth of every child she sinks into domestic slavery', reflects her understanding of the experience of pregnancy by the Maoist women 'as disciplinary action' (2003a: 2–3).

The brave new social world of the revolution that Prachanda had hailed in his statement, celebrating a 'cultural revolution' that had turned upside down 'questions of marriage, questions of love, questions of family, questions of relations between people' has turned out to be less than a field of possibilities, and more a reproducing of traditional gender relations. Nepal's Maoist revolutionaries too have chosen to postpone the resolution of the woman's question for after 'the freedom of all other communities and classes', as Hsila Yami advised.

REWORKING GENDER RELATIONS: LEADERSHIP ISSUES

The Maoist leadership made a most emphatic statement about the leadership role of women when during the two rounds of peace talks in 2001 and in 2003, they put forward an all-male team. It was all the more surprising as the Maoist team for the 2003 peace talks had been carefully constituted to be fully representative. Despite the brave front, the head of the negotiating team, Baburam Bhattarai, slipped-up with the following statement: 'You do not have to have a woman to represent woman'. The oversight speaks volumes about the constraints in the field of the possibility for articulating an emancipatory politics for women in the movement. The borders of this field are further reinforced by the fact that the politburo of the party has no women.

For activists associated with Nepal's mainstream women's movements, it was a disillusioning blow. Aruna Upreti, a women's health and reproductive rights activist, was particularly outspoken. '[You're] behaving no differently than our 'men-stream' political parties. We never expected our male dominated government to involve women in the peace process but we thought you were going to be different' (Upreti 2003).

In the early days of the Maoist movement among the top leadership there were women like Pampa Bushal, co-leader of the United People's Front, the political platform of the Maoists, with accomplished political qualifications. Hsila Yami, an architect, was head of the ANWA(R) and also in the circle of the top leadership, both being upper-caste social groupings. Since then there has been a huge influx of women who are visible at every level in the movement. With the majority likely to be between fifteen and eighteen years old, it remains questionable what level of agency they enjoy. Are they seen, in the military ranks, as fodder for the young boys' cannons? As the struggle grows increasingly militarized and hierarchically structured, it is not clear whether the visibility of senior Maoist women as area commanders and district party secretaries actually translates into power to shape policy and programmes or whether an insidious ghettoization is produced and perpetuated. Parvati, the head of the women's department in the Central Committee, is openly critical of the party's lack of attention to the women's question and gender issues.

In 1998, four years after the People's War began, Hsila Yami asserted in an interview with me that women were enjoying due representation in the exercise of political power of the 'embryonic new democratic state'. Women were visible everywhere in the Central Committee, in positions as party secretaries, as office bearers in the People's Government, as area commanders and among militia in the fighting units. However, at the level of elected people's government, it is conspicuous that in mid-2001, when people's governments were set up in twenty-one districts, none was headed by a woman, although there were four women vice chairs. In the

United Revolutionary People's Council there are only four women out of thirty-seven members. The people's government of Magrat autonomous region set up in January 2004 has no women in its top leadership despite the fact that, in the Magrat area, women's participation comprises a third of all armed rebels.

Prachanda acknowledged in an interview with Li Onesto the initial difficulties of developing the leadership of women comrades to effect new relations of equality between men and women. Writing in 2003, Parvati admitted that male cadres still have difficulty in relinquishing 'the privileged position bestowed on them by the patriarchal structure'. In the movement, women's role is conceived of as supportive (Parvati 2003a: 5); the 'traditional' division of labour is reproduced within the movement, witnessing men maintaining responsibility for the mental work while women are expected to do the 'everyday drudgery work'. Women in the political wing and in particular those associated with propaganda work and located much closer to the home seem to have fewer opportunities for transcending gender-specific roles than women in the fighting units. Moreover, Maoist publicists, in describing the naturalized way in which women engaged in propaganda work access homes in a new area easily, unwittingly reinscribe a gendered division of labour that is undervalued by male colleagues. Illustrating the transcendence of gender roles and greater opportunity for equal relations within the fighting units, Pettigrew focuses on a two-women team, a Dalit and a Chettri (cutting across caste), described cleaning their guns. She observes, 'They did not help in preparing food nor in repairing uniforms both of which jobs were carried out by men' (Pettigrew and Shneiderman 2004). The Maoist propaganda discourse publicizes the existence of all women guerrilla units, but the very emphasis prompts scepticism about the possibility of establishing gender-neutral military structures.

CULTURAL DYNAMICS

More fundamentally, what kind of articulation of a rights-based vision or of the women's question is possible when nested in militarized politics and processes? The paradox of the possibility of an empancipatory politics in such authoritarian and violent movements is at the crux of the ambivalence towards the LTTE women in Sri Lanka and the Maoist women in Nepal. What kind of social transformation has been enabled for these women? What is its impact on the radicalization of the social agenda and, in extended scope, the women's question in Nepal as a whole?

The hallmark of the Maoist cadres in Nepal are their running shoes, but amongst girl cadres a quiet revolution of a different kind is taking place in the rural areas. Manjushree Thapa, in her travels in search of the girls in the Maoist movement, remarks that Comrade Binita and her young colleague 'stood out as Maoist cadres'. They were wearing plain *kurta surals* and no jewellery. The younger girl's hair was cut in a rough modern style. Both were carrying backpacks. Their counterparts would have been wearing traditional finery and jewellery and carrying on their backs baskets laden with grass or firewood. I was reminded of the LTTE women whose androgynous style of dress and short hair make a powerful cultural statement in a social environment where the *sumangal* (auspicious) Tamil woman is weighed down by ritually defined dress, jewels and flowers. In Nepal, did this signal a shift in the cultural signifiers of identity?

It needs to be emphasized that, in view of the myriad identities of Nepal's social groupings, the implications of the participation of girl-women in the Maoist movement would necessarily vary depending on the nature of their culturally defined identities. Evidently for women whose identity is defined in terms of a Brahminical cultural frame, the challenge of the Maoist cultural frame will be of a different revolutionary position than for the Tibeto-Burman women, whose identity is less bound up in rituals of taboo and pollution. As with all analyses of identity, one must simultaneously chart the intersections of class, religion and ethnicity.

It can be argued that the quiet (social) revolution which has been catalysed by the Maoist movement is taking place in the midst of contradictions, or, at best, ambivalences. For example, the Maoists have discouraged—even banned—ritual mourning, especially for their victims. When the Maoists killed Navraj Sharma, editor of *Kadam Saptahik*, his widow Rita Sharma (thirty-five years old) had not seen the body of her husband, nor had she been able to perform the funeral rites and achieve emotional or legal closure; she remained stuck in a cultural limbo between marriage and widowhood. When I met her, Rita Sharma was not wearing the traditional white saree. 'It is not obligatory in our village (Kalikot district). We are poor people.' In another instance, Thakma KC, widow of Krishna Sen, the editor of the pro-Maoist publication, was wearing a version of a *mangalsutra*, the married women's ritually solemnized necklace and a couple of glass bangles. Thakma explained she was not a great believer in the rituals and had never worn the vermilion mark. But then added, 'I never saw his body. I have no proof. I haven't observed any of the funeral rites, so how can I be a ritual widow?' (Manchanda 2003a). Yet both women belong to upper-caste Hindu families. Even while the dominant cultural model is Hindu, life cycle rituals and attitudes are different for the women from the Janjati communities and for the oppressed castes.

In Tebang (Rolpa) a Tibeto-Burman populated village, the Maoists had boarded up the temple and put an end to the celebration of the life cycle rituals and the accompanying *melas* (public gatherings). The women who spoke to us seemed to approve of the social changes—end of dowry and the heavy expenses at births, weddings and funerals. Most important was the end of the pollution taboos that sequestered a woman as ritually impure during menstruation and childbirth.[19]

Comrade Parvati claims that the phenomenon of women's participation in the party has effectively shifted the locus of Nepal's women's movement from the urban centres to the rural areas, from middle-class women to Janjati and lower castes (Parvati 2003b). It is a claim that Sujita Shakhya of the UML trivializes: 'Injustice, tyranny, exploitation and oppression faced by women cannot be overcome by beating someone with 500–1000 bamboo sticks and breaking a pot of wine'(Shakhya 2003).

Significantly, there has been little forging of solidarities on the women's question between the Maoist women and the myriad women's organizations in the country even when the ANWA(R) was above ground. However, the impact of the Maoist movement in radicalizing the social agenda is evident in the reform proposals forwarded by the government during the ceasefire negotiations in 2003. Specifically on the women's question, the government proposed 'to remove all kinds of discrimination and at least 25% of seats in all representative institutions to be reserved for women and special reservation for them should be constitutionally ensured in education, health administration and other employment sectors'.[20]

Within the Maoist movement, it is the grass-roots dynamics that has produced sites of contestation and resistance. That Parvati has the political space to be so critical is a testimony to the exigencies that oblige a patriarchal movement to reinvent itself. For disempowered rural women, despite the contradictions of the competing priorities of the 'anti-feudal revolution' and the paradox of the possibility of an emancipatory politics amidst an authoritarian militarized culture, their lives have been changed by the political opportunities offered by the Maoist revolutionary vision.

POSTSCRIPT

On 3 August 2005, *Jana Astha*, a Nepali weekly, reported that four women 'Maoists' were sexually tortured and killed in army custody in Kathmandu. These women had 'disappeared' more than two years ago. The report confirmed Amnesty International's warnings about the widespread potential of sexual abuse in Nepal's spiralling human rights crisis that has been further exacerbated by the king's assumption of absolute power and the Royal Nepal Army's virtual takeover of governance. As a consequence, Nepal's democratic middle ground has been hollowed out, and the two authoritarian forces—the Palace and the Maoists—are directly pitted against each other, precipitating an intensification of a conflict that has seen widespread human rights abuses on both sides. Many civilians who have been trying to stay out of the conflict will be forced by the security forces into the arms of the Maoists, producing an increasing polarization of society, greater violence, and making the search for peace more elusive.

In February 2005, King Gyanendra assumed direct control through a royal coup, ending Nepal's untenable experiment in balancing a political system poised on the twin pillars of multi-party democracy and a constitutional monarchy that had not accepted a figurehead role. The king clamped down emergency powers, suspended fundamental rights— especially freedom of speech and dissent—and arrested hundreds of politicians, journalists and human rights activists. It was the culmination of a series of royal moves precipitated by the king's removal in October 2002 of an elected prime minister following the dissolution of parliament and the marginalization of political parties.

Under pressure from the international community to revive democracy or forgo aid, particularly military aid, the king lifted the emergency on 30 April 2005 but the curfew on fundamental rights continues, escalating opposition, especially by journalists, and student protests.[21] So far the crippled 'political parties' have not thrown in their lot with the Maoists despite the latter's overtures, even while there is an irreversible swing towards Republicanism. Meanwhile, rather than politics being in control, the Maoists are being challenged from within by the contradictions of the gun. It has not diminished their ability to mount blockades or attack army camps. The army is under pressure to make good its claim to defeat the Maoists within six months. Given its clear inability over three years to hurt the ever-more-powerful Maoist forces, there is the danger that civilians will bear the brunt of government military operations.

Prospects for peace look most dismal. The king's seizure of absolute power has not brought with it any new strategy to address the challenge of the insurgency. Restrictions on freedom of information make it difficult to grasp the changing dynamics in the Maoist-controlled rural areas. Experience elsewhere has shown that the escalation of violence and the narrowing of the space for democratic politics are likely to push back the social transformation agenda as violent politics seizes the day and produces greater militarization and hierarchical disempowering structures. However, with the middle ground disappearing and brutal sexual abuse of 'suspects' widespread, more women will be drawn into violent revolutionary politics. How will that impact the shaping of new cultural identities and transforming social structures? Will Nepal be subsumed in the politics of violent insurgency?

NOTES

1. I am indebted to Darini Rajasingham-Senanayke for drawing my attention to this aspect. See Rajasingham-Senanayke (2001).
2. The concept, which is akin to agency, is developed in Cordero (1998).
3. Among the many contributions that have shaped this discourse, mention may be made of Jayawardena (1986), Chatterjee (1989), Sangari and Vaid (1989), Menon and Bhasin (1998), Manchanda (2001), and De Mel (2001). Also, see, Manandhar and Bhattachan (2001) and Meintjes et al. (2001).
4. Nepal has sixty ethnic groups. For an analysis of the ethnic profile of Nepal see Gellner et al. (1997).
5. For an insightful analysis of the heterogeneity of women's identities in Nepal, see Tamang (2002).
6. On the issue of women in various militarized movements in India see Custers (1987), Lalitha and Kannabiran (1998). For Sri Lanka see Adele (1993), Coomaraswamy (1997) and Mulniari (1998).
7. For perspectives on the Maoist revolution see Bhattarai (1998), Thapa (2003) and Thapa and Sijapati (2003).
8. Interview with Hsila Yami, New Delhi, 1998.
9. Also see *The Worker*, February 1998 at http://www.insof.org/w8/aritcleParvati.htm. Last accessed June 2004.
10. Interview with Hsila Yami, New Delhi, 1998.
11. Interview with Hsila Yami, New Delhi, 1998.
12. Prachanda's interview with Onesto (2000). Senior Maoist women leaders like Pampa Bushal and Hsila Yami are professional women from bourgeois backgrounds. Pampa Bushal fell foul of the leadership and had to be re-educated.
13. *Kantipur*, 23 February 2004.

14. Interview with Hsila Yami, New Delhi, 1998.
15. *Kantipur*, 30 May 2004.
16. Interview with Hsila Yami, New Delhi, 1998.
17. 'Maoist Post Conflict Vision for Position of Women', no. 8, *The Worker*, 2003. Available at www.cpnm.org/worker/issue. Last accessed June 2004.
18. Media reports describe condoms found in the pockets of young guerrilla fighters. Moreover, sacks of condoms have been found in their hideouts and in the pockets of dead guerrillas. Sources close to the Maoists explain three quite novel uses of condoms freely distributed by NGOs: (*i*) for antiseptic purposes on a cut; (*ii*) for carrying water; and (*iii*) as a protective cover for a musket-rifle.
19. Based on a field visit to Tebang in July 2002.
20. Text of proposals in *Nepal Samacharpatra* (Nepali daily), Kathmandu, 18 August 2003.
21. *Times of India*, 2005.

REFERENCES

Adele, Ann (1993). *Women Fighters of Liberation*. Jaffna: Publication Section LTTE/ Thasan Printers.

Bhattachan, Krishna (1999). 'Nepal: Minority Rights in a Predatory Nepalese State', in Sumanta Banerjee(ed.), *Shrinking Space: Minority Rights in South Asia*, pp. 38–58. Kathmandu: SAFHR.

Bhattarai, Baburam (1998). *Politico-Economic Rationale of People's War in Nepal*. Available at: www.maoism.org/misc/Nepal. Last accessed June 2004.

Chatterjee, Partha (1989). 'The Nationalist Resolution to the Women's Question', in Kumkum Sangari and

Sudesh Vaid (eds), *Recasting Women: Essays in Colonial History*, pp. 233–53. New Delhi: Kali for Women.

Coomaraswamy, Radhika (1997). 'Women of the LTTE', *Frontline*, 10 January, Chennai, p. 61.

Cordero, Isabel Coral (1998). 'Women in War: Impact and Responses', in Steve Stern (ed.), *Shining and*

Other Paths: War and Society in Peru 1980–1995, pp. 345–74. Durham, NC: Duke University Press.

Custers, Peter (1987). *Women in the Tebhaga Uprising*. Calcutta: Naya Prakashan.

De Mel, Neloufer (2001). *Women and the Nation's Narrative: Gender and Nationalism in 20th Century Sri Lanka*. New Delhi: Kali for Women.

De Sales, Anne (2003). 'The Kham Magar Country, Nepal: Between Ethnic Claims and Maoists', in Deepak Thapa (ed.), *Understanding the Maoist Movement in Nepal*, pp. 59–88. Kathmandu: Martin Chautari.

Dixit, Kanak Mani and Sashtri Ramachandran (eds) (2002). *State of Nepal*. Kathmandu: Himal Books.

Gautam, Shobha (2001). *Women and Children in the Periphery of the People's War.* Kathmandu: IHRICON.

Gautam, Shobha, Amrita Banskota and Rita Manchanda (2001). 'Where there are No Men: Women in the Maoist Insurgency in Nepal', Rita Manchanda (ed.), *Women, War and Peace in South Asia: Beyond Victimhood to Agency*, pp. 214–51. New Delhi: Sage Publications.

Gellner, David, Johana Pfaff-Czarnecka and John Whelpton (eds) (1997). *Nationalism and Ethnicity in a Hindu Kingdom.* Amsterdam: Harwood Academic Publishers.

Global IDP Project (2003). *Nepal IDP Research Initiative Findings.* Kathmandu: GTZ, INF, SNV, UNDP/RUPP and NHRC.

INSEC (1997) 'The Maoist People's War and Human Rights', in *Nepal Human Rights Yearbook 1996.* Kathmandu: INSEC.

———— (2004). *Nepal Human Rights Yearbook 2004.* Kathmandu: INSEC.

Jayawardena, Kumari (1986). *Feminism and Nationalism in the Third World.* London: Zed Books.

Karki, Arjun and David Seddon (eds) (2003). *The People's War in Nepal: Left Perspectives.* Delhi: Adroit Publishers.

Lalitha, K. and Vasantha Kannabiran (eds) (1998). *'We were Making History': Life Stories of Women in the Telegana People's Struggle.* New Delhi: Kali for Women.

Manandhar, Laxmi Keshari and Krishna B. Bhattachan (eds) (2001). *Gender and Democracy in Nepal.* Kathmandu: Central Department of Home Science—Women's Studies Program, Tribhuvan University.

Manchanda, Rita (ed.) (2001). *Women, War and Peace in South Asia: Beyond Victimhood to Agency.* New Delhi: Sage Publications.

———— (2003a). 'A Tale of Two Widows'. Inter Press Service.

———— (2003b). 'Gender Conflict and Displacement', presentation at 'Women and Migration' conference, Delhi University, December.

Martinez, Esperanza (2002). *Conflict-related Displacement.* Kathmandu: USAID.

Maycock, Matthew (2003). 'Whose Revolution? Can the Maoist Movement in Nepal Lead to Women's Empowerment?', unpublished MSc dissertation, School of Oriental and African Studies (SOAS), University of London.

Meintjes, Sheila, Anu Pillay and Meredith Turshen (2001). *The Aftermath: Women in Post Conflict Transformation.* London: Zed Books.

Menon, Ritu and Kamla Bhasin (1998). *Borders and Boundaries: Women in India's Partition.* New Delhi: Kali for Women.

Molnar, Augusta (1981). 'The Kham Magar Women of Thabang', in *Status of Women in Nepal*, 2(2).

Mulniari, Diana (1998). 'Broken Dreams in Nicaragua', in Lois Ann Lorentzen and Jennifer Turpin (eds), *The Women War Reader*, pp. 157–63. New York: New York University Press.

National Network Against Girl Trafficking (NNAGT) (2003). *Women's Voice: A Compendium of Articles on the Status of Women in Nepal.* Kathmandu: NNAGT.

Onesto, Li (1999). 'Report from the People's War in Nepal', reprinted in Deepak Thapa (ed.), *Understanding the Maoist Movement*, p. 167. Kathmandu: Martin Chautari.

———— (2000). 'Red Flag Flying on the Roof of the World: Interview with Prachanda', *Revolutionary Worker*, 1043, 20 February. Available at: www.rwor. org. Last accessed June 2004.

Parvati, Comrade (2003a). 'The Question of Women's Leadership in People's War in Nepal', *The Worker*, 8 January. Available at: www.cpnm.org/worker/ issue. Last accessed June 2004.

———— (2003b). 'Women's Perspectives in the Maoist Movement', in Arjun Karki and David Seddon (eds), *The People's War in Nepal: Left Perspectives*, pp. 165–72. Delhi: Adroit Publishers.

Pettigrew, Judith and Sara Shneiderman (2004). 'Women and the Maobaadi: Ideology and Agency in Nepal's Maoist Movement', *Himal Magazine*, 17 January, pp. 19–29.

Pradhan, Suman and Indrani Bagchi (2005). 'Nepal King Lifts Emergency', *Times of India*, 30 April 2005. Available at: http://timesofindia.indiatimes. com/articleshow/1094209.cms. Last accessed September 2005.

Rajasingham-Senanayake, Darini (2001). 'Ambivalent Empowerment: The Tragedy of Tamil Women in the Conflict', in Rita Manchanda (ed.), *Women, War and Peace in South Asia*, pp. 102–30. New Delhi: Sage Publications.

Sangari, Kumkum and Sudesh Vaid (eds) (1989). *Recasting Women: Essays in Colonial History*. New Delhi: Kali for Women.

Shah, Saubhagya (2002). 'From Evil State to Civil Society', in Kanak Mani Dixit and Sashtri Ramachandran (eds), *State of Nepal*, pp. 137–60. Kathmandu: Himal Books.

Shakhya, Sujita (2003). 'The Maoist Movement in Nepal: An Analysis from Women's Perspectives', in Arjun Karki and David Seddon (eds), *The People's War in Nepal: Left Perspectives*, pp. 375–404. Delhi: Adroit Publishers.

Tamang, Seira (2002). 'The Politics of "Developing" Nepali Women', in Kanak Mani Dixit and Sashtri Ramachandran (eds), *State of Nepal*, pp. 161–75. Kathmandu: Himal Books.

Thapa, Deepak and Bandita Sijapati (eds) (2003). *Understanding the Maoist Movement in Nepal*. Kathmandu: Martin Chautari.

Thapa, Manjushree (2004). 'Girls in Nepal's Maoist War', *Himal Magazine*, 16 June, pp. 49–59. Available at: http://www.himalmag.com. Last accessed June 2004.

Upreti, Aruna (2003). 'Letter to the Maoist Leadership on Women's Day', *Nepali Times*, 7 March, Kathmandu.

4

Sexualizing the State

Sodomy, Civil Liberties, and the Indian Penal Code
Jyoti Puri

MOBILIZING AGAINST SECTION 377

On 2 September 2004, the Delhi High Court ruled against a public interest litigation (PIL, Civil Writ Petition No. 7455 of 2001) challenging the scope of Section 377 of the Indian Penal Code (IPC).[1] Section 377 can be described as the 'sodomy law' that criminalizes sexual practices—mostly oral and anal sex—and, despite its emphasis on sexual practices, is widely interpreted to make same-sex sexual lives illegal in India.[2] Naz Foundation (India) Trust, a Delhi-based organization working with Human Immuno-Deficiency Virus (HIV)/Acquired Immuno-Deficiency Syndrome (AIDS) issues, petitioned the court to 'read down'[3] Section 377 to exclude same-sex private adult consensual sexual practices from its purview.[4] The court turned it down on the grounds that Naz (India) did not have the locus standi to file the PIL since it was not directly affected by the law, contrary to the point that a PIL may be filed by anyone, including those not directly impacted.[5]

These events are significant not least because the Naz (India) PIL was the second of two courageous attempts to decriminalize same-sex sexual practices and, by extension, same-sex sexual subjectivities in India. The AIDS Bhedbhav Virodhi Andolan (ABVA, AIDS Anti-discrimination Campaign) led the way with the first petition filed in the Delhi High Court in 1994.[6] At the time, state agents, including the then superintendent of Tihar Jail in Delhi, Kiran Bedi, prevented the distribution of condoms to protect inmates against sexually transmitted diseases, especially HIV/AIDS (Bhaskaran 2001; Kapur 2004). For Naz (India), the hindering of much-needed HIV/AIDS outreach efforts due to the criminalization of same-sex sexualities was the primary motivation against Section 377.[7] As a community-based organization, Naz (India) does HIV/AIDS outreach work, promoting awareness, providing care and support for those infected with, and those affected by, the virus. Although the Naz (India) petition was turned down, the legal process is still underway; a special leave petition[8] was filed with the Supreme Court on 17 February 2005 to reconsider the grounds upon which the Delhi High Court rejected the PIL.[9]

Mobilization against Section 377 has deepened and widened across India since the two petitions were filed, and the law has become the lightning rod of protests against social and state discrimination of same-sex sexualities. Voices Against Section 377 is forged out of a coalition of Delhi-based groups, including women's and feminist groups, sexuality rights groups, child rights groups, and individuals united in their struggle to change the law.[10] The Million Voices Campaign is underway to gather and document a million voices opposed to the law.[11] The National Campaign for Sexuality Rights, coordinated through the Bangalore-based sexuality rights organization, Sangama, is primarily oriented against Section 377. On 16 August 2005, in the aftermath of India's 58th independence anniversary, a coalition of Mumbai-based groups and individuals courageously rallied in Flora Fountain, the city's centre, to protest for legal change. These are among the vivid but not only examples of the widening circles of the struggle to change or repeal the law and, in effect, to decriminalize same-sex sexuality. Even though the law affects all sexually active persons in India, anyone who might consider anal or oral sex, the immediate impact is on same-sex sexualities.

Same sex sexualities is shorthand for gendered and sexual subjects insufficiently described through the terminology of gay, lesbian, bisexual, queer, transgender, Kinnar/Aravani/Hijra, Kothis, and men who have sex with men (MSM). These terms are contested ones. MSM was coined to signal the many and varied circumstances under which men will have sex with men and to contest the ostensibly class-based and Westernized connotations of the term 'gay' (S. Khan 2000, 2001). However, others have objected to its implicitly behaviourist and depoliticized connotations while defending the salience of gay, lesbian, and bisexual as not always already Westernized and as the basis for political mobilization of sexuality rights (O. Khan 2000; Vanita 2001). Sexuality-rights based groups, Prism in New Delhi and LABIA (Lesbians and Bisexuals in Action) in Mumbai, incorporate the term queer as a means of forging political alliances.[12] Among the most socially and sexually marginalized, Hijra is a long-standing, changing, and hybrid cultural identity within the subcontinent. Partly due to the derogatory use of the term and partly due to regional variations, the terms transgender, Kinnar (in the Delhi area), Aravanis (in the Chennai area) circulate along with Hijra.[13] Although some may self-define as neither man nor woman, most identify as women, and a few will refer to the self in masculine terms. A few are born intersexed, some voluntarily castrate, and almost all wear women's clothing at least some of the time and in most cases wear their hair long. Most importantly, they are expected to live by the cultural codes of their community (Cohen 1995; Jaffrey 1996). Often incorporated under the aegis of MSM, Kothis are largely described as feminine-identified men from the working classes who have sex with normatively gendered or hypermasculine men. Sexual partnering with men and women (some are married) varies according to circumstance and while some choose to cross-dress occasionally or mostly, others do not. This brief overview of the terms is not meant to suggest clear-cut differences for the terms circulate freely.[14] Rather, they are reminders of the gendered, sexuality- and class-based, regional and historical variations among same-sex sexualities and highlight that sexual violence is differently inflicted by state institutions, a point that is explored in the subsequent section.

State-based discrimination against same-sex sexualities cuts across South Asia and law is only one of its aspects. Similar laws exist in Bangladesh (Section 377 Bangladesh Penal Code), India (Section 377 IPC), Pakistan (Section 377 Pakistan Penal Code), and Sri Lanka (Sections 365 and 365A of the Penal Code). Activists in Sri Lanka have been at the forefront of challenges to sodomy laws in the subcontinent and their struggle has yielded important lessons about the redoubtable power of state institutions and legal structures. As a result of a legislative effort to undo the British colonial law criminalizing sodomy incorporated into Sri Lanka's legal regime, Section 365 was not repealed and, to make matters far worse, members of parliament voted to expand the scope of the law to include women and worsened the possible penalty.[15] But the effect of law extends beyond court prosecutions. In fact, as will be explored in this article, few cases of same-sex consensual sexualities are prosecuted in the higher courts in India. Rather, state institutions, such as the police, abuse the law to commit physical violence, extort, blackmail, and harass.[16] Feminized males/men are the most frequent targets of state and extra-state violence.[17] This targeting is powerfully captured in the accounts of the Blue Diamond Society, an organization for sexual minorities in Nepal, where police abuses of sexual minorities are widespread and most often aimed against Meti (feminized males).[18] Section 377's egregious impact in India extends beyond physical violence to enabling a culture that defends discrimination of same-sex sexualities as public morality and supports intolerance and violence committed in intimate spaces of the family as maintenance of social order. The law and its prohibitions may be said to be widely internalized to defend people's prejudices against same-sex sexualities and, thereby, give false justification for violence against these sexualities (Narrain and Bhan 2005). Section 377 not only criminalizes some sexualities as non-normative but also *institutionalizes* unequal rights and lack of protections of citizenship. The importance of undoing Section 377 cannot be overemphasized for it is the first step towards ensuring legal recognition, rights and protections for same-sex sexualities.

This article calls for a thorough scrutiny of the state and the role of state institutions in perpetrating social injustice through law and its enforcement. My analytical and political intervention here is not only to raise the issue of direct and indirect state violence against same-sex sexualities, which I do. It is also to see the state as a contested site. Critical activists and scholars are keenly aware of how state policies and laws thoroughly mediate citizenship as sexual and gendered. Recent challenges to national laws that criminalize homosexuality (Sri Lanka, Sections 365 and 365A of the Penal Code; United States, *Lawrence et al.* v. *Texas*, 26 June 2003) demonstrate the impact of the state on matters of sexuality, especially for those denied equal access to the rights of citizenship.

Yet, we do not similarly attend to the conceptualization of the state, to state institutions and structures, their interrelations, from the lens of sexuality. As scholars and activists of sexuality and gender, our struggle is to not reproduce the state as monolithic, unified, and coherent. Rather our aim is to demonstrate the state as an unstable and complexly related set of structures, institutions, agencies, and discourses that are saturated with sexuality but also with the inconsistencies of power. The challenge is to identify the institutional arrangements of power while identifying the 'internal' inconsistencies as well as consistencies of operations. Such approaches help dispel the fiction of the state as overarching and encompassing (Ferguson and Gupta 2002) and avoid lending the state further strength.

Feminist scholars, especially those speaking to postcolonial contexts have been at the forefront of gendering analyses of the state (Enloe 2000; Hasan 1994; Kandayoti 1991; Peterson 1992; Radcliffe and Westwood 1996; Stevens 1999; Yuval-Davis and Anthias 1989). The significance of state policies and effects on women, the gendered, race-, religion-, and class-based inequalities of citizenship, and the gendered masculinist politics of state institutions, such as development and the military, are underscored in these contributions. While considerations of sexuality are implicitly part of these analyses, they are often seen as corollaries of gender. Exchanges across sexuality and gender studies illuminate the importance of not collapsing or separating considerations of these two constructs (Butler 1994; Sedgwick 1990). Sexuality and gender, like gendered and sexualized violence, are by no means interchangeable constructs (Abelove 1993); yet, neither are they disconnected.

The analytics of violence as gendered are crucial to the recognition of how women, transgenders and men survive state policies and ideologies in the everyday and the exceptional. The violence that is nation state takes multiple forms—economic, ideological, physical, sexual—and is inflicted in ways that recognize persons—whether women, transgenders, men— as deeply and differently gendered selves and symbols of collectivities (Agnes 1999; De Mel 2001; Hasan and Menon 2004; Rouse 2004). In their instructive essay, Banerjee et al. (2004) show how a gendered analysis of violence reveals the commonality of women's experience across sexual brutalization, displacement, death, property, and more. How state violence is inflicted and experienced by women of numerous ethnic, caste, religious, and class groups varies but what holds together the custodial rape of Dalit women with that of the disenfranchised upper-caste Hindu widow are women's bodies as metonyms of sexuality, family, of community, and of nation. A gendered analysis of sexual violence tells us much about the deeply entrenched ideologies of gender and (hetero) sexual difference that make only women and girls the subject of rape laws in the IPC to the exclusion of boys, transgenders and males/men.[19] That marital rape is not recognized under rape law, that rape rather than sexual assault is codified in law further reflects on the importance of questioning the gendered nature of violence and its institutionalization in the state in India.

A subtext of this article is the importance of also attending to the analytics of sexual violence in ways that are not grounded in unrelenting assumptions of heterosexuality. State violence rests not only on ideologies and regimes of gender difference. It also rests on relentless reproduction of the violence that is heteronormativity.[20] What gives force to heteronormativity is its normalization through social institutions and structures, especially the nation state, and its active re-production as natural and eternal. Determining who belongs to the national community, the privileging of normatively gendered, heterosexual women and men from the dominant social classes as the bearers of respectable sexuality, and the precariousness of same-sex sexualities are directly shaped by the nation's heteronormative underpinnings (Aarmo 1999; Gopinath 2005; Puri 2004). The citizen-subject of the national state is constituted through the social arrangements predicated on *'compulsory heterosexuality'* (after Adrienne Rich) and its conjunctions with ethnicity, radicalization, caste and class processes (Alexander 1997, 1991; Luibhéid 2002). Having to pass as a single heterosexual woman in order to retain one's flat and one's job in New Delhi, for example, to live in fear of physical and emotional violence should one's sexual orientation become known, denial of the gamut of rights of citizenship as a result of criminalization and invisibilization of lesbian sexuality, lack of state protections against discrimination give some indication of the tremendous costs exacted from women by the heteronormative mandate. Yet, as the presence of women who seek sexual intimacy with other women makes plain, 'compulsory heterosexuality' is neither unchallenged nor the only possibility.

Between June and August 2003, I started researching the mobilization against Section 377. The Naz (India) PIL had served to bring the injustices of Section 377 into focus for the second time since ABVA's petition in 1994. Its outcome, the government response, the legal proceedings, and the role of the Delhi High Court in mediating a matter of potential public controversy were of urgent concern. The grounds upon which the Naz (India) PIL petitioned the state for legal amendment, the strategies used, the gendered and class-based sexualities that were the subjects of the petition, the process through which the petition was developed, the support and the criticism expressed by sexuality rights organizations and activists were of as much concern to me as the petition's outcome. The Naz (India) PIL, the court hearings, the government's response filed a year and a half later in September 2003, the positions taken by the various agencies indicted in the petition provided invaluable insights into not just state power but also inconsistencies and fractures thereof. This research was expanded and deepened in the summer of 2005, from which I draw selectively, here.

For the purpose of this article, I highlight the Naz (India) PIL as one example of the mobilization against the sodomy law in India. I draw on interviews conducted with Shaleen Rakesh, then coordinator of the MSM Project and person appointed as the organizational representative on the PIL, among others, and relevant documents and minutes of meetings. Particularly interested in the question of the state, I met with several of the official spokespersons of the various state agencies named in the Naz (India) petition. These included then police commissioner of New Delhi, a representative from the police commissioner's office, and an official from the judicial section of the Ministry of Home Affairs. The director of the National AIDS Council was unavailable despite repeated requests to meet. Though they are not named in the Naz (India) petition, I also met with a representative from the National Human Rights Commission. To this, I add research from the summer of 2005, which involved additional interviews with staff of the Ministry of Home Affairs and discussions with members of the Delhi police, especially constables. Formal recorded and informal interviews were the primary means of data collection, along with court documents and statements.

The Naz (India) PIL foregrounds questions about sexual and gendered subjectivities, law as a site of contestation, and state policies that promote sexual and gender- and class-based forms of violence. It presents questions not sufficiently contended with: how is the state conceptualized, imagined as the arbiter of rights, sexual and gender normality, and legality and criminality, and organized through the discourses of sexuality? This is the point of departure of this article. What critical readings of the state might the Naz (India) PIL against Section 377 enable? What insights about the nature and functioning of the state, how we conceptualize 'it', might be derived by looking at the state through the framework of sexuality? Posed as such, these questions hearken Michel Foucault's (1978) framing of sexuality as a transfer point of power; how and in what ways do discourses of sexuality densely organize and permeate state institutions and agencies, their frequently fraught inconsistent interrelations, state agents and representatives, state policies, and, indeed, the terrain of governmentality?[21] The understanding of sexuality used here draws directly from Foucault's (1978, 1980) insights that it is no obdurate biological drive, but a historical construct, instrumental to the enactment of power through formation of knowledge, the simulation of bodies, pleasures, and the incitement of discourses of subjectivity, control and resistance. Sexuality's instrumentality in the dispersal of power, especially at the level of institutions, is of concern in this article.

What is at stake, here, is the issue of resistance to state violence and effective challenges to strategies of power. By turning the lens on the unjust criminalization of some sexualities, the Naz (India) PIL takes an important step in that direction. I believe that the imagination of the state and approaches to the state that would help undermine its power, regardless of the legal outcome, are useful to consider. Inasmuch as the Naz (India) attempt to bring social change through legal reform may be read as failure due to the Delhi High Court's 2004 decision, such a reading lends further strength to the state; the imagination of the state as a cohesive, rather than a composite and unstable hegemon, is unwittingly reasserted. In contrast, the PIL gives us a necessary glimpse into the numerous points of fractures and inconsistencies that help undermine the reproduction of state power.

To analyse state structures from the intertwined lens of sexuality and gender, I draw upon queer theory, the insights of postcolonial feminist theory on law and violence against women, and critical, feminist approaches to conceptualizing the state. The intention is to underscore the heteronormative and masculinist moorings of not just state policies but also state institutions, agencies and authorities. Insofar as analyses of sexuality leave the concept of the state unexamined, its hegemony may be reproduced and the analyses become unwittingly complicit with state power. In a nutshell, my purpose is to 'sexualize the state', or in the language of queer theory, to 'queer the state' (Duggan 1994: 1). Building on critical approaches to the state and sexuality, this article argues the importance of seeing the state as a fragmented, inconsistent set of institutions and relations, both reproductive of domination and open to contestation. This analysis examines strategies for combating sexual and gendered violence materially and symbolically encrypted in Section 377. The regrettable outcome of the Naz (India) petition at the Delhi High Court makes these considerations and critical interventions especially urgent.

LEGACIES, CONTEXTS AND CONCERNS

Section 377 is rooted in the legacies of the British colonial state and the interlaced colonial anxieties of national, socio-sexual, and racial purity at home and in the colonies. In her informative essay, Suparna Bhaskaran (2001) locates the first British civil injunction against sodomy in 1533 by Henry VIII, thereby making sodomy a secular rather than ecclesiastical crime and challenging the Catholic Church and papal authority. Although an 1860 revision, implemented in 1862, reduced the punishment for sodomy from execution to ten years' imprisonment in Britain, its introduction into the subcontinent a year later served to institutionalize what was in pre-colonial India a minor strand of homophobia (Vanita 2001; Vanita and Kidwai 2000). In their ground-breaking collection, *Same-Sex Love in India*, editors Ruth Vanita and Saleem Kidwai charge the introduction of this anti-sodomy law as Section 377, along with the suppression of Rekhti (Urdu poetry written in the vernacular that represents sexual intimacy among women) and the heterosexualization of the *ghazal* (often extolling passion among men), as a key marker of the broadening scope of homophobia and its institutionalization under the state in colonial India. The intersecting vectors of racial, class and sexual differences mark some of the early case law under Section 377, and work to specify and preserve a hierarchal colonial social order. Bhaskaran (2001) analyses early cases to show that racial differences are maintained between the colonizer and the colonized, aggressive masculinity and sexual degeneracy is imputed to the colonized labouring classes in contrast to the effeteness ascribed to the colonized elite, and relentlessly heterosexist reasoning is used to decide cases.[22] The criminalization of same-sex sexual practices, regardless of age and consent, was symbolic of the gradual suppression and partial erosion of rich and varied traditions of same-sex eroticism, sexual practices and representations within the subcontinent.

That this law was seamlessly incorporated into the legal structures of the postcolonial national states in the subcontinent disturbingly reflects dominant nationalism and normative sexuality. The imbrications of dominant nationalisms and sexualities in contemporary India have been particularly troubling. Perhaps no postcolonial nationalist myth on sexuality is more pervasive than the belief that homosexuality is alien to India (read as: Hinduism), and the outcome of Mughal invasions and Westernization. The questionable position taken is that the Indian, seen synonymous with Brahminical, past was devoid of expressions of homoeroticism and same-sex sexual practices until it was introduced through Mughal invasions (Bacchetta 1999). The trope of Westernization is also used to disavow rich histories of same-sex sexuality as un-Indian. Much needs to be and has been said to challenge this Hindu right wing nationalist stance. One counter expression is the writing of alternate sexual cultural histories (Thadani 1996; Vanita and Kidwai 2000). These alternate histories seek to challenge dominant nationalisms by revealing an ancient and pre-modern past replete with expressions of same-sex love, desire and behaviours, which, while sometimes disapproved and punished, were nonetheless tolerated, and survived.

The Naz (India) PIL, as well as the 1994 petition by ABVA, signals a parallel political mobilization against state policies and laws. How the state institutionalizes heteronormativity, heterosexism and homophobia through laws and their enactment (especially Section 377), through policies discrepantly enforced by its various agencies and representatives (for example, the National AIDS Control Organization's handling of the issue of HIV/AIDS) are of particular concern to the gathering momentum of sexual minority rights' activism in India. The state as a purveyor of violence against same-sex sexualities is a key target of the mobilization. Exhorting the Supreme Court to intervene against Section 377, long-standing gay activist Saleem Kidwai (2005) recently noted that the defunctness of the law makes it dangerous, for it is used to inflict material and sexual violence. He rightly observes that it is difficult for the state to prosecute people for same-sex sexual acts without vindictiveness. Section 377 has become a conductor for the mobilization against violence towards same sex sexualities that often stretches seamlessly across putative distinctions of state and civil society beyond the realm of law. The immediate purpose of the legal challenge presented by the Naz (India) PIL, however, is the decriminalization of same-sex sexualities in India.

An important point to underscore is that legal decriminalization of same-sex sexual practices would not mean the lack of regulation of same-sex sexual subjects or that same-sex sexual subjects are no longer under the purview of the state. State regulation of sexuality is mediated by but extends beyond law. Counter-intuitively, legal reform can serve to strengthen the state and give greater force to some institutions through changing and adding legislation. Feminist scholars Flavia Agnes (1999) and Nivedita Menon (2004), writing on law, gender and sexuality in India, have carefully and compellingly pointed out the limits of what appear to be legal successes for women in the courts. For example, Menon problematizes the feminist argument that what's needed to protect women in India, and elsewhere, from sexual assault are better formulated laws by noting the decreasing number of successful convictions and the deeply misogynist assumptions underlying even favourable decisions and successful convictions. Critical race studies scholars, such as Kimberlé Crenshaw (1995) and Mari Matsuda (1996), have made a parallel argument about the institutional biases of law in the United States, which favour the privileges of whiteness, wealth and maleness, and the limits of seeking justice through legal reform.

The Naz (India) PIL against Section 377 was filed in the Delhi High Court on 6 December 2001. Legal representation was provided by Lawyer's Collective HIV/AIDS Unit, under the stewardship of the director, Anand Grover.[23] Since Naz (India) was willing to serve as the petitioner, the case was filed in the Delhi High Court. A favourable decision by the court would have had nation-wide legal impact, contingent on final approval by the Supreme Court to amend the law. As Vivek Diwan at the Lawyer's Collective suggested, the overall strategy was that should the Delhi High Court reject the petition, there would be recourse to the Supreme Court since it was a question of fundamental rights. While the upper courts may rule on any laws, matters of fundamental rights may be brought before the Supreme Court. This strategy is being explored as a subsequent petition to review the Delhi High Court's unfavourable decision was also turned down (3 November 2004, Review Petition No. 384/2004).[24]

Organizations such as Naz (India) and ABVA stay clear of state-based funding. In the case of Naz (India), it has deliberately sought to protect itself from state scrutiny and tried to avoid compromising advocacy work on behalf of sexual minorities by looking for funding elsewhere. Naz (India) is currently supported by funds from MacArthur and Ford foundations, United States, and Lotteries Commission, United Kingdom (now known as Community Fund), among other sources.[25] Ironically but expectedly, Naz (India) frequently finds itself at odds with the state on behalf of vulnerable groups, as Rakesh explained.[26] This paradoxical situation repeats and endures, despite the fact that the state relies heavily on organizations such as Naz (India) to do the necessary HIV/AIDS outreach work. Naz (India) does not see itself as a rights-based organization but chooses to position itself as intervening primarily in sexual health-related matters. Still, as is well stated in the petition, matters of health, life and rights are closely related.

While a thoroughgoing analysis of the petition, its possibilities and pitfalls, is outside of the scope of this article, a summation gives insight into the strategies and orientations that shaped it. Developed over a three-year period, the PIL's legal strategy to petition the Delhi High Court to 'read down' Section 377 (see note 3) to exclude private adult consensual sex was based on two factors. To repeal Section 377 of IPC, a bill would have to be introduced, debated and voted upon favourably in the parliament, an unviable option due to the lack of sufficient support in the legislature, according to Rakesh.[27] The second factor has to do with recourse to Section 377 in order to prosecute sexual assault against children. Existing laws narrowly address forcible sexual intercourse or rape committed by men against women and girls (under sixteen years of age, or fifteen years if married) and altogether ignores sexual assault against boys. Violence against women, girls and boys is selectively recognized by the law, which, in turn, perpetuates it; ignoring marital rape or sexual assault that goes beyond forcible penile penetration of the vagina paradoxically renders rape law another site of the normalization of violent sexuality. The ambiguous language of '*carnal intercourse against the order of nature*' (see note 2) oddly is the only recourse to prosecute sexual assault on boys and aggravated sexual assault on girls that extends beyond the scope of penal-vaginal penetration.

The PIL was strategically shaped by an emphasis on health, which stages and subsumes issues of fundamental rights. It suggests that Section 377 jeopardizes the health of MSM and gay men and, in effect, their lives by promoting social stigma, enabling abuse by the police, and pushing homosexual acts underground. Thus, the constitutional validity of Section 377 is challenged on the grounds that it violates fundamental rights guaranteed by the state, namely Article 14 (Equality before Law), Article 15 (Prohibition of Sex Discrimination, argued to include sexual orientation), Article 19 (Fundamental Liberties), and Article 21 (Right to Life and Privacy).[28] Of these, the right to privacy, under the ambit of ordered liberty and individual autonomy, and the violation of right to life, at once protected under Article 21, are emphasized. Sexual relations are among the most private aspects of a person's life and selfhood, which, according to the PIL, this law continually jeopardizes even when no harm is done to others.

The PIL highlights the material, endangering impact of Section 377 alongside its oppressive symbolism; the law promotes homophobia and discriminates against homosexuals by creating a class of people continually victimized in society and by state agencies, such as the police. As a legal code introduced under the British colonial state, Section 377's anachronistic, aberrant nature is outrightly criticized in the petition. The PIL argues that the law is Judaeo-Christian[29] in orientation and inconsistent with Indian cultural history, which makes it especially egregious in its promotion of homophobia (Civil Writ Petition 7455 of 2001). Section 377 is also noted to be inconsistent with international law (Article 12 of the Universal Declaration of Human Rights and Article 8 of the European Convention for the protection of Human Rights and Fundamental Freedoms) by which India abides. Although more could be said about the deleterious impact of Section 377, this is a damning and needed indictment of the state from the perspective of same-sex sexualities by any count.

If the decision that a health-based, right-to-private-consensual-sexual-activity approach against Section 377 was likely to be better received by the courts, by the government, and the various respondents named (identified below) in the Naz (India) PIL, then it was not a decision without consequences. The limits of this approach are not only reflected in the language and positioning of the PIL but are reasons for reservations expressed by other sexuality rights activists and groups. For example, an autonomous feminist group in Mumbai challenged the absence of a fundamental, civil rights approach in the petition against Section 377.[30] A health-based approach does not sufficiently unsettle the structural and institutional underpinnings of heterosexism. It might solicit a practical logic to consider the legal recognition of adult, consensual same-sex sexual activity in private on the grounds that criminalization of same-sex sexualities is making them and others more vulnerable to the transmission of HIV. This, even if granted by the courts, would not build an adequate case for the recognition of civil liberties, fundamental rights, and, therefore, the assurance of equality of citizenship, and protection from discrimination. The logic that citizenship rights accrue to normative heterosexuality, insofar as it intersects with privileges of gender, class, ethnicity and religion, would remain intact. Not only do the problems of heterosexism confound the health-based focus of the PIL but it is also marked by tensions of gender, of class, and of the variations among same-sex sexualities. The language of privacy becomes embattled from the perspective of groups who do not fit the profile of gay, relatively privileged men.

The petition focused on gay men and MSM, groups identified as especially vulnerable to the spread of HIV and AIDS-related complications. Lesbian women, as a low-risk group for HIV infections, are sidelined in the petition. Nevertheless, lesbian women are not as well inured from the threat of Section 377. Only one case involving two consenting women has been prosecuted in the higher courts (Bhaskaran 2001), but the threat of Section 377 and the social sanctions against homosexuality saturate daily life with the violence of heteronormativity. Especially since the language of the law emphasizes penetration in its explanation section of 377, it leaves open the possibility of prosecuting lesbian women[31]; would the law emphasize *penile* penetration, women would be excluded from its purview (Vanita and Kidwai 2000). Thus, even though lesbian, bisexual, or transgendered women are vulnerable to the threat of Section 377, the health-rights strategy of the PIL makes them partially invisible.

The language of privacy in the petition inadvertently foregrounds class privilege. Men without access to same-sex sexual activity in the privacy of a home or a hotel, especially those who are economically marginal, are directly vulnerable to the threat and enforcement of Section 377. Indeed, accounts of state and extra-state violence are told by men/ males from the working classes.[32] The petition foregrounds HIV/AIDS outreach workers and MSM, who are frequently though not always, from less resourced social class backgrounds. But, the language of privacy undermines the degree of protection that a possible amendment to Section 377 would allow these men/males. The paradoxical legacies of the hyper-sexualization of working class manliness and the presumption of sexual access to those who are not seen as conventionally male and conventionally heterosexual makes the threat of Section 377 all the more real for these males/men.

What goes frequently unstated but is not unrelated is the threat of Section 377 to transgenders/Hijras/Kinnars/Aravanis. In yet another postcolonial twist to the persistent legacies of the colonial state, castration, whether forced or voluntary, is illegal under Sections 320 and 322 IPC (Gupta 2002b; Talwar 1999). Further, due to the pervasiveness of normative sexual dimorphism—two biological categories of female and male—in state laws and policies related to subjectivity and citizenship, the social and political status of transgendered people in India is constantly at risk; the lack of a systematic policy towards transgenders means an ambiguous civil and political status for them. This combination of lack of full recognition by the state, the criminalization of voluntary castration, and the tendency to perceive Hijras as erstwhile, and therefore essentially males/men, makes them especially vulnerable to the homophobia and heterosexism underlying Section 377. Relentless perceptions of transgenders—whether castrated, male-bodied or intersexed—as males prevents them from filing a complaint of sexual assault with the police for fear of being booked under Section 377. Despite reports of wide prevalence of sexual violence against them, they are afraid that their complaints of sexual assault will be unjustly interpreted by the police as falsified accounts of a failed commercial sex transaction and they will, instead, be accused of homosexual activity.[33] How they are simultaneously recognized and rendered invisible within the terminology of MSM is relevant here. The PIL and other discussions of MSM arguably include Hijras (Khan 2001). But insofar as transgenders are subsumed under this category of same-sex sexualities the particularities of how Hijras become vulnerable to allegations against 'unnatural sex' differently from males/men are lost and the significance of the laws against castration are sidelined.

The Naz (India) PIL represents a necessary and courageous move against the legalization of homophobia and heteronormativity in Section 377 towards the decriminalization of same-sex sexualities in India. As a result of intense deliberations and strategic considerations, the PIL took a health-based, rather than sexual rights, approach against Section 377, which coincided with the organization's mission and orientation. The PIL rightly indicted the state on its failure to protect the lives, interests and the rights of those most vulnerable to HIV/AIDS. The petition and the process through which it was developed are not without significant criticisms, which are shadowed above. The PIL, the Delhi High Court hearings, and the responses of other state institutions present the nexus between state and sexuality. The petition against Section 377 is an opportunity to interrogate the state through a queer lens, to question the nature of the state, its inconsistencies across institutions and agencies, and effective ways in which to undo its predominance.

SCRUTINIZING THE STATE

What does it mean to scrutinize the state from the framework of sexuality, to sexualize the state? This speaks foremost to how the state is imagined. In their introduction to the book, *States of Imagination: Ethnographic Explorations of the Postcolonial State*, Thomas Hansen and Finn Stepputat (2001) note that in addition to the material aspects, modern states are also defined by the *'imagination of the state'* (p. 8); the idea of the state and its existence. The authors draw on Foucault to describe the materiality of the state as vivid and violent; the state is characterized by claims of territorial sovereignty through a monopoly over violence, the gathering and control of knowledge about the population, and the generation of resources through a national economy towards the well-being of the population. What Hansen and Stepputat underscore is how important the idea of the state as a normal and permanent feature is to its continued existence. The institutionalization of law as the source of state authority, the materialization of the state in permanent signs, rituals, monuments, letterheads, etc., and the nationalization of the territory and state institutions through the writing of history and notions of a national community perpetuate the idea of the state (ibid.).

The imagination of the state is produced not just through state discourses and institutions but is collectively shared. Attempts to bring about social change through legal reform are important but also part and parcel of the shared production of the state as the overarching arbiter of rights and protections. Hardly limited to the Naz (India) PIL, this is true of the myriad and innumerable attempts at securing rights through state institutions and agencies. One of the initial points of criticism against the PIL, noted by sexuality rights activists not associated with it, questioned the value of directing resources towards legal rather than cultural change. Notwithstanding this criticism, the Naz (India) PIL to amend Section 377 and decriminalize homosexuality filed against state bureaucracies reflects how the imagination of the state as the permanent overarching authority is collectively sustained and how inescapable it may be.

Even though the idea of the state is preserved through recourse to legal reform, it becomes a ready icon of power's egregiousness that extends well beyond the putative boundaries of the state. Rallying against Section 377 may not only decriminalize same-sex sexualities in India. The PIL helps stage Section 377 as the predominant symbol of state *and* social injustices against same-sex sexualities around which a broad coalition of groups, individuals and organizations can come together. For example, despite the reservations of several sexuality rights-based groups in Bangalore, Mumbai and New Delhi against the Naz (India) petition, there is widely shared consensus that a collective movement against Section 377 could help create the awareness and sensitization necessary for change in social attitudes in civil society and state institutions, among ordinary people as well as state agents. According to Rakesh, setting into motion a gay and lesbian movement across India was part of the intended strategy of the Naz (India) PIL;[34] although, unpredictably, it was the government's response to the PIL in September 2003 that rallied together a coalition of groups across the country and triggered the formation of Voices Against Section 377 in Delhi, and National Coalition of Sexuality Rights in Bangalore. In her interview, a member of the group Voices Against Section 377 expressed her enthusiasm at this national mobilization but also her concern that the coalition would fragment once same-sex sexualities were decriminalized.[35]

Perhaps no site is more implicated in how the state is imagined than scholarly writings. Few would dispute the point that the state is not a monolithic organization or a thing. Yet, conceptually and empirically the state is often treated as an 'it'; what Philip Corrigan (1994: xvii) has aptly called 'thingification' (borrowing from Césaire [1972] who coined the term). Insofar as part of the power of the state rests on *its* imagination, scholarly analyses that treat the state as a monolith unwittingly lend further force to this idea. Curiously, debates on the state, in particular how to theorize the relation between state and civil society, have helped sustain imaginations of the state.[36] Notwithstanding well-established criticisms, the misleading distinctions between state and civil society continue to circulate widely, and lend weight to the state as a normal and necessary feature of society. In contrast, Timothy Mitchell (1991, 1999) insightfully notes that the state is a structural *effect*—not a real structure, but a powerful and metaphysical effect that sustains the myth of its coherence, unity and distinction from society. Moreover, assuming the distinctions between state and civil society obscures the point that these are hierarchical distinctions in which one is granted power (state) over the other (civil society). The hierarchy of state power is forcefully evident in James Ferguson and Akhil Gupta's (2002) important caution that the state is implicitly imagined and empowered as both the highest authority and the natural container of culture, society and politics.

While some scholarship and theorizations may preserve state imaginations and power, critical interventions help unravel these imaginations, and denaturalize the state. I refer to the growing contributions of political anthropological work grounded in careful ethnographies of the state. Drawing strength from Philip Corrigan and Derek Sayer's (1985) approach to the state as cultural production, these ethnographies are also influenced by the theorizations of Antonio Gramsci (1971) and the insights of post-structuralism, especially Foucault's (1994) work on governmentality. The writings focus on the intricacies and nuances of state-making, the possible existence of more than one state, mundane routinized effects of the state, consistencies and inconsistencies, and hegemonic and contested aspects of the state, as well as the blurred boundaries between state, civil society and community in numerous cultural contexts (Ferguson and Gupta 2002; Gupta 1995; Hansen and Stepputat 2001; Joseph and Nugent 1994; Ong 1999; Scott 1998; Steinmetz 1999). Foucault's work (1978, 1980, 1985) linking sexuality to nation has afforded numerous feminist excavations exploring the relation of sexuality and gender to larger contests (Diamond and Quinby 1988; McClintock et al. 1997; Rubin 1993; Sawicki 1991; Stoler 1995a). Other arguments attend to gender, such as Gupta (2001) and Seider (2001).

Seeing the state as disaggregated, possibly marked by fractures and disjunctions between and among the various parts whose internal consistencies and coherence cannot be prejudged is crucial to unravelling state power (Gupta 1995; Hansen and Stepputat 2001). The Naz (India)

PIL exemplifies the promise (and pitfalls) of such an approach to the state. The petition takes the inconsistencies and disaggregations of the state as its starting point in two ways. First, the language of the PIL points out irregularities among the laws and rights guaranteed by the state. By juxtaposing Section 377 with the fundamental rights stated in Article 14 of the Indian Constitution (see discussion in section entitled, Legacies, Contexts and Concerns), the PIL reveals how Section 377 is incompatible with the guarantees of fundamental liberties provided by the Constitution to all citizens. Insofar as such incompatibilities are strategies of power and state regulation, the PIL takes the position that this is outside the scope of the state's function, especially because the state ought to have no compelling interest in curtailing private sexual relations among consenting adults. Second, the PIL is directed against specifically named respondents, disaggregating 'the state' for those who see fundamental rights, including the right to life, in jeopardy. The respondents are listed in the following order: Government of National Capital Territory of Delhi, Police Commissioner of New Delhi, Delhi State AIDS Control Society, National AIDS Control Organization (NACO), Union of India's Ministry of Home Affairs, Ministry of Health Welfare, and Ministry of Social Welfare.

In his article on the discourse of state corruption in a north Indian village, Gupta (1995) similarly notes how regional newspapers and their readers, of necessity, are less likely to reify the state as a monolithic organization, to explicitly name the various state bureaucracies, and to highlight stories of corruption. While Gupta's observations are a useful reminder about polysemic interpretations, it helps me underscore the point that a disaggregated state is ineffective or weakened; rather, inconsistency and incoherence may not only characterize modern states, but also make them more powerful (Hansen and Stepputat 2001). That state inconsistencies and state power are not mutually exclusive is ironically illustrated through the PIL. The PIL observes that though the Union government does not recognize MSM, the same cannot be said of NACO, another state agency. Contrary to Section 377, NACO recognizes the presence of MSM and their susceptibility to HIV/AIDS, and directs prevention efforts toward them, attempting to protect and promote their rights, thereby making it incumbent on the Union government and the law also to acknowledge and legitimize same-sex sexual subjects. The PIL and the broader mobilization for legal reform seek a just though uniform state policy towards same-sex sexualities. Each of respondents named in the petition is argued to bear responsibility for the protection of the fundamental rights of life, privacy and human dignity for every member of the national community, including gay men and women. Political exigencies of decriminalizing same-sex sexualities invoke state inconsistencies only to encourage state coherency. The state is unravelled and reassembled toward a just cause.

Critical theorists have been long concerned about sexuality as a historical construct that deeply pervades and organizes nations and nationalisms (Berlant and Freeman 1993; Eng 1997; Gopinath 1997; Mosse 1985; Parker et al. 1992; Puri 2002; Stoler 1995b). Whether as eroticized nationalism or in the guise of respectable sexuality, this scholarship compellingly speaks to the imbrications of nationalism and sexuality. What must figure prominently is the role of the postcolonial state in perpetuating and perpetrating homophobic policies and laws. For the most part, the focus of activists and academics writing on these topics has been on cultural texts to the exclusion of material aspects, where the former is equated with the terrain of nationalism and the latter with the state; this, despite the usefulness of seeing the state as a cultural material/discursive site. Indeed, while nations and nationalisms are consigned to the realm of affect and emotion, rationality is ascribed to the state (Stoler 2004). The nation and dominant nationalisms overlap, but are not synonymous, with state structures and institutions, and the messy terrain of sexuality is just as deeply relevant to the state (Alexander 1991, 1997; Banerjee 2005; Bhaskaran 2001, 2004; Duggan 1994; Enloe 2000; Herrell 1996; Kapur 2004; Luibhéid 2002; Menon 2004; Stevens 1999; Uberoi 1996). How the state serves as the material/symbolic site through which law, policies and discourses on sexuality are produced cannot be subsumed in an exclusive focus on nationalisms and the terrain of cultural politics.

It would not do to disregard the significance of gender to 'sexualizing the state'. The dangers of detaching sexuality from gender within the context of state policies were amply evident in my own research, especially in how gender politics are deployed to bolster heteronormativity. In the interview with an official in the Delhi police commissioner's office, undertaken in July 2003, when asked about the PIL against Section 377 the official said that he wasn't aware of it and deflected the issue. He attempted to minimize and implicitly justified the violence encoded in Section 377 on the basis that few people fall under its purview. He referred to same-sex sexual activities as crimes, even as he took the position that as peripheral to the total volume of crime, they garner little police attention. Instead, what he focused on was the issue of (heterosexual) violence against women. Strongly and repeatedly, he instructed me to pay attention to Section 376, or rape against women and girls, rather than Section 377. His point was that (hetero)sexual violence against women is not only more widespread and threatening but also ought to be of greater interest to me as a (feminist) scholar. The official's concerns about violence against presumably heterosexual women are not unimportant but they are troublingly used to turn attention away from forms of violence against sexual minorities, including non-heterosexual women. Heterosexualized forms of violence are used to draw a wedge between matters of gender and sexuality. Yet, even within the context of heterosexual violence, only some forms of sexual violence could be acknowledged; and when pressed that Section 376 egregiously does not acknowledge marital rape, he chose to ignore my argument.

Another key point is that sexuality is not marginal to the state. Here, I find especially useful parallels to Stoler's (2004) attention to affect as not incidental or a mere side-effect of the rational, bureaucratic state. Against the grain of the Weberian rational state predominant in colonial studies, Stoler details how ascertaining affect, managing sentiments, 'private' feelings, 'public moods', assessing their beneficial and subversive effects was, indeed, a central function of the late colonial state in the Dutch East Indies. Stoler challenges the idea of the rationally-minded, bureaucratically driven state where affect and sentimentality are seen merely as smokescreens of state rule that mask reasoned calculations or as factors of the state's racist ideologies towards colonized people. Invoking Foucault, Stoler argues that the Dutch state's concerns with affect and sentimentality, in fact, were not missteps of rule or metaphors for something else; rather, they were *dense transfer point[s] for relations of power*,[37] akin to discourses of sexuality. Social policy on educational reform, citizenship requirements, marriage laws, among others, political stances, the tone and content of archives produced about these issues were charged with calibrating and regulating sentiment and affect as instruments of power.

Indeed, state institutions, agencies and relations in India are saturated with discourses of sexuality. Through the myriad laws that regulate sexuality (Section 377) but also through those that are not ostensibly about sexuality (Article 21/Right to Life), through the innumerable policies on matters of sexuality (population control) and those that regulate sexuality indirectly (educational materials), and through the innumerable agencies that impact sexuality (Family Planning Association of India), and institutions that appear to have little to do with it (Ministry of Home

Affairs), material and discursive aspects of sexuality are articulated by the state. Not merely an arbiter of sexual rights and sexual citizenship, state institutions and structures serve as 'dense points of transfer of power'.

Even as Foucault (1978) cautions against focusing on the state as the only source of power, when the state is seen as a powerful symbolic and cultural site of discourses of sexuality, a part of the wider historical shift that Foucault (1994) indicts as governmentality, state institutions undoubtedly emerge as dense transfer points, though not the only ones, of power and regulation. These myriad discourses, sometimes consistent and inconsistent at other times, are routinely generated whether it is through law, through its representatives and agents, through specially appointed commissions, through the regulation of film and other forms of media, and through the prosecution and persecution of certain sexual subjects. What is sexuality, what is normal sexuality, what is appropriate, indeed, respectable sexuality, under what circumstances, for which subjects, at what ages, how to manage this messy aspect of human life, how to channel it toward socially-productive ends, how to contain sexual excesses that might be inherent to sexuality are all key points of concern for the state in India and elsewhere.

In re-examining imaginations of the state, sexuality, a concept notoriously difficult to define, cannot be reified. Foucault's approach to sexuality as a historical construct, described above, is especially useful in seeing sexuality as not just including the discursive and material realm of sexual desires, practices, identities, beliefs, institutions, and structures thoroughly infused by relations of power and agency; sexuality is also the dense matrix that enables the proliferation of power through the production of knowledge and truth. The thoughtful contributions of Lesbian and Gay Studies (for example, Abelove et al. 1993; Nardi and Schneider 1998), attention to the production of heterosexuality (Katz 1990; D'Emilio and Freedman 1988; Halley 1993), and the early insights of queer theory (Butler 1990; De Lauretis 1991; Fuss 1991; Sedgwick 1990) have further complicated any attempts to treat sexuality as unitary or monolithic, or as binary—homosexual and heterosexual—points that serve as useful cautions for how we see the state.

Sexualizing the state from a critical stance would mean eschewing binaries of homosexuality and heterosexuality. Lisa Duggan (1994: 1) called for 'queering the state' in response to Christian right wing backlash against sexual and gender minorities in the United States in the 1990s, which continues unabated but not unchallenged. By way of a response that would effectively sidestep the pitfalls of identitarian politics, Duggan insightfully calls for disestablishment strategies.[38] Drawing a parallel to the debates about religion and the (assumedly secular, see Shapiro 2006) state in the United States, Duggan explains the framework of disestablishment strategies: to show how the state systematically and constantly privileges heterosexuality; and to argue that the state should, in fact, divest itself of the promotion of heteronormativity. Duggan's approach is useful to further a critical politics of sexualizing the state, one that draws its inspiration from the insights of queer politics and the need to engage the state creatively and assertively.

The Naz (India) PIL provides insight into the nexus of sexuality and state. Not only does it become a lens through which to examine the gendered and class-based nature of this nexus, it also becomes an occasion to examine how we imagine the state as a cultural/historical effect where power is organized through the framework of sexuality. The open-ended grids of institutions, agencies and agents that make up what we collectively think of as the state, partly secured through discourses, law and its enforcement, and policies, fraught with the unevenness of power, are realized through the continually produced imaginations of the state as enduring, unified and overarching. The framing of the PIL, the encounters with state representatives and the conjunctions of critical literature on state and sexuality alert us to the consistencies and inconsistencies across relations of power. Perhaps more than anything else, the Naz (India) PIL becomes a means to be reflexive about how we conceptualize state power so as to not lend further strength thereof. The fundamentals of queer studies, by which I refer to a profound scepticism towards the binaries of heterosexuality and homosexuality and the caution against reinforcing heteronormativity, help further unsettle strategies of power at the nexus of sexuality and the state (De Lauretis 1991; Fuss 1991; Sedgwick 1990; Patton and Sánchez-Eppler 2000; Somerville 2000).

QUEER STATES, QUEER SUBJECTS

A queer analysis of the state demands that we go beyond accepting homophobia as the primary explanation for state resistance to decriminalizing same-sex sexualities in India towards a thoroughgoing critique of heteronormativity. The issue of how sexual subjects are constituted through Section 377 reflects their regulation through the regime of law. The language of '*against the order of nature*' (see note 2) in this code provides little indication that it is directed towards particular sexual subjects. The commentary (see note 2) attached to Section 377 indicates that the law is meant to punish sodomy, buggery and bestiality; in other words, targeting sexual practices rather than sexual subjects who come to embody socially constituted perversities in the form of the homosexual. What underlies this discrepancy is a shift in the exercise and proliferation of power through the deployment of sexuality. Foucault (1978, 1985) documents the shifting modes of power by the early eighteenth century and through the nineteenth century in Europe whereby the discourses of sexuality become instrumental to the surveillance of the individual but also the social body. Away from the site of ecclesiastical authority, medical science, psychiatry and pedagogy, and increasingly the state, became the sites of producing new knowledges and 'truths' about sexuality. Alongside the rendering of people as desiring subjects and subjects of desire was also the elaboration of perversity in new ways—whereby practices such as sodomy were no longer mere acts perpetrated by their doers but embodied in the 'perverse' self. By the time Section 377 is introduced under the colonial state in India, concerns about the importance of regulating the subjects of vices, whether sodomy or prostitution, were part of state attempts not just to surveil sexuality and contain anxieties about race, gender and class (Bhaskaran 2001), but also part of the broader concern of the state with sexuality and the social body (Foucault 1978). The language of the law may have been shaped by the legacy of a different space, but the question of 'perverse' sexual and colonial subjects was very much part of the colonial state's concern, and remain so in the postcolonial era.

The current continuance, and interpretation of the language, of the legal code of Section 377, therefore, is entirely relevant to understanding the postcolonial state's reach to determine sexuality and morality. Through questions of what constitutes unnatural sex, whether consent was involved, and what constitutes penetration, the present day courts read subjectivities into a law which essentially criminalizes practices. In her overview of Section 377, Bhaskaran (2001) argues that whenever children and animals are involved or if forcible sex can be proved, only the perpetrators are punished and the assaulted are considered victims. Yet, according to her, in the few cases concerned with two adult men engaging in mutual sexual activity if either of them is shown to be a 'habitual sodomite', both men are automatically punished. In other words, if one of the men is seen to be 'homosexual', both are assumed to have consented. The point is that law is a means not just to adjudicate but also to produce sexual subjectivities through its application—both 'homosexual' and, by implication, normative.

However, there is a nagging inconsistency between seeing Section 377 as a node in the production of state power and arguing that it is a prevalent site for the legal regulation of same-sex sexual subjects. Section 377 case law suggests that few cases of same-sex adult sexual activity are prosecuted in the higher courts. Shamona Khanna (2002) observes that since 1830 there have been only four cases involving consensual acts of anal sex, of which three cases occurred before 1940. Although its threat is indisputable, there appears to be little indication of the persecution of adult same-sex consensual sex under this law. Indeed, Alok Gupta (2002a) notes that of the forty-six cases involving prosecution under Section 377, the vast majority of the cases, thirty out of the forty-six, involve sexual assault on children. Statistics from the lower courts are not available to know the extent to which this is consonant across the court system. What is certain is that Section 377 is wielded as a threat against sexual minorities by the police, another state agency; the police and others in positions of authority, as well as thugs and goons, use Section 377 to harass, blackmail, threaten, assault vulnerable men. Of that, there is little doubt. This became disturbingly obvious in the attack on Bharosa Trust, an organization that works to prevent HIV/AIDS among MSM, and the persecution of its members in the city of Lucknow in July 2001. At the time, police raided a cruising park in Lucknow and arrested a Bharosa Trust outreach worker. Subsequently, they raided and sealed the Bharosa Trust office as well as the office of Naz Foundation International, a Britain-based organization that supports and assists Bharosa Trust. The police arrested and imprisoned for several weeks the acting director of Bharosa and staff member of Naz Foundation International, Arif Jafar, and two other staff members. Among the criminal codes under which they were charged was Section 377 on the preposterous grounds that Bharosa Trust was running a 'sex club', despite the fact that it is recognized by the Uttar Pradesh State AIDS Control Organization and the state relies on it for HIV/AIDS prevention work. This case of state violence received unusual attention due to its scope and the ensuing nation-wide protests and anti-state coalitions, and exemplifies the quotidian and arbitrary abuse of Section 377 to harass those seen to be associated with sexual practices '*against the order of nature*' (see note 2).

The higher courts do not appear to be the active site of regulation of sexual subjects or their prosecution under Section 377. This point, in fact, is used in the Naz (India) PIL to show that the law is archaic and anachronistic. Then why is there not sufficient support across the respondents named in the PIL to 'read down' Section 377? Does its use (perhaps) at the lower court justify the need for state agencies to retain this code and its injunction against sexual practices regardless of age and consent? The answer is not clear since, as mentioned earlier, statistics from lower courts are not available. One obvious response for the lack of state support to amending Section 377 is: homophobia and the state's role in preserving heteronormativity. The state is and ought to be indicted for systematically preserving and promoting heteronormativity; of this, and the promotion of heterosexism there is overwhelming evidence. Still, I believe the matter is more tangled than the expression of homophobia.

I caution against reading state practices as always already fully heteronormative and homophobic for two reasons. One, starting from the position that state practices are solidly and unrelentingly heteronormative assumes coherency and re-imposes ideological and material uniformity onto the state. Second, if state practices are unambiguously heterosexist and homophobic, it prematurely forecloses the state as an arena of resistance in which transformations may and have occur(ed), where heteronormativity may be not unrelenting, and where homosexuality may be decriminalized. Unquestionably reading heteronormativity into state practices ironically privileges the very problem. My point is not that criticism of the promotion of heteronormativity or the repression of non-heteronormativity is unjustified. My point, instead, is to raise the question: is it always already so? At stake, I argue, is the need for 'denaturalizing' the state as a site of unjust social policies and laws, and for unmaking this seemingly monolith, opaque, overarching state. If the Naz (India) PIL offered some direction in this regard, the government's reply provides some indication of the fractures in state power.

THE GOVERNMENT'S REPLY

On 6 September 2003, after significant delay and repeated injunctions from the Delhi High Court, the government filed a reply to the Naz (India) petition on behalf of the Union of India and its various subsidiaries, Ministry of Home Affairs, Ministry of Health Welfare, Ministry of Social Welfare, and none was filed on behalf of the other respondents, notably NACO. The court's decision delivered approximately a year later on 2 September 2004 proceeded without NACO's response. The statement, filed by the Judicial Division of the Ministry of Home Affairs, highlighted that Section 377 is not arbitrarily used, it is used to complement gaps in child rape laws, that the social disapproval of homosexuality in India is strong enough to criminalize it, that the law does not distinguish between procreative and non-procreative sex in its punishment of unnatural sex, and despite the tolerance towards homosexuality in the United States and the United Kingdom, it is not accepted in India (counter affidavit filed by respondent number 5 in the matter of Civil Writ Petition 7455/2001). Clearly, the reply is riven with homophobia and justifies heteronormativity, and supports a simplified history of heterosexuality in India.

Yet, notable in the government's reply to the Naz (India) petition is its degree of dissonance. On the one hand, the reply takes the unequivocal position that it objects to the writ petition to exclude same-sex consensual adult sexual activity from the purview of Section 377. So, the grounds upon which the reply objects to the Naz (India) PIL are that: consent to a crime does not make it lawful and Section 377 serves to protect public safety and defend health and morals; that proposed changes in law can well open the flood gates of delinquent behaviour and be construed as providing unbridled license for the same; rights named in the petition are not infringed and are subject to reasonable restrictions; Naz (India) has no locus standi since only those whose rights are directly affected by the law can challenge its constitutionality; the Naz (India) writ petition relates to the policy of law rather than its legality.

On the other hand, the government's objections to the petition are laced with what appears to be conciliatory logic. The reply reiterates that the law is used only when a complaint is filed by a victim (implicitly excluding consenting adults) and to fill a lacuna in child rape laws. It also suggests that private homosexual activity between consenting adults is not criminally prosecuted. Arguably, the government's reply is taking the position that adult, consensual, same-sex private sexual activity is implicitly and practically excluded from Section 377. It notes that Section 377 is always understood in the context of particular cases and not in the abstract, as suggested in the petition. Courts are said to use contemporary meanings and consider changes since the law was passed to ascertain whether an alleged offence is covered by Section 377. Further, where there is doubt about the relevance of Section 377 to a particular subject, preference is given to the subject and those accused under this law can petition that the law is not relevant to the facts of the case, according to the government's reply. Section 377 is said to be applied only upon a complaint by a victim and is not arbitrarily used.

To say that the government reply is inconsistent is to understate the case. Inconsistency implies lack of coherence, something without consistence or firmness, incongruence. The reply takes a heteronormative nationalist stance in its position that *that the law does not distinguish between procreative and non-procreative sex in its punishment of unnatural sex, and despite the tolerance towards homosexuality in USA and UK, it is not accepted*. This is hardly unexpected if part of the state's function is to manage the conjunctions of nationalism and (respectable, normal) sexuality. But the response also suggests that private homosexual activity is not, in fact, prosecuted under the law, that courts use discretion in light of contemporary (perhaps, liberal) standards, short of guaranteeing that such prosecutions would not occur. A critical reading of the government's response to the PIL reinforces the point that inconsistencies across the government's reply, among or across state institutions does not connote weakness of the state or is simply an outcome of homophobia; points obscured when the state is treated as a monolith. This became compellingly evident in fieldwork at the Ministry of Home Affairs and among the Delhi police, described below. A 'queer' reading highlights the fractures and dissonances in the reproduction of heteronormativity at the site of state bureaucracies.

Ministry of Home Affairs

One straightforward analysis of the government's reply is that it is illogical precisely because the state has the power to be so. However, research persuasively suggests the need to understand more precisely the operations of state power and the messiness of reproducing heteronormativity. By this, I mean the process through which the formal reply was developed in the Judicial Division of the Ministry of Home Affairs. According to the current director of the Judicial Division, who had custody of the folder related to the Naz (India) PIL, the Division is charged with the responsibility of overseeing matters related to the IPC or the Criminal Procedure Code wherever there is a question of amending or interpreting a law or the procedural code.[39] In June 2003, and between May–August 2005, I met with the two bureaucrats who served in the capacity of director at the Judicial Division, and interviewed the joint secretary, and the desk officer, and deputy secretary, who helped draft the government's response.

In June 2003, the then director, who has since been transferred to another state institution, agreed to speak confidentially so that his identity would be protected. I met him again in May 2005. His responses give some insight into the process through which the response was developed, which was confirmed by subsequent interviews in the department. The former director's position on the Naz (PIL) was equivocal; a curiosity mitigated with fear of retribution for seeming sympathetic. Since the first interview occurred before the government filed its reply in September 2003, he did not feel at liberty to divulge its contents. What he did reveal is that junior-level bureaucrats craft a response usually. Further research revealed that a desk officer and his supervisor, the deputy secretary, had formulated the first draft after some discussion within the department. Typically, and in this case, the director and the joint secretary reviewed the response, making comments and notes. When the joint secretary considered it appropriate, it was shared with the politically appointed minister of home affairs. The interviews confirmed that as each bureaucrat in the hierarchy of the department reviews the government response being crafted, not only do they leave a trail of their notes and comments in the folder, but also they can record their dissent, if any, to aspects of the statement. Also confirmed is that the final approval to the response comes from the minister, who may ask for it to be significantly modified, even reversed.

What these interviews suggest is that many different opinions on this law prevail in the Ministry of Home Affairs. It was independently confirmed through the various interviews that the decision to not support the Naz (India) petition for amendment to Section 377 was endorsed by the minister. The former director nonetheless acknowledged that some privately believed that homosexuality should not be illegal but were afraid to be seen promoting this view in the Ministry of Home Affairs. Examining the folder on Section 377, the current director summarized:

> Internally (it appears that) some felt that Indian society is laid back, resistant to change. Naz is asking for unnatural sex, promiscuity, and society is resisting. It is like sati; Indian society was resistant to change and it would not have been abolished had the law not been changed. But unnatural sex is a reality; we cannot simply put it down. It's very internal to human beings and will come up one way or another.[40]

It is hardly possible to describe the director's analysis of the previous discussions, likely mixed with her personal positions, as liberal. She and other officials speak in their capacity as state agents but also as cultural subjects influenced by contested social attitudes. The expressions of homophobia are intertwined with questions of the responsibility of the state in difficult social matters. The analogy to sati speaks to perceptions of a society with deeply entrenched attitudes that marginalize same-sex sexualities but also reflects on the progressive role of law. The government's reply may have taken a counter-position to the Naz (India) PIL, but the insights into the process makes it likely that the apparent inconsistencies register the messiness of successive drafts, building on various sets of comments. They also register the messiness of inconsistently heteronormative and homophobic discourses rife *within* the Ministry of Home Affairs.

The government's response underscores, in part, what is clearly reflected in case law: that Section 377 is not used to prosecute adult consensual private same-sex sexual activity. The fact that case law supports the government's position that Section 377 is not used to prosecute adult consenting homosexuals does not mean that they are not persecuted—either by the police, through other state bureaucracies (for example, by the National Human Rights Commission and the Ministry of Home Affairs). The police are assigned the primary responsibility of enforcement of criminal laws, including Section 377.

The Police

The most consistent and troubling charge by same-sex sexualities against the state is police violence and brutality. When I tried to delve into this with the presiding New Delhi police commissioner in June 2003, the interview was terminated within a few minutes. At first, the commissioner admitted that he wasn't aware of the Naz (India) PIL or its status even though this interview occurred approximately eighteen months after the petition was filed, and the court had repeatedly directed the state respondents to file their replies. When asked, he vehemently denied charges of police abuse against sexual minorities and insisted that the institution's role is merely to enforce the law; a point that would be hotly disputed by those who bear the brunt of this enforcement. The position that the police merely enforce law was repeated almost to the letter two years later in June 2005 by the New Delhi Commissioner of Police, who said 'We come into the picture only if there is something repugnant to the law; we enforce the law'. What is being evaded in these denials of police brutality is how enforcement of law serves as an active production of sexual and gendered subjects, who is subjected to law enforcement, and how ought he/she to be treated.

A subsequent group discussion with twenty-five policemen at a police station in New Delhi in June 2005 about Section 377 was productive and disturbing. My purpose was to understand police perceptions, those charged with the direct enforcement of law, of what it means to exercise

Section 377. All male, ranging from six years to thirty-two years of service, these policemen have served or continue to serve the beats—the streets, the parks, the neighbourhoods, etc. Notably, as a group, they were divided in their positions on the relevance of Section 377. A handful of vocal constables took the position that same-sex sexual activity is 'unnatural' and 'against nature'. To the question of whether Section 377 should be deleted or modified to exclude consensual same-sex activity, several responded, 'sex among men or women is wrong', 'this is against our culture', 'if this is removed it will increase in homosexual behaviour; what will happen to the population if everyone is doing unnatural sex, especially in the next 100 years?'. They were emphatic. An equally vociferous group took the position that Section 377 should not be applied to two consenting adults. In a conversation entirely in Hindi, a police constable said surely: '*Har ek ko sexual satisfaction ka adhikar hai*' (translation: all have the right to sexual satisfaction). A second constable said to his colleagues in Hindi: 'This law is wrong in the case of two adults who consent to sex. This law should change'. Another said, 'This law should be changed as now we are free from colonialism'. A few constables supporting deletion or modification of Section 377 took the following position: 'There should be a difference between forced and consensual sex.' The discussion and disagreement among the constables flowed through the discussion. Rather than predictably and overwhelmingly homophobic reactions, their responses as a group were tempered with differences.

In contrast, their responses to how Section 377 is enforced were cohesive and all the more troubling reflections on the conditions of police violence. They chorused that Section 377 is deployed *only* when there is a complaint (by implication, consenting adults are excluded), echoing the government's reply filed in court. Hypothetical examples of two gay men holding hands in a public park were responded to unambiguously, even from those who expressed reservations on homosexuality, that there would be no question of Section 377 being utilized to harass. The position that they enforce the letter of Section 377 was shared and police abuse of gay men or MSM was categorically denied. Why Kinnars are consistently harassed elicited a different, disturbing set of responses. They said vehemently: 'Kinnars have sex in public places; they do it for money; they are doing wrong by having sex for money in a public place. Kinnars will take someone into a car and rob them of his clothes and money.' The policemen did not have trouble conceding that sometimes Kinnars are beaten up by clients or the police. Rather, they openly admitted that police will threaten Kinnars in anticipation of sex work and to prevent them from committing petty and serious crime. Perhaps what could not be articulated in the hypothetical case of two gay men could be openly expressed and defended in the case of transgenders. These reactions reveal how strategies of enforcement are unevenly expressed and borne by subjects of law. The necessary qualifier is that violence against Kinnars is committed under the aegis of laws against public nuisance (Sections 268 and 290 IPC) and Sections 7 and 8 of the Immoral Traffic (Prevention) Act of 1956 (amending Act of 1986, entitled, Suppression of Immoral Traffic in Women and Girls Act), which criminalizes soliciting and having sex in public places and *not* under Section 377. What emerges from the government's reply is an equivocal defence of Section 377 and tempered resistance to modification in the law. That the response is marshalled against the decriminalization of homosexuality is reprehensible. However, fieldwork complicates facile analyses that such resistance can be reduced primarily to homophobia, even though one is not hard pressed to find evidence. Fieldwork across the Ministry of Home Affairs and the police in New Delhi suggests that the reasons for the government's resistance to the Naz (India) PIL cannot be attributed to a single overarching factor. Rather, the government's response reveals the messiness of heteronormative reinforcements. Underlying its response to the petition is a process which elicits a range of competing, uneven positions on the decriminalization of same-sex sexualities. Even though the government's reply, similarly echoed by the New Delhi police commissioners, is rife with homophobia, fieldwork points towards a more complex analysis of heteronormativity across state institutions.

In interviews and discussions, state agents do not speak with one voice. While not devoid of homophobia and heterosexism, these responses reveal the fractures and dissonances in the reproduction of heteronormativity within these state institutions. The responses of police raise the challenging question of how to theorize heteronormativity and, more importantly, what counts as fissures and dissonances thereof. If the constables who oppose the modification or deletion of Section 377 can be seen as homophobic, rooted in heteronormative understandings of society, then can the views of the others who are critical of Section 377 be read more hopefully? Does the constable's affirmation that each of us has a right to sexual satisfaction signal lessening homophobia and does it unsettle heteronormative reasoning—that gender dualism and heterosexuality are elemental to nature and society—while acknowledging equal citizenship and belonging to all?

Lessening homophobia may not entail a weakening of heteronormativity; indeed, the reverse may be true. Police violence that is directed against transgenders presents a chilling example of the power of the heteronormative amidst possibly declining homophobia. Still, the examples of support for changes in Section 377 are grounds to stake the claim that state support for Section 377 is neither uniform nor unquestioned and point towards the possibilities of engaging state agents and institutions. HIV/AIDS-related and sexual minority rights activists in India have long recognized the need to engage the institution of police, re-train members of the police force, to sensitize and educate them about same-sex sexualities, even though the work has proved to be arduous and frustrating.[41] The Naz (India) PIL and a critical queer analysis of the state suggest that at the least law enforcement as well as the courts are the primary battlegrounds for state legitimization of same-sex sexualities. They are also the battlegrounds for thoroughgoing challenges to heteronormativity and its material and symbolic violence directed towards transgenders.

CONCLUSIONS AND SPECULATIONS

Critical writers have been sensitive to the effects of the state on sexual subjects and sexual policies. The story of the PIL, its process, the production of sexual subjects fraught with the limits of gender and class are important, and will be explored and expanded upon elsewhere. Here, I chose to turn the lens on state institutions, including the courts, in order to bring the state under more careful scrutiny, and by sexualizing the state, to explore how discourses of sexuality unevenly criss-cross state institutions, policies and laws in the operations of power, but not in consistent or unified ways. The Naz (India) PIL against Section 377 exposes a disjunction in the tangle of sexuality-state. The state-sexuality nexus is thriving through state policies and laws that institutionalize homophobia and heteronormativity. The material/cultural site of state violence is all too frequently ignored or simply subsumed through an emphasis on nationalism. The Naz (India) PIL helps reveal how state policies and law are not only a source of domination but also a site of resistance to state power and violence against sexual and gender minorities.

An analytics of the contemporary postcolonial state, specifically through a critical framing of sexuality, is central to this essay. It proceeds on the grounds that critical analyses of state-sexuality are a step in undermining images of the monolithic, impenetrable state. At the same time, these analytics ask that we go beyond justifiable critiques of the unitary state's implication in the production and perpetuation of homophobia/heteronormativity. Anything less would strengthen the scope and power of the state, and render invisible the struggles for justice of sexual minorities. My point is hardly to redeem the state, for state violence articulated through homophobia and heteronormativity is rife. Still, state institutions, relations, agencies, and state agents are surfeit with fractures and disjunctures in terms of sexual discourses, policies and stances. The Naz (India) PIL provides useful direction in challenging and disaggregating the state even though the imagination of the state as an overarching and cohesive container of society endures and the legal outcome is still unclear. Such tensions and tactics continue to be relevant to the process of mobilizing for the legal recognition of homosexuality. Given the experiences of the first ABVA petition and the one brought by Naz (India), the next steps are being formulated by the Lawyer's Collective HIV/AIDS unit. If the Supreme Court rules in favour of returning the PIL to the Delhi High Court for review, as it probably will, another decision by the Delhi High Court will be in process.[42]

A final point about the nature of state power revealed through the government's response to the Naz (India) PIL. The Bharatiya Janata Party (BJP) was the government in power at the national level while this petition was in the Delhi High Court. The BJP government's and Hindu nationalist positions on social and sexual minorities are a matter of record and have been addressed in this volume and elsewhere (Bacchetta 1999; Chatterji 2004). Yet, I am not at all confident that the government's response and subsequent court decision would have been substantially different under the present Congress regime. Extending well beyond the governments in charge at any given moment are enduring effects of state institutions and ideologies that must be called into question. I believe that the government's reply filed in the Delhi High Court to the Naz (India) PIL, after significant delay, indicates the messy but rife nature of heteronormativity across and within state institutions. This response and related fieldwork also points us towards the fractures and disjunctions in the relentless reproduction of heteronormativity. Theorizing the state's inconsistent but not necessarily attenuating role in the reproduction of heteronormativity as well as theorizing the inconsistencies of heteronormativity are crucial if heteronormativity is to be undermined within and beyond the courts.

AUTHOR'S NOTE

This chapter was completed in 2005 and captures an earlier moment in the legal process of the Naz Foundation challenge to Section 377. Although much has changed since then, including the 2009 Delhi High Court judgment decriminalizing homosexuality, the overall argument of the chapter still holds because its point of intervention are the conjunctions of sexuality and state.

ACKNOWLEDGMENTS

My deep gratitude to the editors, especially to Angana Chatterji, and to Richard Shapiro, for their painstaking reading and careful comments that make this a richer text. I also thank Colin Danby for his insightful and incisive feedback on a draft, which has left its imprint on various parts of this essay.

NOTES

1. See Sen (2004); also, letter from Naz Foundation (India) Trust & Lawyers Collective HIV/AIDS Unit, 2004, at http://www.aanchal.org/News/Letter_from_NAZ/letter_from_naz.html (last accessed November 2005).

2. The law, its explanation and the attached general commentary states: 'Whoever voluntarily has *carnal intercourse against the order of nature* with any man, woman or animal, shall be punished with imprisonment for life, or with imprisonment of either description for a term which may extend to ten years, and shall also be liable to fine.'

   Explanation: Penetration is sufficient to constitute the carnal intercourse necessary to the offence described in this section.

   General Comments: This section is intended to punish the offence of sodomy, buggery and bestiality. The offence consists in a carnal knowledge committed against the order of nature by a person with a man, or in the same unnatural manner with a woman, or by a man or woman in any manner with an animal.

   For a website with a listing and language of sections of the Indian Penal Code, see India Law Info (2000).

3. Rather than the deletion of the law, the Naz (India) PIL asked that the law be 'read down', which is to say instead of asking for the law to be repealed, the petition asked for it to be modified to exclude same-sex adult consensual sex conducted in private from its purview.

4. Naz Foundation (India) Trust is a separate organization from the Britain-based Naz Foundation International, which is described later in this article.

5. See Mohapatra (2003) on this point about PILs.
6. By the time that the Naz (India) PIL was submitted in the courts on 6 December 2001, the ABVA petition had been dismissed. This fact was not widely known and the exact date of its dismissal by the court is not clear.
7. Interview with Shaleen Rakesh, the Naz (India) organizational representative in the courts.
8. As per the rules of the Supreme Court of India, a special leave petition may be filed when an appeal to a High Court/Tribunal to review its decision is turned down and a petitioner wishes to challenge the order. See the Supreme Court website (Supreme Court, circa 1999) for further details. See Supreme Court of India (circa 1999) 'Rules' at http://supremecourtofindia.nic.in/new_s/rules.htm. Last accessed November 2005.
9. The Supreme Court is asked to deliberate on the grounds of the Delhi High Court decision, not directly speak to the merits of amending Section 377.
10. Interviews, New Delhi, May–June 2005.
11. This campaign was launched by Voices Against 377 on the eve of Human Rights Day, 9 December 2004. Interview, New Delhi, May 2005.
12. Based on personal observations and consultations of their writings.
13. These terms are not exhaustive and many more such terms circulate within India and across South Asia. I will alternate between these terms, including transgender.
14. Kinnars in Delhi will playfully refer to each other as 'Kothi' (interview, New Delhi, June 2005). Self-identified Kothis are not always from the working classes (for example, interview, New Delhi, August 2005) and some working class men will identify as 'gay' rather than Kothi or MSM (interviews in Mumbai, July 2005).
15. See the website www.lines-magazine.org/textmay03/yasmin.htm for the precise language of Sections 365 and 365A. In an amendment to the subsection, 365A, the language of 'male persons' was changed to 'persons', thereby expanding the scope of prosecution to women. Also, see Thompson (2001), and related stories on Sri Lanka on this point. Based on my conversations, I learned that sexual rights activists, such as Vivek Diwan, Elarvathi Manohar, and members of the lesbian group, Humjinsi, Mumbai, were concerned about the possibilities of a backlash to the PIL against Section 377 in India, similar to the one that occurred in Sri Lanka.
16. In the case of India, see the report by the People's Union of Civil Liberties (PUCL), Karnataka; see PUCL (2003). Also see Gupta (2002a). See Bondyopadhyay and Khan (2003) for violence against MSM in Bangladesh.
17. Based on interviews conducted in Chennai (August 2005), Mumbai (July 2005), New Delhi (August 2005).
18. For details of some of the incidents, see Blue Diamond Society's website: http://www.bds.org.np/. Last accessed November 2005.
19. See Sections 375 and 376 of the IPC; see India Law Info (2000).

20. By heteronormativity, I draw partly upon Michael Warner's (1993) explanation: '...as the belief that heterosexuality is an elemental form of human association, is a model of inter-gender relations, is the indivisible basis for community, and the means of reproduction without which society would not exist' (p. 21).

21. By the term governmentality, Foucault refers to the modern disciplinary forms of state power that operate by producing knowledge about populations and their justifying regulation by state institutions and bureaucracies. See the chapter on governmentality in Foucault (1994) for further discussion on this concept.

22. By heterosexism I mean the privileging of the belief that the world is composed of two sexes/genders—women and men—who are naturally and consistently heterosexual, and the concomitant marginalization of all others. Seen this way, heterosexist beliefs and practices are part of the broader normalizing framework of heteronormativity. Examples of the heterosexist reasoning in case law under Section 377 include Bhaskaran's (2001) point that in one case (AIR 1982, 48), the judge grants a woman the right to divorce her husband on the grounds that she did not consent to sodomy and in another case (*Ratan Mia v State of Assam*), since the victim is determined to be a 'catamite', the charges against the perpetrator are dropped. I will return to the latter point shortly.

23. Lawyer's Collective HIV/AIDS Unit is based in Mumbai; see http://www.lawyerscollective.org/

24. During the time that this article was being revised the Supreme Court still had not set a hearing date to announce its likely decision to return the case to the Delhi High Court.

25. The Infinity Foundation, with Hindu nationalist leanings, in New Jersey, United States, initially provided a small amount of funding to Naz (India) for the outpatient department. This is surprising given the group's leanings. However, this funding was inexplicably withdrawn later, according to Anjali Gopalan, director of Naz (India); personal communication, 2005.

26. Personal interview, July 2003.

27. Personal interview, June 2003.

28. For descriptions of the articles of fundamental rights, see Bakshi (2005).

29. Judaeo-Christian refers, in fact, to ideologies and practices that are often Christian, and obscures the history of European anti-Semitism.

30. Here, the purpose is not to identify particular groups and their criticisms but to identify the positions taken.

31. See note 2.

32. See the citations mentioned in Footnote 16.

33. Based on interviews with Kinnars in New Delhi and Aravani in Chennai, June–July 2005.

34. Personal interview, July 2003.

35. Personal interview, May 2005.
36. For useful summations of the state versus society debates, see Mitchell (1991) and Steinmetz (1999).
37. Foucault (1978: 103) in Stoler (2004: 7). Insert [] is mine.
38. The term identitarian politics encapsulates Duggan's concerns about how responses to right wing homophobia all too easily fall into the trap of having to claim gay and lesbian sexualities as biological given the difficulties of advancing constructionist arguments in the popular domain. Duggan also notes the problems with politics that proceed on the assumptions that categories of sexual identity—gay, lesbian, bisexual, heterosexual—are mutually exclusive and stable.
39. Interview, New Delhi, May 2005.
40. Interview, New Delhi, May 2005.
41. Personal communication with Shaleen Rakesh about the training sessions he conducted with the police in New Delhi.
42. While this article was being revised, the Ministry of Home Affairs filed a response to the Naz (India) Special Leave Petition (SLP) in the Supreme Court on behalf of the Union of India [Special Leave Petition (Civil) NO. 7217-7218 OF 2005]. The response did not support the Naz (India) SLP.

REFERENCES

Aarmo, Margrete (1999). 'How Homosexuality became 'Un-African': The Case of Zimbabwe', in Evelyn Blackwood and Saskia E. Wieringa (eds), *Female Desires: Same-sex Relations and Transgender Practices across Cultures*, pp. 255–80. New York: Columbia University Press.

Abelove, Henry, Michele Aina Barale and David M. Halperin (eds) (1993). *The Lesbian and Gay Studies Reader*. New York; London, Routledge.

Agnes, Favia (1999). *Law and Gender Inequality: The Politics of Women's Rights in India*. New Delhi: Oxford University Press.

Alexander, M. Jacqui (1991). 'Redrafting Morality: The Postcolonial State and the Sexual Offences Bill of Trinidad and Tobago', in Chandra Talpade Mohanty, Ann Russo and Lourdes Torres (eds), *Third World Women and the Politics of Feminism*, pp. 133–52. Bloomington: Indiana University Press.

———— (1997). 'Erotic Autonomy as a Politics of Decolonization: An Anatomy of Feminist and State Practice in the Bahamas Tourist Economy', in M. Jacqui Alexander and Chandra Talpade Mohanty (eds), *Feminist Genealogies, Colonial Legacies, Democratic Futures*, pp. 63–100. New York and London: Routledge.

Bacchetta, Paola (1999). 'When the (Hindu) Nation Exiles its Queers', *Social Text*, 17(4): 141–67.

Bakshi, P.M. (2005). *The Constitution of India*, sixth edition. New Delhi: Universal Law Publishing Co.

Banerjee, Sikata (2005). *Make Me a Man: Masculinity, Hinduism, and Nationalism in India*. Albany, New York: State University of New York Press.

Banerjee, Sukanya, Angana P. Chatterji, Lubna Nazir Chaudhry, Manali Desai, Saadia Toor, Kamala Visweswaran. (2004). 'Engendering Violence: Boundaries, Histories, and the Everyday', in Angana P. Chatterji and Lubna Nazir Chaudhury (eds), *Gendered Violence in South Asia: Nation and Community in the Postcolonial Present, Cultural Dynamics: Theory Cross-Cultures*, 16(2/3): 125–39. Thousand Oaks: Sage Publications.

Berlant, Lauren and Elizabeth Freeman (1993). 'Queer Nationality', in Michael Warner (ed.), *Fear of a Queer Planet: Queer Politics and Social Theory*, pp. 193–229. Minneapolis: University of Minnesota Press.

Bhaskaran, Suparna (2001). 'The Politics of Penetration: Section 377 of the Indian Penal Code', in Ruth Vanita (ed.), *Queering India: Same-sex Love and Eroticism in Indian Culture and Society*, pp. 15–29. New York and London: Routledge.

———— (2004). *Made in India: Decolonizations, Queer Sexualities, Transnational Projects*. New York: Palgrave Macmillan.

Bondyopadhyay, Aditya and Shivananda Khan (2003). *Social justice, human rights and MSM*, Naz Foundation International, Briefing Paper No. 7, Delhi, The Naz Foundation.

Butler, Judith (1990) *Gender Trouble: Feminism and the Subversion of Identity*. New York: Routledge.

———— (1994). 'Against Proper Objects', *Differences: A Journal of Feminist Cultural Studies*, 6 (2–3): 1–26.

Césaire, Aimé (1972). *Discourse on Colonialism*. New York, Monthly Review Press.

Chatterji, Angana, P. (2004). 'The Biopolitics of Hindu Nationalism: Mournings', in Angana P. Chatterji and Lubna Nazir Chaudhury (eds), *Gendered Violence in South Asia: Nation and Community in the Postcolonial Present, Cultural Dynamics: Theory Cross-Cultures* 16 (2/3): 319–72. Thousand Oaks: Sage Publications.

Cohen, Lawrence (1995). 'The Pleasures of Castration', in Paul R. Abrahamson and Steven Pinkerton (eds), *Sexual Nature Sexual Culture*, pp. 276–304. Chicago, University of Chicago Press.

Corrigan, Philip (1994). 'State Formation', in Gilbert M. Joseph and Daniel Nugent (eds), *Everyday Forms of State Formation: Revolution and Negotiation of Rule in Modern Mexico*, pp. xvii–xix. Durham: Duke University Press.

Corrigan, Philip, and Derek Sayer (1985). *The Great Arch: English State Formation as Cultural Revolution*. New York: Blackwell.

Crenshaw, Kimberlé (ed.) (1995). *Critical Race Theory: The Key Writings that Formed the Movement*. New York: New Press.

D'Emilio, John and Estelle Freedman (1988). *Intimate Matters: A History of Sexuality in America*. New York: Harper and Row.

De Lauretis, Teresa (1991). 'Queer Theory: Lesbian and Gay Sexuality: An Introduction', *Differences: A Journal of Feminist Cultural Studies*, 3(2): iii–xviii.

De Mel, Neloufer (2001). *Women and the Nation's Narrative: Gender and Nationalism in Twentieth Century Sri Lanka*. Lanham, M.D.: Rowman and Littlefield.

Diamond, Irene and Lee Quinby (1988). *Feminism and Foucault: Reflections of Resistance*. Boston: Northeastern University Press.

Duggan, Lisa (1994). 'Queering the State', *Social Text*, 39: 1–14.

Eng, David L. (1997). 'Out Here and Over There: Queerness and Diaspora in Asian American Studies', *Social Text*, 52/53, Autumn-Winter: 31–52.

Enloe, Cynthia (2000). *Maneuvers: The International Politics of Militarizing Women's Lives*. Berkeley, Los Angeles, and London: University of California Press.

Ferguson, J. and A. Gupta (2002). 'Spatializing States: Toward an Ethnography of Neoliberal Governmentality', *American Ethnologist*, 29(4): 981–1002.

Foucault, Michel (1978). *The History of Sexuality. Volume I: An Introduction*. Trans. Robert Hurley. New York: Random House.

———— (1980). *Power/Knowledge: Selected Interviews & Other Writings, 1972–1977*, ed. Colin Gordon. New York: Pantheon.

———— (1985). *The Use of Pleasure: The History of Sexuality, Volume 2*. Trans. Robert Hurley. New York: Vintage Books.

———— (1994). 'Governmentality', in *Power: Essential Works of MichelFoucault, 1954–1984*, ed. James Faubion, pp. 201–22. New York: New York Press.

Fuss, Diana (ed.) (1991). *Inside/Out: Lesbian Theories, Gay Theories*. New York: Routledge.

Gopinath, Gayatri (2005). *Impossible Desires: Queer Diasporas and South Asian Public Cultures*. Durham and London: Duke University Press.

———— (1997). 'Nostalgia, Desire, Diaspora: South Asian Sexualities in Motion', *Positions*, 5(2): 467–89.

Gramsci, Antonio (1971). *Selections from Prison Notebooks*. Quintin Hoare and Geoffrey Smith trans. New York: International Publishers.

Gupta, Akhil (1995). 'Blurred Boundaries: The Discourses of Corruption, the Culture of Politics and the Imagined State', *American Ethnologist*, 22(2): 375–402.

———— (2001). 'Governing Population: The Integrated Child Development Services Program in India', in Thomas Blom Hansen and Finn Stepputat (eds), *States of Imagination: Ethnographic Explorations of the Postcolonial State*, pp. 203–20. Durham and London: Duke University Press.

Gupta, Alok (2002a). 'Trends in the Application of Section 377', in Bina Fernandez (compiled and ed.), *Humjinsi: A Resource Book on Lesbian, Gay and Bisexual Rights in India*, pp. 66–74. Mumbai: Indian Centre for Human Rights and Law.

———— (2002b). 'Transgender, Law and Civil Rights', 2005. Available at: http://www.lawyerscollective.org/lc-hiv-aids/magazine_articles/april _2002.htm. Last accessed August

Halley, Janet (1993). 'The Construction of Heterosexuality', in Michael Warner (ed.), *Fear of a Queer Planet*, pp. 82–102. Minneapolis and London: University of Minnesota Press.

Hansen, T.B. and F. Stepputat (eds) (2001). *States of Imagination: Ethnographic Explorations of the Postcolonial State*. Durham and London: Duke University Press.

Hasan, Zoya (ed.) (1994). *Forging Identities: Gender, Communities and the State*. New Delhi: Kali for Women.

Hasan, Zoya and Ritu Menon (2004). *Unequal Citizens: A Study of Muslim Women in India*. New Delhi: Oxford University Press.

Herrell, Richard K. (1996). 'Sin, Sickness, Crime: Queer Desire and the American State', *Identities*, 2(3): 273–300.

Jaffrey, Zia (1996). *The Invisibles: Tales of the Eunuchs in India*. New York: Pantheon Books.

Joseph, G. M. and D. Nugent (eds) (1994). *Everyday Forms of State Formation: Revolution and Negotiation of Rule in Modern Mexico*. Durham: Duke University Press.

India Law Info (2000). 'The Indian Penal Code'. Available at: http://www.indialawinfo.com/bareacts/ipc.html#_Toc496764830.   Last   accessed November 2005.

Kandayoti, D. (ed.) (1991). *Women, Islam and the State*. Philadelphia: Temple University Press.

Kapur, Ratna (2004). *Erotic Justice: Law and the New Politics of Postcolonialism*. Portland, Oregon: Glass House Press.

Katz, Jonathan (1990). 'The Invention of Heterosexuality', *Socialist Review*, 20(1): 7–34.

Khan, Owais (2000). 'A Rose by Any Other Name…? Gays vs. MSM', *Trikone Magazine*, 15(3), 31 July, p. 15.

Khan, Shivananda (2000). 'Kothi, Gays and (other) MSM', *Trikone Magazine*, 15(4), 31 October, p. 14.

——— (2001). 'Culture, Sexualities, and Identities: Men Who Have Sex With Men in India', in Gerard Sullivan and Peter A. Jackson (eds), *Gay and Lesbian Asia: Culture, Identity, Community*, pp. 99–115. Binghamton, Harrington Park Press.

Khanna, Shamona (2002). 'Gay Rights', in Bina Fernandez (compiled and ed.), *Humjinsi: A Resource Book on Lesbian, Gay and Bisexual Rights in India*, pp. 56–65. Mumbai: Indian Centre for Human Rights and Law.

Kidwai, Saleem (2005). 'Time to Break Shackles', *Outlook: The Weekly Newsmagazine*, 25 April, p. 52.

Luibhéid, Eithne (2002). *Entry Denied: Controlling Sexuality at the Border*. Minneapolis/London: University of Minnesota Press.

Matsuda, Mari J. (1996). *Where is Your body? And Other Essays on Race, Gender, and the Law*. Boston: MA: Beacon Press.

McClintock, Anne, Amir Mufti and Ella Shohat (1997). *Dangerous Liaisons: Gender, Nation and Postcolonial Perspectives*. Minneapolis: University of Minnesota Press.

Menon, Nivedita (2004). *Recovering Subversion: Feminist Politics Beyond the Law*. Urbana, ILL: Permanent Black/University of Illinois Press.

Mitchell, Timothy (1991). 'The Limits of the State: Beyond Statist Approaches and their Critics', *American Political Science Review*, 85(1): 77–96.

————— (1999). 'Society, Economy, and the State Effect', in George Steinmetz (ed.), *State/Culture: State-formation after the Cultural Turn*, pp. 76–97. Ithaca, NY and London: Cornell University Press.

Mohapatra, Arun (2003). *Public Interest Litigation and Human Rights in India*. New Delhi: Radha Publications.

Mosse, George (1985). *Nationalism and Sexuality: Respectability and Abnormal Sexuality in Modern Europe*. New York: Howard Fertig.

Narrain, Arvind and Gautam Bhan (eds) (2005). *Because I Have a Voice*: Queer Politics in India, New Delhi: Yoda Press.

Nardi, P. and B. Schneider (eds) (1998). *Social Perspectives in Lesbian and Gay Studies: A Reader*. London; New York: Routledge.

Ong, Aihwa (1999). *Flexible citizenship*. Durham, North Carolina: Duke University Press.

Parker, A., M. Russo, D. Sommer, and P. Yaeger (eds) (1992). *Nationalisms and Sexualities*. New York and London: Routledge.

Patton, C. and B. Sánchez-Eppler (eds) (2000). *Queer Diasporas*. Durham, N.C.: Duke University Press.

People's Union for Civil Liberties (PUCL)(2003). 'Human Rights Violations against Sexuality

Minorities in India'. Available at: http://pucl.org/Topics/Gender/2003/sexual-minorities.htm. Last accessed November 2005.

Peterson, V. S. (ed.) (1992). *Gendered States: Feminist (Re)visions of International Relations*. Boulder, Colorado: Lynne Rienner Publishers.

Puri, Jyoti (2002). 'Concerning Kamasutras: Challenging Narratives of History and Sexuality', *SIGNS: A Journal of Women in Culture and Society* 27(3): 603–39.

Puri, Jyoti (2004). *Encountering Nationalism*. Malden, MA: Blackwell Publishing.

Radcliffe, Sarah A. and Westwood, Sallie (1996). *Remaking the Nation: Place, Identity and Politics in Latin America*. London; New York: Routledge.

Rouse, Shahnaz (2004). *Shifting Body Politics: Gender, Nation, State in Pakistan*. New Delhi: Women Unlimited (an associate of Kali for Women).

Rubin, Gayle (1993). 'Thinking Sex: Notes for a Radical Theory of the Politics of Sexuality', in Henry Abelove, Michele Aina Barale and David M. Halperin (eds), *The Lesbian and Gay Studies Reader*. New York; London: Routledge.

Sawicki, Jana (1991). *Disciplining Foucault: Feminism, Power, and the Body*. New York, Routledge.

Scott, James (1998). *Seeing Like a State: How Certain Schemes to Improve the Human Condition Have Failed*. New Haven and London: Yale University Press.

Sedgwick, Eve (1990). *Epistemology of the Closet*. Berkeley and Los Angeles, California: University of California Press.

Seider, Ruth (2001). 'Rethinking Citizenship: Reforming the Law in Postwar Guatemala', in Thomas Blom Hansen and Finn Stepputat (eds), *States of Imagination: Ethnographic Explorations of the Postcolonial State*, pp. 203–20. Durham and London: Duke University Press.

Sen, Ayanjit (2004). 'India Court Rejects Gay Petition', BBC, 2 September, available at http://news.bbc.co.uk/2/hi/south_asia/3622418.stm. Last accessed November 2005.

Shapiro, Richard (2006). 'Religion and Empire: Secular Christian Cultural Dominance in the United States', *International Journal of the Humanities*, 2(3).

Somerville, Siobhan (2000). *Queering the Color Line: Race and the Invention of Homosexuality in American Culture*. Durhan, North Carolina.: Duke University Press.

Steinmetz, George (ed.) (1999). *State/culture: State-formation after the Cultural Turn*. Ithaca and London: Cornell University Press.

Stevens, Jacqueline (1999). *Reproducing the State*. Princeton, New Jersey: Princeton University Press.

Stoler, Ann, Laura (1995a). *Race and the Education of Desire: Foucault's History of Sexuality and the Colonial Order of Things*. Durham: Duke University Press.

——— (1995b). 'Sexual Affronts and Racial Frontiers: European Identities and the Cultural Politics of Exclusion in Colonial Southeast Asia', in Frederick Cooper and Ann Stoler (eds), *Tensions of Empire: Colonial Cultures in a Bourgeois World*, pp. 198–237. Berkeley, Los Angeles, California: University of California Press.

——— (2004). 'Affective States', in David Nugent and Joan Vincent (eds), *A Companion to the Anthropology of Politics*, pp. 4–20. Malden, MA: Blackwell Publishing.

Talwar, Rajesh (1999). *The Third Sex and Human Rights*. New Delhi: Gyan Pub. House.

Thadani, Giti (1996). *Sakhiyani: Lesbian Desire in Ancient and Modern India*. London and New York: Cassell.

Thompson, Ben (2001). 'Sri Lanka Gays Eye Canada', in Sodomy Laws'. Available at: http://www.sodomylaws.org/world/sri_lanka/slnews010.htm. Last accessed November 2005.

Uberoi, P. (ed.) (1996). *Social Reform, Sexuality, and the State*. New Delhi: Sage Publications.

Vanita, Ruth (ed.) (2001). *Queering India: Same-sex Love and Eroticism in Indian Culture and Society*. New York: Routledge.

Vanita, Ruth and S. Kidwai (eds) (2000). *Same-Sex Love in India: Readings from Literature and History*. Palgrave.

Warner, Michael (ed.) (1993). *Fear of a Queer Planet: Queer Politics and Social Theory*. Minneapolis: University of Minnesota Press.

Yuval-Davis, N. and F. Anthias (eds) (1989). *Woman-Nation-State*. New York: St. Martin's Press.

5

Afghan Women

Stranded at the Intersection of Local and Global Patriarchies

Huma Ahmed-Ghosh

This article investigates the shifting roles of Afghan women in relation to practices and policies of governance in modern Afghanistan.[1] It explores constructions of masculinity to situate the oppression, exploitation and resistance of Afghan women in a historical context of internal and international socio-political struggles.[2] My intent is to trace how such conditions and contestations have produced Afghan women's bodies as 'globalized property' against a range of multilayered social and political factors, including control by local patriarchies, expansionist policies of communist states, legacies of Cold War rivalries between superpowers, symbolic value and deployment for the benefit of fundamentalist regimes, western rhetoric of women's rights, the quest for oil pipelines, and, in the context of response and reaction following 9/11. Women's bodies and lives have been repeatedly subjected to censures and violence as warring displays of masculinity and forms of patriarchal power vie to express strongmanship at the local and global levels. Strategically manipulated to justify and claim masculinist hegemony, women struggle at the intersections of patriarchy, territory, religion, and nation.

INTRODUCTION

This article examines the multiplicity of Afghan women's oppressions and exploitation in Afghanistan's recent history of internal and international socio-political struggles through local and global patriarchal agendas. Historically, Afghan women's lives and experiences have been circumscribed by the 'use', and abuse, of their bodies in local practices[3] and in contexts of foreign occupation where gendered norms and behaviours are imposed in order to meet or mark international standards.[4] While the former have controlled women through the continual (re)invention[5] and implementation of customs deemed traditional, including polygamy, early marriages, bride-price and forced veiling, the latter have taken on as their project the 'modernization' of Afghan women, actualized through processes of unveiling, secular education and public employment. Although seemingly contrary in their impulses, those deploying tradition and those promoting emancipation as their justifications for defining how Afghan women should live and be are similar in their disrespect and disregard of Afghan women's wishes and realities.

Feminists[6] writing about women in contexts of conflict have emphasized how women's bodies become the terrain on which masculinist battles for supremacy, at material as well as discursive levels, are enacted. Here, I will trace the history of such patriarchal contestations as they have unfolded over time in a country torn by inner conflict and repeated external occupation in order to illuminate Afghan women's[7] bodies as 'globalized property' over which women themselves have limited control (Gregory 2004; Magnus and Naby 1998; Moghadam 1997).

Although my emphasis is on the violence determining and framing women's lives, the discussion in this article incorporates an attention to Afghan women's agency in terms of how it is impacted and constrained by various patriarchies as well as its manifestations in the form of resistance to various bids for control. It has been customary to dismiss and even erase Afghan women's agency and resistance in the face of oppressive discourses and conditions. Khattak (2004: 228) states, 'The Taliban government as well as the international donor community is characterized by viewpoints and approaches that denigrate or reduce Afghan women's agency and resistance, and in the case of donor agencies, racism intersects with their subtle misogyny'. Khattak continues, 'While the manifestations might be different, the intention and impact are very similar because the well-being and real emancipation of Afghan women gets discounted' (ibid.: 228). As Emadi (2002) emphasizes, Afghan women have not been silent objects throughout history. They have resisted, though, as I describe later, their achievements have been tempered through a rationalization/ negotiation and maximization of their position at various socio-political historical junctures.

This article is based on primary and secondary sources as well as field-work conducted in Afghanistan in 2003 and 2004. I travelled to Kabul and Jalalabad to conduct research on the role of women-run non-government organizations (NGOs) in the reconstruction of Afghanistan.[8] Detailed interviews with Afghan women have been described in an earlier paper (Ahmed-Ghosh 2006). The objective of this article is to contextualize Afghan women's complex positioning in contemporary geopolitics by undertaking a critical analysis of how they have been constructed through various points in history. A key motivation is to propel a shift away from an analysis of gendered violence against Afghan women that overemphasizes the Taliban disparagement of women. As I elucidate here, Afghan women's contemporary experiences and circumstances of violence stem from an entrenched, albeit dynamic, local patriarchal order that precedes the Taliban and that has been shaped as a response to threats posed by various internal and external incursions.[9] Following Khan (2001), the intent is to render Afghan women as historical subjects in the geopolitical arena, thereby resisting the impulse to cast Afghan women's suffering as a mere consequence of either the timeless patriarchal urges inherent in Afghan men, or the Islamic fundamentalist tendencies of the Taliban. This article explores the historical framing and complex layering that structure Afghan women's experiences of violence in the post 9/11 era, asking what forces—international, regional, national— colluded over time in various contexts to create the lived realities of the present. Three distinct yet interlocking strands of feminist thought motivate my project in this article. I briefly present them here as the conceptual and theoretical underpinnings of my analysis.

Firstly, I am indebted to feminist writings emerging from the so-called 'Third World'/women of colour quarters that have highlighted the linkages between First World feminist theorizing and colonialist thought.[10] As Mohanty (1988) eloquently delineates, analysis of women's oppression in the Global South cannot be divorced from an investigation of women's experiences and constructions as colonized subjects, and as inheritors of an imperialist reality whereby colonial relationships have persisted to form the postcolonial present.

Secondly, my analysis is grounded in feminist theorizing on the body that stresses how violence against women in different contexts, including contexts of conflict, is perpetuated by perceptions and readings of female bodies that are created and maintained structurally in relation to power over time (Price and Shildrick 1999). Violence targeted at different bodies is *gendered* in its intention and manifestation. This means that women experience violence differentially, not just because their bodies are different but because violence against women is inextricably intertwined with assertions of masculinity, nationhood and honour, whereby the control of women—whether 'ours' and 'theirs', whether through physical violence or other forms of oppression that can be seen as indirect violence—becomes an end in itself (Sangari 2006).

Thirdly, and most saliently for this article, I work with the conception of a 'gendered continuum of violence' that has been advanced by feminists to capture the nuances, range and intersections of the different types of violence faced by women (for example, Cockburn 2004; Moser and Clark 2001). Feminists concerned specifically with women's experiences of violence in contexts of conflict use this notion to emphasize the shortcomings of an approach that restricts itself to discussions of the atrocities women suffer during war. These feminists argue for a perspective that 'tends to represent war as a continuum from the bedroom to the battlefield, traversing our bodies and our sense of self' (Cockburn 1998: 4). Resisting 'any division between public and private domains' (Giles and Hyndman 2004a: 3), such a viewpoint highlights how gendered violence in militarized war zones is in many ways a continuation, or at least a mutation, of expressions of violence in so-called peacetime contexts. Conversely, war-time violence, gendered and otherwise, gets carried over to contexts such as refugee camps and everyday living in the private sphere of home (Chaudhry 2006), an arena not traditionally considered as maintaining any consistency with the battlefield. Even when technically there is no active war, men continue to participate in the culture of honour tied to conflict. Here, enactment of a desirable form of masculinity takes place at the expense of women: women and children are not only disproportionately killed and injured in contemporary conflicts, they bear the brunt of other war-related experiences and crimes (Giles and Hyndman 2004b).

Without interrogating how women are variously positioned within this continuum, feminist analyses cannot comprehend the particularity of women's experiences of violence and the relationships between commonly accepted distinctions between wartime violence and peacetime crimes. Nor can these analyses comprehend the centrality of patriarchal and masculinist discourses emanating from different quarters but united in their denigration of women to the initiation and perpetuation of multiple forms of violence. Patriarchy,[11] which has been historically more or less a global phenomenon despite the heterogeneity of its antecedents and permutations, plays itself out in culturally specific ways by ritualizing masculinities primarily through the control of women's bodies and their sexuality. In order to address the kinds of alliances we need to form with Afghan women to effect/influence feminist change, we need to be 'capable of acting in many places, at many levels, and on many problems simultaneously' (Cockburn 2004: 44).

Through a focus on Afghan women's circumstances in the present, with a particular focus on the gendered continuum of violence framing Afghan women's lives and experiences, I attempt to introduce such an approach. After this, a relatively longer section approaches contexts of gendered violence by delineating trends evidenced during several key historical phases in Afghanistan's history. I then revisit the issue of Afghan women's agency and oppression, using this discussion as a bridge to move back from the past to the present to explore more fully the range and depth of violences in recent and contemporary Afghanistan. The final section weaves together the threads of my argument through the voices of Afghan women, to convey the hope and promise they continue to find even after living through the abysmal conditions of the past decades.

AFGHAN WOMEN'S DISMAL PRESENT

Soraya Parlika, head of the All Afghan Women's Union, testifies, 'Brutal gang rapes and violence continue to keep Afghan women living in fear' (Troup 2005).[12] In another interview, while commenting on the increased kidnapping of women and children, Parlika states, 'I am against the *burqa*,[13] but until security is secured completely, I do not think women will take them off'.[14] Parlika's pointed comments, even as they respond to the western obsession with the so-called 'Muslim veil' as the most visible sign of Muslim women's oppression,[15] serve to foreground the severity of the security issues facing Afghan women in the present. Her remarks also point to how Afghan women negotiate available options to protect themselves in the face of intense threats within the patriarchal society of present-day Afghanistan.[16] The burqa is one such option.[17] This section will address the persistent threat to safety faced by Afghan women, as well as the political and cultural underpinnings of their lack of security; a discussion of Afghan women's agency follows in a later section.

What became clear through my visits to Afghanistan between 2003 and 2004 was that the country was still engaged in conflict under the thin veneer of so-called democratic stability. Afghanistan had at that point been at active war for twenty-seven years[18] with no end in sight. As a result of this enduring period of political instability and war, as of 2006, an estimated one million Afghans had lost their lives, and almost the same number of people were rendered disabled.[19] Sources suggest that at least seven million Afghans were forced to flee their homes, and of these, at least five million have become international refugees, mainly in Pakistan and Iran, with the remaining two million falling into the category of internally displaced persons (IDPs). According to United Nations Development Fund for Women (UNIFEM), only a quarter of Afghans in 2006 had access to clean water and approximately one-tenth of the population had access to adequate sanitation.[20] Such conditions compound the incidence of disease, particularly tuberculosis, which takes 15,000 lives a year in Afghanistan, a disproportionate 64 per cent of them women (UNIFEM).

Trafficking of Afghan women and children continues to increase at alarming rates. Its escalating incidence can be attributed to the vicious cycle of war, poverty and cultural and political oppression spanning more than two and a half decades. According to the 2004 International Organization for Migration (IOM) Report, 'forced prostitution and prostitution of minors, forced labour, abductions for forced marriage for debt relief, and exchange of women for dispute settlement continue to thrive in Afghanistan' (2004: 7). Other atrocities on the rise, according to the above report, include sexual and domestic servitude of women and slavery of men, women and children. The report notes that the majority of those subjected to such atrocities are 'displaced, destitute, and indebted persons and families, and young people seeking economic opportunities abroad, and rural women' (ibid.: 8).

In Afghanistan, 90 per cent of births take place at home, which, in conjunction with other issues like the above statistic regarding sanitation, contributes to the country earning the second highest maternal mortality rate in the world, with about 15,000 women dying of causes related to pregnancy each year.[21] Additionally, infant mortality in Afghanistan for the years spanning 2000–5 was 168.1 deaths to 1,000 live births,[22] a figure that likewise positions Afghanistan dismally on a global health scale. Life expectancy has plunged to forty-two years for both men and women,[23] and by 2006, literacy rates for men had dropped to 51 per cent, while for women the figure stood at 21 per cent.[24] The US' commitment to any kind of reconstruction or implementation of human rights and raising of women's status is squarely reflected in where the funds are allocated: between 2002 and 2006, approximately US$13 billion poured into Afghanistan, only 9 per cent ($1.16 billion) of which was used for humanitarian aid, and a paltry 4 per cent ($504 million) of which was directed towards international peacekeeping. Meanwhile, 85 per cent of the dollars ($10.2 billion) were committed to fighting al-Qaeda and the Taliban. This leaves 3 per cent ($365.5 million) for reconstruction assistance for a country that has been ravaged by nearly three decades of war and a decade of drought.[25]The rhetoric framing US policies in Afghanistan stressed issues of safety and security for women to justify an ongoing armed presence and cooperative governance with the Northern Alliance. Yet according to Human Rights Watch, 'Many women blamed the failure of disarmament, the entrenchment of warlords in both regional and central governments, and limited reach of international peacekeeping troops as the reasons why they felt unsafe'[26]

Even though semi-successful attempts at unification, starting in 1880, have been made through different periods in history, Afghanistan has always been a conglomeration of provinces loosely held together by a fluid central government in Kabul (Ahmed-Ghosh 2003; Moghadam 1997). Kabul exists as an island unto itself: in political as well as economic and cultural terms. As a city, it has witnessed periods of institutional modernization and increased opportunities for women. During the decades of the 1950s to the 1980s[27] local elites in Kabul experimented with liberal and co-educational institutes and modernized social programmes. Women experienced greater mobility, going out in public unveiled and in western clothes, while significant numbers of women participated in the workforce in a range of jobs and marriages of choice increased. This period in Kabul witnessed a rise in the average age of marriage for both men and women simultaneous with diminishing rates of bride-price. These emerged as urban privileges, while the reality in the countryside has always been different. In the countryside, the situation remains much more conservative, with women's lives dictated by tribal laws. Such laws restrict access to education and limit mobility for girls and women, and frequently adhere to practices of marrying off daughters at young ages. In addition, the largely unabated practice of polygamy and prevalence of bride-price have further contributed to oppressive conditions for women in rural Afghanistan historically and into the present (Emadi 2002). Rural women have always been very active in agricultural processes, from farming to livestock maintenance. However, agency afforded through participation in such labour is mediated by demarcations of public and private spheres by a well-entrenched kinship system based on honour and prestige and vested in the women of the family. This dual system has existed in Afghanistan for centuries, with women's position in society largely unchallenged in rural areas (ibid.).

PATRIARCHY AND GENDERED VIOLENCE: CONTEMPORARY AFGHANISTAN

In the spring of 2005, an article reported the stoning to death of a twenty-nine-year-old Afghan woman named Amina in Urgu district, Badakshan province.[28] This report is neither unexpected nor atypical. Such acts perpetuate forms of masculinity that are tied to the honour of the community. According to the Afghanistan Independent Human Rights Commission Report (AIHRC)[29] 2003–4, and the Women and Children Legal Research Foundation (WCLRF)[30] the prime suspects are the legal courts. Particularly in rural Afghanistan, most settlements are arrived at through decisions by the *jirga* or *shura* (both are local political bodies) that are controlled entirely by senior men. AIHRC claims local bodies control 70 per cent of the justice system, though informal conversations with Afghans placed this figure closer to 90 per cent.[31] This, coupled with the continuing power and elevated status of 'traditional practices and customary law' in Afghanistan, renders the justice system virtually impenetrable for Afghan women. Justified through tradition to encode gender norms and shape rural societies in the present, these forms of female subjugation are mostly ignored by the West's human rights' rhetoric. Such crimes are sustained through a culture based on 'honour and shame' and often legitimated by Western Orientalist views to inform policies of 'respecting local cultures'.

The continued oppression of women through systems of justice in rural communities across Afghanistan extends beyond egregious sentences for 'shameful' behaviour. Through conflict resolution exchanges such as *bad* (the giving away of women and girls to victims' families to resolve disputes) the perpetrator's family recuperates honour. WCLRF (2004) estimates that 25 per cent of these transactions involve children. These transactions can occur to resolve issues ranging from murders, elopements, inter-tribal animosities, and land disputes.

Similar reports also highlight the increase in domestic violence, deterioration in women's mental health, and a rise in suicides among girls and women, especially in cases of forced marriages. Self-immolation is mounting among women and has reached a proportion of national concern. A news release from Amnesty International points to a 'worsening situation in which women are afraid to leave their homes for fear of abduction and are even imprisoned for their own protection'.[32]

While representing a range of contexts for violence against women, these practices and present realities are similar in the ways that masculinities are deployed in Afghanistan's present, and in their subordination of Afghan women's bodies. In addition they highlight how despite lip service to the emancipation of Afghan women, the present US-backed regime has no commitment to the amelioration of violence against Afghan women (Khattak 2002). Although the cases above reflect the entrenched culture of patriarchy in Afghanistan, they also indicate how this culture has been sustained at structural levels, both through the implementation and the negligence of institutions tied to the modern nation-state.

There is a long history of rhetoric that balances the barbarism of 'honour and shame' with the noble pursuits of a civilized empire, as the position and condition of 'other' women are cited as cause for intervention.[33] In the era preceding 9/11, the West expressed their cultural supremacy by, 'belittling local cultures, emasculating local men, and by referring to [Afghan] cultural norms pertaining to women as barbaric or backward' (Ahmed-Ghosh 2005: 104). In the wake of US intervention following 9/11, however, the evasion of the issue of gendered violence in Afghanistan can be observed in the interplay of local and international masculinist contests for hegemony. This was evidenced in the April 2005 decision to eliminate the job of the top investigator on human rights in Afghanistan (Rupert 2005: 1). This decision, taken by the UN, 'under USA's pressure in a situation where the official criticized violations by U.S. forces in the country'. According to US sources, this was done because 'the human rights situation in Afghanistan is no longer troubling enough to require it [the senior position]' (ibid.). As a statement, it is difficult not to read this as Afghan women's actual conditions in the present not warranting the attention from high-level human rights officials. Is it surprising that women I talked to in Afghanistan were bitter about the West using them as pawns, as part of the 'package' for the justification of the post 9/11 bombing of Afghanistan, their dire issues consigned to oblivion once a regime supportive of US agendas was in place? Given the current situation in Afghanistan, then, one has to be wary of how gendered identities, both masculine and feminine, are played out, and, as

Enloe warns, 'If the government continues to privilege masculinity, then even those policies it may enact to widen women's spheres of activity can be reversed as soon as it decides such a reversal is politically convenient' (2004: 198). Enloe continues, pointing out that the 'broadening of women's autonomy is secure only when that broadening actually rolls back the masculinization of both local and foreign interventionist political cultures and government power' (ibid.).

As witnessed in the above case of the stoning death, and countless and continuous other atrocities and abuses, Enloe's 'rolling back' is nowhere in sight. Numerous reports from UNIFEM, Amnesty International, Feminist Majority and other UN and independent agencies carefully catalogued the atrocities against women in Afghanistan in the five years following US intervention in Afghanistan,[34] but, as of 2006, their efforts have not had significant impact on either foreign policy in the US or on considerations for funding by foreign agencies, including the World Bank.

In Afghanistan, culture and tradition are seen as crucial markers of high status; family is the reflection of such status, and women must uphold the status of their families through appropriate behaviour (Emadi 2002). Most women continue to be responsible for reinforcing gender, and explicitly for upholding clear demarcations between men and women and their appropriate roles in society (Ahmed-Ghosh 1998; Enloe 1989, 2000, 2004). Honour becomes a masculine concept, and femininity is about shame. Men's dishonour does not necessarily bring shame to the community to the extent that women's does; women's behaviours bring shame on not just herself, but her family and community as well. This difference in dishonour is reflected in the forms of censure that exist in such societies, notably, honour killing and exchanges of blood money.[35] Women are not recognized as having an individual identity, rather, they derive status through their relationship to a male: fathers, husbands and sons. A woman in this context is expected to conform to her role as the dependent, one which complements the status of the male. There are no special behavioural expectations of her outside of her relationships that would signify honour (Ahmad 1992; Ahmed-Ghosh 1998; Tapper 1991; Weidman 2003; Wikan 1984).

For men, honour can be earned, and is rewarded by society through participation in a cultural masculinity that is in all instances superior to cultural femininity (Ahmad 1992; Ahmed-Ghosh 1998; Tapper 1991; Weidman 2003; Wikan 1984). Men establish their own honour and patriarchy is reinforced through participation in war, protection of their women, entitlement to citizenship and through various contests of bravery and strength that allow for the display of expertise. In the name of honour and for the preservation of patriarchal institutions, control over women's lives and bodies are deemed essential. Through war, honour can be won or reclaimed by dishonouring 'other' men and women through the undermining of the enemy's masculinity. Actions that retrieve masculine honour are prevalent in Afghanistan's present, and include gendered violence through rape of women in war, kidnapping of the enemy's women, destruction of the enemy's home base, and deprivation of basic human rights to women (Christensen 1990; Donini et al., 2004; Khattak 2002; Mertus 2000; Physicians for Human Rights 1998;Skaine 2002).

Different societal contexts have their own histories of how women's bodies and the functions of their bodies become tied to a nation's honour and used to signify purity (see, for example, Eisenstein 1996). In multi-ethnic areas of the world where nation-states can not be easily mapped onto homogenous populations that claim a united past and present, women's bodies in patriarchal discourses come to acquire multiple connotations of shame and honour, as well as identity and otherness (see Welchman and Hossain 2005). Women are not only rendered as agents of purity of nation-states, but also of other collectivities such as tribes or ethnic groups. So the two-fold task of protecting 'our' women's honour and attacking the enemy through 'other' women's honour translates into complex and profuse enactments of oppression and violence. In the Afghan context, this has meant strict confines on women's lives on the one hand, and, on the other, the prevalence of various forms of sexual violence emerging in particular manifestations at certain junctures in history. Such an excavation allows that the stoning of women for alleged transgressions, although often justified in the present as justice by tradition, is better understood as a feature of a post 9/11 struggle for power, identity, and survival than as a form of national justice in Afghanistan. The justice levied in this instance does not reflect a historically consistent mode of sentencing within a functioning state legal apparatus. Further, while its occurrence, like any murder or misogynistic or sadistic act, may share historical precedents, such repetitions as punishment or discipline must be seen as distinct from a juridical legacy, whether state or local. It should no more be considered as acceptable jurisprudence in Afghanistan than it should as a tenant of Islam. It becomes important to consider who benefits from readings that seek to cast or interpret these acts outside the realm of local practice, practice that must be intervened upon by communities in conjunction with larger, accountable governing bodies.

In discourses of protection, violation and vulnerability, Afghan women's bodies thus represent the 'weak spots' in a nation or tribe's body politic. While seen as crucial to the future of a collectivity, women are the ones responsible for the enculturation of the younger generation to nationalism, patriotism and citizenship—they can also bring dishonour to it. Ivekovic and Mostov aptly address the conundrum of the 'common fate of women' who are 'members of the community, but not equal political subjects in (ethno) national contexts'; while considered vital to the perpetuation of 'the nation', 'they are in some way, always suspect; they are a symbol of purity of the nation, but always vulnerable to contamination; they embody the homeland, but are always a potential stranger' (2002: 13–14).

Afghan women have over the years become 'globalized property' as their bodies become sites of inscription by/for multilayered patriarchies. Local level patriarchies intersect with transnational, international and intra-national masculinist imperatives to compound gendered violence, oppression and restrictions in the lives and on the bodies of women. The following section traces a history of patriarchal structural dominance and women's responses within and against the Afghan social structure.

AFGHAN PATRIARCHY: A HISTORICAL PERSPECTIVE[36]

The Reign of Amirs

It is no longer the jurisdiction of Islamic laws to decide gender roles in the region. It is tribal laws and sanctions that jeopardize the position of women through tribal power plays, institutions of honour and inter-tribal demonstrations of machismo (Ahmed-Ghosh 2001: 2). During his reign, Abdur Rahman Khan (1880–1901), referred to as the 'Iron Amir' abolished the custom of levirate and raised the age of marriage for both men and women. The Amir still considered women subservient to men, but felt that they should be treated fairly (Dupree 1986). It is on the reign of Amir Khan that Afghanistan stakes its own modernity, though many of the changes instituted were not necessarily adopted by the larger population.

After Abdur Rahman's death, his successor and son, Amir Habibullah Khan, continued the modernization process in his father's footsteps, a process steeped in western influence and most readily accessible among metropolitan elites. Habibullah Khan, too, enacted legislation aimed to address the situation of women in Afghanistan, including placing a ceiling on extravagant weddings. Under the influence and advice of Mahmud Beg Tarzi, a liberal-modernist who had been educated in Syria and Turkey, and recalled from exile by Habibullah Khan, he opened a school for girls with an English curriculum, while his wives set the example of liberation through the wearing of western clothes and entering the public unveiled. The sovereign's reforms in the education of women and the interference in marriage institutions were not eagerly accepted across the nation, however. Among tribal leaders and those who supported and lived according to patrilineal and patrilocal kinship systems, such actions were seen as challenging tribal leaders' power and threatening the very systems people traditionally lived by and relied on for security and identity (Ahmed-Ghosh 2003: 4). The project of modernization as manifested in the Khan legacy was experienced by the tribal leaders as one which undermined their political, economic and social authority; it is in this context that the assassination of Habibullah Khan occurred in 1919. What became apparent is that a perceived threat to patriarchy and masculinity within the household and community resulted in strong censure of the royalty. It must be noted here that under no regime was there ever an objection to industrialization and modernization through education for boys.

Amir Amanullah took the throne following his father's assassination and continued the modernization agenda set by his grandfather and father. In this task he depended even more on Mahmud Beg Tarzi, whose daughter Soraya was also Amanullah's wife. Amanullah is widely regarded as a great leader, for he was the first king to finally succeed in defeating the British in the Third Anglo-Afghan War in 1919, thus ridding the Afghans of further British attempts at colonization in this region. Amanullah was also commended for instituting laws 'liberating' women, as well as putting Afghanistan on the global stage through his foreign travels.

With support from his wife Queen Soraya and her family, Amanullah campaigned against the veil and polygamy, and encouraged education of girls, not just in Kabul, but also in the countryside. Women from the royal family brought out women's magazines, and hospitals and schools were built for girls and women. Amanullah's sister encouraged civic participation and politicization of women through the creation of an organization structured to address women's concerns (Dupree 1986). Amanullah judiciously evoked Islam as an egalitarian faith to set forth his liberal agenda for women. Thus, historically, elite women in Afghanistan were positioned to not only leverage institutional access towards a more emancipatory feminist agenda, but to leverage modernity's signifiers of visible resistance as well. The emerging policies and practices contributed to a reshaping of rural-urban tensions with diverse effects. As cosmopolitan influence and women's struggles for empowerment emerged more perceptibly at the centre, the countryside witnessed a strengthening in tribal leaders' conservative agendas. Traditional tribal patriarchies were forced to engage the challenges to patriarchal structures made public in urban politics.

During Amanullah's reign, modernization of the nation, and specifically the move towards women's independence, undermined the socio-political and economic power of tribal patriarchies within the family and the community. In a system where women were used as pawns for political alliances, where their marriage brought wealth to the family through bride-price and where their complete subservience was seen as complimentary to male authority, shifts that allowed for the education of their daughters, their faces unveiled on the streets, and their increasing ability to take individual decisions in marriage left the power of their fathers compromised. As this power was increasingly eroded, it became difficult to maintain their patriarchal tribal authority within the community and their dominance in the family according to the traditional ways they were familiar with. Also, a sense of alienation may have permeated the system, with the royalty living a life that was not just elite, but was becoming culturally and economically difficult to comprehend for the common folk. Coupled with rumblings from other tribal leaders, a resentment and antagonism against the king built up. This antagonism accelerated into a revolt, which ultimately led to Amanullah's exile to Italy in 1929.

It is interesting to observe that in the later years of his reign Amanullah tried to regain his grasp on political power by reversing some policies that directly affected women. He shut down girls' schools, reinstituted the veil, and even took a second wife. It was too late; he had to flee the country, and Afghanistan was taken over by a leader who reversed every single modernizing policy affecting Afghan women and girls (Dupree 1986). It would be decades before a ruler in Afghanistan would once again bring up issues pertaining to women's empowerment or visibility in society.

Other Rumblings: The Soviet Union

In the 1950s, a discourse emerged among the ruling elite and the middle classes that emphasized the need for greater labour power in order to expedite Afghanistan's development (Emadi 2002). This felt need, in conjunction with influences that valorized the model of development in the Soviet Union, paved the way for the easing up of restrictions on women's education and employment. In the drive for development, by 1959, women were once again asked to abandon the veil, marriage expenses were curtailed, and women were encouraged to contribute to the economy. This ideology involved socialist-style 'liberation' of women to legitimize their economic policies in the region (Khattak 2004). Women were strategically deployed to reflect and symbolize the need of the economic and political hour (Ahmed-Ghosh 2003), while once again, the public status of their bodies began its pendulous swing between covered and uncovered, with external forces defining the direction and momentum. By 1964, in the third constitution created that year, they were recognized as powerful enough to earn the right to vote. A year later, in 1965, the first women's organization, the Democratic Organization of Afghan Women, was formed. It should be pointed out here that these developments, as welcome and as necessary as they were, were at the behest of the Soviets and the modernized elite Afghans (Emadi 2002). The tribal and religious leaders continued to resist these changes, thus preventing rural and urban women from conservative families from gaining benefits accrued through such progressive steps.

In 1979 the Soviets physically occupied Afghanistan, in a move that had more to do with the patriarchal hegemonies of Cold War politics between competing superpowers than it did any threat to power perceived on the part of the Afghan nation. (Khattak 2002). The US and the Soviet Union alike had been asserting their muscle across the globe through wooing alliances with Third World countries (aimed at either preventing or facilitating the development of socialist states), and as part of a race extending from arms and weapons to the moon! Somewhat ironically, in the context of an enduring contest between patriarchal powers for world domination, Soviet occupation had the effect of generating spaces of empowerment as women across Afghanistan moved more substantially into the public sphere.

Soviet occupation also saw the rise in literacy and employment among women. This was partly because education was made mandatory in accordance with a socialist ideology, and partly because Afghan men were leaving to fight the Soviets. More and more women joined the ranks of various professions. In averaging various sources, the following figures attest to the high incidence of women's participation in Afghanistan's personal and professional development sectors during the Soviet era.

Women accounted for approximately 70 per cent of all teachers, 40 per cent of university students, 40 per cent of physicians, 50 per cent of all public officials, with similar figures for other professions (Ahmed-Ghosh 2003). Not out of any commitments to feminism but rather given the absence of men, the Soviets ensured that women were educated because they needed women's labour. Women were able to empower themselves significantly through this Soviet push for education and employment (ibid.) even as simultaneously Soviet presence and power undermined an Afghan masculinity contingent on women's subordination and lack of mobility.

Attempts at land reforms, abolition of bride-price, and raising of marriage ages once again took centre stage, but this time the resistance was magnified two-fold—firstly, reform efforts were instituted by a foreign power, the Soviets; and secondly, such reforms were considered in opposition to 'Afghan' culture and traditions. This time, resistance to modernization came not just from the tribal leaders, but also from the newly emerging nationalist class (ibid.). The Soviets, with their ever-expanding control of the nation and mandatory implementation of land reforms, literacy and other projects in the name of socialism, contributed to destabilizing the nation, leading to the creation of the Mujahideen.[37]

The Regime of the Mujahideen

The Mujahideen, who were, practically speaking, in control of Afghanistan from 1992 to 1996, were a collective of tribal leaders united only in their efforts to rid the country of the Soviets. Backed by aid specifically from the US, the Mujahideen played out Cold War animosities on behalf of the US by fighting a Communist regime. Physicians for Human Rights has documented the severe problematics that characterize the involvement of the US (1998: 22). As stated in Hans (2004), according to Ahmad's claim, 'Washington alone supplied an estimated $10 billion in arms and aid [to] the freedom fighters' to dethrone the Soviets. With the departure of the Soviets, the US abandoned the Afghans, leaving the country in chaos that gave way to civil war.

With the mission to push out the Soviets achieved, a struggle arose among the various tribal leaders to take over the leadership of the nation. There was large-scale destruction of property, indiscriminate bombing of Kabul and other cities, mass scale raping of women, looting and inter-tribal acts of vengeance. Norah Niland describes the descent into anarchy, noting thus: 'The willingness of different commanders to raze much of the capital city, and the lawlessness of the Mujahideen who killed, pillaged and raped with abandon ...marked a new phase in the war' (2004: 64). The Mujahideen were supported and financed by the US, Saudi Arabia, Iran and China, a conglomeration of nations with contradictory discourses on democracy and women's rights. This conglomeration of nations maintained a policy of 'least resistance' to the Mujahideen. President Rabbani[38] declared Afghanistan as an Islamic state, and his government introduced strictures against women requiring them to wear burqas, as also an interdiction on women leaving the house without the accompaniment of a male relative, and that too, only with their father's or husband's permission (Ahmed-Ghosh 2003).

The Rule of the Taliban

In 1996, it was not surprising that when the Taliban, an organization of young religious students of Afghan origin brought up in Pakistan, entered the city of Kabul they were received with much jubilation. The Taliban did bring about some law and order, but proceeded to enforce an extremist interpretation of Islam to rule. They legitimized the gendered social order started by the Mujahideen by creating the infamous *Amar Bil Maroof Wa Nahi An al-Munkar* (Department for the Promotion of Virtue and Prevention of Vice) to monitor and control women's lives.

While men were expected to conform to visible Islamic ideals of dress and appearance, including the beard, the Taliban's radical policies had a much harsher impact on women. Using Radio Sharia on a daily basis to remind Afghan citizens of their duty to the newly formed ultra-Islamic state, the Taliban issued various dictates. Among these were requirements for a strict dress code for women, insisting that a burqa be worn when leaving the home. Additionally, women needed to be accompanied by a *mahram* (male relative) when out in public. Women and girls could only go to female doctors, girls' schools were closed down, and women were forbidden from employment. The Taliban took sole credit for redefining the Islamic roles of men and women, and, within this framework, reconstructed expressions of gender to empower and legitimize their own masculinity. This was done not only through the oppression of women, but also through meting out cruel punishments to both women and men who did not conform to 'their' Islamic tenets. Images of public floggings and killings for crimes began filtering out of Afghanistan raising awareness of the atrocities committed by the Taliban in the name of Islam (Khattak 2004).

Even then, much of what was happening in Afghanistan would have gone unnoticed by the US were it not for European sources that began internationally publicizing the atrocities perpetuated by the Taliban against women. The feminist majority pressured the US government to intervene by boycotting their business interests in the country. Despite the US government's history of levying censure against other nations for human rights violations even as they refuse to acknowledge their own atrocities, it had to bow out of a Unocal deal to build oil pipelines in Afghanistan for fear of international condemnation. Given the global knowledge of the oppression of Afghan women under the Taliban regime, the US could not afford to blatantly contradict its rhetoric of freedom and liberty. This strategic stance would serve them well three years later when they bombed Afghanistan on the pretence of the liberation of Afghan women. Once again, the world was exposed to the masculinist rhetoric of protection of the 'weak' and 'oppressed' (read: women), and was largely complicit in affirming the West's masculine domination via the US-led war begun in 2001 October (Khattak 2003; Azarbaijani-Moghaddam 2004).

GENDERED VIOLENCE, WOMEN'S AGENCY AND MASCULINIST AGENDAS

Despite the draconian governance of the Taliban, this era too saw resistance from women (Armstrong 2002; Emadi 2002; Khattak 2004). Soraya Parlika ran underground schools for girls and training centres for widows.[39] She was one of the few women leaders of Afghanistan from the 1960s who chose to stay in Kabul despite the struggles. The Revolutionary Association for Women of Afghanistan (RAWA), Humanitarian Assistance for Women and Children of Afghanistan (HAWCA) and many other groups also conducted underground schools, as well as skill training centres and clinics for children and women in Afghanistan in defiance of the Taliban. Khattak cites surgeon Suhaila Sidiq to demonstrate how 'Some women doctors were able to negotiate with the more moderate mullahs to continue their work in hospitals' (Khattak 2002: 21). Khattak continues, contending 'there were thousands of ghost schools for girls in people's homes' (ibid.). In addition, women deftly used the burqa and adherence to other visible norms of 'good Muslim women behaviour' to strategically navigate through the Taliban's rules and regulations, gaining some semblance of control over their lives, a control that had been denied them during the physically punitive and harsh Mujahideen era, and a control that was then blasted away by the post 9/11 bombing (Armstrong 2002; Brohi 2004/2005; Khattak 2004).

The Mujahideen reign of terror is also notable because it represents a time when some Afghan women were more actively supportive of extremist, so-called Islamic policies. Afghan women have historically enacted prolific resistances to masculinist forms of gendered violence, direct and physical as well as indirect and structural, that was perpetrated through imposition of patriarchal traditions. However, during the time of the Mujahideen, Afghan women have themselves been implicated in wars and conflict, and any discussion of their resistance needs to take into account their roles in conflict as expressions of agency (Azarbaijani-Moghaddam 2004).

Throughout the 1980s Afghan women were split in their co-operation with the Soviets and the Mujahideen. Some women supported the Soviet regime because of the freedoms it promised them as women. Other women chose to be part of the freedom struggle to remove Soviet occupiers at any cost. Numerous accounts of women leaders and heroines weave through the narratives and chronicles of history of the Mujahideen war against the Soviet invasion (Azarbaijani-Moghaddam 2004; Hans 2004; Mayotte 1992; Rubin 1997). Supporting the Mujahideen to fight the Soviets became the battle cry of these Afghan women, who maintained that this war was about Islam, Afghan culture and national identity against a foreign/western occupier. For Mujahideen women, this was a holy war, and gender issues were not the focus. If gender issues were considered important, they would be in accordance to the tenets of Islam, and any positions that were taken on gender would stand in definite contrast to the western values of the occupiers. Thus, even if it meant denying education, jobs and healthcare to girls and women, the women supporters of the Mujahideen had a one-point agenda of driving the infidels out of Afghanistan. It was this sense of infidel occupiers that resonated most with Afghan women. Azarbaijani-Moghaddam (2004), in an interview with Nancy Hatch Dupree in 2002, discusses how many Afghan women willingly joined the 'Jihad effort' because of their belief that Prophet Mohammad had sanctioned 'equal obligation' for men and women to participate in Jihad. The call for women to join the Jihad was justified as protection from infidel occupation and liberation for their fathers, husbands, and most importantly their sons. Enloe elaborates on formations of gender difference, stating, 'Constructing ideals of masculine behaviour in any culture cannot be accomplished without construction of ideals of femininity that are supportive and complimentary' (2004: 106). For Ivekovic and Mostov (2002: 11), 'Women's bodies serve as symbols of the fecundity of the nation and vessels for its reproduction, as well as territorial markers. As markers and as property, mothers, daughters and wives require the defence and protection of patriotic sons' (ibid.:10).

Simultaneously, however, Afghan women, especially during the Mujahideen era in the country, were also subjected to rape, torture, kidnappings, resulting in a high rate of suicides among women. Suicide, then, given the intensity of the oppression, often became the only way women could protect themselves from continued violation and oppression, or the only tolerable act of agency. At that time, unlike later, under the Taliban reign, even wearing the burqa was not a deterrent to violence (Khattak 2002). Azarbaijani-Moghaddam points out that the Mujahideen period 'was marked by double standards' where 'women were expected to be veiled and housebound, but were often victims of unbridled lust of commanders and their troops, who were responsible for violent rapes, multiple forced marriages, and pressure to provide sexual favours in return for humanitarian assistance' (2004: 99).

More men than women recall crimes during the Soviet-Communist period, whereas more women recall crimes during the Mujahideen period.[40] Paradoxically, the US chose not to recognize the atrocities perpetuated by the Mujahideen when they took over Afghanistan.[41] Yet abuses perpetuated by the Mujahideen would frequently become a topic of discussion when, during my trips there, we drove by the huge billboards displaying Ahmad Shah Masood.[42] Masood was part of the Mujahideen that had in 1992 engaged in the massive plunder, rape and bombing of Kabul. Stories of rape and of men indiscriminately entering homes to kidnap girls and exact violence on the bodies of those inside were common, and accounts of Mujahideen violence are replete with instances of gendered violence along recurrent themes—removal of women's breasts, tearing open of wombs of pregnant women, and others[43] (Ahmed-Ghosh 2003). One of the women whom I interviewed told me about hearing screams at night and finding out the next morning that her neighbour's daughter had jumped out of the window. She looked away from me and said, 'She was only 13 and it was her parents who told her to jump'.[44] This does not downplay the strictures and abuse perpetrated by the Taliban, but brings to the forefront the atrocities committed by the Mujahideen and made invisible by their key collaborator, the US. Absent from the US's discussion was the abuse of women by their main ally, the Northern Alliance (which largely consisted of the Mujahideen). Despite their celebrated mission of intervention for the liberation of women, US operations against the Taliban aligned with former Mujahideen, irrespective of the violence they perpetuated against Afghan women. Women, their bodies, and their status are sacrificed to forge patriarchal alliances. This was witnessed in the case of the US and the Northern Alliance, and later by the US and Hamid Karzai's regime, which still harbours many warlords in its government (Azarbaijani-Moghaddam 2004).

Empowering men's masculinity through patriarchal power has been well defined by Enloe (2004) who, in her discussion on Borislav Herak, a working-class Serbian tried in court for murder and mass rape, tries to understand how a once shy man 'unpoliticized' and with an 'undistinguished career' could commit such horrific crimes. Struggling to think violence in contexts of state power and entrenched structures of patriarchy, Enloe explores 'how ethnicity gets converted into nationalistic consciousness, how consciousness becomes organized, and how organized nationalism becomes militarized' (2004: 101). In Afghanistan, the rampage of the Mujahideen and the ensuing Civil War were reflective of similar ethnic rivalries, which were reshaped through the emergence of modern forms of nation state and international geopolitical tensions, and soldered into religious alliance through foreign intervention and massive foreign funding. It was in this context that thousands of young men were drawn into battle by their warlords to perpetuate atrocities against their adversaries, both men and women. The Taliban too, who were primarily Pushtuns, furthered agendas of ethnic cleansing begun under the Mujahideen. Enloe continues: 'There is evidence that the warrior is a central element in the modern cultural construction of the Serbian ideal of masculinity' (ibid.: 106). For centuries in Afghanistan, masculinity has been defined by and tied to a sense of 'warriorhood'. Besides inter-tribal struggles, Afghans have been faced with streams of foreign invasions over the centuries, including Persian, British, Soviet, and US. The defence of the nation has legitimized the primacy of masculinity as related to might and power, and ultimately to the 'protection' of honour through 'protection' of women, through previously mentioned restrictive traditional norms of segregation, marriage institutions and limited access to education and mobility.[45]

With Afghanistan, the West that continues to exploit Afghan women to further their economic and political agendas has reinforced subordinate constructions for women, with cooperation from local tribal cultures and various interpretations of Islam. While post-9/11 discourses exploited

Afghan women's misery and suffering to justify further violence against them and their families (Khattak 2002), over the years neither Afghan women's oppression nor their negotiation of that oppression has been comprehensively addressed. In the instances where this oppression is addressed, there is a paucity of political discourse that links masculinist agendas, ranging from the global to the local, as they impact Afghan women. Afghan women's lived experiences of violence and threats to their security persist into the present, while these issues remain peripheral to the project of the modern democratic nation-state of Afghanistan (Azarbaijani-Moghaddam 2004). Despite the range and depth of the violence they encounter, Afghan women across many contexts valiantly strive to survive and resist the multilayered power relations that attempt to determine their lives. However, the barriers to their well-being are innumerable and even policies and interventions designed to help them often have the effect of adding to their burden (Brohi 2004/2005).

TOWARDS A MORE HOPEFUL FUTURE?

Situations of conflict produce conditions for further exploitation, particularly among women, who have already been accorded low status. Despite individual and collective resistances, continuing conflict in Afghanistan has rendered women globalized property. Patriarchies that alternately challenge and then dictate cultural and religious identities leave Afghan women in flux as to what their position in the larger society can or should be. Given Afghan women's economic and social dependency on men, kin and community, tribal identity has taken precedence over gender identity through much of Afghan history. With Soviet occupation, religious (Islamic) identity gained stature and continues to do so under the current government, largely enabled by the US, but this shift has not significantly alleviated women's subordinate positioning or their multi-faceted experiences of violence. A gendered approach to Afghanistan's history has shown how, as in other cultures, masculinity continues to be defined through violent cultural and political inscriptions on women's bodies. These inscriptions are legitimized and sustained through patriarchal discourses and practices.

Despite the intensity and range of violence in Afghan women's lives, it is important to reiterate the ways Afghan women have negotiated available discourses and options to enable their own survival and the survival of loved ones even in the direst of circumstances. Such an approach is vital in deconstructing dominant stereotypes about Afghan women, but also in locating potential for equitable and peaceful societal transformation. When talking about violence against women, many women in Afghanistan that I spoke with felt that it was the result of extreme poverty, ignorance and, depending on their ethnicity, the fault of the Mujahideen (Northern Alliance: Tajiks, Uzbeks, others) or the Taliban (mainly Pushtuns). Afghan women continue to live in the hope that improvement will occur, even if it is very slow. They ascribed these acts of violence to 'corrupt and power crazy tribal leaders', 'foreign occupiers', and 'fundamentalists' and not necessarily to 'Afghan culture and Islam'.[46]

Most interviews with Afghan women in Afghanistan and India reflected a serious concern with security in the country. A strong sense of patriarchal oppression through tribal culture as palpable was recurrent in the testimonies of the interviewees, but they were careful to point out that this patriarchal order was not based on Islam.[47] Public dissent against gendered violence continues to grow in Afghanistan. In June 2005, an e-mail signature campaign was sent out worldwide by twenty-six Afghan women's groups to protest the lack of action by President Karzai to the stoning death of Amina, and the rape and murders of three Afghan women working for NGOs. These are positive signs of the women's movement in Afghanistan gaining strength publicly.

Afghanistan today remains poised amid power struggles and contestations on a global and local scale—for economic domination of the region; between East and West, Christian and Islamic, modern and traditional—largely through control over women's bodies. Denigration then, of Afghan/Islamic society is framed in a traditional versus modern discourse that gauges treatment of women in the West and in Afghanistan to legitimize the superiority of the West. The impact is one that escalates many of the most strident features of traditional patriarchal cultures, perpetuating old and enabling new forms of domination of women by local Afghan tribal leaders. As Dr Habiba Sorabi, the ex-minister for women's affairs and the current governor of Bamiyan, succinctly put it in a recent interview, 'We have a long way to go. Changing the attitudes of men rather than women [is necessary] because this is a male dominated country and men should change their minds towards the women' (North 2005).

The task ahead in supporting Afghan women is to map out spaces for alliance and intervention. What actions erode global, regional and local structures that have sustained the treatment of Afghan women as globalized property? How might scholarship and discursive frames shift to reflect a more nuanced understanding of the continuum of violence framing Afghan women's lives? How do we address the larger issue of national sovereignty and peace for Afghanistan, even as we attempt to express solidarity with Afghan women, especially those living in Afghanistan? These are some of the questions that loom large in my mind as I write.

NOTES

1. Modern Afghanistan dates itself back to the reign of Abdur Rahman Khan (1880–1901).

2. In employing the term 'masculinity' or 'masculinities' throughout this article, I refer to the expression of manhood as a particular construction at the intersection of complex processes of collective identity building, including nationalist projects and ethnic and tribal communities. Such ideas about what it means to be a man play a critical role in the formation and maintenance of nations and other collectivities. See, for example, Banerjee (2005).

3. Local traditions that have kept women oppressed at different levels and in different ways include institutions of bride-price, early marriage of girls, practices of polygamy, levirate marriages (practice where a widow marries her dead husband's brother or next of kin), and the institution of forced veiling, to name a few.

4. Western insistence on the abandonment of the veil, as well as demands for secular education and employment of women, though seen as progressive in the West and by many Afghans, continue to be perceived as assertions that challenge and denigrate local cultures and religion. Foreign occupiers, including the Soviets (1979–89) and the US (2002 to the present), have also contested Afghan patriarchal institutions by insisting on norms for women that are contrary to traditional roles.

5. Sangari (2006) posits the notion of 'retraditionalization' in order to capture the revival or reinvention of supposedly historical practices in various societies. While evidence of the value or status of these practices in the actuality of history or collective memory remains minimal, these instances of retraditionalization more often than not are born out of a response to perceived external or internal threats to ideational and structural hierarchies, and are generally inimical to women as well as those deemed as 'minorities' on ethnic, religious or ideological grounds. Also, see Saigol (2000) for a discussion of how the reassertion of tradition and culture is inextricably bound with the working of multilayered power structures, and how these invariably involve women's bodies. Rejuvenation of specific 'cultural' discourses at various points in the history of South Asia have been tied to various bids of control and authority initiated by local and global forces, often in collusion with each other.

6. See, for instance, Eisenstein (1996).

7. It should be pointed out that the country has different tribal and ethnic groups. In Afghanistan the Pashtuns are 44 per cent of the population, followed by the Tajiks (25 per cent), Hazaras (10 per cent), Uzbeks (8 per cent), and other minorities (13 per cent). Sunnis are the majority (84 per cent); Shias account for 15 per cent; and others, 1 per cent (www.afghansite.com). In this article I rely on a certain homogenization of women in Afghanistan to discuss their oppression and/or resistance. While recognizing some of the problematics inherent in such a choice, I nonetheless argue for its relevance as well, because in the last twenty-seven years, for those women who stayed back in Afghanistan and were refugees especially in Pakistan and Iran, the situation has been uniformly harsh. I am aware of tribal, religious and class differences but overall, with the exception of the elite that moved to the West, the struggles of most Afghan women share commonalities across contexts.

8. In addition to conducting interviews with women in NGOs, universities, and with the minister of women's affairs, I participated in meetings and workshops held in Kabul for women's issues. I was also able to visit and evaluate schools, clinics and canal projects in and around Jalalabad as part of a short-term assignment for an international NGO working in Afghanistan. Further insights on women's situation were garnered from interviews with Afghan women in 2005. In January 2005, I organized and conducted a workshop, 'Skill Development and Economic Empowerment: Afghanistan, Pakistan and India' in New Delhi. Ten Afghan women leaders of NGOs based in Kabul and Jalalabad attended the workshop.

9. See Emadi (2002).

10. See, for instance, Frankenberg and Mani (1993) for a pithy summary of this literature.

11. According to Enloe (2004: 4), 'Patriarchy is the structural and ideological system that perpetuates the privileging of masculinity'.

12. Soraya Parlika is one of the founding members of the first women's organization, the Democratic Organization of Women started in 1964. She currently heads her own NGO and is very active in Kabul in issues of women's rights and the legal system.

13. A garment that covers from the head to the toe.

14. See www.deseretnews.com. Last accessed 5 June 2005.

15. See also Brohi (2004/2005) for an overview of historical and contemporary perspectives on Muslim women's veil; see Lewis and Mills (2003) for an insightful selection of articles on the subject.

16. See Rajagopalan (2005) for a recent and comprehensive discussion on security issues that are salient in the lives of South Asian women. This discussion also provides a thorough critique of current theorizing on the topic.

17. Especially after the Taliban came into power, wearing a burqa became a woman's way of communicating that she was a good practicing Muslim, and, therefore, deserving of cultural (read 'male') protection.

18. Further in the article, a brief historical context is presented. Please see section entitled 'Afghan Patriarchy: A Historical Perspective'.

19. The total population of Afghanistan is twenty-eight million. See (www.odci.gov/cia/publications/factbook/geos/af.html). Last accessed 25 April 2004.

20. See www.unifem.org/index.php?f_page_pd=37. Last accessed 25 April 2004.

21. See www.unifem.org/index.php?f_page_pd=37. Last accessed 25 April 2004.

22. See http://data.un.org/Data.aspx?d=PopDiv&f=variableID%3A77. Last accessed 25 April 2004.

23. This places Afghanistan among the lowest ten nations in the world according to the United Nations World Populations Prospects for 2006. It is noteworthy that while Afghanistan is the only nation from this region that consistently ranks so low on international scales, the nations by which it is flanked are consistently African. See: http://www.un.org/esa/population/publications/wpp2006/WPP2006_Highlights_rev.pdf. Last accessed 25 April 2004.

24. For a discussion on shifts in education and the gendered implications, please see the section in this article entitled, 'Afghan Patriarchy: A Historical Perspective'.

25. See (www.feminist.org/afghan). Last accessed 23 April 2005. The decade-long drought must also be considered in the context of inadequate and disrupted infrastructure, destruction of the natural terrain, and misappropriation of development funds common to nations ravaged by war. Further, the ongoing conflict has rendered an already vulnerable population increasingly so, as families are displaced from their farms and local support structures by the violence, as roads and other supply networks become more disrupted and inconsistent, and as villagers must make difficult decisions to sew crops for food or for cash (for example, poppies) as the nation is engulfed by poverty.

26. See www.hrw.org/campaigns/afghanistan, p. 11. Last accessed 23 April 2005.

27. Please see section entitled 'Afghan Patriarchy: A Historical Perspective' for an elaboration of this period in the context of a larger history of modern Afghanistan.

28. See www.afghan@yahoogroups.com. Last accessed 26 April 2005.

29. See http://www.aihrc.org.af/. Last accessed 26 April 2005.

30. See http://www.wclrf.org.af/. Last accessed 26 April 2005.

31. Personal conversations, 2003–4.

32. "Women Treated Worse Than Dogs' as Ignorant Judges Fail to Protect Victims and Punish Criminals', Amnesty International News Release, at W4wafghan@egroups.com or www.Afghan.com. Accessed 11/22/2004.

33. British colonialism in India was justified on the basis that Indian men were not capable of self-rule because they ascribed a low status to their women (Ahmed-Ghosh 2005; Sinha 1998).

34. See, for example, the following Human Rights Watch publications: 'Between Hope and Fear: Intimidation and Attacks against Women in Public Life in Afghanistan', October 2004; '"We Want to Live As Humans': Repression of Women and Girls in Western Afghanistan', 17 December 2002. Available at: http://www.hrw.org/en/publications/reports?page=1&filter0=%2A%2AA LL%2A%2A&filter1=130 and http://www.hrw.org/legacy/backgrounder/ asia/afghanistan1004/afghanistan1004.pdf. Last accessed 26 April 2005.

35. This refers to financial reparation made to a victim's family by the perpetrator of the crime, usually a monetary compensation for murder. Also known in Pashtun as *saz*.

36. I draw from diverse sources for this history, including Ahmed-Ghosh (2003), Armstrong (2002), Azarbaijani-Moghaddam (2004), Dupree (1986), Emadi (2002) and Khattak (2002).

37. Freedom fighters and a fundamentalist Islamist group.

38. Berhanuddin Rabbani served as president of Afghanistan from 28 June 1992 to 27 September 1996, and was succeeded by Hamid Karzai.

39. Personal conversation, 2003.

40. According to the Afghan Independent Human Rights Commission Report of 2003–4, 17 per cent of the male respondents reported violations during the Soviet period in comparison to only 9 per cent of the females. Twenty per cent of the females reported violence against them by the Mujahideen compared to 16 per cent of the men. The report did not offer a gender breakdown of figures for the Taliban era. Of the total population of men and women reporting abuse, 30 per cent reported some kind of abuse under the Mujahideen, 16 per cent under the Soviets, 11 per cent under the Taliban, and 25 per cent under two or three of the above mentioned eras. The remaining said that they were not sure which regime was worse (www. aihrc.org.af, p. 11). Last accessed 26 April 2005.

41. However, these atrocities were unparalleled to those later committed by the Taliban, according to the perceptions of those I interviewed in Kabul and Jalalabad in 2003and 2004.

42. Ahmad Shah Masood belonged to the Shura-i-Nazar wing of Jamiat-i-Islami, part of the Northern Alliance that resisted the Taliban in northern Afghanistan. Masood's death at the hands of the Taliban and his resistance to the Taliban has led to deification by the current government.

43. Shaheen and other women I interviewed confirmed these stories.

44. Personal conversation, 2003–4.

45. See www.feminist.org/afghan. Last accessed 23 April 2005; www.hrw.org/ campaigns/afghanistan, p. 11, last accessed 23 April 2005; www.aihrc.org.af. p.10; www.deseretnews.com, last accessed 5 June 2005.

    Another interesting theory about the violence perpetuated against women by both the Mujahideen and the Taliban in Afghanistan was the lack of 'maternal care' through their upbringing and socialization in refugee camps in Pakistan. Derek Gregory has also recorded this in his latest work, *The Colonial Present* (2004), with reference to the Mujahideen: 'Many of them had been shaped by the hybrid, exilic, and profoundly patriarchal culture of the refugee camps on the border around Peshawar in north-west Pakistan' (2004: 34). Gregory, in an almost apologetic tone continues that the Mujahideen were 'orphans of the war', growing up 'without women—mothers, sisters, cousins', in an intensely masculinist culture where the space for the participation of women in almost every area of non-domestic life (including education) was severely restricted (ibid.). I heard similar justifications from a few young people in Kabul who claimed similarly, that the Taliban 'had no mothers' and that it was this history that led to such harsh strictures against women. While accepting the above reality, such apologetic justifications verge on rationalizations of masculinities at many levels of discourse. On the one hand, an attempt is made to absolve perpetrators of heinous crimes against women by painting them as pathological characters because of their single-gendered childhood. On the other, women are once again held responsible for their own victimization because of their absence in 'mothering'. Another implication of the above discourse is that women are not only responsible for, but can acculturate boys to grow up to be non-violent citizens, an argument which historically has been unfounded. Finally, it hints at a legitimization of violence due to an 'intensely masculinist culture', by correlating the presumed inevitable violence to masculinity. Though the intention of the author may not have been to absolve the Mujahideen of the carnage they carried out, such explanations remain problematic in their practical implications for feminist understandings and interventions against gendered violence.

46. Personal communication, 2003–4.
47. Personal communication, 2003–4.

REFERENCES

Ahmed, Leila (1992). *Women and Gender in Islam: Historical Roots of a Modern Debate.* New Haven: Yale University Press.

Ahmed-Ghosh, Huma (1998). 'Women Trapped in a Web of Hierarchy: Life Cycle of a Woman in India', *INSTRAW News*, no. 29: 10–17.

——— (2001). 'Feminist Perspective: September 11 and Afghan Women', *Lemar-Aftab*, afghanmagazine.com. pp. 1-2.

——— (2003). 'A History of Women in Afghanistan: Lessons Learnt for the Future', *Journal of International Women's Studies*, 4(3): 1–14.

——— (2005). 'Deconstructing the Human Rights Discourse: Relevance for Afghan Women', in SDPI (ed.), *Sustainable Development: Bridging the Research/Policy Gaps in Southern Contexts*, Volume 2: Social Policy, pp. 98–110. Karachi: Oxford University Press.

————— (2006). 'Voices of Afghan Women: Human Rights and Economic Development', *International Feminist Journal of Politics*, 8(1): 110–28.

Armstrong, Sally (2002). *Veiled Threat: The Hidden Power of the Women of Afghanistan*. New York and London: Four Walls Eight Windows.

Azarbaijani-Moghaddam, Sippi (2004). 'Afghan Women on the Margins of the Twenty-first Century', in Antonio Donini, Norah Niland and Karin Wermester (eds), *Nation-Building Unraveled? Aid, Peace and Justice in Afghanistan*, pp. 95–116. Bloomfield: Kumarian Press.

Banerjee, Sikata. (2005). *Make Me A Man!: Masculinity, Hinduism, And Nationalism In India*. Albany: State University of New York Press.

Brohi, Nazish (2004/2005). 'Study of the International Response to Afghan Women Refugees in Pakistan: The Gendered Crisis', *South Asia Refugee Watch*, 6/7, 16-49.

Chaudhry, Lubna N. (2006) 'Salient Contours of Structural Violence in the Lives of Rural Women: From Fieldwork in Sindh and Punjab', in SDPI Staff (ed.), *Troubled Times: Sustainable Development and Governance in the Age of Extremes*, pp. 460–82. Islamabad and Karachi: SDPI & Sama Editorial and Publishing Services.

Christensen, Hanna (1990). *The Reconstruction of Afghanistan: A Chance for Rural Afghan Women*. UN Research Institute for Social Development.

Cockburn, Cynthia (1998). *The Space Between Us: Negotiating Gender and National Identities in Conflict*. New York: Macmillan.

————— (2004). 'The Continuum of Violence: A Gender Perspective on War and Peace', in Wenona Giles and Jennifer Hyndman (eds), *Sites of Violence: Gender and Conflict Zones*, pp. 24–44. Berkeley and Los Angeles: University of California Press.

Donini, Antonio, Norah Niland and Karin Wermester (eds) (2004). *Nation-Building Unraveled? Aid, Peace and Justice in Afghanistan*. Bloomfield, CT: Kumarian Press.

Dupree, Nancy Hatch (1986). *Women of Afghanistan*. Stiftung-Foundation.

Eisenstein, Zillah (1996). *Hatreds: Racialized and Sexualized Conflicts in the 21st Century*. New York and London: Routledge.

Enloe, Cynthia (1989). *Bananas, Beaches and Bases: Making Feminist Sense of International Politics*. Berkeley: University of California Press.

————— (2000). *Maneuvers: The International Politics of Militarizing Women's Lives*. Berkeley: University of California Press.

————— (2004). *The Curious Feminist: Searching for Women in a New Age of Empire*. Berkeley and Los Angeles: University of California Press.

Emadi, Hafizullah (2002). *Repression, Resistance, and Women in Afghanistan*. New York: Praeger Publications.

Frankenberg, R. and L. Mani (1993). 'Crosscurrents, Crosstalk: Race, "Postcoloniality and the Politics of Location', *Cultural Studies*, 7(2): 292–310.

Giles, Wenona and Jennifer Hyndman (2004a). 'Introduction: Gender and Conflict in a Global Context', in Wenona Giles and Jennifer Hyndman (eds),

Sites of Violence: Gender and Conflict Zones, pp. 3–23. Berkeley and Los Angeles: University of California Press.

Giles, Wenona and Jennifer Hyndman. (2004b) 'New Directions for Feminist Research and Politics', in Wenona Giles and Jennifer Hyndman (eds), *Sites of Violence: Gender and Conflict Zones*, pp. 301–15. Berkeley and Los Angeles: University of California Press.

Gregory, Derek (2004). *The Colonial Present*. Malden,MA: Blackwell Publishing.

Hans, Asha (2004). 'Escaping Conflict: Afghan Women in Transit', in Wenona Giles and Jennifer Hyndman (eds), *Sites of Violence: Gender and Conflict Zones*, pp. 232–48. Berkeley and Los Angeles: University of California Press.

International Organization for Migration (IOM) (2004). *International Organization for Migration Report*. Kabul: IOM.

Ivekovic, Rada and Julie Mostov (2002). 'Introduction. From Gender to Nation', in Rada Ivekovic and Julie Mostov (eds), *From Gender to Nation*, pp. 9–25. New Delhi: Kali for Women.

Khan, Shahnaz (2001). 'Between Here and There: Feminist Solidarity and Afghan Women', *Genders*, no. 33. Retrieved from www.genders.org/g33/g33-khan.html, 19 June 2006.

Khattak, Saba Gul (2002). 'Afghan Women Bombed to be Liberated?' *Middle East Report*, no. 222, pp. 18–23.

——— (2004). 'Adversarial Discourses, Analogous Objectives: Afghan Women's Control', *Cultural Dynamics*, 16(2/3): 213–36.

Lewis, R. and S. Mills (eds) (2003). *Feminist Postcolonial Theory: A Reader*. New York: London.

Magnus, Ralph and Eden Naby (1998). *Afghanistan: Mullah, Marx, and Mujahid*. Boulder, CO: Westview Press.

Mayotte, Judy (1992). *Disposible People: The Flight of Refugees*. New York: Orbis Books.

Mertus, Julie A. (2000). *War's Offensive on Women: The Humanitarian Challenge in Bosnia, Kosova, and Afghanistan*. Bloomfield, CT: Kumarian Press.

Moghadam, Valentine M. (1997). 'Nationalist Agendas and Women's Rights: Conflicts in Afghanistan in the Twentieth Century', in Lois West (ed.), *Feminist Nationalism*, pp. 75–100. New York: Routledge.

Mohanty, Chandra (1988). 'Under Western Eyes: Feminist Scholarship and Colonial Discourses', *Feminist Review*, 30: 61–88.

Moser, Caroline and Fiona C. Clark (2001). *Victims, Perpetrators, or Actors?: Gender, Armed Conflict and Political Violence*. New York: Palgrave.

Niland, Norah (2004). 'Justice Postponed: The Marginalization of Human Rights in Afghanistan', in Antonio Donini, Norah Niland and Karin Wermester (eds), *Nation-Building Unraveled? Aid, Peace and Justice in Afghanistan*, pp. 61–82. Bloomfield, CT: Kumarian Press.

North, Andrew (2005). 'Silence over Afghan Women's Rights', BBC News Online. Last accessed 10 January 2005.

Physicians for Human Rights (1998). *The Taliban's War on Women: A Health and Human Rights Crisis in Afghanistan*. A report. Boston: Physicians for Human Rights.

Price, J. and M. Shildrick (eds) (1999). *Feminist Theory and the Body: A Reader*. New York: Routledge.

Rajagopalan, Swarna (2005). 'Women and Security: In Search of a Paradigm', in Farah Faizal and Swarna Rajagopalan (eds), *Women, Security, South Asia: A Clearing in the Thicket*, pp. 11–88. New Delhi: Sage Publications.

Rubin, Barnett (1997). 'Women and Pipelines: Afghanistan's Proxy Wars', *International Affairs* 73(2): 283–96.

Rupert, James (2005). 'U.N. Cuts Human Rights Job', W4wafghan@egroups. com, 23 April.

Saigol, Rubina (2000). *Symbolic Violence: Curriculum, Pedagogy, and Society*. Lahore: SAHE.

Sangari, Kumkum (2006). 'Violent Acts: Cultures, Structures, and Retraditionalization', paper presented at the LACAS Lecture Series, State University of New York at Binghamton, 18 April.

Sinha, Mrinalini (ed) (1998). *Selections from Mother India: Katherine Mayo*. New Delhi: Kali Press for Women.

Skaine, Rosemarie (2002). *The Women of Afghanistan Under the Taliban*. Jefferson, NC: McFarland and Co.

Tapper, Nancy (1991). *Battered Brides: Politics, Gender, and Marriage*. Cambridge: Cambridge University Press.

Troup, Christina. (2005). 'Women's Advocate Eyes Afghan Seat', *The Oakland Tribune*, 1 April.

Weidman, Amanda (2003). 'Beyond Honor and Shame: Performing Gender in the Mediterranean', *Anthropological Quarterly*, 76(3): 519–25.

Welchman, L. and S. Hossain (eds) (2005). *'Honor': Crimes, Paradigms, and Violence against Women*. London & New York: Zed Books.

Wikan, Unni (1984). 'Shame and Honor: A Contestable Pair', *Man*, 19(4): pp. 635–52.

Women and Children Legal Research Foundation (WCLRF) (2004). *Bad Painful Sedative–Final Report*. Kabul.

6

Women Negotiating Change

The Structure and Transformation of Gendered Violence in Bangladesh

Meghna Guhathakurta

The mid-1980s witnessed a spate of literature on violence against women in Bangladesh (Guhathakurta 1985; Islam and Begum 1985; Jahangir and Khan 1987). This occurred against the backdrop of an increase in the reportage of gender-based violence in the media, which caused subsequent response from the women's movement as well as from political circles. The reason for this sudden media interest was due to policies pursued by the then autocratic regime of General Ershad which had restricted political activity and issued strict censorship of the news media to prevent political criticism or dissent (Guhathakurta 1985). Thus media attention was directed to gender-based violence as a way to critique the government without appearing to be partisan. This was the context that shaped the discourses of gender-based violence.

The mainstream discourse approached the question of violence from a functional viewpoint. Since the problem of violence was treated as an issue and not as a trend, causes of gender-based violence were perceived and analysed in an isolated manner. Economic causes were among those most frequently cited by the establishment and mainstream political parties while deterioration of law and order and the degradation of moral values were used as arguments by the opposition (Guhathakurta 1985). Only a few women's groups chose to relate the incidence of violence to structures of patriarchy and class (Jahangir and Khan 1987: i–iv). Patriarchal structures and ideology were seen to create conditions of male privilege especially within social institutions such as the family, whereas class equality in a peripheral capitalist system was seen to marginalize women in the more specific politics of gender.

In the context of present-day realities, however, it has become imperative to understand that some of the recent trends of violence emerge not out of static social structures, but in the way that these structures themselves get constructed and reconstructed in the battlefield of politics, specifically feminist politics. Having taken an active role in helping to generate a feminist discourse of gendered violence in Bangladesh from the 1980s onwards and contributed to its polemics, my approach has been to focus on the structured nature of violence in society, to distinguish it from the statist or mainstream discourse of looking at acts of violence as 'incident' or 'issue'. But as will be explained, I do not consider these structures in any deterministic sense of cause and effect but as norms, values and processes underlying gender relations, which may be negotiated variously by victims and perpetrators. In this article I look more specifically at parameters of gendered violence as experienced by women at the margins of society; for example, in the struggle of the indigenous women's resistance movement in the Chittagong Hill Tracts (CHT). This article explores the abduction and murder of Kalpana Chakma, organizing secretary of the Hill Women's Federation (HWF), a local network addressing issues of gendered violence in the CHT of Bangladesh. The article reflects on Kalpana Chakma's views of life and struggle, the incident, and its consequences. Analysing the response of the mainstream women's movement to the event, I foreground contesting notions of violence and victimization upheld by the state and the women's movement in Bangladesh. Engaging the processes through which ethnic women have been victimized, this article addresses issues of agency and resistance, and the means by which women, as individuals and in movements, negotiate and resist the subject position of 'victim'.

CONCEPTUAL FRAMEWORKS: VICTIMS AND VICTIMIZATION

In Bangladesh, the feminist debate on gender-based violence has shifted somewhat from the 1980s, although the statist and mainstream discourse remains much the same. In dominant mainstream discourse, it is only the physical manifestation of gender violence that receives prime concern: rapes, murders and kidnappings. This perspective only succeeds in disassociating the results or immediate factors from the deep-seated causes embedded in social structures. The Bangladesh feminist debate in the 1980s focused on foregrounding the structures underlying gender-based violence, including those of patriarchy and class. This has been a continuing trend evident in the agendas of many non-governmental organizations (NGOs) working with women, for whom patriarchy or class become standard, but not fully examined, categories for women's oppression. However, as poststructural and feminist frameworks have shown, the examination of structures must be mediated by historical analysis or the claims remain superficial and over-determined (Butler and Scott 1992; Kumar 1994). My outline here suggests a conceptual framework to help overcome objectifying tendencies, and develop a feminist understanding of gender-based violence in the context of Bangladesh.

Norms and values underlying and affecting gender relations such as 'patriarchy' or 'tradition' are constructed and reconstructed as women and men enact them in their individual lives, and through institutions and cultural and social processes. In this sense women and men are not merely passive recipients or 'victims' of tradition but actors/agents who choose (consciously and subconsciously) to maintain, reaffirm and strengthen or to resist, challenge and creatively reshape structures of existing gender relations. For example, while men may act to strengthen their positions of power and privilege, women may try to contest and challenge them in various ways.

However, women and men are actors with different access to power and, often informed by this access, with very different interests in processes of shaping and reshaping gender constructions. Familiar categorical constructions of men as superior and dominant against women as inferior and subordinate do not only vest power in men over women, they also help sustain these divisions. While this may take the form of violence against women, more often it operates in more subtle ways as an aspect of institutional ideologies, rules and practices (Mohanty et al. 1991; Rajchman 1995). The inheritance laws of Bangladeshi institutions, as they concede male dominance in terms of rights and resources, simultaneously perpetuate and legitimate domestic violence against women by designating a male 'right' to control property, including women.

But these notions and practices of male dominance may be challenged, negotiated and radically transformed not only from positions of dominance, but from subordinate (and resistant) positions, by women. It is in this latter sense that an analysis of the processes of victimization[1] may also generate understandings of how a woman may negotiate agency and her subject position as victim altogether. From here, one may evaluate the advantages and/or limitations of such responses from the perspective of the women's movement.[2]

I now attempt to look at this politics by engaging the processes through which women have been victimized, exploring the case of the abduction and subsequent disappearance of Kalpana Chakma. I will engage the subtext of gendered violence as experienced by women at the margins of society in the struggle of the indigenous women's resistance movement in the CHT.

The Chittagong Hill Tracts: The Marginalization of Ethnic Groups

The Chittagong Hill Tracts or CHT, situated to the southwest of the country, occupies a physical area of 5,093 square miles, constituting 10 per cent of the total land area of Bangladesh. The region comprises three districts—Rangamati, Khagrachari and Banderban—and its hilly topography, with its innumerable ravines, cliffs interspersed with fast-flowing mountain streams and rivers, and dense vegetation rise in contrast to most other districts of Bangladesh, which consist mainly of flat deltaic alluvial lands. For this reason, people residing in the hills were\are often called Paharis (Hill People) as opposed to the Bengalis who dwelt in the plains. At the time of the incorporation of the Hills of Chittagong into the British administration in 1860, the region was inhabited by thirteen ethnic groups: Chakmas, Marma, Tripura, Tanchangya, Riang, Murang, Lushai, Bawm and Pankhos, Kukis, Chak, Khumi, Mro, and Kheyang. Together these groups identify themselves as *Jumma* (a Chakma word), stemming from their traditional practice, *jum*, meaning swidden cultivation.[3] Jumma is a collective term used to denote the ethnic groups residing in the CHT. During the recent movement for autonomy, 'Jumma' has been reinvented as an identity for those engaging in jhum cultivation as opposed to plough cultivation predominant among Bengalis of the plains. In 1991, the population of the CHT was estimated to be 0.974 million (Mohsin 1997: 11). Jumma people constituted 0.5 million and Bengalis 0.47 million. Ethnically, the Jumma people are of Sino-Tibetan descent, belonging to Mongolian groups, and hence racially distinguishable from Bengalis.

The predicament of the Jumma people began with the building of a hydroelectric dam in the early 1960s, which flooded 1,036 sq. km of land, submerged some of their best agricultural land, and displaced about 100,000 people from their ancestral lands. In 1964, about 40,000 displaced Chakmas and other indigenous people were forced to migrate into India and were settled in the state of Arunachal Pradesh (Mohsin 1997). After the liberation of Bangladesh in 1971 from Pakistani rule, the founder of the Jana Samhiti Samiti (JSS) Manabendra Narayan Larma was elected to the Bangladesh parliament from the CHT in the first general election held in Bangladesh. As an elected member of parliament, he demanded constitutional safeguards and rights for the Jumma, but his petitions were ignored. Following this effort, he led a Jumma delegation and submitted a written memorandum to Sheikh Mujibur Rahman, the then prime minister, with a four-point charter of demands for regional autonomy for the CHT. Not only was this proposal rejected outright, but the Jumma leaders were charged with secession and indicted as anti-Bangladeshi. After the assassination of Sheikh Mujibur Rahman, President Ziaur Rahman, the military general who came to power, designated the CHT a security zone under threat of insurgency and further militarized the situation. The JSS responded by forming the armed resistance group, Shanti Bahini, and the situation rapidly transformed into that of counter-insurgency operations under President Ziaur Rahman's regime. From this point on, the history of the CHT has included a series of military occupations, killings and human rights violations, including the displacement of thousands of villagers from their homes and land. In the early 1970s, the entire CHT was brought under military control through state policies aimed at undermining the local civil administration. In 1976, the Chittagong Hill Tracts Development Board (CHTDB) deeply strengthened military occupation and the development of military infrastructure in the CHT (Mohsin 1996). Between 1980 and 1993, the Bangladesh army and Bengali settlers committed eleven massacres, evicted countless villagers, and plundered and destroyed innumerable homes and villages in the CHT. Counter-insurgency operations produced fresh waves of refugees into India, most notably in 1979, 1981, 1984, and 1986 (Timm 1992), further devastating individuals and fragmenting ethnic groups.

Despite a 1997 accord, reached between the JSS (the armed wing) and the Bangladesh government, the struggle of the Jumma continues. Three decades of forced evictions, terrorization through 'counter-insurgency', and the planned settlements of plains Bengalis in the CHT have caused havoc among those who refused to flee to India. Following the accord, many refugees returned to find their land occupied by Bengali settlers and the military. They now join the ranks of the internally displaced. According to the Global IDP Database set up by the Norwegian Refugee Council (NRC 2003), an estimated 50,000 to 100,000 people were internally displaced during the conflict, while 75,000 fled to the neighbouring state of India as refugees.

Military oppression also resulted in armed resistance in the guise of the Shanti Bahini. In response to the government's formidable 'counter-insurgency' military presence, the Hill People, through organizations such as the Pahari Gono Parishad (PGP), the Pahari Chattra Parishad (PCP) and the HWF have demanded the right to self-determination under the rubric of 'Jumma nationalism'.

An analysis of the gendered agency of power must also include its reciprocal gendered effects: structures and institutions that shape dominance and subordination also shape the reality that power produces (Foucault 1980). The militarized situation in CHT constituted Jumma women as the most vulnerable section of the population, and engendered the formation of the HWF. Among the many crimes committed against the people of the CHT, sexual violence of rape, molestation and harassment was especially prevalent. In 1990 information from one refugee camp in India indicated that, in the CHT, one in every ten Jumma women had been raped by security forces between 1991 and 1993.[4] Of these rape allegations, over 40 per cent of the victims were women under the age of eighteen. These figures are denied by the military authorities.[5]

Together with these outward manifestations of violence, women were affected in a number of ways during military rule, not least in the daily activities of household chores, procuring food and looking after children, all in an environment that became hostile to their very existence (Guhathakurta 2001). It was women's experiences of struggling against this hostile environment that led to the formation of the HWF, which emerged in the 1980s and became the most organized expression of women's resistance in the area. The powerful response of the HWF to the brutalization of the state, as witnessed in the following case of abduction and alleged murder of Kalpana Chakma, the organizing secretary of the HWF, is testimony to the breadth and depth of agency that the members of this organization attained in their negotiation with the Bangladeshi state.

The Incident

I will try to reconstruct the incident as it happened that night by using information collected by a human rights investigation team sent by the legal aid organization Ain O Salish Kendra. Part of this finding was also published in a national daily, *Bhorer Kagoj*, offering exceptional coverage of (and visibility to) the issue as it occurred (Akhter 1996). The team interviewed Kalpana Chakma's family (her brothers and mother) and other neighbours in the vicinity.

After the midnight of 11 June 1996, on the eve of the national elections of 12 June, Kalpana Chakma, the twenty-three-year-old central organizing secretary of HWF, was abducted from her home in New Laillaghona village of Baghaichari Thana of CHT. Kaplana was a first-year graduate student of Baghaichari College and a vocal and dedicated activist committed to her work with the HWF. She and her two brothers lived together with her mother and sister-in-law in the not-too-well-off neighbourhood of New Laillaghona village. Her brothers Kalindikumar also known as Kalicharan (thirty-two years of age) and Lalbihari Chakma also known as Khudiram (twenty-six years of age) were farmers who could not afford an education for themselves, but were committed to it for their only sister.

On 11 June, sometime after midnight, as Kalpana's household slept, a group of men circled the family's house and started calling out, waking the family. When the door was not opened promptly, the men broke open the bamboo bolt. The men gathered everyone into the drawing room and forbade them to put the light on. They started asking names and calling for Kalpana's younger brother, Lalbihari. They dragged him outside. They announced that he had to be taken to the 'Boss' (Sir), repeatedly flashing a torch on his face in order to identify him. As the torch light was not falling directly in his eyes, he was able to recognize some of the men, whom he later identified as Lt Ferdous, Kojoichari Camp Commander, 17 East Bengal Regiment, who was wearing an army vest; Nurul Huq, Village Defense Party (VDP) Platoon Commander, and Saleh Ahmed, VDP.[6]

Lt Ferdous then ordered Khudiram to be taken to the water's edge of a stream about 150 yards from Kalpana's house. At the edge of the stream, he was blindfolded and his hands were tied. After ten or fifteen minutes, Kalpana and her elder brother Kalicharan were brought to the same place. Kalicharan's eyes were blindfolded at that time. Kalpana was holding his hand. They were taken further west towards a water reservoir.

They could guess where they were—Khudiram was told to go knee deep into the water. Someone caught hold of his hand and another person gave the order to shoot. On hearing this, Khudiram freed his bound hand and jumped into the water. Although guns were fired, Khudiram managed to escape. When Kalicharan heard the shot, he thought his brother dead, so he left Kalpana and made a dash for his life. Another shot was fired, and he could hear Kalpana crying out: *Dada! Dada!* (Brother!). Thinking it unsafe, Khudiram did not return home that night. When he returned in the morning he went with the Union Parishad (local government) chairperson to the Ugalchari army camp nearby to look for Kalpana. Lt Ferdous chased them away with threatening words. A search party from the village started to look for Kalpana and found Khudiram's lungi in the lake and an ammunition pouch, which Kalicharan claimed he deposited at the thana (police station). The Thana Nirbahi Officer (TNO) later denied this.

When the TNO was informed of Kalicharan's claim, he met with Kalicharan, the eldest brother, to take a verbal statement. Initially there was a misconception that this also constituted a First Information Report (FIR), but this was later denied by the TNO. Kalicharan's FIR was taken by the officer in charge.[7] However, in the verbal statement given by Kalicharan, Lt Ferdous and Khudiram's recognition of him and others were not mentioned, perhaps for the reason that it was Khudiram and not Kalicharan who recognized him, and at the time of taking Kalicharan's statement, Khudiram had gone with the Union Parishad chairperson to the army camp in search of Kalpana. The ammunition pouch, which Kalicharan claimed he deposited with the TNO, was also not found. The human rights team that investigated the incident noted the complicity of the local police with the military administration, which from the very beginning was bent on denying the incident had occurred at all.

A protest strike was staged by the joint coalition of PCP, PGP and HWF in the Hill Tracts on 27 June 1996. During the strike, clashes occurred between the law enforcement agencies and the protesters, where a school student, Rupam Chakma, was shot dead and his body taken away. Three more people, Monotosh Chakma, Sukesh Chakma and Somor Bijoy Chakma, disappeared and could not be traced.[8]

In the aftermath of these crises many allegations and counter allegations were made as to who or what caused this incident. The military and their collaborative organizations tried to link up the incident with pre-poll violence in an attempt to portray the role of the PCP, PGP and HWF as anti-people and anti-democratic before, during, and after the elections. They denied all charges of involvement and claimed that Kalpana's disappearance was staged by her own people. The Bangladesh Manobodhikar Commission (a human rights organization with alleged links with the government) asserted that Kalpana Chakma had been found in a village in Tripura, India. These reports remain unverified.

Another independent human rights group based in Chittagong contended this was not an isolated incident but part of the continuous communal tension in the Hill Tracts. They had testimony of military involvement in the abduction of Kalpana Chakma. My personal interviews with Kalpana Chakma's friends and colleagues corroborated the view that Kalpana's skills in organizing and speaking against injustice rendered her a target for military violence. Her friends related an incident on 19 March of the same year involving Lt Ferdous, who allegedly participated in carrying out an army raid that burned down seven houses in a village in the vicinity of Kalpana's house. This operation was purportedly to track down members of the armed Shanti Bahini. During the raid, Kalpana Chakma had gotten into a heated argument with the lieutenant, and her friends believe that, as a result of this exchange, she had been targeted for revenge.[9]

KALPANA CHAKMA AND RESISTANCE POLITICS IN THE HILLS

Systematic and pervasive military presence in the Hill Tracts had heightened awareness among Pahari women of their rights (Guhathakurta 2001: 277–84). This is borne out by vivid statements made by Kalpana Chakma in her diary, recovered from her home by journalists after her disappearance. Parts of this diary were serially published in the Bengali Daily *Bhorer Kagoj*, and much later, the HWF brought her words to public attention, in conjunction with writings about her in the anthology *Kalpana Chakma's Diary* (Chakma 2001). Kalpana's writings confirm her determination to fight a dual struggle against politico-military and male oppression in the CHT.

Kalpana introduces her 'daily notebook' with the following lines: 'Life means struggle and here are some important notes of a life full of struggle.' In depicting the life of a woman in the CHT, she writes,

> On the one hand, the woman faces the steam roller of rape, torture, sexual harassment, humiliation and conditions of helplessness inflicted by the

military and Bengalis, on the other hand she faces the curse of social and sexual discrimination and a restricted lifestyle.

At one point she writes, 'I think that the women of my country are the most oppressed', and later,

> When a caged bird wants to be free, does it mean that she wants freedom for herself alone? Does it also mean that one must necessarily imprison those who are already free? I think it is natural to expect the caged bird to be angry at those who imprisoned her. But if she understands that she has been imprisoned and that the cage is not her rightful place, then she has every right to claim the freedom of the skies! (Chakma 2001).

In expressing her yearning for freedom, Kalpana struggles to contextualize her local experience within the broader range of structural domination and oppression that encompasses so many women in Bangladesh, ethnic and Bengali.

We see from the quotations that Kalpana's reading of the woman question is a feminist one. It allows her to look at the position of women with regard to Bengali-Pahari domination, and in relation to sexual politics within her own community. This is quite striking and unique since in the majority of nationalist and ethnic movements, the gender question exists as a subtext to the larger 'national' one. In interviewing women in resistance politics it will be usual to find them speaking of gendered violence across racial or ethnic boundaries (for example Bengali men raping Chakma women rather than Chakma women being raped by men of their own community).[10] Kalpana's views are not only extraordinary in their erudition, but, as we shall see in another section, in their ability to energize others. Her writing, as with her speaking before her abduction, succeeded in generating a debate within the student movement with regard to the woman question. But Kalpana's feminism also differs sharply from that of her middle-class Bengali sisters because unlike them her life struggles force her to confront and engage military and ethnic\racial domination in a way that is not easily comprehensible to the privileged Bengali.

That Kalpana Chakma was a frontline activist in the struggle for self-determination of the Pahari people is clear from her writing. In paying respect to the leader of their struggle, the late Manabendra Narayan Larma, she writes as part of her speech on the occasion of the anniversary of his death,

12 years has passed by. Every year, regardless of the 'combing eyes of the olive brigade' (the army), a memorial service is held, furtively, beneath a plum tree on a hilltop where thousands of students and public flock together to pay their respect. His name is celebrated from the hillsides to the jail... A leader dies, but new leadership emerges at the need of the hour. The struggle continues. It becomes more intense. Very inevitably so. (Chakma 2001).

On another occasion that commemorated the martyrs of the Naniarchar massacre of November 1993, Kalpana stresses the need for the youth to shake off the inertia that has descended on them. Again, we see that her call is all-embracing: she calls upon all students and she situates the student movement in the larger context of other historical struggles. She writes: 'A section of our youth are without direction. In losing their creative force they are being turned into pawns in the hands of the Army and the *Zilla Parishad*. But we are part of the students' movement who had created '52, '69, '71. And '90!' This is an interesting claim to make, especially since the movements mentioned above showed no signs of incorporating the demands of the Hill People in their nationalist agendas (Mohsin 1996). But if one looks at the time when this statement was made, 17 November 1995, then one can perhaps understand its significance. The country was at that time on the verge of a civil disobedience movement led by the main opposition parties in their demand for a caretaker government as an assurance of a free and fair election. The Pahari organizations too therefore voiced their preference for the democratic process, which they saw as being part of the movements of 1952, 1969, 1971 and 1990. We thus see that despite the many allegations of treason or secession hurled at them, these Pahari organizations had expressed their partiality for a democratic struggle for self-determination within the confines of Bangladesh.

But for Kalpana Chakma, democracy does not merely mean free and fair elections. It means participation in the political process and more specifically participation as a Chakma and a woman. She therefore stridently voices a critique of her own student movement, which remains male-dominated. She writes:

Despite the fact that women constitute half the population, they are not taken seriously in any movement for social change. As an example one can point out that the numerous demands voiced during the current movement, even the ten-point demand of the *Chhatro Shongram Parishad* does not speak specifically of problems faced by the woman! Many conscious men seem to think that such problems are not important enough to be dealt with at this

> hour. Therefore the issue of woman's emancipation has remained neglected in agendas for class struggle and political change. (Chakma 2001)

Kalpana's observations are not the first of their kind in the history of social change nor are they likely to be the last. One is rather uncannily reminded of words which the brave freedom fighter of Chittagong, Pritilata Wadeddar wrote in her last statement to the world before she died in combat against the British: 'The discrimination between men and women in the struggle for our liberation had wounded me. If my brothers can go to war to liberate our motherland, then why can our sisters not do so?' (Dastidar 1956: 114). Kalpana and her sisters had progressed one step further. They no longer have to fight to get included in the struggle, but they still have to struggle to get their agenda incorporated.

Kalpana's tragic disappearance is still shrouded in mystery, as the inquiry commission report is yet to see daylight, even in a situation where the government has entered into a peace agreement with the JSS. Every year, 12 June is celebrated by the HWF as the Kalpana Apaharan Dibosh (Kalpana's Abduction Day) and demands are repeatedly made for transparency of the justice system. But in successive regimes we have seen that the military enjoys complete impunity and cases such as Kalpana's are not investigated properly or else lack transparency. If such a situation persists, the mounting anger of the Hill People does not bode well for the peace of the region.

The peace accord reached with the Bangladesh state (during Sheikh Hasina's regime) was rejected by the main opposition as giving in to the 'terrorists', thus leaving the government to defend it tooth and nail. It was also opposed by other factions of the movement, especially one part of the unarmed wings of PCP, PGP and the HWF, consequently creating a polarization within the Jumma people. The demand for trial of Kalpana's abductors therefore became marginalized, although it was still taken up by those groups who criticized the accord. Since the accord was nationally and internationally hailed as a marker of peace, it became even more difficult to question army-led massacres and crimes against humanity, since no such mechanism of justice was built into the peace process or instrument. Civil society organizations, including women's organizations, are ill equipped to respond to this complicated scenario since none of them had seriously analysed, outside the dominant national discourse, questions of ethnicity, gender and national identity which the Jumma people's movement for self-determination has raised, of which

Kalpana Chakma was an integral part. Let us now turn to the dynamics of this movement.

THE MOVEMENT FOR KALPANA:
THE ROLE OF CIVIL SOCIETY ORGANIZATIONS

The movement which campaigned to bring the issue of Kalpana Chakma's abduction into the national and international arena was spearheaded primarily by the coalition of Pahari organizations, the HWF, PCP and PGP, but also involved sympathizers from the left, human rights and women rights activists with whom the former group worked closely in areas such as Dhaka. Mention has been made of the resistance politics of the Pahari organizations, especially the HWF.

Civil society organizations have been flourishing in Bangladesh, particularly since the collapse of the autocratic Ershad regime (1980–89). Most of these organizations are development oriented, though in the last few years some of them have been increasingly concerned with human rights violations and giving legal aid to vulnerable sections of the population. However, until the signing of the treaty between the Bangladesh state and the rebel Shanti Bahini only a small proportion of these organizations have been concerned with the Hill Tracts.

The CHT issue has remained a delicate and touchy one for the Bengali middle class, even after the polity of Bangladesh had attained a formal democratic character. Human rights violations have remained the concern of a handful of lawyers, academics and human rights activists and left party workers and students. Many Pahari activists complain that civil society organizations are reluctant to take up frontline activity. The National Committee for the Protection of Fundamental Rights was formed in 1991 as an advocacy organization for both Pahari and Bengali scholars and activists.

Recently, however, the Hill Tracts issue has also been receiving the attention of the women's movement, as was reflected in the Kalpana Chakma case. The women's movement too had been and still is largely development oriented and the issue of women's rights as human rights proliferated among organizations as an instrument of development (Guhathakurta 2000). Although women's organizations registered as NGOs were limited by their manifestos that prevented them from actively getting involved in political situations, in recent times the movement has been getting more 'political', that is, taking up issues which had direct repercussions on the state. Women's organizations and NGOs formed a common platform, the Sammilita Nari Shomaj, which enabled them to bypass the limitations of their organizational agendas and protest state-instigated violence against women in general. The Sammilita Nari Shomaj later took up the Kalpana Chakma case.

It may be mentioned that the HWF had participated in the 8 March 1994 rally of the women's movement with their slogan Autonomy for Peace. They also went to the NGO Forum of the Women's Conference in Beijing in 1995 with the same slogan. However, although the National Preparatory Committee Towards Beijing, NGO Forum '95, constituted a separate task force on indigenous women, barely two lines were included on the topic in the summary of the official NGO report. This reflected the hesitation on the part of some NGOs to deal with an issue that had become a matter of political controversy. On the other hand, the larger movement, which rallied behind Kalpana Chakma, was exceptional to the extent that many human rights and women's organizations demonstrated on the streets and joined hands with the left and trade union activists in protesting the kidnapping in unambiguous terms.

Nonetheless, it cannot be understated that the position and status of Bengali middle-class activists fighting for their rights on the streets of Dhaka are very different to those fighting for their rights and dignity in the frontline of existence, the CHT. Needless to say the stakes are much higher in the latter case. The fate of Kalpana Chakma is a sad reminder of this.

There is also a failure of Bengali middle-class-led organizations to engage with questions of ethnicity and, more seriously, nationality. The following incident bears this out.[11] After the CHT accord was signed in 1997, while celebrating 8 March, International Woman's Day, the same Sammilita Nari Shomaj which had campaigned actively for the Kalpana Chakma issue, turned on a group of indigenous women representing the HWF who had brought with them a banner saying that their struggle would stop only with autonomy! The organizers of Sammilita Nari Shomaj asked the HWF members to put down their banner as the slogan was 'too political'! It seemed that what was really meant was that it went against the sovereignty of the Bangladesh state, an argument very close to the one being offered by the Bangladesh state and its military establishment, especially in denouncing any Pahari voices who critiqued the peace accord! What had the women's movement learned from its engagement with the Kalpana Chakma issue? It seemed that they had rallied their support to HWF on the basis of a very abstract construction of human rights without looking at the specificity of politics in which these rights were based. This specificity entailed taking a hard look at notions of citizenship, nation, national self-determination and ethnicity. The hard realities which Kalpana Chakma faced as a woman of her community taught her more about these things than all the rhetoric deliberated at the Beijing Conference, a conference which she had wanted to attend but had not been able to as she did not have enough money to pay for her registration (Guhathakurta 2001).

RECENT DEVELOPMENTS: KALPANA'S LONG-TERM IMPACT

A new development has taken place outside the mainstream women's movement, which has had important consequences for the CHT activists as well as other indigenous peoples such as Garos.[12] Two of the more centrally located university campuses of the country, Dhaka University and Jahangirnagar University, experienced some of the worst incidents of sexual harassment ever reported. But in both universities, first in Jahangirnagar and then in Dhaka University, it was the female students who were in the frontline of protests. Most students' branches of mainstream political parties not only steered away from them but also vehemently attacked such attempts, thus revealing the ruthless patriarchal culture of traditional student politics. The young students who protested (both male and female) were supported by a few students groups of the left who were willing to take on board the issues of sexual harassment in their political agenda. After the crisis was over, the networks developed during these times endured and an effort was made to translate this into a sustained social movement. Networks and alliances were contracted in response to other incidents of sexual violence which rocked the country and a kind of loose network of organizations and individuals were formed under the banner of the Jouno Nipiron Protirodh Mancha (Platform Against Sexual Harassment). Although in its formative stage, the movement is unlike Sammilita Nari Shomaj in at least two ways. First, the Mancha constitutes both men and women, and therefore in a real sense it is not part of the women's movement. Second, it takes into consideration both the class and the nationality question and hence associates itself with, as well as supports, both left-oriented groups and indigenous peoples' movements like the PCP, HWF and the upcoming Bangladesh Garo Chattra Shongothon (BAGACHAS).

But this platform has also served groups like the PCP and HWF (those still contesting the Bangladesh state) as a forum in which they can demonstrate solidarity with issues of general concern. Some of these issues have been sexual harassment, eviction of slums and brothels, environmental policies of the state, and the politics of oil exploration. As such the same groups who had been concerned solely with issues of ethnic discrimination are broadening their participation and thereby strengthening their democratic foundations in the wider body politic. Simultaneously, the PCP and HWF who have had a longer and more arduous history of struggle than the other indigenous peoples' organizations are now actively involving themselves in building up networks among indigenous students groups such as the Garos. Interestingly, the BAGACHAS made its debut in national politics by effectively protesting the rape and murder of a Garo domestic worker in Mymensingh. They are effectively networking with PCP, HWF and other member organizations of the Mancha on specific gender concerns as well as other issues that link up with their agenda. In a leaflet demanding proper investigation and justice for the alleged rape and murder of Garo domestic worker Levina Howie, their demands included, among others, issues such as constitutional recognition of all nationalities, solution to land-related problems, investigation and justice for all crimes committed against women.[13] This is perhaps an indication that some of the issues connecting gender and ethnicity that were previously absent from the mainstream women's movement are being compensated for in this forum.[14] It seems that though Kalpana Chakma has disappeared from our midst, she has clearly left a legacy.

It is evident from Kalpana Chakma's quotes that Hill women had argued the case for greater participation of women in the movement as well as for the inclusion of the gender issue within the agenda of the party. But at the same time they realized that they needed to be free of ethnic discrimination as well. Kalpana Chakma in an article talked of their vision of a peaceful world: 'We want a society where men and women would enjoy equal rights. Also where one class of people would not exploit another class of people or where one community will not be able to dominate and abuse another community' (Chakma 2001).

WOMEN NEGOTIATING CHANGE: USING VICTIMHOOD AS AGENCY

At the beginning of the article, I stated that an analysis of the processes of victimization would help generate an understanding of how a woman may negotiate her subject position as a victim and at the same time resist or reject the role of the victim altogether. In the case of Kalpana Chakma, we have seen that happening, both in her individual case as well as in the movement that demanded justice for her abduction and among subsequent movements in Bangladesh that championed the cause of ethnic groups in general and ethnic women in particular.

Kalpana Chakma and people of her community were victims of state oppression. But their resistance against these structures of domination was both physical and symbolic. The movement of which Kalpana was a member used victimhood as a way to draw sympathy from other organizations and actors (both national and international) to their cause as well as to mobilize themselves. A beautiful poem written by Kabita Chakma, a young activist in the movement, typifies this process of transformation and provides a shining example of how Chakma women have negotiated change. The poem 'Joli No Uddhim Kitteye' (Why shall I not resist!) was originally written in the Chakma language and Bengali and is translated by the author.

> Why shall I not resist!
> Can they do as they please -
> Turn settlements into barren land
> Dense forests to deserts
> Mornings into evening
> Fruition to barrenness.
>
> Why shall I not resist
> Can they do as they please -
> Estrange us from the land of our birth
> Enslave our women
> Blind our vision
> Put an end to creation.
>
> Neglect and humiliation cause anger
> The blood surges through my veins
> Breaking barriers at every stroke,
> The fury of youth pierces the sea of consciousness.
>
> I become my own whole self
> Why shall I not resist![15]

Kalpana Chakma's abduction and disappearance took place within a general environment of increasing violence in Bangladesh. It was near to this time that the then home minister on 22 November 1993 disclosed in Parliament that of 21,622 reported suicides since January 1992, women accounted for 12,470. These suicides were largely consequences of dowry and other domestic violence.[16] Another report stated that, in 1984, out of 1992 recorded murder incidents, 273 victims were women, which was 14 per cent of total incidents. In most cases such incidents are underreported or not reported at all. According to a study, from January 1996 to June 1996, out of eighty-six reports of violence in the media, 52.32 per cent were reported as suicides, 47.67 per cent were reported as single rapes and gang rapes. Next came murder by husband and then torture because of dowry.[17]

Laws relating to violence against women are also often ambiguous and difficult to implement. But more relevant to our concern are the social and political codes of a male dominant society, which are often manifest in its legal structure. Women in Bangladesh are subject to both personal laws sanctified by religion and public laws, that is, the Penal Code (Guhathakurta 1985). The Prevention of Cruelty to Women (Deterrent Punishment) Ordinance 1983, later changed into an Act in 1995, was first introduced by an autocratic regime that wanted to dilute women's resistance in the face of increasing violence. Although by no means a perfect law, it has enabled more women victims to seek redress in the courts of law than previously possible. But the dual standards followed by our legal system have often succeeded in disguising or camouflaging acts of violence against women. Hence redress by judicial means remains an elusive option for many.

In Kalpana Chakma's case, the state itself was involved as perpetrator of the crime. Gender ideologies as manifest in the workings or policies of the state therefore appeared negatively. The military tried to trivialize the abduction of Kalpana Chakma by trying to link the incident to pre-poll violence, by fabricating ulterior motives for the other party, and concocting 'red herrings' in order to diffuse resistance politics (for example, more than once Kalpana Chakma was reported found!). In Kalpana's disappearance and her conversion into an icon, both victimization and symbol-making were processual. Agency between the individual and the (temporary) whole in relation to structures of resistance, as Kabita's poem explores, enables a rising together and a fluctuating. Likewise, the movement which campaigned to bring the issue of Kalpana Chakma's abduction into the national and international arena, also used Kalpana's victimization in the hands of the state and military to negotiate issues of democracy, transparency and even citizenship. It may have had limited success in effecting a proper inquiry publicizing and in punishing those responsible. But the long-term effects of Kalpana's victimhood have been evident in the subsequent struggles of other ethnic groups such as the Garos in addressing gendered violence in their communities. It is tragic and yet undeniable that it was Kalpana's victimization at the hand of the state and military, which enabled the women's movement, both in the mainstream and at the margins, to take the discourse on gendered violence to new heights.

A note of caution for the women's movement: women's voices in the protest against gender-based violence were raised within a milieu of general political protest, for example, in a setting that promised democratization. The women's movement too acknowledged this and worked simultaneously with the movements such as the anti-autocratic movement against General Ershad. There are both advantages and disadvantages inherent in this. The advantages are that women find a ready support base in mainstream political discourse. In a society which usually trivializes issues relating to women this is of great significance. But the disadvantages are that, if the women's movement does not retain a certain amount of distance or autonomy in their analysis, then the dangers of getting co-opted by either the ruling or oppositional mainstream is inevitable. Women's perspectives on issues of nationalist ideologies, democratic participation and state policies such as militarization, ethnic discrimination and legal structures have therefore become imperative for the future.

NOTES

1. Here, we must acknowledge certain important distinctions between 'victimization' and 'victimhood', the former as a process, the latter as a state.
2. See Manchanda (2001: 15–41) for a discussion of victimhood and agency.
3. Another name for slash and burn agriculture, where communities clear forest land on a hill slope preferably covered with bamboo. The bamboos are cut and the smaller trees felled, but larger trees only denuded of their lower branches. The land is allowed to dry and then put to fire so that all but large trees are reduced to ashes. The ash spread on the land serves as fertilizer. Crops are then sown as rain falls on the land. 'Jhum' can only be cultivated for two successive years and the land then is left to fallow for two successive years. See Mohsin (1997: 82) for details.
4. HWF leaflet distributed in NGO Forum, Beijing, 1995.
5. For a detailed analysis of the militarization and gendered violence in the CHT, see Mohsin (1997) and Guhathakurta (2001: 252–93).

6. Village Defense Party was comprised of paramilitary forces stationed in villages purportedly to help maintain law and order, but primarily to keep vigil.
7. Memorandum to the home minister, presented by twelve civil society organizations, 14 July, Bangladesh.
8. Memorandum to the home minister, 14 July, Bangladesh
9. Personal communication with Kabita Chakma, the then president of HWF.
10. This is from personal communication with members of the HWF. For details see Guhathakurta (2001: 282–84).
11. I was an eyewitness to this incident and have subsequently spoken at length about it to both members of the HWF and leaders of the Sammalita Nari Shomaj.
12. Garos are a matrilineal indigenous community that occupies the Modhupur tract in central Bangladesh. See Burling (1997) for a classic account of their history and livelihood.
13. Leaflet distributed to demand justice for the rape and murder of Garo domestic worker, Levina Howie, BAGACHAS, 25 August 1999, Dhaka.
14. While it is beyond the scope of this article, it is important to bear in mind the history of civil society organizations in Bangladesh.
15. Translated from Chakma (1992: 7).
16. 'The 1994 Sub Editorial Report', *Daily Star*, 4 January 1994.
17. *ASK Bulletin*, Ain O Salish Kendra (ASK), September 1996.

REFERENCES

Akhter, S. (1996). *Kalpana Chakma Udhao Keno?* (Why has Kalpana Chakma Disappeared?), *Bhorer Kagoj*, 17 July.
Burling. Robbins (1997). *The Strong Women of Modhupur*. Dhaka: UPL.
Butler, Judith and J.W. Scott (eds) (1992). *Feminists Theorize the Political*. New York: Routledge.
Chakma, Kabita (1992). *Joli No Uddhim Kitteye* (Why Shall I Not Resist?). Dhaka: Nari Grontho Probortona.
Chakma, Kalpana (2001). *Kalpana Chakma's Diary*, ed. Hill Women's Federation. Dhaka: HWF. (Also published serially in *Bhorer Kagoj*, 24 July, 29 September and 6 October 1996.)
Foucault, Michel (1980). *Power/Knowledge*. New York: Pantheon Press.
Guhathakurta, M. (1985). 'Gender Violence in Bangladesh: The Role of the State', *Journal of Social Studies*, vol. 30: 77–90.
——— (2000). 'Human Rights in Development Policy', in A.K.M. Abdus Sabur (ed.), *Development Cooperation at the Dawn of the Twenty First Century*, pp. 167–81. Dhaka: Bangladesh Institute of International and Strategic Studies.
——— (2001). 'Women's Narratives from the Chittagong Hill Tracts', in Rita Manchanda (ed.), *Women, War and Peace in South Asia: Beyond Victimhood to Agency*, pp. 252–93. New Delhi: Sage Publications.

Islam, Shamima and Zakia Begum (1985). *Women: Victims of Violence, 1975–1985.* Dhaka: Centre for Women and Development.

Jahangir, B.K. and Zarina Rahman Khan (eds) (1987). *Bangladeshey Nari Nirjaton* (Violence Against Women in Bangladesh). Dhaka: Centre for Social Studies.

Kumar, Nita (ed.) (1994). *Women as Subjects. South Asian Histories.* Delhi: Bhaktal Books.

Manchanda, Rita (ed.) (2001). *Women, War and Peace in South Asia: Beyond Victimhood to Agency.* New Delhi: Sage Publications.

Mohanty, Chandra, Talapade, Ann Russo and Lourdes Torres (eds) (1991). *Third World Women and the Politics of Feminism.* Bloomington: Indiana University Press.

Mohsin, A. (1996). 'The Nationalist State and the Chittagong Hill Tracts 1971–1994', *Journal of Social Studies*, 74: 32–61.

——— (1997). *The Politics of Nationalism: The Case of the Chittagong Hill Tracts, Bangladesh*, Dhaka: UPL.

Norwegian Refugee Council (NRC) (2003). 'Profile of Internal Displacement: Bangladesh', in Global IDP Database (updated Dec.). Available at: http://idpproject.org. Last accessed 4 June 2004.

Rajchman, John (ed.) (1995). *The Identity In Question.* New York: Routledge.

Timm, R.W. (1992). *The Adivasis of Bangladesh.* London: Minority Rights Group International.

7

Reconstituting Selves in the Karachi Conflict

Mohajir Women Survivors and Structural Violence

Lubna Nazir Chaudhry

FRAMING THE PROJECT

This article focuses on Mohajir women's attempts to reconstitute[1] their selves as they rebuild their lives in the wake of conflict-generated violence that hit their homes during the 1990s in Karachi, Pakistan.[2] Following Patai (1988: 150), the emphasis here is not on learning the facts of women's lives, but on comprehending 'how a person verbally constructs an image of her life, how she creates a character for herself, how she becomes the protagonist of her own story'. Using life-history interviews, I present and analyse two self-identified poor Mohajir women's self-representations that are post-conflict and post-trauma. These women, in addition to other deprivations, each faced the death of a family member. In a vein similar to the 'practice theory of self' proffered by Skinner et al. (1998: 5),[3] I see selves as sites of struggle, whereby these women survivors attempt to constitute themselves as agents, even as this agency remains constrained and circumscribed by their positioning in a society fraught with multiple forms of violence (Chaudhry 1998). For disempowered women in urban society, the reconstruction of self divulges particular nuances in the face of structural violence. How do these women represent themselves as agents within the life-worlds they inhabit? How do postcolonial constructions of ethnicity, gender and class play out in these representations? Highlighting how agency remains delimited by social positioning and circumstances, this article argues for complex understandings of women's agency in contexts of armed conflict.

Following encounters with violence, pain and loss, survivors have to reconfigure their lives and selves in drastic ways (Das and Kleinman 2000; Nordstrom 1997). Armed conflict causes the taken-for-granted everyday quality of the world to implode. When the world changes, the major players change, and the self also changes in relation to the world and others. The reconstruction of self is not linear and straightforward, and this process has particular nuances in settings characterized by resurfacing conflict and persistent structural violence, the everyday forms of violence that become normalized and naturalized. Despite the relentlessly severe nature of circumstances, survivors display a remarkable creativity in creating conditions under which they continue to survive and cope.[4] What kinds of selves are enacted in this bid for survival? What types of meaning-making processes underpin these enactments? What possibilities of societal transformation, of movements towards peace, equity and justice, emerge, if any, as survivors forge new selves and lives from within and against their violent worlds? In this article I explore these and related questions in the light of Mohajir women's experiences in the Karachi conflict.

My concern is especially with Mohajir women survivors at the lowest rung of urban society, those who, so to speak, inhabit the margins. The lives of poor Mohajir women survivors, as I will elaborate in the next section, are embedded in postcolonial[5] contexts of structural violence that are classed, gendered and ethnicized. That is to say, if we understand structural violence to be the systematic production of suffering,[6] then the structural violence in the lives of these women is generated, experienced and resisted within categories of class, gender and ethnicity, in response to the shifting geopolitics of social stratification in a Third World urban centre.[7] The intent, then, is to delineate how intersections of ethnicity, gender and class play out in Mohajir women survivors' constructions and understandings of selves as they struggle on the fringes of Karachi.

Srinivasan posits the survivor of violence as a repository of invaluable knowledge, since the 'mechanisms of remembering and forgetting, describing and classifying, recounting and recreating, explaining and expressing, reflected in the survivor's testimony, all led back to the social fabric itself'. This 'movement of history away from events to structures' (1990: 307) in the Karachi context of conflict enables us to understand how the construction of marginalized selves is inextricably bound with the working of multilayered power structures.[8] As Smith (1987) contends, individual cases are also points of entry into broader social and economic processes. My reading of interviews with two Mohajir women is meant to illustrate the manner in which the impacts of global relations of domination, regional politics, repressive state apparatuses, diverse nationalisms, local hierarchies, and multileveled patriarchies, from the transnational to the familial, converge and intersect in the telling of a life story leading to the presentation of a self that can be contradictory and multifaceted.[9] A focus on only two women survivors permits an in-depth look at the various manifestations of self and the systems of meaning, simultaneously making for a comparative base to demonstrate the heterogeneity of women's constructions, experiences, and realities in contexts of conflict, even when ethnicity, class and geographical location are not disparate.

The approach[10] to selves and agency in this article is perhaps best characterized by the conjoining of Third World poststructuralist feminist understandings of relational, hybridized, multiple selves[11] with materialist feminism, the brand of anti-capitalist feminism that links class analysis to *all* aspects of women's lived experiences.[12] The constitution of selves, from such a perspective, entails an ongoing negotiation (Alarcon 1990). Agency can be achieved through relationality (Joseph 1999), and the capacity to dexterously utilize multiple identities through a consciousness of the differential impact of power relations in different contexts (Sandoval 1991, 2000). Consciousness of multiple selves, however, many times a consequence of ruptures caused by forces of domination, might not always entail agency or resistance, as the workings of power relations in certain contexts might foreclose the array of options available for the constitution of selves. I, therefore, locate enactments of selves in the linkages between history, and intersecting and contradictory, yet discrete, axes of domination/resistance, such as class, gender and ethnicity (Frankenberg and Mani 1993; Mohanty 1987). This study of how economics and multilevel patriarchies define selves and agency takes into account historical and contemporary global relations of power, and the colonial and neocolonial politics of lasting inequalities within and between nation states.

This piece of writing continues the work undertaken by Khattak (2002), Saigol (2002) and de Mel (2003) by utilizing feminist lenses to examine selected themes emerging from interviews collected for the *Archive on Women, Conflict, and Security* (SDPI 2001).[13] The Sustainable Development Policy Institute (SDPI) study, which included data collection in Karachi,[14] was designed to privilege women's standpoints about conflict situations.[15] What distinguishes the SDPI initiative from the few other efforts[16] to write about Mohajir women's experiences in the Karachi armed violence is the attempt to achieve an understanding of the genesis, proliferation and impact of violence through the elicitation of life-histories from women survivors. By the incorporation of an approach that encouraged self-reflection,[17] the emphasis was shifted from a mere recounting of the effects of violence to an analysis of experiences, allowing for connections across spatial and temporal contexts.

The articles based on the SDPI data set, including the present one, at the most claim to *highlight* and *foreground* the research participants' perspectives. In the ultimate analysis, the privileged voice in each of the papers is that of the researcher-writer. The survivor women's words, educed through interviews undertaken in hierarchical contexts,[18] were subjected to an analytical scrutiny, and interviews were selected, themes were extracted, theoretical frameworks were developed, and language choices were made, in order to put forth insights motivated by the writer's agenda.[19]

This article is divided into four sections. The next section provides the historical, geographic and economic contours of the politics underlying Karachi's conflict, and its impact on Mohajir women. This leads into a discussion of the selves and agency of Mehr-un-Nisa and Ayesha Begum, the two Mohajir women survivors I am choosing to write about. The final section sums up issues raised, posing questions for feminist theorizing and praxis.

ON THE KARACHI CONFLICT

Karachi, despite the recurrent violence, with an average of 630 violent deaths (95 per cent male) per year from 1990 to 2000 (Khattak 2002), remains the financial capital of Pakistan, holding 50 per cent of the bank assets in the country (Gayer 2003). Karachi, presently the seat of Sindh's provincial government, is Pakistan's largest city, with a population of around ten million, according to the 1998 census.[20] In Karachi, 50 per cent of the population live in *basti*s (squatter settlements) on the outskirts of the city, where amenities such as electricity and clean water are not a given.[21] Whereas postcolonial Karachi does not retain the 'black' and 'white' divisions of the British era, the contrast between the elite parts of town and these bastis is striking (ibid.). The middle- and lower middle-class localities lie between these two extremes, in the geographical sense as well as level of material comfort.

Before the British occupied Karachi in 1839, it was just a small fishermen's village, but it was already an important point in a sea route linking China and parts of India to Africa and Europe (Lari and Lari 1996). The British developed Karachi's port, and exploited its strategic location in the world wars[22] to their advantage (Gayer 2003). Just before Partition, Karachi had 450,000 inhabitants, of which 61.2 per cent claimed Sindhi as their mother tongue and 6.3 per cent spoke Urdu-Hindu (Hasan 1999). Also, 51 per cent of the population was Hindu, and 42 per cent was Muslim (ibid.). Hasan writes:

> By 1951, all this had changed and Karachi's population had increased to 1.137 million, because of the influx of 600,000 refugees from India. In 1951 the Sindhi speaking population was 8.6 per cent, the Urdu speaking population was 50 per cent, the Muslim population was 96 per cent, and the Hindu population was 2 per cent. (ibid.: 24)

Karachi was declared the newly formed nation's capital in 1948, partly because the other strong contender for the position, Lahore, like the rest of Punjab, was still reeling from the impact of Partition violence (Tan and Kudaisya 2000). This involved taking Karachi out of Sindh, and turning it into a centrally administered area (ibid.). Sindh received no compensation, and lost control of their most thriving area. The fact of the geographically reconfigured province coupled with the radically shifting demographics, whereby Sindhis became a minority in what had been the urban centre of their province, set the stage for the conflict between Sindhis and non-Sindhis, including the group who were later to call themselves Mohajirs, the Urdu-speaking Muslim immigrants from India (Jalal 1990). The Sindhis, mostly rural, came to resent the largely urban Urdu-speaking population, while the immigrants set themselves up as the civilized, enlightened urbanites against the feudalistic, backward Sindhis (Verkaaik 2004).

Post-Partition, Karachi also became Pakistan's industrial centre, and, initially, its workforce was mostly drawn from the working-class Urdu-speaking Muslim immigrants from India. Karachi's demographics continued to shift in the 1950s and 1960s, and the city became increasingly multi-ethnic. While Balochi workers were already present in the city at Partition, Pathans from the North West Frontier Province (NWFP) also migrated to Karachi in the 1950s and 1960s, and so did the Punjabis in the 1960s. The Pathans were mostly involved in construction, and were awarded the transport business in Karachi as part of state patronage during Ayub Khan's regime (1958–69).[23] The 1998 census shows the following population breakdown in terms of mother tongue: Urdu, 48.52 per cent; Punjabi, 13.94; Pushto, 11.42; Sindhi, 7.22; Balochi, 4.34; Seraiki, 2.11; and others, which include speakers of Bengali, Gujarati and Brahui, are 12.4 per cent (Government of Pakistan 1998). The different working-class groups were settled along ethnic lines in the bastis on the periphery of Karachi from Partition onwards (Gayer 2003).

According to Wright (1991), 1947–51 represents the era of the dominance of Urdu-speaking immigrants in Pakistan (Ahmar 1996; Shaikh 1997; Verkaaik 2004). A segment of this population, the Muslim elite that had received the benefits of a colonial education, comprised 55.6 per cent of the Civil Service of Pakistan (Shaikh 1997). This Muslim elite had also been the most fervent supporter of the Pakistan movement and, therefore, could lay claim to a high degree of political involvement with the new state (Tambiah 1996). The claim of ownership translated into Urdu being the national language of the country (Rahman 1996). By the early 1950s, however, the Urdu-speaking elite had to share their hegemony with the Punjabis, the largest group in Pakistan, who had already constituted 85 per cent of the Pakistani army at Partition,[24] and are now dominant in the Civil Service by virtue of their sheer numbers (Tambiah 1996). When the capital of Pakistan shifted from Karachi to the new city of Islamabad, the balance started to shift towards the Punjabis (Tan and Kudaisya 2000). The position of Urdu-speaking immigrants declined under Zulfikar Ali Bhutto (1971–77), a Sindhi, who decentralized the power of the bureaucracy, and uplifted the Sindhis by creating rural quotas in jobs and education (Wright 1991). Also, by this time, the state after successive military-led governments had become very militarized, and Punjabi hegemony had become entrenched (Rizvi 2000). This decline continued, when another military dictator, Zia-ul-Haq, came to power, in 1977 (Tambiah 1996). Zia-ul-Haq, in his eleven years of rule, further consolidated the power of the Punjabis (Jalal 1994). The tentative attempts to regain power through a coalition with Benazir Bhutto in 1988–90 did not prove to be very fruitful (Tambiah 1996). Also, with the rise of the Mohajir Qaumi Mahaaz (Mohajir Nationalist Front/Movement), the leadership for the Urdu-speaking immigrant communities originating from India now began to be drawn from the middle classes rather than the elite (Verkaaik 2004). The manner in which the Urdu-speaking elite was increasingly sidelined in the Pakistani political and bureaucratic scene was utilized by the middle- and lower middle-class Mohajirs as a symbol of the decline of the entire population of those whose families had originated in northern, central and western India.

It is customary to frame the contemporary phase[25] of the armed violence in Karachi, beginning in 1985, in the reign of military dictator Zia-ul-Haq (1977–88), and extending into the present as an ethnic conflict, which then produced a sectarian, religion-based, offshoot, culminating in the post-9/11 hotbed of terrorism.[26] It is also customary to frame this violence, in its various permutations, as oppositional to the project of modernity represented by processes of industrialization, urbanization and the formation of a democratic nation state. However, as Bowen (2002: 336) reminds us, 'ethnic thinking in political life is a product of modern conflicts over power and resources, and not an ancient impediment to political modernity'.

Alavi (1989: 246), in his analysis of the 1985 and 1986 riots, sees the 'ethnic conflict explanation' as insufficient. Ethnic solidarities, he writes, 'were … exploited', but the 'powerful organized interests that were at work' need to be taken into account. I would add that the urban struggles in which the politics of ethnicity were deployed by powerful organized groups have to be contextualized in the specific set of historical and political conditions characterizing post-independence Pakistan.

The riots of 1985 that marked the onset of Karachi's contemporary conflict started in Orangi, the largest basti. These riots initially occurred between transport-users, Mohajirs and Punjabis, and transporters, often Pathans, and escalated into protracted armed violence between Mohajirs and Pathans.[27] Shaikh (1997) cites the strain placed on Karachi's population as a result of the congestion and inadequate public transportation system as a major cause of this violence. Although Karachi had witnessed anti-Ahmedi riots in the 1950s and 1969–70, anti-Pathan riots in 1965 and Sindhi-Mohajir riots in 1972–73, the 1985 riots, and the subsequent 1986 riots between Pathans and Mohajirs, were unprecedented in the level of cruelty exhibited as well as the extent of the death and destruction. The influx of weapons into Karachi, on their way north to support the United States-backed, and Pakistan-assisted, Mujahideen (braves) in Afghanistan, was responsible for the scale of the brutality (Gayer 2003; Jalal 1994; Khattak 2002; Shaikh 1997). The intervention by the state security forces in 1985, with the deployment of the army against the so-called rioters, also set the tone of subsequent crackdowns by the repressive state apparatuses, which in the mid-1990s, during Nawaz Sharif's and Benazir Bhutto's tenures,[28] were at their most brutal, earning Pakistan the charge of severe human rights violations

(Amnesty International 1996; Gayer 2003; Shaikh 1997). For Hussain (1990), the rioting and the state brutality represented the failure of the state to provide the political mechanism for its citizens to express and redress their grievances. For others, this was yet another reincarnation of the militarized, coercive state that had so ruthlessly sought to put down the perceived insurgency in 1971 in what was then East Pakistan (Rizvi 2000; Shaikh 1997).

The group in Karachi that has been continuously exposed to the changing configurations of the violence in their city began to call itself Mohajir around the time of this explosion in violence (Khattak 2002; Saigol 2002). Literally meaning 'one who has migrated',[29] Mohajir, in the context of the politics of identity in Pakistan, has come to designate a collectivity primarily comprising of lower middle-class and working-class Muslim immigrant families from India (the elite Muslim immigrants from India have not identified with this label), who after the 1947 Partition of the subcontinent were settled mostly in Hyderabad and Karachi[30] in a bid to create electoral constituencies for certain members of the Muslim League, including Liaqat Ali Khan, the first prime minister of Pakistan. This settlement of Urdu-speaking immigrants in Sindh was also part of a Punjabi move to preserve the homogeneity of the Punjab province, which had accommodated the immigrants moving from Eastern Punjab (Alavi 1989). The term Mohajir also encompasses Muslim immigrants who came to Karachi from India after 1947 as well as the Biharis who migrated to Pakistan during or after the 1971 struggle for independence in the former East Pakistan. Mohajirs are primarily Urdu-speaking, although members originated from diverse places in what is now the nation state of India.[31] Before the ascendancy of the MQM, in the 1980s, the middle- and lower-class Urdu-speaking population in Karachi had preferred the identity label Hindustani (Shaikh 1997).

Altaf Hussain, a Mohajir student at the Karachi University, conceived the All Pakistan Mohajir Students Organization (APMSO) in 1979.[32] Central to the political ethos propagated by Altaf Hussain was the idea that the Mohajirs be accorded the status of the 'fifth nationality' on par with the four 'national' groups, the ethnic entities, Punjabi, Sindhi, Baluchis, and Pathans, that had laid claim to the four provinces of Pakistan, Punjab, Sindh, Baluchistan, and the NWFP. When Zia-ul-Haq banned all student organizations in 1984, the MQM was born. According to various reports, MQM was a recipient of state patronage in its initial years, since the Zia regime wanted to counter the power of the Sindhis, the ethnic group of Zulfikar Ali Bhutto, the ruler Zia-ul-Haq had ousted (Khattak 2002). The MQM's attempt to construct a political identity through a collective sense of disenfranchisement and alienation among a heterogeneous group of religious sects and classes did enlist a great degree of support. The MQM was especially attractive to the large body of lower middle- and working-class young men[33] disillusioned by the unequal life chances available to them in the urban metropolis (Hasan 1987). The MQM established itself politically in the 1988 and 1990 elections, and Benazir Bhutto's Pakistan People's Party (PPP) had to form a coalition with them in order to take the reins of control. The coalition ended with violence between Sindhis and Mohajirs (Tambiah 1996).

The devastation in Karachi in the mid-1990s, with around 2,000 people killed in 1995 (Amnesty International 1996), and approximately the same number of deaths in 1996, as well as the mass arrests and persecution of alleged MQM activists, their families, and even their entire localities, by the state security forces (Shaikh 1997; Tan and Kudaisya 2000; Verkaaik 2001), was the continuation of the earlier culture of violence that had set in, in the 1980s, but there were also new developments. For one, in 1991, the MQM split into two factions, with MQM Haq Parast (literally, the lovers of truth) still under the leadership of Altaf Hussain, and the splinter group calling itself MQM-Haqiqi group. Verkaaik (2004) traces a rise in the militancy of the MQM in this division. The militancy also took the form of brutal killings of members of the rival faction, through shoot-outs, ambushes and bombs. Second, in 1992, the Pakistani Intelligence services declared MQM a terrorist group, emulating other contexts of state-sanctioned violence, where such a charge was used to justify excessive force against citizens (Zulaika and Douglass 1996). Third, there were reports that the Research and Analysis Wing (RAW), the Indian intelligence agency, was funding MQM's organized violence in retribution for Pakistan's contribution to the conflict in Kashmir.[34]

While Altaf Hussain and other high-ranking leaders left Pakistan to avoid state persecution, and the elite moved their businesses and themselves to other parts of Pakistan or abroad (Verkaaik 2004), the brunt of the violence from various sources was faced by the communities, mostly Mohajir, living in the bastis (Khattak 2002; Shaikh 1997). Innumerable families were rendered destitute, when they lost homes, breadwinning members, and livelihoods in a city torn apart by armed conflict (SDPI 2001; Shah 1998). The lack of adequate medical services and disaster-mitigating programmes, coupled with unchecked persecution by the state security agencies, deepened the experience of chaos and vulnerability (SDPI 2001; Shah 1998). The conflict-generated violence thus intensified the structural violence that had circumscribed the lives of the women and families in the bastis. Even during the relative lull in the violence after the 1999 coup in Pakistan, whereby the current president of Pakistan, General Musharraf, seized power from Nawaz Sharif, the so-called reconstruction of the urban metropolis has mostly involved the re-adornment of elite spaces, for instance, through the building of western-style malls. The women who are at the centre of discussion in this article continued with the tasks of grieving and surviving with little or no change in the material fabric of their lives or the conditions of their surroundings.

RECONSTITUTING SELVES IN THE URBAN MARGINS

Here I write about/from my interviews conducted in the spring and summer of 2000 with Ayesha Begum and Mehr-un-Nisa, both of them residents of Orangi, Karachi's largest basti with an estimated population of about one million, which provided a significant percentage of the blue-collar workforce as well as employees for the informal sector, especially during the heyday of Karachi's economy before the current violence (Gayer 2003). The majority of Orangi residents are Mohajir, and the contemporary Karachi conflict started here in 1985. At the time of the interview, Ayesha Begum, whose teenaged son was reportedly shot by the police for keeping company with terrorists, was in her early sixties, while Mehr-un-Nisa, whose nineteen-year-old brother was apparently caught in the crossfire between rival MQM factions, was somewhere in her late teens to early twenties. The difference in age between the two women, although significant, cannot be conclusively linked to all the differences evidenced in these women's presentation of selves during the interviews. However, the fact that Ayesha Begum migrated to Karachi in 1948 as part of the earlier influx of post-Partition immigrants from India, and Mehr-un-Nisa was born in Karachi a few years after her family moved here in 1970 from what was then East Pakistan, does make for quite different relationships to the term Mohajir. The two women also differed with respect to their caste identities and their family's points of origin in India.

We interviewed the research participants in their homes. Given the nature of the insecurity in Orangi, even in that time of relative peace in

2000, interviews were conducted in only one sitting of two to three hours, since follow-up visits were considered risky for the research participants as well as the research team. Interviews were tape-recorded. I also took copious notes during the interactions, jotting down my reflections about the people and the setting. The interviews were conducted in Urdu, the home language of the research participants, and Pakistan's national language. My notes were in a mixture of Urdu and English. The recorded material was first transcribed in Urdu, and then translated into English.

The interviews were semi-structured, and, therefore, relatively open-ended. We generated a list of broad topics around which questions would be asked, but there was neither a prescribed order nor a compulsion to adhere to any rigid wording of questions. Our goal was to listen to the life-stories of research participants as those experiencing, and living, violence, but also as those who had lives beyond that experience of violence. Also, we wanted to facilitate a listening space, where research participants were encouraged to share with us their meaning-making processes, their analysis of their lives and experiences in contexts of violence as well as through connections they made between different aspects of their lives, before and after the violence affected their families and communities. I focused on the kinds of selves participants constructed during the course of the interview. In other words, when the research participant said 'I', what subject position was she speaking from, what story was being told, and what spaces of agency could be located in theses constructions and stories? Although we did not get narratives of self in the strictest sense, we did get representations[35] and constructions from research participants. The interaction style was contingent on the particular research participant, and the circumstances under which interviews were conducted. The research design was not participatory in nature.[36]

In my writing about the interviews I have tried to reflect the complexity that the interviews had conveyed: women's constructions of themselves in different times and spaces were not linear or unitary. I am also looking at the interviews as a Third World feminist committed to understanding the scope of women's agency and using that understanding as a point of departure to locate possibilities of equitable and peaceful social change.

The following discussion about Ayesha Begum and Mehr-un-Nisa by no means claims to be an exhaustive account or analysis of their lives and experiences. I analyse the manner in which both women represented themselves during the course of the interview. Encapsulated within the interviews were women's representations of selves spanning the past, the continuous present, and even the perceived or desirable future, but these representations were constructed from the vantage point of the 'now'. Although I was welcomed graciously, even warmly, in most homes I visited, and the trusting attitude of the survivors I interviewed never failed to amaze me, I still wondered what was said or not said, because I was a Punjabi—maybe not 'like the ones who lived in Karachi' as one research participant put it, but, nevertheless, a member of the most powerful ethnic group in Pakistan.[37]

Ayesha Begum

> Only a mother can understand the grief and pain of losing a child, only the one who gives birth and brings up a child with so much care and difficulty can understand … (Ayesha Begum, 2000)[38]

The interview with Ayesha Begum took place in the small room she shared with her three unmarried children in the two-room house built of unbaked bricks and metal sheets. Ayesha sat on the bed against the wall, upright, without leaning against the pillow her son placed behind her back. I sat on a chair next to the bed, with my recording equipment rather precariously balanced on my lap. As the interview unfolded, Ayesha's children and her neighbours drifted in and out of the room we sat in, sometimes on the pretext of bringing us tea, and sometimes without giving any reason at all. We drank a lot of very strong tea and, for the most part, it was Ayesha who talked. Her initial reserve lasted only two questions into the session, and very soon it became difficult to even utter questions. Ayesha alternated between animated story-telling and passionate lecture modes, although she would politely, even if very briefly, provide a response to my specific queries. Overall, I was left with a lasting impression of a vibrant woman with a keen intellect, who tempered her anger and bitterness with humour and practicality.

What emerged from the interview was a strong sense of Ayesha Begum, the mother, and Ayesha Begum, the citizen-subject, struggling to meet her obligations and responsibilities towards her children, severely disappointed with the treatment meted out to her by structures that were supposed to support and protect her, but still not disillusioned enough to give up entirely on the promise of deliverance that these structures held for her children and herself. Ayesha the mother and Ayesha the citizen-subject were, at times, distinct from each other, but mostly they worked together, voicing Ayesha's paradoxical anticipation of safety and trauma from the patriarchal family and the masculinist nation state. While sometimes acutely aware of the impossibility of her desires for security and stability—she was, after all, poor, a woman, and the member of a group targeted by repressive state apparatuses—her incessant critique of the larger socio-historical processes in which her circumstances were situated pointed to her faith in the possibility of change rather than the immutability of structures. Motherhood, a site of continual strife and painful loss, and citizenship, a state of unmet expectations and seething rage, nevertheless, provided anchorage in a chaotic world typified by recurring violence and ongoing displacement.

Ayesha Begum told me that she was taking medicine for high blood pressure as well as tranquilizers to help her sleep. The transportation situation in Karachi made it difficult to go to the hospital from where she got her medicine, and the medicine was also expensive, so she had learned to spread out the doses to last a long time. Thoughts of her children, the dead and the alive, raised her blood pressure and kept her awake. Since her husband had passed away a few years ago, she was the only one responsible for keeping the household together. Her older sons had only part-time employment in a nearby factory; her youngest son was too afraid to go outside after his brother died; her youngest daughter, having given up her dream of getting a science degree, after her high school was teaching in a private school for very little money; the three married daughters were not happy at all; and she had to somehow arrange matches for the unmarried children.

Ayesha Begum cast herself as a mother from a particular class background. 'How very hard is it for the poor to bring up their children!' she exclaimed at more than one juncture in the interview. Yet, Ayesha Begum's positioning of herself as a mother who was poor was not merely an expression of abject helplessness. The mother who mourned the unlawful killing of her son, and lamented the lack of opportunities for her other children, was also a mother who voiced a trenchant protest against the system that had abused her, and others occupying the margins, rendering them powerless:

> Every new government needs votes to get elected. We make queues all day long and cast votes. If we do something for them, what do they do for us? They kill our children. The police enter the houses by force and harass people. The police demand money in return for freeing our children. But how can we poor manage it? They pick the locks and break the doors. Where do we get the money to fix them? Do we vote to get maltreatment from the elected government? They should take care of people rather than harming them.

Even when narrating the event of her son's death, intense grief was juxtaposed with forceful indignation against the denial of rights to her son and herself as citizen-subjects:

> If my son had done anything wrong at all, he should have been put behind bars. If he were sentenced, there would have been hope for his release after the punishment was over....If the killers had ever come to me, I would have requested them to probe into the matter first. The question is, why did they lift my son? If any wrongdoers accompanied him, they should have made inquiries. Suppose a child does something wrong to anybody, the parents first ask him about it; and if the child is at fault, only then they scold him. What a blind reign this is. They kill without inquiry or investigation.

The pain of the bereaved mother and the outrage against the violation of citizens' rights was a cry for due process, and desirable state apparatuses that would offer justice and nurturance rather than violence and inhumanity. Ayesha Begum refused the interpellation of herself as the mother of a 'terrorist', reverting the charge of lawlessness on to those who would brand her son thus. Her challenge to the perpetrators of the crime against her son, the cogs in the bureaucratic wheel intent on getting rid of supposed threats to the peace and security of the state, was couched in terms of a reminder of the humanity they shared with her rather than any declaration of retaliatory desire.

> ...my family did not inform me about it ... If I were aware of it I would have gone to the police station and asked what would happen to them if they killed their own son! Don't they feel sorry by doing so with the children of others?

Ayesha Begum's powerful articulation against structural violence derived from her identification with her social space, even as it gendered the citizen-subject as a mother and a widow. Since the populations in the bastis on the outskirts of post-Partition Karachi were initially settled along ethnic lines, and the segregation intensified as other groups came into the city, the 'we' used by Ayesha Begum was classed as well as ethnicized:

> We vote for them with the hope that someone of our locality might get elected as the councillor and we would go to him to get our problems redressed. But no one from our locality gets elected, no one from whom we can request something. We are totally helpless. These days it is the rule of the police, and they inflict cruelties.... How can the poor have any peace? The poor are born just to die. Now, where can the widows go? .... The police harass the widows

more. They enter the houses without permission and upset everything…and demand money. They threaten us if we don't pay them. We did not vote for this. There is neither electricity nor water in our area. Whom do we approach for this?

In speaking of her ethnicity, however, Ayesha Begum used the relatively apolitical identity label 'Hindustani' which was employed to designate Urdu-speaking immigrants from northern India before the ascendancy of MQM and the term Mohajir. Despite Ayesha Begum's elision of her identity as Mohajir, Ayesha Begum's construction of herself as a citizen-subject of Pakistan was predicated heavily on a narrative of arrival that underscored her Muslim identity, and the hardships faced during the migration, resonating with what is put forth as the quintessential Mohajir experience by the MQM (Shaikh 1997). However, Ayesha's incorporation of classed and gendered dimensions, as well as an attention to the power dynamics that infused the settlement process, did fissure the myth of the educated Mohajir, who claimed that sacrifices earned them their due in the Muslim country, till their position was usurped by other less deserving ethnicities:

> Many Muslims also accompanied us to this land.…We stayed there at the border for about fifteen to twenty days. Then the government sent tickets with the order stating how many refugees would go to Karachi, Sindh, or other places. We were sent to Shikarpur. My father had no income then. First he left India, then Shikarpur, and went to Karachi. I was not married at that time. Beyond Jail Road, …we put up our tents.… We stayed there like that for a year and then proper plots were allotted to us where we made our huts and also my husband (made his hut) … I was fourteen or fifteen and got married … my father-in-law had a desire to marry his son early so that children would be born and the race would increase …I studied up to fourth and fifth class in addition to Holy Quran. I had to shoulder household responsibilities as a child.

Ayesha's description of her family's multiple displacements in the early years in Pakistan is mirrored in her account of fleeing her home, and finding refuge in various rented homes in different parts of Karachi to avoid police persecution during Benazir Bhutto's second tenure (1993–96) as prime minister. This was the time period when Ayesha's son was killed, and her other sons were repeatedly harassed, because of their dead brother's supposed connections with the MQM.[39] At one point, the police, under trumped-up charges, took all of her four remaining sons into custody. Ayesha arranged the release of her sons by paying off the police through borrowed funds, but the police incursions into their home continued, so leaving home was the only recourse. Ayesha drew a parallel between the violence that led to her migration into Karachi, and the brutality that triggered the more recent internal migration: 'Such cruelty and lawlessness shouldn't exist. We left our home in India because the Hindus and Sikhs had started looting and killing.'

The crucial difference for Ayesha Begum, however, between leaving home in 1948 and the series of displacements in the 1990s was that 'Liaqat Ali Khan Sahib was alive at that time. He helped us a great deal. We were provided with mats and ration.' As she elaborated later on in the interview when I asked her if and how it was possible to put a stop to the conflict in Karachi: 'If Liaqat Ali Khan or Quaid-i-Azam had lived a little longer ... there would not have been such killings and destruction. When the heads of the state keep on changing abruptly, it causes destruction just like it has happened.' This perspective was analogous to Ayesha's presentation of the trials and tribulations faced by herself and her children, first because of her husband's ten-year-long chronic illness, and later on because of his death:

> ...when their father could not get well, the children started doing petty jobs. Our children could not get educated. Whatever material came from the factory, my daughters and myself cleaned that and cut its threads. This is how our children were brought up. They studied and learnt their work alongside each other... there are still three to be married.... There is neither my husband nor any guardian to take care of them. One year after the death of my husband, my son was murdered, and since then I have been ill.

Things fall apart at home as well as in the nation state when fathers are absent or ineffectual:

> ...a house is destroyed without its head.... At times it is said to vote for this and then for that.... Now the military is in rule; perhaps they might give us justice. They should slash the prices, so that the poor might earn their bread peacefully.

Ayesha Begum's conception of the authority figure necessary to ensure safety and well-being was gendered *and* ethnicized. Bhutto, a woman and a Sindhi, of rural feudal origins, served as the foil for the first rulers of Pakistan, male, Urdu-speaking immigrants from India, embodying the spirit of the educated, civilized urban elite.[40] Ayesha Begum said she returned home when Sharif, a Punjabi male, came into power, but in pinning her hopes on Musharraf's army regime, Ayesha Begum was expressing her confidence in a man and in a fellow Hindustani. The Pakistani state had let her down earlier, but that was only because the ruler did not have the right credentials.

In a similar vein, Ayesha Begum's dissatisfaction with her own marriage or the realization that her married daughters were not happy did not lead to a dismissal of marriage as a worthwhile institution. She wanted her youngest daughter to earn a higher degree and make some money, so she could be independent in the eventuality 'that her husband turned out to be bad'. At the same time, Ayesha Begum was on the lookout for a match for her daughter with an appropriate Hindustani with a 'government job or his own house'. Yet, to view Ayesha Begum's stance on the state and marriage as indicative of her inability to think beyond the status quo, in spite of her defiance, would be too simplistic a reading of the matter. In adhering to societal imperatives for marriage and locating the potential for positive change in the state apparatuses, if they were 'manned' by those who shared her ethnic affiliation, Ayesha Begum was crafting a vision of life for herself and her loved ones within the constraints and opportunities afforded for well-being and safety by existing power structures.

Using ethnicity as a building block for self-constitution, as a citizen-subject, and as a mother, enabled Ayesha Begum to achieve agency in a context where the politics of ethnic identity, at local and national levels, even when not made explicit, remained overpowering.[41] Ayesha Begum and her family experienced physical violence because they were Hindustanis and/or Mohajirs. Also, a space for contesting the relentless structural violence impacting her life was available through a politicized reworking of the Hindustani identity, thanks largely to the MQM. In Ayesha Begum's life-world, the possibilities of other forms of coalitions and alliances, where other modalities, such as class or gender, could be utilized as grounds of mobilization, remained minimal, ironically, because of the gendered and classed nature of her reality. Despite enjoying the relative mobility of an older woman living in an urban metropolis, there were still restrictions on Ayesha Begum's freedom. These gender-based boundaries, hand-in-hand with the class-based experiences of a problematic transport system, limited her contact to the people sharing her ethnic affiliation, since they were the ones who shared her physical space, a circumstance arranged and facilitated by the powers-that-be.

Still, the limited interaction with people from other ethnic backgrounds only partially accounted for Ayesha Begum's blatant ethnocentrism: 'I don't know where have these people of various ethnicities come from and settled in Karachi…. In fact the situation got worse as more and more races moved in here.' At another point in the interview, Ayesha Begum attributed the conflict in Karachi to the ethnocentrism evidenced in people of different ethnicities. When I asked her if she was ethnocentric, she replied, 'Earlier on my children and myself were all right, but since the death of my husband and my son I have become so.' Reconstituting the self after violence shattered it apart had also involved incorporating some form of that violence into the process of reconstitution. An acknowledgement of class-based suffering was a salient theme in Ayesha Begum's representation of her life. She did recognize, for instance, that 'it is the children of the poor who get murdered', even if 'poor and rich Hindustanis are all harassed by policemen of other ethnicities'. The implications of Ayesha Begum's highly ethnicized agency, as a poor mother, and as a citizen-subject, in a postcolonial context of violence does not allow for either valorization or romanticization. Nor, however, can this agency be disavowed, if we want to think with/through Ayesha Begum's life in all its complexity.

Mehr-un-Nisa

> After my brother's death, we ended contact with everybody. I wanted to become a doctor. It was not fated to happen. (Mehr-un-Nisa, 2000)[42]

We sat in one of two rooms in a house that was made of a mixture of baked and unbaked bricks. The only two articles in the room were the straw mat and a brass glass. While Mehr-un-Nisa and I talked, her mother lay on the side, a newspaper rolled into a pillow underneath her head, occasionally fanning herself with another newspaper. At times, she would interject into the conversation, but Mehr-un-Nisa was my primary respondent. Mehr-un-Nisa assiduously answered all my questions, but her answers, even to my broadly framed queries, were brief, and to the point. I was struck, however, by her wisdom, for her somewhat terse responses were uttered after careful deliberation. I also noted a deep sadness in her eyes, which was in contrast to the haziness I could see in her mother's gaze. Mehr-un-Nisa told me, in the course of the interview, that the doctor gave her mother sleeping pills to help her with the psychological illness that had set in after her brother's death.

Mehr-un-Nisa dropped out of school four years before the interview after her older brother, Iqbal, was killed. Her family could no longer afford her education, since Iqbal was the chief breadwinner. Iqbal had quit school after his matriculation (tenth standard), to take on the job in a shop where electronics were repaired, since their father's health had started to deteriorate, and he could not work everyday. Her father, who was seventy years old at the time of the interview, had first worked in a lawyer's office, but for the past ten years had been working, at a salary of Rs 100 per day (approximately $2.00) for the Nimco Centre, a store where they sold savoury snacks. Her mother had never worked outside the home. Her brother, who was a year younger than her, dropped out of school after their older brother died as well, but could only find temporary part-time work. Three of the four younger sisters went to school, but the fourth 'cannot learn anything' after the death of her brother, so she stopped going to school. Mehr-un-Nisa and her sisters contributed to the household income by sewing clothes for people in the neighbourhood, but sewing jobs were only available intermittently, usually around the times of festivals.

Although the presence of Mehr-un-Nisa, the sister and daughter, was felt during Mehr-un-Nisa's representation of her life before her brother died, it was in the post-violence context of her life that these selves, and hence her relationships with her immediate family, seemed to become all-consuming.

> Lubna: 'What were your feelings at your brother's sudden death?'
> Mehr-un-Nisa: 'I fainted. I had no consciousness.'
> Lubna: 'What happened after you gained consciousness?'
> Mehr-un-Nisa: 'I was very sad after seeing my brother's face. Our brother had gone out after eating food ... at 1 o'clock at night we saw his dead face.'

Mehr-un-Nisa was under a doctor's care for a few weeks after her brother was buried. She had to terminate the treatment, since the medicines were too expensive, and her mother's cure was the priority. Her mother, however, had barely recovered since then. Since Iqbal's death she had not been able to continue the job of running the household. Mehr-un-Nisa and her older sister took on the responsibility for household chores, while her sister had the additional task of taking care of their mother. Since her sister's wedding, which took place a month before I interviewed her, Mehr-un-Nisa was in charge of the home and her mother's care. Mehr-un-Nisa, the sister, reasserted herself in the face of emptiness, and an aborted desire:

> Lubna: '… you cannot go to college on your father's income. Did you think about working for the exam as a private student who could study at home?'
>
> Mehr-un-Nisa: 'I have thought about it a lot of times, but they say leave it.'
>
> Lubna: 'Who says leave it?'
>
> Mehr-un-Nisa: 'The heart and mind say that. The rest of the sisters should study, and we should try to get them educated.'
>
> Lubna: 'When you left school, did anyone, a teacher, come to find out why?'
>
> Mehr-un-Nisa: 'Give the fee, then study. Otherwise not.'
>
> Lubna: 'Was there a way for you to get a scholarship?'
>
> Mehr-un-Nisa: 'No, nobody said anything.'
>
> Lubna: 'Were you studying science?'
>
> Mehr-un-Nisa: 'Yes.'
>
> Lubna: 'Why did you want to become a doctor?'
>
> Mehr-un-Nisa: 'When I used to see Dr. Khurshid, I would get that desire.'
>
> Lubna: 'What was it about Dr. Khurshid that you liked?'
>
> Mehr-un-Nisa: 'He talks very wisely. His words are very good. That is why I thought I should become a doctor. Then one of our teachers was becoming a doctor. She has become a doctor. She used to live in this block. Now she has gone to the city.'

For Mehr-un-Nisa, the desire to become a doctor had represented attaining wisdom and the chance to move to the city, a move symbolizing upward mobility, and perhaps freedom from class- and gender-based constraints.

Towards the end of the interview, when asked if it was possible to bring peace to Karachi, she answered: 'If we get good education and good jobs, then maybe all this will end.' Very early in the conversation, when I asked her for an analysis of who was responsible for the violence, she replied succinctly, 'It is the whole society's fault. We should give our children pens, not guns.'

Mehr-un-Nisa's selves as sister and daughter were fundamentally relational selves, deriving their agency through identification with various family members. Hierarchical power relations structured the parameters of relationality as well as the agency it enabled.[43] Mehr-un-Nisa's reminiscences about her brother, Iqbal, as the one who 'was very humorous', and without whom 'the evenings do not seem like evenings anymore', for 'when he used to come home, it was great', pointed to the joy he brought her. However, the relationship with Iqbal was imbued with meanings drawn from specific patriarchal constructions of what it meant to be a good brother or a good sister in Mehr-un-Nisa's family.[44] Iqbal worked outside the home in order to provide for the family. He was also the one to escort his sisters to school, or wherever the girls went. For Mehr-un-Nisa, he was also a window to that other world of seeming openness and liberty, and listening to his stories about work, and the people he met, afforded a vicarious pleasure. In turn, Mehr-un-Nisa, as would have behoved a good sister, reciprocated by personally taking care of Iqbal's needs at home.

Although Mehr-un-Nisa identified herself as ethnically Mohajir, it was the classed and gendered dimensions of her selves that came to the forefront in the interview. She did inhabit an ethnicized space, for all her neighbours were Mohajir, and her family was strict about finding matches within the Mohajir community. Her friends at school, however, had been Mohajir, Punjabi and Pathan. She preferred to remain immersed in her housework, and not engage with the world around her. 'Sometimes, when I think then my mind goes crazy, that why are there so many killings in the last three-four years. Why is this happening?' While Mehr-un-Nisa's relative isolation, in physical and mental terms, was the outcome of circumstances interfacing with structures, it was also, to a certain degree, a preference, representing a coping mechanism in a life-world rendered unfamiliar and chaotic by violence: 'It did not seem like this was Orangi Town anymore. Everyday, all the time, we heard the noise of firing.'

Mehr-un-Nisa also appeared uninterested in her family's history. She knew very little about her parents' migration to Karachi around the time when East Pakistan declared its independence as Bangladesh, and knew nothing at all about her family's first migration from the Indian state of Bihar to East Pakistan in 1947 (her mother told me they were from Bihar). When I asked her if she ever asked her parents about their lives before they moved to Karachi, she simply stated, 'We have got everything here, so what is the point in asking about it.' Her mother responded in a comparable, though slightly more definitive tone, when I asked her if she shared stories from her previous homes with her children: 'They do not want to hear about it. I do not want to talk about it. We are here now.' A pact seemed to exist, across generations, whereby the past was deemed redundant, irrelevant or taboo.

On the whole, the interview with Mehr-un-Nisa left me with an overwhelming impression of the starkness of it all: Mehr-un-Nisa's unembellished words; her mother's uncompromising grief and letting go of life after her son's death; the unqualified sadness in Mehr-un-Nisa's eyes; the austerity of the room where the interview took place; the harshness of the physical violence that can ravage a family; and the unmitigated burden of continuing an existence in an unjust, unfair, and inequitable world. Mehr-un-Nisa came across as a determined young woman, but her determination manifested itself in striving towards the absolute acceptance of the limits in her life. This determination was based on a realistic appraisal, from the vantage point of her knowledge and social positionality, of the gendered, classed and violent world around her.

If consciousness could be simply equated with agency, then Mehr-un-Nisa was an agent, not just in her role as sister and daughter or through her assumption of a self-contained persona, but also in her attempt to make sense of her place in the world she inhabited. However, from Mehr-un-Nisa's perspective, these particular exercises of agency—the diligent realization of household responsibilities, the self-imposed isolation, and the consciousness of limits—were the aftermath of a brother's untimely death in an unjust system, that not only allowed that death but, then, made no provisions to support the healing and financial stability of her family.

CONCLUSION

This article adds to the body of literature that explores the nature and scope of women's agency in conflict situations (for instance, Khattak 2001; Manchanda 2001; Moser and Clark 2001), through the scrutiny of two Mohajir women survivors' enactments of selves in the light of macro socio-historical and political processes and structures. The interviews with Ayesha Begum and Mehr-un-Nisa revealed different experiences of direct and structural violence as well as different reactions and responses to those experiences. Although the reading/writing of these interviews was not meant to yield generalizations about even the lives of Mohajir women survivors in Karachi, let alone women in all conflict situations, the glimpses and insights into the two women's lives raise some provocative issues about women's agency in contexts of armed conflict and violence in postcolonial nation states, where processes of ethnic, class and gender formation intersect with colonial histories and neocolonial realties.

While Ayesha Begum's constructions of her self, suffering and response to violence were grounded in history, Mehr-un-Nisa's reconstitution after the encounter with violence involved a professed detachment from history. This difference, to a certain extent, could be attributed to the age disparity between the two women. After all, Ayesha Begum had witnessed the Partition violence, personally undertaken the migration to Karachi, lived through the time of Mohajir ascendancy and decline, and was determined to ensure the betterment of her children, despite her own deprivations in the present and the past. Also, as a married woman with a sick husband, and later as a widow with children, she had enjoyed a higher degree of mobility and decision making, and had, therefore, been exposed to various opinions and perspectives in her interactions with various people. Mehr-un-Nisa was born in Karachi, too young to remember the intricacies of the politics underpinning the creation of the Mohajir identity, and as a young unmarried woman, with more restrictions on her movement, was afforded little opportunity for exposure to varied perspectives. Also, as a young woman she remained more invested in her personal future, and the present, rather than the past, offered an apparently more useful point of departure. Mehr-un-Nisa's disengagement from history, however, also stemmed from her family's way of dealing with their dual migration in 1947 and 1971, during two bloody partitions, each hailing the birth of a postcolonial nation state. The erasure of the past, for Mehr-un-Nisa's parents, and herself, allowed for a fresh start with the prospect of a future where the violence would not repeat itself, even if the everyday reality of trying to survive with some measure of dignity in the present left very little room for future plans and aspirations.

Mehr-un-Nisa's turn inwards, her deepened introspection after her brother's death, was simultaneously a rejection of the primacy of history, and a bid to accept the stark reality of her limits without any illusions. Within a socio-cultural context, where the vision of the life she had wanted could not be realized, the reassertion of her agency took the shape of reworking herself as the perfect sister and daughter, integral to the smooth running of a household with very little resources, coping with death and illness. In spite of Mehr-un-Nisa's laudable courage and clarity, this exercise of her agency did serve to reinforce gendered modes of existence. Ayesha Begum, on the other hand, was vociferous in her protests against the direct and structural violence impacting her life, with history informing her project of self-constitution as citizen-subject and mother, placing her firmly within discourses of entitlement emanating from political quarters. Ayesha Begum's agency as ethnicized citizen-subject enabled her to speak out against the injustice perpetrated against herself and her family by state apparatuses and structures, but her utilization of a politics of identity defined by boundaries of hatred, albeit in a less virulent form, for her own purposes, had repercussions for the perpetuation of xenophobia in already violent geographies. Also, her agency exhibited through a trenchant critique of her circumstances had not led to a change in her circumstances, even if it had proved to be an effective survival mechanism. In the final analysis, neither Mehr-un-Nisa nor Ayesha Begum, despite their compelling personalities, and remarkable determination, could fulfil their desires, and the enactment of their agency had the potential to lead to an entrenchment of the violence, direct or structural, in their life-worlds.

The aim here is to question our constructs of agency, as feminists of colour writing/theorizing women's agency in dire circumstances, as we attempt to debunk the myths of passive Third World women by paying attention to their agency and resistance (Mohanty 1988). While in accordance with the importance of effecting a change in the discursive representations of Third World women, I also want to reiterate Abu-Lughod's (1990) proposal that the everyday forms of women's subversions be used as a point of entry to study the working of power relations. How can our alliances with women like Mehr-un-Nisa and Ayesha Begum, who might not even consider alliances with the likes of us as useful, help us work towards postcolonial futures where agency does not translate into mere survival?

ACKNOWLEDGMENTS

I would like thank the following friends for valuable inputs during the writing of this paper: Rajib Akhter, Angana Chatterji, Kate Elder, Saba Khattak, Joshua Price, and Karen Watson-Gegeo.

NOTES

1. By 'reconstitute', I mean how women respond to circumstances and conflict in ways that change their self-understanding and relation to the world.
2. The mid-1990s was an intensely violent period in Karachi. Factions of militant groups ambushed each other and state security forces, while the state security forces clashed with alleged militants in so-called police encounters, arresting thousands of people in one day without a warrant, mostly from

the poorer areas. In addition, there were bomb blasts that killed innocent bystanders. The official death count for 1995 alone was around 2,000 people (Amnesty International 1996). See the next section in this article for the origin and history of the conflict.

3. According to Skinner et al. (1998: 6), the practice theory of selves views selves as 'grounded in history, mediated by cultural discourses and practices, and yet makers of history, of culture, of selves'. This approach embraces both social constructivism and the idea of human agency, seeing selves as being constituted through powerful discourses that are mediated, contested, and even co-produced by people as they create their selves. From such a perspective, self-making is a dynamic process, resulting in selves that shift across time and space. While an understanding of structures remains central to an understanding of how selves are constructed, it also becomes crucial in analysing people's activities and struggles.

4. Nordstrom (1997: 15) cautions against subscribing to the thread in western thought that prescribes violence as a necessary precondition for creativity. She writes, 'To make violence the font of creativity essentializes and naturalizes violence… to survive, people are forced to create… but these are not the best conditions under which to be creative.'

5. I am aware of the painful irony underwriting the use of the word 'postcolonial'. I use the term here not to signify an unequivocal state of decolonization, but merely to indicate a historical period that began when the colonizers left the subcontinent formally and physically after supposedly handing power over to the natives. While I agree with Shohat (1992) that the very idea of the end of colonialism is problematic in this neocolonial era, I still find the term useful if we read/write postcoloniality as a condition which subsumes, continues, and extends the multidimensional violence of colonialism.

6. For Anglin (1998: 145) structural violence is 'normalized and accepted as part of the status quo', even as it 'is experienced as injustice and brutality at particular intersections of race, ethnicity, class, nationality, gender, and age'. My understanding of structural violence is chiefly based on Anglin (1998), Farmer (1997), Galtung (1969, 1990, 1996), Kleinman (2000), Pilisuk and Tennant (1997), Scheper-Hughes (1992, 2002), and Uvin (1998). While these authors work from distinctively nuanced definitions of structural violence, they all utilize the concept to draw 'our attention to unequal life chances, usually caused by great inequality, injustice, discrimination, and exclusion and needlessly limiting people's physical, social, and psychological well-being' (Uvin 1998: 105). They also agree that various forms of structural violence are 'products of social arrangements created by people in ways not easily noticed' (Pilisuk and Tennant 1997).

7. While structural violence has come to be equated mostly with suffering resulting from poverty, feminist writing on the subject (for example, Anglin 1998), analyses of contexts in Africa (for example, Uvin 1998) and a strand

in recent anthropological discussions (for example, Scheper-Hughes 2002) have broadened the scope of its usage to encompass a consideration of the unequal distribution of suffering and brutality due to additional measures of social stratification, such as ethnicity, religion, gender, and age.

8. I find 'structure' a useful construct, even as I recognize the ambiguity of 'structure' as an overarching concept, which despite recent sophisticated attempts at reinvention, particularly by feminists, remains beset with problems of ahistoricity and intractability (Edgar and Sedgwick 1999). Social hierarchies do operate through structures and institutions, but societies change, structures and institutions are not completely deterministic, and individuals can intervene (see Connell 1987, for an exhaustive discussion). What is key is that structures be regarded as dynamic and that an appraisal of structures should be accompanied by an understanding of historical and geographical underpinnings.

9. Grewal and Kaplan (1994: 17) stress the urgency to locate women's issues around the world in the 'historicized particularity of their relationship' to 'scattered hegemonies'. While concurring with the imperative to situate women's concerns in the multilayered power relations within which their lives are embedded, I believe the scattered hegemonies only appear to be scattered. They can be linked together in certain times and spaces through the effects they produce in people's lives and experiences.

10. I do not claim a 'clean slate' approach to the interviews. While I am cognizant of the need to constantly interrogate theoretical frameworks in the light of empirical data, and not to use theory as a container into which the data must be poured (Lather 1991), I read and write women's constructions of self in this article through particular scholarly and experiential lenses, including the feminist lens which insists on the highlighting of women's constructions (ibid.; Phillips 1990). I work from the assumption that grounded research requires a 'reciprocal relationship between theory and data' (Lather 1991: 62), whereby a priori theoretical frameworks are used in a dialectical manner, and theoretical frameworks are not rigid, but dynamic, subject to revision and modification. Also, I do not subscribe to the idea of theories as reified discourses, generated through processes of abstraction in purely academic pursuits, offering metanarratives with ultimate explanatory power, but see them as 'frames of intelligibility' through which the world is perceived and interpreted (Ebert 1991: 122). These frames, according to this alternative viewpoint, can be formulated by anyone interested in making sense of specific aspects of reality, do not necessarily require an academic discourse for their articulation, and can draw upon sources not usually regarded as legitimate scholarship, such as narratives based on authors' personal experiences. See Davies (1994) for details about the feminist engagement with the role and place of theory.

11. While poststructuralist feminism in general has utilized notions of multiple, discontinuous and contradictory identities to decentre the humanist model of

the unequivocally rational, autonomous and unified (white) feminist subject, thereby creating spaces for hitherto unacknowledged different voices (for example, Alcoff 1988; de Lauretis 1990), it is mostly feminists of colour who have formulated a credible place for agency and resistance in a framework where the emphasis on fragmentation poses the danger of a nihilistic eschewing of political action. White feminist poststructuralists, such as Davies (1991) and Butler (1997), building on Foucauldian ideas about the unequal, heterogeneous effects of power relations as well as the viewpoint that power enables even as it constrains, do point to the possibility of resistance. For women of colour writing on the subject, selves are sites of 'struggle, effort and tension' (Alarcon 1990: 365). Multiplicity, then, translates into hybridization rather than fragmentation, and affording the potential for reconfiguring racialized, classed and gendered selves through knowledge of contexts, and their demands of identification and disidentification, paving the way for coalition-building across differences (Sandoval 2000). Also, I undertake in Chaudhry (2004a) a critical scrutiny of my own self as a postcolonial feminist researcher 'studying' women in conflict situations. As this self exists for the most part in relation to my research participants, issues with respect to their voice and agency also come up in the course of discussion. Chaudhry (1998, 1999, 2004b) also addresses the issue of agency.

12. Materialist feminism distinguishes itself from earlier Marxist feminisms by emphasizing the intersection of class with other vectors of differentiation among women, imploding monolithic conceptions of patriarchy, and exposing the linkages between the unequal distribution of resources, the making of meanings, and subjectivity (Belsey 2000; Hennessy and Ingraham 1997).

13. The project, funded by the Ford Foundation, was developed as a contribution to feminist and alternative security scholarship about South Asia by South Asian scholars. It entailed the creation of an archive of interviews with women in conflict situations as well as the publication of articles based on those interviews. I was one of six researchers who participated in the project. Although the structure of the project remained hierarchical—two of the researchers served as coordinators, and most of the interviews were conducted by research assistants 'trained' for the purpose—the entire process did reflect a remarkable spirit of collaboration among the six researchers. Besides writing our individual papers, we facilitated the workshop for the research assistants, co-developed the interview protocols, and gave our input at different stages in the project. Three of us also participated in the fieldwork. I conducted interviews with seven women survivors. The project's culmination was marked by a two-day workshop in August 2001 where the researchers in the project joined other activists and scholars in an intensive discussion around the study's findings and their relevance to feminist movements for peace.

14. Fifty-eight women were interviewed within the Karachi context of violence. The interviews were tape-recorded. In addition, the interviewers took extensive notes about the settings and interactions during the interviews. The research focused primarily on women impacted by the ethnic violence that was generated after April 1985 and has persisted in various forms to this date, but also encompasses the later sectarian killings that were an offshoot of the ethnic violence.

15. Smith (1987) and Collins (1986) provided useful starting points for the conceptualization of the research design.

16. As Saigol (2002) notes, the gender dimension and questions related to women's roles in the conflict remain missing from most accounts of the Karachi violence. Verkaaik's (2004) ethnographic study of the Mohajir Qaumi Mahaaz (MQM) in Hyderabad does incorporate a gendered analysis in its scrutiny of the masculinist underpinnings of MQM members' identities. Women, however, are absent from the narrative, and the author pleads inaccessibility to female spaces as the reason. Of the four available analyses of women in the Karachi context of violence, Shah (1998) is the only study that claims to be research-based. Shah's collection of testimonies, which includes the voices of Mohajir women, yields themes that are similar to the SDPI study when it comes to the impact of violence on women, but its analytical scope does not allow for an understanding of women's constructions of their life-worlds and their place in these worlds. Farrukh (1994), Haroon (2001) and Mumtaz (1996) write about the place and roles of women in the MQM movement. All three articles provide useful activist-oriented reports, and Haroon's story of a peace-building initiative by the Pakistani Women's Action Forum (WAF) in Karachi is especially instructive. Nevertheless, Mohajir women's perspectives are not the key focus of these papers, and even Mohajir women's experiences beyond the movement or conflict are not a concern.

17. Phillips (1990: 99–100) posits self-reflexive life stories, 'gathered in a self-critical way', as a key vehicle in the understanding of women's constructions of their selves, lives and experiences.

18. I am thankful to Oakley (1981), one of the earlier feminist critiques of the interview process, for helping me articulate the discomfort I felt with the research situation.

19. In the spirit of feminist writing (for example, Chaudhry 1999; Lather 1991; Minh-ha 1989; Visweswaran 1994), at certain junctures in this article I make myself exist as a social subject who shapes the process of inquiry and is in turn shaped by what transpires. Space restrictions do limit my exercise of self-reflexivity, since the focus here, I have decided, should be primarily on the analysis of women's realities. See also Chaudhry (2004a) for further thoughts on the issue of conducting research with women in conflict situations.

20. These official figures (Government of Pakistan 1998) have been contested from various quarters. Some sources list Karachi's population as over twelve

million (Hasan 1999). The census data remain imprecise because of a significant population of undocumented, so-called illegal immigrants from Bangladesh, Afghanistan and other countries of origin. Also, there are no exact figures available for 'legal' Afghan refugees.

21. The squatter communities, the bastis, are built on illegally occupied land along the city's drainage channels, railway lines and inside riverbeds. Most of the houses in the bastis are made of a mixture of baked and unbaked bricks, or with bricks (baked and otherwise) and metal sheets (Gayer 2003; Hasan 1999; SDPI 2001).

22. Food and equipment to British and allied troops went through Karachi. Karachi also served as a ship reparation port in 1942–45 (Gayer 2003; Hasan 1997 1999; SDPI 2001).

23. Here I draw from the history of Karachi's conflict synthesized in Khattak (2002).

24. The British recruited Punjabis heavily into the Indian army, because they were considered as a martial race (Ali 1984).

25. See Gayer (2003), Khattak (2002), Shaikh (1997), Tambiah, (1996) and Verkaaik (2004) for exhaustive and critical analyses of Karachi's conflict.

26. See, for instance, John (2003). This is also very typical of the western media's representation of Karachi's violence in general. See also Gayer (2003) for a brief on how Karachi's violence is generally viewed.

27. The riots in 1985 were triggered when a road accident involving a Pathan driver killed a young Mohajir woman. See Shaheed (1990) and Gayer (2003) for a full account.

28. 'Operation Clean-Up', meant to eradicate the militant groups who were now labelled as 'terrorists', was launched by Nawaz Sharif's government, which took power in 1990 from Benazir Bhutto, and was ousted in 1993, when Benazir Bhutto took power again after a brief period in which there was an interim, caretaking government. The game of musical chairs continued with Nawaz Sharif becoming prime minister again in 1997, after Benazir Bhutto's assembly was dissolved yet again. However, despite their differences, Benazir Bhutto persisted with 'Operation Clean-Up' in Sindh.

29. I borrow this translation from Shaikh (1997: 3). The use of the identity label Mohajir is meant to evoke the first migration of significance in Islamic history, that of the Prophet Mohammed and his followers' migration from Makkah to Madina in the wake of persecution by non-believers.

30. See Saigol (2002) for insights into the deployment of the term Mohajir as an ethnic and political label; Gayer (2003) and Shaikh (1997) for analytical histories of the evolution of the Mohajir identity; and Alavi (1989) for a discussion of ethnic formations in Pakistan. All these writings highlight the constructed nature of the Mohajir identity.

31. Gujarati and Madrasi are examples of other languages spoken by some Mohajirs (SDPI 2001; Shaikh 1997). Punjabi-speaking populations crossing

the border into Pakistan from the Indian side of the Punjab are not included in this usage of Mohajir as a proper noun, although in certain parts of Punjab these populations are still referred to as Mohajir to distinguish them from people inhabiting those areas before Partition (World Bank 2002).

32. My account of the genesis and rise of the MQM is based on Gayer (2003), Shaikh (1997), Tambiah (1996), Tan and Kudaisya (2000), and Verkaaik (2004).

33. The MQM also has a Women's Wing, although the women members of the party do not enjoy the same status as men. Also the female membership of MQM has never equalled the male membership numerically. Still, as Haroon (2001: 183) notes, 'Since 1947, there has not been such a mobilization of women'. See also Farrukh (1994) and Mumtaz (1996) for earlier accounts of women in the MQM.

34. This was brought to my attention by journalist colleagues in India during a discussion at a three-day seminar entitled 'Reflections on Violence' organized by the Seminar Foundation, Neemrana, India, 1–3 December 2001. See also Ahmar (1996) for this theory.

35. Here I echo DuPlessis (1990) who suggests that representation itself becomes a site of struggle in the works of twentieth-century western women modernists. These women are faced with the challenge of expressing themselves in an aesthetic tradition that has colonized female figures. DuPlessis compellingly details the ambiguous power of these women writers as they attempted to rupture and disturb the very systems of meaning from which they were drawing.

36. See Lather (1991) for a perspective on participatory research whereby the research participants co-construct the parameters defining a project and are involved in the entire project, from the conceptualization stage to the writing up of the analysis and application as well as dissemination of findings.

37. Although Musharraf, the army general, who seized power through a coup in 1999, is a Mohajir in that his Urdu-speaking family immigrated from the Indian side of the border to Pakistan, Punjabis still constitute a heavy majority of the army and bureaucracy. According to Tambiah (1996), Punjabi hegemony started to take shape in the 1950s, for the Pakistan movement was spearheaded mostly by north Indian Urdu-speaking Muslims. He writes, 'Punjabi dominance in contemporary Pakistan's politics is one of the factors in the discontent of certain provinces and lies behind the stress on the need for provincial autonomy and for keeping the federal government in check. Punjabi dominance is the inevitable backdrop to any study of Pakistan's ethnic conflicts' (pp. 165–66). The predominance of Punjabis in the Pakistani military, however, was a post-independence continuation of a colonial practice. In the context of the Karachi violence, being a Punjabi also meant sharing the ethnicity of the police contingent reputed to be the experts in torture. During the 1990s, the Punjab Police was sent out to

Karachi on several occasions to help curb the violence. The 'Rangers', a national paramilitary force, also deployed during armed violence in Karachi, was heavily Punjabi.

38. I received permission to use her first name.

39. See Shaikh (1997) for the impact of police and army action against supposed MQM activists and their communities in the 1990s. Also see Amnesty International Reports on Pakistan.

40. See earlier section. See Tan and Kudaisya (2000) and Shaikh (1997) for detailed accounts of the origins and history of the Sindhi-Mohajir strife.

41. I touch upon this issue in the section entitled 'On Karachi's Conflict'. See Verkaaik (2001).

42. I received permission to use her first name.

43. Joseph (1999: 2–3) writes, 'Relational selfhood and patriarchy are not seen to be inimical to the coexistence of agency and the self. ... The agency of the self emerges experientially and existentially although it may not be the agency of the bounded, separative individual.'

44. Joseph (1994) presents an analysis of how patriarchy underwrites and infuses relationality between brothers and sisters in the context of Lebanon.

REFERENCES

Abu-Lughod, Lila (1990). 'The Romance of Resistance: Tracing Transformations of Power through Bedouin Women', *American Ethnologist*, 17(1): 41–55.

Ahmar, Moonis (1996). 'Ethnicity and State Power in Pakistan: The Karachi Crisis', *Asian Survey*, 36(10): 1031–48.

Alarcon, Norma (1990). 'The Theoretical Subject of *This Bridge Called My Back* and Anglo-American Feminism', in Gloria Anzaldua (ed.), *Making Face, Making Soul/Hacienda Caras: Creative and Critical Perspectives by Women of Color*, pp. 356–69. San Francisco, CA: Aunt Lute.

Alavi, Hamza (1989). 'Politics of Ethnicity in India and Pakistan', in Hamza Alavi and John Harris (eds), *Sociology of Developing Societies: South Asia*, pp. 222–46. New York: Monthly Review Press.

Alcoff, Linda (1988). 'Cultural Feminism versus Poststructuralism: The Identity Crisis in Feminist Theory', *Signs*, 13(3): 405–36.

Ali, Tariq (1984). *Can Pakistan Survive?* London: Pelican Press.

Amnesty International (1996). 'Pakistan: Human Rights in Karachi'. Available at: http://www.amnestyusa.org/countries/pakistan/document.do. Last accessed October 2003.

Anglin, Mary K. (1998). 'Feminist Perspectives on Structural Violence', *Identities*, 5(2): 145–51.

Belsey, Catherine (2000). 'A Future for Feminist Materialist Criticism?', in Anna Tripp (ed.), *Gender*, pp. 29–41. New York: Palgrave.

Bowen, John (2002). 'The Myth of Global Ethnic Conflict', in Alexander L.

Hinton (ed.), *Genocide: An Anthropological Reader*, pp. 333–43. Malden, MA: Blackwell Publishers.

Butler, Judith (1997). *The Psychic Life of Power: Theories in Subjection*. Stanford, CA: Stanford University Press.

Chaudhry, Lubna (1998). 'We Are Graceful Swans Who can Also be Crows: Hybrid Identities of

Pakistani Muslim Women', in Shamita Das Dasgupta (ed.), *A Patchwork Shawl: Chronicles of South Asian Women in America*, pp. 46–61. Newark, NJ: Rutgers University Press.

———— (1999). 'Fragments of a Hybrid's Discourse', in Sangeeta Gupta (ed.), *Emerging Voices: Writings by Women of South Asian Origin*, pp.79–91. Thousand Oaks, CA: Sage Publications.

———— (2004a). 'The Postcolonial Feminist as Conductor/Reader of Interviews with Women in Conflict Situations', SDPI Working Paper Series, 88. Islamabad: Sustainable Development Policy Institute.

———— (2004b). 'Women and Poverty: Salient Findings from a Gendered Analysis of a Quasi-Anthropological Study in Rural Punjab and Sindh', SDPI Research Report Series, 28. Islamabad: Sustainable Development Policy Institute.

Collins, Patricia Hill (1986). 'Learning from the Outsider Within: The Sociological Significance of Black Feminist Thought', *Social Problems*, 33(6): 14–32.

Connell, R.W. (1987). *Gender and Power: Society, the Person, and Sexual Politics*. Stanford, CA: Stanford University Press.

Das, V. and A. Kleinman (2000). 'Introduction', in Veena Das, Arthur Kleinman, Mamphela Ramphele and Pamela Reynolds (eds), *Violence and Subjectivity*, pp. 1–18. Berkeley: University of California Press.

Davies, Bronwyn (1991). 'The Concept of Agency: A Feminist Poststructuralist Analysis', *Social Analysis*, 30: 42–53.

Davies, Carole Boyce (1994). *Black Women, Writing, and Identity: Migrations of the Subject*. New York: Routledge.

de Lauretis, Teresa (1990). 'Eccentric Subjects: Feminist Theory and Historical Consciousness', *Feminist Studies*, 16(1): 115–50.

de Mel, Neloufer (2003). 'Fractured Narratives, Totalizing Violence: Notes on Women in Conflict: Sri Lanka and Pakistan', SDPI Working Paper, 83. Islamabad: Sustainable Development Policy Institute.

DuPlessis, Rachel (1990). *The Pink Guitar: Writing as Feminist Practice*. London: Routledge.

Ebert, Teresa (1991). 'Political Semiosis in/of American Cultural Studies', *American Journal of Semiotics*, 8(1–2): 113–35.

Edgar, A. and P. Sedgwick (1999). *Key Concepts in Cultural Theory*. New York: Routledge.

Farmer, Paul (1997). 'On Suffering and Structural Violence: A View from Below', in Arthur Kleinman, Veena Das and Margaret Lock (eds), *Social Suffering*, pp. 261–85. Berkeley: University of California Press.

Farrukh, Sheen (1994). 'Women and Ethnic Identity: A Case Study of MQM', in Nighat Said Khan, Rubina Saigol and Afiya Shehrbano Zia (eds), *Locating the Self: Perspectives on Women and Multiple Identities*, pp. 205–11. Lahore: ASR Publications.

Frankenberg, R. and L. Mani (1993). 'Crosscurrents, Crosstalk: Race, "Postcoloniality" and the Politics of Location', *Cultural Studies*, 7(2): 292–310.

Galtung, John (1969). 'Violence, Peace, and Peace Research', *Journal of Peace Research*, 6(1): 167–91.

———— (1990). 'Cultural Violence', *Journal of Peace Research*, 27(3): 291–305.

———— (1996). *Peace by Peaceful Means: Peace and Conflict, Development and Civilization*. London: Sage Publications.

Gayer, Laurent (2003). 'A Divided City: "Ethnic" and "Religious" Conflicts in Karachi, Pakistan', Paper presented at the 1st Pakistan Seminar organized by the International Institute for Asian Studies and the International Institute for the Study of Islam in the Modern World, Amsterdam, 24 March.

Government of Pakistan (1998). *Population Census Report*. Islamabad: National Statistics Bureau.

Grewal, I. And C. Kaplan (1994). 'Introduction', in Inderpal Grewal and Caren Kaplan (eds), *Scattered Hegemonies: Postmodernity and Transnational Feminist Practices*, pp. 1–33. Minneapolis: University of Minnesota Press.

Haroon, Anis (2001). '"They Use Us and Others Abuse Us": Women and the MQM Conflict', in

Rita Manchanda (ed.), *Women, War and Peace in South Asia: Beyond Victimhood to Agency*, pp. 177–213. New Delhi: Sage Publications.

Hasan, Arif (1987). 'A Generation Comes of Age', *The Herald*, October, pp. 52–53.

———— (1997). 'The Growth of a Metropolis', in Hamida Khuhro and Anwer Mooraj (eds), *Karachi: Mega-City of Our Times*, pp. 171–96. Karachi: Oxford University Press.

———— (1999). *Understanding Karachi: Planning and Reform for the Future*. Karachi: City Press.

Hennessy, R. and C. Ingraham (eds) (1997). *Materialist Feminism: A Reader in Class, Difference, and Women's Lives*. New York: Routledge.

Hussain, Akmal (1990). 'The Karachi Riots of December 1986: Crisis of State and Civil Society in Pakistan', in Veena Das (ed.), *Mirrors of Violence: Communities, Riots, and Survivors in South Asia*, pp. 185–93. Delhi: Oxford University Press.

Jalal, Ayesha (1990). *The State of Martial Rule: The Origins of Pakistan's Political Economy of Defence*. Cambridge: Cambridge University Press.

———— (1994) 'The State and Political Privilege in Pakistan', in Myron Weiner and Ali Banuazizi (eds), *The Politics of Social Transformation in Afghanistan, Iran, and Pakistan*, pp. 152–85. Syracuse, NY: Syracuse University Press.

John, Wilson (2003). *Karachi: A Terror Capital in the Making*. New Delhi: Observer Research Foundation.

Joseph, Suad (1994). 'Brother/Sister Relationships: Connectivity, Love, and Power in the Reproduction of American Patriarchy', *American Ethnologist*, 21(1): 50–73.

———— (1999). 'Introduction', in Suad Joseph (ed.), *Intimate Selving in Arab Families: Gender, Self, and Identity*, pp. 1–17. Syracuse, NY: Syracuse University Press.

Khattak, Saba G. (2001). 'Home as Space and Home as Place: Women's Agency during Times of Conflict', Paper presented at the SDPI Workshop on Women, Conflict, and Security, Islamabad.

———— (2002). 'Violence and the Centrality of Home: Women's Experiences of Insecurity in the Karachi Conflict', SDPI Working Paper Series, 73. Islamabad: Sustainable Development Policy Institute.

Kleinman, Arthur (2000). 'The Violences of Everyday Life: The Multiple Forms and Dynamics of Social Violence', in Veena Das, Arthur Kleinman, Mamphela Ramphele, and Pamela Reynolds (eds), *Violence and Subjectivity*, pp. 226–41. Berkeley: University of California Press.

Lari, Y., and M.S. Lari (1996). *Karachi: The Dual City under the Raj*. Karachi: Heritage Foundation and Oxford University Press.

Lather, Patti (1991). *Getting Smart: Feminist Research and Pedagogy with/in the Postmodern*. New York: Routledge.

Manchanda, Rita (ed.) (2001). *Women, War and Peace in South Asia: Beyond Victimhood to Agency*. New Delhi: Sage Publications.

Minh-ha, Trinh T. (1989). *Woman, Native, Other: Writing Postcoloniality and Feminism*. Bloomington and Indianapolis: Indiana University Press.

Mohanty, Chandra T. (1987). 'Feminist Encounters: Locating the Politics of Experience', *Copyright*, 1(1): 30–44.

———— (1988). 'Under Western Eyes: Feminist Scholarship and Colonial Discourses', *Feminist Review*, 30: 61–88.

Moser, C.O.N. and F.C. Clark (eds) (2001). *Victims, Perpetrators, or Actors? Gender, Armed Violence, and Political Violence*. New Delhi: Kali for Women.

Mumtaz, Khawar (1996). 'The Gender Dimension in Sindh's Ethnic Conflict', in Kumar Rupesinghe and Khawar Mumtaz (eds), *Internal Conflicts in South Asia*, pp. 144–63. London: Sage Publications.

Nordstrom, Carolyn (1997). *A Different Kind of War Story*. Philadelphia: University of Pennsylvania Press.

Oakley, Ann (1981). 'Interviewing Women: A Contradiction in Terms', in Helen Roberts (ed.), *Doing Feminist Research*, pp. 30–62. London: Routledge and Kegan Paul.

Patai, Daphne (1988). 'Constructing a Self: A Brazilian Life Story', *Feminist Studies*, 14(1): 143–66.

Phillips, Lynne (1990). 'Rural Women in Latin America: Directions for Future Research', *Latin American Research Review*, 25(3): 89–107.

Pilisuk, M. and J. Tennant (1997). 'The Hidden Structure of Violence', *ReVision*, 20(2): 25–27.

Rahman, Tariq (1996). *Language and Politics in Pakistan*. Karachi: Oxford University Press.

Rizvi, Hasan-Askari (2000). *Military, State, and Society in Pakistan*. New York: St. Martin's Press.

Saigol, Rubina (2002). 'The Partition of Self: Mohajir Women's Sense of Identity and Nationhood', SDPI Working Paper, 77. Islamabad: Sustainable Development Policy Institute.

Sandoval, Chela (1991). 'US Third World Feminism: The Theory and Method of Oppositional Consciousness in the Postmodern World', *Genders*, 10(1): 1–24.

Sandoval, Chela (2000). *Methodology of the Oppressed*. Minneapolis: University of Minnesota Press.

Scheper-Hughes, Nancy (1992). *Death without Weeping: The Violence of Everyday Life in Brazil*. Berkeley: University of California Press.

———— (2002). 'The Genocidal Continuum: Peace-Time Crimes', in Jeannette Mageo (ed.), *Power and the Self*, pp. 29–47. Cambridge: Cambridge University Press.

SDPI (2001). *Archive on Women, Conflict, and Security*. Islamabad: Sustainable Development Policy Institute.

Shah, Nafisa (1998). *Blood, Tears, and Lives to Live: Women in the Crossfire*. Lahore: Human Rights Commission of Pakistan.

Shaheed, Farida (1990). 'The Pathan-Muhajir Conflicts, 1985–6: A National Perspective', in Veena Das (ed.), *Mirrors of Violence: Communities, Riots, and Survivors in South Asia*, pp. 194–214. Delhi: Oxford University Press.

Shaikh, Nermeen (1997). 'Migrant Nation: Ethnicity and Ethnic Violence among the Mohajirs of Karachi', unpublished MPhil dissertation, Cambridge University.

Shohat, Ella (1992). 'Notes on the "Post-colonial"', *Social Text*, 31(2): 99–113.

Skinner, D., D. Holland and A. Pach III (1998). 'Selves in Time and Place: An Introduction', in Debra Skinner, Alfred Pach III and Dorothy Holland (eds), *Selves in Time and Place: Identities, Experience, and History in Nepal*, pp. 3–16. New York: Rowman & Littlefield.

Smith, Dorothy (1987). *The Everyday World as Problematic*. Toronto: University of Toronto Press.

Srinivasan, Amrit (1990). 'The Survivor in the Study of Violence', in Veena Das (ed.), *Mirrors of Violence: Communities, Riots, and Survivors in South Asia*, pp. 305–20. Delhi: Oxford University Press.

Tambiah, Stanley J. (1996). *Leveling Crowds: Ethnonationalist Conflicts and Collective Violence in South Asia*. Berkeley: University of California Press.

Tan, T.Y. and G. Kudaisya (2000). *The Aftermath of Partition in South Asia*. London: Routledge.

Uvin, Peter (1998). *Aiding Violence: The Development Enterprise in Rwanda*. West Hartford, CT: Kumarian Press.

Verkaaik, Oskar (2001). 'The Captive State: Corruption, Intelligence Agencies, and Ethnicity in Pakistan', in Thomas Blom Hansen and Finn Stepputat (eds), *States of Imagination: Ethnographic Explorations of the Postcolonial State*, pp. 345–64. Durham, NC: Duke University Press.

——— (2004). *Migrants and Militants: Fun and Urban Violence in Pakistan.* Princeton, NJ: Princeton University Press.

Visweswaran, Kamala (1994). *Fictions of Feminist Ethnography.* Minneapolis: University of Minnesota Press.

World Bank (2002). *Pakistan Qualitative Poverty Survey 2001.* Washington, DC: World Bank.

Wright, Theodore P., Jr. (1991). 'Periphery-Periphery Relations and Ethnic Conflict in Pakistan: Sindhis, Muhajirs, and Punjabis', *Comparative Studies in Society and History*, 22(4): 576–96.

Zulaika, J. and W.A. Douglass (1996). *Terror and Taboo: The Follies, Fables, and Faces of Terrorism.* New York: Routledge.

8

The Erotics and Politics of Militarization

Communalism and Sexual Violence in Gujarat

Kavita Panjabi

'On 28th morning our entire area was attacked with people swaying in matadors, scooters, trucks, and even private cars. They were about 20–25,000. Suddenly they attacked us; we are residents of Naroda Patia. First they started beating the young people with various types of weapons. They also killed them brutally. We started running on our own. I hid myself behind a bush…. My mother too was running, and no sooner had she stopped for breath…. After killing my uncles their eyes fell on us. They started pulling my sister. My grandmother begged for their mercy, asked them to spare my sister as her marriage had been fixed. They killed my grandmother with a sword. Then they asked her sister to say "Jai Sia Ram".[1] She refused. Many policemen were standing watching the crime. We were pleading with them to give us protection but they were indifferent to all our cries and tortures. On the contrary they started shooting at us. To save myself I hid behind a bush. From there I noticed that they had pulled my sister towards them and were doing something forcefully on her… I wanted to cry for help; someone closed my mouth. Then I watched them burn my sister along with my grandmother and her sister.' (Reshma: 7 years, Resident of Naroda Patia, Ahmedabad)[2]

'On February 28, 2002 the mob started chasing us with burning tyres…. We saw about 8–10 rapes. We saw them strip [a] 16-year-old…. We saw a girl's vagina being slit open. Then they were burnt. Now there is no evidence.' (Kulsum Bibi, Shah e Alam Camp, 27 March 2002)[3]

It is to emphasize the complex power of testimonies of sexual violence, that I begin my paper by citing two such testimonies—that are discomfiting precisely because they represent the experience of violation of self, dignity and identity that sexual violence effects. The collective, public, celebratory, performative, and ritualized nature of the sexual abuse of Muslim women by Hindutva (Hindu extremist) militants in Gujarat in 2002 necessitates a rethinking of the dynamics of sexualized violence. There is an intimate connection between violence as a sexual act, and sexuality as an intimate aspect of our emotional, aesthetic, intellectual, even spiritual selves and formations of identity. It forces us to reflect on the schism that divides analyses of sexual violence from sexuality as a realm of pleasure and desire in understanding the powerful erotic content of violence against women.[4]

Theorizations, which conceptualize sexual violence solely as an attribute of power asserted over women, to the exclusion of considerations of sexuality, are often motivated by a justified need to highlight its exploitative and oppressive dimensions. Yet they miss the point that sexual violence not only impinges upon sexuality at the deepest and most intimate levels of identity, but is also motivated by political constructions of identity that structure hostile and violent acts of sex as necessary, even sacrosanct, in the maintenance of nation and national identity.

Wilhelm Reich (1975: 17) states that 'Fascism countenances that religiosity that stems from sexual perversion, and it transforms the masochistic character of the old patriarchal religion of suffering into a sadistic religion'. This article explores how Hindu nationalism incorporates sexual violation as the cornerstone of militancy, developing intimate connections between sexuality and the project of nationalism. It investigates the ideological constructions that form the rubric of a Hindu authoritarian regime that is premised on the sexual violation of minority women. In *Fascist Virilities*, her study of fascism in Italy, Spackman asks: 'How…are different interpellations—religious, political, familial, racial and gendered—bound together to form a unified fascist discourse?' (1996: xi), and demonstrates how it is that the interpellation of virility fulfils a role of condensation with respect to the 'other'. While this is of central relevance to a analysis of events in Gujarat in 2002 too, I argue that in order to understand the nature of socio-political constructions by which regimes continue to enlist consensus, both active and passive, of increasingly militant populations in more and more horrific forms of sexual violence, it is crucial to understand the connections that are structured between sexual violence and notions of pleasure, desire and the sacred.

The study of nationalism and sexuality yields some insights into the nature of such conjunctures between identity, sexuality and sexual violence, precisely because both nationalism and sexuality are sites where catalytic connections are forged between political and public contexts and intimate, private realms. Parker points out, 'Whenever the power of nation is evoked...we are more likely than not to find it couched as a love of country: an eroticized nationalism' (Parker et al. 1992: 1). They assert that both nationalism and eroticization function as 'volatile sites for condensing and displacing the ecstasies and terrors of political life' (ibid.: 14), as the scripts of both are routinely rewritten across history.

This article elaborates the connections between constructions of a militant communal[5] (Hindu) fascism, repressed erotic sensibilities, and the systematic sexual abuse of women from minority (Muslim) communities in Gujarat 2002. It examines how the Gujarat genocide marked one such recasting of both nationalism and sexuality into a militant Hindu nationalism and the perversely eroticized sexual abuse of Muslim women in the service of a brutally violent communal fascism. I draw links between fascism and genocide, in elaborating on the genocidal violence in Gujarat.

The carnage that took place in Gujarat in 2002 constitutes a genocide: the communal violence unleashed in Gujarat was neither spontaneous, nor a backlash; the majority community had been prepared for it; and there was direct and public incitement to violence. Organized mobs of Hindus *systematically* butchered and burnt Muslims and Muslim-owned property across Gujarat, including the major cities of Ahmedabad, Vadodara, Rajkot, Bharuch and Gandhinagar. The police and other law-enforcement agencies were prominent in their complicity, and at best in their absence and inefficacy. And even though the army was called in eventually, the violence continued to spread to rural areas and continued into the month of May (Chenoy et al. 2002; Hameed et al. 2002; Panjabi et al. 2002). Gujarat was a marker of much more than ordinary militarization (by this I refer to militancy enacted by Hindu groups)—it represented the consolidation of a fascism premised on a programmed sexual violence that buttressed all its levels of functioning. Banaji argues, 'Fascism is a politics of spectacles. As such, it belongs to the repertoire of forms of manipulation through which all authoritarian movements seek to reinforce their hold over the masses' (2002: 5–7). In addition to performativity and interpellation through spectacle, she elaborates three critical aspects of fascism: 'nationalism as the core of fascist ideology, involving a deification of the nation; …a culture of authoritarianism and repression; … and a form of genocide or ethnic cleansing [that] is implicit in the programme of every fascist movement' (ibid.). We are confronted by these aspirations in the Rashtriya Swyamsevak Sangh's (RSS, the umbrella organization of the Hindutva forces) mandate and its idealization of the Holocaust in Nazi Germany.

Nationalism, repression, genocide, and their reinforcement through spectacle in both discourse and action in Gujarat were integrally constructed on the grounds of sexuality, and geared towards sexual abuse of the 'other'. The triumph of such fascist populism does not rest upon rational or scientific appeals to the popular mind; in Gujarat its success derived from the inculcation of sexual terror of the Muslim as other, and from a vengeful ecstasy of sexual abuse displaced onto the site of a sanctified Hindu nationalism. In Gujarat, the macabre of sexual violence was enacted in a context where the pursuit of domination was marked, and enabled by, its simultaneous eroticization.

WEAPON OF WAR

What marks the massacres of Gujarat as distinctly different from the carnage that erupted between Hindus and Muslims during the Partition that heralded the emergence of the nation states of India and Pakistan is that, in Gujarat, mass violence was unleashed by fundamentalist political parties and systematically perpetuated by a majoritarian state machinery against its own minority citizens (Chenoy et al. 2002; *Communalism Combat* 2002; Grover 2002; Hameed et al., 2002). In the genocidal programme in Gujarat in 2002 (the beginnings of which were already evident in Surat in 1992 Agrawal (1995), sexual abuse became one of the *chief* weapons of war and was fully premeditated and planned, with a stress on the *necessity* of rape (ibid.); an act of power in an individual context was transformed into a *public spectacle* and a *ritual performance* in a collective context; and, far from any feeling of guilt, shame, or embarrassment, there was unashamed elation, public *celebration*, and a glorified narration of brutal acts of sexual violence—all in the name of 'Hindu' nationalism. Such sexual violence, including rape and butchery of women and girls of all ages, followed by burning to destroy evidence (Hameed et al. 2002; People's Union for Democratic Rights 2002; Chenoy et al. 2002; Panjabi et al. 2002), has not only become *central* to forms of militarization, it is also an instance of the shifts that are taking place in relation to gendered violence as a weapon of war.

Even in a nation founded on the violence of Partition, which marked one of the most horrendous histories of sexual abuse and gendered violence of both Hindu and Muslim women, the events that took place in Gujarat in 2002 evoke unprecedented outrage. The nature and degree of brutality against a minority community, especially women, as well as the fact that it was a state-sponsored pogrom, posed perhaps the greatest challenge—to both the women's movement and the basic principles of democracy—that India has witnessed since independence. The response of civil society too was unprecedented, resulting in no less than forty-five citizens' reports testifying to eyewitness accounts of the carnage. I was part of a three women citizen's team from Calcutta that went to Gujarat two months after the carnage, and reported on the ways in which children and the young had been affected. Our report, *The Next Generation: In the Wake of the Genocide* (Panjabi et al. 2002), recorded the immediate, visible and palpable impact of the pogrom on children, both boys and girls, from affected communities. Yet there was more that remained unexplored, that I had learnt through conversations and interviews with victims, local activists, educationists and lawyers, as well as through my own experiences of having to confront the responsibility of having a Hindu identity by birth (that I had so far considered irrelevant in a secular democratic nation) that allowed me the privilege of a security denied Muslim women and men in India. Above all, questions regarding the *subjective* transformations that have been wrought, to enable the 'normalizing' of such grotesque violence, continue to haunt me to this day. This essay is an attempt to return to some of these questions.

THE SOCIO-ECONOMIC CONTEXT

Gujarat is also a terrifying augury of a grim future. The build up to the pogrom, which ran parallel to the process of enhanced economic liberalization in India, was accompanied by a localized but severe form of militarization that now threatens to spread across the country. This included, as we found through our work, equipping hundreds of thousands of Hindu households with swords and *trishuls* (tridents) beginning at least as early as November 2001, establishing hundreds of youth camps across the state for training in the use of these weapons, and the intensification of a militant ideology in right wing women's organizations in the name of 'empowerment'. The Gujarat government's complicity with the Sangh Parivar groups of Hindu extremist organizations, which has been well documented,[6] left over 2,000 people massacred, 500 missing, and approximately 250–300 girls and women gang-raped and killed. Almost 200,000 Muslims were hounded out of their homes, of whom approximately 61,000 remained displaced four years after the massacre.[7] In addition, the economic losses of the Muslim community were estimated to be Rs 4,500 crores (*Communalism Combat* 2002).

The severe communal violence of 2002 is significantly rooted in the changing political economy of Gujarat. Jan Breman (2001) has demonstrated the ways in which the regime of neo-liberalism has worsened the plight of labour at the bottom of Ahmedabad's urban economy. The events of 2002 became possible in the context of a policy regime that has not addressed the brutal consequences of a market-led mode of capitalist production, and the eclipse of Gandhian values that has led to the shrinking of social space needed for humanizing economic growth. The rapid decline of the textile industry, with more than fifty mills closing down and at least 100,000 workers losing their jobs within the last twenty years, has resulted in the creation of a huge labour reserve that is now pushed into the informal sector, thoroughly depriving citizens of their former economic dominance and vitality. The sites of the worst violence were ex-mill localities populated by the social segments of subaltern Hindus and Muslims. It is from these lumpenized subaltern castes that the front organizations of the Sangh Parivar were able to mobilize mercenaries to assist in the operation of killing, burning and looting (ibid.).

In addition, the trade union movement, which at one time had more than 150,000 members, used to play a central role in defusing clashes through appeals to working class solidarity. The closure of textile mills has now reduced the movement to less than one-tenth of its former strength and depleted of significant economic and political power. Neither have other social movements been able to stem the rising tide of communalism (Breman 2002). Throughout much of the twentieth century, the social life of the industrial working class had also been organized in ways which facilitated interaction between people of different identities: 'The "Other" was not at a distance but highly visible and touchable as a workmate, a neighbour or a friend with whom close contact was maintained both within and outside the mill' (ibid.). But in the aftermath of the 1969 riots in Ahmedabad, organized by the RSS, the ghettoization of Muslims and growth of mafia-like bodies within Hindu and Muslim communities has intensified both crime and communal conflict.

The year of the riots, 2002, also witnessed the first widespread attacks by lower caste and Adivasi (tribal) communities on Muslims. The success of the KHAM, the Kshatriya Harijan (former 'untouchable' caste)-Adivasi-Muslim combination, mobilized by the Congress as an election strategy in 1980, had been perceived by the upper castes as a threat to their political and economic domination, and resulted in anti-reservation (affirmative action) agitations in 1981 and 1985 (Yagnik 2002: 20). The last two decades, however, were marked by the mobilization of low and intermediate castes by Sangh Parivar organizations to broaden the base of communal Hindu forces. To achieve social acceptance into the Hindutva-fold, these previously denigrated segments had played an actively antagonistic role against the Muslim population during the 2002 violence (Breman 2002). It is significant that the tribals of south Gujarat did not participate in the violence, unlike their northern counterparts who had been actively mobilized by the Hindutva forces (Yagnik 2002: 22).

However, while the underprivileged of both urban and rural society were incited to engage in looting, and in violent combat with Muslims, it is the urban middle class that is the most communalized. The middle and entrepreneur class not only justified the open violence and the role of the state, they too took active part in the mass looting of Muslim establishments. Accounts of men and women on the rampage in departmental stores testified to the role that the consumerist culture of globalization had played in intensifying economic tensions that were then played out between the Hindu and Muslim sections of the middle class. It has also been observed that this same class is perpetrating increased violence in the private sphere in the form of female foeticide and infanticide, for the dismal sex-ratio revealed by the 2001 Census, of 879 females to 1,000 males, is as much an indication of violence within the family as it is of the increase in male migrant populations (ibid.: 22).

A diverse ideological, educational, political, and economic apparatus is harnessed in the process of 'normalizing' the rabid communalism and violent masculinity of the Hindutva groups. The organization of pervasive militant forces, including that of women, that perpetuate orgies of violence, an extensive educational system for spreading the ideology of hate, an aggressive anti-Islamic and anti-Pakistan ideological apparatus, an efficient network of foreign funding, and a sophisticated technology of terror have become *integral* to the very notion of nationalism for millions of men and women across India, and continue to remain firmly in place to ensure its continuity and spread.

Activities were not restricted to Gujarat alone. A year later, in March 2003, there was news of 100,000 trishuls having entered even West Bengal, the bastion of the left, as well as of a retaliatory mass distribution of other weapons, such as the *panchshuls* (five pronged weapons resembling tridents),[8] amongst Muslims across the country. It has also been observed that Gujarat represents a condensed culmination of the activities of the Hindutva forces in the decade beginning with the demolition of the Babri Masjid in Ayodhya in 1992. Individual features of Gujarat have been anticipated and experimented with since the Ramjanmabhoomi movement began: in Meerut, Maliana, Bhagalpur, Ayodhya, Mumbai, Surat, Bhopal, Manoharpur in Orissa, and countless other places (Agrawal 1995; Chatterji 2004; Sarkar 2002).

Even if we do develop intellectual clarity regarding these issues, the practical immensity of tackling them is confounding—it involves confronting decades of ideological training that has continued to proliferate across the country in over 30,000 *shakhas*[9] and 20,000 RSS schools.[10] The genocide in Gujarat was perpetrated by various mobs of 5,000 to 15,000 who collected swiftly to execute the massacre (*Communalism Combat* 2002). No other organization or political party in India currently has such a massive base, efficient infrastructure or sustained history of training.

The communalization of education, and a systematic crackdown on minority children had begun in Gujarat months, even years, prior to the pogrom,[11] jeopardizing the future of Muslim children in the state. People talked to our fact-finding team/our citizen's inquiry team about minority children being forced to withdraw from private schools, of the differences in the numbers admitted in municipality schools and the corresponding phasing out of these schools in stages in minority areas, and of the pressure to conform to the appearance and dress codes of the majority community in colleges in the build up to 27 February. Community members discussed the looting of computers and equipment from the better-off institutions by largely Hindu mobs in the direct aftermath of the Godhra train incident,[12] and spoke of the large-scale arrests and torture of school children and college students, and of the continued problems relating to the examinations (Panjabi et al. 2002: 25–35). In addition, the Bharatiya Janata Party (BJP), while it was in government at the centre, launched a proposal to introduce compulsory military training in schools.[13] The women's wing of World Hindu Council (Vishwa Hindu Parishad, VHP) currently holds training camps in several locations in India, which, according to journalists reports, are 'cauldrons of hostility and inject hatred against Muslims and Christian minorities' and where 'girls too learn martial arts, are trained to use guns, leap through rings of fire, fight with knives and wooden truncheons, and are "ordained" with metal tridents'.[14]

The international dimensions of the situation are significant to understanding the context of violence in Gujarat, in terms of discursive formations and economic backing. In addressing various dimensions of violence, Das and Kleinman's work explores how a transnational flow of images can lodge itself in the subconscious of a relatively peaceful culture and alter the experience of social suffering (Das and Kleinman 2001: 4). School textbooks in Gujarat were marked by an admiration for Hitler and Nazism for years prior to the pogrom,[15] while the local iconography of hostility against Muslims is increasingly sustained by an international anti-Islamic sentiment. Strategic linkages drawn between such select international perceptions and local representations 'validate', normalize and reinforce a culture of hate, and simultaneously desensitize populations to the lived suffering caused by the violence of such hatred.

The international dimensions of the situation are also significant. After 9/11, the identification of Indian Muslims with Pakistan, as virulent enemies of the Indian nation, was amplified (Chenoy et al. 2002; *Communalism Combat* 2002). In a strategic move to posit Muslims as national 'enemies of the nation', the burning of a bogie on 27 February 2002, of the Sabarmati Express carrying Hindu *karsevak*s in which fifty-eight people were killed in Godhra, upheld as 'justification' for the three days of 'riots' that followed, was posited as a Pakistani ploy to destabilize India (Chenoy et al. 2002). After 9/11, the identification of Indian Muslims with Pakistan, as virulent enemies of the Indian nation, was amplified (ibid.; *Communalism Combat*, 2002). The 'enemy without' had come to bear on the 'enemy within', while anxieties about Pakistan were deployed to reinforce constructions of Indian Muslims as enemies of the nation, and to spread fear which could later be mobilized towards communal violence.

The 2002 report, *The Foreign Exchange of Hate* (Sabrang Communications 2002), compiled by academics and activists within and outside India, in focusing its inquiry on economic backing from abroad, situates the violence of 2002 outside the 'local' of communal strife. It reveals the exorbitant amounts of funding flowing into the coffers of the RSS and other such 'Hindu' organizations, including the India Development and Relief Fund (IDRF) in the US, to sustain these and other activities in Gujarat. All this allowed for the establishment of a cycle of terror in which 'the anomie (in the sense of the violent normlessness) of the perpetrator, unites with the anomie (in the sense of violent powerlessness) of the violated' (Baxi 2002: 19), facilitating the re-election of the perpetrators into power in the last month of 2002.

DILEMMAS FOR THE WOMEN'S MOVEMENT

The Gujarat experience demonstrates that gender and sexuality are much more central to social and political problems than has been acknowledged, and that violent masculinist ideologies pose the greatest challenge to feminist movements today. Hindutva's apparatus of militarization is based on the establishment of an ideology that weaves militant nationalism and violent masculinity, and that 'logically' *necessitates*, through modes of legitimization, the public, ritualized, sexual abuse of Muslim women.[16] Another deeply disturbing aspect of this militarization is that it is *literally centred in men's bodies*. It is premised on the violence exercised by the human body; and millions of human bodies have become the most fearful weapons of attack. Gujarat has literally taken us down to the basic denominators of militarization and disarmament. This is the gruesome 'human' face of militarization, that men and women cannot be 'disarmed' of their bodies. Also extremely disturbing is the consolidation of forces of militant women who actively participate in the violence against other women, including inciting the rape of other women (Chenoy et al. 2002; Hameed et al. 2002; *Communalism Combat* 2002).

Resistance in such a context poses severe problems for the women's movement. The events of Gujarat 2002 marked a regression for Muslim women back into the folds of patriarchy in no uncertain terms. In the face of severe militancy and sexual abuse women had no alternative but to retreat into the community. It was as much a literal, physical retreat into the *dargahs*[17] for shelter as it was a symbolic retreat into a patriarchal 'protectionism'. What power, even relevance, can 'secular' women's movements or egalitarian feminist values have in such a situation? These predicaments highlight the lacuna in the women's movement in terms of a virtual silence on the role of religion in the lives of a majority of women in the country. There is clearly a dire need to develop more effective feminist, anti-communal solidarities across religious communities.

Yet another aspect of domination relates to fear, silence and the impossibility of securing justice. In Gujarat 2002, acts of militant nationalism and violent masculinity that targeted the bodies of women for public and collective violation and abuse were rendered possible, permissible and legitimate through an apparatus of impunity and consent. Approximately 250–300 women were raped (*Communalism Combat* 2002), but the number of First Information Reports (FIRs) amounted to only four or five. A complicit police force refused to file FIRs which record the information basic to all cases. They refused to record details about the criminals or recorded nameless mobs of 5,000 and more as the culprits. In other cases, they filed 'omnibus' reports which club incidents relating to different times, places and accused persons all together in a manner that is generalized, vague and bereft of details (Grover 2002). Thousands of FIRs were finally filed with the police, but the majority of them have been rendered ineffective for these reasons. This is not an unprecedented situation.[18] This situation points to yet another lacuna in law, in terms of penalties for policemen refusing to write specific and detailed FIRs. In addition to the fear and sense of futility of filing complaints with the very police who were assisting the rapists, there was also an impasse, one of disclosure versus silence: legal recourse necessitates disclosure, but the fear of social castigation imposes silence. In fact even activists would find themselves trapped in this bind, as they recalled the example of a village in Kashmir where, after the rapes of women were made public, no one from another village would want to marry any woman from there for the next ten years.[19] It was *not enough to refuse* that sense of shame, as the history of Bangladesh and her *'viranganas'* proves to us. The issue is one of countering the ideological violence of rape in the Hindutva context and challenging the very basis of the social constructions of victory and shame that overdetermine this act of sexual violence. The legal dilemmas that confronted us in Gujarat were confounding too. The fact that we have not yet come to terms with the shifts in the gendered violence of militarization became evident in the grave constitutional crisis that confronted India.[20] Yet, while there is a critical need to press for justice in the courts of law and for legal reform,[21] it is equally important to simultaneously guard against the possibility of feminist politics remaining circumscribed within the legal domain. Along with the institutional failures of the state and the Constitution, it is critical to address not only the violent cultural transformations that have been legitimized by communal forces, but also a pervasive *subjective* transformation that endorses communalized militancy and sexual abuse.

VIOLENT MASCULINITIES

The scope and dangers of fascism are not limited to the political realm. The deep resemblance between the structuring of nationalism and the construction of the religious in Hindutva, and the structuring of sexual relations in everyday life is not fortuitous, for fascist violence has its roots in sexuality. What we have witnessed in Gujarat is an appropriation of sexuality as the central site for a politico-cultural transformation that stretches far beyond the purview of the law, and runs far deeper than the now commonplace views that explain the effectiveness of rape as a weapon against another community because women are considered to be property, or because the community's honour is perceived as being vested in its women. Compounding the attack on one's religion and religious space, as in the demolition of Babri Masjid, the destruction, literally, of property and, figuratively, as one's sense of home, as has been experienced by large segments of the population time and over again since the days of the Partition, this deliberate and concerted public attack on sexuality has been effective in crushing the confidence of the Muslim population. It is premised on the desecration of the most intimate sense of self, nurtured by sexuality. In the training of Hindutva forces and in the devastation of Muslim populations, Hindu communal forces in India have capitalized on an extreme vulnerability associated with the perceived threat or actual violation of sexuality. The most disturbing questions are those regarding the degree of cruelty and normalization of a fascism developed to work at multiple levels of signification—of Eros and Thanatos, physical and symbolic, psycho-sexual and purportedly religious, impacting present and future, in a network of related aims. This layering functions, as Tanika Sarkar (2002: 9) tells us: 'To possess and dishonour ... and what, according to their understanding, explains Muslim virility ... physically destroy the vagina and the womb, and, ... symbolically destroy the sources of pleasure, reproduction and nurture for Muslim men, and for Muslim children.' Sarkar explains the sequence of perpetration, from beatings that damage female fertility to physically destroying children to end Muslim reproduction, to the 'cutting up [of] the foetus and burning it, to achieve a symbolic destruction of future generations, of the very future of Muslims themselves' (p. 9). She continues: 'The burning of men, women and children ... served multiple functions: to destroy evidence, ... make Muslims vanish ... by denying them an Islamic burial, ... forcing a Hindu cremation upon them; [establishing] a ... macabre post-mortem forced conversion' (p. 9). What made such cruelty acceptable is an even more difficult question. I can only begin to address here the cultural processes that have been at work in the 'normalization' of such grotesque violence.[22] Compelling modalities of legitimation, religious, historical and ethno-sexual, in symbolic and 'empirical' modes, and modes of incitement, respectively, have been pressed into a pernicious project of an ideological and powerful cultural transformation.

SYMBOLIC CONSTRUCTIONS—POLITICAL GOALS IN SEXUAL TERMS

Hindu nationalism incorporates sexual violation as the cornerstone of militancy, developing intimate connections between sexuality and the project of nationalism. Cultural representation plays a critical role in making the abstract nation visible. The iconography of the ascendant nation as a violated mother or beloved, the graphic 'historical' representations of Hindu women purportedly abused by Muslim men, and the visualized sexual fantasies of lustful aggressive Muslim rapists, and overfertile, oversexed, Muslim women all contributed to the dominant perception of the Muslim as an 'inherently violent other'. As Sarkar asserts, 'There is a dark sexual obsession about allegedly ultra-virile Muslim male bodies and overfertile Muslim female ones, that inspire and sustain the figures of paranoia and revenge' (2002: 8). Das and Kleinman argue that 'Such representation effaces the concreteness of relationships and replaces them by imagined 'realities' of sexual threat and violence; it distorts identity in face to face relations' (2001: 4). This process facilitates the emergence of a passionate and violent subjectivity on the part of the Hindu.

Hindutva ideology has constructed its 'political goals in sexual terms', with the crisis of identity expressed as a crisis of masculinity (Chenoy 2003: 173–81). This translation of political goals into sexual terms has been wrought through the manipulation of symbolism[23] of the nation, portraying Bharat *mata* (Mother India), already an integral aspect of nationalist discourse and familiar on Indian terrain, as wounded. Veena Das has gone further to suggest that the nation was also visualized as a magnified image of the beloved worshipped in the abstract. The desire for icons allows the nation as an abstract object to be made magically visible through an investment in this magnified sexuality (Das 1998: 74). What is common to both images, however, is the investment in sexuality, with the mother as progenitor whose sexuality is sanctified. Das observes that the potential for violence is written in this very construction of the nation: 'Nationalism gives birth to its double—communalism. If one deified women so that the nation could be imagined as the beloved, the other makes... the bodies of women the surfaces on which their text of the nation is written' (ibid.: 75).

This integral linkage of such masculinity with the symbolic representation of the nation as Bharat mata and goddess had already facilitated the linking of nationalism with spirituality through nationalist discourse in the colonial period (Bagchi 1990), and in Hindutva politics (Sarkar 1993). What is new is the introduction of a deliberate and premeditated technology of violent eroticism that facilitates a distinct shift within this political symbolism, and is also markedly different from the unplanned violence of Partition. The RSS presents Bharat mata as 'a chaste mother, victimized (by Muslims), and declares that she needs the protection of her "virile" sons...' (Bacchetta 1996: 143). Interviews with RSS men in Lalit Vachani's film, *The Men in the Tree*, reveal a clear internalization of this ideology—the self-image of the RSS workers as *pracharak*s or preachers is premised on protecting the honour of Bharat mata from the attacks of the Muslim enemy. The passion of spirituality metamorphoses into a zealous sexual abuse of women of the other community, 'sanctified' as revenge for the defilement of Bharat mata. The rape of Muslim women in Gujarat was constructed as a 'sacred' duty. As Sarkar has observed, 'In Gujarat, mobs who raped, sometimes came dressed in khaki shorts or in saffron underwear, rape being obviously seen as a religious duty, a Sangh duty. In times of violence, Hindu male sexual organs must function as instruments of torture' (1993: 9).

Further, it is an eroticized passion that enables the Hindutva brigades not merely to die, but to rape and kill in ritualized public frenzy, and then celebrate these acts. The shattering irony of the idealistic pracharak in Vachani's film is that it was with an evocation of Bharat mata and a look of complete devotion on his face that he justified the sexual abuse of Muslim women. It was part of his passionate idealism to live in the right way, for the right reasons, and with the right desires, as a holy and sacred force.

'EMPIRICAL'/HISTORICAL VALIDATION—RAPE AS NATIONAL DUTY

The site of historical interpretation is a crucial one for comprehending how acts such as mass rapes and killings that are normally held to be morally reprehensible have found such wide acceptability. Through the widely disseminated writings of V.D. Savarkar, one of the chief ideologues of Hindu communalism, the stereotype of an 'eternally lustful Muslim male with evil designs on Hindu women' has been reiterated and 'made part of a historical common sense' (Sarkar 1995: 185).

Savarkar's role in intensifying the focus on gendered violence in Hindu-Muslim relations, and ensuring that protection slides into rape and killing was strategic. Purushottam Agarwal's analysis of Savarkar's *The Six Glorious Epochs of Indian History* (published in 1963) demonstrates that the replacement for God with nation as the ultimate source of morality creates the ground for the communal-fascist attack on female sexuality. In his 'nationalist' approach to rape, Savarkar attempts to prove the validity of the image of the Muslim as rapist, and berates the tolerance and passivity of Hindu men as a 'perverted sense of Hindu virtue'. Citing the impact of the Muslim lust for carnage, in a strategic move he targets none less than Shivaji, the prime hero of Hindu nationalism, for not taking revenge on the Muslim women he captured, holding the cowardice and femininity of the Hindu male responsible for the defeats, humiliation and decline of the Hindu nation.

Thus, 'Savarkar breaks down this resistance [to upholding rape as a 'moral' act] in one decisive stroke by removing the conflict between virtue and perversion… by systematically turning virtue itself into perversion' (Agrawal 1995: 52). With nation replacing God as 'primary referent of moral discourse', rape in retribution, or pre-emption, is designated a valid weapon in the warfare with Muslims. Hindus are exhorted to violently defile women of the other community as national duty, even as they would consider it their national duty to save the flag from the enemy (ibid.: 52–54).

The public discourse of Sadhvi Rithambara, a pioneer amongst militant Hindu women and a precursor to their forces in Gujarat, lends insight into the virtual impossibility of mobilizing even women's resistance within the Sangh Parivar against rape, since its 'normalization' by the Hindutva forces in their construction of a Hindu communal patriarchal history hinges on male sexual honour or *izzat*. This history is mobilized by the need to prevent repetition of the rape and pillage which supposedly characterized medieval India, and now 'justifies' retribution and violence against 'other' women. Analysing this discourse, Sangari explains how rape cannot be challenged as an institution from such a position: 'Rape here is … not a routine exercise of patriarchal power …; rather it is [in] the unique history of Hindu women's sexual vulnerability, [that] rape represents a violation of the community's proprietorship of its women by other men' (1999: 388). Thus legitimized, this masculinist ideology of rape pre-empts resistance by women in the name of anything other than community or communal hatred, pitting Hindu women against Muslim women and men.

The macabre ritualized sexual abuse of women witnessed in Gujarat in 2002 had a precedent in Surat in 1992, albeit not in numbers. *The Survivors*

Speak reports that in 2002, 'The murder and rape of Hindu women, emblazoned in banner headlines across the vernacular press became the excuse, the emotional rallying point, the justification for brutalizing Muslim women and children in ways not ever seen in earlier communal carnages' (Hameed et al. 2002: 11). Ideological constructions such as those popularized by Savarkar and Rithambara clearly have nothing to do with religion; they form the rubric of a Hindu fascist authoritarian regime that is premised on the sexual violation of minority women.

FANTASIES OF SEXUAL VIOLENCE AS BASIS OF 'HINDU' IDENTITY

Political oratory, symbolic action and incendiary pamphlets incited the Hindutva brigade to a frenzy, capitalizing on fantasies of sexual fear as well as sexual fantasies of violence against Muslims. As Spackman observes, 'the coupling of the terms "fascism" and "fantasy" is by now no surprise' (1996: ix).[24] She observes that 'ideological fantasy names a reality structured by disavowal, in which the fantasy acts as a structuring illusion' (ibid.: xi), and this was confirmed in Gujarat in 2002, with the central fantasy being that of sexual violence.

Praveen Togadia, international general secretary of the VHP called for action that was to follow the burning of the train in Godhra: 'Hindu Society will avenge the Godhra killings. Muslims should accept the fact that Hindus are not wearing bangles. We will respond vigorously to all such incidents' (Chenoy 2003: 175–76). This firm assertion of masculinity as militancy was not only constructed in contrast to femininity as a signifier of the weak and docile, in fact those men who refused to participate in the violence were mocked for their lack of masculinity; newspaper and other reports told of 'how bangles and saris were distributed to villages that were peaceful and to men who did not participate in the carnage. This was central to the construction of masculinity linked to the warrior image' (ibid.).

Given that sections of the Muslim population in Gujarat were relatively well off, the economic attack on them too was couched in sexual fantasies of fear. A leaflet distributed in Kalol ended with the exhortation: 'Before buying the goods from the Muslim shops think. Won't you be helping these Muslims indirectly in murdering your own Hindu brothers and in raping your own Hindu sisters?' (Chenoy et al. 2002: Appendix 2). In another widely circulated pamphlet, *Jehad*, the celebrated *brahmacharya* (which technically implies celibacy) of the Gujarat chief minister and Sangh Pracharak, Narendra Modi, is dramatically reversed in a lauded elevation of his status to a rapist. Imaged in full virility, with sexual prowess harnessed in vengeance, Modi is feted for delivering an imagined and savage justice—an eye for an eye, a tooth for a tooth—the rape of living mothers of Muslims in revenge for the violation of the symbolic Bharat mata: 'Narendra Modi you have fucked the mother of miyas'.[25] Narendra Modi is celebrated as a rapist of Muslim women during the progrom. Celibacy is played out as political theatre: the sexual restraint of the preacher unleashed as terrifying sexual fury in retribution.

In the contemporary Hindutva cult of violent masculinity, the self-image of a docile, almost feminine Hindu male is transformed into the 'new' Hindu male: sexually aggressive, virile, masculine and violent. Masculine identity and the sense of self of the Hindu male is now predicated on exerting dominance and control over Muslim women (Gupta 2002), symbolized through the sexual opening of Muslim women: 'We have widened the tight vaginas of the bibis'.[26] Thus, women, nation, religion, history are all welded together in seamless fantasies of sexual violence.

Further, as a counter to the threat of the virile Muslim male, what we have is not merely gender violence, that is, violence against women, but also the gendering of violence, in the feminization of the Muslim community, and the Muslim male, where rape not only takes on metaphoric dimensions but is also extended to homosexual rape (ibid.):

> The volcano which was inactive for years has erupted...
> We have untied the penises which were tied till now
> Without castor oil in the arse we have made them cry[27]

Finally, Adivasis have also been initiated into this privileged clan through a ritualized sexual abuse of maulvis:

> Now even the adivasis have realised what Hinduism is
> They have shot their arrows into the arses of mullahs[28]

Given the unsettled nature of class, caste and gender issues, communalized sexual abuse has become a major axis of internal unification and public consensuality, a vector for the reinterpretation of social contradictions (Sangari 1999: 405). Adivasis are incorporated and elevated to the elite 'Hindu' cult of violent masculinity in an ironic

'Sanskritization'—in this case a community created through violence—that detracts attention from the continued denial of rights, equality and social justice.

RELIGION, REPRESSED SEXUALITY AND EROTICIZED MILITANCY

Underlying these events of Gujarat are deeper issues regarding the 'commerce between eros and nation' (Parker et al. 1992: 1). A recognition of this linkage raises numerous questions, among them: Is the nation self-evidently the model of political legitimacy? Why is there a linkage between nation and sexuality? Why is it that the politics of nationalism inevitably signals the subordination if not demise of women's politics?[29] While Anderson's theorizations on nationalism are marked by an absence of discussions on gender and sexuality, *Imagined Communities* does open up one way of approaching these questions via his radical claim, that is extremely relevant in the Indian context, that nationalism must be conceived not as 'an ideology' (that is, as an effect of false consciousness), but 'as if it belonged with kinship or religion...' (Anderson 1983: 15). With these cultural conceptions of antiquity being transferred to the site of the nation, nationalist unity is symbolically modelled on gender and sexual norms. In a strong parallel to the modalities of kinship and religion, the trope of nation as woman is drawn in the image of woman as chaste and maternal on the one hand, and as elevated to the level of a goddess (Bagchi 1990) or worshipped in the magnified image of the beloved (Das 1998: 74) on the other.

In fact, M.S. Golwalkar, the general secretary of the RSS, wrote as far back as 1938 that 'The Nation is to be conducted 'as one of the commands of Religion'' (Noorani 2000).[30] Gujarat could become a laboratory of the Hindutva forces, through the incitement of frenzied passion for Bharat mata, the nation as violated mother and goddess, embodying a spiritualized Hindu rashtra transcending the boundaries of time and space. Ironically it is the love of Bharat mata that became the ground not only for the vengeful rape of Muslim women, but also for the collective ecstasy and transcendental 'sanctity' it inspired in the rapists. Reich's theorizations (1975) on religion, sexuality and fascism offer one way of understanding this connection between religion, erotic pleasure and sexual violence that is so powerfully operative in the Hindutva context. Drawing attention to the unity of religious and sexual cults in antiquity, and locating the split between them in the transition from matriarchal organization based on natural law to patriarchal organization based on the division of classes, he asserts that 'at that moment when sexual experience ceased to constitute a unity with religious cult and indeed became its antithesis, religious excitation also had to become a substitute for the socially affirmed sexuality that was lost' (ibid.: 178).

Elaborating the connection between sexual pleasure, repression and religious ecstasy, he observes that the separation of sexual feelings and religious feelings from one another, and the designation of the sexual as infernal and diabolical resulted in pleasure anxiety, that is, the fear of sexual excitation, which in turn is destructive and torturous if not allowed to achieve release. 'Thus ... the religious conception of sex as an annihilating diabolical force.... is rooted in actual physical processes.... The deep longing for redemption and release—consciously from sins, unconsciously from sexual tensions—is warded off' (ibid.: 181).

It is not surprising that Hindutva forces are marked by an ideology of sexual suppression, and that there has been an enormous proliferation of religious sects and lavish celebrations (Shah 2002: 59), and *satsangs* specializing in the performance of religious music that lead 'devotees' to heights of ecstatic experience. This ideology of suppression draws upon and intensifies already existing elements of sexual repression in South Asia, where, as in many other parts of the world, sexuality experienced as domination and control is still associated with shame, and simultaneously linked with the 'honour' of the community; complicating this further is a traditional Hindu cultural privileging of male celibacy in *brahmacharya* as a virtue. Hindutva forces build on these elements of sexuality— domination and possession of women, shame and honour, along with an intensification of sexual repression in everyday life—with the purpose of harnessing sexuality for political ends. Sexual suppression, glorified in the name of celibacy, has been one of the tenets of Hindutva ideology, a tenet practised by and identified with the most important leaders, from Narendra Modi, Sadhvi Rithambara, Uma Bharati, and Vijayaraje Scindia, who are all celebrated for their abstinence.

The question however is of the relation of the connection between sexual suppression and the eroticism of sexual violence enacted/ exercised on the 'Other', that is, Muslim women. Drawing on Reich's argument that 'Fascism countenances that religiosity that stems from sexual perversion, and it transforms the masochistic character of the old patriarchal religion of suffering into a sadistic religion' (1975: 17), in the context of contemporary Gujarat, a more specific explanation is possible. Gujarat is not only the most communally fraught, but also one of the most economically advanced, states of India, marked by a highly globalized consumerist culture. In such a sexually repressive context where the globalized media promotes desire and the pleasures of sexuality in no uncertain measure, the success of a strategy of transference of sexual excitation into religious ecstasy is highly dubitable. Thus, in an insidious twist into 'this worldliness', the rape of Muslim women is constructed as a national duty, which in turn is attributed with 'other-worldly', 'sacred' and 'religious' signification, as retribution for the violation of 'Bharat mata'. Sexual excitation is allowed to achieve release; this physical 'release' is achieved through the rape of Muslim women. As Marcuse asserts, 'the release of repressed sexuality within the domination of institutions has been used time and again as a prop for suppressive regimes' (1956: 202). Sexual repression continues to be preserved within the community, harnessed in the service of 'religious (read political) ecstasy', while sexual violence is sanctioned against the 'Other' community, also harnessed in the service of a 'religion' that is purportedly the very basis of the Hindutva collective.

Sexuality is suppressed within the community in Gujarat, while masculinist militancy is structured as *jouissance* (Accad 2001). Sexuality is centrally involved in militarization, in the connections forged between constructions of a militant masculinity, systematic sexual abuse of women of 'other' communities, and repressed erotic sensibilities. Further, violence becomes central not only to the construction of masculinity, but to the very experience of freedom itself, in sports, military, in 'accultured sexuality' (ibid.), in 'the history and mythology of heroism, it is taught to boys until they become its advocates' (ibid.: 25). Accad continues, 'Men become advocates of that which they most fear. In advocacy they experience mastery of fear. In mastery of fear they experience freedom.' This fear transforms into a metaphysical commitment to male violence, as, 'Violence itself becomes the central definition of any experience that is profound and significant' (ibid.). This transformation into an authoritarian regime of violence structures sexuality, masculinity and identity as gendered to the core.

MILITANT WOMEN: INCITEMENT AND AGENCY

The active complicity of militant Hindutva women in the rapes and killings occurred in the context and at the behest of a communal patriarchy. Militant women's complicity in patriarchy now constitutes a severe break in possible alliances for survival and resistance, in what Sangari explores as an 'axis of division amongst women who could potentially unite in a common opposition to patriarchies' (Sangari 1999: 365). This represents one of the most difficult quandaries confronting the women's movement in India today. It is usually claimed that even women who enter the political field as militants are victims of patriarchal politics, as they have few options but to 'retreat to the kitchen' after the war is over. However, viewing women as merely victims of war or patriarchy elides women's agency in violence (Rajasingham-Senanayake 2004: 151). The pitfalls of such claims too are grave as they tend to reinforce masculinist ideologies as well as detract attention from what Sangari (1999) terms the 'convoluted' nature of militant women's agency.

On the other hand, to privilege women's consent to forms of patriarchal oppression over their will to contest these is to play into the trap of anti-feminist claims that hold women responsible for their persistence (ibid.: 365). It is also to play into the dead end of an either-or situation: either women are helpless pawns of patriarchy, or they 'choose' complicity with it in a deliberate and ambitious move towards opportunistic politics. The more useful approach is to understand the dialectical relationship of militant women's consent with the determining conditions within which such consent is obtained.

In an apparent paradox, such consent works through appropriating a language of feminism, and simultaneously instating women as guardians of (patriarchal) social values. The vocabulary of women's empowerment is extremely relevant to militant women of the Hindu right in relation to their emergence from the invisibility of the kitchen into the prominence of nation making, the value placed on their public roles and their heightened sense of self as active members of the community. What the headiness of such empowerment elides is the distinction between the agency delegated to women within patriarchal structures, and the agency of women to contest these very structures. It obscures the distinction between being an emancipation that empowers one as capable of exerting independent feminist values, and being 'empowered' pawns in a violent game, one which will inevitably affect their lives for the worst in situations of scarcity and danger.

The fact that ideologies are not necessarily coherent, and that 'fascist discourse works precisely by binding together the progressive and the reactionary' (Spackman 1996: 40), allows us a way to understand the contradictory position of women within fascism, as well as develop some sense of their motivations and agency. Hindu women were reported to have cheered the rapes of Muslim women by Hindu men. One 'reason' could be their internalization of the fear of Muslim men as past and future violators of Hindu women. Bacchetta (1996) shows that Sangh literature repeatedly conjures up demonized images of Muslim men raping Hindu women, especially in the context of Partition, and constructs them as representing a threat of future violence as well (p. 145). A more complex explanation of the agency of militancy in Hindu women can however be found in the contradictory logic of RSS and BJP nationalism. The RSS 'celebrate[s] brave and powerful women who use violence if necessary to protect their communities' (Basu 1995: 171), even as it idealizes women from epic literature who embody notions of suffering and self-sacrifice.

Further, while the BJP is deeply patriarchal, it has simultaneously advanced women's rights in particular ways in its attempts to alienate and vilify the Muslim community. Such negotiation and manipulation was evident in their move to introduce a Uniform Civil Code purporting to grant equality to all women, but with the underlying implication that this would also challenge the Personal Laws. Nor had the BJP (until 2002) opposed 'women's legal and political rights that would accord them greater equality with men' (ibid.: 171). The BJP's engagement with issues of women's rights has evidently been a mere vehicle for attacking the interests of the Muslim community, or has been limited to a tacit policy of non-opposition geared towards appeasing women. It has never been a proactive engagement, and even the BJP women's organization, as Basu asserts, 'has not organized around issues like rape, female foeticide, and dowry deaths, the real violence that women confront in their everyday lives' (ibid.: 173).

It is not paradoxical then that the power of militant Hindu women derives from their conferred status as custodians of patriarchal value. As Sangari has demonstrated in her incisive analysis of the public speeches of Sadhvi Rithambara, the agency of militant Hindutva women is at best 'convoluted' (1999: 387), and, far removed from concerns of women's equality, it actually serves as buttress to a violent patriarchy of communalism that hinges upon the sexual abuse of 'other' women. Militant Hindu women 'act' through female incitement, by calling upon men to act, exercising situational control over man's status through an insistence on patriarchal codes of 'honour'.

It is here that the hazards of depicting all (Hindu) women as past and future victims of sexual abuse are revealed, for such incitement is based on an insistence of Hindu men's duty—of 'protection' of Hindu women from sexual abuse, and retribution on 'other' women—and reinforces violent masculinist ideologies by drawing upon anxieties of male emasculation and impotence. As such, it simultaneously adds force to Hindu communal patriarchy hinging on male sexual honour, and validates, even demands, a specific masculinity revolving on competition and retaliation, in which protection of one's 'own' women involves violation of 'other' women' (Sangari 1999: 398–99). In fact, Sangari further demonstrates how such insistence upon codes of male 'protection' from sexual abuse facilitates the consolidation of a fascist nationalism: 'consent [that is elicited] for patriarchal values on the basis of defence of "nation" and "religion" ... simultaneously uses existing social consent for patriarchies to get consent for Hindu rashtra' (ibid.: 408). The power delegated to militant Hindu women to insist that their men protect the 'honour' of the nation vested in its women in turn becomes patriarchy's justification for militancy and the basis of a fascist nationalism.

SEXUALITY, FASCISM AND FEMINISM

It is now evident that fascism in Gujarat has been premised on a violent eroticized militancy that is integrally masculinist. This however raises perplexing questions about the discourse of sexuality and its impact on subjective transformation among militant women. Though they too may be schooled in such violence in training camps and *mahila* shakhas, yet, how do they locate themselves in relation to the sexual violence that informs this masculinity? In a context where the erotic dimensions of militancy are linked to a feminization and sexual subjugation of the other, where violence against a feminized 'other', or even feminine 'other', is built on everyday experiences of sexuality as 'masculine' possession and control of the 'feminine', how is the sexuality of militant women structured? The majority of them are not forged in the image of the purportedly celibate *sadhvi* or *sanyasin* like Rithambara or Uma Bharati, the female leaders and most powerful orators of Hindu nationalism, who stage 'celibacy as political theatre'[31] and use chastity, with all its associations in Hinduism of spirituality, purity and other-worldliness (Basu 1995: 161), to heighten their iconic status. The majority of these women are ordinary homemakers entrenched in the norms and mores of community life. The contradiction between their 'feminine' experience of sexual relations in everyday life and their 'masculinist' living out of the erotics of militarization as militant women deserves to be explored, as do its possible implications for the future of Hindutva women's politics.

Feminist scholarship has already established that militancy itself seems closely connected with the way people perceive and act out their desires and power, as well as relations with their partners, families and within general society in terms of love, power, violence, intimacy, and notion of territory attached to the feelings of oppression and jealousy. One tries to obtain material goods and territory not in order to enjoy them, not out of need, but to enlarge one's domain and authority (Accad 2001). It has also been argued that patriarchal sexual relations are not built on pleasure, intimacy or love, but on reproduction, the preservation of a girl's virginity and the 'honour' of the family, and the confinement and control of women for the increase in male prestige. Everyday sexuality is structured as domination and possession, and the heterosexual act experienced as possession and control of man over woman is central to the experience of masculinity and femininity at the most intimate and ontological levels. This marks an area of critical overlap between sexuality and nationalism: both are structured in terms of heterosexual relations, domination of the 'other' and territorial possession.

On the other hand, it is precisely because sexuality is a critical foundational site of an authoritarian order that the sexual politics of feminism posits the greatest threat to fascism. As Reich has pointed out, the roots of authority lie deep within the institutionalized repression of sexuality and the manipulation of desires, which through pedagogy, the family and other institutions and practices create an artificial interest that actively supports the authoritarian order.[32] As early as the 1930s, Reich argues, 'Sexually awakened women affirmed and recognized as such would mean the complete collapse of the authoritarian ideology' (1935: 138).[33] Historically too, the emergence of a strong feminist movement with a focus on sexual politics seems to have coincided with a relative tempering of the power of fascism in Europe: 'The emergence of sexual politics in the shape of feminism does contribute to the fight against fascism as an ideology....Had feminism not been on the scene, neo-Nazism would be much stronger in Europe than it is today' (Banaji 2002: 7). Historical precedents such as this make it imperative to rethink the agenda of the women's movement in India today. For what is at stake is the transformation of the basic values that forge social relationships; such a transformation would demand the implementation of radical alternatives to ownership and possession as final goals.

Yet what is the starting point for transformation? Accad tackles the issue at the basic level of the very structuring of militancy: '[It is claimed] that if the 'right' side in a war were to win, women's problems would automatically be solved. I would like to argue the reverse' (2001: 17). Because violence is entrenched in everyday relations and the 'normal' patterns of daily life, for fascism to lose its critical foundational base, sexual politics has to be envisioned anew. As Banaji also asserts: 'Sexual politics is equally important because it is in the interests of conservative, right-wing establishment forces to mould individuals, to control and manipulate their desires, and make the young in particular feel guilty and repressed about their sexuality' (2002: 7). She continues, 'This suppression of sexuality is a powerful factor in the reinforcement of authoritarianism and the rise of fascist movements, and there is no way we can respond to such movements without encouraging reciprocity and an active stake in freedom' (ibid.). It emerges then that feminism and democracy—for it is the very principles and culture of democracy that are at stake as is the well-being of women—will not only have to press for adequate constitutional and legal measures at the national and international levels, but also for the reconceptualization of patriarchies, and more effective and autonomous agential modes for women, as well as work towards transformations of erotic sensibilities at the most personal levels, in order to break this vicious chain of masculinity creating fascism and fascism recreating masculinity.

NOTES

1. Jai Sita and Ram.
2. In Panjabi et al. (2002: 14). I chose to retain the original names of those who gave testimony without asking for their names to be withheld, as a tribute to their courage (and of their families) and their will to fight the violent injustice of their times. Their testimonies were published in their original names in the face of the immediate dangers of 2002, in the citizens' reports I cite here.
3. The Survivors Speak p. 9. Insert(s) [ ] within quotes are the author's.
4. While these concerns regarding sexual violence and appropriations of sexuality clearly pertain to men too (as was recently evident in the context of Abu-Ghraib), and especially to violence against homosexual men, each of these deserves specific in-depth analysis, and are outside the purview of this current essay, which focuses on sexual violence against women.
5. Communities defined by faith.
6. Section 3: 'State Complicity? Penetration of the Gujarat State', Chenoy et al. (2002: 11–17); Section II: 'Women's Experiences of the State', Hameed et al. (2002: 18–26); Section 2: 'Role of the State and Political Parties: Through the Prism of the Young', Panjabi et al. (2002: 18–22); and large sections of

the document 'The Foreign Exchange of Hate: IDRF and the American Funding of Hindutva', Sabrang Communications (2002)

7. Citizens for Justice and Peace, Press Release, 16 April 2005.
8. 'Muslim League to Distribute 'panchshool'', *The Hindu*, 14 March 2003.
9. 'RSS Membership Falling', *Hindustan Times*, 21 April 2002.
10. 'The Need for a Law against Genocide', *The Hindu*, 25 March 2002.
11. The National Steering Committee on Textbook Evaluation, Recommendation and Report II, National Council for Educational Research and Training (NCERT) 1999; Publications of Vidya Bharati (Section VI of the report), which clearly states that: 'Much of the material in these books is designed to promote blatantly communal and chauvinist ideas....' A detailed analysis of the communalization of education by Teesta Setalvad has been much cited, both by the Parliamentary Committee on Education and Culture in 2000, and by various newspapers across the country since March 2002. Reports on communal indoctrination in examination papers also appeared in various newspapers, including *The Telegraph*, Wednesday, 24 April and Monday, 29 April 2002; and on the 'psychological fear created in children, that could result in carnage and destruction' in *The Telegraph*, Wednesday, 24 April 2002.
12. The burning of a compartment on 27 February 2002, of the Sabarmati Express carrying Hindu *karsevaks*, in which fifty-eight people were killed.
13. 'Latest from Joshi lab: Moral Grooming', *Indian Express*, 17 March 2003.
14. 'Training Camps Worrying India's Minorities', *Los Angeles Daily News*, 12 July 2003.
15. Analysis of the communalization of education in Gujarat, including textbooks, by Teesta Setalvad much cited both by the Parliamentary Committee on Education and Culture in 2000, and by various newspapers across the country since March 2002.
16. Elaborated in the third section of this article.
17. As the attacks and killings began, thousands of Muslims flocked to the dargahs for shelter; whatever safety there was, was in numbers. The camp in the Shah-e-Alam dargah in Ahmedabad housed approximately 12,000 victims. The dargahs became sites of community living and decision making, with the safety of women being one of the priorities of the community.
18. These strategies are an uncanny repeat of the Delhi anti-Sikh Riots in 1984 (Grover 2002). In the latter case, no less that twenty thousand FIRs, had been filed; there has not been even one significant conviction to date.(Those of us who have been following the reports in the media note that the press keep reporting about aborted cases, but not, so far, about a single conviction.
19. Private communication with an activist in Ahmedabad in May 2002.
20. In the absence of adequate laws there are no signs of the political parties and the state being convicted for either the brutal intimidation and massacres of genocidal nature, or for the mass sexual abuse, rape and butchery of women

that continued for over three months in Gujarat. The International Criminal Tribunals that were set up in Bosnia and Rwanda recognize such rape as a crime against humanity, a form of torture and an act that contributes to genocide. The Rome Statute of the International Criminal Court (ICC) now codifies this, but the problem is that India has not signed the Conventions of the ICC. Lack of implementation of laws where they do exist, due to reasons such as deliberately inadequate FIRs filed by a complicit police force, creates other dead ends. Further loopholes, such as the absence of facilities for the protection of witnesses, which drive them into turning against their own testimonies under force, as has been revealed in the case of a prime witness in the violence in Gujarat, Zahira Sheikh ('Is She a Liar?', *The Telegraph*, 30 August, 2005; 'Nailed', *Tehelka*, 3 September 2005), further complicates matters. Zahira, having turned against her own testimony in a move that safeguards the interests of the accused, has alienated her Muslim community (which, in response to her turn, has burnt an effigy of her in public) as well as angered activists. There have even been suggestions regarding filing suits of perjury against her for bearing false witness in court citation. Obviously caught in the crossfire of opposing pressures, this is a woman who is now isolated from all but those who burnt her own people to death—You might speak to the absence of adequate physical and psychological rehabilitation and the context in which Zahira recanted her testimony, to therefore set a context that does not allocate 'blame' but speaks to the impossibility of the situation. Zahira has been doubly victimized,—once in 2002, the second time in the interstices of the law. Witness protection should be made the responsibility of the court; there is a dire need for a law on witness protection that considers the need for protection of all classes of witnesses. Three years down the line, it is yet to be seen if the recommendations of the Human Rights Commission, Amnesty International, The Women's International Initiative for Justice in Gujarat, The Citizen's Tribunal comprising eminent judges and professionals, and over forty reports by other citizen's groups will ever be implemented.

21. Asserting the need for a law against genocide in the aftermath of Gujarat 2002, eminent jurist and national president of the People's Union for Civil Liberties, K.G. Kannabiran wrote: 'There are no provisions in the old penal code to cope with this kind of large scale violence and killings.' Further, citing the complicity between the central and state governments as a major obstacle to justice, he elaborates aspects of the Convention on Genocide and asserts that: 'it has, unfortunately, become necessary to translate this covenant into national law' ('Manufacturing Believers', *The Hindu*, 10 February 2002).

22. For an impressive analyses of the organizational and ideological apparatus of the VHP up to 1993, see 'The VHP: Organizing Mass Communalism', in Basu et al. (1993); also see Sarkar (1993).

23. Anuradha Chenoy refers to this as 'metaphoric' uses of gender representation,

but the point is that there is no one-to-one correspondence between the abstract notion of nation and the figure of mother or beloved. In fact, the notion of nation has been materialized through a 'filling in' of a feminine figure as a symbolic representation of the nation.

24. Cf. Theweleit (1987).
25. English translation of pamphlet (*Jehad*) in the genocide issue of *Communalism Combat* (2002: 77–78). (Henceforth *Jehad*.)
26. *Jehad*.
27. *Jehad*.
28. *Jehad*.
29. Cf. R. Radhakrishnan (1992) for a critical analysis of the normative criteria by which the nation 'becomes the binding and overarching umbrella that subsumes other and different political temporalities'.
30. See Noorani (2000: 18–39), for a detailed analysis of Golwalkar's, 'We or Our Nationhood Defined'.
31. See Sangari's impressive analysis of Rithambara in 'Consent, Agency and the Rhetorics of Incitement' in Sangari (1999: 364–409).
32. Cited in Banaji (2002: 7).
33. Cited in Agrawal (1995: 29).

REFERENCES

Accad, Evelyn (2001). 'Guns and Roses: On Sexuality and War', *The Little Magazine*, 2(1): 14–25

Agrawal, Purushottam (1995). 'Surat, Savaarkar & Draupadi: Legitimizing Rape as a Political Weapon', in Tanika Sarkar and Urvashi Butalia (eds), *Women and the Hindu Right*, pp. 29–57. New Delhi: Kali for Women.

Anderson, Benedict (1983). *Imagined Communities: Reflections on the Origins and Spread of Nationalism*. New York: Verso.

Bacchetta, Paola (1996). 'Hindu Nationalist Women as Ideologues: The Sangh, the Samiti and Differential Concepts of the Hindu Nation', in Kumari Jayawardene and Malathi de Alwis (eds), *Embodied Violence: Communalizing Women's Sexuality in South Asia*, pp. 126–67. New Delhi: Kali for Women.

Bagchi, Jashodhara (1990). 'Representing Nationalism: Ideology of Motherhood in Colonial Bengal', *Economic and Political Weekly*, XXX: 42/3, *Review of Women's Studies* 20-27, WS 65–72.

Banaji, Jairus (2002). 'The Political Culture of Fascism', Talk delivered at a Gujarat seminar organized by the Vikas Adhyan Kendra in Bombay, September 2002. Available at: http://www.mnet.fr/aiindex/2002/BanajiSept02.html

Basu, Amrita (1995). 'Feminism Inverted: The Gendered Imagery and Real Women of Hindu Nationalism', in Tanika Sarkar and Urvashi Butalia (eds), *Women and the Hindu Right*, pp. 158–80. New Delhi: Kali for Women.

Basu, Tapan, Pradip Datta, Sumit Sarkar, Tanika Sarkar and Sambuddha Sen

(1993). *Khaki Shorts Saffron Flags*. New Delhi: Orient Longman: Tracts for the Times/1.

Baxi, Upendra (2002). *The Future of Human Rights*. New Delhi: Oxford University Press.

Breman, Jan (2001), 'An Informalised Labour System: End of Labour Market Dualism', *Economic and Political Weekly* 29 December. Available at: www.epw.org.in

——— (2002). 'Communal Upheaval as Resurgence of Social Darwinism', *Economic and Political Weekly* 20 April. Available at: www.epw.org.in.

Chatterji, Angana P. (2004). 'The Biopolitics of Hindu Nationalism: Mournings', in Angana P. Chatterji and Lubna Nazir Chaudhury (eds), *Cultural Dynamics: Theory Cross Cultures*, 16(2/3), October, pp. 319–63.

Chenoy, Anuradha (2003). 'The Politics of Gender in the Politics of Hate', in Ammu Joseph and Kalpana Sharma (eds), *Terror Counter-Terror: Women Speak Out*, pp. 173–81. New Delhi: Kali for Women.

Chenoy, Kamal Mitra, S.P. Shukla, K.S. Subramanian and Achin Vanaik (2002). *Gujarat Carnage 2002: A Report to the Nation by an Independent Fact Finding Mission*. Ahmedabad: Concerned Citizen's Tribunal.

Communalism Combat (2002). Genocide Issue, March-April, Year 8, No. 77–78.

Das, Veena (1998). 'Language and Body: Transactions in the Construction of Pain', in Arthur Kleinman, Veena Das and Margaret Lock (eds), *Social Suffering*, pp.67–92. New Delhi: Oxford University Press.

Das, Veena and Arthur Kleinman (2001). 'Introduction', to Veena Das, Arthur Kleinman, Mamphela Ramphele and Pamela Reynolds (eds), *Violence and Subjectivity*, pp. 1–18. New Delhi: Oxford University Press.

Grover, Vrinda (2002). 'Peace sans Justice? The Elusive Quest For Justice 1984–2003'. Available at: www.amanpanchayat.org. (Originally published as 'The Elusive Quest for Justice: Delhi 1984 to Gujarat 2002', in Siddharth Varadarajan (ed.), *Gujarat—The Making of a Tragedy*. New Delhi: Penguin.)

Gupta, Charu (2002). 'Hindutva Celebration of Rape', *Mainstream*, 7 September.

Hameed, Syeda, Malini Ghose, Sheba George, Farah Naqvi and Mari Thekaekara (2002). *How Has the Gujarat Massacre Affected Minority Women? The Survivors Speak*. Ahmedabad: Citizen's Initiative.

Marcuse, Herbert (1956). *Eros and Civilization: A Philosophical Inquiry into Freud*. London: Routledge and Kegan Paul.

Noorani, A.G. (2000). *The RSS and the BJP: A Division of Labour*. New Delhi: Leftword Books.

Panjabi, Kavita, Krishna Bandopadhyay, and Bolan Gangopadhyay (2002). *The Next Generation: In the Wake of the Genocide. A Report on the Impact of the Gujarat Pogrom on Children and the Young*. Ahmedabad: Citizens' Initiative and Kolkata: Action Aid India.

Parker, Andrew, Mary Russo, Doris Sommer and Patricia Yaeger (eds) (1992). 'Introduction', *Nationalisms and Sexualities*. New York: Routledge.

People's Union For Democratic Rights (PUDR) (2002). *'Maaro! Kaapo! Baalo!'* *State, Society, And Communalism in Gujarat*. Delhi: PUDR.

R. Radhakrishnan (1992). 'Nationalism, Gender and the Politics of Identity', in Andrew Parker, Mary Russo, Doris Sommer, and Patricia Yaeger (eds), *Nationalisms and Sexualities*, pp. 77–95. New York: Routledge.

Rajasingham-Senanayake, Darini (2004). 'Between Reality and Representation: Women's Agency in War and Post-Conflict Sri Lanka', in Angana P. Chatterji and Lubna Nazir Chaudhury (eds), *Cultural Dynamics: Theory Cross Cultures*, 16(2/3), October, pp. 319–63.

Reich, Wilhelm (1975). *The Mass Psychology of Fascism*. London: Pelican Books.

Sabrang Communications & Publishing and The South Asia Citizens Web (2002). 'The Foreign Exchange of Hate: IDRF and the American Funding of Hindutva', Sabrang Communications & Publishing Private Limited, Mumbai, India, and The South Asia Citizens Web, France. Available at: http://www.stopfundinghate.org. Last accessed November 2005.

Sangari, Kumkum (1999). *Politics of the Possible: Essays on Gender, History, Narrative, Colonial English*. New Delhi: Tulika.

Sarkar, Tanika (1993). 'Heroic Women, Mother Goddesses: Family and Organization in Hindutva Politics', in Tanika Sarkar and Urvashi Butalia (eds), *Women and the Hindu Right*, pp. 181–215. New Delhi: Kali for Women.

——— (1995). 'Heroic Women, Mother Goddesses: Family and Organization in Hindutva Politics', in Tanika Sarkar and Urvashi Butalia (eds), *Women and the Hindu Right*, pp. 181–215. New Delhi: Kali for Women.

——— (2002). 'Semiotics of Terror: Muslim Children and Women in Hindu Rashtra', *Economic and Political Weekly*, 37(28): 2872-76.

Shah, A.M. (2002). 'For a More Humane Society', *Seminar*, 513, May, pp. 58–60.

Spackman, Barbara (1996). *Fascist Virilities: Rhetoric, Ideology and Social Fantasy in Italy*. Minneapolis: University of Minnesota Press.

Theweleit, Klaus (1987). *Male Fantasies*, 2 vols. Minneapolis: University of Minnesota Press.

Yagnik, Achyut (2002). 'The Pathology of Gujarat', *Seminar*, 513, May, pp. 19–22.

9

Democratizing Bangladesh

State, NGOs and Militant Islam

Lamia Karim

In 1990, Bangladesh saw its transition to democracy after fifteen years of military rule, from 1975 to 1990. The transition to democracy came with a sharp rise in reported crimes against women perpetuated by militant Islamic groups and rural power elites. The first set of organized nation-wide attacks against women occurred in 1993–94. In 1993, several rural women who were accused of adultery by the local clergy were publicly stoned, and one woman was burned to death.[1] During this time, the clergy ostracized 5,000 families of women who worked with non-governmental organizations (NGOs), forbade women to appear in public without the burqa, and forcibly divorced fifty women whose marriages they deemed 'un-Islamic' (Hashmi 2000: 131). While these attacks on poor women spread, militant Islamic groups also targeted NGOs that worked with poor women by burning NGO offices, primary schools and mulberry trees that were used in certain NGO-operated sericulture projects, a cottage industry that primarily hired poor women.[2]

In 1998, while I was conducting research in Bangladesh, the clergy of a local madrasah attacked an NGO-sponsored public rally of 5,000 poor women and men by accusing the rally of non-kin men and women as being 'contrary to the teachings of Islam'. The clergy attacked the women with sticks, knives and stones, and publicly shamed them by calling them 'whores' and tearing off their clothes.

This article analyses the conflicts and contradictions released by the processes of democratization and globalization in Bangladesh as they are played out between two competing groups of rural patrons: the clergy and the developmental NGOs. Both groups vie for rural dominance by fighting over the role of women in society. By investigating the violent circumstances surrounding the poor women's rally in 1998, I examine how, in this conflict, these women were vulnerably situated in relation to the clergy and the NGO. The Bangladeshi state, which has fostered an Islamic ideology, remains complicit in this violation of women. I further argue that the good intentions of feminist NGOs are constrained in their ability to offer an autonomous critique of NGO practices because of their structural dependence on the NGOs. This article locates this rise of violent crimes against women committed by the clergy and rural elites against the complex and shifting landscape of democratic rights for women in Bangladesh, a landscape that gets intersected by the interests of the state, the modernizing forces of development in rural areas (the NGOs), and by militant Islamic groups.[3] All of these groups are vying for political power within the emerging framework of democracy in Bangladesh, and these ongoing struggles over the nature of the Bangladeshi state (will it be a secular or an Islamic state?) are often played out within 'a gendered symbolic politics to secure political legitimacy and authority in Bangladesh' (Feldman 2001: 209). In the post-independent phase of Bangladesh, as elsewhere in the Muslim world, developmental failures are not seen as technical failures but as a moral corruption of cancerous proportions, and, in Kandiyoti's words, a condition that has produced calls for a just Islamic society in many quarters of civil society, 'invoking notions of an authentic Muslim womanhood as part of a larger critique of Westernization and consumerism' (Kandiyoti 1995: 23–24).

I suggest that we locate the study of the kind of violence I discuss here at the intersection of three forces that are reshaping the economy and politics of contemporary Bangladesh, and assess how they have simultaneously strengthened and eroded the sovereignty of the traditional power base of the clergy and the rural power elites. These three forces are: (a) the culture of political Islam in Bangladesh that developed during military dictatorship, 1975–90; (b) the forces of economic globalization that target poor women as cheap labour in the rural sector and integrate them with productive forces that lie outside the control of rural patriarchy; and (c) the rise of the NGO sector as a modernizing force in rural life, whose work with women has begun to gradually dissolve the private/

public distinctions that have traditionally guided and guarded gender roles in rural society.

Violence is a complex and entangled terrain, and as this article will demonstrate, the sources of the conflict are multilayered and complex. In analysing these gendered atrocities, it is essential to remember that the local clergy and the rural elites, the village headmen and rural propertied males, often collude in violating the poor, particularly women, to exercise their domination over rural people. The use of rape, torching of houses, repossession of animals, denial of access to water for irrigation, and other forms of physical and material abuse are regularly meted out to poor villagers as punishment for refusing to accept the mandates of the rich landlords. The village headmen and rural elites often use the mullah at the local mosque or madrasah to pass supposed Islamic judgements that benefit their interests, whether it be the acquisition of land or women or the disciplining of more radical elements in rural society.

The right of a woman to free speech, to free assembly, to vote, and to work are rights under the Constitution of Bangladesh, and the function of the democratic state is to protect the rights of its (female) citizens. Yet, in the face of threats by the clergy, the state retreats, often becoming a silent abettor of these atrocities committed in the name of religion against women. It is important to note that the class dimensions of these conflicts, that is, the socio-economic status of *who violates rights and whose rights are violated* is significant because it is poor women, and not middle-class women, who bear the social costs of democracy and gender-defined modernization in Bangladesh.

In reviewing the violence of 1998, one is compelled to ask, where is the shaming of women by disrobing them in public sanctioned in Islam? Pointing to this disjuncture between Islamic jurisprudence and local interpretations that pass as Islamic law, Taj Hashmi (2000: 131) has termed these violent actions the effects of a *'narod* culture', that is, misogynistic behaviour rooted in rural society, and one that has little or no connection to Islamic ideals or jurisprudence. As Hashmi points out, these interpretations have their roots in existing misogynistic patriarchal norms towards women, and they are often the result of local land disputes and the exercise of power by rural elites to gain access to poor women. However, Hashmi does not extend his critique to explain why such barbaric customs are repeatedly sanctioned against women, and are accepted as 'Islamic law' by many in various Muslim societies.

This article has three parts. In the first part, I discuss the role of the Bangladeshi state in promoting two competing ideologies: women's full citizenship through economic and democratic participation, on the one hand, and on the other, the nurturance and growth of Islamic parties and madrasah education that place restrictions on women's full democratic rights, that is, on their participation as political and economic subjects in the economy. In the second part, I talk about the contested relationship among development NGOs, clergy and women; and in the third and final part, I locate the conflicts between the clergy and NGOs through an examination of the violent circumstances surrounding rural women's public participation in an NGO-sponsored rally.

RELIGIOUS IDEOLOGY OF THE STATE

Bangladesh, with a population of 130 million, is the third most populous Muslim country in the world. Bangladesh is also the only Islamic country in the world where the prime minister and the leader of the main opposition political party are both women. The Bangladeshi state terms itself as a 'moderate' Muslim nation by pointing to the public roles of women in the country. Government officials note that women in Bangladesh have been granted full rights in the Constitution. Bangladeshi women can vote, they can work, they are visible in the public sphere, and although Islam was made the state religion in 1988, sharia laws have not been implemented in the country, and the rights of minority religions have not been curtailed.[4]

When Bangladesh became independent on 16 December 1971, it celebrated four pillars of its Constitution: nationalism, socialism, democracy and secularism.[5] The 1972 Constitution extolled the virtues of secularism, which translated into *dharmo niropekhota* or the neutrality of the state towards all religions. What was less clear though was to what extent 'secularism' as a value was embraced by the majority of Bangladeshi Muslims. According to the 1991 census, Bangladesh is close to 90 per cent Muslim.[6] A majority of Bangladeshi Muslims consider themselves pious and god-fearing Muslims, and one could thus argue that they would not favour a secular state.[7] Thus, secularism as a value was not based on a consensus of the population but was imposed from above by the secular ruling party, the Awami League, whose client base was urban and middle class.

What then is secularism in the context of Bangladesh? The first democratically elected prime minister of Bangladesh, Sheikh Mujibur Rahman,[8] was sharp enough to note that values that are contradictory to Islamic ideals or the teachings of the Prophet Muhammad would not be acceptable to the people of a Muslim majority country. On 7 June 1972, Sheikh Mujibur Rahman clarified his position on secularism by stating:

> Secularism does not mean the absence of religion. You are a Mussulman, you perform your religious rites. The Hindus, Christians, Buddhists all will freely perform their religious rites. There is no irreligiousness on the soil of Bangladesh but there is secularism. This sentence has a meaning and the meaning is that none would be allowed to exploit the people in the name of religion or to create such fascist organizations as the al-Badr, Razakaars, etc.[9] No communal politics will be allowed in the country. Have you understood my four pillars? (Connell 2001: 188)

With the enactment of secularism, the Awami League banned all religiously affiliated political parties, such as the Muslim League and the Jamaat-i-Islami, from electoral politics, although these parties continued to exist clandestinely. Both the Muslim League and the Jamaat-i-Islami had collaborated with the Pakistani military forces against the independence struggle of the Bengali nationalists, and both parties were known for their divisive communal and Islamic politics. Sheikh Mujibur Rahman wielded secularism as a political tool to disempower those political forces that might threaten the stability of his rule. Thus, secularism was in actuality a political tool of the Awami League, and not a humanistic ideal that was promoted by the state. Surely then, it is not surprising that secularism as an ideal disintegrated with the assassination of Mujibur Rahman.

In 1975, the military came to power following a coup that killed Sheikh Mujibur Rahman along with members of his family. The first military dictator, Ziaur Rahman, who came to power through illegitimate means (he was not elected to office) began the steady Islamization of the polity. Zia made systematic changes in three areas of state governance——constitutional, administrative and symbolic—the effects of which were to be far-reaching for social life and politics in Bangladesh.[10]

On the constitutional level, Zia removed secularism from the Constitution and replaced it with 'absolute faith and trust in Allah'. He also included a phrase in the Constitution that Bangladesh was part of the Islamic ummah (the brotherhood of Islamic nations) with an aim to develop fraternal ties with Muslim nations worldwide.

On the administrative level, Zia opened a new Ministry of Religion whose role was to promote and protect the religious life of Bangladeshi citizens. The Islamic Academy, which was formerly a small institution, was transformed into the Islamic Foundation, the largest umbrella organization of research on Islam in the country. He also opened an Islamic University with a Research Centre for students from Bangladesh and overseas Muslim countries. Zia also reinstated the Jamaat-i-Islami and several other Islamic political parties that had been banned after the independence of Bangladesh and allowed them to again participate in electoral politics, thereby establishing a religious constituency for his rule. These changes enabled him to appease local Islamic groups in the country, and helped him gain legitimacy as a Muslim leader among Islamic countries.

Zia also changed the national identity of the people from the ethnolinguistic category 'Bengali' to 'Bangladeshi'. Although the category 'Bangladeshi' was supposedly a more inclusive category that embraced all citizens, whether Bengali-speaking or not, it effectively narrowed the definition of what it meant to be a Bangladeshi, and introduced an Islamic wedge into the national consciousness. It also drew a religious demarcation between the Bengali Hindus of West Bengal (India) and the Bengali Muslims of Bangladesh. The province of Bengal was divided by the British in 1947 into two parts along religious lines: predominantly Muslim East Bengal became East Pakistan in 1947, and separated from Pakistan and became Bangladesh in 1971. Through his policies, Zia introduced a new discourse of religion-inflected nationalism, one that broke with the earlier linguistic nationalism upon which the country was inaugurated, and brought in a new identity of being a 'modern' Muslim the Bengali way (whatever that may mean).

Moreover, in order to consolidate his power base, Zia started his own political party, the Bangladesh National Party (BNP), which took as its founding principle Bangladeshi nationalism, which in other words was the commingling of religion with ethnicity. The creation of BNP also bifurcated electoral politics in Bangladesh along religious lines; BNP supporters are overwhelmingly Muslim, with few Hindus and members of ethnic minorities, whereas overwhelmingly Hindus and other religious and ethnic minorities support the Awami League.[11]

On a symbolic level, Zia introduced the hanging of framed sayings from the Quran and the Prophet Muhammad in government buildings. State symbols and authority were manipulated to privilege Islam as the religion of the country. The state flag flew on Muslim holidays, and special prayers and messages from Zia as the head of the state were broadcast to the people. Quotations from the Quran, Hadith (the sayings of the Prophet) and Sunna (the life of the Prophet) were daily features, and the Muslim call to prayer was broadcast five times a day on state-owned radio and TV.

While Zia was shifting Bangladesh towards an Islamic ideology, he also turned to western donors for development dollars. Zia's coming to power coincided with the beginning of the UN Decade for Women in 1975 and the new policy mandates of Women-in-Development (WID) programmes in USAID offices worldwide that required women to be an integral part of the development process. In order to garner development funds, Zia promoted women's participation in public works programmes (Food for Work programmes undertaken with UN Food and Agricultural Organization assistance) and NGO activities that targeted women. He established a Ministry of Women's Affairs, recruited women into the police force, and reserved 15 parliamentary seats for women. This number was raised to 30 by the second military dictator where it currently stands. In order to legitimize his rule and to create his own ruling bloc within the country, Zia introduced contradictory and incompatible impulses into the body politic whose effects have been far-reaching.

The second military dictator, Hussain Muhammad Ershad, took the Islamization of national life further. He established a national zakat board to raise the poor tax in accordance with Islamic teachings, made Friday the weekly holiday, made mosques exempt from paying utility bills, introduced prayers on national TV, and in 1988 made Islam the state religion through an amendment to the Constitution. Ershad even attempted to make Arabic language instruction mandatory in the school curriculum but this proposal was defeated by a coalition of feminist, nationalist and secular groups.

CONTRADICTORY POLICIES: MADRASAH AND NGO SCHOOLS

The power of the clergy is dispersed through a wide network of madrasahs and mosques in the 65,000 villages of Bangladesh. Different national governments have not attempted to displace this clerical sovereignty; instead they have brokered local power-sharing agreements with them, letting the clergy have their own fiefdoms as long as they pay allegiance to the ruling party. Although several prominent clergy have placed fatwas on both the female leaders of the two major political parties, calling female leadership contrary to the teachings of Islam, both female leaders curry favour with Islamic parties in order to enlist their voters. The Islamic parties carry huge vote banks and an alliance with them assures the BNP or the Awami League of a victory in the elections. In the 2002 elections, Begum Khaleda Zia, who is the widow of the assassinated military dictator Ziaur Rahman, came to power with an alliance with Islamic parties. Her party, the BNP, gave two ministerial positions to Islamic party leaders, a first in the history of Bangladeshi politics.

In order to consolidate their power base, both military dictators, Zia and Ershad, wooed the Islamic parties, and simultaneously promoted madrasah education alongside the secular state education. The military dictators bifurcated secular education in Bangladesh by diverting funds meant for public sector education to madrasah education.[12] In Bangladesh, the government funds both secular and religious education: the public and madrasah schools. In Bangladesh, there are two types of madrasahs, the government madrasah known as the Alia Moderesin Madrassah and the private madrasah system known as Quomi (People's) Madrassah.

At the time of Zia's rise to power in 1975, there were 1,976 government madrasahs with an enrolment of 375,000 students (Table 9.1). By the year 2002, the number had risen to 15,661 and the enrolment had jumped to 2,824,672. Between 1975 and 2002, student enrolment had jumped by 653 per cent and madrasahs had increased by 692 per cent.

TABLE 9.1   Government Madrasahs and Student Enrolment

	1977/78	1981/82	1990/91	1991/92	2002
Madrasahs	1,976	2,846	5,959	6,025	15,661
Students	375,000	388,000	1,028,000	1,735,000	2,824,672
Teachers	21,579	29,608	83,761	94,941	133,445

Source: The figures for 1977–92 are from Murshid (2004); the figures for 2002 are from BANBEIS (2003).

In addition to Islamic teachings, the government madrasah curriculum includes science, math, English, and vocational training, and their graduates are competitively placed with students from the national public schools in an otherwise very tight labour market.

The military dictators also supported the growth of the Quomi (People's) Madrassah that follows a curriculum from the Deoband School, established in 1857 in Uttar Pradesh in north India.[13] The Deoband School strictly enforced Islamic jurisprudence based on medieval scholarship of Hanafi scholars and any departure from that path was considered heresy.

This refusal to adjust to modern times and changing circumstances kept the followers of the Deoband school trapped in an imagined vision of the golden age of Islam (the time of the Prophet Muhammad and his Four Caliphs), the establishment of which was their goal.

Following the legacy of the Deoband school, the Quomi madrasahs in Bangladesh only teach the Quran, Hadith, Sunna, and an orthodox interpretation of the sharia to its students. Its students are taught to recite the Quran in classical Arabic. English language, math and sciences are not taught in these madrasahs. It is estimated that the Quomi madrasahs number around another 15,000 (there is no official number available) and unofficial sources estimate that they have an enrolment of more than two million students.

The funding structure of Quomi madrasahs remains shrouded in mystery. While these madrasahs do not accept any government funds, they have received patronage from Iraq, Saudi Arabia and Libya in the past (Kabeer 1991: 134). They also receive private donations from overseas Bangladeshis residing in the United Kingdom and the Middle East. In the 1970s, oil companies in the Middle East had recruited Bangladeshis as labour to work in the oil fields. For the majority of these men, travel to the Middle East was their first global contact. Many of them returned home with a new sense of Islamic values, one that was closer to the norms of Wahhabi Islam practised in Saudi Arabia than to the syncretic Islam of Bangladesh. Upon their return home, they were keen on reforming the folk Islamic tradition[14] of rural Bangladesh through their patronage of the Quomi madrasahs. In addition to this, patrons also establish and donate money to madrasahs in order to garner votes in local elections. These religious actions are considered as acts of piety by villagers, and earn politically ambitious patrons the goodwill and the votes of rural people.

Madrasah students are usually male orphans. Apart from economic reasons, the poor also give their children to madrasahs because villagers consider it an act of godliness to dedicate a child to the work of Allah. These male children live their entire childhood under the tutelage of the madrasah clergy and develop a loyalty akin to familial loyalty towards them. Brought up within the strict orthodoxy of the madrasah, many graduates develop revulsion for what they see as the wantonness of modern life and, along with it, women's emancipated roles in society. Most significantly though, graduates of the madrasahs do not possess the skills to function in the competitive global economy of the twenty-first century, and thus it is not surprising that they resist what they see as the modernizing influences in the rural economy. This loss of relevance for these men in a rapidly changing global economy in turn becomes a vengeful wrath on women as 'trespassers' of Quranic and sharia dictates.

The twin policy of secular and religious education introduced strife and competition between the clergy and the NGOs in the rural sector where both groups struggled to define autonomous spheres of influence among the rural population, and competed for the same clientele: the children of the poor. In a move to garner western donor funds, the military dictators allowed NGOs to run secular primary schools for poor children in the rural economy. The lead was taken by BRAC, the largest NGO in the country and in the world, which has an impressive record of providing basic education to rural children.[15] In the 1990s, BRAC, with support from its donors, began to lobby for the privatization of rural primary education, which would bring rural education under NGO (and indirectly, donor) jurisdiction.

This shift in policy, which both enraged the clergy and allowed them to form an alliance with government primary school teachers who also feared the loss of their employment with the NGO takeover of education, led to the torching of BRAC schools in the 1993–94 nation-wide attacks on NGOs. This emphasis on privatization in the early 1990s made many secular-minded teachers of government primary schools form an alliance with the clergy to target NGO schools in 1993. In other words, these attacks were not solely the work of militant Islamic groups but of different groups forming alliances with Islamic groups when their interests were threatened.

The NGOs formed a powerful institution that was richly endowed with donor funds, which they did not share with the clergy or their mosques and madrasahs. It was only after the clergy-led attacks on their offices and schools in 1993–94 that the power and network of the clergy became evident to NGO leadership. Some NGOs, such as BRAC, made an effort to accommodate the demands of the clergy. Until the 1993–94 attacks, BRAC schools did not have religious education as part of their curriculum. After that point, it introduced Islamic studies into their curriculum, tempered some of its legal education programmes, and hired madrasah graduates in its schools.[16] As a result, the NGOs operating in rural areas were disciplined and normalized by the structures of rural patriarchy within which they have to operate.

THE NGO AS A MODERNIZING FORCE

The acceleration and growth of the NGO sector occurred after the military dictator, Zia, came to power in 1975. In order to garner development funds and to gain legitimacy among western nations as a modern Muslim leader, Zia promoted women's participation in public works programmes and NGO activities that targeted women. His policies also linked Islamization with dictatorship, and dictatorship with development, creating new networks of patronage and dependencies among the state, Islamic parties and NGOs.

The result of these calculated political moves by the leading political parties was paradoxical to say the least. One side of the official face of Bangladesh took on an Islamic appearance, while the other side brought women into the public sphere as head of state, public servants, police, members of parliament, labour, activists, and as NGO beneficiaries in loan and voter education programmes. These moves were made to ensure a constituency for the party in power, but they also strengthened the hands of different Islamic groups in the country that are opposed to women's participation in public life.

The developmental NGO sector in Bangladesh began its work in war relief and rehabilitation efforts soon after the war of independence in 1971. Over the years, it has grown into a lattice of more than 13,000 NGOs in an integrated network, of which at least 1,200 NGOs are directly funded by foreign aid. Of this number, 549 NGOs work directly with women, which is a result of the WID mandate of western aid organizations.[17] The NGOs service thirty million people in over 80 per cent of the villages in Bangladesh. The development NGO has stepped in to provide many of the services traditionally provided by the state, such as credit, education, reproductive healthcare, child immunizations, potable water provisioning, diarrhoeal rehydration programmes, prevention of environmental degradation, rural road construction, and voter education.

In Bangladesh, developmental NGOs have been among the most able service providers to the rural population. But NGOs are not mere service providers; they are also producers of social meanings and identities for actors associated with them. In rural society, NGOs have introduced modern consumption patterns and are purveyors of new ideas and symbols. For example, BRAC female fieldworkers ride motorbikes and bicycles to work. The image of an unveiled woman whizzing by on wheels, as the local mullah walks to his mosque with villagers watching his humiliation, creates enormous prestige and tension issues for the clergy. NGOs have starkly delineated the asymmetrical power and material distinctions between them and the rural clergy, and have become symbols of immense resentment for the clergy who feel diminished by the NGOs' work with the poor, and by the arrogance of some NGOs that refuse to include them in their systems of patronage.

At the rural level, which is what I am concerned with here, the work of development NGOs and feminist organizations has challenged rural patriarchy in three areas of traditional male authority: economy, law and politics. In the economic realm, women who are targeted by NGOs are reinscribed into western capital markets and, in the process, they become consumers of products manufactured by multinational corporations (finance capital, cell phones), on the one hand, and on the other, as producers who remain dependent on multinational corporations for physical inputs (hybrid seeds, fertilizers, pesticides). NGOs distribute these commodities to their members through their loan programmes. High indebtedness (often due to NGO loan programmes with their unstated high interest rates) and loss of arable land from flooding have forced many rural Bangladeshi women to migrate to the cities to work either as domestic help or as labour in the export-oriented garment industry.[18] In rural areas, women work as contract labour on various development schemes, such as sericulture, operated by NGOs.

The work of development NGOs that targeted women as their beneficiaries challenged the authority of rural patriarchy and changed the dynamics of rural power by introducing the NGO as a new patron into the community, and, at the same time, by mainstreaming poor women as labour and consumers into the economy. While these NGO programmes have created limited opportunities for women and their families to earn a living, they have also created parallel conditions of violence and domination against poor women who are willed into this process not as informed agents but as clients of these NGOs. The most important work of NGOs in this area is in micro-credit operations, that is, the extension of small loans to women to start income-generating projects from the home. The NGO sector provides two-thirds of the total institutional credit in rural areas (Sobhan 1997: 133). It is this power over access to credit for financially strapped poor people that gives NGOs tremendous power to bring rural people into new structures of subordination, altering existing codes of conduct for women, and enlisting poor female loan recipients in their own political work and priorities. I have discussed elsewhere that, as more and more poor families have become indebted to the NGOs, the heavier debt burden has resulted in increased violence against women debtors at both family and community levels.[19]

It is important to note that the problems of redefining the social in Bangladesh are embedded in a rural/urban divide. Bangladesh has a two-tiered social structure, a small coterie of western-educated urban elites who advocate women's rights, secularism and issues of social justice (the NGO camp belongs to this group), alongside a large rural population that is poor, illiterate, unemployed/underemployed, and that is not part of the nation-making project.

In the urban areas, positive and strong images of women abound. As noted, the prime minister and the leader of the opposition are both women. Bangladesh is one of the few countries with a Ministry of Women's Affairs, established soon after its independence in 1971. There is a national women's organization (Bangladesh Jatiya Mahila Sangstha) entrusted with improving the conditions faced by working women. Moreover, 10 per cent of all professional government posts and 15 per cent of all non-professional (clerical and custodial) posts are reserved for women. However, these changes benefit educated urban women. The majority of women in Bangladesh live in the rural sector and they have access neither to education nor to public sector jobs. The prime minister and the leader of the opposition in Bangladesh are women who identify themselves as 'pro-women' leaders. Both claim that under their respective leadership the conditions facing Bangladeshi women have improved. Being pro-women in their terms refers to pro-development programmes that target women, and do not include a critique of development policies that exploit women's social vulnerabilities.

The last fifty years have seen a rise in international human rights treaties and standards designed to protect the vulnerable members of society. While Bangladesh is a signatory to all these treaties, and has 'clear treaty obligations to protect human rights, in addition to its obligations under customary international law' (Hossain and Turner 2001: 2), the various successive governments continue to manipulate the religion card for their own political agendas.

Feminist NGOs (Ain-o-Salish Kendro, Sammilito Nari Samaj, Nari Pokkho, Nijera Kori) have been able to exploit the globalizing force of the liberal ideology of human rights and women's rights by taking on the issue of the ratification of the Convention on the Elimination of all Forms of Discrimination Against Women (CEDAW) with the state. Despite the avowal of women's equality, successive Bangladeshi governments have refused to ratify CEDAW without reservations.

The ongoing conflict between local feminist NGOs and the Bangladeshi state over the ratification of CEDAW warrants some comment. Bangladesh has ratified CEDAW with reservation to Article 2, which is an important umbrella provision in which discrimination against women is unequivocally condemned by signatory states, claiming that Article 2 goes against sharia laws based on the Quran and Sunna.[20] In a statement that reveals these tangled politics, the law minister in Bangladesh in 1999 defended the position of his government by saying that, although his government supported equal inheritance rights for women, it was 'impossible to take a step that would hurt the religious faith of the people'. He also added that constituents must be ready to accept change before the government can make changes, thereby shifting responsibility of discrimination against female citizens from the domain of the state to civil society (Harrison 2002: 4). What is erased in his statement is that there are women of other religions—Hindus, Christians, Buddhists—who are citizens of Bangladesh, and whose rights are subsumed under the overarching category of Muslim women.

In justifying their policy, state officials often claim that they cannot hurt the religious sentiments of the people. Bangladesh does not have sharia laws on the books. The religious sentiments to which the officials refer do not speak to either the views of women or religious minorities. In fact, by endorsing Islam as the privileged site of state policy, the state effectively discriminates against women belonging to religious minorities. While feminists have raised this question, successive governments have ignored the validity of the critique by making the astonishing claim that religious minorities do not suffer discrimination in Bangladesh (Pereira 2003)!

In their bid for equal rights, feminist NGOs have also aggressively pursued the establishment of a Uniform Civil Code (UCC) that would grant women equality with men in matters of inheritance, marriage, child custody, alimony, rapes, spousal abuse, and divorce. Bypassing the rural elites/clergy who refused to cede ground, Ain-o-Salish Kendro (ASK) has begun to appropriate the concept of the *shalish* or village adjudicating board run by rural elites, and has begun to run parallel adjudication hearings on divorce and maintenance issues on behalf of poor women.

While ASK has conducted parallel legal processes in rural areas dealing mostly with women's rights according to constitutional family laws, one is reminded that these feminist disputations are largely symbolic enactments of women's rights, and are still restricted to poorer members of the community who happen to be clients of these feminist NGOs. The ability of feminists to change rural power dynamics is constrained by their ideology, which is perceived by rural propertied males as an affront to their power and masculinity, and additionally, by the clergy as a tool of western imperialism to undermine Islam. Nonetheless this process has begun to impart knowledge to poor women about their rights and legal remedies which they may not be able to exercise fully or substantially.

The power of the clergy is a moral one based on their authority to interpret religious texts and Islamic law, and their authority to guide rural society according to their interpretations. However, the establishment of a UCC, the takeover of the shalish, and the illegality of fatwas would effectively shift the power of adjudication away from the clergy to the modern court system, reducing both the clergy's social relevance and economic power.

In a major feminist victory against the clergy, the highest court in Bangladesh declared all fatwas illegal in 2001,[21] stating that only the courts have the authority to pass legally binding judgements, posing a further challenge to the traditional power of the clergy. This was a frontal challenge to the authority of the clergy by feminist groups.

NGOs have also strategically moved into the political sphere since the 1990s, aligning their vote banks with political parties that endorse their work. The transition to democracy has given NGOs muscle to aggressively sponsor their own female candidates in local government elections called Union Council elections. These elected rural officials play a vital role in distributing scarce resources to their constituents, and they also maintain primary rights to these resources in a weak economy. For example, in the 1988 election seventy-nine women contested and one was elected chairperson.[22] In 1992, 115 women candidates contested the elections in 4,401 Unions and fifteen were elected chairpersons. In the 1997 Union Council elections, 44,138 NGO-sponsored women contested for 12,894 seats in 4298 Union Councils. Out of this figure, 12,822 were elected to 4,274 Union Council seats (*Adhuna* 1998).

One should not take these data to mean that a revolution is taking place in rural Bangladesh through NGO interventions. In the unfolding of this process, the political ambitions of several individual NGO leaders have also become evident as they try to carve out political territory through their established networks of patronage. These activities challenge the gender and class composition of rural local government, and begin to create new fissures and disturbances within the hierarchical world of the clergy and rural elites. These are small inroads into the entrenched power structure of rural patriarchy, but nonetheless these changes have begun to challenge rural authority and have begun to rupture deeply held views about women and their social roles. The clergy and the rural elites respond to these changes by scapegoating poor women, the most vulnerable members of rural society, for their alleged un-Islamic behaviour in adopting modern roles.

In her work on globalization, Saskia Sassen (1998) shows that economic globalization is a process that weakens territoriality and sovereignty of the nation state. In replacing the concept of the nation state with the clergy/rural elites who have traditionally functioned as the sovereign power in the rural economy (the clergy as the word of God, the richer peasants as landlords), we observe a similar process in the gradual weakening in the established power hierarchies through the work of the developmental NGOs. NGOs link the rural with the global by creating new markets locally as well as integrating women's labour into international global production (the garment industry, for example). These changes have created new forms of anxieties with rural men over their loss of economic power and the threat to their social control over their women.

THE NGO RALLY OF WOMEN

I want to now move into the final section of my article, which is a discussion of the conflicts between the third largest NGO in the country, and the local clergy of the Jamia Islamia Yunisia Madrassah over the democratic right of women to participate in a public rally. I analyse how the processes of democratization and globalization intersect and impinge on the lives of poor women, women caught in multiple structures of subordination through their debt relations with Proshika Human Development Forum, the social mobilization NGO.[23] I explore the contestations between the 'democratic' impulses of Proshika leadership under Qazi Faruque and the 'sharia-based' impulses of the local clergy of Jamia Islamia Yunusia Madrassah over the democratic right of women to participate in a public rally.[24] The clergy and NGOs often express competing and conflicting ideologies about the nature of Bangladeshi society, and women's role in it (Karim 2001b: 103).

On the surface, the leadership of Proshika expresses more modernist and democratic impulses that come in direct conflict with the sharia-based impulses of the clergy. But as this analysis shows, the 'democratic' impulses of Proshika were grounded in its non-democratic clientelist relationship with its constituents—the poor borrowers—who were forced to act according to the dictates of the Proshika leadership. And paradoxically, both parties, whether champions of more progressive/ modernist ideas of women's rights, or as guardians of purdah, end up brutalizing the bodies and souls of the women they seek to 'empower' and 'protect'.

The events I narrate took place on 7, 8 and 9 December 1998. The NGO decided to have a winter *mela* (fair) in the town of Brahmanbaria. I visited Brahmanbaria a month after the events in question took place. I was able to spend several days interviewing the affected women, their families, ordinary civilians, left party members, and the clergy. My analysis is grounded in conversations with these different groups of people.

Proshika organized a winter mela for its women members in the conservative town of Brahmanbaria on 7 December 1998. Proshika, as part of its democratic initiatives, sponsored rural fairs and folk theatres as pedagogical tools for instructing their members in democratic norms. Their folk theatres dealt with issues pertaining to social justice, gender discrimination, and critiques of the clergy and rural elites who were depicted as exploiters of the poor.

Brahmanbaria is home to a Quomi madrasah, the Jamia Islamia Yunusia Madrassah. The madrasah controls fifty-four smaller madrasahs in the surrounding areas. The leader of the madrasah was known as Boro Huzoor (Elder Mufti) who was reputed to be 134 years old, a distinction earned by being a highly pious man rather than referring to his real age.

When Boro Huzoor found out about the mela, he issued a fatwa against any fair within the town of Brahmanbaria, saying that melas were blasphemous events that allowed free mixing, gambling, drinking, dancing, puppet shows (considered idolatrous). Melas are historically associated with Hindu festivals, and are eschewed by the more orthodox elements of society.

Not to be outdone, the NGO declared that it was a constitutional right of women to free assembly, and changed the winter mela to a public rally of women to commemorate the spirit of the war of independence of 1971. The clergy declared that a women's public rally was against the teachings of Islam (what need did women have to come outdoors and shout slogans?) and threatened that mayhem would break lose if a public assembly of women and men were held in their town.

The Bangladeshi state played the part that it has continually scripted for itself over time. Local government officials deliberately chose not to take any action against the clergy even after the clergy had violated the Constitution by issuing a fatwa against the right of female citizens to assemble in public, and instead appealed to a nineteenth-century colonial law Section 144 to prohibit the gathering of more than four people in a public place. The local District Commissioner (DC) refused to deploy police in substantial numbers to maintain law and order. Later the government refused to take any action against the clergy for their crimes. By whitewashing the crimes of the clergy, the state not only retains its friendly ties with the Islamic political parties, it also becomes complicit in these crimes against women.

Despite warnings from both the clergy and the District Commissioner, the Proshika leadership gathered between 8,000 and 10,000[25] poor women and men in Brahmanbaria on 7 December 1998. As soon as the first speaker started to speak, youths and clergy from the madrasah attacked the rally with sharp sticks, axes and large knives. They tore down the stage, chased away the bureaucrats and NGO workers (Qazi Faruque and others ran to seek shelter in nearby homes), beat the women attendees, injuring many of them, and publicly humiliated them by tearing off their clothes. Many women said that the clergy had shouted at them that they were 'shameless women' and had ordered the madrasah students to tear off their clothes because 'such shameless women might as well be bare for all to see'.[26]

Thereafter, widespread looting and destruction of commercial and NGO property occurred in town for two and a half days.[27] NGO offices and schools were looted and burned. In a nearby village, twenty-six houses belonging to NGO members were specifically targeted and burned. In the eruption of violence, Proshika leaders who had gathered the poor women as a symbolic march against the clergy, fled to Dhaka in their imported SUVs, and began to hold seminars aimed at raising donor funds to prevent the takeover of Bangladeshi society by militant Islamic groups. Proshika also tried to reify itself as the leader within the NGO community in fighting Islamic extremism in the country. Such a 'progressive' role would grant both symbolic and material benefits to Proshika (or for that matter to any other NGO) from the western donor community, whose policies try to shape Bangladesh as a moderate Muslim nation.

In analysing gendered violence that occurs in the public sphere, the class position of those whose rights are violated is significant because it highlights how poor women often shoulder the costs of social adjustments, in this case, NGO-led democratization. For example, only two days after violence erupted against the women's rally, a local female member of parliament led a procession of twenty middle-class women in the town of Brahmanbaria to observe Rokeya Day.[28] Not a single middle-class woman was assaulted by the clergy of Yunusia Madrassah. One is compelled to ask then, what was this violence about? Against women? Against a specific class of women?[29] Against NGOs? Or was it entwined in more complex issues of ongoing social transformation in rural society?

I went to Brahmanbaria to investigate the incidents of domestic violence that had increased against women who had participated in the rally. My travel to Brahmanbaria as a single woman warrants some comments. I travelled with my research assistant, a young man in his twenties. While I did face some problems at the hotel where they would not initially let me register as a single woman, these problems did not prevent me from moving around town with several young men who willingly assisted me in my work. This behaviour towards me reveals some of the attitudinal changes brought on by the work of NGOs that have introduced many middle-class women like myself as NGO fieldworkers and officers in rural and provincial areas. It is now grudgingly acknowledged by many that in order to do NGO work, women are sometimes required to travel with non-kin men on official work. And women *who work* outside bring financial relief to their families, an important consideration that puts many families with conservative attitudes towards women's work in an ambivalent situation. Having said that, probably the most important factor in my reception was that I was an outsider. I was a middle-class woman from the city who did not belong to their social group, and the community did not consider their 'honour' besmirched by my behaviour.

In the villages, I told people that I was a researcher interested in the events surrounding the mela. Very few people believed that to be my true intent. I was seen as an investigator sent by the government or an NGO to uncover the events and to perhaps collect evidence to 'punish' the culprits. Alternately, I was seen as a journalist who had come to do investigative reporting. I was also seen as an aid worker who had come to assess the damage in order to calculate relief assistance for the affected families. While I repeatedly told people that I had no power or authority to provide them with relief assistance, my pleas went unheard. Given the various ways I was positioned in these interactions with the women, the stories I heard emphasized more the victimization of women than the underlying rural tensions (pre-existing feuds over land or women for example) within these villages that may have played a decisive role in the targeting of specific families as 'transgressors' by the clergy.

As I walked through the different villages, there was a certain aura of fear that permeated the area. In one village where twenty-six houses had been torched, one could still see the burned houses, hacked corrugated tin, singed wood poles used in house construction, broken mud walls. Families had assembled their few remaining assets into some semblance of 'normalcy'. Some families had constructed makeshift homes with saris stretched between two poles to give them some privacy. Women were seen cooking their evening meals with the few remaining pots and pans that the madrasah youths had left behind. While it was clear that the clergy had violated these women's rights and their human dignity by publicly beating them, this knowledge was mingled with fear. For it was evident to the women that if the clergy came back, no one—not the police, rural authorities or the NGOs—would protect them. So, when I asked the women to analyse the events, their comments were confined to Proshika or to their husbands. In conversations, it was revealed that even a month after the incident, some women had not been able to return to their homes because their husbands refused to accept them back. While in some instances, the husbands in question were willing to take back their wives if they paid additional dowry, some of the women confided that their husbands continued to abuse them physically and verbally for bringing 'shame' on them. The women noted that they faced increased verbal abuse from relatives who called them 'spoiled goods'.

While some women blamed Proshika leadership for making them attend the rally, other women contradicted them by pointing out to me, 'Why should our husbands beat us? Do they not take NGO money? How can they eat NGO money and beat us?' The husbands of the affected women had in effect become objects of ridicule, and were taunted in public by other men. They were no longer seen as real men because they could not protect the honour of their women.

The husbands told me that Proshika officers had threatened to withhold future loans if the women did not attend. Several men pointed out that they may be poor and they are forced to take NGO money but that did not give Proshika the right to take their women to rallies. Women, operating inside the patriarchy of the home, are not autonomous agents who make independent choices (in this case, the rally) but are dependent on their husbands' will, and the will of the NGO that had invaded the privacy of the home.

In my conversations with the women victims, they revealed that none of them were aware of the fatwa against the rally. Had they known, they claimed, they would not have attended the rally. In fact, most of the women were not even aware that the mela had been changed to a rally. The women were not only critical of the role played by the clergy, they also drew a distinction between religion as a spiritual practice ('we didn't go against Islam, we went to the rally in modest attire'), and Islam as an ideology, which is instrumentally deployed by the clergy to exercise power over its subject populations ('we do not follow the mullah parties').

The extent to which this was a democratic rally is open to question. Entrapped in debt relations to Proshika, the women were deployed as foot soldiers by Proshika in its ideological struggle with the clergy. These women were neither informed nor willing participants of the rally. Their desires to attend the rally were not grounded in democratic impulses. They saw it as recreational—as a day off from the daily grind of their existential reality (Karim 2001b: 103).

In the clientelistic culture of Bangladesh, rich and important folks from Dhaka city coming to visit them is an acknowledgment of their importance as *people*, recognition that the poor matter. As several women said to me, 'NGO sirs told us that rich people were coming all the way from Dhaka to see us. We had to go and greet them.' The NGO leaders and representatives and the poor beneficiaries stand in opposition to each other: they are unequal 'partners' in development. NGOs may deploy the rhetoric of equality and democracy, but careful analysis shows that they inaugurate themselves as rural patrons by ingeniously appropriating and exploiting these unequal social relations. For many of these women the rally was really a *darshan*—a pilgrimage to pay respects to a holy man, Qazi Faruque, who as the new patron occupied this role in their worldview (ibid.: 103).

It was alleged by local people and newspaper reports[30] that the clergy were instigated by local moneylenders to attack the rally because moneylenders were losing their clients to NGOs that work in micro-credit. I find this reasoning disingenuous, because it makes a simplistic causal connection between the oppression of moneylenders and micro-credit NGOs as liberators of the poor. In fact, as I have argued elsewhere, the work of micro-credit NGOs has created increased usury in the rural economy, which has actually benefited rural moneylenders by increasing their network of possible clients (Karim 2001a).

It was also pointed out that the real culprits were two male rival members of the Awami League. It was alleged that members loyal to both men had variously instigated and manipulated the local administration and the clergy to create a situation of lawlessness to make a political statement that the current member of parliament (MP) could not maintain law and order.[31]

Without fully discounting the merits of these accusations, I want to entertain some different motivations for the actions of the clergy. I want to speak to the motivations that underpinned the actions of the clergy, which extrapolate on the observations I made at the beginning of the article about the processes of globalization and democratization. It need not be emphasized that the clergy were acting out their misogyny towards women, poor women (and not middle-class women) who are subjects of their patriarchal authority. For them, women are 'rubbish little things'.[32] How dare they (women) assemble in public, march by their madrasah in broad daylight, and chant slogans against them? For the clergy, women's voices are duplicitous, designed to lure men from the faithful path into un-Islamic conduct, that is, drinking, gambling, sexual gratification. The clergy alleged that women were marching into town in raised voices shouting 'I will give my body to whomever I please', 'down with fundamentalism', 'I will not live in a broken house, I will not listen to my husband'.[33]

The fact that thousands of rural women could march by their madrasah in broad daylight against their mandate (fatwa) makes the clergy lose face and displaces their authority in front of the community that they are supposed to guide as moral guardians. If they do not react to this challenge posed to them by the NGO and by 'insignificant' women, how will they face their constituents the next day—their students, the people of Brahmanbaria who look to them for moral leadership—and command their respect?

The clergy repeatedly made two comments that I found illustrative about how the forces of economic globalization and the work of NGOs are undermining rural patriarchy. In the first instance, the clergy justified their actions against the rally (although they denied that they or their madrasah students had touched the women in any way or form) by saying that these women were marching into town half-naked in 'denim shorts and Sandoz undershirts', on 'motor-bikes', and as moral guardians they were forced to protect the morality of Islamic life by intervening.

In the second instance, they remarked that NGOs have started to convert poor women into Christianity by giving them loans in exchange for 'Christian seals',[34] and that they had to stop the proselytization of poor Muslims by these 'western and imperialist NGOs'. Both of these comments warrant some discussion.

The NGOs have brought perceivable change in local consumption patterns among the poor. In some instances, the poor are able to have some of the same commodities as the clergy, thereby gradually levelling the material distinctions that maintain a hierarchical society. Thus, while the comment referring to Bangladeshi women in 'denim shorts and Sandoz undershirts' on the surface is absurd, careful consideration will allow us to see that the clergy are really making a critique of Westernization, consumerism, and the control over poor people, particularly women. In rural communities, elite men normally wore undershirts under thin cotton *panjabis* (a long shift-like garment worn by Bengali men). Poor men either wore short-sleeve shirts or they kept their torsos bare. The use of the term 'Sandoz undershirts' (Sandoz is a time-honoured manufacturer of men's undershirts in South Asia) refers to the adoption of elite culture by the village people.

Similarly, denim shorts are synonymous in Bangladesh with the West and the export-oriented garment industry where poor women work as labour. As more and more women join the garment industry and the NGO as contract workers, it symbolizes a loss of male power over women's bodies and their labour, and effects a new source of income for poor people. Women, by acting like men (in symbolic language, women now wear 'half-pants'), are moving into traditional spheres of male influence and privilege, and are displacing male economic power and authority.

The Yunusia clergy also alleged that NGOs were converting poor Muslim women into Christians by giving them loans, and then they were forcibly placing a 'Christian seal on the woman's underbelly'. The underbelly here refers to the sexual organs of a woman, and a 'Christian seal' refers to sterilization, which is widely practised and associated with the work of a number of NGOs.[35] The clergy thus uses the words Christian and West interchangeably.

Women whose reproductive tubes have been tied are explosive females—sexual free agents in the eyes of the clergy—who will fornicate at will. The loss of male authority over the sexual control of women leads to potential loss of future generations of Muslims. These actions are seen as a conspiracy against Muslim men by the Christian West to take away their right to produce Muslims who would go on to establish the golden age of Islam[36] on earth once again. These fears of the clergy of women acting outside the norms of an 'authentic' Islamic womanhood were also exposed in the comment that, if thousands of men and women assembled together for three days, 'where would they sleep and defecate? Under the open sky?'[37] Thus, this form of behaviour can only lead to the contravention of all sexual rules and morality.

Women who have moved away from the control of rural authority into a new sphere controlled by the NGO/capitalist forces are the actors actively engaged in the undermining of Muslim male authority. From the clergy's perspective, such women must be punished severely. Poor women, as agents of transformation in rural society and as vulnerable targets, thus become the symbol of an incitement to violence for the clergy.

The forces that colluded and intersected in creating this violence against women cannot be analysed as an isolated event or as an erratic action by crazed Quran-waving fanatics. In an effort to resist this undermining of their authority, the clergy use acts of public violence to assert themselves. Violence reifies their power, and forces their adversaries (NGOs in this instance) to negotiate with them the contours of emerging structures of power and rural authority.

In terms of analysing community responses to the violence perpetrated against the women, there were very few supporters of the women who had been victimized. In fact, the women whose houses were burned did not receive any support from their neighbours who blamed them for bringing the clergy into their village. Given the hierarchical organization of rural social life, this is not surprising. However, it is equally important to note that, through their work in micro-credit, NGOs have enmeshed rural people in multiple levels of financial dependency that have weakened existing forms of social solidarity and community building.

Women targeted as loan recipients are individuated from the group (the extended family and kin group), so they can be brought more easily into NGO structures of domination. NGO micro-credit loans are given collectively to five[38] or more women, usually kin members, who are *collectively held responsible for the repayment of individual loans.* When defaults occur, and they do routinely,[39] the NGOs pressure the group members to extract money from the defaulting woman by withholding future loans from all of them.

These NGO practices of isolating the individual woman from the group, and then holding the group responsible for individual breaches of contract, allows the NGO to use the social group as its enforcer and police. Pressure by the NGO on the group (to recover the money or pay up) results in group strife, and domination of individual members and their families by the larger unit, and the repossession of their assets for loan recovery.

The social group has incorporated these NGO methods of isolating and violating individual women borrowers. When women are subjected to violence, the social group (village members) incorporates the strategy of the NGOs by isolating these women as individual 'trespassers' who have breached their social contract by acting against the wishes of rural authority, and for bringing chaos and shame into their village.

If events had gone as planned, Proshika leadership would have garnered kudos from their donors and media for advancing the democratic process far into the Muslim heartland. In fact, Proshika employed the rhetoric of development and the techniques of bureaucracy and transformed the failed rally into a social disaster management project by claiming that a 'social disaster' was looming in Bangladesh. How 'social disasters' are sometimes manufactured by NGO actions went unremarked.

What one finds in the context of Bangladesh is the NGO-ization of dissent.[40] That is, the possibility of dissent itself has become dependent on the 'largesse' of the NGO sector. To understand this phenomenon one has to realize how the NGO network has inducted different groups into its structure in Bangladesh. NGOs are the primary providers of employment for college-educated young men and women, and they hire university professors, bureaucrats and researchers as consultants on high-paying NGO projects. This structural dependency makes it difficult for dissent to occur in certain public spaces, or when it does occur, for it to be heard as a legitimate form of social critique. Thus, it is not surprising that the feminist critique of this violence was partisan. On 5 July 1997, three Proshika women borrowers along with a child were killed in a road accident on their way to the local police station. This happened in Matikata village in Kuliachar thana in Bhairab district. Of the three, one woman was pregnant. These women were members of Proshika Bhumiheen Samity No. 1 (Landless Society No.1). The police arrested the women because Proshika had lodged a criminal complaint against them as defaulters. At the time of the arrest, the group owed Taka 2,400 in arrears ($52 in 1997 exchange rate). While this report was widely publicized in the vernacular dailies, not a single feminist NGO spoke out against the use of police coercion in harassing and intimidating women.[41] The public feminist response was a denouncement of the clergy, and of the state for failing to prosecute the clergy. However, there was no public criticism of Proshika leadership. In fact, leaders of two leading feminist NGOs in Dhaka were shocked to hear from me that 'women who had been violated by the clergy were now facing domestic abuse and abandonment'.[42] Remarks like this indicate the divide that exists between the worlds of urban, Dhaka-based elite feminists and the rural women.

In my research in Bangladesh, I found that the relations between urban feminists and rural women were often based on a clientelist relationship. This is said not to diminish the hard work of feminist NGOs but to recognize that middle-class feminism is often trapped in its own class privilege, and in the clientelist culture of Bangladesh feminist practices often take on a patron-client relationship, which stands in direct opposition to the culture of equality that informs a feminist ideology and practice. The difficulties facing feminists working with the NGO paradigm in Bangladesh have to be analysed against the limits that such an organizational structure may impose on feminist practice. Several feminists expressed their frustration with the leader of Proshika for creating enormous difficulties for them. As one of them pointed out, 'We, as members of the NGO community, have to keep an united front against the clergy.'

While NGO loans are given to women, it is the *men who really use the loans*, while women who do not use the loans remain liable for repaying the loans to the NGOs.[43] For my analysis, it is the method of loan recovery that reveals how loan relationships, which are structures of interlocking dependencies, weaken social bonds and cohesion. What we find here is an example of Aiwah Ong's notion of a 'double patriarchy'.[44] Rural women are trapped inside the patriarchy of the home (their men insist that they join NGOs, and bring home loans for the men to use) and the patriarchy of NGOs, institutions that have a clientelist relationship with their members and often use women members for the furtherance of their own goals, as is evidenced by Proshika in this case.

The role of the Bangladeshi state is crucial in understanding how and why these kinds of actions go unpunished in Bangladesh. In Bangladesh, the process of democratization has released all forms of violent, competing and incompatible forces in the country. The leading political parties, BNP and Awami League, play the religion card to woo the Islamic political parties, thereby unleashing religiously charged disturbances in the polity.

The Bangladeshi state has solidified neither its earlier secular character, nor its later Islamic character. It calls itself a 'moderate Muslim state' but it tolerates, and often abets, all forms of excesses in the name of religion (Islam). To be 'moderate' in Bangladeshi official jargon means not to be 'Taliban-like'.[45] But surely, not being like the Taliban government is not saying much about the nature of democracy or about the rights of women and religious and ethnic minorities. I would argue that one step would be to go back to the Constitution and rethink what it means to claim that 'Islam is the state religion'. If Islam is to remain the state religion, what will be the rights of female citizens? Religious minorities? How will the state reconcile democratic laws (laws that are made by people) versus Islamic laws (laws that are given by God)? In order to contain the Islamic militant genie in the bottle, a real concerted effort has to be made by the state to address some hard questions about the nature of democracy in Bangladesh.

It is a long road to equality for women in Bangladesh, that it is not a chimera. In this respect, the role of feminists, particularly Muslim feminists, is critical. For many Bangladeshi women secularism does not have any relevance, and Islam is seen as a religion of social justice and equality for the poor. Thus, critiques of society have to come from within an Islamic interpretive frame. There are Muslim feminists who have begun to reinterpret the Quran in feminist terms, arguing that Islam grants equality and justice to women (Barlas 2003). Feminist NGOs and activists could include feminist interpretations of the Quran as part of their legal literacy programmes, educating the poor with tools to interpret religious texts. It is also equally important that as a first step towards a feminist rethinking of the patriarchal state, we, as middle-class feminists, have to overcome our own class bias and privilege, and acknowledge our own limits in knowing what poorer women want. This is, as feminists are aware, a continual process of unlearning and learning.

This is an important lesson to bear in mind: feminists are working within the vexed contours of democracy in Bangladesh, and inside the structure of the NGO with its links to the government, donors, and other NGOs. This relationship, which is the status quo in Bangladesh, makes it difficult for bold feminist critiques of the NGO way of doing things to emerge in public. These institutional structures provide feminists with alliances and possibilities but they may also impede the making of a feminist practice and ideology that is autonomous of any structural dependence on NGOs.

ACKNOWLEDGEMENTS

Writing of this article was made possible by a Rockefeller Postdoctoral Fellowship at the Kroc Institute for Peace Studies at the University of Notre Dame in 2003. The research on which it is based was undertaken in Bangladesh in 1998–99, and was supported by the following grant agencies: US Fulbright Fellows Program, Wenner-Gren Anthropological Foundation and the Harry Frank Guggenheim Foundation. I would like to thank the following people for suggestions and comments: Riyad Koya, Kamala Visweswaran, and the editors of this collection. As always, my thanks are to my research assistant, Chauhan, for facilitating conversations with the clergy, and the women of Brahmanbaria who shared their stories. A preliminary version of this article was presented at the 'Women and the Contested State' conference held at the University of Notre Dame in April 2003, and is forthcoming in an edited volume of conference papers published by the University of Notre Dame Press.

NOTES

1. For a discussion on the attacks of 1993–94, the following texts provide useful information: Feldman (1998); Hashmi (2000); Shehabuddin (1999).
2. Mannan (1994). The two NGOs that were specifically targeted were the Bangladesh Rural Advancement Committee (BRAC), whose most significant work is in rural primary education, and the Grameen Bank that has made micro-credit for women internationally famous.
3. By militant Islamic groups I refer to the clergy of the various madrasahs and mosques in the country that are affiliated with several of the major Islamic political parties in the country, such as the Jamaat-i-Islami, Islamic Oikye Jote, Harkat-ul-Jihad-al-Islami (HUJI). These groups, taken loosely together, envision an Islamic state based on a literal interpretation of the Quran and the sharia, and one that would have restricted rights for women and religious minorities.
4. Although the Constitution has not restricted the rights of religious minorities, these rights are increasingly under threat with the growth of political Islam.
5. For a historical background on the politics on Bangladesh, the following provide useful information: Mascarenhas (1986); Muhith (1978).
6. The population of Bangladesh is approximately 129 million: Muslims 88.3 per cent, Hindus 10.5 per cent, Buddhists 0.6 per cent, Christians 0.3 per cent, and animists 0.1 per cent. See http://banbeis.org/bd_pro.htm, 1 July 2004.
7. I make this statement not to make a causal connection between Islam and anti-secularism. Based on my own interactions with Bangladeshis, it emerged that the majority of the people did not view Islam as the source of any political problem. They viewed the corruption of various governments as the real source of conflicts, poverty and lawlessness in the country.
8. Sheikh Mujibur Rahman was the leader of the Awami League, and the Father of the Nation.

9. These were paramilitary organizations created by the Pakistani army during the war in 1971 to kill Bangladeshi civilians.

10. Much has been written on the topic of Islamization in Bangladesh. The following articles provide more details: Ahamad and Nasrin (n.d.); Kabeer (1991); Murshid (1995).

11. I make this observation based on conversations with Bangladeshi scholars, and from my own research among the Garos, an ethnic minority, who overwhelmingly supported the Awami League. In my research area, Hindus supported the Awami League.

12. This was done in an effort to create an Islamic ideological state.

13. The Dar-ul-Ulum Madrassah in the town of Sahranpur, Uttar Pradesh (India) was opened in 1857 after the failed independence struggle by sepoys against the British. It is the second largest Islamic seminary in the world. Thousands of madrasahs are attached to it in South Asia. For a discussion on madrasah education in South Asia, see Sikand (2001).

14. Folk Islam in Bangladesh has many features of Hinduism and Buddhism, such as participation in Hindu religious festivals, worship of certain harvest deities, and consultation of astrologers. The Deobandis forbid the worship at Sufi shrines, claiming that only Allah can be worshipped, and ban Sufi musical and dance performances as un-Islamic.

15. BRAC started operations as a relief provider in 1972. It gained international recognition for its innovative primary school instruction for rural children. It started credit operations in 1986. In 1998, BRAC covered 42,033 villages in all sixty-four districts and membership stood at 2.75 million. BRAC is a corporate NGO with interests in all aspects of industry and social life. In addition to work in micro-credit, sericulture, breeder chicken, chicken feed industry, hybrid seed cultivation programmes, it recently opened a private university (BRAC University) and a commercial bank (BRAC Bank), and has multiple commercial enterprises like Aarong (its international handicrafts store).

16. While BRAC will not openly admit to these changes, in private, BRAC officials note that they are an institution dedicated to long-term transformation, which necessitates accommodations with different power brokers.

17. These figures are from the NGO Affairs Bureau, Bangladesh (1998). The figure has probably gone up significantly.

18. Hidden costs include such unstated fees as entrance fees, late fees, service charges, mandatory savings deposits that members cannot withdraw from automatically, fees for breeder chickens (BRAC) and other products that are sold as mandatory loan tie-ins, etc. Calculations of all these various charges show a very high rate of actual interest charged to the borrowers.

19. For critiques of the micro-credit model in Bangladesh, please see Karim (2001a). My research, conducted over eighteen months in Bangladesh, was on the micro-credit model and its effects on gender, social and political

relations. I studied the four largest NGOs in the country: BRAC, Grameen Bank, Proshika Human Development Forum, and the Association for Social Advancement (ASA). My findings contradict the much-heralded miracles of micro-credit for rural women in Bangladesh, and document instead how debt relations have subordinated poor women and their families to increased domination and exploitation by the NGOs and community members. See also Goetz and Rina (1996: 45–64), Karim (2001b) and Rahman (1999: 67–82). For arguments in favour of micro-credit for Bangladeshi poor women's empowerment, see Counts (1996) and Todd (1996).

20. Bangladesh signed CEDAW on 6 November 1984 with two reservations: Article 2.12.1 Rights to Family Benefits and 2.12.2 Reservation on Article 13 (a) which does not recognize welfare benefits for citizens (Harrison 2002).

21. 'Fatwa Illegal, Declares HC', *Daily Star*, Dhaka, 3 January 2001.

22. The lowest rung of state government is at the village level and is known as the Union Parishad, which is made up of nine members with a chairperson. Three of these member seats are reserved for women.

23. In 1998, Proshika was the third largest NGO in the country. Its membership stood at 8,639,180. The funding of Proshika was suspended by the BNP when it came to power in 2002, alleging 'financial irregularities' by Proshika management. The leader of Proshika, Qazi Faruque, is currently in jail. The actions against Proshika leadership were taken because of its support of Awami League, and the use of its resources and members to vote for the Awami League. The early work of Proshika in the 1970s and 1980s was on conscientization of the poor, training landless farmers about their rights, fighting for government land redistribution among the poor, and focusing on the inequalities of rural society. In the 1990s, it expanded its micro-credit programmes and became more enmeshed in loan services. During my research in Bangladesh when these events in question occurred, Proshika was aggressively pursuing a 'grass-roots political mobilization' ideology, and actively lobbying for the Awami League. In my research area, I found female members belonging to Proshika to be most exploited. There were seventy-four police cases against women who had defaulted on loans. In response to my question, how could the organization reconcile its women's empowerment rhetoric with throwing them in jail, the local Proshika manager retorted 'For such women, police is the best solution'.

24. The leader of Proshika, Qazi Faruque, is politically aligned with the Awami League. He is reputed to have political ambitions of his own. However, my analysis is not focused on the personal ambitions of individual NGO leaders (these are papers in their own right) but on the structural causes of violence.

25. The figure is from Aksir Chowdhury's *Human Rights Report* (1999). *Samaj Chetona* (a socialist monthly published in Dhaka, Bangladesh) puts the figure at 4,000–5,000.

26. Comments made to me by affected women, NGO workers and eye-witnesses present at the rally.

27. 'Brahmanbariar NGO Shanggitio Ghar-Bari Loot Hoyechey' (Houses of NGO Members Looted in Brahmanbaria), *Prothom Alo*, 12 December 1998.

28. The date was 9 December 1998. Rokeya Day commemorates the achievements of Begum Rokeya Sakhwat, a late nineteenth-century Bengali Muslim feminist author who advocated Muslim women's education, and was a vocal critic of Muslim patriarchy.

29. When I posed this question to the clergy of the Yunusia Madrassahs, I was reminded that 'We are not the government. We cannot be in charge of the moral responsibility for everyone.'

30. 'Brahmanbaria: Fatwa Brittanto O Dadan Brittanto' (Brahmanbaria: Fatwa and its Relationship to Moneylending), *Samaj Chetona*, December 1998, pp. 12–15.

31. 'Brahmanbariay Shohinshutar Pechone Sharther Khela' (The Play of Personal Politics behind the Brahmanbaria Melee), *Prothom Alo*, 13 December 1998.

32. The Bengali term for it is 'mohilara abar manush naki'. It could be translated to mean 'women are not even human'. I find the comment 'rubbish little things' closer to the sentiments expressed.

33. Comment made by Mufti Kefayetullah of Yunusia Madrassah to author. Women borrowers of Grameen Bank, BRAC, Proshika, are taught slogans like 'I will not live in a broken house, I will not leave Grameen Bank', that the clergy routinely distort to suit their goals.

34. A frequent allegation brought by the Muslim clergy.

35. The Bangladeshi state implemented family planning programmes in the 1970s, and they have been widely accepted by the rural population. There have been many undocumented incidents of sterilizations of unmarried men and women but since this programme was accelerated during military dictatorship, no organized political dissent was possible. Many rural women have had sterilizations after three/four children down from seven/eight only a generation ago. From my conversations with rural people, I did not find any stigma attached to sterilization. The clergy resist family planning strategies but they have not used it as an organized strategy against NGO work.

36. The time of Prophet Muhammad and his Four Caliphs.

37. Author's interview with Mufti Kefayetullah of Yunusia Madrassah. Kefayetullah also alleged that NGOs teach women that verbal divorce (the Islamic practice of triple *talaq*) is illegal, which is against the sharia. Verbal divorce (talaq) was made illegal by the former Pakistani dictator, Ayub Khan, in 1963.

38. The number five pertains to the Grameen Bank micro-credit model; other NGOs have larger groups but the ideology is the same, group responsibility for individual loans.

39. I documented that in almost all the collection meetings of the Grameen Bank, BRAC, Proshika and ASA, at least 10 per cent of the women were struggling with the payments, and there were frequent defaults.
40. I am grateful to Angana Chatterji for suggesting this term to me in reference to this article.
41. See Bengali daily, *Bhorer Kagoj*, 1997. Also, Karim (2001a: 141–42)
42. Comments made to me during my research.
43. In my research, I found that over 95 per cent of micro-credit loans were used solely by the men.
44. In her work on Malaysian factory women, Aiwah Ong analyses how, instead of becoming empowered, women are trapped inside the feudal patriarchy of the home and the capitalist patriarchy of the factory. She dubs this entrapment of working-class women 'double patriarchy' (Ong 1987).
45. This sentiment is found in popular discourse.

REFERENCES

Adhuna (1998). 'Grass-Roots Democracy'. Dhaka: ADAB Publications.

Ahamad, Emajuddin and Dil Roushan Jinnat Ara Nasrin (n.d.). 'Islam in Bangladesh'. Available at: http://www.power-xs.de/delta/islam.html. Last accessed June 2004.

Bangladesh Bureau of Education and Information Statistics (BANBEIS) (2003). http://www.banbeis.org/db bb/ins prol.html. Last accessed February 2003.

Barlas, Asma (2003). *'Believing Women' in Islam: Unreading Patriarchal Interpretations of the Quran*. Austin, TX: University of Texas Press.

Connell, Joseph (2001). 'The Bengal Muslims and the State: Secularism or Humanity for Bangladesh', in Rafiuddin Ahmed (ed.), *Understanding the Bengali Muslims*, pp. 179–208. New Delhi: Oxford University Press.

Counts, Alex (1996). *Who Needs Credit?* New Delhi: Research Press.

Feldman, Shelley (1998). 'Representing Islam: Manipulating Gender, Shifting State Policies, and Class Frustrations in Bangladesh', in Patricia Jeffrey and Amrita Basu (eds), *Appropriating Gender: Women's Activism and Politicized Religion in South Asia*, pp. 33–52. New York and London: Routledge.

——— (2001). 'Gender and Islam in Bangladesh: Myth and Metaphor', in Rafiuddin Ahmed (ed.), *Understanding the Bengal Muslims*, pp. 209–35. New Delhi: Oxford University Press.

Goetz, Anne-Marie and Sengupta Rina (1996). 'Who Takes the Credit? Gender, Power and Control over Loan Use in Rural Credit Programs in Bangladesh', *World Development*, 24(1): 45–64.

Harrison, Christine M. (2002). 'Tough Row to Hoe: Can CEDAW's Optional Protocol Help Muslim Women in Rural Bangladesh Realize their Right to Development?', *Praxis, Fletcher School Journal of Development Studies*, 18(4).

Hashmi, Taj-ul (2000). *Women and Islam in Bangladesh: Beyond Subjection and Tyranny.* New York: St. Martin's Press.

Hossain, Sara and Suzanne Turner (2001). 'Abduction for Forced Marriage: Rights and Remedies in Bangladesh and Pakistan', *International Family Law*, April: 15–24.

Kabeer, Naila (1991). 'The Quest for National Identity', in Deniz Kandiyoti (ed.), *Women, Islam and the State*, pp. 115–43. Philadelphia, PA: Temple University Press.

Kandiyoti, Deniz (1995). 'Reflections on the Politics of Gender in Muslim Societies: From Nairobi to Beijing', in Mahnaz Afkhami (ed.), *Faith and Freedom: Women's Human Rights in the Muslim World*, pp. 19–32. Syracuse, NY: Syracuse University Press.

Karim, Lamia (2001a). 'Development and its Discontents: NGOs, Women and the Politics of Social Mobilization in Bangladesh', dissertation, Rice University: Houston, TX.

——— (2001b). 'Politics of the Poor? NGOs and Grass-roots Political Mobilization of the Poor', *Political and Legal Anthropology Review*, 24(1): 92–107.

Mannan, Manzurul (1994). *Fatwabazz Against BRAC? Are They Alone?* Dhaka: BRAC, Research and Evaluation Department.

Mascarenhas, Anthony (1986). *Bangladesh: A Legacy of Blood*. London: Hodder & Stoughton.

Muhith, A.M.A. (1978). *Bangladesh: Emergence of a Nation*. Dhaka: Bangladesh Books International.

Murshid, Tazeen (1995). *The Sacred and the Secular: Bengali Muslim Discourses, 1877–1977*. Calcutta and New York: Oxford University Press.

——— (2004). 'Women, Islam and the State: Subordination and Resistance'. Available at: http://www.lib.uchicago.edu/e/su/southasia/Tazeen.html.

Ong, Aiwah (1987). *Spirits of Resistance and Capitalist Discipline: Factory Women in Malaysia*. New York: State University of New York Press.

Pereira, Faustina (2003). 'Legislating Justice in the Postcolonial Subcontinent', Paper presented for the Jeremiah Lecture Series, University of Oregon, Eugene, OR.

Rahman, Aminur (1999). 'Microcredit Initiatives for Equitable and Sustainable Development: Who Pays?', *World Development*, 27(1): 67–82.

Sassen, Saskia (1998). *Globalization and its Discontents*. New York: New York Press.

Shehabuddin, Elora (1999). 'Contesting the Illicit: Gender and the Politics of Fatwas in Bangladesh', *Signs*, vol. 24: 1011–44.

Sikand, Yoginder (2001). 'Madrassah Education in South Asia', *Himal*. Available at: http://himalmag.com. Last accessed June 2004.

Sobhan, Rehman (1997). 'The Political Economy of Micro-Credit', in Geoffrey Wood and Iffath Sharif (eds), *Who Needs Credit? Poverty and Finance in Bangladesh*, pp. 131–41. Dhaka: University Press.

Todd, Helen (1996). *Women at the Center*. Dhaka: University Press.

10

Playing Off Courts

The Negotiation of Divorce and Violence in Plural Legal Settings in Kolkata

Srimati Basu

Say the number '420' to anyone who has grown up in India, and there is instant recognition of its connotation—it refers to a shady person, a cheat, a thief; the concept refers to the section number for the offence of fraud in the Indian Penal Code (IPC), but is so naturalized that the link to the category signified is all but forgotten, making for hilarious cross-cultural misunderstanding on occasion. A more recent signifier, marked also by its Penal Code section number, fast assuming equivalent potency, is '498'—this section of the IPC refers to 'torture' of women (domestic violence both physical and mental is to be prosecuted under this), but it erupts frequently in common parlance to signify a new order of choices for women, a new slate of sanctions for men, and a new way of using courts, police and community mediators. In my ethnographic investigations of Family Courts and Women's Grievance Cells of the Police in Kolkata, India, I began to be struck by how often my observations of divorce proceedings were infused with references to '498': male litigants in the social camaraderie of the courtroom corridor would check in with each other, 'How did your 498 go?', assuming a shared legal torment; 'you can't save the marriage once there's a 498' was the most frequent phrase I heard from police officers; 'How can she blame me for the marriage failing when she has filed a 498?', a Family Court 'counsellor' (mediator) asked rhetorically. Yet, when judges, counsellors and police dealt with '498s', they often were not managing/punishing violence per se, but rather negotiating a range of issues related to the social and economic entitlements of marriage.

The Indian state's management of divorce and domestic violence, driven by disparate forces such as postcolonial discourses of equity and modernity and demands refracted through social movements as well as customary notions of kinship and equity, is enacted through a number of potentially contradictory fora, including civil and criminal remedies and formal and informal mediation. This article focuses on Section 498 of the IPC which legislates against 'torture' and has been the primary criminal law governing domestic violence. 'Domestic violence' emerges notionally in international feminist discourse in the 1970s, challenging the normativity of intra-family disciplining of women—typically, domestic violence is discussed under the rubric of 'Violence Against Women', juxtaposed against rape, sexual harassment, trafficking, etc.; it is rarely grouped under discussions of women's economic survival needs or changing forms of kinship entitlements. In this article, I present a number of recent cases of domestic violence allegations in India by way of problematizing categorizations of family violence, highlighting the ways in which violence is marked as a strategy of negotiating economic and other kinship needs in marriage.[1] Domestic violence emerges, thus, both as a condition of marriage and as a lever of destabilizing its material and symbolic power. The postcolonial state's struggle to preserve customary notions of kinship while balancing emergent notions of conjugal equity in marriage law, as well as increasing state involvement in the control of children and payments in the dissolution of marriage, are foregrounded in the process.

Two contesting images vie for prominence in recent depictions of domestic violence in India. One, as reflected in National Crime Records Bureau (NCRB) statistics and some other studies, points to rising numbers of domestic violence incidents (Table 10.1; Pande 2002). Here family violence may be read as ubiquitous and systematic, related to women's economic marginalization and their isolation within virilocal affinal households.[2] For example, recorded examples of 'cruelty by husbands and in-laws' and 'death by negligence' outpace murders (of both men and women). As later examples reveal, these recorded numbers reflect a very small number of complaints. The other perspective, an evocative example of which is the 'Save Indian Family Foundation' webpage where blood drips from the glowing red letters '498A', parallels other accounts from men testifying that they have been humiliated, dragged through courts, and incurred severe financial losses because of the vengeance and greed of women and their natal families. These two perspectives set the discursive stage for discussions of legal provisions around violence. Is physical violence ubiquitous in married women's lives? If not, or even if so, what (non-physical) violations are perceived by women to be equally troubling? Or, is it men who are systematically victimized through the evocation of domestic violence? If not, what are their complaints interpellating?

TABLE 10.1   Incidence of Cognizable Crimes (IPC) Under Different Crime Heads, 1953 to 2004

Year	Dowry Deaths	Cruelty by Husband or Relatives	Causing Death By Negligence	Total Cognizable Crimes u/IPC	Murder
1995	4,648	28,579		1,695,696	37,464
1996	5,513	35,246		1,709,576	37,671
1997	6,006	36,592		1,719,820	37,543
1998	6,975	41,375		1,778,815	38,584
1999	6,699	43,823		1,764,629	37,170
2000	6,995	45,778		1,771,084	37,399
2001	6,851	49,170	57,182	1,769,308	36,202
2002	6,822	49,237	64,044	1,780,330	35,290
2003	6,208	50,703	60,672	1,716,120	32,716
2004	7,026	58,121	69,423	1,832,015	33,608

Source: NCRB, Government of India (Available at: http://ncrb.nic.in/cii2007/cii-2007/1953-2007.pdf).

In this article domestic violence complaints serve as a way to think through the uses of multiple forums for (gender) justice: criminal complaints to police, civil remedies and community mediation forums work to address the problem with overlapping but often contradictory imperatives, and each is used to negotiate kinship structure and socio-economic sustenance as well. As scholars of legal pluralism have evocatively demonstrated in the last two decades, courts and law enforcement venues are only a very partial component of 'law' in any given society—'law' is broadly and creatively interpreted by users, both by fashioning legal norms from cultural or moral norms, and by making use of legal norms that fit cultural needs. While the contemporary nation-state puts forth mechanisms of governance of law and order[3], they are transformed both legally and culturally, often being used to mediate and translate a variety of other issues. In this case, the emergence of multiple venues to address domestic violence does not necessarily mean that domestic violence is thereby rendered docile and manageable—rather, the cases are used (for men) to mark unease with their affinal kin and their sense of entitlement to marital property, and (for women) to process marital property and kin negotiations in extended households. Police, arrest, bail, etc., transform the space of marriage through an unprecedented apparatus of governance, but also play out dominant cultural conceptions. The discourse of litigants, judges, police and mediators analysed in this article delineates the significance of domestic violence in the political economy of marriage: the tensions between looking to marriage for economic sustenance and undoing marriage through invocations of violence, the salience of social class in claiming the harm of violence, and the radical potential of laws of gender justice that may be contrarily deployed to secure dominant notions of domestic order.

THEORETICAL FRAMEWORKS: LAW AS CULTURE AND POWER

Law is both the realm of intensely practical strategy and also that of diffuse symbolic connotation. Clifford Geertz famously conceptualized law as primarily a symbolic map, 'a cultural system of meanings', 'part of a distinctive manner of imagining the real', 'a species of social imagination' (Geertz 1983: 184). According to Geertz, legal reasoning is one of the most significant ways in which people try to make explicit sense of their world, and it is itself partially constitutive of that world, notably through law's capacity to relate general concepts to particular cases (Fuller 1994: 232).

Geertz's perspective, while underemphasizing relations of power and repression (Fuller 1994) that gain significance in later analyses, provides for a focus on the polyvalent meanings inherent in legal manoeuvres, a reminder that engaging with the legal realm always also entails specific entanglements with family and state and that law is metaphorically or metonymically working out those dramas. Foucauldian analysis urges attention to ways in which relations of power are diffused and ubiquitously met with resistance, becoming both changed by resistance and resilient to it (Abu-Lughod 1993). Contemporary legal anthropology heavily favours such study of law as a discursive system, an arena where the interplay of hegemony and resistance might be examined particularly well. In this vein, Mindie Lazarus-Black and Susan Hirsch characterize law as 'simultaneously a maker of hegemony and a means of resistance' (Lazarus-Black and Hirsch 1999: 9), presenting instances where marginal subjects' use of legal tools both destabilizes and emphasizes the resilience of hegemonic norms, as well as cases where recourse to the law is empowering even as legal categorization proves limiting and coercive. In both Geertzian and Foucauldian analyses, law is a space to examine meaning-making and power structures, providing a window on fundamental cultural struggles.

As Sally Engle Merry ably summarized in a now classic article, anthropologists have broadened their notions of legal pluralism beyond colonial customary law boundaries to examine evocations (and systematic avoidance) of law in a variety of rural and urban settings: 'Plural normative orders are found in virtually all societies. This.... places at the center of investigation the relationship between the official legal system and other forms of ordering that connect with but are in some ways separate from and dependent on it' (Merry 1988: 873).[4]

Important here is that 'normative' orders vie for salience with the legal order, but also what Griffiths has called the 'semiautonomy' of the two realms and their mutual constitutiveness (1986: 38). Anthropologists have continued to ponder the definition and salience of law, and the mechanisms through which state and kin realms are melded and separated, with definitions getting ever broader in scope. Revealing the interplay of custom and law in various Papua New Guinea settings, Demain claims that 'it is now widely recognized that anything presuming to call itself 'law' is a product of a specific moment in the history of a society' (2003: 99). Tamanaha reviews a wide range of literature, seeking a definition of law that will be neither functionalist (pre-specifying that law maintains a certain form of social order) nor essentialist (defining what should count as law), and concluding that 'Law is whatever people identify and treat through their social practices as 'law'' (2000: 313). Law, thus, must be explored with ethnographic and historical specificity if its meaning in a given context is to be determined.

The focus of inquiry in this article is the motivation behind approaches to legal fora, and the meanings assigned to various fora.

Merry demonstrated that people (working-class Americans in her sample) may approach courts with ideas of justice being both abstract or idealistic and situational. Thus, while law acts to make 'the power of ruling groups' seem 'fair and acceptable', for non-hegemonic subjects 'some aspects of the ideology of the dominant society are incorporated and others are not' (Merry 1986: 255). Seeming manipulations of the law can thus be read as attempts to put law to complex use rather than fetishizing it. Engel studied an American small town where both engaging with and refraining from legal engagement carried significant cultural connotations, but there was often a 'double translation' of sense making in and out of legal categories:

> To 'go to the law' means typically to assert an interest through the formal juridical apparatus....To assert the same interest elsewhere implies the selection of different rules, procedures and forums in keeping with the system chosen. The decision to go to court may, in some instances, imply a deliberate choice to step outside the local culture, to translate the subject matter from the language of local customs into the language of the formal legal system, to obtain an outcome based on the premises and procedures of the court, and then to return to the existing system of relationships with a resolution obtained externally (Engel 1980: 430–31).

The following cases illuminate this process of double translation rather vividly, showing people negotiating around various legal spaces for extra-legal outcomes. However, as Erin Moore's study of one Muslim woman's legal engagements shows, approaching law is a limited form of resistance when 'law legitimizes ideologies and asymmetrical power relations, particularly between genders' (Moore 1999: 30).

DISCERNING THE SHAPE OF DOMESTIC VIOLENCE

What counts as family or domestic violence? It must be emphasized that data only exist in very specific categories and provide an incomplete picture, although the categories in existence reveal evidence of a substantial problem in South Asia. As gatherers of data we are well aware that we often lack language to define and ask questions about violence. For example, while gathering data on domestic violence in Bangladesh and West Bengal, the words *nari nirjaton* (roughly translated as torture of women) are often used, also the English word 'torture', indicating ways in which legal entities work themselves back into interpellating cultural practices, generating new interpretations of existing phenomena; how people understand these terms colloquially is an inquiry beyond the scope of this article. Suffice it to say that categories generated in development discourse are used to name certain forms of violence and to seek their corresponding remedies.

The Indian NCRB reports in 2004 that the rate of crimes against women in Delhi is slated to rise higher than the population growth rate by 2010. There are 7,000 reported domestic violence complaints in Delhi annually (UN Wire 2000). In 1995 'torture of women' was recorded as 29.2 per cent of crimes against women. Leela Visaria's report on Gujarat showed that two-thirds of the women surveyed reported some physical, psychological or sexual abuse (including 42 per cent who reported beatings or sexual assault, and 23 per cent who reported 'abusive language, belittlement and threats'), echoing previous findings where 36–38 per cent of women in a Tamil Nadu study and 42–48 per cent of women in an Uttar Pradesh study reported violence (Visaria 1999: 10). As Pande summarizes, three studies from different states in India have shown that 'violence cuts across caste, class, religion, age and education boundaries. Regardless of the level of economic prosperity or literacy rate, two out of every five wives in India experience physical abuse' (Pande 2002: 344). Another estimate is that nearly 50 million women are victims of domestic violence, of which only 0.1 per cent cases are reported (Centre for Social Research 2005a: 2).

Coomaraswamy's UNIFEM report traces the trajectory of legislation on violence against women. International feminist mobilization against such violence acquired momentum in the 1980s, and was further spurred by the CEDAW[5] Committee's response to feminist demands to count violence against women as a form of gender discrimination in 1991, and the UN Declaration of the Elimination of Violence against Women in 1993. The Report contends: 'The violence against women movement is perhaps the greatest success story of international mobilization around a specific human rights issue, leading to the articulation of international norms and the formulation of international programs and policies' (Coomaraswamy 2005: 2).

Gathering data on domestic violence was a feminist political act of naming forms of silence and oppression, arising out of such political mobilization. Government and other agency statistics began to be collected at about the same time that the following civil and criminal remedies became operational. There is, thus, some coherence between the statistics and the envisaged solutions (although these are often quite transformed as they work their way through political processes) in terms of feminist theory, but more dissonance at the level of practice, particularly because those working in the remedial structures may be resistant to feminist critiques of violence.

There are three principal routes for addressing domestic violence in India: civil, criminal and community mediation. In order to avoid the publicity of legal venues, individuals or families may seek pre-litigation mediation through a variety of community organizations, and even through the police or the courts. Secondly, in the course of divorce cases, women may make allegations of domestic violence as a form of cruelty constituting grounds for divorce, and a rationale for claiming 'maintenance' costs while living away from spouses. (Men may do so too, but given the gendering of economic protection, I did not observe any such cases). In the lawyer-free Family Courts where I started my participant observation, judges evaluate claims of abuse and nutritional neglect (typically brought by women) against claims of domestic unadaptability and incapacity to pay (typically brought by men). Thirdly, besides these civil remedies (which principally provide monetary compensation), criminal complaints may also be lodged under Section 498 of the IPC, a broad provision against 'torture' as already mentioned. S. 498 owes its existence to persistent feminist campaigning: in the PROWID report, Nishi Mitra reminds us that S. 498 was seen as groundbreaking because it identified family violence as criminal behaviour, and provided that the accused (both husbands and affinal families) may be arrested without a warrant and held without bail,[6] and that charges could be filed on the testimony of the tortured person without other witnesses (Mitra 1999: 21).[7]

However, there have been persistent allegations that, because such slight evidence is required to file a 498 arrest warrant, it is widely misused for revenge by women, to humiliate the affines. Various 'men's groups' have sprung up specifically to protest this (Solanki 2001; UN Wire 2000). I remember getting a pamphlet in 1992 in the Indian Law Institute library showing a man and his parents in tears while his wife took all their money and had them thrown in jail.[8] A corresponding cry is now raised, for example, by the website 'Save Indian Family Foundation', which foregrounds alleged narratives of numerous men who 'suffered' patiently for years, acceding to their wives' demands for money and for moving out of the virilocal extended family, until one day the wives (and their families) had the husband and his frail relatives put in prison on a 498 charge.

Some of the headlines—'3-year-old girl arrested in a false dowry case in India', 'Bollywood Godmother Nirupa Roy brutally slandered before her death', 'Raped girl arrested on dowry torture charges'—alongside the invocation of high suicide rates for men (remember the much higher NCRB figures for women!), and the claim to be working primarily to stop 'elder abuse' by false imprisonment, delineate women as powerful and vengeful, and men and their families as helpless, in an ironic reversal of the images usually associated with dowry harassment. The primary author of this website, Peco Chakravatru, describes this phenomenon with his neologism 'S.O.W.R.Y (Son-in-law's Own Wealth Released to You) Harassment', and places the blame squarely on S. 498 for providing women with a supposedly unfair advantage.[9] It is, obviously, impossible to ascertain the veracity of the claims on the website. Even if we deem the individual narratives to be true, however, the framing of the issue is similar to the disproportionate hype attached to false allegations of rape in the US. While erroneous or malicious accusations may be made in a very small number of cases (1–2 per cent of rape cases in the US, 6.5 per cent of dowry and cruelty against women cases in India [Centre for Social Research 2005b: 1], the systemic and widespread nature of existent violence gets downplayed in the process.[10]

More importantly, representatives of groups addressing violence against women have acknowledged that S. 498 can be capricious in its application. Maitreyi Chatterji of Nari Nirjaton Pratirodh Mancha (Forum Against Torture of Women) contended that elite women have been able to use their influence to have police act on S. 498 and have succeeded in creating dramatically humiliating scenarios for their husbands and in-laws (she cited a case of a politically well-connected woman married to a prominent actor), but that women without socio-economic resources continue to have a very hard time getting police to file complaints. She recalled a case where a woman's in-laws bribed the police, who refused to press charges.[11] The CSR Report cited police, lawyers and judges who claimed there is misuse by 'educated and independent minded women' (ibid.: 10). As Madhu Mehra's analysis of judicial decisions reveals, this duality is mirrored in case law, where certain women (often elite) are believed to be entitled to a broader slate of rights, while for non-elite women, 'domestic violence has often been legitimized as natural to the institution of marriage' and the idea that women should be more forgiving and 'have a greater biological capacity to tolerate adversity' are put forward (Mehra 1998: 68, 71). Nishi Mitra also identifies several 'practical constraints' on filing a case under S. 498:

The complainant cannot realistically hope to gain access to her matrimonial home once she files a case. Thus, women without alternate shelter and financial support cannot exercise this option. The husband's family also often proposes withdrawing the case as a precondition for an easy divorce. (Mitra 1999: 22)

The construction of an appropriate 'battered' gendered subject, associated standards of evidence and action, alongside questions of caste and class, are thus salient in interpreting S. 498 prosecutions.

Even so, while a certain number of arrests may take place, the number of convictions is extremely low. Solanki (2001: 84) found 100 per cent acquittals among the cases that were filed in a particular Women's Cell. The Report on Delhi Crime Cell shows that 53.98 per cent of complaints recorded under S. 498 and S. 304B (related to dowry) do not become formal cases; 74 per cent of S. 498 and S. 304B cases combined are challenged in court, and 87 per cent of cases decided by courts result in acquittals (Pande 2002: 346). In one district of Maharashtra, 2.2 per cent of cases between 1990 and 1996 resulted in convictions (Mitra 1999: 22). In the Women's Grievance Cell, where I undertook participant observation in Kolkata, 2004 figures were even more dramatic: 470 petitions were received, and only four were recorded as cases (about 230 becoming 'counselling' or mediation cases). The Centre for Social Research Report found no convictions that relied solely on S. 498 (although there were a few where S. 498 was combined with S. 302 for murder and S. 304 for dowry death), the biggest legal obstacles being the difficulty of providing concrete evidence of torture and evidentiary proof of cruelty, especially mental cruelty. An important practical problem for feminist groups has been the facts mentioned by Nishi Mitra as quoted above, that a woman effectively loses access to her matrimonial home by filing a complaint, and that there is often pressure to withdraw the case as a condition for easy divorce.

Still, Nishi Mitra argues that the deterrent value of S. 498 is critical, and that it should be recognized under best practices to address domestic violence. A 2005 Supreme Court decision against a claim to strike down the law for potential abuses also held

… that the mere possibility of abuse of a provision of law does not invalidate the law. In cases of abuse, it is the 'action' and not the 'section' that may be vulnerable. The court, while upholding the provision of law, may still set aside the action, order or decision and grant relief to the aggrieved person. (Shukla 2005)

Gopika Solanki has a more tentative scope in conclusion, that S. 498 'offers a small section of women some leverage to negotiate for their rights at the time of marriage. This is particularly important given the fact that there is no concept of matrimonial property rights for women in Indian law' (Solanki 2001: 84).

FAMILY COURT: JUDGE-FRAMED PRIORITIES

In India, the establishment of Family Courts is tied to demands arising out of the feminist movement of the 1970s and 1980s, as well as the prominence of 'Alternative Dispute Resolution' (ADR) methods to counter bureaucratic complication, delays and corruption in the courts. The Family Courts Act, 1984, decreed that special courts were to be created for the disposal of divorce, maintenance, adoption and custody cases. These were to be courts where litigants would express their concerns to judges in 'plain language'; lawyers were generally excluded, although they could appear on petition as *amicus curiae* (friend of court). Importantly, it is this mode of operation or speaking that is different; the legal apparatus, including evidence, rights of appeal and reference to case law, apply as in conventional courts. Clients were to work first with 'counsellors' (paralegals or social workers, not lawyers), who would help negotiate settlements, try to bring the parties back together, and advise about legal issues. The Kolkata court came into being on 12 September 1994. It currently has positions for two judges and handles cases for about one quarter of the city. Its jurisdiction is based on where litigants live, and cases in other areas go through conventional 'mixed' civil courts.

In various Indian venues, Family Courts are talked about as spaces where women have an advantage (although this view is strongly contested by both judges and counsellors who see themselves being fair to both genders). In Mumbai, they are referred to as *baikanche* courts (women's courts). There may be said to be a few advantages, such as speedier disposal of cases.[12] Processes for obtaining maintenance are also fairly streamlined, although there are many gaps between getting the maintenance award and receiving the money in hand. But though generated from feminist demands, the courts have been a controversial venue for gender justice. While reports have described the ease of access to the courts, they have also pointed out that women are often vulnerable to judges' mercies in these courts, and that these courts do not necessarily have a supportive atmosphere free from expectations of gendered behaviour (Das 1996; Singh 1996; Anjali 1995). My ethnography of the

Kolkata court has also emphasized the unchanged structures of power in a superficially changed venue.

According to the 1984 Act, Family Courts are set up 'with a view to promote conciliation in, and secure speedy settlement of disputes related to marriage and family affairs' (S. 1 of the Act). 'Conciliation' is a slippery concept here. While a few practitioners take it to be a mode of conflict resolution, an antonym of 'adversarial process',[13] it is commonly interpreted to mean that 'reconciliation' must be tried to the utmost extent before divorce. The language of the Act (S. 9), and the Parliamentary Introduction to the Bill both ambiguously refer to 'conciliation in marriage' and the latter frames it in terms of 'preserv[ing] the institution of marriage and promot[ing] the welfare of children'.[14] Thus, not only might these two stated purposes—efficiency and preservation of marriage—be seen as contradictory interests for the state, but the goals of preserving marriage and serving women's best interests are also potentially contradictory—the management of domestic violence is of crucial importance here. Elsewhere, I have recorded numerous cases in Kolkata where conciliation as process is taken to mean 'reconciliation into marriage' as outcome, where court counsellors describe horrific tales of axe-wielding husbands and family torture to narrate how they proudly worked out happy 'reunions' and persuaded husbands to be not quite as controlling, often citing women's lack of other economic options to marriage in addition to the glory of reunion per se. This may be chilling as legal process, but is consonant with community responses to domestic violence. Judges, too, see themselves as intervening to better facilitate marriages in ways that they would not in other courts—they cite talking people through their problems and ensuring speedy resolution of cases as the most important features of their jobs.[15]

Domestic violence emerges in these niches around reconciliation, but is also often addressed by judges in terms of economic compensation. While norms of gendered behaviour were graphically present in adjudicatory decisions, in general the judges were very careful to pay attention to issues of women's economic maintenance. I witnessed one case where the woman had left her husband and was living with another man, another where there were numerous reports (and evidence in court) of a woman's querulous and erratic nature: the judges were annoyed by these women who were clearly not models of ideal feminine behaviour (in the latter case she was even removed from the courtroom), but always insisted that the bottom line was providing her a liveable allowance as part of the solution. Indeed, judges described their role in ensuring speedy and just economic sustenance as the most significant part of their jobs.[16]

Yet the knowledge that women may additionally have filed parallel charges of 'physical and mental torture' in the criminal courts under S. 498 was cause for great suspiciousness, the implication from judges (and counsellors) being that the woman's invocation of S. 498 was a wilful destruction of her marriage and an unforgivable embarrassment to her husband and affinal family, as well as an arbitrary demonstration of power. One of the celebrities seen in court, Pratima, a singer (and teacher), exemplified such power in the case she brought against her husband, a prominent senior government official, with the ensuing publicity believed to have brought them to the brink of extreme vendetta and bitterness. Observation of this case, both in court and in counselling sessions, showed clearly that Pratima sought full advantage of legal provisions and articulated a desire for public retribution. Moreover, neither judges nor counsellors sought to interrogate her on her claim even though they expressed wariness about her motivation, in a perfect example of the difference that social class makes.

In contrast, the judge countered a more middle-class homemaker litigant Sudha's allegation that she had been slapped when she refused to go out with her husband (the husband claimed the wife was insane and had hit him as well) by asking her jocularly: 'Are you sure you didn't smack him (*chor mara*) about something? We women do this to our husbands, all the time.' Sudha's rhetorical and legal strategy was to seek to return to her affinal home despite the violence (or to claim maintenance in the alternative). Her mother's rendition of this claim to me foregrounded the notion of domestic violence as a condition of marriage and marriage as the only possible living situation: '*ki ar hobe, morey geley morey jabo, meyeder to shoshurbaritei jayga, biyer por baperbarite thakte nei, ar Hindu meyer ek bar-i biye hoi*' (roughly translatable as 'so what, if I die I die. Women belong in their affinal homes, and ought not to live at their parents' after marriage. A Hindu woman gets married only once'). This picture-perfect articulation of Hindu women's ideological assent should be framed in the context of several levels of translation and vested interests, such as the mother's inability to support the daughter financially or to speak up for her to be supported by her brother in the long term, as well as the best possible rationale for seeking to return to a home where routine violence had already been claimed. The S. 498 case registered a protest against violence, although not necessarily an intention to end the marriage, while the parallel civil suit sought financial support within the marriage, but they were treated as incompatible in the counsellor's question, 'how can she blame me for the divorce if she filed a 498?' Thus, Sudha's 498 claim was regarded dismissively as a question of miscommunication by the judge and failed strategy by the counsellor, in contrast to that of the powerful Pratima whose status had ensured a public fracas.

The following case provides a somewhat thicker description of the suspicion accorded to invocations of S. 498, as well as the succession of strategies deployed by litigants. It began in this session with the judge K.B.'s queries to the husband Hemanto, about part of a house he owned in Chandannagar, a town a few hours away from Kolkata. She asked whether they had two separate rooms, and if the kitchen could be made separate. That is, she was asking about possibilities for the wife Shibani to move into a space where she would be free of interference from her affinal kin, implying that this was central to the solution. It was unclear who was being protected from whom in this process. Hemanto agreed but said the bathroom could not be really separated, whereupon the famously loquacious K.B. talked at length about her own experience of north Kolkata houses where the downstairs bathroom was for women and the upstairs for men. Hemanto, perhaps trying to get back to matters legal, tried to strike a note of compliance, saying he was willing to increase the interim maintenance slightly, 'whatever you decide', and showed his railway department salary certificate for Rs 3,000 per month as proof of earnings, with additional earnings in months when he got a travel allowance. Judge K.B., reviewing his documents, kept referring to his wife as having 'axed' him, *kop diyechche*, by having filed an S. 498, following which he had been suspended from his government job and almost fired. The charge was dismissed because none of the neighbours finally testified.

K.B. then initiated the process of cross-examination by the wife, by inquiring of Shibani if she had anything to ask him. She was silent—litigants often seem intimidated by the thought of being cross-examiners in court. K.B. repeated the query a couple more times, then yelled, '*ei meyeder karbar*' ('these things women do!). Shibani finally said in a very low voice that she left the house because she was '*nirjatito*' ('tortured', a word brought into this discourse primarily through feminist activism), to which K.B. responded: 'But you're the one who was able to give him the axe (*kurul diyechchilen*), you filed the 498. Because of you he was about to lose his job, and this is a Railways job. If I send a qualified person to you, can you get them a Railways job? Is it so easy to get?' Here, Shibani's allegation of violence was not only minimized, but this violence was also treated as being less than a 498 charge. The judge then paused dramatically, smiled broadly, and said with an ironic twinge,

> But you want your maintenance claim, don't you? (*Khorposh ta to chan?*) You're not willing to live with him under any circumstances [referring to what Shibani had said in her claim, and what K.B. had been trying to ascertain in her questions about residential arrangements to separate the conjugal unit], but you still want maintenance. You tried to have it both ways by filing a 498 while the other case is going on. If he was convicted you would have lost all the money so this strategy of playing both things would not work. You're not some simple dumb woman (*sadashidhey bokashoka non*), you were able to put him through this process so I know you know what's going on and you must respond in court.

K.B. switched gears and asked her about how much interim maintenance she wanted. Shibani said Rs 500 instead of the present Rs 225 (K.B. had asked Hemanto earlier if he could raise it perhaps to Rs 300 in response to her petition). Then K.B. asked how much permanent alimony she wanted, that is, 'from now till the end of your life', she explained. Shibani was silent for a long time and K.B. was getting visibly angrier at this, iterating her query about how much she needed for food and clothes, when Shibani suddenly burst out in a rush that she wanted Rs 2,500 per month. 'What do you eat?,' K.B. inquired rhetorically, and then asked what lump sum payment Shibani would settle for instead. She thought for a minute and said '10 lakhs'.[17] There was an audible gasp throughout the courtroom, and the judge's clerk surreptitiously flashed his palms in surprise to me ('Ten?! Ten?!!'). Even K.B. paused a bit and then said to Hemanto sarcastically, 'So, do you have 10 lakhs in your Provident Fund?[18] It would have to be a very different sort of government job than mine!' Hemanto merely smiled in agreement. (Meanwhile Shibani's brother had been saying from his bench: 'We don't want anything at all, we're just happy she got out of the torture', but only we could hear him). K.B. gave out two dates in the following month when the case would be finished. When Shibani asked if it could be a little later because her brother was not well, K.B. was unsympathetic: 'Your brother's health is no concern of the court. You must be there, you can't rely on your brother for the rest of your life, you need to know what's going on.'

It is, of course, impossible to determine the veracity of the domestic violence claim, nor to deny that filing S. 498 charges can provide a level of threat and leverage beyond the usual civil remedies that are highly dependant on the judge's mercies. However, the situation reveals some paradoxes involving recourse to these legal forums. Legally 'enterprising' behaviour is accorded suspicion, and becomes grounds for insisting on a whole new package of legal and cultural subjectivity from the woman. If there were to be a presumption that the S. 498 complaint was genuine (rather than the usual a priori assumption that it was false, manipulative or both), then the filing of the dual claim, using the appropriate channels, should be an entirely valid act, and the recommended corollaries of job suspension and possible job loss should signal the seriousness of the offence, rather than being typified as revenge. Given women's economic dependence on marriage for survival (lack of natal and marital property shares, labour market inequities, and ideologies of women's domestic responsibilities all contributing to this), the legal conundrum is, indeed, that claims for maintenance are made to the person against whom one is filing criminal charges. The potential conviction negates the very earning power that is relied upon in the maintenance claim, and the two legal provisions are located in separate conceptual niches meant to provide very different kinds of remedies. The onus of resolving the contradiction seems to fall upon the female litigant here. Each remedy works only if the other fails, and thus either violence complaints must be foregone in order to maintain the cash flow, or economic support must be foregone if symbolic redress of violence is deemed to be more important.

Scripts of femininity and female agency also weigh heavily in the balance in this judgement. K.B. treated Hemanto with apparent sympathy, not inquiring into the veracity of the S. 498 claim and validating his sense of entrapment with the ironic metaphor of his wife 'axing' him, which casts the verbal claim against physical violence as the violent act. Nor did she inquire whether the lack of participation of neighbours as witnesses was a sign of disinclination to be involved in legal process rather than a testament to the lack of violence. She devoted quite some time to residential arrangements, exploring with Hemanto options for his wife's return: she tried to work out a way for him to be able to offer his wife a conjugal space without extended family, such that Shibani's refusal to move back there could then be read as a failure of her domestic duties, and her maintenance claim a further burden upon marital resources. It also opened up a way for him to claim desertion as a ground of eventual divorce, and then to pay little by way of maintenance because desertion would put her at 'fault' in the divorce.

The amount of maintenance Shibani asked for seemed to turn courtroom opinion against her, as if that made the torture claim spurious, because she shouldn't be thinking about money if she was indeed a genuine victim. It is relevant to point out here that she was paid a pittance at the time, the equivalent of a few days' food costs for her family. His seemingly generous gesture to double it (which would make it a sixth of his stated income) makes him appear amenable to the judge but is still grossly inadequate to live on. Most people in the room would be aware that a railway salary would, more often than not, be plentifully supplemented by an under-the-table income, so the norms of determining evidence by salary certificates further diminishes her entitlement. Shibani's brother, in this scenario, publicly protested about the violence, and wanted her 'home', without any money demands (possibly sensitive to the ways the claims cancel each other, possibly also to avert criticisms of his own role in financially supporting her). But her financial dependence was also constructed by his own entitlement, sons being preferred heirs of natal property, despite laws to the contrary.

The transformation of subjectivity presumed to occur here is also predicated on assumptions of agency in using legal provisions. The judge's irritation with Shibani (shown, for example, when she exclaimed 'you're not some simple dumb woman') is addressed to her silence, seemingly contradicted by her having approached the criminal court. The judge's refusal to change the hearing schedule and the admonition that she should be independent and not rely on her brother also implicitly rebukes her for the other case. However, the maintenance amounts deemed suitable are so low that they do, ironically, make her reliant on her brother or presume new training and skills for the labour market.[19]

There is an explicit sense in such cases that the judge's role as sole authority has been insulted because litigants have taken some matters into their own hands, and also that women litigants have asserted themselves in ways that are at odds with their roles as economically vulnerable entities in need of the court's protection. The implication is that women's empowerment can best be achieved second-hand, through the judge's benevolent patronage. The Family Court process of apportioning maintenance or evaluating physical violence as part of the divorce grounds of cruelty were regarded by judges and counsellors as fairer ways of getting adequate maintenance for women, without embarrassment all around. Thus domestic violence was both assigned a compensatory value and effaced as crime in the process.

THE POLICE CELL: AVERTING DIVORCE

The Women's Grievance Cell of the Kolkata Police was also, like the Family Court, started in 1995, but, unlike the courts, was not related to any feminist demands. As Mitali Samaddar, the Officer-in-Charge (OC) of the Cell in 2005, narrated to me, in 1988 the Deputy Commissioner (DCDD) Gautam Chakravarty decided counselling would be a good idea for some violence cases: 'He said to us, "listen to them, hear their problems"; and I soon understood too when I applied my own smarts to it that a third party intervention often resolves things (*mitey jai*).' The staff of four takes on both investigation and counselling, but seems especially proud of the reconciliations they have effected. Samaddar knows right away that she has done twenty-one in her present position, and that only four cases were officially registered in 2004 though 470 petitions came to them. The staff at the unit are candid and indeed proud of their un-police-like tasks, and sanguine about the roles they play in the process. Samaddar's assertion that 'we prefer counselling because you can't have a home if there is a 498' (*498 case holey ar ghar-ta hoi na, tai counselling prefer kori*) is iterated often by her staff as common-sense knowledge. She described to me that often the 'counselling' process lasts five to six months, and then they often see that 'there is a home again' (the Bangla phrase *ghar boshey gelo* evoking both home and settling in spatial terms). Alternatively, they might see 'not torture but problems with adjustment' and advise divorce by mutual consent and reasonable (*shushthu*) compensation. If they see right away that there is a lot of 'torture', she said, they might call the husband in a few times, or if it is very severe, they might arrest him right away before he gets tipped off. Samaddar insisted about S. 498 that 'they [litigants] do it to apply pressure' (*pressure debar jonyo korey*), evoking a metaphor of performance and manipulation: 'let me tell you how the game works' (*khelata apnakey boli*).

In the following case the performances of both litigants and investigator reveal the salience of economic claims in the dissolution of marriage, and claims of violence as a discursive strategy for framing such claims. When I arrived one morning, I saw a woman (I call her Rekha here) in her late twenties or early thirties, in a pink-and-blue salwar kameez, sitting with Samaddar describing the details of her marriage. She married in 1999 and had a three-year-old child. Her husband had a temporary job in British Airways at the time paying about Rs 6,000 per month, which had progressed at the time of recounting the story to a permanent job paying Rs 25,000. Her father-in-law was a bank manager, her husband's brother a dentist in the US, her own father a retired college professor in Midnapore, a small town in West Bengal (that is, his family appeared to be considerably stronger financially). She claimed her husband's family had been very opposed to the marriage, that her father-in-law used to say they were a bad (*kharap*) family, and that his son ought not to have suddenly got married while his sisters were still unmarried. After living by themselves for a bit, they moved into her father-in-law's flat, but she alleged that her father-in-law wanted her generally confined to her room and often cursed her as ill-behaved and unruly (*oshobhbho beyadob*). He wanted her to have an abortion when she was pregnant and simultaneously had a gallstone, and did make her have an abortion for her second pregnancy. By her account, her husband was at first castigated for being caring towards her when she was ill, but his behaviour had changed a lot in the last few years, especially since his brother had visited. After the brother's visit they demanded that she leave the house, and she had been at her parents' since then, locked out of the matrimonial home and considering whether there should be a divorce proceeding.

The OC checked and confirmed that there was actually a divorce case underway, wherein her father-in-law had accused her of 'behaving badly' (*kharap byabohar*) in his plaint. She also told Rekha that she had called the husband's family three times to come in. They made excuses twice, and once there was a time conflict. At this point, Samaddar's interrogative mode changed physically and verbally—looking too casually at her ring while cleaning it out, she asked Rekha: 'What do you want out of this?' (*ki chaichchen?*). Rekha replied with the English word 'settlement'. The word seemed to imply divorce by mutual consent, because Samaddar reminded her that it took a year for the divorce, and that settlement was difficult in cases such as this where she had an 'irritative' nature and there had been disputes (*jhograjhanti*).

Rekha's only allegations of physical violence emerged at this point. She said she had been thrown down in the bathroom, and had not told her parents she cracked her head. But the OC, like the judge who ignored the only evocation of violence in Shibani's case, went on with her earlier thought: 'Your case is legally weak, so now all we can try is counselling.' It emerged that there was no substantive record of any violence, other than a 'GD' (general diary or account of an offence written down at a police station, not necessarily investigated) filed shortly before the divorce was filed; Rekha's father who had come in recounted: 'The local police station wanted to use counselling to make him less rigid, that's why they recommended filing a case.' The Grievance Cell's response at this point illuminates the power dynamics of the criminal/ civil binary divide. Samaddar rebuked, 'The *thana* (police station) don't know these things, they don't need to know, but *we* know that filing a case creates more rigidity'. Another staff member chimed in: 'When you make a report at the *thana* that means the husband promptly puts in a 'mat suit' [matrimonial suit or divorce case] to counter the police claim.' Samaddar further interrogated Rekha:

> Tell me the truth, what did you say to your father-in-law? How did you talk to him? Marrying someone because you were in love (*Prem korey biye korlam*) doesn't mean they are your property, he has parents too. No one's real personality comes out during romance—tell me the truth now, how did you react (to them)? Did you force him into marriage? If you reacted [badly], the son will not go against the father, I would not either.

The final advice to Rekha and her father significantly invoked both the strategic powers of legal fora and the new agency interpellated for women who appear in these fora: 'You can't just start a criminal case in a naïve way (*bokar moto*), you have to win it. She should have been more 'intelligent' and patient (*shohonshil*), now she has poisoned her husband's mind against herself.' Her scant offer of help was that they would try to 'set up the home again, since there is a child—but everything has been delayed because of the case'. Rekha and her father asked for the OC to talk with the other parties before the court hearing in two weeks, since they could not talk directly while the matrimonial suit was underway. She promised they would try, and that a 498 case could be filed later if the counselling failed, but that this would not go well if the divorce judgement went against them in court. The final question from Rekha's father, seemingly in response, was: 'How much could maintenance be?' The answer again was deeply circuitous: 'Time will be needed. If the police try to achieve something good then it takes time, we have to show the police are involved in 'social welfare'.'

This case exemplifies the confusion around the two legal provisions, and the inseparable connection between domestic violence, alimony and divorce. The Police Cell entrusted with monitoring S. 498 claims puts forth the analysis that launching a case under S. 498 delays matters, precipitates divorce proceedings and wreaks irreparable damage; the only good 498 case is one that does not quite become a 498 case. Both divorce and criminal suits appear here as a carefully choreographed set of call-and-return responses of which all participants have slightly different readings. Rekha's father's question about maintenance at the end is thus not, as it seems, a non sequitur to Samaddar's suggestion about a 498 case down the line if the divorce hearing goes badly. It is, on the contrary, the heart of the whole conversation, because what is fundamentally sought is a home and financial sustenance for Rekha and her child.

As in the courtroom cases, women's behaviour is held to be responsible for the demise of a marriage, on the slightest of suspicions. The 'counselling' cell turns into its most interrogative form here. To call it tough love would be the kindest explanation. While I have no evidence as to how the in-laws in this case were treated (although I did watch interviews with several husbands where they were asked to undertake some behaviour modifications consistent with their gender roles), the onus of responsibility for ill-feeling and violence was put upon Rekha with no trail of evidence. The implication was that the only conditions under which she could lay claim to property and resources were if she showed self-effacing pleasantness no matter what came her way.

There was remarkably little discussion of the details of violence throughout the whole interview. The police officers discussed it merely in terms of relative strategy and never queried the facts. Even Rekha invoked physical violence only incidentally, implying that it would worry her parents. This may be consonant with the shameful silences of domestic violence survivors which are all too common across cultures. Again, while there is no way to ascertain the facts of violence, it is ironically significant that the whole legal apparatus is constructed around this little-mentioned aspect, and yet this was the one subject that Rekha seemed unwilling to articulate, and was the only possible leverage, double-edged though it was, for better terms in divorce. Unlike other divorce provisions, S. 498 is delineated as a space to resist the habitually unfavourable terms of divorce for women—hence the unusually fierce rhetoric against it, as also the confusion amongst those who invoke it seeking a range of expansive remedies.

Community Mediation: Leveraging Admitted Violence

There were very high hopes for community mediation, called *shalishi* in Bangla, during my 2004–5 fieldwork. Encouraged by the proliferation of alternative dispute resolution methods in courts and among non-governmental organizations (NGOs), and invoking customary village-level arbitration forums, the state government and the ruling party at that time had envisaged a network of shalishi forums at various local levels to supplement *and* complement formal legal settings. Given that people often took their complaints first to locals known to have influence and authority, or to neighbourhood [political] party offices or women's organizations, long before they sought formal legal sanction, there was a move to have some structured venues where semi-formal mediation could take place.[20] Some non-governmental women's organizations also got involved in 'women initiated community dispute resolution mechanisms' where 'responses emerge from culturally consistent solutions informed by the gradual increase in the organization's and women's collective power' (Talwar 2002: 2).

One of my fieldwork sites was the ambiguously-named *Paribarik Paramarsho O Shahayata Kendra* (Family Advice and Assistance Center would be a rough translation) in a medium-sized town about an hour from Kolkata, where arbitration sessions lasting about three to four hours were held every Friday. The unit was actually located inside one of the police posts in the town, advertising the *Mahila Pulish Tadanta Kendra* (this title can be translated as 'Police Investigative Centre for Women', but there is also a punning sense in which it could be read as 'Women Police Investigative Centre', given the prominence of female police officers). There was a different police station in town which functioned as a Women's Grievance Cell of the kind described in the previous section, where criminal complaints were to be investigated. The unit I observed was meant to be focused on shalish or arbitration and sent people off to the other police unit when necessary.

On one of my first visits, when I was being shown around by one of the constables, a motorcycle pulled up with two women and a man. Approaching the constable, one of the women introduced herself as being with a NGO in town, and said of the other woman, 'she is having some trouble at home and wants to report it'. The constable responded '*Ekhaney, jara shongshar korben tader jonyo*' (my translation: 'this place is only for those who want to pursue marriage' does little to capture the sense of *shongshar/sansar* as embodying notions of family, domesticity, worldliness), and said that she needed to go to the other police station for registering a complaint or seeking maintenance. To approach this unit, thus, is to foreground reconciliation as a putative outcome. While almost every case I observed here dealt with domestic violence, these cases do not even count in the record-keeping of the local Women's Grievance Cell, because in this town the two occupy mutually exclusive spaces.

The 'counselling' (their term) board consisted of a local female magistrate (of the lower courts), a male doctor, a female lawyer, the male supervisor of the centre and the female OC of the Cell. The 'board' had been given the authority to summon witnesses and draw up arbitration agreements but had no civil or criminal enforcement authority beyond that. However, given that the OC and a magistrate served on it, they seamlessly invoked these other formal roles during proceedings. The spatial configurations were conspicuously different from the previous settings. The board members sat on a row of chairs behind a wooden screen, across the table from a bench for the couple. But every other available seat was occupied by other family members and even neighbours, and over the top of the screen was a continuous row of heads peering in. In this setting, these families and community members were allowed, indeed encouraged, to attend.[21] This centre thus provides yet another semi-autonomous domain that deploys formal legal provisions even as it circumvents them, incorporating community sanctions and surveillance to extend its reach—an unofficial venue within a formidably official setting.

There were some marked differences from the previous two settings. Domestic violence allegations were often front-and-centre in women's complaints here, not merely obliquely evoked as part of legal strategy, nor contested by the accused or their families. The counsellors/arbitrators also took the violence seriously rather than minimizing or doubting it, perhaps because denial was impossible. The formal position was to condemn it in the strongest terms and emphasize its criminal nature. And yet, while their solutions contained provisions to reduce violence, they used outrage against violence to reconfigure socio-economic realms. These limitations were also present for Talwar's study of women-centred NGOs which used the main activist as facilitator and sought to foreground women's voices: 'if the intention is restoration of family life which is what the women want most often, it becomes necessary to deal sympathetically with the perpetrator' (Talwar 2002: 20). The challenge for this group was to balance feminist principles with cultural norms of the villages and arrive at consensus through persuasion (ibid.: 22).[22]

The following case is distinguished by the brash defiance of the husband Mirza, who readily admitted to drunkenness, drug use, battery and bigamy (the last being legally valid for Muslim men). The wife Fariza listed her complaints about eighteen years of marriage as follows: '*nesha bhang, khisti, maar, bochor bochor jomi bikri*' (being drunk/drugged, cursing her, beating her up, selling off their [family] land each year). Thus the physical violence was seen as part of a linked chain of behaviour, at least on par with economic abuse. She foregrounded two main triggers of the violence: her objection to her husband's family marrying off their daughter too young and to the particular groom; and her everyday complaints upon his return home that there was no food at home. Bigamy did not feature in her list of complaints. Mirza, on the other hand, foregrounded equitable treatment of his two wives and the need to provide for his second wife as well, possibly in some space in the same house if the children agreed: 'one lives in a two-storey hut and one in a two leaf-hut' (it rhymes in Bangla!), he kept muttering.

The adjudicatory board responded to a variety of issues rather than keeping a narrow focus, perhaps in line with their stated purpose of working towards a holistic community solution. Various members expressed regret at length about the daughter's marriage: 'She could have got a good job as a Muslim girl, have you seen the [good] jobs other girls are getting?' They began with the proposition that they would try for a *mimangsha* or solution, but that there would have to be a legal case if they failed to resolve matters. Mirza said he didn't want a legal skirmish at all costs, whereupon the doctor reminded him that in that case he should attend to what they said, suggesting that it would be in his best interest to do so because he had admitted to domestic violence and thus the very first step in a legal case might be a jail sentence. Occasional bouts of strong-arm negotiation followed from this, with a defiant Mirza saying, 'Fine, jail's what I want', or 'Now they'll see how much I can drink', and the police OC, the magistrate and the doctor making moves as if to put him away immediately, openly irritated and saying that a night in jail would do him a lot of good. These transactions indicate that none of the parties lacked knowledge of domestic violence as a criminal offence, and that it could always be called upon as an imminent threat. Its legal sanction provided a spectral yet capacious space in which other needs could be negotiated.[23]

The solution involved economic sustenance for Fariza by recourse to landed property that Mirza had been selling off systematically, such that only 6 bighas (about 2 acres) were left. Mirza was notionally willing to let his children from Fariza, though not Fariza herself, have access to half of his land, claiming the other half would be for the other wife and his business. The board examined the land documents closely, deciding that much of this family land had not even been his to sell, and rejecting his notion of making an informal transfer mediated by his father. Instead, they came up with a strongly patrilineal solution (far below the *de jure* gender equity of property law). He should formally pay to register two-thirds of the land in his son's name, with his daughter having access to it until marriage, and his wife in her lifetime. Mirza was to return to the board with legal documents showing he had completed the registration in his son's name. Other conditions included: the second wife was not to be brought back to this marital residence; Mirza was to be responsible for providing food for the household; and Fariza was to be able to choose or consent to her daughter's marriage partners. Both the husband and in-laws protested vehemently at this last condition, among other reasons saying, 'what if she picks a dark person?', but the board prevailed, at least in writing.

The board gave Fariza much overt support to use their resources, and to come back whenever there were problems, and also urged relatives on both sides to report any domestic violence to them. But they simultaneously negotiated a set of conditions which buttressed patriarchal authority over her mobility and decision making. While Fariza was to have access to the land, and a monthly maintenance amount, this was on condition that she return to her marital residence immediately, that she stay there peaceably (*shantimoto*), and that thereafter she get permission from her husband or in-laws when she wanted to visit her natal home. Mirza's discursive strategy was to speak to the rights of his absent second wife and her deprivation. His counter-offer was to allow Fariza to visit her parents only if the other wife could come to the marital residence as well. He protested by claiming that Muslim wives were not to leave home by themselves, but promptly followed that up by refusing to shop for food for her, saying she could go to the market herself. He was roundly berated for the latter and told he was liable for providing food, but the former injunction was never directly challenged. Even as the magistrate said to Mirza, 'remember you've signed things here, if you beat her up again you'll find out what the results are for you (*petaley bujhbey ki phol*)', she followed this up by advice to Fariza to 'get along with others (*maniye nao*)' and 'be less agitated/ rambunctious' (*lomphojhompo kom diyo*, which might literally be translated as 'don't jump up so much over everything').

Despite these complicated contractual exchanges, uneasiness prevailed as the group left. Fariza said that she was afraid he would beat her a lot because she had brought these issues to the board. 'Why did you do it then?' a married female neighbour chimed in, even as Fariza was urged by the board to calm down and seek help when necessary. The magistrate commented wistfully at their departure: 'Let's see them 'united' first, let them stay together first—there are a lot of problems from 'broken families'.' I asked in the interlude between cases whether they thought their intervention was going to stop Mirza's domestic violence: 'It may decrease a bit', the doctor responded.

The possibilities and circumscriptions of community mediations through official boards are exemplified here: the board has the skill and police resources to leverage criminal legal sanctions, and the civil authority to design a contract about maintenance and property that mirrors remedies constructed in venues such as the Family Court.[24] They articulate righteous if jaded outrage at domestic violence, consistently condemning it in all public declarations (and hoping some injunctions will stick as a result). The optimal conjugal family and the companionate marriage where partners have an equal say in family decisions, as imagined at the heart of postcolonial Family Law, is also reflected in their ancillary negotiations to allow women a say in their children's marriages, to imagine that sharing a home with a co-wife is humiliating to a first wife, and to refuse to sever women's relationships with their natal families. But correspondingly, they are governed by the ideological correlates of those same constructs of conjugality: that a 'united' family is optimal for mental health and social harmony, that women need to defer to authority structures in their affinal homes, and that women fare best when they act without undue agitation or strident claims.

CONCLUSION

The World Health Organization (WHO), which identifies violence as a critical problem of health and tabulates the costs of violence to various nations, uses an 'ecological model' to try to understand correlations and risk factors. In this model, biological and personal issues which influence individuals, relationships with family and friends, 'community contexts for social relationships', and broader social norms where violence is encouraged, form ever-broader concentric circles within which violence becomes realizable (WHO 2002: 9). Domestic violence easily spans all of these realms. As the UNIFEM report points out, the effects of domestic violence are harmful on various fronts: 'This normalization [of violence against women] prevents men from seeing the violence as wrong, prevents women from asserting that the violence is wrong, and paralyzes the criminal justice system in trying to attain justice' (Coomaraswamy 2005: 13).

Much effort has been expended on tracing the causes or correlations of such violence. Thus the WHO report tabulates correlations such as alcohol abuse or economic hardship, but analyses often come around to the notion that domestic violence is a fundamental ideological mirror of patriarchal relations: 'Women are particularly vulnerable to abuse in societies where there are marked inequalities between men and women, rigid gender roles…and weak sanctions against such behavior' (WHO 2002: 16; similarly, Coomaraswamy 2005: 8). Suggested solutions, correspondingly, have been, alongside the gathering of data, the formulation of a national plan, and 'strengthening responses for victims', broader attempts to 'integrate violence prevention into social and educational policies, and thereby promote gender and social equality' (WHO 2002: 31–33). In the cases discussed here legal sanctions are not inconsiderable, but social sanctions defuse legal accountability.

The cases discussed also illustrate perfectly the relationship between discourses of masculinity and violence. A comparative study of various regions in India affirmed that domestic violence was often linked to the inability to 'fulfill a hegemonic masculinity' (ICRW 2002: 2). Socio-economic or political disempowerment may be seen to threaten the salience men attach to the provider-protector role and thus they use violence 'in order to express their masculine dominance' (ibid.).[25] Another facet of this hegemonic discourse is 'controlling women in their family and ensuring that women fulfill expected roles', such that wives' complaints against men's behaviour or perceptions of their non-compliance in domestic duties become the commonest triggers of violence (ibid.). An alternative version of this formulation is 'adhering to perceived expectations, such as maintaining order in the family and being the primary decision maker' (ibid.: 69). In this article the cases where domestic violence was rendered invisible, as well as Mirza's case where it was admitted, centred on anxieties over husbands' economic abilities and wives' transgressive complaints. Affinal family control over women's mobility and men's decision-making power were often affirmed in decisions. While overt violence was condemned, the hegemonic ideologies through which such violence is justified continued to be validated.

S. 498 cases exemplify the difficulties of using law as an instrument of radical gender justice. While the clause individually names domestic violence, its placement in the corpus of other laws and cultural expectations undermines any hope of its effectiveness. At best, it allows for a strategic leverage of economic entitlements and a modification of certain forms of behaviour, but the manipulation involved does not serve to empower women as equal subjects in marriage. On the contrary, S. 498 processes can subject them to backlash and restrictions on their behaviour even as it provides minimal legal shelter. The power of the state is deployed to destabilize the structures of kinship, but acts principally to validate its behavioural norms. Unlike some other countries, leaving the conjugal home and moving into a shelter is not an optimal alternative for most women, given prevailing residence and occupational conditions. Consequently their 'decisions' to stay married mark poignant economic and ideological choices. Furthermore, they must often act by deploying the one lever that is designed to be disharmonious. Domestic violence thus continues to have lethal consequences whether it is relegated to silence, or articulated as a strategic solution.

Why, then, are numerous women and their families resorting to using this provision? Like Merry and Engel's studies, the examples here also show people moving themselves in and out of law in ways by which they can best optimize their socio-cultural and economic options. Law is not a formidable, ideal sphere but rather one of strategic translation. Even when the outcomes are statistically unfavourable, the effort is undertaken in order to attempt the best negotiation possible. These attempts at playing off different settings and provisions are not illegal or even extra-legal. In the sense recognized by Tamanaha, they have been culturally incorporated as a form of behaviour associated with law. However, the process against violence becomes rendered a mere strategy here—the fundamental protection recognized in S. 498 is sacrificed in favour of achieving sustenance goals.

NOTES

1. The research draws on my fieldwork in Kolkata in 2001 and 2004–5. I observed the Family Courts, the Women's Grievance Cell associated with the Kolkata Police, and several other organizations that informally undertook mediation and counselling related to family law, and interviewed related personnel. The project started as an ethnography of the Family Court and expanded to include an exploration of the management of family violence. Some names are drawn from public court records; other names are assigned. Translations are my own.

2. A note of caution: images such as 'dowry deaths' have often come to stand metonymically for the plight of Indian women, rather than, as Uma Narayan (1997) points out, supporting a case for global similarities in forms of domestic violence.

3. I set aside the question of customary law here, tempting though it is to explicate in the context of a postcolonial state, because family and domestic violence have been more prominent issues in recent times, having come into

discourse primarily in the 1970s, working their way from feminist analyses into state policies.

4. See also: Auerbach (1983), Basu (1999), Demain (2003), Greenhouse et al. (1994), Just (2000), Merry (1986), Moore (1999).

5. Convention on the Elimination of All Forms of Discrimination against Women.

6. The S. 498 offence is a 'cognizable' (police may arrest without a warrant), 'non-bailable' (getting bail is not the right of the accused, and bail may only be obtained later from a court and not from the police) and 'non-compoundable' (prosecution cannot be withdrawn or settled between parties) offence. These severities may cause reluctance to deploy the law.

7. The newly passed Domestic Violence Act, while controversial in other ways, addresses some of the provisions of S. 498 with more specific scope and remedies. It has already, however, become an incendiary point of controversy in the media and among some groups, with familiar notes about men's 'everyday' interactions being misunderstood and the potential for men's economic devastation and humiliation being trotted out.

8. The focus in those days was also on opposition to S. 304 of the IPC related to dowry deaths, and to the Dowry Prohibition Act, which has effectively failed as a punitive or deterrent measure.

9. On the home page, globalization and development are cited as factors contributing to the rising divorce rate (the 'West' is blamed), and the primary problem is phrased thus: 'The least [sic] we want is a large scale single parenting and resultant massive crime rate in another 15 years time. Is this the kind of society we plan to hand over to our children?' Here particular sociological phenomena, for example, single parenting, are arbitrarily juxtaposed with crime rate, implying causality, and suggesting that women's attempts to dissolve marriage are the root of these disparate processes.

10. On the website, assorted diatribes against 'feminism' displaying rather virulent misogyny—'Towards Greater Gender Sensitivity in India', 'Say No to Feminism', 'Feminist Activism'—further dilute the validity of the narratives as forms of objective evidence.

11. Maitreyi Chatterji, Interview, September 2001.

12. Between 1997–2001, the Kolkata Family Courts cleared about 200 cases a year (Family Court information gathered for parliamentary question), and while separate statistics are not maintained for divorce in 'mixed' civil courts, it seems likely that rates are typically faster—most cases seem to have been resolved within a year and a half (based on data in court), whereas divorce cases in regular courts often take years to come to the docket and have taken up to twenty-five years for resolution.

13. Pratibha Gheewala, Retired Chief Counsellor of Mumbai Family Courts, Personal Communication, December 2002.

14. *The Family Courts Act 1984: Bare Act 2001*. Allahabad, Law Publishers, 2001,

p. 192. For parliamentary debates see Family Courts Bill. 1984. Lok Sabha Debates 15th Session. V LI #25: 181-241

15. Interviews, October 2001.

16. Interviews, October 2001.

17. One lakh = Rs 100,000. Though this would amount to about four-years' income at Rs 2,500 per month, it sounds like a lot for a middle-class person to have in raw savings. The suddenness of the claim also indicated that it may have been a symbolically high number presented in order to negotiate.

18. Savings and Pension schemes contributed to by employer and partially by employee, that can be borrowed against or even withdrawn in crises.

19. Purna Sen (1999) argues that it is education, rather than wages per se, which enable women to resist violence.

20. The move was ultimately turned down by the legislature. Among various protests about the scope and nature of authority of these units, there was a prominent concern among those not affiliated with the ruling party that the units might be overly influenced by the political connections and interests of litigants. Talwar (2002: 8) affirms the profound influence of political alliances in shalishi cases.

21. In the other settings, while an occasional family member was called to mediation sessions, the focus was on talking to couples individually and then jointly.

22. Typically, each case in Talwar's study involved multiple shalishis, and the activists tried to stay in touch with the couple over time to check on issues. The study reports highly positive results for these forms of mediation: 65.7 per cent women reported they were definitely better off after the shalishi, and 86 per cent women said they had more self-confidence. Ninety per cent of women said there was less physical violence, and 87 per cent women reported fewer problems with deprivation of basic needs. But the figures on reduced emotional and sexual violence were less positive. Fifty-seven per cent women reported a recurrence of problems and 46.4 per cent reported new problems after the NGOs' intervention (Talwar 2002: 24–25).

23. Talwar also reports that activists found the legal provisions to be useful in that fear of legal action could be used to negotiate modifications in behaviour (ibid.: 27).

24. As previous accounts showed, configuring alimony or maintenance is one of the principal tasks of the Family Court. For Muslim women under the prevailing laws in India, this could take the form of monthly payments for sustenance before divorce and 'fair and reasonable' provisions for some amount of time after divorce, or the payment of deferred dower or settlement of property in lieu of monthly payments.

25. In the WHO study, 'disobeying or arguing with the man, questioning him about money or girlfriends, not having food ready on time' were among the top triggering events for violence (WHO 2002: 15). Similarly, Talwar's report

cited 'deprivation of basic needs' including depriving women and children of food and shelter (ibid.: 8, 31) as one of the primary forms of violence against women.

REFERENCES

Abu-Lughod, Lila (1993). 'The Romance of Resistance: Tracing Transformations of Power Through Bedouin Women', in Stevi Jackson et al. (eds), *Women's Studies: Essential Readings*, pp. 102–3. New York: New York University Press.

Anjali (1995). 'The Pathos of Family Courts', *The Pioneer*, 9 April, p. 16.

Auerbach, Jerold S. (1983). *Justice Without Law?* New York: Oxford University Press.

Basu, Srimati (1999). *She Comes to Take Her Rights: Indian Women, Property and Propriety*. Albany: State University of New York Press.

Centre for Social Research (2005a). *Stop Violence against Women: From Womb to Tomb*, Annual Report. New Delhi: Centre for Social Research.

———— (2005b). 'A Research Study on the Use and Misuse of Section 498A of the Indian Penal Code: Study Summary?' New Delhi: Centre for Social Research.

Coomaraswamy, Radhika (2005). 'The Varied Contours of Violence Against Women in South Asia', Report Prepared for the Fifth South Asia Regional Ministerial Conference Celebrating Beijing Plus Ten, Jointly Organized by Government of Pakistan and UNIFEM South Asia Regional Office, 3–5 May.

Das, Prafulla (1996). 'For and Against Family Courts', *The Hindu*, 30 September, p. 4.

Demain, Melissa (2003). 'Custom in the Courtroom, Law in the Village: Legal Transformations in Papua New Guinea', *Journal of the Royal Anthropological Institute*, (N.S.): 97–115.

Engel, David (1980). 'Legal Pluralism in an American Community: Perspectives on a Civil Trial Court', *American Bar Foundation Research Journal*, 5(3): 425–54.

Fuller, Chris (1994). 'Legal Anthropology: Legal Pluralism and Legal Thought', *Anthropology Today*, 10(3): 9–12.

Geertz, Clifford (1983). 'Local Knowledge: Fact and Law in Comparative Perspective', in Clifford Geertz, *Local Knowledge: Further Essays in Interpretive Anthropology*, pp. 167–233. New York: Basic Books.

Greenhouse, Carol J., Barbara Yngvesson and David M. Engel (1994). *Law and Community in Three American Towns*. Ithaca: Cornell University Press.

Griffiths, John (1986). 'What is Legal Pluralism?' *Journal of Legal Pluralism*, 24: 38.

ICRW (International Center for Research on Women) (2002). *Men, Masculinity and Domestic Violence in India: Summary Report of Four Studies*. Series: Domestic Violence in India: Exploring Strategies, Promoting Dialogue #5. Washington, DC: International Center for Research on Women.

Just, Peter (2000). *Dou Donggo Justice: Conflict and Morality in an Indonesian Society*. Oxford: Rowman and Littlefield.

Lazarus-Black, Mindie and Susan F. Hirsch (1999). 'Performance and Paradox: Exploring Law's Role in Hegemony and Resistance', in Mindie Lazarus-Black and Susan F. Hirsch (eds), *Contested States: Law, Hegemony and Resistance*, pp. 1–31. New York: Routledge.

Mehra, Madhu (1998). 'Exploring the Boundaries of Law, Gender and Social Reform', *Feminist Legal Studies* 6(1): 59–83.

Merry, Sally Engle (1986). 'Everyday Understandings of Law in Working-Class America', *American Ethnologist*, 13(2): 253–70.

————— (1988). 'Legal Pluralism', *Law and Society Review*, 22(5): 868–96.

Mitra, Nishi (1999). 'Best Practices among Responses to Domestic Violence in Maharashtra and Madhya Pradesh', in PROWID, *Domestic Violence in India: A Summary Report of Three Studies*, pp. 18–27. Washington, DC: International Center for Research on Women.

Moore, Erin P. (1999). 'Law's Patriarchy in India', in Mindie Lazarus-Black and Susan F. Hirsch (eds), *Contested States: Law, Hegemony and Resistance*, pp. 88–117. New York: Routledge.

Narayan, Uma (1997). 'Cross-Cultural Connections, Border-Crossings and "Death by Culture": Thinking about Dowry-Murders in India and Domestic-Violence Murders in the United States', in Uma Narayan, *Dislocating Cultures: Identities, Traditions and Third-World Feminism*, pp. 81–118. New York: Routledge.

Pande, Rekha (2002). 'The Public Face of a Private Domestic Violence', *International Feminist Journal of Politics*, 4(3): 342–67.

PROWID (1999). *Domestic Violence in India: A Summary Report of Three Studies*. Washington, DC: International Center for Research on Women.

Sen, Purna (1999). 'Enhancing Women's Choices in Responding to Domestic Violence in Calcutta: A Comparison of Employment and Education', *The European Journal of Development Research*, 11: 65–86.

Shukla, Rakesh (2005). 'SC Upholds Constitutionality of S 498A', *InfoChange News and Features*, August. Available at: http://www.infochangeindia.org/analysis86.jsp

Singh, Kirti (1996). 'Family Courts', *The Pioneer*, 17 April, p. 6.

Solanki, Gopika (2001). 'Women's Experiences through the Police Lens: Analysis of Cases Registered under Section 498(A)', *Journal of Gender Studies*, 10: 83–86.

Talwar, Anuradha (2002). 'The Shalishi in West Bengal: A Community Response to Domestic Violence', in *Women Initiated Community Level Responses to Domestic Violence: Summary Report of Three Studies*, pp. 14-30. Series: Domestic Violence in India: Exploring Strategies, Promoting Dialogue #5. Washington, DC: International Center for Research on Women.

Tamanaha, Brian Z. (2000). 'A Non-Essentialist Version of Legal Pluralism', *Journal of Law and Society*, 27(2): 296–321.

UN WIRE (2000). 'India: Domestic Violence Rates Rising', *Women's International Network News*, 26: 62.

Visaria, Leela (1999). 'Violence Against Women in India: Evidence from Rural Gujarat.' in PROWID, *Domestic Violence in India: A Summary Report of Three Studies*, pp. 9–17. Washington, DC: International Center for Research on Women.

WHO (WORLD HEALTH ORGANIZATION) (2002). *World Report on Violence and Health: Summary*. Geneva: World Health Organization.

11

The Land of Lalla-Ded

Negation of 'Kashmiriyat' and Immiseration of the Kashmiri Woman

Nyla Ali Khan[1]

In a post 9/11 world, in which the uncritical essentializing of people from the 'Third World' has been legitimized, Iraq and Afghanistan have been dehumanized in an attempt to disseminate enlightenment in those 'dark' regions; the discourse of 'honour killings' is prevalent in the North West Frontier Province of Pakistan and has carved a niche in western academic discourse as another instance of the incorrigible bestiality of the Orient; inciters of communal riots on the Indian subcontinent enjoy the patronage of political bigwigs as evidenced by the relentless persecution of Muslims during the riots in the Indian state of Gujarat in 2002; the rhetoric of hate and binarisms pervades the politics of the 'Third World' and of the West. In such a scenario, feminist activist-scholars seek to reinterpret the repressive frameworks of military occupation, nationalism, patriarchy, and fundamentalism that essentialize the identities of postcolonial and transnational subjects.

Using self-reflexive and gendered frameworks, drawing on my heritage and kinship in Kashmir, this article explores the construction and employment of gender in secular nationalist, religious nationalist, and ethno-nationalist discourses in the former princely state of Jammu and Kashmir. I question the victimization and subjugation of women selectively enshrined in the social practices and folklore of Kashmiri culture, such as limited educational and professional opportunities; the heterosexual and patriarchal right of a husband to prevent his wife from making strides in the material world; the kudos given to the 'hapless' wife who agrees to live in a polygamous relationship; the bounden duty of the woman to bear heirs; the unquestioned right of a husband to divorce his 'barren' wife; confinement of the woman to her home where she is subjected to material and emotional brutality; the hallowed status of the woman who conforms to such cultural dogmas; the social ostracization of the woman who defies them; the status of woman as a fiefdom facilitating political and feudal alliances; the exclusivity of cultural nationalism; the erosion of cultural syncretism; the ever-increasing dominance of religious fundamentalism; and the irrational resistance to cultural and linguistic differences (Butalia 2002; Kishwar 1998; Rai 2004; Whitehead 2004). At the same time, I do not advocate the abandoning of Kashmiri culture as a regressive discourse in favour of uncritically adopting a unified and cohesive notion of culture without critically engaging with the engendering of dynamic identities by the discourses of colonial historiography, nationalist historiography and unofficial historiography. I attempt to critically examine the linkages between Kashmiri culture and the cultural, social and political institutions created by secular nationalist, religious nationalist and ethno-nationalist discourses. I interrogate nationalist historiography by recording the vivid and verifiable details of individual lives and memories that do not necessarily correspond with the documented version of history. I do this by delineating the agonies and ruptures caused by challenging traditional gender roles, ambiguous citizenship and nationalisms.

I contextualize my argument by underlining the significance of the syncretic ethos of Kashmir that has been violated by the outburst of religious nationalism, secular nationalism and ethno-nationalism, which have facilitated political and social structural violence. My emphasis on the syncretic ethos of Kashmir is neither an attempt to silence religious, class and ethnic differences nor is it an attempt to glorify a bygone era. Instead, I wield this concept in my argument as a strategic tool to deconstruct the discourses of a unified Indian nation-state and a Pakistani nation-state, and to demystify the Orientalist trope of the paradisiacal Kashmir valley. I highlight the threatening nature of nationalism when its means are internecine, sundering Kashmiri from Kashmiri. The series of irregular wars have polarized these groups into Muslims and Hindus who are required to disaffirm their cultural, linguistic and social unities. I consider the shape of women's agency in the syncretic ethos of Kashmir and the new languages of resistance, negotiation and empowerment it adopts in the cacophonous social and political situation created by various nationalist discourses.

I draw from the cultural and ideological spaces I was raised in; the cherished verses of the Sufi poetess, Lalla-Ded, in whose immortal poetry the legendary beauty of Kashmir endures pain and strife but lives on; conversations with my maternal grandmother that are etched in my memory; informative and enlightening discussions with my parents, who have continued to live in the strife torn valley through years of unbearable hostility and the psychological trauma of armed conflict with an unparalleled stoicism; informal conversations with friends and acquaintances who were victims of the politics of dispossession; the extensive reading that I have done over the years on the conflictual history and politics of Jammu and Kashmir. I also draw from the fieldwork conducted during my annual trip to Kashmir in July 2005 among predominantly agricultural communities in areas bordering the Line of Control (LoC) between India and Pakistan.

I was raised in a secular Muslim home where we were encouraged to speak of the 'liberation of women' and of a culturally syncretic society. I was taught that Islam provided women with social, political and economic rights, however invisible those rights were in our society. It was instilled in me that Islam gave women property rights—the right of Mrs Ghulam Kabra, a Kashmiri state subject, to inherit the property to which she was the legal heir was challenged as early as 1939 because she had married a non-state subject, but the High Court legislated that she could inherit the property bequeathed to her by her parents; the right to interrogate totalizing social and cultural institutions; the right to hold political office—Khalida Zia and Sheikh Hassina in Pakistan, Benazir Bhutto in Pakistan, Najma Heptullah and Mohsina Kidwai in India, my maternal grandmother, Begum Sheikh Mohammad Abdullah, in Kashmir, who represented Srinagar and Anantnag constituencies in Jammu and Kashmir in the Indian parliament from 1977 to 1979 and 1984 to 1989, respectively, and was the first president of the Jammu & Kashmir Red Cross Society from 1947 to 1951 (Lok Sabha 2000); the right to assert their agency in matters of social and political import; and the right to lead a dignified existence in which they could voice their opinions and desires so as to 'act upon the boundaries that constrain and enable social action by, for example, changing their shape or direction' (Hayward 1989: 27).

Although my maternal grandfather, Sheikh Mohammad Abdullah, was a nationalist and an idealist, the notion of 'Kashmiriyat' wasn't handed down to me as an unachievable and an abstract concept. 'Kashmiriyat' was the secular credo of Sheikh Mohammad Abdullah's All Jammu and Kashmir National Conference, which was popularized in the 1940s and 1950s to defeat the centralizing strategies of the successive regimes of independent India (Rai 2004). This significant concept does not attempt to simplify the ambiguity and complexity of religious, social and cultural identities. The notion of 'Kashmiriyat' neither attempts to assert a fixed identity nor does it reinforce the idea of the purity of culture. I would veer away from adopting an image of this secular credo that is created by the unitary discourses it deplores. On the contrary, 'Kashmiriyat' brings about a metamorphosis in the determinate concept of the Indian nation-state and creates a situation in which the nation-states of India and Pakistan are forced to confront an alternative epistemology. At a time of political and social upheaval, this notion engendered a consciousness of place, which offered a critical perspective from which to formulate alternatives. Without negating the historicity of the notion, this theoretical fiction was deployed by Sheikh Abdullah's National Conference in order to forge a strategic essentialism that would enable the creation of a sovereign Kashmiri identity. It certainly wasn't a flawless notion, as Mridu Rai is quick to point out: '... this notion of cultural harmony was predicated on the requisite condition of protecting Kashmiri Pandit privileges and a consequent subsumption of the interests of the majority Muslims' (ibid.: 296). But this well-crafted theoretical fiction by the advocates of a Kashmiri polity empowered them in a circumscribed fashion to choose an idiom within which they could arbitrarily remove the distinction between religion and politics.[2] This articulation of the supplementary and unstable structure of the nation-states of India and Pakistan is a deconstruction of an originary source of identity. 'Kashmiriyat' was crystallized for me as the eradication of a feudal structure and its insidious ramifications; the right of the tiller to the land he worked on; the unacceptability of any political solution that did not take the aspirations and demands of the Kashmiri people into consideration; the right of Kashmiris to high offices in education, bureaucracy and government; the availability of medical and educational facilities in Jammu, Kashmir and Ladakh; the preservation of literatures, shrines and historical artifacts that defined an important aspect of 'Kashmiriyat'; formation of the Constituent Assembly of Jammu & Kashmir to institutionalize the constitution of the state in 1951, which was an enormous leap towards the process of democratization; the fundamental right of both women and men to a free education up to the university level; equal opportunities afforded to both

sexes in the workplace; the nurturing of a contact zone in social, political
and intellectual ideologies and institutions; pride in a cultural identity
that was generated in a space created by multiple perspectives and the
ability to look beyond one particular location in order to locate myself
in a social world.[3] For me, the process of identity formation has been
and still is one of perpetual struggle in which discursive communities
produce narratives of belonging, resistance or escape. This narrative of
self-imagining is a self-conscious rewriting of history, a rewriting derived
from the intersubjective spaces I occupy. Having been raised within
the framework created by the liberatory discourse of 'Kashmiriyat', I
learned to view with suspicion cultural myopia and state-sponsored
monologic identities. I understood that the creation of the sovereign
Kashmiri subject rested upon a fragmented subjectivity that is dispersed
over several dominant and peripheral practices rather than existing as a
homogeneous and monolithic entity.

My maternal grandfather returned to Kashmir in 1975 after a long
period of incarceration. He returned to much adulation and cult worship
in a Kashmir that had witnessed the insensitivity of legitimized pillage and
rapine. For the layperson, Sheikh Mohammad Abdullah embodied the
'new Kashmir' in which the hitherto peripheralized Muslim population
of the valley would reinsert itself into the language of belonging.
Abdullah, with his socialist politics sought to challenge the safely guarded
domain of privilege and power, which had disenfranchised the Muslim
majority and made their support irrelevant for the Dogra sovereigns and
later for regimes installed by New Delhi. Despite the popularization of
'Kashmiriyat', which sought to engender a strategic essentialism, as I
mentioned earlier, the privileges that the Pandit population enjoyed in
the princely state of Jammu and Kashmir by affiliating itself with the
Hindu maharajah and with the Hindus of post-independence India, is
a well-established fact (Copland 1991; Ganguly 1997; Rai 2004; Singh
1995). Although the National Conference was founded on socialist
principles, it was the centralization that occurred in the organization
towards the late 1970s that did not enable the engendering of a second-
generation mature and responsible leadership. Perhaps, it was Abdullah's
age, failing health and the mammoth task of bolstering the self-image of
Kashmiris that prevented him from grooming the younger generation in
the National Conference cadres, and he was forced to resort to the law
of primogeniture.[4] At the risk of sounding presumptuous, I will not deny
the sense of entitlement I had to feeling a part of a system designed by a
new elite to interrogate the hegemonic and manipulative powers of the

successive regimes in post-independence India and Pakistan. The social, cultural and intellectual spaces that I had access to taught me not to accept a life of mediocrity with the resignation and endurance of a silent victim. As a child, I was entitled to privileges that nurtured a selfhood, which ran contrary to the traditional representation of the girl child as the silent symbol of an embryonic nation. My life in a 'Third World' country did not deprive me of the wondrous beauty of being privy to the intricacies of global movements. I learned to shadow my mother and my maternal grandmother early in life (an only child suffers from a dearth of companions) and realized that the role of women in the Kashmir polity was a well-defined one: these women were clearly not marginalized in the body politic but, on the contrary, were involved in direct action as national citizens. Within this discourse, which I would distinguish from that version that has been enshrined in official historiography, patriarchy wasn't deified whilst rendering women powerless and superfluous. Although the appellation of 'Madr-e-Meherban' or 'Benevolent Mother' was affixed to my maternal grandmother, Begum Akbar Jahan, which she embraced with panache, this appellation reinforced the claim that the image of woman as powerful mother underlines economic independence for women and reinforces her strength and courage of conviction to sacrifice for the nation. I see this as an attempt to inspire the kind of self-assurance that the Kashmiri polity required in that period of social, cultural and political redefinition. As a benevolent mother, my maternal grandmother endeavoured to negotiate the undulating terrain of Islam and modernity. Because of her privileged position as first lady, she could without fear of chastisement publicly advocate gender equality and equal opportunities for men and women in the workplace as social and political virtues reinforced by Islamic teachings. The work that I saw my grandmother do for disenfranchised Kashmiri and Gujjar women within the bounds of societal and cultural norms enabled me to imbibe and practise a politicized form of Islam in which selfhood could be imagined. This worldview enabled the creation of a dialogue between tradition, represented by my father's family, who were considered to be from old money, and representative of modernity. Although my father's family is immersed in tradition, their faith in and loyalty to the 'new Kashmir' represented by the socialist politics of Sheikh Mohammad has been unwavering. I have witnessed the gradual amenability of that clan to other paradigmatic structures and their diminishing insularity from the complex position of insider/outsider. Had I not had access to the echelons of privilege, the havoc that new social and political phenomena can wreak on social relations would, perhaps, have left me with recourse to the abstractions of faith and a fantastic hope in the creation of an earthly paradise. I will admit that this access came with its own set of problems, one of which was the scathing sense of being tokenized, particularly in school and later in college. This need to be the authentic representative of an elite political culture created a disconnection between me and other people who didn't belong to that group. At that point, I didn't realize that identity fluctuates as the spaces through which people move change, enabling the subject to interpret the world through specific identities of history, culture and links to land. The ethnographic field research, which I undertook, was a method of seeking reconnection by simultaneously belonging to, and resisting, the discursive community of traditional Muslim Kashmiri and Gujjar rural women. I was further motivated by the desire to critically observe the socio-political discourse in Kashmir through an oblique focus from the margins, instead of from an elitist centre. The way I see it now, my personal identity was embedded in socially structured and politically mediated processes of group formation. It was much later that I began to conceive of identity construction as a deliberate process of individual self-formation within the porous boundaries created by one's social, political and cultural discourse. This perception of an alternative discourse as well as of an alternative epistemological structure was enhanced by my study of the complex demythologized history of Lalla-Ded, the Sufi mystic whose verses were deployed in nationalist discourse and literature as embodying the syncretic ethos of Kashmir. After engaging with the iconicized figure of Lalla-Ded in nationalist historiography, I learned of the complexities of her identity, which underlined the dialectical interplay between Brahminism, Islam and indigenous culture. This contiguity among disparate histories engendered a historical identity formed in a hybrid space as well as a pluralistic vision of the world, not the fixity of a glorified vision of the past in terms of gender roles, societal roles or cultural identities.

Most nationalist movements and literatures of independence have portrayed women as icons of cultural preservation. In the nationalist and postcolonial phase of nations, gender divisions have been reinforced by the hallowed figure of the 'native woman' (Gandhi 1998: 83). The complexity in the varying positions of women is ignored to preserve nationalist portraits of the 'native woman', which do not concede to the female subject the right to foreground her own 'distinct actualities' (Minh-ha 1989: 5). For instance, the iconicization of Lalla-Ded as goddess-mother in nationalist literatures circumscribes her sphere of the influence within Kashmiri folklore and social practices. Lalla-Ded de-emphasized the roles imposed by conjugality and motherhood in order to widen her identity without totally dismissing its cultural definition. The Sufi mystic located agency in possibilities created in the variability of spaces in which identity is formed. Lalla-Ded's unsurpassed Sufi mysticism and the eloquent verse that ensued from it led to her being owned by the Pundits of the valley as Lalla Ishwari and by the Muslims of the valley as Lalla Arifa (Bamzai 1994; Jha 1996; Khan 1994; Ray 1970). Lalla-Ded is a fitting symbol of the syncretic ethos of Kashmir, a figure revered by both the Pundits and Muslims. Lalla-Ded was born in 1334 into a Kashmiri Brahmin home in village Simpur, about 4 miles from Srinagar, the summer capital of Kashmir. Lalla-Ded was brutalized in a marriage that was arranged for her by the elders once she crossed the threshold of puberty. Unwilling to acquiesce to constraints placed on the 'traditional' woman and questioning the self-abnegation of women that disallows them from reconciling their private selves with their roles as public contributors to the community, Lalla-Ded disavowed the psychosocial narratives inscribed on the female body in defiance of the continued immiseration of women (Bhatnagar et al. 2004: 30). I would argue that by committing the sacrilegious act of crossing the threshold of the husband's house in order to choose a life of asceticism, Lalla-Ded subverted the reliance on male authority.

Although a Sufi mystic, childless Lalla-Ded eroded the construct of woman as goddess or mother that binds her to a form of subordination that is the ultimate paradigm of social relationships in traditional societies (Nandy 1998: 30). Most historians are of the opinion that Sheikh Noor-ud-Din Wali, the founding father of the predominant Sufi sect in the Kashmir valley, Rishiism, acknowledged Lalla-Ded as his spiritual mentor. The recorded poems and paradigmatic sayings of Lalla-Ded and of Sheikh Noor-ud-Din Wali enrich Kashmiri literature and add layer upon layer to the culture (Kaul 1999; Murphy 1999; Parimoo 1978; Sufi 1974). It is also believed that she met and held discourses on mysticism and on the different schools of Sufi thought with Mir Syed Ali Hamadani, a regal central Asian Islamic scholar and mystic, who disseminated and perpetuated Islamic teachings in predominantly Brahminical fourteenth- and fifteenth-century Kashmir (Bamzai 1994; Murphy 1999; Parimoo 1978). She chose to break the mould of patriarchy in a stiflingly traditional society by not allowing her intellectual and spiritual freedoms to be curbed. Lalla-Ded's complex legacy represents, for me, the ability of women to work through the past in order to encourage a self-imagining that incorporates profound social, cultural and political differences necessary in the process of nation-building. Such women have the wherewithal to create alternative, socially structured bases. I see this as an effect that the doctrine of 'Kashmiriyat' can have. These details of Lalla-Ded's rich life do not correspond with the documented version of history. Neither history alone nor a single theory sufficiently explain the multiple inheritances of her subjectivity. The distinct subjectivity of this historical figure manifests itself in the profundity of her verse:

> Shiv chuy thali thali rozaan
> Mav Zaan Hyound ta Mussalman
> Trukhay chukh ta panunuy paan parzaan
> Ada Chay Saahibas Zaani Zaan (Lalla-Ded, n.d.)

> (Shiva abides in all that is everywhere
> Then do not discriminate between a Hindu and a Muslim
> That is true knowledge of the Lord)[5]

The sentiment of syncretism in the above verse is linked to my exposure to various cultural, religious and educational influences, which have been instrumental in forming my belief that culture is shaped and shapes in multiple ways. I was educated in a Catholic school run by Irish missionaries, although proselytization was never a concern and I learned to respect the richness of other cultural, religious and literary traditions. Having been influenced by my maternal grandmother, who was part European and part Gujjar, I have never been quite sure who had the authority to say which cultural mores were enforced.[6]

ETHNOGRAPHIC SETTING

Against the backdrop of my history and of the politically tumultuous situation in Jammu and Kashmir which has led to an increase in gender-based violence, I attempt to show that women's muted voices haven't been raised loud enough against the atrocities to which they are subjected by Indian paramilitary forces, Pakistan sponsored insurgents, counter-insurgency forces, and religious fundamentalists (Kashmiri Women's Initiative for Peace and Disarmament 2002). I also emphasize the necessity of foregrounding women's perspectives on issues of nationalist ideologies, religious freedom, democratic participation, militarization, intellectual freedom, and judicial and legal structures in a milieu that does not co-opt them into mainstream political and cultural discourses or First World feminist agendas. My research is undertaken from complicated spaces. I am a politically connected Kashmiri Muslim woman, educated in Delhi and in the West, located in the conservative heartland of America, the Midwest. My research, at the crossroads of postmodern and postcolonial theoretical frameworks, seeks to reconnect to 'home', questioning the complexities and power dynamics that have made Kashmir, my history, struggles and normalizations, from intersubjective spaces (Karim 1993: 248;). In order to explore women's empowerment in some militancy ravaged rural areas of Kashmir, I travelled to the villages of Mahiyan and Qazipora in July 2005.[7] These villages are in Tangmarg, a sub-district of Indian-occupied Kashmir, which borders Pakistan. The Kashmiri and Gujjar women I met with in predominantly agricultural communities are workhorses on the lands they cultivate but lack the tools to critically understand their reality and the causes creating structural poverty, and do not have the privilege of turning to discourses that subvert the one that brands them as stoic and austere cultural icons who maintain an unsullied homely space.[8] While conducting my research, I found myself constantly beleaguered by the following question: Is the rich complexity in the social and cultural positions of 'native women' ignored in order to retain the remnants of colonialist power-knowledge in '[the] appropriation and codification of "scholarship" and "knowledge" about women in the third world by particular analytic categories . . .'? (Mohanty 1991: 196). How is the version of those women absent from the official record relegated to the archives of memory and history?

Indigenous ethnographers who might be 'partial insiders', like me, are able to raise questions about the boundaries of understanding and interpretation: 'insiders studying their own culture offer new angles of vision and depths of understanding' (Clifford and Marcus 1986: 9). My work enabled me to become more sensitive to my informants' perspectives and experiences. My research enabled me to realize that despite being unable to overturn the structural determinants of their oppression, the Kashmiri and Gujjar women I talked with are able to negotiate in small spaces.[9] The importance of context must be understood and used to identify items within each boundary appropriate to local circumstances. All of them had no qualms about functioning as the main socializing agents for their children and considered the constitution of the mother-son relationship as the nexus of every social relationship in that culture. With their faces turned away from the camera, Hafeeza Begum, Fareeda

Akhtar and Rifat Ara controlled their shy laughter after being berated by their mother-in-law, feisty Haneefa Begum, and sang a medley of folk songs for me in the intimacy of their hut. The folk songs, which were translated for me by Shabeer Ahmad, a Gujjar lawyer, were a doleful rendition of the self-abnegation and loneliness of a young bride who is severed from everything familiar to her and finds herself being ruthlessly moulded to fit her new environment. The most articulate of the group was Shabeer's mother who was content to understand historical and social events within the explanatory frameworks of religious and filial obligation. Her stance to the contexts that formed her identity displayed a capacity to act upon the social boundaries that 'define fields of action for all actors' (Hayward 1989: 27).

The women I talked with had cultivated a learned nonchalance to the cruel treatment meted out to women in their husbands' homes and did not think to, or could not afford to, reprimand the disrespect shown to women who were either barren or widowed, without a male protector. This ostensibly compliant attitude seems to be a strategy of survival in a social setting in which relationships are hierarchically structured, maintaining social and political stasis. The notion of uncompassionate in-laws was a part of their folklore. But it might be easier to imagine the survival strategies that women deploy in that environment if we think of power 'not as instruments powerful agents use to prevent the powerless from acting freely, but rather as social boundaries that, together, define fields of action for all actors' (ibid.: 27). The agency that enables Haneefa, Fareeda Akhtar and Rifat Ara to survive involves 'bargaining and negotiation, deception and manipulation, subversion and resistance' (Kabeer 1999: 438).

This aspect of Kashmiri and Gujjar folklore that I mentioned earlier is not exclusive to rural areas and the burden of preserving the notion of its innateness to the culture is taken on by the urban women as well. Subsequent to the dismantling of the feudal economic and social structure in Kashmir in the early 1950s, feudal clans and the emasculated nobility clung to their decadent traditions with an unparalleled ferocity. The lack of exposure in those clans to other paradigmatic structures, their insularity and hollow arrogance encourages the perpetuation of regressive notions like confinement of the woman to the home, her role as mute spectator, her ostensible lack of agency while manipulating the householder to do her bidding by deploying a cunning that would be difficult to vie with, and a bridgeable distance between the woman of a decrepit feudal clan and her upper middle-middle class counterpart.

The womanly virtues of devotion, submission, chastity, and patience are still viewed as the social forms that tradition inculcates in women. Nationalist discourse creates a framework that confers upon women the pre-lapsarian mythological status of a selfless, asexual, benevolent, and maternal entity. As Chakravarti theorizes, because the edifice of national culture was propped up by the ideals of purity, selfless love and sacrifice, the decapitation of women was the result (1989: 143). A woman who does not conform to that construct generates contradictions in the seamlessness of predominant cultural and social discourses because the very definition of nationhood has been made contingent on the male recognition of female identity. The iconicization of woman as goddess-mother circumscribes her movement within society. Women who choose to break this mould are denied even the meagre freedom that the domestic image has bestowed and are dislocated to the margins of society.

My articulation of the complexities and power dynamics of Kashmiri culture and politics uses Lalla-Ded as a figure who defied traditional gender roles. It is an attempt to understand the complexities of my history by rescuing the term 'Kashmiri Woman' from the homogenizing power of the culture industry? Kashmiri women are positioned in relation to their own cultural realities, their own socio-economic conditions, their political affiliations, their own histories, their sensitivity to the diversity of cultural traditions and to the questions and conflicts within them, their own struggles not just with the discourses of the Indian and Pakistani nation-states but also with the centralizing hegemony of the ethno-nationalism propagated in the state, their interpretations of religious law, and their concepts of the role of women in contemporary societies.

POLITICAL DISCOURSES INSCRIBED ON THE KASHMIRI LANDSCAPE

Kashmir is a space in which conflicting discourses have been written and read.[10] Cultural notions of Kashmiris in image and word have been reconstructed to emphasize the bias that reinforces the propagandist agenda of the hegemonic powers involved in the Kashmir dispute, India and Pakistan. In establishment Indian and Pakistani thought, Kashmiris are defined as different from the nationals of the two countries. The various fractions in the state of Jammu and Kashmir—Kashmiri Muslims, Kashmiri Pundits, Dogras, and Ladakhis—have tried time and again to form a national consciousness in order to name its cultural alterity through the nation, as 'Kashmiriyat'. The construction of 'Kashmiriyat' involved culling selected cultural fragments from an imagined past that would enfold both the Pundits and the Muslims. The coexistence of Muslims and Hindus, mutual respect for their places of worship, and an ability to synthesize not just cultural but religious practices as well created a syncretic space in Kashmir (Kaw 2004; Kishwar 1998; Razdan 1999; Rushdie 2005; Whitehead, 2004). The deep reverence for each other's shrines and the relics housed in those shrines is a well-entrenched aspect of the culture. Salman Rushdie describes the sentiment of 'Kashmiriyat' succinctly in his fictionalized account of the history of Jammu and Kashmir: 'The words Hindu and Muslim had no place in their story…. In the valley these words were merely descriptions, not divisions. The frontiers between the words, their hard edges, had grown smudged and blurred' (2005: 57). Rushdie's romanticized description of the secular credo blurs the historical necessity of this theoretical fiction. The notion of 'Kashmiriyat' has more facticity in Mridu Rai's account. As Rai points out in her well-researched book on Kashmir, 'This espousal of a "secular" ideology, read through a secularly written history, was intended also as a way to keep at bay a centre in Delhi that had begun to encroach upon Kashmiri "autonomy" increasingly in the early 1950s' (2004: 284–85). But due to the regional sentiments that are so well entrenched in the psyche of the people, this attempt is still in a volatile stage. The symbols of nationhood in Jammu and Kashmir—flag, anthem and Constitution—have thus far been unable to forge the process of nationalist self-imagining. Although, separatist movements have been surfacing and resurfacing since the accession of Kashmir to India in 1947, the attempt to create a unitary cultural identity bolstered by nationalist politics has been subverted by regional political forces and the comprador class, backed-up by the governments of India and Pakistan. The revolutionary acts of demanding the right of self-determination and autonomy for Jammu and Kashmir have not been able to nurture a unity amongst all socio-economic classes (Ganguly 1997: 78–79; Rahman 1996: 148–49).

Kashmiris have tried, time and again, to translate themselves from passive recipients of violence legitimated by the foreign legislations of the physically and psychologically removed parliaments of India and Pakistan into subjects who recognize that they can exercise agency and take control of their destinies. They march forward with a refusal to allow history to be imposed on them; now the people of Kashmir attempt to take charge of their social and political destinies. The confluence of religious nationalism, secular nationalism and ethnic nationalism create the complexity of the Kashmir issue. For India, Kashmir lends credibility to its secular nationalist image. For Pakistan, Kashmir represents the unfeasibility of secular nationalism and underscores the need for an Islamic theocracy in the subcontinent. Currently, a large part of Jammu and Kashmir is administered by India and a portion is administered by Pakistan. China also annexed a section of the land in 1962, through which it has built a road that links Tibet to Xiajiang (Rahman 1996: 5–6; Schofield 2002). In an attempt to resolve this conflict, Sir Owen Dixon, the United Nations representative for India and Pakistan, noted in 1950 that the Kashmir issue was so tumultuous because Kashmir was not a holistic geographic, economic or demographic entity but, on the contrary, was an aggregate of diverse territories brought under the rule of one maharajah (Schofield 2002). Sir Owen Dixon propounded the trifurcation of the state along communal or regional lines or facilitating the secession of parts of the Jhelum Valley to Pakistan (Ganguly 1997: 3–4, 43–57; Rahman 1996: 4). The insistence on rejecting the trajectory charted out for them by the power structures of India, Pakistan and the West and the urge to proclaim themselves a nation that is capable of exercising the right of self-determination has been haunting the psyche of the Kashmiri people for decades.

NATIONALISM AND GENDERED VIOLENCE

What are the traditional freedoms and prerogatives of Kashmiri women in the land of a spiritual luminary like Lalla-Ded? Over the years, tremendous political and social turmoil has been generated in the state by the forces of religious fundamentalism and by an exclusionary nationalism that seeks to erode the cultural syncretism that is part of the ethos of Kashmir. These forces are responsible for the shutting down of dissenters who voice cultural critique, repression of women, political anarchy, economic deprivation, lack of infrastructure, and mass displacements that have been occasioned by these events. Since 1949, the United Nations and Pakistan have consistently demanded that a plebiscite be held in order to determine the wishes of the Kashmiri people. India has denied this wish for fear of losing the vote in the predominantly Muslim Kashmir valley. India uses Pakistan's reluctance to withdraw its forces and the decision of the United States government to supply arms to Pakistan in 1954 to justify its denial (Ganguly 1997: 43–57; Rahman 1996: 4; Schofield 2002). Nearly 400,000 Indian army and paramilitary forces have been deployed in the state, in India's most beefed up counter-insurgency operation till date. Financing these operations has taken an enormous toll on the annual administrative budget of the state (Ganguly 1997: 1–2). Since the inception of the secessionist movement in 1989, more than 38,000 Kashmiris have been brutally murdered by Indian forces, 100,000 Pundits have migrated to other parts of India for fear of persecution, over 5,000 women have been violated, innumerable people have been incarcerated and held incommunicado. United Nations experts on extrajudicial, summary and arbitrary executions have not been invited to Kashmir and international human rights monitoring organizations have been prevented from entering the state (Amnesty International 1995; Schofield 2002). In such a conflict situation, the law and order machinery is rendered dysfunctional, increasing the vulnerability of women and children.

Kashmir lives in the unpleasant reality of Indian and Pakistani dominance, which is full of redoubtable paramilitary troops, barbed wire and invasive searches; dispossessed youths trained in Pakistani training camps to unleash a reign of disorganized and misguided terror in the state; custodial killings in detention centres and mothers whose faces tell tales of woe waiting outside those gloomy detention centres to catch glimpses of their unfortunate sons (an exercise in futility); burqa-clad women afraid of the wrath of fundamentalist groups as well as of paramilitary forces bent on undercutting their self-respect. The military has carte blanche under the Jammu and Kashmir Public Safety Act of 1978 and the Terrorist and Disruptive Activities [Prevention] Act of 1987 (Puri 1995; Schofield 2002; Widmalm 2002; Wirsing 2002). The traditional communal harmony in Kashmir has been eroded by Pakistan's sponsorship of terrorism in the state, India's repression of every demand for local autonomy and shelving self-determination for Kashmiris, the eruption of ethno-religious fervour as the central government disregarded democratic institutions in Jammu and Kashmir (Ganguly 1997: 14–20). The anarchy that pervades the cultural and political fabric of Kashmir has been stoked by government-sponsored militants and foreign mercenaries. In such an unwieldy situation, women are psychologically incarcerated (Butalia 2002). Such occurrences do not enable an autonomous Kashmiri life, devoid of the pressures that Kashmiris have been subjected to since 1947. The brutalization of the culture has been rendered more lethal by the socialization of Kashmiri boys and men into military culture. Within such a masculinist discourse and praxis the rigidly entrenched hierarchical relationship between men and women is inextricably linked with sexualized violence. For instance, more than 5,000 rapes were reported to have been committed by Indian security forces in the state since the inception of the secessionist movement in 1989 (Prasad 1999: 478–506). A number of women have been ruthlessly violated by members of the paramilitary troops deployed in Kashmir as a tool to avenge themselves and indelibly scathe the consciousness of the culture that dared to raise its insurgent head against the two mammoth nuclear powers on the Indian subcontinent. A large percentage of rape victims and war widows are afflicted with post traumatic stress disorder and are prone to suicidal tendencies (Kashmir Human Rights 2002).

In contemporary Kashmiri society, the question of the role of women in the nationalist scenario remains a vexed one. As Ann McClintock observes about the role of the subaltern woman in Third World societies: 'Excluded from direct action as national citizens, women are subsumed symbolically into the national body politic as its boundary and metaphoric limit' (1997: 345). For instance, the only women's reactionary organization in Kashmir, Dukhtaran-e-Milat, claims that the image of woman as a burqa-clad faceless and voiceless cultural icon, devoid of the agency to pave a path of her own choosing, is sanctioned by the versions of religious scriptures that this vigilante group subscribes to and reinforces her strength and courage of conviction to sacrifice for the family. The Dukhtaran-e-Milat is a pro-Pakistan organization which believes that the salvation of Kashmir lies with the theocratic nation-state in which the impassioned appeals of the clergy to an outdated concept of Islam breed rancorous hate against the former imperialist occupiers of the Muslim world and exploit the pitiful poverty and illiteracy of Muslims who are unable to study the progressive concepts of the religion for themselves. This vigilante group, affiliated with other pro-Pakistan organizations like the Jamaat-i-Islami, uses intimidating and questionable tactics to raid houses that allegedly have been converted into brothels and brutally censors romantic liaisons between college-going boys and girls (based on information that I have gathered by talking with politicians, academics and students in the Valley). The women members of Dukhtaran-e-Milat would perhaps never identify the modern Kashmiri woman with the liberated woman of the western world. On the contrary, they make a facile attempt to reconstruct historical and cultural discourses in order to inspire the kind of cultural nationalism that fundamentalist politics requires. This organization advocates the creation of a homogeneous culture devoid of the freedoms that Kashmiri women have traditionally enjoyed. Their draconian methods to enforce purdah, reinforce a patriarchal structure in which an unaccompanied woman is rendered vulnerable, and curtail the mobility of the technology savvy youth is an attempt to Arabize the syncretic ethos of Kashmir (Schofield 2002). There seems to be an insensitivity in such reactionary organizations as well as in former and current regional and national administrations, such as the Congress and People's Democratic Party coalition government in the state and the centralizing regimes of the Congress, the Bharatiya Janata Party (BJP) and the National Democratic Front (NDF) in the centre, of the diverse interpretations of religious laws regarding the institutions of marriage, divorce, inheritance rights, etc.; of the rich heterogeneity of cultural traditions and to the paradoxes within them. In its initial years, Sheikh Mohammad Abdullah's National Conference enabled the emergence of a well-educated, politically aware generation of Kashmiris. But in the 1970s and the 1980s, Indira Gandhi's Congress regime characterized every demand for local empowerment as potentially insurgent, discouraging the growth of a progressive generation of Kashmiris (Ganguly 1997: 84–85; Kohli 1997: 341–42; Rai 2004: 295). The vociferous members of the Dukhtaran-e-Milat would better serve the female population of the state by campaigning for quotas for women in the legislative assembly, legislative council, parliament, and the judiciary. An increase in female representation in these institutions of authority would facilitate a cultural shift in terms of gender role expectations, legitimizing a defiance of the normative structure. The intrusion of women in traditionally male domains would cause perceptible erosion in the structural determinants of sexualized violence. This form of empowerment would 'frame and facilitate the struggle for social justice and women's equality through a transformation of economic, social, and political structures' (Bisnath and Elson n.d.; Porter and Verghese 1999). In the present scenario, no thought is given either by the state authorities or by insurgent groups to women who have been victims of the paramilitary forces and/or of militant organizations. Horrifying narratives of women and adolescent girls being humiliated and brutally interrogated in remote villages are absent from the official record, and are fearfully voiced in the atmosphere of paranoia that pervades the Kashmir valley. For instance, in 1991, more than 800 soldiers of the fourth Rajput Regiment raped twenty-three to sixty women in the course of one night in the village of Kunan Pohpura in Kashmir. These soldiers raided the village on the pretext of interrogating the local men who were allegedly insurgents. Another gruesome incident of a similar nature occurred in Handawara village in 2004, where a mother and her minor daughter were sadistically defiled by a major of the Rashtriya Rifles. In Mattan in south Kashmir, an Indian army subedar and his bodyguard of seven Rashtriya Rifles were involved in a spine-chilling rape case against which the necessary governmental action is yet to be taken.[11]

Women representatives of the then ruling People's Democratic Party (PDP) and those of its ally, the Congress, were quick to make visits accompanied by their entourages to isolated villages or towns in which the Indian army had trammelled on the sensibilities of the female population. The PDP, while in opposition, raised the issue of human rights abuses which, until then, hadn't been given much credence by the National Conference government. But they were unable to advocate reforms specific to women. No stringent and timely measures were taken to redress those wrongs. In effect, the Kashmiri woman is constructed as a parchment on which the discourses of religious nationalism, secular nationalism and ethno-nationalism are inscribed, and the most barbaric acts are justified by Indian paramilitary forces as means to rein in uncontrollable separatist forces and by militant organizations as a means to restore the lost dignity of the 'women'.

Secular as well as ethno-nationalists assert that as long as the inner or spiritual distinctiveness of the culture is retained, an autonomous Kashmiri 'nation' can equip itself to cope with a globalized world without losing its essential identity. Nationalist discourse creates the dichotomy of the inner/outer in order to make the inviolability of the inner domain look traditional. For example, ethno-nationalists assert that a Kashmiri woman who marries a non-Kashmiri loses her legal right to inherit, own or buy immovable property in the state. By inhabiting the metaphoric inner domain, the Kashmiri woman embodies the virginal purity of the culture and ethnicity which would get tainted by her stepping outside the cultural threshold. As a strategy to maintain the inviolability of the cultural sanctum sanctorum, ethno-nationalists problematize the law concerning state subjects which was promulgated in Jammu and Kashmir on 20 April 1927 by Maharajah Hari Singh. This injunction was meant to protect the interests of the local landed class and the peasantry against wealthy people from outside the state who had the wherewithal to buy the locals out of hearth and home. In 1957, the new constitution of the state changed 'state subject' to 'permanent resident'. Permanent resident status was accorded to individuals who had been living in the state for at least a decade before 14 May 1957. On 25 March 1969, the state government issued an injunction requiring all deputy commissioners to issue certificates of permanent residence to

Kashmiri women with the stipulation that status was valid till marriage. After that, women who married permanent resident men would need to get their certificates reissued and those who married outside the state would automatically lose their permanent resident status, whereas, a male permanent resident would have the privilege of endowing his non-state subject spouse with the ability to own and inherit property in the state as long as she didn't leave the state for permanent residence elsewhere (Abdullah 1993; Zutshi 2004).

In 2002, the state High Court declared that this proviso had no legislative sanction because it violated the gender equality clause of the constitution of the state as well as of India. The High Court held that the proviso relied on section 10 of the British law which governed pre-Partition India, and that law had itself been amended (Bhagat 2002; Puri 2004). The bench quoted section 4 of the Sri Pratap Consolidation Law Act to declare that the only legislative prohibition was that the property inherited by a non-state subject could not be sold to a non-state subject. But this decision created a furore in which the opposition National Conference asserted that the declaration of the earlier proviso invalidating the permanent resident status of women who married outside the state as outmoded was an attempt to erode the distinctive cultural identity of the state. The National Conference accused the then ruling PDP of having made a compromise by withdrawing its appeal from the Supreme Court against the judgement of the state High Court. The angst of power caused the PDP, including its women members, to immediately draft a Permanent Resident Bill in the assembly thus reinforcing the earlier stipulation. The High Court's decision was supported by the PDP's coalition partner at the time, the Congress. The issue of permanent residence was hijacked by Hindu fundamentalist originations, the BJP and the Rashtriya Samaj Sevak, to inflame regional divisiveness by condemning the opposition of the National Conference and the PDP to the High Court's decision as acts of Muslim secession, excluding the predominantly Hindu Jammu. The representatives of the National Conference and the PDP in the legislative assembly and legislative council opposed the decision of the High Court that declared the earlier proviso archaic and outmoded, and the representatives of the Congress and the BJP supported it (Puri 2004). In effect, women were deployed as a political tool not just by regional political organizations but by national ones as well.

Women politicos in the current legislative assembly and legislative council of Jammu and Kashmir play the role of tokens who bolstered the social, cultural and moral institutions that maintain a male-dominated power structure (Amnesty International 2004; Kashmiri Women's Initiative for Peace and Disarmament 2002). Even those with access to the echelons of power refuse to engage 'more effectively with the politics of affiliation, and the currently calamitous dispensations of power' (McClintock, 1997: 396). Despite its firm promise, the current state government has been unable to incorporate the Special Operations Group (SOG), a paramilitary division of the police accused of heinous human rights violations, entirely into the regular police force. The SOG continues to run amok and functions as an entity that only obeys the law of the jungle. Alongside the SOG, the Special Task Force, a militia group comprising renegade militants, has been incorporated into the regular police force as well but has not been disbanded, a promise the then PDP government had made at the time of its installation in office. These forces have been deployed to handle extrajudicial matters in arbitrary ways and are responsible for gross misdemeanours against women (Amnesty International 2004).

Why is gender violence such a consistent feature of the insurgency and counter-insurgency that have wrenched the Indian subcontinent for about decades? In nationalist rhetoric the equation of the native woman to the motherland has in recent days become more forceful. In effect, the native woman is constructed as a trough within which male aspirations are nurtured, and the most barbaric acts are justified as means to restore the lost dignity of the 'women'. The story of India's partition in 1947 into two separate nation-states, India and Pakistan, is replete with instances of fathers slaughtering their daughters in order to prevent them from being violated by the enemy; and women resorting to mass suicide to preserve the 'honour' of the community (Kaul 1999; Kumari and Kidwai 1998; Jayawardena 1986; Ray 2000). If a woman's body belongs not to herself but to her community, then the violation of that body purportedly signifies an attack upon the honour (*izzat*) of the whole community.

In one instance, the crime of a boy from a lower social caste against a woman from a higher upper caste in the Meerawala village in the central province of Punjab in Pakistan in 2002 was punished in a revealing way by the 'sagacious' tribal jury. After days of thoughtful consideration, this jury gave the verdict that the culprit's teenage sister, Mai, should be gang-raped by a group of goons from the wronged social group: The tribal jury ruled that to save the honour of the upper-caste Mastoi clan, Mai's brother, Shakoor, should marry the woman with whom he was accused of having an illicit relationship while Mai was to be given away in marriage to a Mastoi man. 'The prosecution said that when she rejected the decision she was gang-raped by four Mastoi men and made to walk home semi-naked in front of hundreds of people' (Reuters 2002). Such acts of violence do occur in the Indian subcontinent and bear testimony to the intersecting notions of nation, family and community.

The horrific stories of women that are in most instances attributed to folklore underscore the complicity of official and nationalist historiography in perpetuating these notions. I might add that the feminization of the 'homeland' as the 'motherland' for which Indian soldiers, Kashmiri nationalists in Indian-occupied Kashmir and Kashmiri nationalists in Pakistan-occupied Kashmir are willing to lay down their lives serves, in effect, to preserve the native women in pristine retardation. Although this essentialist portrayal of the Kashmiri woman is clearly suspect, it is embedded more deeply in the quasi-feudal culture of Pakistan-occupied Kashmir. Pakistan-occupied Kashmir has been a fiefdom of feudal lords whose only concern is with the impregnability of their authority and the replenishment of their coffers. Tribal women in 'Azad' Kashmir are still circumscribed within the parameters created by the paternalistic feudal culture that disallows the creation of a space for distinct subjectivities (Cohen 2004; Talbot 1999; Ziring 2000).

Do women embody the history of a culture and community only as it is remembered in the murky corridors of officialdom? The on-going story of trouble torn Kashmir is replete with instances of fathers forcing their daughters to live in marital unions of psychological, sexual and material frustration to prevent them from being violated by the paramilitary forces or by trigger-happy militants; women accepting physical and emotional torture in their marital homes to preserve the 'honour' of the family and the community; and women who were 'dishonoured', either by being violated or by asserting their political and sexual agency, being ruthlessly shunned by their families (Amnesty International 2004; Kashmiri Women's Initiative for Peace and Disarmament 2002). Consider Gayatri Chakravorty Spivak's delineation of the contexts in which the politics of representation renders mute the figure of the 'Third World woman', which would apply to the situation in Kashmir:

> Between patriarchy and imperialism, subject-constitution and object-formation, the figure of the woman disappears, not into a pristine nothingness, but a violent shuttling which is the displaced figuration of the 'Third World woman' caught between tradition and modernization. (1999: 304)

Culture inscribes a wide range of experiences, which centralizing institutions attempt to render invisible and homogeneous. Women in Kashmir, as in other postcolonial countries, are positioned in relation to their own class and cultural realities, their own histories, their sensitivity to the diversity of cultural traditions and to the questions and conflicts within them, the legacies of Sufi Islam, their own struggles not just with the devastating effects of Indian occupation and Pakistani infiltration, but also with the discourses of cultural nationalism and religious fundamentalism propagated in the valley, their own relations to the West, their interpretations of religious law, their beliefs in the different schools of Islamic and Hindu thought, and their concepts of the role of women in contemporary societies.

WOMEN AND AGENCY

My attempt to theorize women's agency involves framing the concept in cognitive, psychological, economic, and political aspects. I borrow eminent educationist, Nelly Stromquist's assertion regarding agency which involves taking decisions that deconstruct cultural and social norms, and beliefs that structure seemingly intransigent traditional gender ideologies; the psychological aspect refers to developing self-esteem for which some form of financial autonomy is a basis; the political aspect involves the ability to organize and mobilize for social change, which requires the creation of awareness not just at the individual level but at the collective level as well (Stromquist 1995). For me, empowerment is a process which enables the marginalized to make strategic life choices regarding education, livelihood, marriage, childbirth, sexuality, etc., which are critical for people to lead the sort of lives they want to lead and constitute life's defining parameters (Kabeer 1999: 437). It is important to keep in mind, however, that women are constrained by and grapple with the normative structures through which societies create gender roles.

Women have more or less power depending on their specific situation and they can be relatively submissive in one situation and relatively assertive in another. Assessing women's agency requires identifying and mapping power relations, the room to manoeuvre within each pigeonhole and the intransigence of the boundaries (Hayward 1989). A woman's level of empowerment also varies according to factors such as class, caste, ethnicity, economic status, age, and family position.

The perception of the requirement for an alternative discourse as well as of an alternative epistemological structure was enhanced by my study of the complex history of Lalla-Ded, the Sufi mystic whose verses were deployed in nationalist discourse and literature as embodying the syncretic ethos of Kashmir. After engaging with the iconicized figure of Lalla-Ded in nationalist historiography, I learned of the complexities of her identity, which underlined the dialectical interplay between Brahminism, Islam and indigenous culture. This contiguity among disparate histories engendered a historical identity formed in a hybrid space as well as a pluralistic vision of the world, not the fixity of a glorified vision of the past in terms of gender roles, societal roles or cultural identities. Lalla-Ded's hybrid identity which annuls the hierarchical purity of cultures does not correspond with the documented version of history. Her identity challenges the inequality between various political, gender-based and religious valences, and constitutes the terrain for the displacement of clearly defined boundaries. Lalla-Ded's cultural identity was never essentialized, but was historically open-ended. Her stance to the contexts that formed her identity displayed a capacity to act upon the social boundaries that 'define fields of action for all actors' (ibid.: 27).

The assertion of an identity that seeks to delegitimize homogenized narratives of society, culture, history, and politics is closely linked to the secular credo of 'Kashmiriyat'. This significant concept does not attempt to simplify the ambiguity and complexity of religious, social and cultural identities. The notion of 'Kashmiriyat' neither attempts to assert a fixed identity nor does it reinforce the idea of the purity of culture. I would veer away from adopting an image of this secular credo that is created by the unitary nationalist discourses it deplores. On the contrary, 'Kashmiriyat' brings about a metamorphosis in the determinate concept of the Indian nation-state and creates a situation in which the nation-states of India and Pakistan are forced to confront an alternative epistemology. At a time of political and social upheaval, this notion engendered a consciousness of place, which offered a critical perspective from which to formulate alternatives.

Since the pervasion of an exclusive cultural nationalism, religious fundamentalism and rampant political corruption in Kashmir, it has become a challenge to lead a dignified existence. The armed conflict has changed political combinations and permutations without either disrupting political, social and gender hierarchies or benefiting marginalized groups. The social, economic, political, and psychological brunt of armed conflict has taken its toll on the populace of Kashmir. The uncertainty created by fifteen years of armed insurgency and counter-insurgency has pervaded the social fabric in insidious ways, creating a generation of disaffected and disillusioned youth. The lack of faith in the Indian polity has caused Kashmiris to cultivate an apathy to the electoral process because it is a given that the person best suited to carry out New Delhi's agenda will be installed in a position of political import, regardless of public opinion. The earlier enthusiasm that accompanied democratization seems totally futile in the current leadership vacuum in the state. On the contrary, it seems to have been replaced by dynastic democracy in which the law of primogeniture prevails. The lack of accountability in the Jammu and Kashmir polity and bureaucracy has caused a large number of people to toe the line by living with the fundamental structural inequities and violence instead of risking the ire of groups and individuals in positions of authority. The glaring lack of a well-equipped infrastructure in the valley makes unemployment rife and underscores the redundancy of the educated segment of the population. The upsurge of gender-based violence has circumscribed the mobility of women who are caught between the devil and the deep blue sea. I, for one, wouldn't have been able to conduct my field research without the armed bodyguard my parents provided for me. As a woman, it would have been difficult and dangerous for me to venture into secluded rural areas which are cordoned by paramilitary troops. I wonder if it'll remain a pipe dream to seek full participation for women and men in professional and political life. I do not conform to the view that women are liabilities without political rights. But the problematic of such a situation is that without a transformation of the social and cultural frameworks which create and facilitate the entrenchment of a gender hierarchy, the burden of maintaining home and hearth will shift onto the women without empowering them in their new roles. Will my daughter, Iman, be able to insert herself from within inter-subjective spaces in the landscape of Kashmir in which the majestic chinars cry in unison, 'We witness this is the land of Lalla-Ded where 'Kashmiriyat' will thrive till the end of time'? Will women be able to construct interstitial identities that undermine hierarchical structures? Will the remembering of cultural identities be propounded as an attempt to challenge the legitimization of patriarchal national imperialisms?

NOTES

1. A version of the article has been published in "The Land of Lalla-Ded: Politicization of Kashmir and Construction of the Kashmiri Woman." *Journal of International Women's Studies* 9.1 (2007): 22-41. And longer versions

of the article have been published in my book, *Islam, Women and Violence in Kashmir: Between India and Pakistan*, under the titles "Negotiating the Boundaries of Gender, Community, and Nationhood" (Tulika, 2009) and "Cultural Syncretism in Kashmir" (New York: Palgrave Macmillan, 2010, pp. 45–62).

2. Rai (2004) and Zutshi (2004). Also conversations with my parents.

3. Sheikh Mohammad Abdullah, popularly known as the Lion of Kashmir, reigned as the prime minister of Jammu & Kashmir from 1948–53. When the pledge to hold a referendum was not kept by the Indian government, Abdullah's advocacy of independence of Kashmir led to his imprisonment. He was shuttled from one jail to the other until 1972 and remained out of power until 1975. During the period of Abdullah's incarceration, Congress Party-led governments in New Delhi made their covert arrangements with puppet regimes installed by them. 'For over three decades, in return for their endorsement of Kashmir's accession, these selected politicians received the most generous grants-in-aid disbursed by the Indian center to any state' (Rai 2004: 289). Prior to the 1975 accord between the Sheikh Mohammad Abdullah-led National Conference and the Indira Gandhi-led Congress, Abdullah demanded the revocation of all central laws extended to the state that delegitimized the popular demand for plebiscite. The then prime minister, Indira Gandhi, forged an accord with Abdullah in 1975 by promising to partially restore the autonomy of the state by revoking certain central laws that had arbitrarily been imposed on Jammu and Kashmir. The same year Abdullah returned as the chief minister of the state. Sheikh Abdullah and his National Conference won an overwhelming victory in the election of 1977 and he remained in office until his death in 1982 (Copland 1991; Lamb 1991; Singh 1995).

4. Fragments of personal memory that I can now form into a composite whole.

5. Kashmiri Saints and Sages: Ancient and Modern Ascetics in Kashmir (n.d.), 'Lalla Ded's Vakhs'. Available at: http://www.koausa.org/Saints/LalDed/ Vakhs1.html. Last accessed November 2005.

6. My maternal grandmother, Begum Akbar Jehan's maiden name was 'Nedou'. She was part Austrian and part Gujjar. Gujjars are a pastoral people who trace their lineage to the Rajputs of Rajasthan (Lidhoo 1987).

7. This project was funded by the College of Fine Arts and Humanities and the Department of English at the University of Nebraska-Kearney.

8. The Gujjar women I met with during my field research were distant clanswomen of my grandmother's.

9. A subject-effect can be briefly plotted as follows: that which seems to operate as a subject may be a part of an immense discontinuous network ('text' in the general sense) of strands that may be termed politics, economics, history, sexuality, language, and so on. Different knotting and configurations of these strands, determined by heterogeneous determinations, which are themselves

dependent upon myriad circumstances, produce the effect of an operating subject (Spivak 1988: 260).

10. The Hindu maharajah of Kashmir, Hari Singh, signed the Instrument of Accession on 26 October 1947, formally acceding to the newly formed nation-state of India. This accession took place under the provisions of the constitution of India which was legitimized on 15 August 1947 and was accepted by Governor-General Lord Mountbatten. The subtext of the Instrument of Accession was that the wishes of the Kashmiri people would be taken into consideration once political stability had been established in the newly formed nation-states of India and Pakistan. The United Nations Commission for India and Pakistan decreed a plebiscite for Kashmir on 13 August 1948 and 5 January 1949. Needless to say, a plebiscite was never held (Chadha 2005; Lamb 1991; Madhok 1963; Rai 2004). A pledge not redeemed was 'that made on behalf of the Indian nation by Jawaharlal Nehru in November 1947 to consult, through a referendum, the wishes of the Kashmiri people on the state's accession to the Indian union' (Rai 2004: 289). See Lamb (1991) for discussions about the legitimacy of the Instrument of Accession.

11. Conversations With human rights activists in the Kashmir valley, 2004; also, Kashmiri Women's Initiative for Peace and Disarmament 2002).

REFERENCES

Abdullah, Sheikh Mohammad (1993). *Flames of the Chinar: An Autobiography*. Trans. Khushwant Singh. New York: Viking.

Amnesty International (1995). 'India Must Prevent Torture'. Available at: http://www.kashmiri-cc.ca/quarterly/kq2-4/AMNESTY2.htm. Last accessed November 2005.

———— (2004). 'India'. Available at: http://web.amnesty.org/report2004/ind-summary-eng. Last accessed November 2005.

Bamzai, Prem Nath Kaul (1994). *Culture and Political History of Kashmir*, 3 vols. Delhi: M.D. Publications.

Bhagat, Pamela (2002). 'Women in Kashmir: Citizens at Last'. Available at: http://www.boloji.com/wfs/wfs110.htm. Last accessed November 2005.

Bhatnagar, Rashmi, Renu Dube and Reena Dube (2004). 'Meera's Medieval Lyric Poetry in Postcolonial India: The Rhetorics of Women's Writing in Dialect as a Secular Practice of Subaltern Coauthorship and Dissent', *Boundary 2* 31(3): 1–46.

Bisnath, S. and Elson, D. (n.d.) *Women's Empowerment Revisited*. UNIFEM. Available at: http://www.undp.org/unifem/progressww/empower.html. Last accessed November 2005.

Butalia, Urvashi (ed.) (2002). *Speaking Peace: Women's Voices From Kashmir*. New Delhi: Kali for Women.

Chadha, Vivek (2005). *Low Intensity Conflicts in India: an Analysis*. New Delhi: Sage Publications.

Chakravarti, U. (1989). 'Whatever Happened to the Vedic Dasi? Orientalism, Nationalism, and a Script for the Past', in Kumkum Sangari and Sudesh Vaid (eds), *Recasting Women: Essays in Colonial History*. New Delhi: Kali for Women.

Clifford, James and George E. Marcus (ed.) (1986). *Writing Culture: The Poetics and Politics of Ethnography*. Berkeley: University of California Press.

Cohen, Stephen P. (2004). *The Idea of Pakistan*. Washington D.C.: Brookings Institution Press.

Copland, Ian (1991). 'The Abdullah Factor: Kashmiri Muslims and the Crisis of 1947', in D.A. Low (ed.), *The Political Inheritance of Pakistan*. London: Macmillan.

Gandhi, Leela (1998). *Postcolonial Theory: A Critical Introduction*. New York: Columbia.

Ganguly, Sumit (1997). *The Crisis in Kashmir: Portents of War, Hopes of Peace*. New York: Woodrow Wilson Center Press.

Hayward, C.R. (1989). 'De-facing Power', *Polity*, 31(1): 22–34.

Jayawardena, Kumari (1986). *Feminism and Nationalism in the Third World*. London: Zed Books.

Jha, Prem Shankar (1996). *Kashmir, 1947: Rival Versions of History*. Bombay: Oxford University Press.

Kabeer, N. (1999). 'Resources, Agency, Achievements: Reflections on the Measurement of Women's Empowerment', *Development and Change* 30: 435–64.

Karim, W. (1993). 'The Nativised Self and the Native', in D.P.C. Bell and W.J. Karim (eds), *Gendered Fields: Women, Men and Ethnography*, pp. 248–51. London: Routledge.

Kashmir Human Rights (2002). 'Impact of Conflict on Children and Women in Kashmir'. Available at: http://kashmirahrchk.net/mainfilephp/articles.45. Last accessed November 2005.

Kashmiri Women's Initiative for Peace and Disarmament (2002). 'Probe Gimmick', *Voices Unheard: A Magazine*. Available at: http://www.geocities.com/kwipd2002. Last accessed November 2005.

Kaul, R.N. (1999). *Kashmir's Mystic: Poetess Lalla Ded, Alias Lalla Arifa*. New Delhi: S. Chand & Co.

Kaw, M.K. (ed.) (2004). *Kashmir and its People: Studies in the Evolution of Kashmiri Society*. New Delhi: A.P.H.

Khan, Muhammad Ishaq (1994). *Kashmir's Transition to Islam: The Role of Muslim Rishis*. New Delhi: Manohar.

Kishwar, Madhu (1998). *Religion at the Service of Nationalism and Other Essays*. New Delhi: Oxford University Press.

Kohli, Atul (1997). 'Can Democracies Accommodate Ethnic Nationalism? Rise and Decline of Self-Determination Movements in India', *Journal of Asian Studies*, 56(2): 325–44.

Kumari, Abhilasha and Kabina Kidwai (1998). *Crossing the Sacred Line: Women's Search for Political Power*. New Delhi: Orient Longman Publishing.

Lamb, Alastair (1991). *Kashmir: A Disputed Legacy, 1846–1990*. Hertingfordbury: Roxford Books.

Lidhoo, Moti Lal (1987). *Kashmir Tribals: Child Rearing and Psycho-social Development*. Srinagar: Minakshi Publishers.

Lok Sabha (2000). 'Obituary References'. Available at: http://parliamentofindia. nic.in/lsdeb/ls13/ses4/24072k.htm. Last accessed November 2005.

Madhok, Balraj (1963). *Kashmir: Center of New Alignments*. New Delhi: Deepak.

McClintock, Ann (1997). *Dangerous Liaisons: Gender, Nation, and Postcolonial Perspective*. Minneapolis: University of Minnesota Press.

Mohanty, Chandra (1991). *Third World Women and the Politics of Feminism*. Bloomington: Indiana University Press.

Minh-ha, Trinh T. (1989). *Woman, Native, Other*. Bloomington: Indiana University Press.

Murphy, Paul E. (1999). *Triadic Mysticism: The Mystical Theology of the Saivism of Kashmir*. New ed. Columbia: South Asia Books.

Nandy, Ashis, Shikha Trivedi, Shail Mayaram and Achyut Yagnik (1998). *Exiled at Home: Comprising, at the Edge of Psychology, the Intimate Enemy, Creating a Nationality*. New York: Oxford University Press.

Parimoo, B.N. (1978). *The Ascent of Self: A Reinterpretation of the Mystical Poetry of Lalla-Ded*. Delhi: Motilal Banarsidas.

Porter, F. and V. Verghese (1999). 'Falling Between the Gaps', in Marilyn Porter and Ellen Judd (eds), *Feminists Doing Development: a Practical Critique*, pp. 124–41. New York: Zed Books.

Prasad, Shally (1999). 'Medicolegal Response to Violence Against Women in India', *Violence Against Women*, 5(5): 478–507.

Puri, Balraj (2004) 'Analysis of the J & K Permanent Resident Bill'. Available at http://www.pucl.org/Topics/Law/2004/jk-pr-bill.htm. Last accessed November 2005.

Puri, Balraj (1995). *Kashmir Towards Insurgency*. New Delhi: Orient Longman.

Rai, Mridu (2004). *Hindu Rulers, Muslim Subjects: Islam, Rights, and the History of Kashmir*. Princeton: Princeton University Press.

Rahman, Mushtaqur (1996). *Divided Kashmir: Old Problems, New Opportunities for India, Pakistan, and the Kashmiri People*. Boulder: Lynne Rienner.

Ray, Sangeet (2000). *En-Gendering India: Woman and Nation in Colonial and Postcolonial Narratives*. Durham: Duke University Press.

Ray, Sunil Chandra (1970). *Early History and Culture of Kashmir*. New Delhi: Munshiram Manoharlal.

Razdan, P.N. (1999). *Gems of Kashmiri Literature and Kashmiriyat, the Trio of Saint Poets*. New Delhi: Samkaleen.

Reuters (2002). 'Pakistan Court Expected to Rule on Gang-Rape Case', *Khaleej Times*, http://www.khaleejtimes.co.ae/ktarchive/270802/subcont.htm. Last accessed August 2003.

Rushdie, Salman (2005). *Shalimar the Clown*. New York: Random House.

Schofield, Victoria (2002). *Kashmir in Conflict: India, Pakistan and the Unending War*, 2nd rev. ed. London: I.B. Tauris.

Singh, Tavleen (1995). *Kashmir, A Tragedy of Errors*. New Delhi: Viking.

Spivak, Gayatri Chakravorty (1988). *In Other Worlds: Essays in Cultural Politics*. New York: Routledge.

——— (1999). *Critique of Postcolonial Reason: Toward a History of the Vanishing Present*. Cambridge: Harvard University Press.

Stromquist, N.P. (1995). 'The Theoretical and Practical Bases for Empowerment', in Medel-Anonuevo, Carolyn (ed.), *Women, Education and Empowerment: Pathways towards Autonomy*, pp. 12–22. Hamburg: UNESCO Institute for Education.

Sufi, Ghulam Muhyi'd Din (1974). *Kashir, Being of History of Kashmir from the Earliest Times to Our Own*, 2nd ed. New Delhi: Light & Life Publishers.

Talbot, Ian (1999). *Pakistan: A Modern History*. London: C. Hurst.

Widmalm, Sten (2002). *Kashmir in Comparative Perspective: Democracy and Violent Separatism in Kashmir.* New York: Routledge.

Wirsing, Robert (2002). 'Kashmir in the Terrorist Shadow', *Asian Affairs*, 33(1): 91–97.

Whitehead, Andrew (2004). 'Kashmir's Conflicting Identities', *History Workshop Journal*, 58(1): 335–40.

Ziring, Lawrence (2000). *Pakistan in the 20th Century: A Political History.* New York: Oxford University Press.

Zutshi, Chitralekha (2004). *Languages of Belonging: Islam, Regional Identity, and the Making of Kashmir*. Delhi: Permanent Black.

12

Memory-Mournings

The Biopolitics of Hindu Nationalism

Angana P. Chatterji

PROLOGUE

> '*Your god has no eyes. He cannot have a soul. Your god is violent, just like you are.*'
> A Hindu neighbour indicts Hasina Begum.[1]

> '*We know that many Hindus hate Muslims and I know that Hindus are in power. I am afraid for my daughter. I want her to stay at home with me. She does not listen. So many times I am afraid for her, I beat her to make her stay at home. She has marks on her back from my beating her. I am ashamed. I feel isolated. If something happens to us, if someone attacks us, robs us, who will be with us? We are asked, "You have no idols, so who is your god? Are you godless?" I know that we are not welcome here. There are stories about us "Pathans"[2] that circulate in the marketplace. We have heard about Gujarat.[3] Will it happen here? Who will prevent it?*'
> Hasina Begum

People tell Hasina that nothing has really happened, that she has not been attacked, that she is overreacting. She responds, 'Fear is attacking me. I feel that they are watching me. This fear is real.'[4] With her technician husband, Hasina's is the only Muslim family in a housing society in a small town in Orissa.[5] They relocated in 2003. Hasina and her husband are isolated with few acquaintances in the area. Geeta,[6] a Hindu woman, befriended Hasina only to be confronted by others about such association with Muslims. Geeta withdrew purposely, saying: 'We like you but we have to live in society here, do we carry you with us, or carry them? What choice do we have?' Geeta and Hasina no longer speak.

EXPLANATIONS

I write at the behest of ever present legacies in 'nationspace' shaped by the riot torn Calcutta of the 1960s and 1970s, reinforced by the presence of Sikh women in relief camps in the Delhi of 1984,[7] and in the hollowed out 'colonies' of Ahmedabad in 2002, as Gujarat introduced an end and a beginning[8] distinctive in the Hindu nationalist movement's malevolent reach for a Hindu state. I write compelled by Adivasi, Dalit,[9] Muslim, Christian women and men in Orissa, whose lives narrate a genealogy of violence before violence in the making of 'nation'. Its dynamics are inscribed on bodies, in language and culture, gender and state (McClintock et al. 1997), affecting community, producing alienation. Displacement and dislocation are its markers, taking place within (and not necessarily outside of) the bounded spaces of village, community, country.[10] Policed via the institutions of patriarchal territoriality, compulsorily heterosexist and sadistic,[11] this violence, as the article describes, powers and makes ordinary, hunger, rape, social abuse, livelihood insecurity, exclusion. It invents and invokes memory, drawing upon intransigent and imagined duplicity from beyond the geographic and historical space of the present nation. Such reprisal, reproduced cross-nation, is useful in constructing and mobilizing the state as immense cultural, ecological, political diversity begins to, is forced to, assimilate (Deshpande 2000). 'Belonging' in disenfranchisement is produced by gradual and episodic erasure and incremental gains,[12] creating an increasingly singular, progressively neutralized, illusory convergence that serves and begets legitimacy from a 'higher' and instrumental authority, the nation. This revolution is bankrupt of spiritual agency.[13] This brutality renders an imagined past hyper-real, making shadows and émigrés of those at the margins of the present. This coincident and ongoing severance and counter-belonging engenders retroactively the promising/furthering of the next violence. Nationspace, as Bhabha (1994: 139) tells us, 'fills the void' lingering in the deracination of history in skin and bone, through remembrances, through the cruelty of (im)possible futures that produce nation as 'essence'.[14]

What are the spaces in which violation occurs? What are its regulatory practices? This work-in-progress explores the govermentalization of Hindutva,[15] the political economy of disequilibrium in which indoctrination takes place, technologies of gendered violence, and militant nationalist mobilizations via development, education and conversions. It selects fragments from the efforts of colleagues,[16] and my own archival, advocacy and policy research on land reform movements and Hindu nationalism in Orissa.[17] It includes issues and concerns made explicit through meetings with individuals, at collective processes in community fora, and at village and district levels, since 1995, focusing extensively on fifty-seven villages over the last five years, and secondarily within others spanning the districts[18] of Karanjia, Ghumsur, Dhenkanal, Mayurbhanj, Angul, Jagatsinghpur, Puri, Cuttack, Rayagada, Bolangir, Sundargarh, and Ranpur. Using local and interdisciplinary methodologies,[19] I have focused on working with social movements and marginalized groups in the state, even as associations with upper-caste communities[20] have allowed complex understandings of privilege. Through this work, I have had the benefit of learning from people refusing to be made objects of history, who are enraged and resilient. I have been witness to deconstructive practise,[21] to struggle and transgression, complicity and grief; a recorder whose language reflects her inadequacy. Politics and alliance made me, as narrator and witness, accountable to excavating disqualified knowledges[22] and the conditions that create, and are shaped by, language, fiction\reality. Knowledge of and as resistance, organized by silence, speech, interpretation, representation and positionality, is immersed in the very wretchedness that produces it. Democratization of knowledge demands a subordination of its production to processes of social change, recognizing the impossibility[23] and absolute necessity of this labour. Working with movement-based organizations and peoples has forced the framework of research to encounter the political capabilities of the disenfranchised in seeking to empower ethical knowledges from hybrid locations—always frail, always ongoing—to act as an intervention in the social world (Chatterji and Shapiro 2011).

I am acutely aware that even as colleagues in village Orissa and I share commitments we are differently impacted by our engagement, its consequences and outcomes. Our differences are embedded in issues of class and politics, in histories that cannot be made monolithic, yet are distinct in relation to privilege and marginality. Such inequities are promised us and protected structurally. The task of intervention is continually problematic as I inhabit the estrangement of bi-national residency.[24] It is a chosen diaspora that seeks continual, if impossible, return. As a woman from postcolonial India, I struggle to presence the political horror of 'First World' inequities in the context of 'Third World' resistance. How might concerns of 'postcoloniality'[25] live within the 'First World' Academy through critical intellectual activity and social action? How might particular forms of knowledge constructed through collective practice in both places question their relevance?[26] What is expected of me? What of me must I interrogate? What rupture, what political perversity, what responsibility,[27] must it facilitate? Research, writing, presence, alliance are made relevant in contexts where complex relationships shape and language scholarship/activism.[28] Allocating labour towards making privilege (mine) accountable[29] (and therefore at risk) is something I struggle with, haunted by the violence of lived events, by irredeemable injustices that produce and maintain power and powerlessness.

HINDU CULTURAL DOMINANCE AND HINDUTVA

Nationalist thought and the practice of nationalism in colonial India shifted from the communal[30] to incorporate the secular in the late nineteenth century (Chatterjee 1986; Pandey 1990). Indian nationalism was built upon the prerogative of the Hindu elite, even as the postcolonial Indian state conferred rights to diverse individuals and communities within its borders. While secular separation of religion and state, and legitimation of the religious and irreligious, was attempted at the constitutional level, Hindu nationalism derives consent from Hindu cultural dominance (Chatterjee 1997). Hindu ascendancy is assisted by the degree to which the authority of the religion, and the enabling cultural and gender hierarchies, are enshrined deep within the popular psyche and cultural practices of the nation (Bacchetta and Power 2002; Hasan 1991). This dominance assumes that to restrict religion to the private realm would deny India its historical 'consciousness' (Hansen 2001; Jaffrelot 1996).

Secularism as a strategy in nation building has been contentious in India. Critics of the modern nation state and purists dispute secularism as impossible and intrusive. Hindu nationalists argue that secularism, if implemented, will force a renegotiation of civic, political, cultural institutions to render incomprehensible 'India', which *is* predominantly 'Hindu'. Hindu nationalists understand secularism as the absurd 'accommodation' of minority demands. Secularism has remained a bargaining tool in national politics, used to advantage by political parties to appease minority groups. Secular reform with a conscience has been marginalized within the Indian polity to accommodate Hindu hegemony, limiting necessary conversations regarding (Hindu and other) religious reform or a meaningful role for faith in these times (Bhargava 1996; Jhingran 1996; Engineer 2003, 1997; Nandy 2003).[31]

In postcolonial nationspace, Hindu nationalists weave communal\ religious nationalism (Jhingran 1996) and cultural nationalism (Noorani 2002) to define majoritarianism, even as these forms function in contradictory and intersecting discursive spaces among secular intellectuals, agrarian and grass-roots movements, self-determination struggles, Gandhian socialists, conservatives, and leftists. The context of economic and political disenfranchisement allows for Hindu ascendancy, strengthening unmarked Hindu cultural dominance in defining polity, ensuring majoritarianism through the imaginary of liberal development and militarization,[32] enhancing inequities, and defusing the diversity of caste, tribe, religion, culture, ethnicity and gender[33] in the emergent nation.

Hindutva is the hyper-practice of Hindu cultural dominance. Hindutva uses the inequities and social capital of Hindu cultural dominance to hierarchicalize difference, even as it invokes difference and plurality in the name of domination.[34] It poses as indigenous to nation keeping (Bhatt 2001), justifying domination in ways that ignore the power dynamics of its discourse. There is no pluralism in its agenda—Hindutva is the *only* 'right' way to be human, citizen, patriot, in relation to (the Indian) nation.

Hindutva defines minority interests as oppositional to Hindu, and therefore national, interest (Bidwai et al. 1996). Intent on demonstrating the incompatibility of according minorities equal citizenship in the state, the Hindu right wing, the Sangh Parivar (family of organizations) popularizes the idea of India as a Hindu nation that 'tolerates minorities even better' than democracy challenged Pakistan or Bangladesh (ibid.). The Vishwa Hindu Parishad (VHP, World Hindu Council), Hindutva's ideological front, in its meeting with Muslim leaders in New Delhi in mid-March 2002, declared that Muslims and other minorities will be subordinate citizens in a Hindu India.[35] The acceptability of a Hindu nation is predicated on the infidelity of non-Hindus, and assumptions of Muslim and Christian treachery are imperative in legitimating Hindutva (S. Sarkar 2002). Muslim minorities are a primary target of Hindutva, whose master narrative creates grievous misrepresentations of the Indian\South Asian Muslim as monolithic, anti-national, violent, and allied with Islamic fundamentalism.[36] In the present Hindutva imaginary, 'the Muslim' whose identity is shaped by kinship, language and culture becomes synonymous with the Taliban.[37]

Hindutva assembles the political, social and economic conditions in which to be non-Hindu (as rigidly defined) in India is no longer tenable, even offering genocide as a 'rational' response to the untruth of betrayal (International Initiative for Justice 2003). Dominant narrations of nation make mute or reluctant necessary confrontations of privilege as they language evidence of unbelonging and non-assimilation, within which to ascribe difference to the classificatory regime of 'other'.[38] They frequently locate the agency of Hindutva's horror as rational, and name where\ what change must occur in ways that serve only to sustain privilege. Hindu extremism, like other xenophobic movements (Sundar 2004), functions through carefully fashioning exclusionary principles whereby all non-Hindus, and dissenting Hindus, identified as traitors, become second-class citizens (Pannikar 1991). The justification of historical inequities, subordination and normalization of Dalits, women (Menon 2000), Adivasis and other minorities, and the consolidation of a cohesive middle-class[39] base are critical to Hindutva's momentum.[40]

Hindutva's narration of history functions in important ways to posit Hindus and Hinduism as under siege and asserts the idea of India as a Hindu nation, legitimizing colonial machinations (Césaire 2000, Said 1978) of religion and culture in the subcontinent.[41] Revisionist history[42] strategically poses that a vengeful justice can be found for the crimes of history committed under non-Hindu rulers (Amin 2002). Retribution is sought by contemporary targeting of the Indian 'other'. Outcry against Hindu cultural dominance and Hindutva often occurs as a response to episodic violence,[43] not in relation to its unacknowledged and persistent presence. Hindutva revivalism in the last two plus decades has sought to consolidate the power of the majority through militant reform that defines Hindu majoritarianism as Indian nationalism. Hindutva organizations oppose the syncretic traditions of Hinduism, assimilating the plural traditions within Hinduism to create a narrow centralized code that promises to unite Hindus (Basu 2002). Philosophically seductive, these Brahminical cultural frameworks are universalistic in principle, segregationist in action.

Brahminism (Thapar 1990, Gupta 2000) organizes the supremacy of Hinduness,[44] and defines and orders norms, values, ethics and morality. Ethnic, minority and marginalized groups are subject to the social and economic violence of Brahminism via which they are forced to frame their political and cultural aspirations. This strategy thwarts the complex search for cultural identity that confronts the vast diversity in India living at the juncture of pre and post modernity, inequitable modernization, and globalism (Ahmad 2002, Roy 1999). Hindutva functions as a meta-narrative in manufacturing foundational truths to build and govern the nation.

Governance functions as a form of power as Hindu nationalism is aided by the postcolonial Indian state as it operates as legatee to its imperial colonizer,[45] inheriting and modifying its biopolitics (Foucault 1994, 1978a, 1978b). Here I draw on Michel Foucault's analysis of biopower (Foucault 1978a) and governmentality (Foucault 1994), where biopolitical states use knowledge and social apparatuses of expertise towards normality, and function to manage, regulate and police the microdynamics of individual lives and whole populations in the production of 'normal', 'healthy', 'happy', docile, producing and consuming subjects.[46] Majoritarian nationalism, imbricated via biopolitical state and cultural ascendancy, hinges upon and facilitates the homogenization of populations and individuals to mobilize human beings as resources for state productivity. The dynamics of nation building include the assimilation of some differences, and the annihilation of others. Dominant identities are constructed to mobilize for the maximization of human and natural resources in ways that police and pathologize those labelled 'other'. The organization of national identity requires the creation of internal enemies, languaged as impure, dangerous and diseased elements that threaten the health and prosperity of the nation (Dutta et al. 1996). In the manufacturing of nation (Bhabha 2002), the use of gendered brutalization[47] across caste and class become simultaneous to state building (Chatterjee 1997). Postcolonial states are immersed in these dynamics in ways that resist colonial legacies and reproduce domination (Pandey et al. 2003).

Hindu nationalist leaders and their cadre in Orissa reiterate that charges of fundamentalism cannot apply to Hindutva. It is not an ideology, they say, but integral practice, a lifestyle for nationhood.[48] Hindutva's doctrine of 'blood, soil and race'[49] rewrites the circumstances and complex histories in a rigged game of 'nation'. Hyper-nationalism, militant majoritarianism lives in-between truth/power relations inseparable from contexts of cultural production, locating and languaging diagnostics and regimes of power/knowledge in the discursive construction of identity (here, that of the nation) (Foucault 1980a and 1980b, 1972). Foucault's archaeology of knowledge (Foucault 1972) interrogates the conditions of possibility for the formation of 'true discourse', examining the rules that regulate its production and circulation, defining spaces of strategic intervention. Genealogy (Foucault 1977) locates discourse in relations of power, linked to institutions and cultural practices, elucidating the effects of 'truth' in the present. Discourse, linked to culture, history, gender, language and power, produces truth, identities and space for strategic intervention. Nationalism asserts truth via the infrastructure of cultural and political institutions, towards defining and regulating hegemony. Nationalism's discourse invites a privileged relation to 'truth' and its production, to 'fact' and 'fiction'. Nationalism's practice establishes a relation to authoritative discourse, manufacturing legitimacy, in part, through distribution of speech and memory in the body politic.[50]

Hindutva's achievement is contingent on civic mobilization that aids in infiltrating, capturing, redirecting state power in constructing the Hindu nation. What multiple and problematic affects result from the intersection of politicized religious culture and globalization/modernization that uses the resources and labour of the poor as collateral to nation making for the privileged (Appadurai 1996)? Hindutva's production of culture and nation is escalated, punctuated, celebrated, by breakdown, rupture and violence. The struggles for justice of marginal groups are depicted as hostile to national unity. What terror and assimilation is produced on the bodies and aspirations of minorities and those vulnerable? How does Hindutva's dominance affect democracy? The Bharatiya Janata Party (BJP)[51] led national government of 1999–2004 was an experimental moment, marked by the consolidation and endurance[52] of Hindutva affiliated state governments across India in Gujarat, Rajasthan, Madhya Pradesh, Maharashtra, Arunachal Pradesh, Goa, Karnataka, Uttaranchal, Chhattisgarh, and Orissa.[53]

ORISSA: CONTEXT FOR HINDU ASCENDANCY

I am a volunteer in the army for Hindu Rashtra [state], I have been watching this army build itself. Gujarat proved to us in Orissa that we can succeed. I hear of Mullas[54] taking over Kashmir, I watch Mullas run around with four wives, and I hate them. This is our motherland, we will not tolerate them here. We will not tolerate the secular people corrupting vanavasis[55] and building up Dalits. We will take back our desh [country].[56]

> Angana Chatterji (AC): 'Do you know of any Muslim man with more than one wife?'
> Hindutva activist: 'Yes, yes.'
> AC: 'Where does he live?'
> Hindutva activist: 'I do not know people like him, but others do.'[57]

And so the script unfolds. Based on extensive communications with the Census Department and Muslim women in Orissa, I would counterpose that Muslim marriages in Orissa are predominantly monogamous, and while polygamy exists,[58] it is infrequent, and, as Kandiyoti offers, its systems may provoke greater autonomy for women rather than be exclusively constitutive of mistreatment (Kandiyoti 1997: 86–92). But even as a familiar script expands, we must ask, 'Why Orissa'? As Hindutva demarcates its recent march across the 'tribal belt',[59] Orissa submits a rich canvas for Hindu nationalism. The state furnishes Hindutva a sculpted conjunction of people and resources in a context of internal social implosion. The strong concentration of Adivasis and Dalits in the state and their deep socio-economic and political disempowerment supply labour for indoctrination. Sharp caste, class, tribal, ethnic and religious inequities leave the state susceptible to militant mobilizations. Vast ecological resources offer immense developmental possibility as a compromised left leadership permits the decay of Hindutva led governmentalization[60] to shatter the political landscape of Orissa.

The Sangh Parivar targets Christians, Adivasis, Muslims, Dalits and other marginalized peoples in Orissa.[61] The network divides its energies between recruitment, developmental/charitable and political work. It aims at incorporating men, women and youth into its fabric through religious and popular institutions. Across the state, the Sangh mobilizes for a Ram Temple among people for whom Ayodhya[62] is a tale from afar. By 2006, the birth centenary of Rashtriya Swayamsevak Sangh (RSS, National Volunteers' Association), architect Madhav Sadashiv Golwalkar, Sangh organizations promise that Orissa will be a poster state for Hindutva. Western Orissa, dominated by upper-caste landholders and traders, is a hotbed for the promulgation of Hindu militancy, while Adivasi areas are besieged with aggressive Hinduization and Sanskritization[63] through forcible conversion to Hinduism.[64] Praveen Togadia, International Secretary of the VHP, visited Orissa in January and August 2003 to rally Hindu extremists. He advocated that Orissa join Hindutva in its movement for a Hindu state in India. '*Ram Rajya*' (rule of Ram, an energizing myth in the discourse of Hindu nation), he promised, would come.[65] In July 2003, in a small room on Janpath in Bhubaneswar (capital of Orissa), workers diligently fashioned saffron armbands.[66] Subash Chouhan, state convenor for the Bajrang Dal, the paramilitary wing of Hindutva, spoke with zeal of current hopes for 'turning' Orissa. Christian missionaries and 'Islam fanatics' are vigorously converting Adivasis to Christianity and Dalits to Islam, Chouhan emphasized.[67] He stressed the imperative to consolidate '*Hindutva shakti*' to educate, purify and strengthen the state.[68]

What are the reasons for Hindutva's conquest in rural and urban Orissa? Over the last decade, the Sangh has amassed thirty major organizations including political, charitable, militant and educational groups, trade and students unions, women's groups, with a massive base of a few million. This formidable mobilization is the largest volunteer enlistment in Orissa.[69] The RSS, responsible for M.K. Gandhi's death, was founded in 1925 as the cultural umbrella of the Sangh. It operates 2,500 *shakha*s (chapters) in Orissa with a 100,000 strong cadre. The VHP, created in 1964, has a membership of 60,000 in Orissa. Born in 1984, at the onset of the Ramjanambhoomi movement,[70] banned and reinstated since the demolition of the Babri Masjid in 1992, the Bajrang Dal (self-described, Warriors of the Hindutva Revolution) has 20,000 members working in 200 *akharas*[71] in the state. The Sangh inaugurated various trusts in Orissa to enable fundraising, such as the Friends of Tribal Society, Samarpan Charitable Trust, Yasodha Sadan, and Odisha International Centre.

Membership in the BJP, the political wing of Hindutva, stands at 450,000. Bharatiya Mazdoor Sangh manages 171 trade unions with a cadre of 182,000.[72] The 30,000 strong Bharatiya Kisan Sangh functions in 100 blocks. Akhil Bharatiya Vidhyarthi Parishad, an RSS inspired student body, functions in 299 colleges with 20,000 members. Rashtriya Sevika Samiti, the RSS women's wing, has eighty centres. Durga[73] Vahini (Army of Durga), centres for women's training and empowerment, has 7,000 outfits in 117 sites in Orissa. In October 2002, a Shiv[74] Sena (Mumbai based, 'Army of Shiva') unit in Balasore district in Orissa declared that it had formed the first Hindu 'suicide squad'. Responding to Bal Thackeray's call, over 100 young men and women signed up to fight 'Islamic terrorism'.[75] The Shiv Sena appealed to every Hindu family in the state to contribute to its cadre. Squad members, it is speculated, will receive training at Shiv Sena nerve centres in Mumbai and elsewhere.[76]

The Sangh's considerable advance in rural and urban Orissa has helped the BJP consolidate its position in the state. The government is shaded in saffron. The BJP-Biju Janata Dal (BJD)[77] coalition acquired electoral power in 1998 in Orissa, with the BJP achieving its first parliamentary win in the state, 7 of 9 seats from western and north Orissa. The BJD won 9 of 11, largely in coastal Orissa.[78] In the 1999 Lok Sabha (parliamentary) elections, the BJP-BJD coalition won 19 seats, and, in

2000, won 106 seats in the state assembly polls.[79] In return, the Sangh expects the government to exonerate its excesses. On 16 March 2002, days after Gujarat, a few hundred VHP and Bajrang Dal activists burst into the Orissa Assembly and ransacked the complex, demanding the construction of the temple in Ayodhya and objecting to alleged remarks made against the two organizations by house members (Das 2002).

Using nationspeak, the BJP has been diligent in building a political base that links village to state and state to nation, manufacturing imaginative agency for nationalism, as Manohar, a Dalit activist from Rayagada, tells us:

> The forest department, and the party [BJP] when they came to our village for an election campaign, tells us to work for our desh. What is this desh? Bharat, Inda [India], Hindustan, they say. I have never travelled to it. Orissa is part of the desh. Our village is part of Orissa. We did not even know this when I was young. What does a desh mean? What does it do? To us, our desh is our village. Even Orissa is too big to understand. It is for the politicians. How can you care for what you cannot see, do not know? Why should you? So, when they have forest rules for the whole desh, how can that work? Does everybody need the same things from the forest? Are all the forests the same? Are all the people the same? Maybe that is why the forest department needs to work with the police to keep us in line, because we are all different, ask different things of them, and they are not prepared to give it to us? Maybe it is too much, even for them, this 'desh'![80]

In May 2003, the Bajrang Dal and VHP declared that they would present 5,000 *trishul*s as part of the Janasampark Abhiyan (mass contact programme)[81] that anticipates reaching 100 million people in 200,000 villages throughout India (Pandit 2003). In June 2003, in preparation for the 2004 elections, the Bajrang Dal announced that it would organize trishul *diksha* (trident distribution),[82] despite Chief Minister Naveen Patnaik's deliberation to ban the same (Gopal 2003). Praveen Togadia planned on launching the trishul distribution campaign in Banamalipur in Korda district to provoke an area with a significant Muslim population.[83] Between July and September 2003, the Bajrang Dal organized intensive programmes in Bhubaneswar, Sundergarh and Jajpur. Invested in securing a 150,000 membership in Orissa, this is part of a larger campaign that targets Gajapati, Phulbani, Keojhar, Mayurbhanj, Koraput, and Nabarangpur districts.[84]

In the 2004 election campaign, the Vanvasi Kalyan Ashram (a Sangh outfit involved in Adivasi education conversion programmes) was the key strategist and organizer for the BJP in the tribal belt. The BJP manipulated the '*jal, jungle, zameen*' (water, forest, land) platform, appropriated from land reform movements (Chatterji 2006), to persuade Adivasis in Orissa to join them (Mohanty 2003). Tribal culture, glorified as artefact, distanced from its political reality, allows the systematic objectification and disfigurement of culture in which Hindutva's mobilization of new identities and affinities is internalized by minorities, acquiring urgency and redemptive capacity.

The BJP-BJD and Sangh Parivar organizations have a significant strategy of manoeuvring Muslims in middle-class neighbourhoods and villages by forming alliances with the local leadership. In Banamalipur and Jadupur village, neighbouring Bhubaneswar in Khurda district, Muslim leaders spoke of their allegiance to the BJP in January 2004, testifying that they would ensure a BJP win in the area.[85] Poor communities in these villages say this allows local Muslim politicians access to electoral seats, leaving the disenfranchised without trustworthy representation.[86]

Praveen Togadia returned to Orissa again to visit Muslim dominated Jajpur on 16 February 2004 and Behrampur on 29 February, continuing his seditious campaign for Hindutva, amid, for the first time (due to mobilizing by activists), rousing protests from local groups.[87] In the 2004 elections, despite the BJP's national defeat, the BJP-BJD coalition was returned to victory in Orissa, winning 18 of 21 parliamentary seats (one less than 1999 which went to the Jharkhand Mukti Morcha),[88] and 93 (of 147) in the state assembly, a long way from one seat in 1985 (Mohanty 2004). In Orissa, Hindutva groups have indicated that the BJP, when it was the Hindu nationalist party in power in the central government, was required to show restraint regarding the practice of far right majoritarian policies, which they can now abandon, especially in Orissa, where they are in power. The cadre of Hindu fundamentalist organizations assert that the BJP in power had been overly lenient in working with non-Hindutva groups and priorities, neglecting to strengthen its 'ideological constituency', and that the agenda for a Hindu state must be aggressively pursued in or out of electoral power (Vyas 2004).

POLITICAL ECONOMY OF VIOLENCE

The Sangh's assault organizes the disenfranchised into a vicious political economy structured by the caste system across Orissa.[89] RSS cadres working in Sambhalpur district stress the significance of converting Adivasis and Dalits into Hinduism. At Sangh organized rallies that marshal Adivasis, '*Garv se kaho hum Hindu hai*' (say with pride that I am a Hindu) pierces the air. Badal Satpaty, an RSS office bearer, stresses the importance of Adivasi conversions for Orissa.

> Vanavasis are given land by the government. If vanavasis see themselves as outside Hinduism, then their lands too are non-Hindu lands that are anti-development and cannot be used for the betterment of the nation. Bharat is a Hindu nation, and these people and their lands are anti-national.[90]

Whose nation? Adivasis are 8.01 per cent of the nation's inhabitants, yet 40 per cent of the displaced population.[91] The National Commission on Backward Areas Development stated in 1980 that mining, irrigation and forest use for development projects submerged and destroyed extensive tracts of forest and tribal lands. In a report on Tribal Development Programmes in 1969, the Planning Commission recorded the non-consensual, illegal passage of tribal lands to non-tribals especially in Orissa, Andhra Pradesh and other Adivasi areas (Rout 1999). Land alienation was enabled by colonial and feudal land structures and tenure systems. It also bore testimony to the systematic reinterpretation of tribal lands as public lands by the state, followed by procedures for nationalization of such lands. Methods of alienation included the reclassification of land, manipulation of land records and non-recognition of Adivasis as landowners, encroachment on tribal lands, and '*benami*' (illegal) transfers, as reported by the Union Home Ministry in 1975 (ibid.). An extensive 'land grab' has resulted from debt bondage and indenturement related to land leasing and mortgage of Adivasi and Dalit lands to large farmers and moneylenders, consolidation of land holdings, strategic marriage alliances, and corruption. While occupations such as agricultural labour necessitate contact between Adivasi and caste groups, Adivasi lives remain predominantly isolated, geographically and socially. Adivasis are often considered, and consider themselves, a subordinate group within the Hindu caste hierarchy. Within politicized spaces, Adivasis and Dalits struggle to rewrite the violent history of assimilation to which they have been subjected, refusing to identify as Hindus in mobilizing for self-determination in opposition to the state and Hindu ascendancy. There are significant distinctions between Hindu and Christian Adivasis, the former relatively less discriminated against within the social hierarchy. Migratory Adivasi communities, labelled 'nomadic', are exceptionally disempowered with few sanctioned economic and political rights (Chatterji 1998, 2006).

Systematic disregard for the human rights of 'lower' caste, Adivasi and Dalit peoples is a social and structural predicament in Orissa. A few years ago a Deori Adivasi activist in Orissa told me, 'We are outsiders to society, threatened by modernization, by the government, by right wing religious forces, by corporations. It is as if we have no history and no place in the nation. If we change, it is to become unrecognizable to ourselves.'[92] Another Adivasi activist reflected, 'We Adivasis are not Hindus. We are being forced to become something we are not, and then fight for it [Hindutva] with our lives. We would rather organize to fight for our own future.'[93]

In December 2000, Rayagada witnessed state repression of Adivasi communities protesting bauxite mining by a consortium of industries in Kashipur that is detrimental to their livelihood. The industries were in breach of constitutional provisions barring the sale or lease of tribal lands without Adivasi consent (Tewatia and Agnivesh 2001). In response, state police fired on non-violent dissenters, killing Abhilas Jhodia, Raghu Jhodia and Damodar Jhodia. Kashipur is a tragic affidavit of the intersections of irresponsible globalization, state complicity in defiling human rights, and police participation in fostering social violence.[94] Further, at the onset of the struggle, the movement was lead by local Adivasis. With the opportunistic intervention of organizations external to Kashipur, the leadership and various local groups have been systematically alienated (Chatterji 2006).

In July 2003, the Orissa government permitted the unconstitutional transfer of lands in Schedule V[95] areas for mining and industrial use. Orissa's decision contradicts the 1997 Samata versus Andhra Pradesh judgement, where the Apex Court had ruled against the government's lease of tribal forest and other lands in Scheduled Areas to non-tribals for mining and industrial operations. Beginning 23 January 2004, four Adivasi villages, Borobhota, Kinari, Kothduar, Sindhabahili, and their agricultural fields, in southeast Kalahandi district, have been razed by Sterlite industries, a multinational corporation building an aluminium refinery near Lanjigarh, adjacent to Kashipur. The villagers were forcibly evicted, without requisite compensation or rehabilitation.[96] The Lanjigarh project will mine bauxite at 4,000 feet from the northwest rim of the Niyamgiri mountains.

As Sudhir Patnaik, a scholar-activist from Bhubaneswar, avows, the state offers disturbing and continued priority to corporations over marginalized citizens, forcing the demise of Adivasi claims to life and livelihood.

After Kashipur, if Sterlite is allowed to succeed, it will be easier for any other corporation to succeed. Their success would mean a total destruction of the rich natural base of southwest Orissa. This will only add to the invasion and growth of the Sangh Parivar.

...The Sangh will use the fear of dispossession Adivasis feel to create a false belonging, they will use the erosion of tribal authority and culture to mobilize Adivasis against each other, against Dalits, offering the promise of development, taking away tribal and Dalit right to self-determination, and leaving them as foot soldiers in the army of Hindutva, for a 'modern', Hindu nation. Scholars will have to prepare themselves to write obituaries about the tribals of southwest Orissa.[97]

Sangh activists have infiltrated deep into state run development agencies such as the Council for Advancement of People's Action and Rural Technology (CAPART), an autonomous institution that works to create rural development partnerships between voluntary organizations and the government. CAPART supports numerous RSS activities in Orissa diverting funds for Hindutva (Chatterji 2006). In Nayagarh district, Dalit communities watch Hindutva's voracious march. They speak of malignant fictions circulated by the Hindutvadis that Christian missionary activity is placing Hinduism at risk. Dalits, Adivasis, Christians, Hindus and Muslims speak of how their villages and watersheds intertwine, and how crops are dependent on the run-off water from each other's lands. They say that they cannot afford to hate each other. As one secular activist states,

> The Sangh Parivar is consolidating its position in the mining belt and in all sensitive and tribal areas in Orissa, where there are popular Dalit or Adivasi struggles for self-determination, trying to undercut them. Several developments are taking place on the mining front, where the Sangh divides poor people, who, driven out by corporations, are organizing to resist. [98]

The state is in disarray as the Sangh infiltrates into civic and political institutions. For the 36.7 million who reside in Orissa, Hindutva's predatory advance aggravates and exploits the social panic of a land haunted by inequity. Orissa houses 577,775 Muslims and 620,000 Christians (Chatterji 2006), 5.1 million Dalits from ninety-three caste groups, and over seven million Adivasis from sixty-two tribes (ibid.; Jena et al. 2002). Eighty-seven per cent of Orissa's population live in villages, 47.15 per cent of the population live in poverty, with 57 per cent of Orissa's rural population living in poverty. Women are the worst affected across tribal, caste and class boundaries as they rarely hold shared or individual titles to either household or agricultural land.[99] While women, in addition to child rearing and supervising the household, are central contributors to household economics and livelihood they continue to be less empowered in relation to men. Such inequity enforces subservience and disables their participation in decision making. State and donor agencies, activist groups and local communities acknowledge that women *should be* vital to development planning. However women's inclusion as a category in macro-micro development agendas, through reassigning development priorities and responsibilities, and diminishing gender inequities, remain largely unsupported by political commitment and resources even as they surface in populist rhetoric.[100]

Twenty-four per cent of the state's population is Adivasi, of which 68.9 per cent are impoverished, 66 per cent are illiterate,[101] and only 2 per cent have completed a college education; 54.9 per cent of Dalits live in poverty (Mahapatra 1999: 139; Kumar 2002). Concentrated in Cuttack, Jagasinhapur and Puri districts, 70 per cent of Muslims are poor (Chatterji 2006). Government of Orissa figures suggest that the intensity of poverty in Orissa is very high. The rate of decline in poverty ratio has been comparatively much lower in Orissa in the 1990s then the national averages. Parallel to a disturbing increase in actual poverty, an emerging middle class masks the reality of despair among the economically marginalized.[102] Infant mortality, 236 in 1000, is the highest in the union (ibid.). In the recent past Rayagada district has witnessed despairing efforts to survive—the sale of children by families (Kumar 2002). In Jajpur district, a mother, a daily wage earner in a stone quarry, sold her forty-five-day-old child for Rs 60.[103] These measures have not evoked reflection and commitment on the part of the state. Rather, unconscionable attempts have been made to show that such action is emblematic of Adivasi and Dalit cultures. The cyclone of 1999, the droughts of 2000 and 2003, and the floods of 2001 and 2003 (which affected three million), pose a formidable challenge for environmental and economic sustainability in the state.

In Orissa, approximately 2.5 acres of irrigable agricultural land (cultivable twice each year) are required by a family of five to cultivate rice for subsistence. The average landholding is about 1.29 hectares per family.[104] Land reforms, inaugurated via the Orissa Land Reforms Act of 1960, have been uneven, followed by the onslaught of state sponsored development in Orissa, linking the aspirations and labour of the poor to dominant development, and their incorporation into the Brahminical social order.[105] This process was enhanced via the British occupation of Orissa in 1803, resulting in the annexation of parts of Orissa to Bengal and the Central Madras Provinces, while the remainder was administered as feudatory states. Development and revenue policies led to a depletion of natural resources and the enhanced colonization and Brahminization of Dalit and Adivasi communities. The Prajamandal (peasant) Movement of the 1930s and 1940s, the Kol insurrection, the Bamanghaty actions, and present movements for public lands reform speak powerfully of Adivasi and subaltern refusal to submit to colonial and Brahminical imposition (Rout 1999; Mahtab et al. 1959).

Despite prolific peasant and Adivasi struggles (Sahoo 2004), their dispossession has been continued by the postcolonial state since 1948, when twenty-four princely states merged to create Orissa (Pati 2001; Senapati 2000 et al.). Mayurbhanj is a district in north Orissa,[106] formed in 1949, with an Adivasi population of 58.5 per cent, including a concentration of Bhunya, Bhumija, Bathuri, Ho, Gond and Santal tribes. Historically, Dalit groups in the district have lived in close relation with Juang and Paudi Bhunya Adivasis, just as Dom and Pano Dalits lived in relationship to Konda and Saora Adivasis in south Orissa. Chronic poverty, illiteracy, Sanskritization, and inequitable relationships between Adivasis and non-Adivasis, as reported by the Tribal Research Bureau, have created ensuing contexts for social fragmentation and Adivasi assimilation (Chatterji 2006).

In response to grass-roots organization, the government of Orissa instated certain checks and balances against Adivasi land alienation, primarily through the Orissa Scheduled Areas Transfer of Immovable Property (by Scheduled Tribes) Regulation of 1956, which legislates against land transfers in Scheduled Areas (Planning Commission of India 1990). There are substantial differences in landholding patterns between districts, such as Sundargarh, Mayurbhanj, Dhenkanal, and Kalahandi, premised on topography, history of settled agriculture, ethnic and class concentrations.

The Green Revolution in agriculture, monocropping, and the increased and damaging use of fertilizers and pesticides has led to a shrinkage and sale of landholdings, escalating debt bondage among poor farmers across the state (Chatterji 2006). Public investment in agriculture has declined since the late 1970s, contributing to the stagnation of agricultural production, a rise in the absolute and relative number of people below the poverty line in rural areas. While schemes and programmes focused on poverty alleviation have been continued in the

Ninth Plan, their capacity to alleviate rural poverty is doubtful (Pandey 1998).

Even as the passage of the 72nd and 73rd Constitutional Amendments in 1992 empowered panchayati rule,[107] enforcing a national mandate for greater democratization and decentralization, land alienation and its concomitant dislocation has dramatically amplified Adivasi and Dalit migration and their dependence on forests for livelihood. There are 46,989 villages in Orissa,[108] of which 29,302, with a population of 15.93 million, record forests as part of their land use (Planning Commission of India 1999). Across Orissa about 15–40 per cent of household income, inclusive of diverse social strata, continues to be dependent on non-timber forest produce, while in some districts it accounts for nearly 50 per cent of the family earnings (Sarin 2003; Singh 2002). With the varied forms of migration, and the dissolution of a rights based, decentralized, framework of resource management across Orissa, the degree of dependence on forests for livelihood has increased dramatically. In turn, deforestation, escalated by industrialization and corporate sponsored globalization, has led to a massive scarcity of subsistence forest products. It has forced people, especially the poor, to migrate inter-state, seasonally and even permanently, to alternate rural areas, nearby towns and far away cities in search of work. While the government stipulated minimum wage is Rs 50 per day for 'unskilled' labour, Rs 75 for 'semi-skilled' and Rs 90 for 'skilled' labour, agricultural and other labourers working in unorganized sectors in Orissa often receive as little as Rs 10–15 daily.[109] Simultaneously, there is out-migration from, and, considerable in-migration to, Orissa from neighbouring states, induced by political factors and poverty. Women, children and (disproportionately) men migrate to semi-urban and urban areas in Orissa, to neighbouring West Bengal, Bihar and Andhra Pradesh, or as far as Delhi and Rajasthan, Tamil Nadu and Kerala, working in recycling, as industrial labour, in building and road construction, head loading,[110] and some in the tertiary sector. The ability to secure employment depends on kinship and familial ties, on connections, on the capacity to become proficient in ever expanding new arenas of labour even as deskilling accompanies the displacement of people from their native lands. Working conditions are horrific for the poor migrant, daily shelter is difficult to locate as pavements substitute for homes. Women and children experience violence, sexual abuse, health perils, meagre and illegal wages, and police brutality, as part of the corruption structuring displacement.[111]

The histories of land reform and redistribution, and of peasant movements have emphasized agricultural (often private) lands and not forest (public) lands, marginalizing and weakening Adivasis who (predominantly) contend for rights to forest territories. While land reforms were instrumental in conferring property rights to the disempowered, the basis of distribution was the individual. The individualization of rights weakened the legal premise for collective mobilization. The state's capacity to recognize property rights was restricted to individual ownership, undermining the very basis of social organization of various Adivasi, Dalit and other forest-user groups that historically functioned within collective structures.

The amputation of tribal tenure to land has contributed to cultural genocide that supports both the consolidation of national territory and the ethic of conservation/development inherent to modern nation states. Adivasis living in forest villages are often evicted, their right to land dismissed by the state's insistence on 'evidence' of ownership and residency. Such demands evince the betrayal of old claims with new boundaries, maps, roads, checkposts that insert violence into the everyday life of the Adivasi. Tribal testimonies are converted into 'lies' by the apparatus of the state. As one Gond male Adivasi elder testifies:

> We live in the village in the forest. We have lived here for generations. Our houses are made of local mud, our roofs from local leaves from the forests. Our diet, our thoughts, our language tells you that we have been living here. You can see the shadows of our ancestors reflected in the pond, our songs mimic the birds, they tell stories of the forest, our feet walk these lands over and over. These [imprints] are our land records. The forester does not believe us. Our lives are lies to them. [112]

Dominant development has failed to address entrenched oppressions as exploitative relations endure between the poverty-stricken and a coterie of moneylenders, government officials, police and politicians in Orissa. The absence of adequate social and economic reform further antagonizes already overburdened minority and disenfranchised groups, pitting them against each other. Hindutva targets the religion and culture of the disempowered as liberalization abuses their labour and livelihood resources. Such conditions and the multiple displacements of place, history and memory produce contexts in which marginalized peoples embrace identitarian and oppositional movements. This is illustrated by the words of a Christian Dalit woman leader from Mayurbhanj, in the monsoon of 2003, who emphasized the violence of forgetting that survival necessitates,

> You ask about resistance, about standing up. It is not so easy. It can happen where there are movements swelling up. Here? I am not sure. We are isolated. Do we have choices? We are Christian Dalits. Our family converted over twenty years ago. RSS workers have been coming to our village since last year to threaten us. They told us that we will have to become Hindus or leave Orissa. They also said that they would put a stop to the earth cutting [project] where we are labourers, and see to it that we do not get any money from the panchayat. We think about converting. So much it takes to keep changing ourselves, to escape fear. We keep our lives through bondage.[113]

ERASURES

The Sangh exploits the architecture of inequity and poverty to weave solidarity built on a mythic Hindu past. Hindutva defames history, speaking of Muslims as the 'fallen traitors' among Hindus who converted to Islam.[114] This revisionist history obfuscates the severity of inequity within Hindu society that led to conversions historically. Hindutva misrepresents Muslims as 'foreigners' and Christians as 'polluted'. Adivasis are falsely presented as Hindus who must be 'reconnected' to Hinduism through Hindutva. Dalit and 'lower caste' people are raw material for manufacturing foot soldiers of dissension. In hunting for the enemy within to blame for India's befallen present, the Sangh demands absolute loyalty to its tyranny, requiring an unequivocal display of obedience. The Sangh dictates rightful gods to worship, prayers to recite, legacies to remember. Hindutva imagines its actions to be above the law. It makes the unification of Hindus central to its mission. To do so, it organizes Hindus to fulfil their 'manifest destiny', fabricating Hinduism as uniform across the immense diversity of India. Elite aspirations in nation making, the annexation of territory and resources from the disempowered, the imposition of violent ideologies and alienating identities, and subaltern resistance, have produced contested meanings and practices of democracy. Through the amassment of identity politics, reinvention of history, production and signification of *volk*, the normalization and pathologization of difference,[115] the extension of its power into private and social life, Hindu majoritarianism exhibits scorn for those it finds unincorporable and inassimilable into its governing imaginary. Majoritarian identity formations and religious nationalism, via Hindutva, operate as projects of cultural reassertion. Questions of ethnic, gender and historical identity are infused with religion in ways that make necessary the organization of religio-cultural movements. These movements live in relation to the state, and intervene in its imaginative, legislative and juridical apparatus, infusing statecraft with the agenda of fundamentalism (Moghadam 1994).

Anti-Christian

> Dalit RSS worker: 'The RSS is helping us build a Hindu samaj. We are poor, we have no assistance, we are fighting Christians and Muslims for development money. The Christians, they have foreign missionary money, what do we Hindu Dalits have? The Sai [Christians] are also converting our people to their religion. They eat meat, they touch leather, they have bad morals. I am scared for my children. We are thankful that the RSS has sworn to protect us.'
> Angana Chatterji (AC): 'Have you seen these Christian missionaries?'
> Dalit RSS worker: 'No, but I have heard that they are nearby.'
> AC: 'How many Hindus have been converted in your village, or in any of the neighbouring villages.'
> Dalit RSS worker: 'Nobody yet, but the RSS tells us that they [the missionaries] might come soon. That is why we go to the RSS meetings, to become informed about the troubles facing us, and how we can be strong and protect ourselves, to become an army against these foreigners.'[116]

Bajrang Dal leader, Subash Chouhan, claims,

> In the country, Orissa is the second[117] Hindu Rajya [state]. Today, Sai [Christian] missionary and Islam, they both want to convert the entire pradesh [state] into Sai and Islam. In the tribal belt they have been planning to convert the people into Christians and Harijans into Muslims. This work is moving with force in Orissa. This is the reason the Bajrang Dal and VHP have taken up the task of consolidating Hindu shakti in Orissa.[118]

An RSS worker adds, 'The Sai have been taking away our language and heritage, replacing them with foreign tongue and customs. How can we tolerate this?'[119] In retelling history, the Sangh infuses events with counter-memory, erasing the fact that Christian missionary use of Oriya[120] facilitated a literary revival in 1822, and that Christian schools today continue to teach both Oriya and English (Senapati et al. 2000).

The Sangh's methods have contributed to violations of life and livelihood. In January 1999, as the vehicle with Australian missionary Graham Staines and his two sons, Philip and Timothy, was torched in Keojhar district (Ramakrishnan 1999), the mob's homage to '*Jai Bajrang Bali*' rent the state.[121] Then followed the murder of Catholic priest Arul Das and the destruction of churches in Phulbani district.[122] After much delay, in September 2003, the Khurda[123] Sessions Court delivered a verdict on the Staines murder case, sentencing Dara Singh, the primary accused, to death,[124] and twelve others to life imprisonment.[125]

Subash Chouhan continues,

> In the entire state we have selected some [key] districts, such as Sai based Sundargarh district, Gajapati zilla, Phulbani, Keonjhar, Mayurbhanj, Koraput, Nabarangpur districts—we are undertaking seva [service] work here, hospitals, one teacher schools, Hari Katha Yojana,[126] orphanage, these types of jojona [planning\development] and seva work are being undertaken all over the state.[127]

Badal Satpaty of the RSS says,

> There is a lot of work to be done in Orissa. There is a lot of underdevelopment and poverty, and social ills. Yes, vanavasis and Dalits are poor and suffering. But it is their own fault. They do not understand or care about our country. It is because these people [Dalits, Adivasis] refuse to integrate that all these problems arise. Why do they ask for special rights? Special land? Special status? The motherland is good to us all. These people are lazy, they live in filth, they are illiterate. How can we take them seriously without civilizing them? The RSS seeks to help in this mission, for the betterment of the poor. The RSS is working with, first, the Hindu Dalits to mobilize them and tell them about the dangers of defection. Then, we are bringing Christian Dalits and Adivasis back to the Hindu fold through education and reconversion.[128] We are also helping them economically. They should be thankful and join us wholeheartedly to prove to us that they belong with us, that they are not terrorists or terrorist supporters.[129]

Where conversions to Hinduism are acquiescent and occur with the complicity of non-Hindus, acquiescence is produced by its intimacy with the dominant. For non-dominant groups, the landscape of Hindu supremacy shapes fear (of the dominant), desire (to acquire privileges), hope (for 'acquittal', to 'pass' as non-other) and thus, internalized oppression. These complex forces create agency on the part of the marginalized (Nair 1994). Such agency is manufactured in relation and response to Hindu ascendancy, as this Adivasi village youth states,

Dalits live in the next sahi [hamlet], are different than us, they do not mix with us. We are poorer than them, they often look down on us. The Sanghis say that if we become Hindus we will be like the Dalits, at their level.[130]

Yet caste oppression prevails in the Sangh Parivar's mistreatment of Dalits in Orissa, who have been assaulted for participating in Hindu religious ceremonies. In April 2001, a Dalit community member was fined Rs 4,000 and beaten for entering a Hindu temple in Bargarh. Dalits continue to suffer social ostracization and economic deprivation as they are manipulated into joining the very Hindutva forces that have historically deprived Dalits of equity in order to use them against other mistreated communities.

Anti-Muslim

In Pitaipura village, in Jagatsinghpur district, a disturbing event occurred in the winter of 2001 after Muslim graveyard lands were placed in dispute. According to Hakim Bhai, a resident of the village,

The land record for the village divides the 25 acres into two plots, one listed as a kabarstan [graveyard] and another as 'gorostan' [also graveyard]. But [Hindu] villagers insisted that 'gorostan' is 'gaochar' [grazing land] not a kabarstan. We were harassed when funeral processions arrived or we read Namaz during Id. We sat down together to resolve the dispute without any success. Then we filed a case in court. The court did not resolve the case for the longest time. The court then began mediating and declared a part of the land as a graveyard, and held the rest as disputed. Once, the night before the official was coming to measure the land, Hindus from the village stole into the graveyard and placed a murti [idol] to mark it as their land. We found out and went inside and took it out. The next morning when the official arrived Hindus were angry that we had taken the murti out. They threw stones at us, we threw stones back at them. The crowd ran from the graveyard pelting each other. We were near the Ma Durga temple. The Hindus started accusing us of throwing stones at the temple. Then it began...[131]

Another resident inserts:

Perhaps our stones had fallen on the temple compound. But we were not destroying the temple, we were responding to each other. Once the word spread that we, Muslims, were destroying the temple, RSS youth arrived from Bhubaneswar and mobilized people from surrounding villages. They went around with loudspeakers to 20–30 Hindu villages accusing us of destroying the temple. Our basti [hamlet] is in the middle of the village, between Hindu hamlets. Five Muslim homes were burnt in our basti and men were beaten. The police could not do anything. For three days during that time we were very afraid, some hid in the forests. A peace rally came to our village. They have not returned. The case is pending. No resolution has happened. If we are left alone things might escalate. Then what?'

Hakim Bhai responds,

The RSS continues its meetings in the Hindu hamlets regularly since the incident. These meetings are not publicized, they spread through word of mouth. We Muslims have now made our own shops in the basti [since the event], we have retreated to ourselves. Our women are afraid and they do not want to go out of the basti. When we go out Hindus call us names. Call us 'Pathans'. We are becoming isolated.

Shazia, one of the neighbourhood women, adds, 'Even our dead cannot rest in peace.'[132]
Poor Muslim communities regularly face social ostracization in Orissa. Cultural and religious differences are diagnosed as abnormal. A Muslim community member from Dhenkanal said,

When Hindus celebrate a puja [prayers] we are expected to pay our respects and even offer contributions. For them this is an example of goodwill, of how we are accepted into their society, indeed we are no different as long as we do not act differently. During Id celebrations in my family, we keep a low profile, no one visits us or celebrates with us. There are so many ways in which we are taught to understand ourselves as different. Some of us practise polygamy. We know the world is changing and there are different views on the matter. But if the family is happy, if there is no abuse, difference should be a matter of debate not segregation.[133]

Against Women

Women fear the Sangh will perpetrate violence on their bodies to attack the social group to which they belong. Violence against women becomes a political act, as in Gujarat, avenging a cultural and ethnic group. The extent to which aggression is inscribed disproportionately on women's bodies and memories is rarely named or given language. One Muslim woman told me,

I think it is violent to deny water to people because they are [considered] 'impure' by caste or religion. I do not have the power to say so. But if I pray to my god or eat certain meats, it is a sin for which I must remain invisible. Women face double discrimination, from men of our own community as well as from the outside.[134]

Another Muslim woman in a different district said,

> We came from Chhota Nagpur, displaced from a mining town. Our village is surrounded by the RSS. We live like moles, I teach my children to be unseen. If we are quiet people will leave us alone. The men, it is not easy for them. Last month there was violence in our village. Bajrang Balis [Bajrang Dal members] called us names, they threatened we would never work again. Said we were dirty, that when we kill cows, we do violence to Hinduism. They said they were watching us. My husband came back, shaken. He brought fear with him into the house. He forced me to have intercourse. It was not about intimacy, it is about power, about feeling helpless and wanting control. So, here it is, in our kitchen, in our bedroom, in our home. Even as we wait for it to strike, it already has.[135]

History is in mourning[136] as the debris of becoming forces complex agency on the part of different groups, proliferating brutality.

As I spoke with women RSS and Bajrang Dal organizers about the scope of unnamed and unmarked aggression, one RSS woman organizer told me: 'I understand that violence is bad, but their [Muslim] women must allow us to control their men, otherwise they [Muslim women] will be inflicted with more violence [from Muslim men].'[137] Intent on constructing the 'ideal' woman who decries 'loose morals', the Sangh seeks to train Hindu women to confront 'undesirable' sexual behaviour '*endemic*' to Muslims and Christians, endorsing the masculinization and misogynization of the Hindu male looking to protect the fictively threatened Hindu woman. When I asked whether violence against Muslim men was acceptable, an RSS male organizer replied: 'Only if they are resisting.'[138] I asked the same question of Subash Chouhan of the Bajrang Dal. He responded that the Dal would engage in militancy if needed to 'get the job done'.[139]

I also asked whether violence against women was acceptable, and the following dialogue ensued with the same RSS male organizer:

> RSS male organizer: 'No, that is not acceptable, but women must not be traitors. If they are traitors, they help bring violence and we cannot stop it.'
> A Bajrang Dal worker: 'Women need to be given power as they

are goddesses, they are like the mother earth. They are also susceptible and need protection, both from themselves and the men who will violate them... Muslim men. They attack our women... Muslim women need protection from their men. They have no entitlement. Their men divorce them as they wish and hide behind their laws. Look what happened to Shah Bano. The Hindutva movement tells Muslims that to belong in this country they have to be of this country. No special deals. We Hindu men have been violated. We have become feeble. We in the Bajrang Dal have sworn to protect our women. We encourage our sisters and mothers to allow the men to be protectors.

Angana Chatterji: 'Have you heard of what happened to Muslim women in Gujarat?'

RSS male organizer: 'There was some violence. It is unfortunate. But most of it is a story, it was organized to malign those working for a Hindu rashtra. Otherwise, where is the evidence? I mean real evidence, not concocted by Mullas or the secular press.'[140]

Hindu majoritarianism intervenes in the construction, mobilization and contestation of gendered roles in the courtyards and fields of rural Orissa, engaging in contradictory scripts that make gender simultaneously monochrome and dangerous.[141] In creating representations of women in Hindu nationalist discourse, the Sangh reinforces a cornerstone of patriarchy that merges motherhood, cultural preservation, morality, patriotism and sanctity in women, functioning to disrupt 'subaltern genders',[142] defacing the expression of women's agency, rights, identity and sexuality.[143] In the performance of nation, cultural reassertion involves a hyper-masculinization from above, (re)constructing the dominant feminine for its repression, synonymously casting the 'other' as sexualized and violent.[144] The performativity of this violence before violence is abiding, as illustrated in Hasina Begum's own beating of her daughter,[145] and by the words of the Muslim woman from Chhota Nagpur (above), 'We live like moles, I teach my children to be unseen'.

Corresponding forms of aggression play out in concert as the internalization of 'overreaction' forbids the articulation of horror and its experience; masking Hindutva's practice of knowledge/power as it operates. Such sadism derives its vigour in Orissa from Hindutva's intervention into civil society as the emissary of the state. Hindutva manoeuvres and reproduces the faint echo of Muslim fundamentalist assertions of threatened Islam in India to evidence Hinduism and Hindus as endangered. Distorted representations of Muslims in Gujarat

(International Initiative for Justice 2003) shifted the structure of gendered violence and extended the limits of the public and possible, to invigorate and intersect the hegemonic aspirations of patriarchy and state with fascistic intent. At a parallel, a discussion of Muslim women's rights, Islam and Islamic personal law, are invariably mediated by references to the Shah Bano case of 1985.[146] Hindu fundamentalists stage the replacement of personal/religious laws with a Uniform Civil Code as critical to national integration (Menon 2000). They pose this as the ultimate test of Muslim loyalty, portraying contemporary Indian feminist critique of the intertwining of religion and law in communalizing Muslim women's rights in the Shah Bano case as heresy (Agnes 1999, 2001; Basu 2003; Kumar 1994). Poor Muslim women's rights are often jeopardized in the prevalent orthodoxy in which they survive the everyday. Najma Bibi, a resident of Bhadrak district in Orissa, was summarily divorced after ten years of marriage by her husband Seikh Sher Ali through a triple *talaq* (a form of divorce). Sher Ali, a poor daily wage labourer who loads cattle onto trucks for transportation to Calcutta, beat up Najma and pronounced talaq in an inebriated condition on the night of 5 May 2003. After which they continued to stay together as before. The incident was witnessed by the crowd that had gathered outside their home drawn to their vocal argument. The couple were resident in Najma Bibi's family home, where her father is a rickshaw puller. Najma Bibi and her husband were driven out of Sher Ali's home by his mother six months after their marriage in a *mehr* (dowry)[147] related dispute. A few days after 5 May, local residents communicated to the couple that the talaq was final and that Najma Bibi must perform *halala*[148] if she and Sher Ali were to remain together. The couple protested and procured a fatwa annulling the talaq.

The All India Muslim Personal Law Board has offered that it will create awareness of the conditions required for talaq, while refusing to take a stand on Najma Bibi's case. Progressive men within the Orissa Muslim community have been largely silent. Some are afraid of drawing attention to internal issues as it may target Islam violently in the substructure of Hindu cultural dominance. The predicament created by the Supreme Court's judgement on the Shah Bano case produces constrained responses on part of feminists in relation to Muslim women's rights under Indian Muslim Personal Law, as evidenced by the National Commission on Women's statement in the Najma Bibi case.[149]

Across India, as in Orissa, the mobilization of women for the nation is used to vilify progressive feminism and amass political authority (amid feminist radicalization of narratives in rethinking/disfiguring 'gender'),[150] bringing into sharp focus the dynamics of power between male militancy and the women they target. There has been a significant increase in women's participation in Hindu right wing movements in recent years (Bacchetta and Power 2002; Sarkar and Butalia 1995). While women's resistance in grass-roots movements linked to land and livelihood security is gaining strength in Orissa (Chatterji 2006), women's right wing movements, especially linked to Hindutva, are undoubtedly more cohesive and commanding.[151] A plethora of xenophobic women's organizations are in position, with women from middle and upper middle caste and class groups offering leadership. As with Hindu majoritarian women who assert the crass logic of sati (Hindu widow self-immolation), these women leaders are often privileged and the least economically, politically, culturally impacted by the capitulation stipulated by Hindutva. The BJP Mahila Morcha and the Rashtriya Sevika Samiti are two principal Sangh organizations in Orissa.[152] Established in 1936, the Rashtriya Sevika Samiti has been active in the crusade against cow slaughter in Orissa. The Samiti organizes state and district level meetings, as well as daily and weekly shakha and prayer meets in villages, towns and cities 'to encourage physical education, intellectual development, mental acumen'. Women's organizations, activists and feminists in Orissa express that Hindutva corroborates the impairment of women's well-being, already structurally limited in the state. These women assert the need to shift from the problematic search for the origins of women's shared oppression to address the diversity of women's needs.[153]

Bidyut Lata Raja, leader of the Rashtriya Sevika Samiti, says that the Parivar helps discipline the mind and wean people from 'pointless' activity. She says that the Parivar functions as a family, each taking care of the other.

> The Parivar seeks to create unity. Dalits and Adivasis say that Hindus are outsiders. How can that be? We must create consciousness that we are all one. Dalits have a lot of grievances. They do not see Hindus as belonging to India. So we say to them that, yes, in the past there has been discrimination. Today, these feelings do not exist in the minds of people. Their major grievance, they say, is that we do not let them into our temples. We say to them that if they [some people] do not let you into the temple, then build a temple in your home.[154]

The Samiti seeks to complement economic development with building moral character to unite India through shared nationalism. The Samiti supervises Balmandirs and Udyog Mandirs,[155] celebrates the anniversaries of influential Sangh leaders and religious festivals, hosts classes on culture and ethics, organizes Bhajan and Kirtan recitals,[156] and runs women's schools and hostels. The Samiti concentrates its volunteer-based social work services in Adivasi areas, seeking to bring 'enlightenment'.

The Rashtriya Sevika Samiti seeks to organize and train women in self-defence, 'to increase their physical and mental capacity to encourage them to protect their nation, dharma and culture'. Stringently heterosexist and mired in sexism, the Samiti is dedicated to supporting women in their youth, in marriage and motherhood, work, and leadership, indoctrinating the practice of Hindutva as patriotic, the saffron flag as the national emblem, insisting on the loyalty of its followers to their husbands, families and the Hindutva leadership. By the end of 2005, the Samiti's mandate was to create and sustain 100 shakhas across Orissa.

The Sangh Parivar asserts that, consequent to its interventions, relations between higher caste, Dalit and Adivasi groups have improved in rural Orissa. In conversations with Sangh members, it was pointed out to me that inter-caste alliances and marriage between non-comparable social castes are more evident today.[157] Sangh members omitted to mention that such liaisons are often socially ostracized, and that underprivileged class and caste and Adivasi people are seldom acknowledged as social equals. In an emblematic display of power, while all residents of a heterogeneous village, including Adivasis, may contribute financially to the major annual Hindu pujas, higher-caste people control the preparations and ceremony. It may be appropriate for a member of the Dalit or Muslim community, if invited, to eat at a caste Hindu home, usually seated in a demarcated space, and (expected to) internalize the invitation as demonstrative of the 'charity' and 'tolerance' of the 'upper caste' towards 'lower caste' people. The reverse is nearly impossible (Chatterji 1998 and 2006). Such invitations are inherently coded in histories of premeditated inequity. Associations among Hindus and non-Hindus remain strained in the state and frequently prohibited. In upper-caste rural Orissa, poor Muslim communities are as socially unacceptable as Adivasis, and constitute a 'lower' social strata than Dalits. Gender and ethnicity are central to how resources and power are allocated and rights disbursed, both nationally and locally, and are salient to the organization of legal, cultural, economic and political infrastructure and institutions. The imposition of Brahminical language, ritual and memory seeks to incorporate the marginal into the dominant polity simultaneous to segregationist arrangements for water use, food and resource sharing.

MOBILIZATIONS

The Sangh uses antagonistic and duplicitous techniques in mobilizing community, primary among them being development, education and forced conversions to Hinduism. In a drive in the mid-1980s the Jaganath Rath Yatra[158] passed through Hindu, Christian, Dalit and Adivasi villages across Orissa. Local people met expenses totalling Rs two to four million. The Yatra traversed a thousand sites between March 1986 and May 1988, drawing 3,000–4,000 people in each place. As an outcome of this process, 1,600 permanent mobilization units managed by 500 committees were established. The VHP and Vanavasi Kalyan Ashrams run these units, carrying out their mission via Kirtan Mandals, Satsangs and Yuvak Kendras.[159] Today, the annual Jaganath Yatra and other Hindutva organized religio-nationalist exhibition continue across the state. Muslims, and Adivasi and Dalit groups connected to self-determination movements in dissent to the Sangh Parivar, are afraid as thundering mobs engulf their villages.[160] On 11 April 2003, communal tensions spiralled in Rajgangapur, an industrial town 400 kilometres from Bhubaneswar, during a procession for Hanuman on Ramnavmi.[161] Two people were killed in police firing.[162]

The Prakalpa Samanvaya Samiti is a pivotal Sangh organization synchronizing the activities of various faith and welfare outfits.[163] The Prakalpa Samiti operates a school at Chakapad, three student hostels, twenty weekly Balwadis,[164] and 300 night schools. It attends to 20,000 patients each month through medicine distribution centres and three mobile vans. The Prakalpa Samiti acts to convert Christians to Hinduism. The Sangh drives spiritual centres that use religious scriptures to incite sectarianism among Hindus. Vivekananda Kendras and Hindu Jagaran Manch are active in Orissa together with Harikatha Yojana centres in 780 villages and 1,940 Satsang Kendras. There are 1,700 Bhagabat Thungis in Orissa, cultural reform centres run by the Sangh that aim at Hindus and Christians.

Another line of attack is to forcibly convert Christians into Hinduism. Churches and members of the Christian clergy are apprehensive. In Gajapati and Koraput, Christians have sought state protection in the past. In Gajapati district, RSS and BJP workers torched 150 homes and the village church in October 1999. A Dalit Christian activist said, 'RSS workers tell me that Christianity brought colonialism to India, and I am responsible for that legacy. How am I responsible? Feudalism, imperialism, postcolonial betrayal. That is written across our bodies. How am I responsible?'[165]

In June 2002, the VHP coerced 143 tribal Christians into converting to Hinduism in Sundargarh district. The Dharma Prasar Bibhag claims to have converted 5,000 people to Hinduism in 2002.[166] Orissa passed a Freedom of Religion Act in 1967 protecting against coercive conversions. The law, open to problematic interpretations, was overturned in 1973 and returned in 1977. In 1989, the state government activated requirements for religious conversion. In 1999, Orissa enacted a state order prohibiting religious conversions without prior permission of local police and district magistrates. Hindu fundamentalists diligently manipulate these provisions to intimidate religious minorities. Sangh organizations work with sympathetic police cadre to ensure that Hindus do not convert.[167]

At the instigation of Sangh organizations, in February 2004, seven women and a male pastor were tonsured by Hindu neighbours against their will in a Dalit *sahi* in Kilipal, a heterogeneous caste village of over 200 households, in Jagatsinghpur district. Forty households inhabit Bauri sahi. Seven Dalit families converted to Christianity (affiliated to the Church on Mount Zion) in the last decade. The conversion had led to progressive ostracization of these Christians from the Hindu Dalit community. Following the cyclone of 1999, non-sectarian humanitarian aid distributed by church organizations to Christian and non-Christian families had repaired the estrangement in some measure. In 2004, Hindu nationalists in the area, with increasing impetus from RSS and VHP organizations, commenced a vociferous anti-minority campaign. Christians in Kilipal were accused of violating Hinduism and were actively targeted; they were deprived of the right to use public water, roads and grazing lands. They were intimidated and pressured to 'reconvert' to Hinduism. Enacted by local Hindus, the event of February 2004 occurred during the day, as Hindu Dalit neighbours watched (People's Union For Civil Liberties 2004). The premonitions of the Christian Dalit woman leader from Mayurbhanj (see section entitled, 'Political Economy of Violence') reverberate as the Sangh looked to enact Bauri sahi across Orissa.

The Sangh Parivar stage manages communities against each other and converts minorities to dominant Hinduism, purposefully confusing distinctions between the right to proselytize, forcible conversions and the use of religion to cultivate hate. The Sangh uses the converted for sadistic ends. The sporadic participation of Hinduized Adivasi and Dalit communities in the brutalization of Muslims was a sad and unexpected distinction of the recent violence in Gujarat (Citizens for Justice and Peace 2002). Divide and conquer, effectively realized. Hindutva propaganda accuses Christian communities of forcible conversion and labels it a crime. The Sangh does not acknowledge that tribal and Dalit conversions to Christianity are rarely directly coercive in the present and occur in response to oppressive and entrenched caste inequities, gender violence and chronic poverty. The Sangh allocates violence against Christians in India by storying them as anti-national. Dalit Christian activists understand 'decastification' as necessary to fighting Hindutva. They also speak of challenging inherent inequities that are often reproduced through the church, where, they say, pews are filled on Sunday mornings with compliant people sitting in rows ordered along caste hierarchies.

The Sangh justifies its use of the conversion in the interests of a higher truth, the 'righteous' action of reuniting Hindus.[168] 'Reconversion' is working well among the Christian community in Orissa, Subash Chouhan says, but not with Muslims.

> Muslim reconversions are going slowly because Mulla, Mulabi people have created mosques and madrasahs[169] in village after village, and guard their children like chickens. That is the kind of people they are and that is why it is not so easy to get them back.[170]

For Muslims, the Bajrang Dal anticipates a different approach. The RSS charges that hostile Hinduization is a 'rational' and necessary response to, among other factors, the growth of missionary activity leading to an increase in the Christian population.

Numerous progressive citizens' groups are conflicted about the need to direct 'equal' energy in assessing Hindutva, Christian missionization and Islamic fundamentalism in India. Violent Islamic fundamentalism certainly requires deep scrutiny in South Asia (Jalal 1995), even as Hindutva must command particular emphasis in India. In Orissa, Hindu nationalism is linked to a state that authorizes Hindutva's actions, lending it dangerous legitimacy. Fundamentalist Christianity, linked to the United States, is endorsed by the current Bush administration (Sutherland 2004). Evidence suggests (United States) evangelist participation in intelligence operations in Latin America and elsewhere.[171] Such activity and its relationship to India should concern us only as it *actually* takes place. Christians constitute less than 3 per cent of the population in Orissa, with a 1 per cent growth since 1981. Neither does the Christian population in India record any appreciable increase from 2.6 per cent in 1971, to 2.43 per cent in 1981, 2.34 per cent in 1991, and 2.6 per cent in 2001 (Pati 2003; Government of India 2001).

Targeting the livelihood of the 'other' is a technique of saffronization.[172] The Bajrang Dal has been strident in the sacralization of the cow (Jha 2002) and disallowing cow slaughter in Orissa, an important source of income for poor Muslims and Dalits who trade in meat and leather. Muslims and Dalits have been beaten and threatened by Hindutva mobs. The participation of government agencies in debating a ban on cow slaughter irresponsibly invokes the debate about animal rights, arrogantly contravening the separation of religion and state in ways that impact poor Muslims, Dalits and Christians.

Gyanendra Pandey (1990) outlines the repertoire of mobilization of the Hindu nation in colonial India to include an aggressive Cow Protection Movement in the 1880s and 1890s, with wide support from a cross-section of the landed and merchant classes across what is today the cow belt of north and eastern India. The movement was militant as guided by a disenfranchised class leadership and moderate as an upper-class Brahminic force, effecting economically underprivileged Muslims, non-Hindus and Hindu 'lower caste' groups.

In Orissa, the Sangh Parivar has revived this legacy in the last decade with apparent and adverse affects on the social and economic health of Muslim and certain poor caste communities. Samshul Amin, a Muslim man from Bhadrak says: 'We trade in leather. We always have. The RSS and Bajrang Dal tell lies about how we slaughter cows to shame Hindus. But we buy the cows from the Hindus. The RSS says that we kill and send the cows to Muslims in Bangladesh.' A Muslim businessman in Jagatsinghpur town confirms: 'They say we are unclean. They threaten and at times beat Muslims on the road, starting from Bhadrak, from Balasore, onwards up to Calcutta, where the Bajrang Dal has a strong presence, there they are violent. They stop cow transportations on Jajpur road.'[173] Subash Chouhan, Bajrang Dal State Convenor, charges,

> There is so much cow slaughter, for example in Sundargarh, Bhadrak, thousands of cows. Every day about 200 trucks leave with cows for Bangladesh. We believe that the cow is our mother, but they want to kill the cow. Also, if the cow stays, it is a financial security for the home. So, if necessary we will use a suicide squad. To save the country and its sanskriti [culture], we will do whatever is necessary.[174]

The use of economic sanctions to assert Brahminical notions of 'pollution' and to label the 'other' as polluting and destructive in order to coerce obedience and unify community, replicates the tactics of terror used in the late nineteenth century (Jha 2002; Pandey 1990).

Development (Sabrang Communications 2002; Awaaz 2004) and education (Sarkar 1996; Sundar 2004) are key vehicles through which conscription into Hindu extremism is amassed. The actions of RSS affiliates Ekal Vidyalaya[175], Vanvasi Kalyan Parishad, Vivekananda Kendra, Shiksha Vikas Samiti, Sewa Bharati and other groups offer incriminating evidence of this. Development implemented by institutions affiliated with the Sangh Parivar lays the groundwork for hate and civil polarization. Adivasis and Dalits assert that development is not a matter of building wells or developing roads, it is also a matter of deciding how needs and priorities are determined, access and decision making is enabled, cultural difference is affirmed and identity politics supported (Chatterji 1998, 2006). Development is the construction of political will towards rethinking inequitable relations of power. It is a mechanism expected to produce equity and ensure the human rights of the poor. Hindutva development violates the premise on which disenfranchised communities seek to determine their right to life and livelihood.[176] The raison d'être for utilizing development as a mechanism for mobilization is complex. A VHP ideologue from Cuttack explains,

> Development is key to strengthening the motherland. Once vanavasis and Dalits receive the benefits of development, they will join our rank and file. Muslims will be exposed and Cristan [Christian] missionaries will have no place to sell their religion. Once the motherland is invincible, both internally, compared with Pakistan and internationally, people will accept that our vision for Hindu Rashtra is the only way.[177]

After the cyclone of 1999, relief work undertaken in a sectarian manner by RSS organizations provided the Sangh a foothold through which to strengthen enrolment in Orissa. As this secular activist states,

> The Rashtriya Swayamsevak Sangh [RSS] and Sangh Parivar sailed in with the cyclone [in 1999], we are now drowning in their midst. They are too many and everywhere. They are kind and giving to people who abide by them, even as they are watchful and intolerant of people who disobey them. They do more than the government; they work hard and say that they are against corruption. But, at what price? They are for a 'clean' Orissa; they are cleaning out the filth, and Christians and Muslims are the filth they want to sweep out.[178]

Today, Utkal Bipanna Sahayata Samiti works with disaster mitigation with facilities in thirty-two villages. Dhayantari Shasthya Pratisthan manages four hospitals and six mobile centres. In offering social services and carrying out rural development work, the Sangh makes itself indispensable to its cadre as a pseudo-moral and reformist force. This continues the Sangh Parivar's long history of implementing sectarian development.

Diasporic charitable organizations affiliated with the Sangh Parivar receive substantial contributions from Hindus in the United States, United Kingdom and elsewhere (Sabrang Communications 2002; Awaaz 2004). A disconnection from what is meaningful compounds the intensity and power of becoming in new worlds, amidst vast differences, racism, forces of homogenization. The greater the alienation, the greater the reach for fiction. In a world intent on placing Islam and Muslims at the centre of 'evil', Hindu nationalism escapes the global imagination, permitting Sangh Parivar groups to function in the United States and United Kingdom as registered charities without political scrutiny. It is noteworthy that while in 1999 the VHP failed to gain recognition at the United Nations as 'a cultural organization' because of its philosophical underpinnings, the VHP of America continues to function as an independent charity registered since the 1970s in the United States. To dissent, as so many do, from the persistence of structural inequities, the horrors of history, the politics of caste and cows in the present, is only to bear incriminating evidence of one's own bastardization, loss of purity, lack of faith and pride in 'Indianness'.[179]

Substantial funds were raised by Sangh organizations during the Gujarat earthquake (2001) and Orissa cyclone, aiding the expansion of Sangh networks in both states. The India Development Relief Fund (IDRF) is one organization that, post cyclone, collected $90,660 for Sookruti, $23,255 for Orissa Cyclone Rehabilitation Foundation, and $37,560 for Utkal Bipanna Sahayata Samiti, as documented in the report 'Foreign Exchange of Hate' (Sabrang Communications 2002).[180] In the United Kingdom, the Seva International UK (the fundraising wing of the Hindu Swayamsevak Sangh, RSS equivalent in UK and US) sent a majority of the £260,000 raised for cyclone relief to Utkal Bipanna Sahayata Samiti, an RSS organization in Orissa, detailed in the report, 'In Bad Faith? British Charity & Hindu Extremism' by Awaaz (2004). Currently, Utkal Bipanna Sahayata Samiti undertakes sectarian disaster relief work, and has been working with approximately 50,000 beneficiaries after the floods of 2001, funded by RSS organizations abroad.[181]

The actions of Sangh organizations are often triangulated, with parallel components for edification, mobilization and service.[132] For example, Vidya Bharati (known as Shiksha Vikas Samiti) directs 391 Saraswati Shishu Mandir schools in Orissa. Sangh students are inducted into the cadre via a formal curriculum that emphasizes Hindu nationalism along with informal training in cultural values and defence. In addition, these students and their families are expected to volunteer in mobilization and developmental work, in local fundraising. They are even expected to participate in temple inaugurations.

Sectarian education campaigns undertaken by RSS organizations systematically seek out minorities in teaching fundamentalist curricula (Sundar 2004). There are 391 Sishu Mandir schools with 111,000 students, preparing for future leadership.[183] Training camps in Bhadrak and Behrampur aim at Adivasi youth. Vanavasi Kalyan Ashram runs 1,534 projects and schools in twenty-one Adivasi districts. The Sangh has initiated 730 Ekal Vidyalayas in ten districts in Orissa, one teacher schools that target Adivasis. The primary purpose of the schools is to indoctrinate villages into Hindutva. The teachers are offered Rs 150–200 per month as honoraria, no salaries. The schools are free, supported through donations from organizations like the IDRF.

History, science, geography, literature and religious texts written in Oriya are translated into Hindutva. The curriculum is increasingly centralized, censored and obscurantist, interpreted to legitimate the sanctity of a 'Hindu worldview' in India. Crafting the imagination of majoritarianism becomes a hyper-deliberate process vacated of ethics, it instantiates fictive memory via each assertion. Adivasis are taught by Ekal Vidyalayas about the 'origins' of Jaganath in Hinduism, as Jaganath, the famed tribal god of Orissa, is Hinduized. Since the inception of Saraswati Sishu Mandirs, the Janata Dal, Congress and other political parties have endorsed the Sangh Parivar's network of educational organizations, interpreting Hindutva education *as* secular. Consecutive governments have abdicated state responsibility in building a quality education system in the state. High levels of illiteracy among Dalits and Adivasis proliferate simultaneous to the denigration of non-Hindu traditions and cultures.

At a 15,000 strong Vanavasi Kalyan Ashram organized rally in Bhubaneswar in December 2003, Dilip Singh Bhuria, Chairperson, National Commission for Scheduled Castes and Scheduled Tribes, commended the BJP for its pro-Adivasi policies.[184] Adivasis have historically voted for the Congress Party in Orissa and have not benefited from this loyalty. Bhuria said, 'We are passing through a governance similar to Ram Rajya', posing Ram as the god, and BJP as the party, of Adivasis. Vanavasi Kalyan Ashram president, Jagadev Ram Oram, insisted that Adivasis converting to Christianity should not be allowed to access the benefits of reservation. Through espousing another religion, he said, Adivasis no longer retain their tribal status. Speakers condemned Christian conversions declaring 'all tribals are Hindus'. The Sangh asserts Adivasi political emancipation is a process of 'tribalism' that jeopardizes the nation.[185]

Orissa remains uncommitted to providing relevant and affordable public education.[186] Social and informal education imparted to children by family and community varies by class and ethnicity. Nuanced with age, children are socialized into gender roles and caste identities, and acquire relevant occupational skills. Affluent villages and sahis increasingly have access to middle and even high schools in Orissa. Formal education holds certain value for many, trusted as a possible means of poverty alleviation. While families feel that formal education is important, parents (many of whom have little or no formal education) are often unable to provide an adequate support system. Schools advocate private tuition in an effort to help students with their homework and compensate for abysmal teacher pay scales. Even as an increasing number of boys and girls are attending and completing school, particularly within general caste communities, the paucity of direct employment opportunities connected to formal education undermines incentive for attendance and completion.

Non-formal and vocational education centres are operated by state and non-governmental organizations (NGOs). Organizations with religious affiliations such as Islamic madrasahs offer orthodox education. With the heightened impetus for privatization of education, Hindu religio-nationalist organizations undertake massive campaigns to inaugurate affordable schools in areas across Orissa where the government fails to provide public funding. Hindu nationalist groups operate informal and formal schools. In the absence of viable educational institutions, Hindutva education offers a free, widely available and rigorous curriculum. Students from these schools succeed in state board examinations. Institutions that facilitate cultural regimentation complement Hindutva schools, run primarily by RSS organizations. The facticity of hate in this curriculum, the dismissal of minorities, the assertion of Hindu supremacy is overlooked by many Hindus. In the current climate, numerous Muslims retreat to madrasahs. These institutions often teach orthodoxy, deliberately mischaracterized by the majority community as uniformly 'fundamentalist'. As Hasina Begum explains,

> My daughter is in a good school but with those other children who do not like her. She wants to play with the neighbours but they curse at her. They physically push her around. Now we think we should find a madrasah for her. The madrasah is orthodox, but they will protect us. The education is better in the school but what if something happens to her?[187]

RSS cadre mobilize shakhas around minority villages in Orissa.[188] Each shakha begins with an organizer and a few members who meticulously monitor the area, teaching people to describe themselves as 'communal', a new identity that denotes Hindu cultural pride. Minorities worry as under the watchful eye of the RSS, a cricket conflict as a harmless fracas between children's winning and losing teams turns into a communal skirmish. Green flags of stars and crescent used by madrasahs are depicted as adhering to Pakistan, linked to terrorism and the Inter Services Intelligence (ISI).[189] Subash Chouhan of the Bajrang Dal says,

> We in the VHP believe that this country belongs to the Hindus. It is not a dharamsala [guesthouse] and people cannot just come here and settle down and do whatever they want. That is not going to happen. We will not let that happen. Whatever happens here will happen with the consent of the Hindus. If you come to another's house and live as a guest and then start doing what you please, that is not going to happen. What ever happens here, say politics happen, it will have to be Hindutva politics, with Hindutva's consent. India is a world power, what is in India is nowhere else, and we want to create India nicely in the image of Ram Rajya.[190]

To domesticate dissent, the Sangh invigorates militant nationalism, threatened by grass-roots democracy and forces of resistance as social movements challenge upper-caste Hindu dominance and contradict elite aspirations. In village Orissa, emulating Gujarat, the Sangh works to create enmity between Dalits, Adivasis, Muslims and Christians. Where Dalits, Adivasis and others are allied in subaltern struggles for land rights and sustenance, Hindutva intervenes, seeking to divide them. Throughout Orissa, such organization for self-determination confronts the devastation of dominant development and globalization, acting as a bulwark against the escalation of the Sangh Parivar. Progressive citizen's groups have initiated campaigns to combat communalism in the state, including the Campaign Against Communalism in Bhubaneswar. Their capacity to contest despotic religiosity is linked to redressing political oppression, redistributing economic resources to ensure well-being and ecological sustainability,[191] and overcome injustice. Since 2002, meetings and marches have taken place in Behrampur, Cuttack, Balasore, Bhadrak, Bhubaneswar, Sambalpur, speaking to the need for rallying progressive, democratic forces across the state and the futility of partnerships with the BJP and Sangh Parivar vigilantes. In January 2004, a state-wide meeting of progressive citizens groups, intellectuals, activists, and NGOs was held in Bhubaneswar to assess the gravity of the situation.[192] At this meeting, and others, citizens have been involved in assessing how the secularization of the polity might be made central to action at the grass roots, within institutions, political parties, trade unions, social movements, schools and universities, NGOs, families and neighbourhoods, in public and private life (Copley 2003).

Citizens debate the continuum of resistance as a repeated commitment to reflexivity, to engendering ethical politics, to alliance, as it expands from livelihood movements in the present to integrate dissent to corporate globalization and militant nationalism. Competing and oppositional identities (local and national) collide to assert counter claims of the marginal-subaltern in rethinking borders (political, cultural, geographic), margins (social, historical), and futures (ethical, accountable).

A Muslim activist from Bhubaneswar states, 'We are isolated. We do not want to identify with the madrasahs and we do not have a mass movement that accepts us'.[193] Isolation reinvents polarization, placing Orissa Muslims at its centre, reverberating a pattern in the post 9\11 world. Rita, a Dalit woman in Orissa, says:

> They stopped my father from taking the cows to sell. They beat him. They said if we do business with Muslims, we are traitors. We have no money to take him to the hospital. We lost business. We should leave, it might be easier in Cuttack, it is a big city, they need labourers there.[194]

Bhuria, an Adivasi Christian woman, says: 'Become a Hindu? Will that change who I am? We are Christians and we are also Adivasis. Hindus don't understand us, they don't have to.' Pushpa Patnaik, a Hindu secular activist, states: 'I did not even know this was happening. What it must take to keep things as they are, to pretend that all is normal. Knowing things does not make them better. I struggle with the responsibility of action. We have to look at ourselves.'[195] Shazia Bibi, a Muslim migrant in Orissa, states:

> A whisper, a comment, a look. Weapons in the hand of the powerful. RSS men, they look at us when they circle our village, they look at the women. They

come in and go as they please. They taunt us in the bazaar. They beat the
men. The women, they whisper about us. They look at me and I feel sick. The
children, they are afraid. When it is time they [Sangh] will act... Sometimes I
think about what they might do. We are prisoners, slowly being pushed into a
darkness. Being at home means not being afraid. Is this home?[196]

Rage, fear and discontinuity, the recurring, fractured narratives of
nationspace. The violence of apathy, desperation in children's eyes, the
hardened laughter of survival. It is pensive in Orissa. I can hear the
disquiet of future ghosts.

POSTSCRIPT

If I am asked to language what in India are intimate silences, for me,
those complex confrontations include prefigured legacies—Bengali class
and caste privilege, woman, 'brown', 'mixed' caste parents, child of
socialists in Calcutta, of Hindu descent.[197] The night is a long journey of
self-reflection as we retell the stories of our becoming.

I recall Lutfera Khatoon, after Gujarat, in Park Street, Calcutta,
surrounded by Hindu fundamentalists, taunting, 'GO BACK TO
BANGLADESH'. Lutuma, family friend, my mother's midwife. She
helped grow me. A Muslim woman whose family emigrated in 1923, a
nurse who laboured with extravagant courage for poor Muslims, Hindus
and any others who happened upon her clinic. 'Small speech,' Lutuma
said, 'but so much power.'[198]

NOTES

1. Personal communication (2004). Pseudonym used. As appropriate, quotations
   are anonymous or pseudonyms have been used, and place names listed
   or omitted, at the request of the contributor. Insertion(s) within [ ] in the
   quotations are mine.
2. Derogatory use.
3. In an arrogant display of militant Hindu dominance, in February and March
   2002, about 2000 people, mostly Muslims, were murdered in Gujarat, aided
   and abetted by the state. Between 120,000–150,000 were rendered homeless.
   Gujarat occurred with the Hindu nationalists in power in New Delhi and at
   the state level in Gujarat. See Human Rights Watch (2002), and Varadarajan
   (2002). I am reminded of a Dalit boy, age 8, in a decimated colony in
   Ahmedabad, in June 2002, who said, 'I am not afraid of death. I am frightened
   by life. Look what happens in life,' as Muslim and Dalit women stared each

other into silence across a boundary wall (Personal communication, 2002).
As I write, justice remains elusive for Muslim minorities in the complex
deception of state negligence, judicial oversight, and the deep fragmentation
of political community.

4. I return to this in the section entitled, 'Erasure'.
5. I withhold the name of the town at Hasina's request.
6. Pseudonym used.
7. The riots in Delhi, October 1984, after the assassination of Indira Gandhi
    that left the Sikh community terrorized. See Chakravorty and Haksar (1987).
    Also see Ansari (1997).
8. I return to this in the section entitled, 'Erasure'.
9. Adivasi (tribal), Dalit ('lower', erstwhile 'untouchable', caste communities).
10. For an account of dislocation, see Samaddar (2003) and Butalia (2000).
11. See Parker et al. (1992), and Puri (2004) for elaborations of ways in which sexist\
    heterosexist nationalist violence impacts gender, gendering and community.
12. India's development record selectively narrates the benefits of enhanced
    industrialization, urbanization, mechanization and militarization, highlighting
    how the quality of life for many in India has significantly improved because
    of the political and economic decisions made as a nation. Yet these very
    indicators of development also tell a discouraging story of the continued
    disempowerment of communities, of persistent and invasive inequities that
    lead to the brutalization of women, children, Adivasi communities, Dalits,
    and ethnic and religious minorities. Struggles over means story the irrevocable
    depletion of the country's natural resource base. They chronicle cultural
    annihilation, toxic pollution levels, appalling working conditions, caste, class
    and religious crimes, and the unequal distribution of livelihood assets. In
    2004, fifty-seven years after independence, the ideals of democracy—food,
    security, self-determination, access to civic and political processes—remain
    elusive for 350 million (Saxena 2000) of India's poorest citizens. Gains in the
    context of economic betterment allow for a certain 'belonging' through entry
    into the middle class.
13. For a discussion of ethics in revolution, see Arendt (1963).
14, I resort to Bhabha's questioning of 'nation' (1994 and 2002).
15. Hindutva: Hindu extremism linked to the movement for a Hindu supremacist
    state in India, through the disintegration of Adivasi, Muslim, Christian, Dalit
    and other minority non-Hindu cultures and groups through their forcible
    incorporation into dominant Hinduism. The movement for Hindutva
    draws inspiration from Nazi and fascistic ideologies. See Jaffrelot (1996) for
    a history of the movement. Also see, Hansen (2001), Noorani (2002) and
    Sundar (2004).
16. Made possible in the context of larger commitments in Orissa to the
    production of radical and subaltern knowledges that dislocate dominant
    ones, my work draws on scholarship by Action Aid, Adhikar, Agragwamee,

People's Institute for Participatory Action Research, Regional Council for Development Cooperation, Vasundhara, and various other organizations. Certain state level coalitions, such as Coalition Against Communalism, Sanahti (coalition of institutions) and Orissa Jungle Manch (Forest Network), allied with village institutions to identify priorities for necessary research and action, have also participated in determining the focus and relevance of research. These organizations and coalitions share a commitment to ethical social action, and while diverse in politics are connected to funding, alliances and prioritization of research and action agendas. My research also draws on movement literature, pamphlets, policy notes, oral narratives produced and continued by people's coalitions.

17. I am most thankful to M.J. Akbar (Editor, *Asian Age*, New Delhi), Ejaz Haider (Editor, *Daily Times*, Lahore) and Teesta Setalvad (Editor, *Communalism Combat*, Mumbai) for carrying a number of articles I authored on Hindu nationalism in 2002–4, specifically on Hindutva in Orissa in October and November of 2003, and in March 2004.

18. Orissa Administrative Boundaries: The state has thirty districts and twenty-eight forest divisions. The districts are administrative boundaries and the district administration oversees legal, jurisdictional, land and rural development matters. The forest divisions are forest boundaries; the forest departments, at the divisional levels, oversee forest jurisdiction and administrative, legal and financial matters related to the specific forest division. See Chatterji (1998).

19. Including oral histories, story telling, ethnographies, narrative analysis, quantitative and qualitative surveys, diagnostic studies, local resource mapping procedures and manual geographical information systems. I have fluency in spoken Oriya. I also speak, read and write in Bengali (fluently) and Hindi (reasonable capacity). I have limited comprehension of certain Adivasi languages, and have solicited the help of colleagues when interacting with some Adivasi colleagues who communicated in these languages. Translations from Oriya, Adivasi languages like Santali, and Hindi and Bengali into the mix of 'subcontinental' English in which I think, are mine, at times with the aid of colleagues.

20. In villages, upper-caste communities are often cautious of my connections with Adivasi and Dalit groups. When found acceptable, it is through translating my association as patronage, 'helping' Adivasis and Dalits. For many upper-caste communities, my reality invariably represents power and socio-economic possibilities that fuel some desire, while my affirmation of self-determination struggles is seen as reactive, even anti-national.

21. I refer to continued reflective action that interrogates the effects of power that circulate in multiple sites and affirms freedom as an ongoing practice. I refer to deconstructive practice not a theoretical stance, but as movement that is continually in action. I draw on Derrida's deconstruction, and Marx's

'ruthless critique of everything existing' (Marx 1972: 7). See Foucault (1977, 1972) and Derrida (1994).

22. I utilize Michel Foucault's explication of genealogy and archaeology, and his delineation of 'disqualified knowledges', those that exist at the margins and operate as resistance, reflecting historical knowledge of struggles and oppression, outside 'scientific' universalizing 'discourses of truth'. (Distinguishing between ideology, as organized within the dichotomy of true and false, and discourse, propositions that circulate within the realms of truth to produce effect, problematic and emancipatory.) See Foucault (1980a: 82–83, 1980b: 118). Also see Foucault (1972, 1977).

23. See Derrida (1993: 194), as he authorizes, 'Only write what is impossible, that ought to be the impossible-rule.'

24. I have been living and working in the United States and India since 1993.

25. 'Postcoloniality' here refers to the diverse conditions, and arena of thinking and action, within the Global South and North, defined by, and in resistance to, legacies of internal and external colonization and continued and new imperialisms, in critical relationship to culture, power and history. In current contexts of state and statelessness, nation building and globalization, postcoloniality is a contested discursive and political space. It does not refer to the 'end' of colonization. See Williams and Chrisman (1994), Said (1978) and Goldberg and Quayson (2002).

26. My use of the term 'Third\First World' (rather than, for example, 'Global South') is deliberate in referring to countries in the Southern Hemisphere, subsumed under the unitary, colonial category of 'Third World' (from the French 'Tiers Monde'), 'less developed', 'underdeveloped' or 'developing'. These terms indicate a hierarchical progression that assumes '... a favourable change, a step from the simple to the complex, from the inferior to the superior, from worse to better....' (Esteva 1997: 10). These frames provide cognitive hegemony for interventionism from the North (countries in the Northern Hemisphere referred to as the 'First World', 'developed', 'modern', 'advanced', 'industrialized') and internal colonization in the South (ibid.: 9).

27. I am, as so many others, compelled by Gayatri Chakravorty Spivak's call to answerability in 'Can the Subaltern Speak?' See Spivak (1994).

28. I am grateful to so many whose lives are dedicated to principled struggle in the villages, towns and cities of Orissa and elsewhere; Ashok Babu who is no more, Kundan Kumar, Tabassum, Sudhir Patnaik, Mohammad Amin, Rabi Ray, Asha Hans, Bijli Begum, Vivekananda Dash, Arif Hossain, Mark Poffenberger, Rajendra K. Sarangi, Madhu Sarin, Mr Farooque, Neera Singh, Pushpa Babu, Shamina Begum, for their guidance, support and generous collaboration; to the Madison Collective (2003), especially Lubna Nazir Chaudhry, for this partnership; my students, for their insistence that these concerns live in the classroom, Annie Paradise for her careful reflections on this text, Pei Wu for her generous support; Srimati Basu, for thoughtful

comments on the essay during its 'delivery'; Harsh Mander, Chittaroopa Palit, Dunu Roy, Smitu Kothari for friendship and shared commitments; Kamala Visweswaran for abundant solidarity; Richard Shapiro for care that permits continued engagement with difficult realities.

29. As I write this I am mindful of Spivak's cautionary interjection on 'ethical singularity'. See 'Translator's Preface' by Spivak in Devi (1995: xxiv).
30. Communalist, communalism: divisive politics based on communal identifications. In India, 'communal' often refers to situations and tensions between groups organized around, and identified with, organized religion. See Pannikar (1991).
31. For a critical read see Desai (2002) and Dutta et al. (1996).
32. See Jalal and Bose (1997) for an account of development and nationalism in India. See Akbar (1985) and Pandey (2001). Also see Escobar (1995) and Sen (1999) for a critique of dominant development.
33. Brink and Mencher (1996) for a cross-cultural critique.
34. I draw on Bacchetta (1996), Bacchetta and Power (2002), and S. Sarkar (2002).
35. See 'RSS Ultimatum To Muslims: A Challenge To All Minorities And Other Secular Forces', Milli Gazette, 15 April 2002 at: http://www.milligazette. com/Archives/15042002/1504200257.htm (last accessed June 2004). Also see, 'NCM Initiative 'Breaks The Ice'', 16 July 2002, *The Hindu* at http:// www.hinduonnet.com/2002/07/16/stories/2002071603951100.htm (last accessed June 2004).
36. For a history of Islam and community in South Asia, see Jalal (2000). For a delineation of Islam's complex legacies, see Majid (2000).
37. The ultra conservative and militant Taliban ruled Afghanistan between 1996–2001. See Moghadam (2002).
38. I draw on Lacan (1982) towards understanding mechanisms of 'othering'.
39. For an explication of structures and processes of dominance, see Chatterjee (1997), Brass (1985) and Hasan (1989).
40. See Partha Chatterjee's rigorous delineation of the contradictory relations that configure and bind people and nation (1998 and 1993).
41. See Habib (1995). Also see Chakrabarty (2002), Dalmia (2003, 1997) and Jalal and Bose (1998).
42. For a formidable elaboration of a history of history, see Thapar (2004).
43. Ahmedabad (1969), Aligarh (1978), Moradabad (1980), Hyderabad (1981), Assam (1983), Bhiwandi (1984), Delhi (1984), Ayodhya (1992), Gujarat (2002). On and on. See Engineer (1997) and Chatterji (2002.)
44. In its upper-caste form.
45. See Pandey et al. (2003) for an examination of continuities in colonial and postcolonial administration of state.
46. Even as Foucault did not extend his analysis to conditions of postcoloniality, his frameworks offer us immense critical possibility. See Stoler (1995).

47. See T. Sarkar (2002) for an exploration of the effects of Hindu nationalism on minority women and children.
48. See Boulton (1979) for a history of nationalism in Orissa.
49. See Thapar (1992), and for history as apology, see Elst (1999).
50. See Foucault (1980a, 1980b, 1972). I am as well indebted to Richard Shapiro in understanding the biopolitics of nationalism.
51. Hindu nationalist party. Nationally, Jana Sangha (People's Organization) was founded as a political party in 1951, and later transitioned into the Bhartiya Janata Party (Indian People's Party). The BJP emerged as a major opposition party and in 1996 as the single largest party in a hung parliament. The BJP acquired power in New Delhi as part of the twenty-four party National Democratic Alliance (NDA) in 1999. In May 2004, the BJP led government alliance completed its five-year term and was defeated in the parliamentary elections with the Congress Party receiving the dominant share, but not the majority, of the votes, to form a Congress-Left Party coalition government at the centre. However, the BJP and its partners remain/are in power at the state level in various states. See Indian Elections at http://www.indian-elections.com/partyprofiles/bharatiya-janta-party.html (last accessed June 2004) and at http://www.indianelections.com/andhrapradesh/index.html (last accessed June 2004). For a history, see Hansen and Jaffrelot (1998).
52. In the 2004 elections.
53. See Indian elections website (2004), www.indianelections.com.
54. Derogatory labelling of Muslims.
55. Derogatory naming of Adivasis. Adivasi (first dweller), Vanavasi (forest dweller).
56. 'Desh' also refers to native village, state, province, motherland, native land, a land.
57. Personal communication (2003).
58. While the sanction of polygamy has, at times, allowed for grievous injustices, as in the case of Najma Bibi of Bhadrak, who was summarily divorced through triple talaq by Sher Ali, her husband, in an inebriated condition in May 2003 after ten years of marriage. As Najma Bibi and her husband attempted to reconcile, they were ostracized by the orthodox Muslim community who demanded that Najma Bibi perform halala [marriage to someone else, divorce, then remarriage to Sher Ali] if she and Sher Ali wish to remain together. Muslim feminists and local leaders say that about 15–25 per cent of Muslim marriages are polygamous, and that this is more frequent in some districts such as Bhadrak. (Personal conversation, 2004, with Muslim leaders in Bhadrak and feminist scholars in Orissa.)
59. In states across (east and west) central India with a concentration of Adivasi peoples, as in Madhya Pradesh, Chhatisgarh, Jharkhand, Uttaranchal and Orissa. See Chattopadhyay (2004).
60. See the use of biopolitics and governmentality in Foucault (1978a, 1994).

61. Adivasi earth- and spirit-based faiths, syncretic monotheistic, idolatrous and non-idolatrous practices, organized Hindu, Muslim, Christian, Buddhist, Sikh, Jain and other religions, as well as the irreligious, co-exist across Orissa. Religion lives, enmeshed in the cultural milieu. Deity, spirit and totem, idol and nature worship through rituals and prayers are often critical to cultural practice, performed daily, as well to mark significant occasions of harvest, birth, marriage, death, and other rites of passage. The practice of Hinduism is increasingly linked to majoritarian ascendancy in the state, leading to Hinduized Adivasis identifying as 'tribal Hindus'. See Pradhan (1999) and Pati (2001).

62. Ayodhya in Uttar Pradesh, a state in northern India, is the alleged\mythic birthplace of Rama, a sacrosanct Hindu deity. In 1992, Hindu militants demolished the 16th century Babri Masjid (mosque), pledging to avenge the history of Muslim conquest in India by building a temple to Rama at the site. The ruin impelled intense communal rioting. See Desai (2002).

63. An anthropological, sociological and political term that refers to the process of acculturation and assimilation of non-Hindu communities into Hindu customs and values, endangering linguistic and cultural diversity.

64. See S. Sarkar (2002) and Pati (2003) for an excavation of conversions historically.

65. Research notes. I attended the meeting at which Praveen Togadia spoke.

66. Saffron (identified with Hindutva). Saffronization implies 'making saffron', the implementation and strengthening of Hindutva. See Hansen (2001).

67. For a history of conversions in Orissa, see Pati (2003).

68. Personal communication (2003).

69. This section draws on Banerjee (2003) and personal communication with VHP, RSS, Bajrang Dal leaders and other informants. Informants that corroborated the information about Sangh organizations in Orissa explicitly requested that I not disclose names.

70. Literally, Ram's birthplace. Movement for a Hindu temple in Ayodhya.

71. Literally, a place for wrestling. Bajrang Dal akharas are centres for Dal activity and training.

72. This draws on Banerjee (2003) and personal communications with VHP, RSS, Bajrang Dal leaders and other informants.

73. Hindu deity.

74. Hindu deity.

75. 'Thackeray's Idea This Dussehra: Let's Have Hindu Suicide Squads', *Indian Express*, 16 October 2002 at http://www.indianexpress.com/full_story. php?content_id=11420. Last accessed June 2004.

76. Personal communication with Sangh organizations and informants in Orissa (2003 and 2004).

77. Biju affiliated People's Party. The BJD was formed by Navin Patnaik, currently chief minister, after he broke with the left inclined Janata Dal.

78. Chaudhuri (1998). Also see Election Commission of India website, http://archive.eci.gov.in.

79. Chaudhuri (2000). Also see Election Commission of India website, http://archive.eci.gov.in.

80. Personal communication, 1999.

81. This section draws on personal communications with VHP, RSS, Bajrang Dal leaders and other informants.

82. Weapon used by the mythological Shiv, it is utilized by the Sangh to signify Hindu militancy. See 'Used Out of Turn', *The Telegraph*, 10 May 2003 at http://www.telegraphindia.com/1030510/asp/opinion/story_1953490.asp. Last accessed June 2004.

83. Personal communication, 2003.

84. Personal communication, 2003.

85. Personal communication (2004).

86. Personal communication (2004).

87. Personal communication (2004).

88. Affiliated with the Naxalilte militant Adivasi and peasant movement constituted of predominantly landless and marginalized cultivators that emerged in the Naxalbari region of Darjeeling in the late 1960s and spread to other areas of West Bengal, and on to Bihar, Orissa, Madhya Pradesh, Andhra Pradesh, less visibly in Uttar Pradesh, and Maharashtra, extensively in the three new tribal states (formed in 2000) of Chhattisgarh and Jharkhand, and parts of Uttaranchal. Initially most of the Naxal leaders came from the pro-Beijing/Peking CPI (Marxist) party. Naxalites acknowledged the inspiration of the Chinese revolution and in May 1969 formed their own party, the CPI (Marxist-Leninist). These demarcations have grown to include over fourteen distinct and often severely fragmented groups, including those with Marxist-Communist and Marxist-Leninist-Liberation affiliations. Targeted by state and central governments and the military as anti-national since the 1970s, Naxalites promoted the organization of working classes for the annexation of state power. The movement has enabled tremendous opportunities for political emancipation even as it has been laden with problems. See Bhatia (2000), Duyker (1987) and Chatterji (1996).

89. For caste and lineage structures in Orissa, see Pati (2001) and Singh (1995).

90. Personal communication (2004).

91. FAO (1998). South Asia is home to 51 million indigenous peoples, a majority of whom live in India (see Bodley 1999, Devi 2002). In September 1958, India ratified the International Labour Organization (ILO) Convention 107 of 1957 relating to Indigenous and Tribal Populations. Convention 107 is integrationist in character and attests to tribal rights based on a framework of indigenous 'populations' rather than 'peoples'. In 1989, ILO revised the provisions of 107, and issued Convention 169, concerning Indigenous and Tribal Peoples in Independent Countries. The ILO Convention 169 acknowledges indigenous cultures as distinct organized societies with specific identities and recognizes

them as 'peoples' (ILO 2004). The recognition of indigenous 'peoples' allows tribes the right to negotiate for 'sovereignty' with states in which they are situated. Sovereignty, in relation to the modern nation-state, was conceptually framed in response to times when society was comprised of rulers and unequal subjects. With the Treaty of Westphalia in 1648, sovereignty became central to determining the sanctity of national and international parameters and relations. For sovereignty to function in the present, it assumes states as egalitarian, democratically responsible to their citizens and peoples. In its infinitude, veritable sovereignty rests with people, attainable through their action, operable constitutionally through (democratically) elected governments. When governments fail to act justly or enforce the rights of citizens and peoples within its borders, resource rests with people, and the interventions of the international community. While international interventions can be necessary, they too function in the context of power dynamics between nations governed by global racism and historically positioned inequities, and can lead to dangerous, unilateral and undemocratic actions, as in the case of United States invasions of Afghanistan (2001) and Iraq (2003), authorizing Empire. Relations that determine action/inaction on the part of the international community are intricate and immersed in realpolitik, customarily invested in the maintenance of the territorial integrity of states. The defining of 'integrity' precludes conceding sovereignty to indigenous peoples, as confirmed by the persistent refusal of the international community to take a stand for the rights of indigenous peoples. In this milieu, Convention 169 is significant in its acknowledgement of the rights of indigenous peoples within states, even as its implementation is scarce. See Soros (2003). Also see Anaya (1996), Dean and Levi (2003) and Niezen (2003).

92. Personal communication (2001).
93. Personal communication (2004).
94. For other examples, see National Alliance of People's Movements, Press Note, 21 February 2003, New Delhi.
95. Constitutional provisions that allow for partial tribal governance in Schedule V areas, while tribal governance through autonomous tribal councils are constitutionally stipulated in areas under Schedule VI. The Fifth Schedule extends to Koraput, Mayurbhanj, Sundargarh (entire districts), and Balasore, Bolangir, Boudhkondmals, Ganjam, Kalahandi, Keonjhar, Rayagada, Sambalpur (parts of districts) in Orissa; personal communication with Vasundhara in 2002 and 2003 (includes conversations held in person, over phone and via electronic mail with various members of the Vasundhara team). Also see Chatterji (2006) and Sarin (2003).
96. Sterlite's finances are generated from its partner company, Vedanta Resources. Vedanta, launched in London in December 2003, and Sterlite, are both operated by non-resident Indians. See Padel and Das (2004). Sterlite has a controversial history. Anil Agarwal, chairperson and managing director, has denied knowledge of the Samata judgement in the past. See Bidwai (2001).

97. Personal communication (2004).

98. Personal communication (2004).

99. Such inequities resonate across the nation where poor rural women labour 1.5 workdays. See Rao (2003).

100. Women's empowerment is a complex process, even when political allocations are made, such as at the panchayat level where government quotas require that a certain percentage of seats be reserved for female occupancy. (Since the 73rd Constitutional Amendment in 1992, 33 per cent of all seats at the panchayat level have been reserved for women.) Men dominate the panchayats, and female panchayat members are usually nominated by local male political leaders, who exercise considerable control over them. Women representatives, often selected from general caste communities, have little political experience or literacy, making it easier for other panchayat members to manipulate them. Women say that this is an important step towards their empowerment, both problematic and necessary, which allows for access and visibility that authorizes the capacity for empowerment. I would submit that the process via which empowerment is 'discerned' must be negotiated to make visible the spaces in which courage is enacted by women.

101. The literacy rate in Orissa is 49.09 per cent, with female literacy rates at 34.68 per cent and male literacy rates at 63.09 per cent. See Chatterji (2006).

102. Figures show that the Eighth and Ninth Plan outlays increased from Rs 10,000.00 crores (Rs 10 million) in 1992–97, to 15,000.00 crores (Rs 15 million) in 1997–2002, as did the net domestic product of Orissa from Rs 4,913 crores (Rs 49.13 billion) in 1994–95, to Rs 6,411 crores (Rs 64.11 billion) in 1999–2000. Tertiary and service sectors have maintained a steady increase since 1993, while primary and secondary sectors have witnessed a spiked performance (Government of Orissa 2000). Yet, in March 2002, Orissa's debt amounted to Rs 240 billion, more than 61 per cent of the gross domestic product of the state. In 2001–2, the government of Orissa signed a memorandum of understanding (MoU) with New Delhi to secure a structural adjustment loan of Rs 3,000 crore (Rs 30 billion) from the World Bank (In December 2003, the World Bank's office in New Delhi announced that it would double infrastructure lending in India within the next two years, including a re-engagement with large dams [See Bossard 2004], and an aid package of Rs 200 crore (Rs 2 billion) from the Department For International Development, the overseas development branch of the government of the United Kingdom [Chatterji 2006]). This is conditional assistance, one that will facilitate further corporatization, laden with extensive and hazardous consequences.

103. Rupee: Between 2000–4, the exchange rate has varied between INR 44–50 = US $1. See 'Mother Sells 45 Day Old Baby for Rs [rupees] 60',

Indian Express, 12 July 2003. Available at: http://www.newindpress.com/ Newsitems.asp?ID=IEQ20030710132755&Page=Q&Title=ORISSA&rL ink=0. Last accessed June 2004.

104. Hectare: A unit for measurement of land. 1 hectare equals 2.47 acres, and 1 acre equals 0.40 hectares.

105. For a discussion of land reforms, see Sinha and Pushpendra (2000).

106. From the former state of Mayurbhanj.

107. See World Bank (2000). In independent India, the panchayat system of government, or Panchayati Raj (rule), refers to the three-tier structure of local governing bodies from village to district level; *gram* (village), *samati* (block—a collective administrative unit constituted a group of villages), and *zilla* (district—an administrative unit constituting a group of blocks).

108. This figure shifts with the demarcation of new villages or the merger of existing ones.

109. Conversations with Rajendra K. Sarangi (2003), and Vasundhara (2003).

110. Carrying (on their heads) bundles of timber and firewood for sale.

111. This information was gathered through personal communication with community groups and non-governmental organizations between 1995–04.

112. Personal communication, 1999.

113. Personal communication, 2003.

114. Personal communication with Sangh Parivar leaders, 2003. Also see, Hansen (2001) and Amin (2002).

115. For an accounting of structures of normalization, see Foucault (1978a).

116. Personal communication, 2004.

117. After Gujarat.

118. Personal communication, 2003.

119. Personal communication, 2003.

120. Language spoken in Orissa.

121. Personal communication, 2003.

122. See 'Murder in the Cathedral', 19 May 2003, Times News Network. Available at: http://timesofindia.indiatimes.com/cms.dll/html/uncomp/ articleshow?msid=46674913. Last accessed June 2004.

123. District in Orissa.

124. Despite international movements to abolish the death penalty and United Nations Commission on Human Rights resolutions (since 1997, signed in 2004 by seventy-six member states) calling for countries using the death penalty to freeze executions, India, like the United States, continues to impose the penalty. See 'The Death Penalty', Amnesty International, 2004. Available at: http://web.amnesty.org/pages/deathpenalty-index-eng. Last accessed June 2004.

125. 'Dara, 12 Others Convicted for Killing Staines: Sentence on September 22', *The Tribune*, 15 September 2003. Available at: http://www.

tribuneindia.com/2003/20030916/main1.htm. Last accessed June 2004. Also see 'Humanity Not Yet Fully Civilized: Judge', Press Trust of India, 23 September 2003. Available at: http://www.rediff.com/news/2003/sep/23staines.htm. Last accessed June 2004.

126. Hari (lit. Hindu deity) *Katha* (lit. words) *Yojana* (lit. planning). Hari Katha Yojana: centres where Hindu scriptures are read and devotional songs are offered in prayer.

127. Personal communication, 2003.

128. 'Reconversion' presupposes that Adivasis and Dalits were 'originally' Hindus.

129. Personal communication, 2004. What defines terror is consecrated to the custody of the state. The landscape of citizenship shifted dramatically post 9\11, aiding the scapegoating of Muslims and other minorities in India. The Hindu nationalist Indian government introduced the Prevention of Terrorism Ordinance in 2002 (later Prevention of Terrorism Act, POTA), a modified security law empowering the government to torture and detain minority groups, and political opponents perceived to engage in terrorism. The Congress Party in its election (2004) manifesto promised to repeal POTA. Post elections, the Congress Party reiterated this commitment in light of the findings of the People's Tribunal on POTA that described the abject misuse of POTA to target minorities across the nation. The resolve of the international coalition of nations committed to fighting 'terror' witnessed instead the revenging of innocent lives, the undermining of civil liberties, and the erosion of international law. See 'People's Tribunal on Prevention of Terrorism Act (POTA) and other Central Security Legislations', 13–14 March 2004, Indian Social Institute, New Delhi.

130. Personal communication, 2004.

131. Personal communication, 2004.

132. All quotes from personal communication, 2004.

133. Personal communication, 1998.

134. Personal communication, 1998.

135. Personal communication, 2003.

136. I write this influenced by Jacques Derrida's evocative *The Work of Mourning* (2001).

137. Personal communication, 2004.

138. Personal communication, 2004.

139. Personal communication, 2003.

140. Personal communication, 2003.

141. For a discussion of gender and power in the construction of citizenship in India, see Thapan (1997). For a discussion of patriarchy and colonial society in the shaping of gender, see Sangari and Vaid (1989).

142. For a conceptual elaboration, see Visweswaran (1996).

143. See Chatterjee (1989) as he speaks to the colonial and Indian nationalist

imaginary of women. Also see, Bacchetta (1996), Bacchetta and Power (2002), Menon (2000), Puri (2004), Sarkar and Butalia (1995), and Visweswaran (1996).

144. For a conceptual elaboration, see Moghadam (1997).

145. See 'Prologue' to this essay.

146. In 1975, Shah Bano, a sixty-two-year-old Muslim woman from Madhya Pradesh, was divorced, after being married for forty-three years, by her husband. She filed a petition in 1978, claiming that she had a right to maintenance under Section 125 of the Code of Criminal Procedure. The Supreme Court, in the *Mohammad Ahmed Khan* versus *Shah Bano Begum & Others case* [A.I.R. 1985 S.C. 945], ruled affirmatively in 1985 on Shah Bano's request to secure maintenance from her husband, contradicting aspects of Muslim Personal Law. In doing so, the Court controversially advocated for a Uniform (Common) Civil Code, stating that: 'A common civil code will help the cause of national integration by removing disparate loyalties in laws which have conflicting ideologies' (Hasan 1999: 126).

147. Orissa passed the Dowry Prohibition Act in 1991, while its implementation remains restricted across class and ethnic groupings in the state.

148. Marry and divorce someone else, before remarrying Sher Ali.

149. I met with members of Najma Bibi's family and Sofia Seikh, a local Muslim feminist leader in Bhadrak, as well as Asha Hans, Professor of Women's Studies at Utkal University and other feminists, and with progressive Muslim men from various organizations in Bhardark and Bhubaneswar, in July 2004.

150. See Bacchetta (2001) for women's resistance to Hindu nationalism. For a discussion of issues relating to the feminist movement in India, see Kumar (1993). 'Disfigure', see Hooks (1994). See Samiuddin and Khanam (2002) for issues in Muslim feminism.

151. This section draws on personal communications with VHP, RSS, Bajrang Dal leaders and other informants.

152. Personal communication with Bidyut Lata Raja, leader of Rashtriya Sevika Samiti, 2004.

153. For allied discussions, see Alexander and Mohanty (1997), Mohanty et al. (1991) and Butler (1992, 1999). Also see, Jayawardena and de Alwis (1996).

154. Personal communication (2004).

155. Education centres.

156. Devotional songs.

157. Personal communication, 2003 and 2004.

158. Hinduized Oriya tribal god. Also spelt Jagannatha. See Mishra (1984).

159. Cultural and youth centres.

160. See 'Re-Animating the Age-Old Faith', 2003. Available at: http://wwww.hindubooks.org/Vision.ch3.html. Last accessed June 2004. This section

draws on personal communications with VHP, RSS, Bajrang Dal leaders and other informants.

161. Celebration of Ram and his revered assistant.

162. Notes from Ashghar Ali Engineer, 2004, and personal communication with Orissa activists, 2003. For an elaboration of police complicity in communal violence, see Khalidi (2003).

163. See 'Re-Animating the Age-Old Faith'. For details see note 160 above.

164. Educations centre(s) for children.

165. Personal communication, 2002.

166. Personal communications with VHP, RSS, Bajrang Dal leaders and informants, 2003.

167. See Anant (2002) and Bhatnagar (2004). Also see, Bureau of Democracy, Human Rights and Labour (2003).

168. Personal communication, 2003, 2004.

169. Islamic schools offering orthodox education. Even while, on occasion, madrasahs offer fundamentalist training, it is critical to caution against generalizations.

170. Personal communication, 2003.

171. Shearer (2003). For history, see Galeano's powerful treatise, *Open Veins of Latin America* (1973), and Chomsky (1988).

172. Personal communication, 2002, 2003 and 2004.

173. Personal communication, 2004.

174. Personal communication, 2003.

175. One teacher schools.

176. Personal communication with Adivasi and Dalit leaders in Dhenkanal and Rayagada, 2002.

177. Personal communication, 2003.

178. Personal communication, 2002.

179. See Rushdie (1991). He speaks of the 'bastard children of history' in the collision of history. Also see Said (1993) and Prasad (2000).

180. The Citizens' Tribunal has charged that such efforts facilitated the mobilization of Adivasis against other minorities in Gujarat, where Vanvasi Kalyan Parishad and Vivekananda Kendra, funded by IDRF, were both held complicit in the communalization of Adivasis. See Citizens for Justice and Peace (2002).

181. Two reports—one entitled 'A Foreign Exchange of Hate: IDRF and the American Funding of Hindutva' assembled by the Campaign To Stop Funding Hate in the United States (in November 2002), and the other 'In Bad Faith: British Charity and Hindu Extremism' by Awaaz, a citizens group, in the United Kingdom (in February 2004)—have highlighted the nature of Sangh Parivar funding from diaspora. The US Commission on International Religious Freedom recently designated India as a 'country of particular concern', asking for US investigations into RSS organizations

registered as charities in the US. See Sabrang Communications (2002) and Awaaz (2004).

182. This draws on Banerjee (2003) and personal communication with VHP, RSS, Bajrang Dal leaders and other informants.

183. Ibid. Also draws from personal communication with VHP, RSS, Bajrang Dal leaders and other informants.

184. This draws on personal communication with the Vasundhara team and journalists in Bhubaneswar in January 2004.

185. Here 'reconversion' is the means of dispossessing Adivasis from the remedial rights provided under the Constitution for 'reserved' class. 'Reservation' refers to provisions for affirmative action for disenfranchised groups.

186. This draws on personal communication with educationists, social movement activists, VHP, RSS, Bajrang Dal leaders and other informants.

187. Personal communication, 2004.

188. This draws on personal communication with Sangh Parivar leaders and other informants.

189. Personal communication, 2004.

190. Personal communication, 2003.

191. People's movements in Orissa elaborate the distinctions between subsistence, well-being and income generation. Leaders confirm that people's aspirations are linked to the achievability and sustainability of well-being. Subsistence refers to minimum requirements for living. Well-being assumes access to resources that permit individual labour and collective energy to devote themselves to the maintenance and development of culture and community. Well-being indicates a space beyond 'survival', from the realm of necessity to that of freedom. For an elaboration on the realm of necessity and the realm of freedom, see Marx (1981). For an explanation of well-being, see Naussbaum and Glover (1995).

192. I participated in this meeting.

193. Personal communication, 2004.

194. Personal communication, 2004.

195. Personal communication, 2004.

196. Personal communication, 2004.

197. And privileged in the context of a Hindu majority state in India.

198. Personal communication, 2002.

REFERENCES

Agnes, Flavia (1999). *Law and Gender Inequality.* New Delhi: Oxford University Press.

———— (2001). *Judgement Call.* Mumbai: Majlis.

Ahmad, Aijaz (2002). *On Communalism and Globalization: Offensives of the Far Right.* New Delhi: Three Essays Press.

Akbar, M.J. (1985). *India: The Siege Within. Challenges to a Nation's Unity*. New Delhi: Penguin Books.

Alexander, M., Jacqui and Chandra Talpade Mohanty (eds) (1997). *Feminist Genealogies, Colonial Legacies, Democratic Futures*. New York: Routledge.

Amin, Sahid (2002). 'On Retelling Muslim Conquest in North India', in Partha Chatterjee and Anjan Ghosh (eds), *History and the Present*, pp. 24–43. New Delhi: Permanent Black.

Anant, Arpita (2002). 'Anti-Conversion Laws', *The Hindu*, 17 December 2002. Available at http://www.hindu.com/thehindu/op/2002/12/17/stories/2002121700110200.htm. Last accessed June 2004.

Anaya, S. James (1996). *Indigenous Peoples in International Law*. New York: Oxford University Press.

Ansari, Iqbal, A. (ed.) (1997). *Communal Riots: The State and Law in India*. New Delhi: Institute of Objective Studies.

Appadurai, Arjun (1996). *Modernity At Large: Cultural Dimensions of Globalization*. Minneapolis: University of Minnesota Press.

Arendt, Hannah (1963). *On Revolution*. Harmondsworth: Penguin Books.

Awaaz, South Asia Watch Limited (2004). *In Bad Faith? British Charity & Hindu Extremism*. London: Awaaz—South Asia Watch Limited. Available at: http://www.awaazsaw.org/ibf/. Last accessed June 2004.

Bacchetta, Paola (1996). 'Hindu Nationalist Women as Ideologues', in Kumari Jayawardena and Malathi de Alwis (eds), *Embodied Violence: Communalizing Women's Sexuality in South Asia*, pp. 126–67. London and New Jersey: Zed Books.

——— (2001). 'Extraordinary Alliances in Crisis Situations: Women against Hindu Nationalism in India', in Kathleen M. Blee and France Winddance Twine (eds), *Feminism and Antiracism: International Struggles for Justice*, pp. 220–49. New York: New York University Press.

Bacchetta, Paola and Margaret Power (eds) (2002). *Right-Wing Women: From Conservatives to Extremists Around the World*. New York: Routledge.

Banerjee, Ruben (2003). 'Spread of Saffron', *India Today*, 27 January, New Delhi.

Basu, Shamita (2002). *Religious Revivalism as Nationalist Discourse: Swami Vivekananda and New Hinduism in Nineteenth-Century Bengal*. New Delhi: Oxford University Press.

Basu, Srimati (2003). 'Shading the Secular: Law at Work In The Indian Higher Courts', *Cultural Dynamics*, 15(2):131–52.

Bhabha, Homi, K. (1994). *The Location of Culture*. New York: Routledge.

——— (ed.) (2002). *Nation and Narration*. New York: Routledge

Bhargava, Rajeev (1996). 'How Not to Defend Secularism', in Praful Bidwai, Harbans Mukhia, Achin Vanaik (eds), *Religion, Religiosity and Communalism*, 57–74. New Delhi: Manohar Publishers.

Bhatia, Bela (2000). 'The Naxalite Movement in Central Bihar', Doctoral Dissertation, University of Cambridge, Cambridge.

Bhatt, Chetan (2001). *Hindu Nationalism Origins, Ideologies and Modern Myths*. New York: Oxford University Press.

Bhatnagar, Rakesh (2004). 'Nobody Has Right to Convert', *The Times of India*, 20 June 2004. Available at http://timesofindia.indiatimes.com/cms.dll/html/uncomp/articleshow?msid=162018. Last accessed June 2004.

Bidwai, Praful (2001). 'Of Sleazy, Criminalized Capitalism', *Frontline*, May 2001, pp. 12–25, New Delhi.

Bidwai, Praful, Harbans Mukhia, Achin Vanaik (eds) (1996). *Religion, Religiosity and Communalism*. New Delhi: Manohar Publishers.

Bodley, John, H. (1999). *Victims of Progress*. Fourth Edition. Mountain View: Mayfield Publishing Company.

Bossard, Peter (2004). *The World Bank at 60: A Case of Institutional Amnesia?* Berkeley: International Rivers Network.

Boulton, John (1979). 'Nationalism and Tradition in Orissa', in R.J. Moore (ed.), *Tradition and Politics in South Asia*, pp. 227–60. New Delhi: Vikas Publishing House.

Brass, Paul R. (1985). *Caste, Faction and Party in Indian Politics*. Volume 1. Delhi: Chanakya Books.

Brink, Judy and Joan Mencher (eds) (1996). *Mixed Blessings Gender and Religious Fundamentalism Cross Culturally*. New York: Routledge.

Bureau of Democracy, Human Rights and Labour (2003). *India. International Religious Freedom Report* Bureau of Democracy, Human Rights and Labour, United States Department of State. Available at: http://www.state.gov/g/drl/rls/irf/2003/24470.htm. Last accessed June 2004.

Butalia, Urvashi (2000). *The Other Side of Silence: Voices from the Partition of India*. Durham: Duke University Press.

Butler, Judith (1992). 'Contingent Foundations', in Judith Butler and J.W. Scott (eds), *Feminists Theorize the Political*, pp. 3–21. New York and London: Routledge.

———— (1999). *Gender Trouble: Feminism and the Subversion of Identity*. London and New York: Routledge.

Césaire, Aimé (2000). *Discourse on Colonialism*. Translated by Joan Pinkham and introduced by Robin D. G. Kelley). New York: Monthly Review Press.

Chakrabarty, Dipesh (2002). *Habitations of Modernity: Essays in the Wake of Subaltern Studies*. Chicago: The University of Chicago Press.

Chakravarti, Uma and Nandita Haksar (1987). *The Delhi Riots: Three Days In The Life Of A Nation*. New Delhi: Lancer International.

Chatterjee, Partha (1986). *Nationalist Thought and the Colonial World: A Derivative Discourse*. London: Zed Books.

———— (1989). 'The Nationalist Resolution of the Women's Question', in Kumkum Sangari and Sudesh Vaid (eds), *Recasting Women: Essays in Colonial History*, pp. 233–53. New Delhi: Kali for Women.

———— (1993). *The Nation and Its Fragments*. Princeton: Princeton University Press.

———— (ed.) (1997). *State and Politics in India: Themes in Politics.* New Delhi: Oxford University Press.

———— (1998). *A Possible India: Essays in Political Criticism.* New Delhi: Oxford University Press.

Chatterji, Angana, P. (1996). *Community Forest Management in Arabari: Understanding Sociocultural and Subsistence Issues.* New Delhi: Society for Promotion of Wastelands Development and Ford Foundation.

———— (1998). *Toward An Ecology of Hope: Community and Joint Forest Management in Orissa.* Berkeley: Asia Forest Network.

———— (2002). 'Gujarat: A Call for Kristallnacht?' *The Daily Times*, 22 December 2002, Lahore.

———— (2006). *Land and Justice: The Struggle for Cultural Survival.*

Chatterji, Angana, P. and Richard Shapiro (2011). 'Knowledge Making as Intervention: The Academy and Social Change', in Bunyan Bryant (ed.), *A Collection on Environmental Justice and Human Rights*, pp. 169–92. University of Michigan, Ann Arbor.

Chattopadhyay, Suhrid, Sankar (2004). 'Saffronizing the Tribal Belt', *Frontline*, 13–26 March, New Delhi.

Chaudhuri, Kalyan (1998). 'Elections '98. Messages from the States', *Frontline*, 15(6), 21 March–3 April, New Delhi.

———— (2000). 'On A Roll In Orissa', *Frontline*, 4–17 March, New Delhi.

Chomsky, Noam (1988). *The Culture of Terrorism.* Boston: South End Press.

Citizens for Justice and Peace (2002). *An Inquiry Into The Carnage In Gujarat: Concerned Citizens Tribunal, Gujarat 2002.* Mumbai: Citizens for Justice and Peace.

Copley, Antony (2003). *Hinduism in Public and Private: Reform, Hindutva, Gender and Sampraday.* New York: Oxford University Press.

Dalmia, Vasudha (1997). *The Nationalization of Hindu Traditions: Bharatendu Harischandra and Nineteenth Century Banaras.* New Delhi: Oxford University Press.

———— (2003). *Orienting India: European Knowledge Formation in the Eighteenth and Nineteenth Centuries.* New Delhi: Three Essays Collective.

Das, Prafulla (2002). 'VHP, Bajrang Dal Men Strom Orissa Assembly', *The Hindu*, 17 March 2002 at http://www.hinduonnet.com/thehindu/2002/03/17/stories/2002031706010100.htm. Last accessed June 2004.

Dean, Bartholomew and Jerome M. Levi (eds) (2003). *At the Risk of Being Heard: Identity, Indigenous Rights, and Postcolonial States.* Ann Arbor: University of Michigan Press.

Derrida, Jacques (1993). 'Circumfession: Fifty-nine Periods and Periphrases', in Geoffrey Bennington and Jacques Derrida, *Jacques Derrida*, p. 194. Chicago: The University of Chicago Press.

———— (1994). *Specters of Marx: The State of the Debt, the Work of Mourning, & the New International.* New York: Routledge.

———— (2001). *The Work of Mourning.* Chicago: The University of Chicago Press.

Desai, Radhika (2002). *Slouching Toward Ayodhya*. New Delhi: Three Essays Collective.

Deshpande, Satish (2000). 'Hegemonic Spatial Strategies: The Nation-Space and Hindu Communalism in Twentieth-Century India', in Partha Chatterjee and Pradeep Jeganathan (eds), *Community, Gender and Violence. Subaltern Studies XI*, pp. 167–211. New York: Columbia University Press.

Devi, Mahasweta (1995). *Imaginary Maps* (Translated and introduced by Gayatri Chakravorty Spivak). New York: Routledge.

——— (2002). 'India's Denotified Tribes', *IndiaTogether*, March 2002. Available at http://www.indiatogether.org. Last accessed June 2004.

Dutta, Madhusree, Flavia Agnes and Neera Adarkar (1996). *The Nation, The State and Indian Identity*. Calcutta: Samya Publications.

Duyker, Edward (1987). *Tribal Guerrillas: The Santal of West Bengal and the Naxalite Movement*. New Delhi: Oxford University Press.

Elst, Koenraad (1999). *Update On The Aryan Invasion Debate*. New Delhi: Aditya Prakashan.

Engineer, Asghar, Ali (ed.) (1997). *Communal Riots in Post-Independence India*. Hyderabad: Sangam Books.

——— (2003). *Communal Challenge and Secular Response*. Delhi: Shipra Publications.

Escobar, Arturo (1995). *Encountering Development: The Making and Unmaking of the Third World*. Princeton: Princeton University Press.

Esteva, Gustavo (1997). 'Development', in Wolfgang Sachs (ed.), *The Development Dictionary: A Guide to Knowledge as Power*, pp. 9–10. New Jersey: Zed Books.

Food and Agricultural Organization (FAO) (1998). *India: Overview of Socio-Economic Situation of the Tribal Communities and Livelihoods in Madhya Pradesh and Bihar*. Available at: http://www.fao.org/tc/tci/SocProj/india.htm. Last accessed June 2004.

Foucault, Michel (1972). *The Archaeology of Knowledge*. New York: Pantheon Press.

——— (1977). 'Nietzsche, Genealogy, History', in *Language, Counter-Memory, Practice. Selected Essays and Interviews by Michel Foucault*. (Edited, with an introduction by Donald F. Bouchard.) Ithica: Cornell University Press.

——— (1978a). *Discipline and Punish*. New York: Pantheon Press.

——— (1978b). *The History of Sexuality, Volume I: An Introduction*. New York: Random House.

——— (1980a). 'Two Lectures', in *Power/Knowledge*, pp. 78–108. New York: Pantheon Press.

——— (1980b). 'Truth and Power', in *Power/Knowledge*, pp. 109–133. New York: Pantheon Press.

——— (1994). 'Governmentality', in James Faubion (ed.), *Power: Essential Works of Michel Foucault, 1954–1894*. New York: The New Press.

Galeano, Eduardo (1973). *Open Veins of Latin America: Five Centuries of the Pillage of a Continent*. Translated by Cedric Belfrage. Mexico: Siglo Xxi Editores.

Goldberg, David, Theo and Ato Quayson (2002). *Relocating Postcolonialism.* Oxford: Blackwell Publishers.

Gopal, Giridhar (2003). 'Orissa May Ban Trident Distribution', *Rediff,* 14 June.

Government of India (2001). *Census Handbook* (Orissa Series.) New Delhi: Government of India.

Government of Orissa (2000). *Industrial Policy Resolution.* Bhubaneswar: Government of Orissa.

Gupta, Dipankar (2000). *Interrogating Caste: Understanding Hierarchy and Difference in Indian Society.* New Delhi: Penguin Books.

Habib, Irfan (1995). *Essays in Indian History: Towards a Marxist Perspective.* New Delhi: Tulika.

Hansen, Thomas, Blom (2001). *The Saffron Wave: Democracy and Hindu Nationalism in India.* New Delhi: Oxford University Press.

Hansen, Thomas, Blom and Christophe Jaffrelot (eds) (1998). *The Compulsions of Politics: The BJP and Competitive Politics in India.* New Delhi: Oxford University Press.

Hasan, Mushirul (1991). *Nationalism and Communal Politics in India: 1916–1928.* New Delhi: Oxford University Press.

Hasan, Zoya (1989). *Dominance and Mobilization: Rural Politics in Western Uttar Pradesh, 1930–80.* New Delhi: Sage Publications.

———— (1999). 'Muslim Women and the Debate on Legal Reforms', in Bharati Ray and Aparna Basu (eds), *From Independence Towards Freedom: Indian Women Since 1947,* pp. 120–34. New Delhi: Oxford University Press.

Hooks, Bell (1994). *Outlaw Culture: Resisting Representations.* New York: Routledge.

Human Rights Watch (2002). *World Report 2002.* New York: Human Rights Watch.

International Initiative for Justice (2003). *Threatened Existence: A Feminist Analysis of the Genocide in Gujarat. Report by the International Initiative for Justice.* Available at: http://www.onlinevolunteers.org/gujarat/reports/iijg/2003/. Last accessed June 2004.

International Labour Organization (ILO) (2004). *Convention No. 169 on Indigenous Peoples.* Available at http://www.ilo.org/public/english/standards/norm/whatare/stndards/indig.htm. Last accessed June 2004.

Jaffrelot, Christophe (1996). *The Hindu Nationalist Movement and Indian Politics, 1925–1994: Social and Political Strategies.* London: C. Hurst and Company.

Jalal, Ayesha (1995). *Democracy and Authoritarianism in South Asia: A Comparative and Historical Perspective.* Cambridge: Cambridge University Press.

———— (2000). *Self and Sovereignty: Individual and Community in South Asian Islam since 1850s.* New York: Routledge.

Jalal, Ayesha and Sugata Bose (1997). *Nationalism, Democracy and Development: State and Politics in India.* Delhi: Oxford University Press.

———— (1998). *Modern South Asian History, Culture, Political Economy.* London: Routledge.

Jayawardena, Kumari and Malathi de Alwis (eds) (1996). *Embodied Violence: Communalizing Women's Sexuality in South Asia*. London and New Jersey: Zed Books.

Jena, Mihir, Padmini Pathi, Jagganath Dash, Kamala Patnaik, and Klaus Seeland (2002). *Forest Tribes of Orissa, Volume 1: The Dongaria Kondh*. New Delhi: D.K. Printworld.

Jha, D.N. (2002). *The Myth of the Holy Cow*. London: Verso.

Jhingran, Saral (1996). 'Religion and Communalism', in Praful Bidwai, Harbans Mukhia and Achin Vanaik (eds), *Religion, Religiosity and Communalism*, pp. 75–86. New Delhi: Manohar Publishers.

Kandiyoti, Deniz (1997). 'Bargaining With Patriarchy', in Nalini Visvanathan, Lynn Duggan, Laurie Nisonoff, and N. Wiegersma (eds), *The Women, Gender and Development Reader*, pp. 86–92. London: Zed Books.

Khalidi, Omar (2003). *Khaki and the Ethnic Violence in India: Army, Police and Paramilitary Forces During Communal Riots*. New Delhi: Three Essays Collective.

Kumar, Radha (1993). *The History of Doing: An Illustrated Account of Movements for Women's Rights and Feminism in India, 1800–1990*. New Delhi: Kali for Women.

———— (1994). 'Identity Politics and the Contemporary Indian Feminist Movement', in Valentine Moghadam (ed.), *Identity Politics and Women: Cultural Reassertions and Feminisms in International Perspective*. Oxford: Westview Press.

Kumar, Sanjay (2002). 'The Adivasis of Orissa' (from a study by the Centre for The Study of Developing Societies), *The Hindu*, 6 November, New Delhi.

Lacan, Jacques (1982). 'Seminar of 21 January 1975', in J. Mitchell and J. Rose (eds), *Feminine Sexuality*. London: Routledge and Kegan Paul.

Mahapatra, L.K. (1999). *Tribal Rights to Land and the State in Orissa. In Contemporary Society: Tribal Studies. Volume III: Social Concern*. New Delhi: Concept Publishing Company.

Mahtab, Harekrishna, Prabhat Mukherjee, Sushil De and Sudhakar Patnaik (eds) (1959). *History of The Freedom Movement in Orissa. Volumes I through V*. Cuttack: Manmohan Press.

Majid, Anouar (2000). *Unveiling Traditions. Postcolonial Islam in a Polycentric World*. Durham: Duke University Press.

Marx, Karl (1972). *The Marx-Engels Reader* (Edited by Robert C. Tucker). New York: W.W. Norton & Company.

———— (1981). *Capital. Volume 3*. New York: Penguin Books.

McClintock, Anne, Aamir Mufti and Ella Shohat (eds) (1997). *Dangerous Liaisons: Gender, Nation and Postcolonial Perspectives*. Minneapolis: University of Minnesota Press.

Menon, Nivedita (2000). 'Embodying the Self: Feminism Sexual Violence and the Law', in Partha Chatterjee and Pradeep Jeganathan (eds), *Community, Gender and Violence. Subaltern Studies XI*, pp. 66–105. New York: Columbia University Press.

Mishra, K.C. (1984). *The Cult of Jagannatha.* Calcutta: Firma KLM Private Limited.

Moghadam, Valentine (ed.) (1994). *Identity Politics and Women: Cultural Reassertions and Feminisms in International Perspective.* Oxford: Westview Press.

——— (2002). 'Women's Rights in Afghanistan: Progress? In Perihelion' (Associated with the European Rim Policy and Investment Council), at http://www.erpic.org/perihelion/articles2002/december/afghanistan.htm. Last accessed June 2004.

——— (1997). 'Gender and Revolutions', in John Foran (ed.), *Theorizing Revolutions,* pp. 137–67. London: Routledge.

Mohanty, Chandra, Talapade, Ann Russo and Lourdes Torres (eds) (1991). *Third World Women and the Politics of Feminism.* Bloomington: Indiana University Press.

Mohanty, Debabrata (2003). 'Sangh Sings BJP Tune to Woo Tribals', *The Telegraph,* 29 December 2003, at http://www.telegraphindia.com/1031229/asp/nation/story_2729415.asp. Last accessed June 2004.

——— (2004). 'New Lease of Life', *The Telegraph,* 1 June 2004 at http://www.telegraphindia.com/1040601/asp/opinion/story_3290299.asp. Last accessed June 2004.

Nair, Janaki (1994). 'On the Question of Female Agency in Indian Feminist Historiography', *Gender and History,* 6(1).

Nandy, Ashis (2003). *The Romance of the State and the Fate of Dissent in the Tropics.* New Delhi: Oxford University Press.

Naussbaum, Martha and Jonathan Glover (eds) (1995). *Women, Culture and Development. A Study of Human Capabilities.* New York: Oxford University Press.

Niezen, Ronald (2003). *The Origins of Indigenism.* Berkeley: University of California Press.

Noorani, A.G. (2002). *Savarkar and Hindutva: The Godse Connection.* New Delhi: LeftWord Press.

Padel, Felix and Samarendra Das (2004). *Niyam Raja: Tribal Villages Bulldozed as the Shadow of Vedanta Looms over One of the Most Sacred Mountains in Orissa,* 9 February 2004 at http://www.minesandcommunities.org/Company/sterlite1.htm. Last accessed May 2004.

Pandey, Balaji (1998). *Depriving the Underprivileged for Development.* New Delhi: Institute for Socio-Economic Development.

Pandey, Gyanendra (1990). *The Construction of Communalism in Colonial North India.* New Delhi: Oxford University Press.

——— (2001). *Remembering Partition.* New York: Cambridge University Press.

Pandey, Gyanendra, Fred Clothey, J. Bruce Long, Peter Gescheire (eds) (2003). *Forging of Nationhood.* Delhi: Munshiram Manoharlal Limited.

Pandit, Tukoji, R. (2003). 'Sangh Parivar's Delhi Conclave Steps Up Hindutva Campaign', *Samachar,* 13 May 2003 at http://www.samachar.com/features/130503-features.html. Last accessed June 2004.

416   ANGANA P. CHATTERJI

Pannikar, K.N. (ed.) (1991). *Communalism in India: History, Politics and Culture*. Delhi: Manohar Books.

Parker, Andrew, Mary Russo, Doris Summer and Patricia Yaeger (eds) (1992). *Nationalisms and Sexualities*. New York: Routledge.

Pati, Biswamoy (2001). *Situating Social History. Orissa. 1899–1997*. New Delhi: Orient Longman.

———— (2003). *Identity, Hegemony, Resistance. Towards a Social History of Conversions in Orissa. 1800–2000*. New Delhi: Three Essays Collective.

People's Union For Civil Liberties (2004). 'A Report on Fact-Finding into the Incident of Atrocities on the Christians in Kilipal Village', April 2004, Bhubaneswar: People's Union For Civil Liberties.

Planning Commission of India (1990) *The Constitution (Sixty-Sixth Amendment) Act, 1990*. New Delhi: Government of India. Available at: http://indiacode.nic. in/coiweb/amend/amend66.htm. Last accessed May 2004.

———— (1999). *Orissa*. New Delhi: Government of India. Available at: http:// envfor.nic.in/fsi/sfr99/chap3/orissa/orissa.html. Last accessed May 2004.

Pradhan, S. (1999). *Orissa: History, Culture and Archaeology*. New Delhi: Bali Nagar.

Prasad, Vijay (2000). *The Karma of Brown Folk*. Minneapolis: University of Minnesota Press.

Puri, Jyoti (2004). *Encountering Nationalism*. Malden: Blackwell Publishers.

Ramakrishnan, Venkitesh (1999). 'An Outrage in Orissa', *Frontline*, 30–12 February, New Delhi.

Rao, Anupama (ed.) (2003). *Gender and Caste*. Series on Issues in Contemporary Feminism. New Delhi: Kali for Women.

Rout, Shyama Prasad (1999). *Land Alienation and Tribal People's Rights: A Case Study of Mayurbhanj District in Orissa*. Dissertation Proposal. Centre for Political Studies, School of Social Sciences, Jawaharlal Nehru University, New Delhi. Available at: http://sos-net.eu.org/red&s/dhdi/amis/rout.htm. Last accessed May 2004.

Roy, Arundhati (1999). *The Cost of Living*. New York: The Modern Library.

Rushdie, Salman (1991). *Imaginary Homelands. Essays and Criticism 1981–1991*. London: Granta Books.

Sabrang Communications & Publishing and The South Asia Citizens Web (2002). 'The Foreign Exchange of Hate: IDRF and the American Funding of Hindutva', France: Sabrang Communications & Publishing Private Limited, Mumbai, India, and The South Asia Citizens Web. Available at: www.stopfundinghate.org. Last accessed June 2004.

Sahoo, Rajib, Lochan (2004). *Agrarian Change and Peasant Unrest in Colonial India. Orissa 1912–1939*. New Delhi: Manak Publications.

Said, Edward (1978). *Orientalism*. New York: Pantheon Press.

———— (1993). *Culture and Imperialism*. New York: Vintage Books.

Samaddar, Ranabir (ed.) (2003). *Refugees and the State. Practices of Asylum and Care in India, 1947–2000*. New Delhi: Sage Publications.

Samiuddin, Abida and R. Khanam (ed.) (2002). *Muslim Feminism and Feminist Movement: South Asia*. Delhi: Global Vision Publishing House.

Sangari, Kumkum and Sudesh Vaid (eds) (1989). *Recasting Women: Essays in Colonial History*. New Delhi: Kali for Women.

Sarin, Madhu (2003). 'Bad in Law', *Down To Earth*, 15 July 2003, New Delhi.

Sarkar, Sumit (2002). *Beyond Nationalist Frames*. Delhi: Permanent Black.

Sarkar, Tanika (1996). 'Educating the Children of the Hindu Rashtra', in Praful Bidwai, Harbans Mukhia and Achin Vanaik (eds), *Religion, Religiosity and Communalism*, pp. 237–47. New Delhi: Manohar Publishers.

——— (2002). 'Semiotics of Terror in India: Muslim Children and Women in Hindu Rashtra', *Economic and Political Weekly*, 13 July.

Sarkar, Tanika and Urvashi Butalia (eds) (1995). *Women and Right-Wing Movements: Indian Experiments*. London: Zed Books.

Saxena, N.C. (2000). 'How Have the Poor Done? Mid-Term Review of the Ninth Plan', *Economic and Political Weekly*, 7 October 2000, XXXV(41).

Sen, Amartya (1999). *Development as Freedom*. New Delhi: Oxford University Press.

Senapati, Fakirmohan, Gopinath Mohanty, Kishori Charan Das, and Manoj Das (2000). *Oriya Stories*. New Delhi: Srishti Publishers.

Shearer, A.R. (2003). 'Evangelicals and the Death Squads', End Times Network, 10 September 2003. Available at http://www.thetruthseeker.co.uk/print. asp?ID=1171. Last accessed June 2004.

Singh, K.S. (1995). *The Scheduled Castes. 2nd Revised Edition*. People of India, National Series, Volume II. New Delhi: Oxford University Press.

Singh, Neera M. (2002). *Towards Democratizing Forest Governance: Creation Of Vertical Social Capital Through Federations In Orissa* [Unpublished manuscript].

Sinha, B., K. and Pushpendra (eds) (2000). *Land Reforms in India. An Unfinished Agenda. Volume 5*. New Delhi: Sage Publications.

Soros, George (2003). *The Bubble of American Supremacy*. New York: Public Affairs.

Spivak, Gayatri Chakravorty (1994). 'Can the Subaltern Speak?' in Patrick Williams and Laura Chrisman (eds), *Colonial Discourse and Postcolonial Theory. A Reader*. New York: Columbia University Press.

Stoler, Laura, Ann (1995). *Race and the Education of Desire. Foucault's History of Sexuality and the Colonial Order of Things*. Durham: Duke University Press.

Sundar, Nandini (2004). 'Teaching to Hate: RSS Pedagogical Programme', *Economic and Political Weekly*, 17 April, pp. 1605-12.

Sutherland, John (2004). 'God Save America...', *The Guardian*, 4 May 2004. Available at: http://www.commondreams.org/views04/0503-11.htm. Last accessed June 2004.

Tewatia, Debi, Singh and Swami Agnivesh (2001). *Police Firing on Tribals. A Report*. Rayagada: Maikanch.

Thapan, Meenakshi (1997). *Embodiment: Essays on Gender and Identity*. New Delhi: Oxford University Press.

Thapar, Romila (1992). 'The Perennial Aryans', *Seminar*, no. 400.

———— (1990). *A History of India, Volume 1*. New York: Penguin Books.

———— (2004). 'The Present in the Past', in *Cultural Pasts. Essays in Early Indian History*. New Delhi: Oxford University Press.

Varadarajan, Siddharth (ed.) (2002). *Gujarat. The Making of a Tragedy*. New York: Penguin Books.

Visweswaran, Kamala (1996). 'Small Speeches, Subaltern Gender: Nationalist Ideology and its Historiography', in Shahid Amin and Dipesh Chakrabarty (eds), *Writings on South Asian History and Society. Subaltern Studies IX*, pp. 83-125. New Delhi: Oxford University Press.

Vyas, Neena (2004). 'Neglect of Hindutva among Reasons for Defeat: Advani', *The Hindu*, 24 June 2004, at http://www.hindu.com/2004/06/24/stories/2004062408190100.htm. Last accessed June 2004.

Williams, Patrick and Laura Chrisman (eds) (1994). *Colonial Discourse and Postcolonial Theory. A Reader*. New York: Columbia University Press.

World Bank (2000). *Entering the 21st Century. World Development Report 1999/2000*. New York: Oxford University Press.

Notes on Editors and Contributors

The Editors

Angana P. Chatterji is a feminist anthropologist and historian of the present. Her recent writings include *Violent Gods: Hindu Nationalism in India's Present; Narratives from Orissa* (Three Essays Collective, 2009); *Land and Justice: The Struggle for Cultural Survival* (forthcoming); a co-contributed anthology, *Kashmir*, with Tariq Ali, Arundhati Roy et al. (Verso Books, 2011); and the report, *BURIED EVIDENCE: Unknown, Unmarked, and Mass Graves in Indian-administered Kashmir* (2009), for which she was the lead author. Chatterji is beginning work on a project on armed conflict and people's rights. Her work spans issues of militarization, gendered violences, and securitization as they contravene human rights, and religion in the public sphere as it shapes minoritization. She has also worked with issues of public forest lands reform and customary and indigenous land rights. Chatterji is also Co-founder of the International People's Tribunal on Human Rights and Justice in Kashmir.

Lubna Nazir Chaudhry is Associate Professor in Women's Studies and Human Development at the State University of New York, Binghamton. She also maintains a Visiting Fellow affiliation with the sustainable Development Policy Institute, Islamabad. Her research primarily focuses on the impact of multi-layered forms of violence on women and other disenfranchised groups in the context of Pakistan and Muslims in the USA.

The Contributors

Huma Ahmed-Ghosh is Professor and Chair, Department of Women's Studies, San Diego State University. Her PhD is in cultural anthropology and women's studies. She has published extensively on the women in Afghanistan looking at issues of human rights, gendered violence and the history of the women's movement. Ahmed-Ghosh has also published on immigrant Ahmadi Muslim women in the USA, and on the dilemmas of Islamic feminisms. Her publications on women in India focus on gendered ageing, domestic violence and widowhood, and on issues of representation of Indian women through beauty pageants. Currently she is working on an edited volume on gender and Islam in Asia.

Sukanya Banerjee is Associate Professor, Department of English, University of Wisconsin-Milwaukee. Her areas of interest include postcolonial studies, Victorian literature and culture, studies of colonialism and empire in the nineteenth century, south asia and gender studies. Her recent publication includes *Becoming Imperial Citizens: Indians in the Late-Victorian Empire*.

Srimati Basu is Associate Professor, Gender and Women's Studies and Anthropology, University of Kentucky. Her current principal project, 'Managing Marriage: Family Law and Family Violence in India', engages with debates about lawyer-free courts, domestic violence and forum-shopping, rape discourse in the context of marriage, reformulating kinship in the postcolonial state, mediation in the context of violence, and transnational engagements with family law reform. Her research on women and inheritance has been published in *She Comes to Take Her Rights: Indian Women: Property and Propriety* (Kali for Women, 2001). She has also edited the *Dowry and Inheritance* volume in the *Issues in Indian Feminism* series (2005), and has written on property, law, religion, kinship, popular culture, violence and resistance in various journals and anthologies.

Manali Desai is Senior Lecturer in Political Sociology, London School of Economics. Her work encompasses the areas of state formation, political parties, social movements, ethnic violence, and post-colonial studies. Her published works include *State Formation and Radical Democracy in India, 1860-1990* (2006) and *States of Trauma: Gender and Violence in South Asia* (co-edited, Zubaan, 2009). In addition, she has been published in various journals and is also the Book Review Editor for the *British Journal of Sociology*.

Meghna Guhathakurta is Executive Director of Research Initiatives, Bangladesh (RIB) and post-doctoral fellow of a collaborative capacity-building project between the University of Dhaka and ISS. Prior to this, she was Professor of International Relations at the University of Dhaka. Her area of specialization is development, gender, minority rights and South Asian politics. She has written extensively on gender issues in Bangladesh, ethnic conflict and peace-building in the Chittagong Hill Tracts, migration and displacement and NGOs in development. She served as member of Netherlands Development Research Council (RAWOO) from 1996 to 2002. She is also a member of South Asian Peoples Commission on Rights of Minorities, a commission formed by the organization, South Asians for Human Rights (SAHR).

Lamia Karim is Associate Director, Centre for the Study of Women in Society, University of Oregon. Her research interests are in globalization, gender, human rights, and social movements. She has published numerous scholarly articles in anthropology journals such as *Cultural Dynamics*, *Political and Legal Anthropology* and *Contemporary South Asia*, on gender and globalization, and has contributed articles to many edited volumes. Her research has been supported with two postdoctoral fellowships from the Rockefeller Foundation and grants from the National Science Foundation, Fulbright Foundation, Harry Frank Guggenheim Foundation and the Wenner-Gren Foundation for Anthropological Research. Dr. Karim has recently published a book entitled *Microfinance and its Discontents: Women in Debt in Bangladesh* (2011).

Nyla Ali Khan is Visiting Professor, University of Oklahoma, where she teaches several courses, including South Asian Studies, Twentieth-Century Anglophone Postcolonial Literature, Postcolonial Theory, and Cultural Studies. She has a PhD in English Literature from the same university and has been Associate Professor at the University of Nebraska-Kearney. Professor Khan, a native of Kashmir, has written extensively on issues related to Jammu & Kashmir. She is also the author of *The Fiction of Nationality in an Era of Transnationalism* (2005) and *Islam, Women, and Violence in Kashmir: Between India and Pakistan* (2010).

Rita Manchanda is Programme Director, South Asia Forum for Human Rights, India. Academically, she trained in International Relations at the Graduate School for International Studies, University of Geneva and is a well known journalist and writer on South Asian security and human rights issues. She is a peace and human rights activist and local partner (for India-Pakistan) of the Women Waging Peace network, a project of the Kennedy School of Government at Harvard University, and a founding member of the Pakistan India Forum for Peace and Democracy.

Kavita Panjabi is Fellow, Indian Institute of Advanced Study, Shimla. Her interests are in the fields of feminist studies, oral history, cultural studies and contemporary Indian and Latin American literatures. She received her PhD in Comparative Literature from Cornell University and has been a recipient of the Mellon Fellowship, USA; the Sephis Post-doctoral Fellowship, the Netherlands; and the South Asia Writing Fellowship of the Social Science Research Council, New York. Amongst her publications are a book entitled *Old Maps and New: Legacies of the Partition*, an edited volume *Nostalgia for the Future in Latin American Literatures*, and essays on violence against women, communalism and gender in Gujarat, testimonial literature, oral narratives of women in the Tebhaga movement, and Latin American literatures.

Jyoti Puri is Professor of Sociology at Simmons College, Boston. She writes and teaches in the areas of sexualities, states, nationalisms, and transnational feminisms. Her book, *Woman, Body, Desire in Post-colonial India* (1999), addresses how constructs of gender and sexuality are shaped across national and transnational contexts. *Encountering Nationalism* (2004) is a feminist sociological exploration of nationalism and the state. She has published a number of related articles and chapters in journals and edited volumes on sexuality and gender. She is the recipient of fellowships and grants, including a Rockefeller Research Fellowship and a Fulbright Senior Research award. She is currently working on a book-length manuscript on Section 377 entitled *Sexual States: Governance and Decriminalizing Sodomy in India's Present*.

Darini Rajasingham-Senanayake is a social anthropologist who specializes in international political economy and culture theory. She received her Bachelor's Degree from Brandeis University, and her MA and PhD are from Princeton University. She is based as the Social Scientist's Association in Colombo, and was formally a Senior Lecturer at the Department of Social Studies, Open University of Sri Lanka. She has written and published extensively on state building, multiculturalism, migration and identity politics as well as gender in development and peace building in South Asia. Her recent research is on developmentalism, the political economy of reconstruction and reconciliation.

Saadia Toor is an assistant professor at Staten Island College, author of *The State of Islam:Culture and Cold War Politics in Pakistan*, and part of the group Action for a Progressive Pakistan.

Usha Zacharias is Associate Professor, Westfield State College, Massachusetts, where she teaches international communication, intercultural communication, media criticism, film and gender, and scriptwriting.